JACAMON & MATZ
THE KILLER.

OMNIBUS VOLUME ONE

JACAMON & MATZ

THE KILLER

OMNIBUS VOLUME ONE

WRITTEN BY **MATZ**

ILLUSTRATED BY **LUC JACAMON**

LETTERED BY MARSHALL DILLON

DESIGN & ADDITIONAL LETTERING BY SCOTT NEWMAN

Edward Gauvin & Matz, *Script Translation*
Paul Morrissey, *Editor*

Archaia Entertainment LLC
Jack Cummins, *President & COO*
Mark Smylie, *Chief Creative Officer*
Mike Kennedy, *Publisher*
Stephen Christy, *Editor-in-Chief*
Scott Newman, *Production Manager*
Mel Caylo, *Marketing Manager*

Published by **Archaia**

Archaia Entertainment LLC
1680 Vine Street, Suite 1010
Los Angeles, California, 90028
www.archaia.com

ARCHAIA™
NEW STORIES. NEW WORLDS.

THE KILLER Omnibus Volume One

Collected Edition Softcover. March 2013. FIRST PRINTING.

10 9 8 7 6 5 4 3 2 1

ISBN: 1-936393-75-1
ISBN 13: 978-1-936393-75-6

Printed in **Korea**.

TABLE OF CONTENTS

I'm writing to you not as a friend of the creators, which in many introduction occasions is exactly what is happening, but as a fan through and true.

I have never met anybody involved in the creation of this amazing omnibus. I am just someone who lucked out and found this book on the shelves, took it home, and, as I always do, hoped for the very best... And this time I got it!

We all hope for the very best from our comic book purchase, but we don't ALWAYS get it. Oh, but when you do... MM! Right?

You sometimes take a shot in the dark based on nothing but your first impression of the art and a cursory enjoyment of the genre that the writer has chosen. In a grocery store they call it an impulse buy, but in a comic book store I think it's something more. Much more.

FOREWORD

When you're in a comic store, you're looking for something special, you're browsing the racks so something will surprise you, knock your socks off, change your mind about something, or remind you why you love comics above all else.

And when you find it -- it's just the best feeling in the world. And all that happened to me when I first found ***The Killer***.

I'm a huge crime comics fan, so that means I'm a huge crime comics snob. But I am an even bigger coloring snob. If I open a book and the coloring doesn't tell me that the colorist knows what they're doing, I put it back. If Jesus and Jack Kirby came down from heaven and made a Buckaroo Banzai comic, but the coloring was "eh," I'd put it back. So when I find a book like the ***The Killer***, that instantly wows me with color choices alone, I'm almost completely sold.

What's that? The colorist and the artist are the same person? I'm all the way sold.

I love an artist like Luc Jacamon. Super stylized, completely original, and completely unique; yet, at the same time, he harkens back to the glory days of Metal Hurlant. I see him in the same vein as Mike Oeming and Alex Maleev, and that's about as high praise as I give.

Beyond the fact that the coloring seems to be the collective dream of the best cinematographers in the world, the choices he makes with his lead character astound me. The almost-never-changing expression on the lead character's face is nearly impossible to pull off in a long-form graphic narrative.

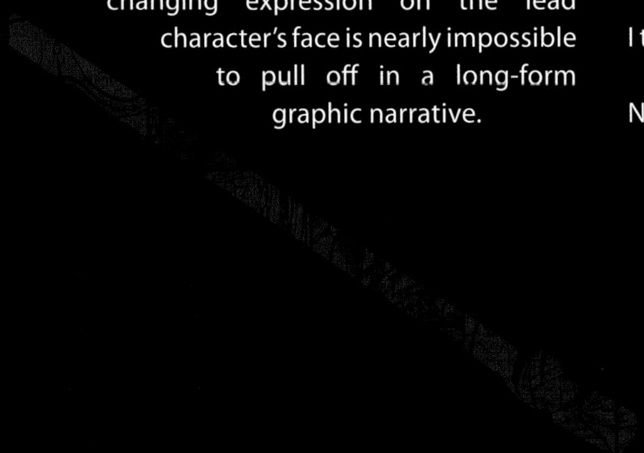

By its nature, it takes away all of the usual tools that an artist has to make the reader follow and fall in love with the character... or, at least, have the reader feel something, anything. Instead, Luc relies on posture and mood lighting. Again, so deceptively simple, yet so hard to pull off.

I was also so impressed by the storytelling choices. He knew when to go "cinematic," and he knew when he take us inside The Killer's mind.

There's another thing that Luc Jacamon has accomplished: he creates a true travelogue. Wherever The Killer goes, we feel we are actually traveling with him. Jacamon takes us to exotic locations around the world that would make James Bond jealous. Lush detail around every corner. That in itself seems to be a dying art form.

And that's where the writing comes in. I cannot express to you my admiration for the quality of Matz's writing. Matz took a well-worn genre and a rather well-worn premise and dove in headfirst with honesty and originality. A writer knows that his moments to shine are in the details and the character's unique perspective. The Killer is a true character study. Jim Thompson would have loved this book.

I'm guessing. I don't know him either.

Well, here it is. ***The Killer***. In all its glory. It was my honor to write this introduction to what I consider to be one of the best graphic novel series of the last ten years.

I toast you, Matz and Luc Jacamon, and I thank you.

Now do it again.

— BENDIS
Portland, Oregon
May 201[illegible]

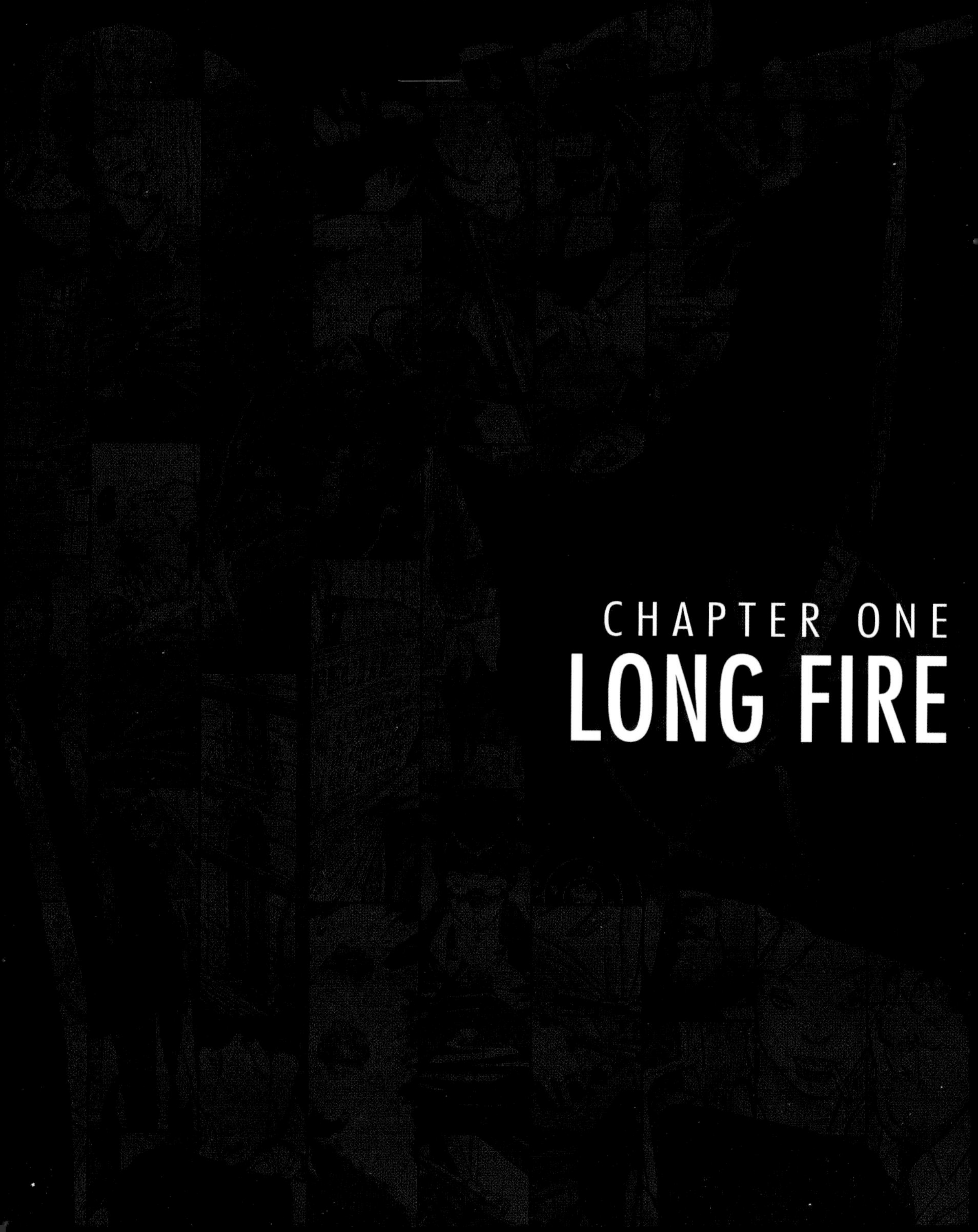

CHAPTER ONE
LONG FIRE

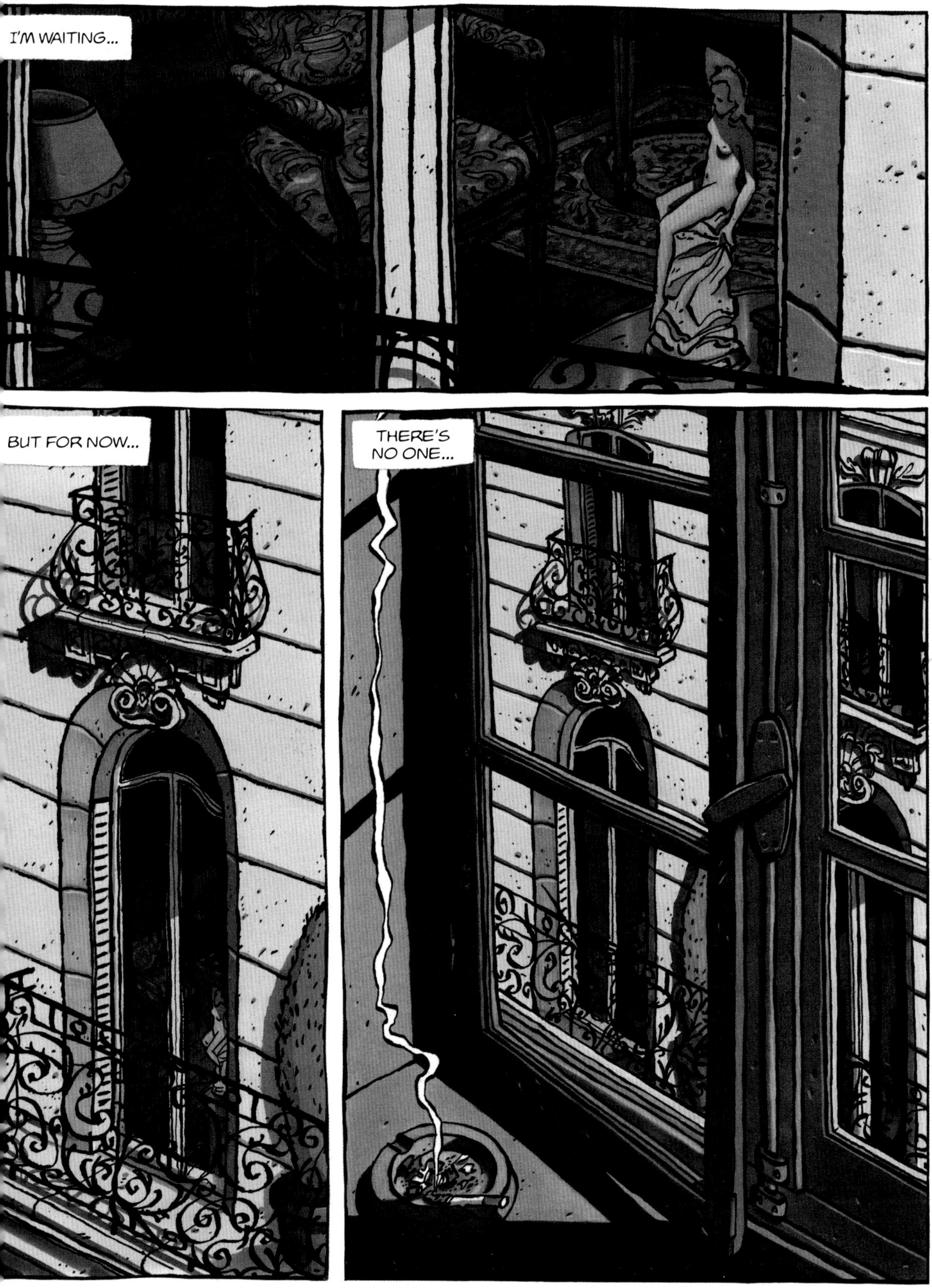
I'M WAITING...
BUT FOR NOW...
THERE'S NO ONE...

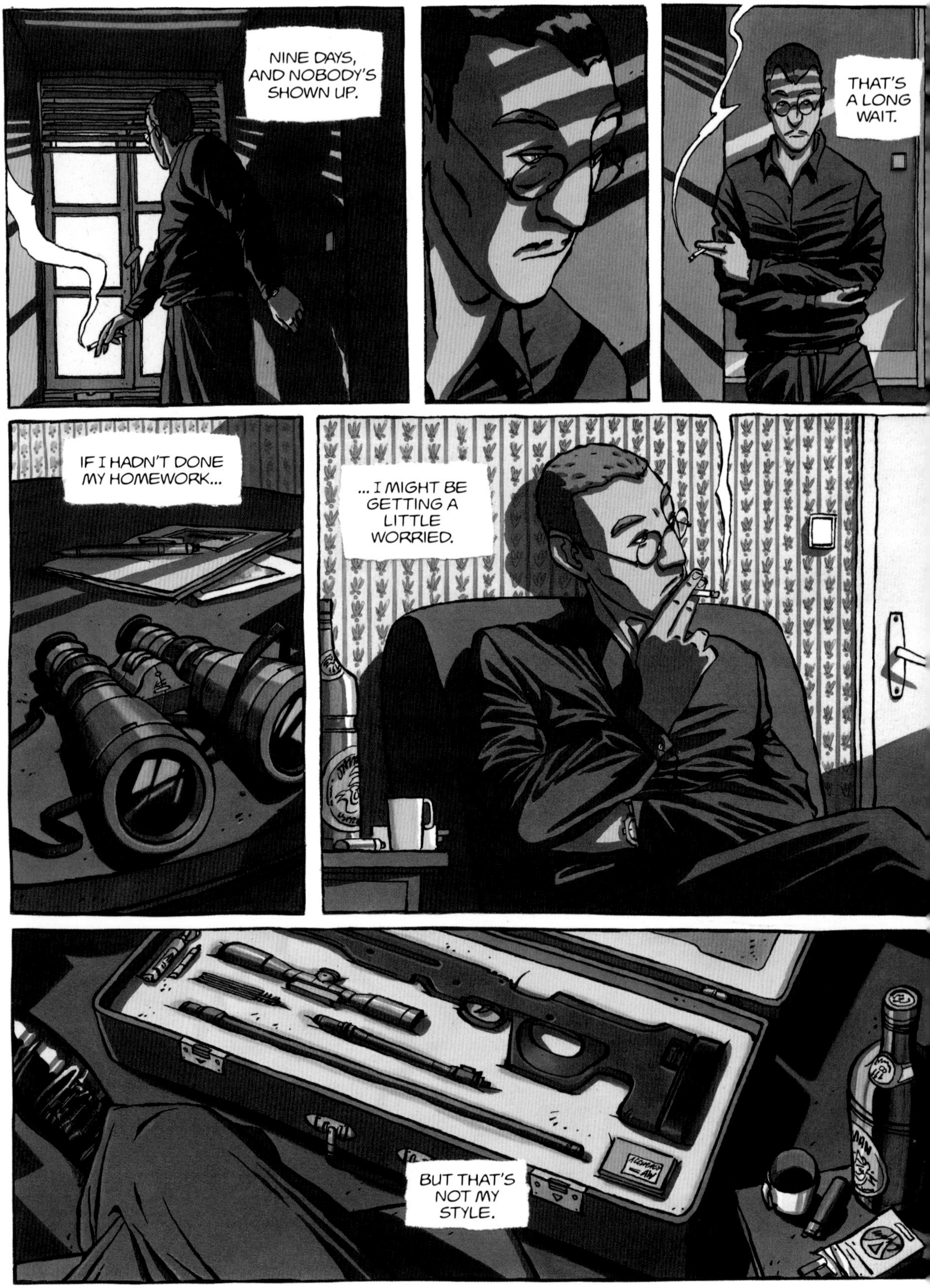
NINE DAYS, AND NOBODY'S SHOWN UP.
THAT'S A LONG WAIT.
IF I HADN'T DONE MY HOMEWORK...
...I MIGHT BE GETTING A LITTLE WORRIED.
BUT THAT'S NOT MY STYLE.

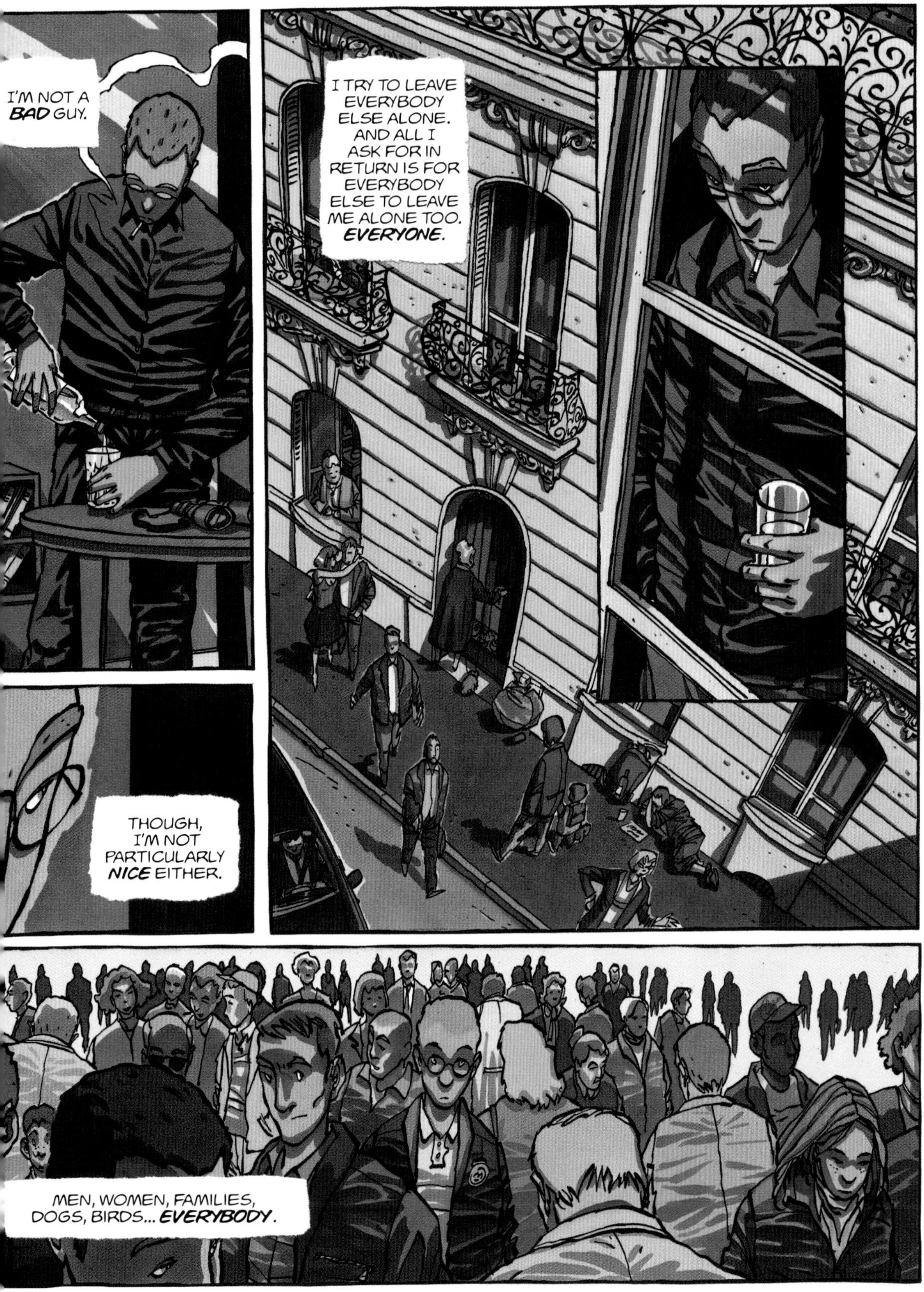
I'M NOT A **BAD** GUY.
I TRY TO LEAVE EVERYBODY ELSE ALONE. AND ALL I ASK FOR IN RETURN IS FOR EVERYBODY ELSE TO LEAVE ME ALONE TOO. ***EVERYONE***.
THOUGH, I'M NOT PARTICULARLY ***NICE*** EITHER.
MEN, WOMEN, FAMILIES, DOGS, BIRDS... ***EVERYBODY***.

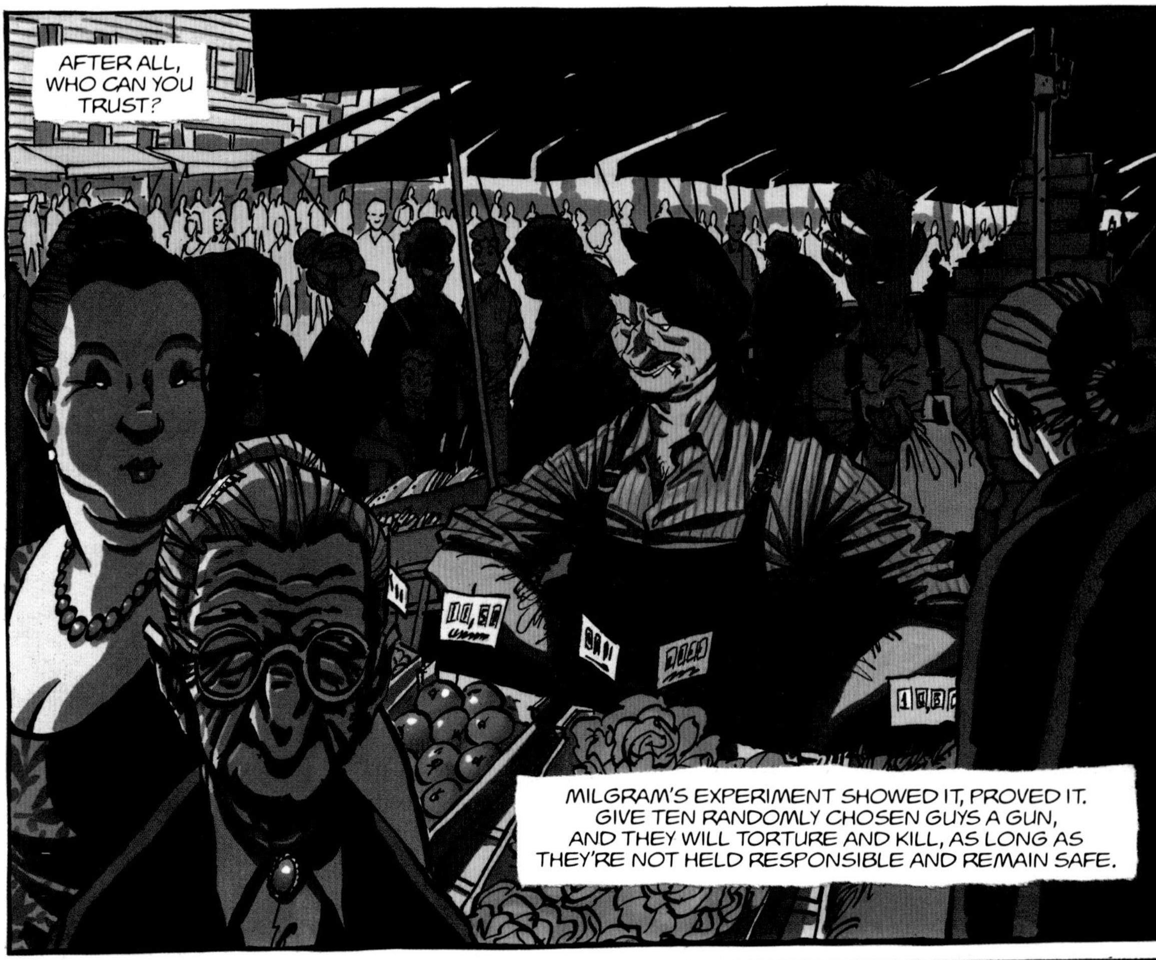
AFTER ALL, WHO CAN YOU TRUST?
MILGRAM'S EXPERIMENT SHOWED IT, PROVED IT. GIVE TEN RANDOMLY CHOSEN GUYS A GUN, AND THEY WILL TORTURE AND KILL, AS LONG AS THEY'RE NOT HELD RESPONSIBLE AND REMAIN SAFE.

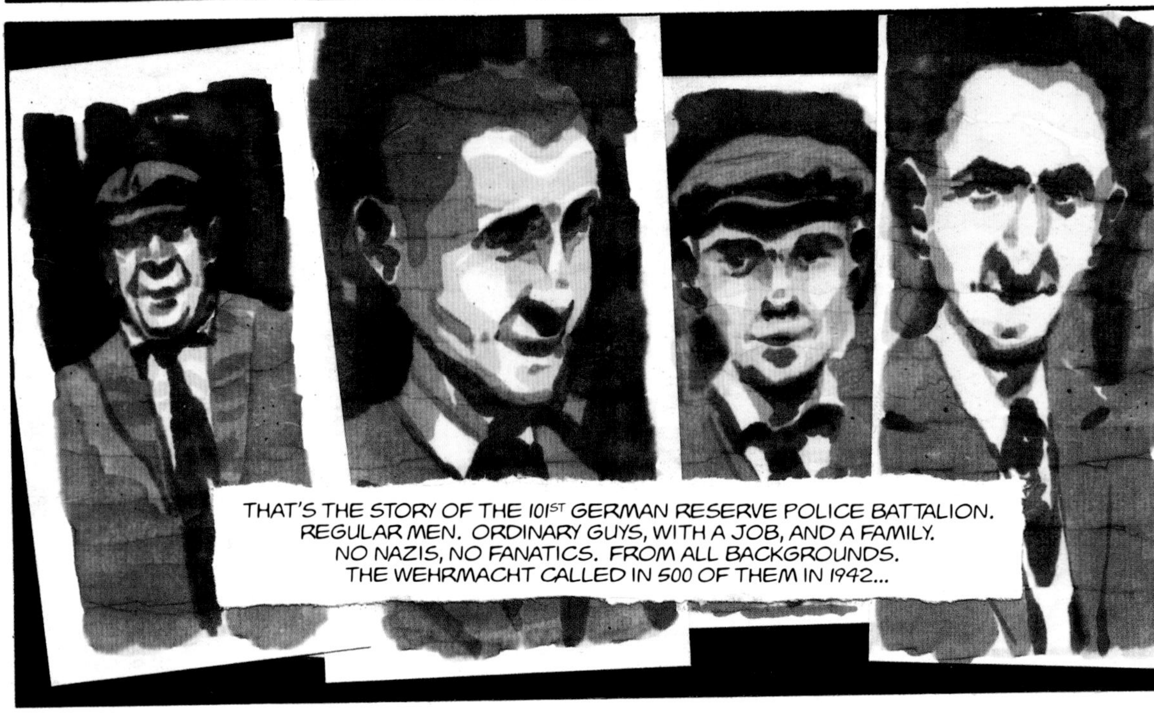
THAT'S THE STORY OF THE 101ST GERMAN RESERVE POLICE BATTALION. REGULAR MEN. ORDINARY GUYS, WITH A JOB, AND A FAMILY. NO NAZIS, NO FANATICS. FROM ALL BACKGROUNDS. THE WEHRMACHT CALLED IN 500 OF THEM IN 1942...

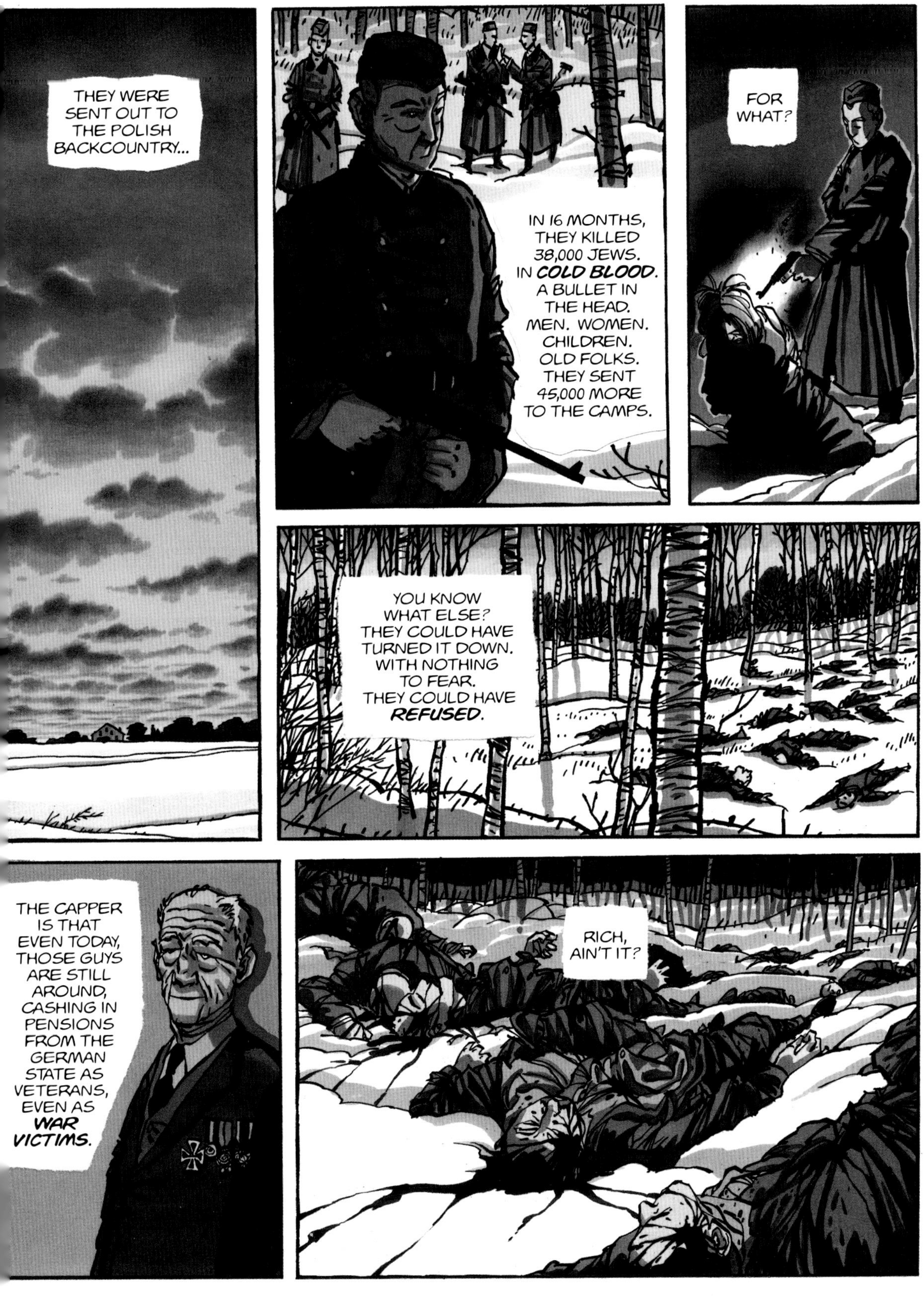
THEY WERE SENT OUT TO THE POLISH BACKCOUNTRY...
IN 16 MONTHS, THEY KILLED 38,000 JEWS. IN COLD BLOOD. A BULLET IN THE HEAD. MEN. WOMEN. CHILDREN. OLD FOLKS. THEY SENT 45,000 MORE TO THE CAMPS.
FOR WHAT?
YOU KNOW WHAT ELSE? THEY COULD HAVE TURNED IT DOWN. WITH NOTHING TO FEAR. THEY COULD HAVE REFUSED.
THE CAPPER IS THAT EVEN TODAY, THOSE GUYS ARE STILL AROUND, CASHING IN PENSIONS FROM THE GERMAN STATE AS VETERANS, EVEN AS WAR VICTIMS.
RICH, AIN'T IT?

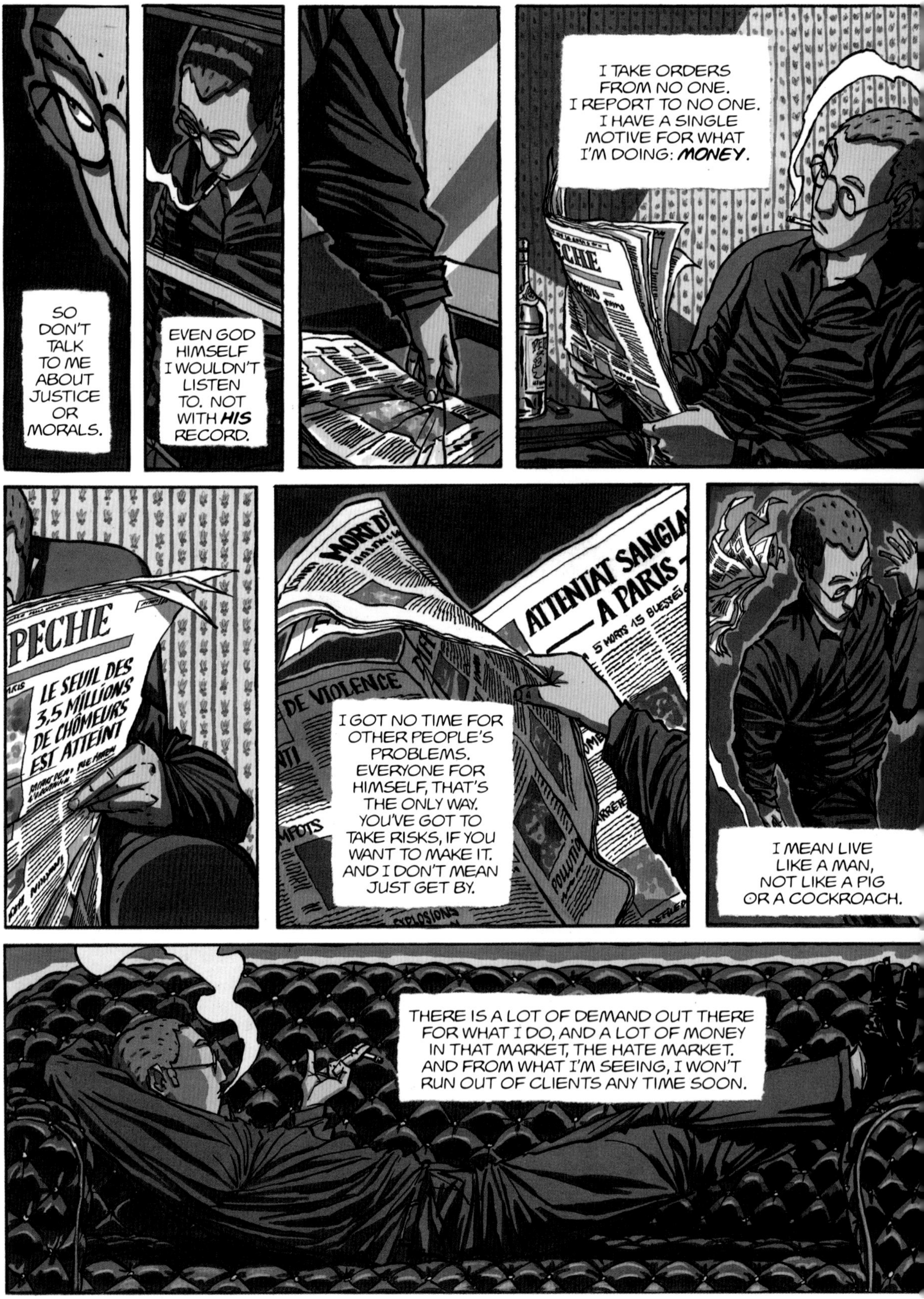
SO DON'T TALK TO ME ABOUT JUSTICE OR MORALS.
EVEN GOD HIMSELF I WOULDN'T LISTEN TO. NOT WITH **HIS** RECORD.
I TAKE ORDERS FROM NO ONE. I REPORT TO NO ONE. I HAVE A SINGLE MOTIVE FOR WHAT I'M DOING: **MONEY**.
PECHE
LE SEUIL DES 3,5 MILLIONS DE CHÔMEURS EST ATTEINT
ATTENTAT SANGLA
A PARIS
5 MORTS 15 BLESSÉS
DE VIOLENCE
I GOT NO TIME FOR OTHER PEOPLE'S PROBLEMS. EVERYONE FOR HIMSELF, THAT'S THE ONLY WAY. YOU'VE GOT TO TAKE RISKS, IF YOU WANT TO MAKE IT. AND I DON'T MEAN JUST GET BY.
I MEAN LIVE LIKE A MAN, NOT LIKE A PIG OR A COCKROACH.
THERE IS A LOT OF DEMAND OUT THERE FOR WHAT I DO, AND A LOT OF MONEY IN THAT MARKET, THE HATE MARKET. AND FROM WHAT I'M SEEING, I WON'T RUN OUT OF CLIENTS ANY TIME SOON.

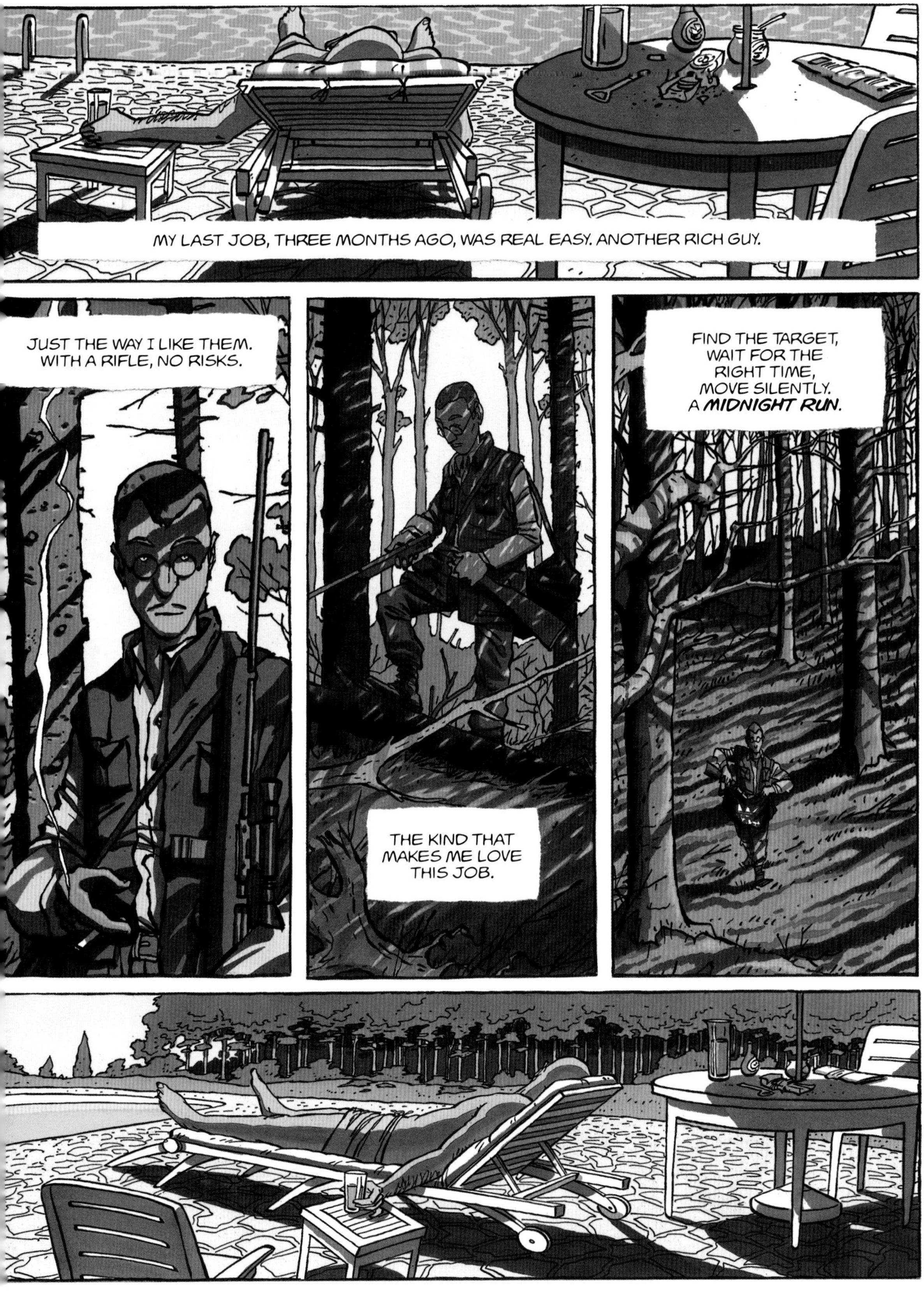
MY LAST JOB, THREE MONTHS AGO, WAS REAL EASY. ANOTHER RICH GUY.
JUST THE WAY I LIKE THEM. WITH A RIFLE, NO RISKS.
THE KIND THAT MAKES ME LOVE THIS JOB.
FIND THE TARGET, WAIT FOR THE RIGHT TIME, MOVE SILENTLY. A **MIDNIGHT RUN**.

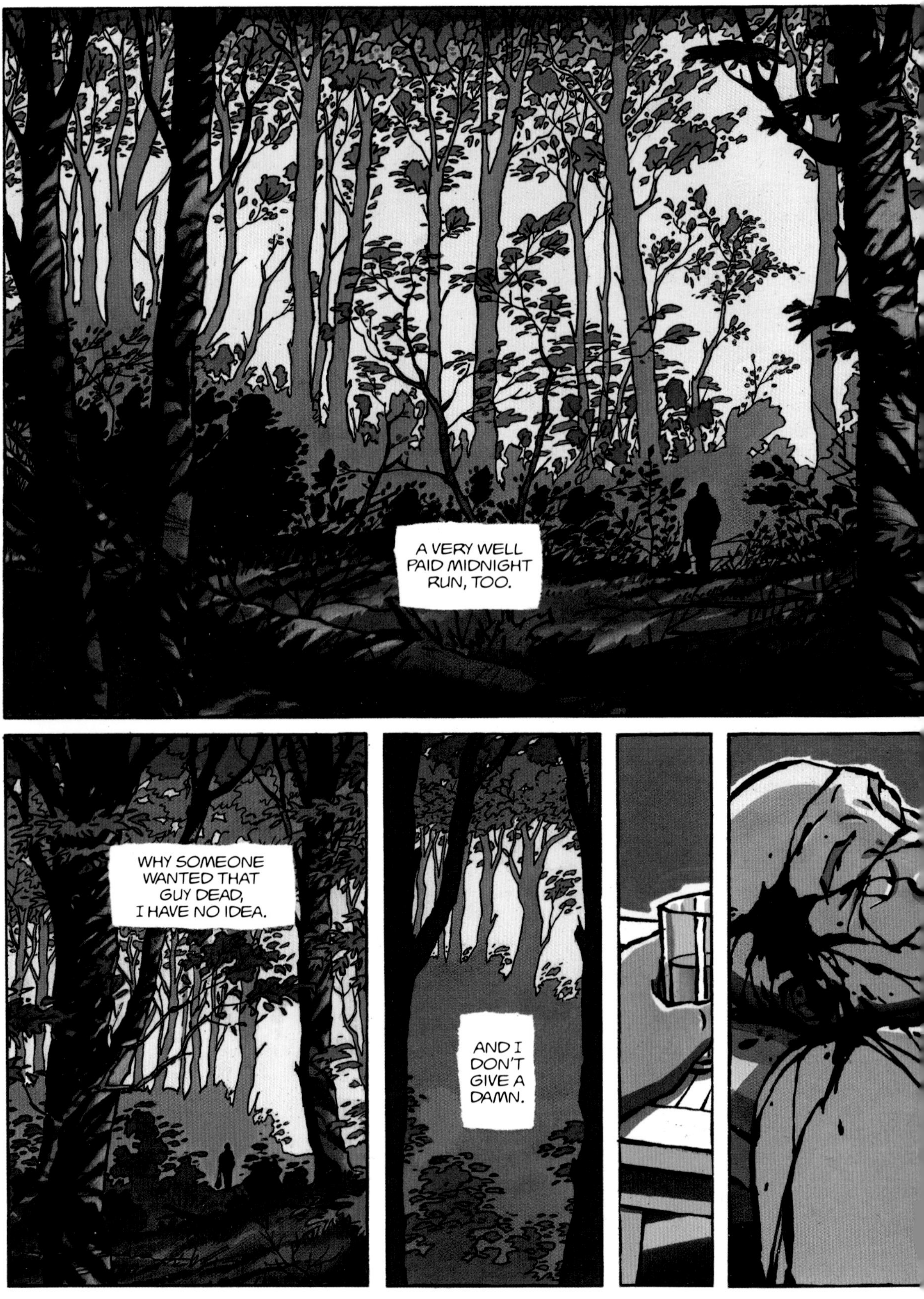
A VERY WELL PAID MIDNIGHT RUN, TOO.
WHY SOMEONE WANTED THAT GUY DEAD, I HAVE NO IDEA.
AND I DON'T GIVE A DAMN.

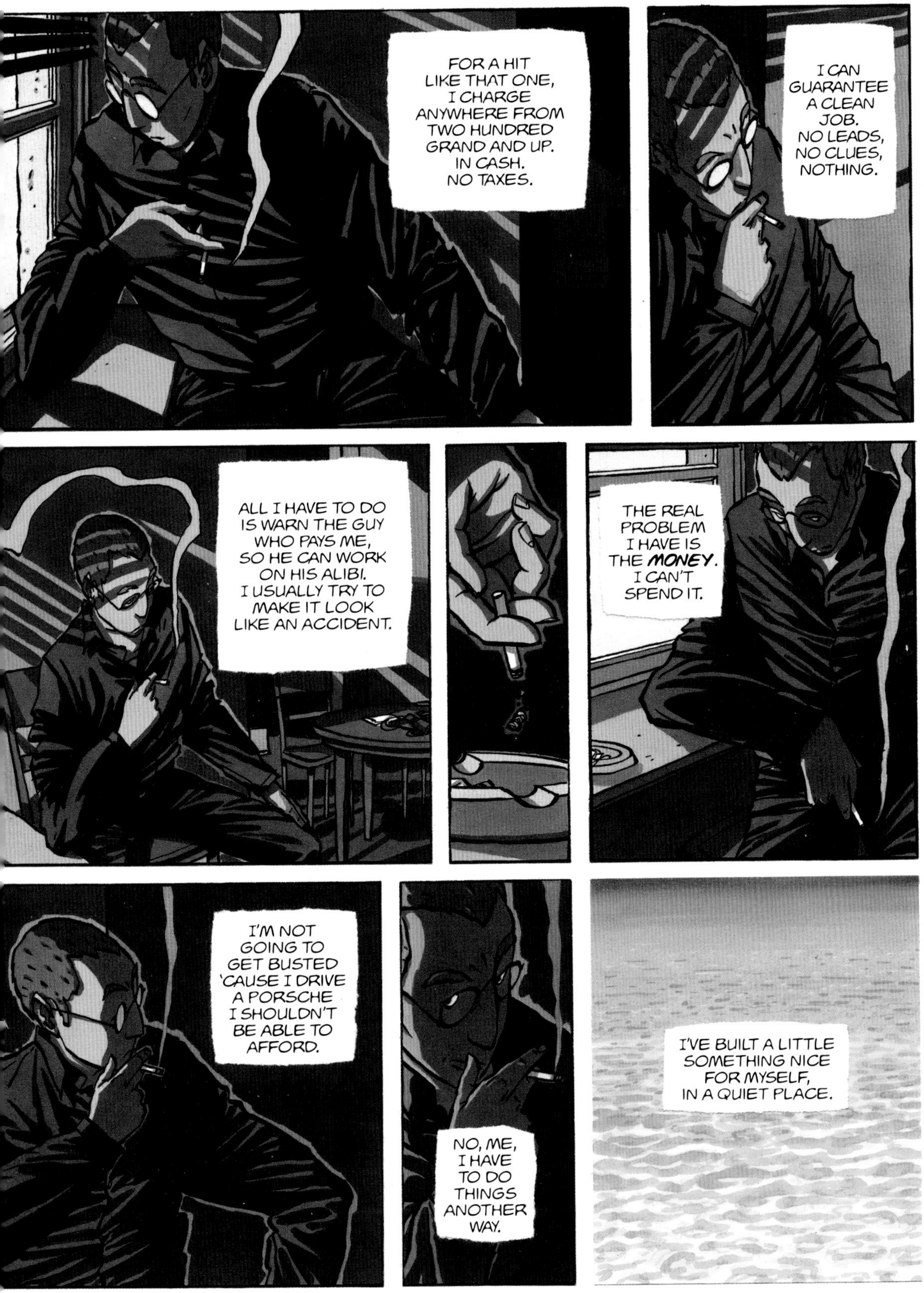
FOR A HIT LIKE THAT ONE, I CHARGE ANYWHERE FROM TWO HUNDRED GRAND AND UP. IN CASH. NO TAXES.
I CAN GUARANTEE A CLEAN JOB. NO LEADS, NO CLUES, NOTHING.
ALL I HAVE TO DO IS WARN THE GUY WHO PAYS ME, SO HE CAN WORK ON HIS ALIBI. I USUALLY TRY TO MAKE IT LOOK LIKE AN ACCIDENT.
THE REAL PROBLEM I HAVE IS THE **MONEY**. I CAN'T SPEND IT.
I'M NOT GOING TO GET BUSTED 'CAUSE I DRIVE A PORSCHE I SHOULDN'T BE ABLE TO AFFORD.
NO, ME, I HAVE TO DO THINGS ANOTHER WAY.
I'VE BUILT A LITTLE SOMETHING NICE FOR MYSELF, IN A QUIET PLACE.

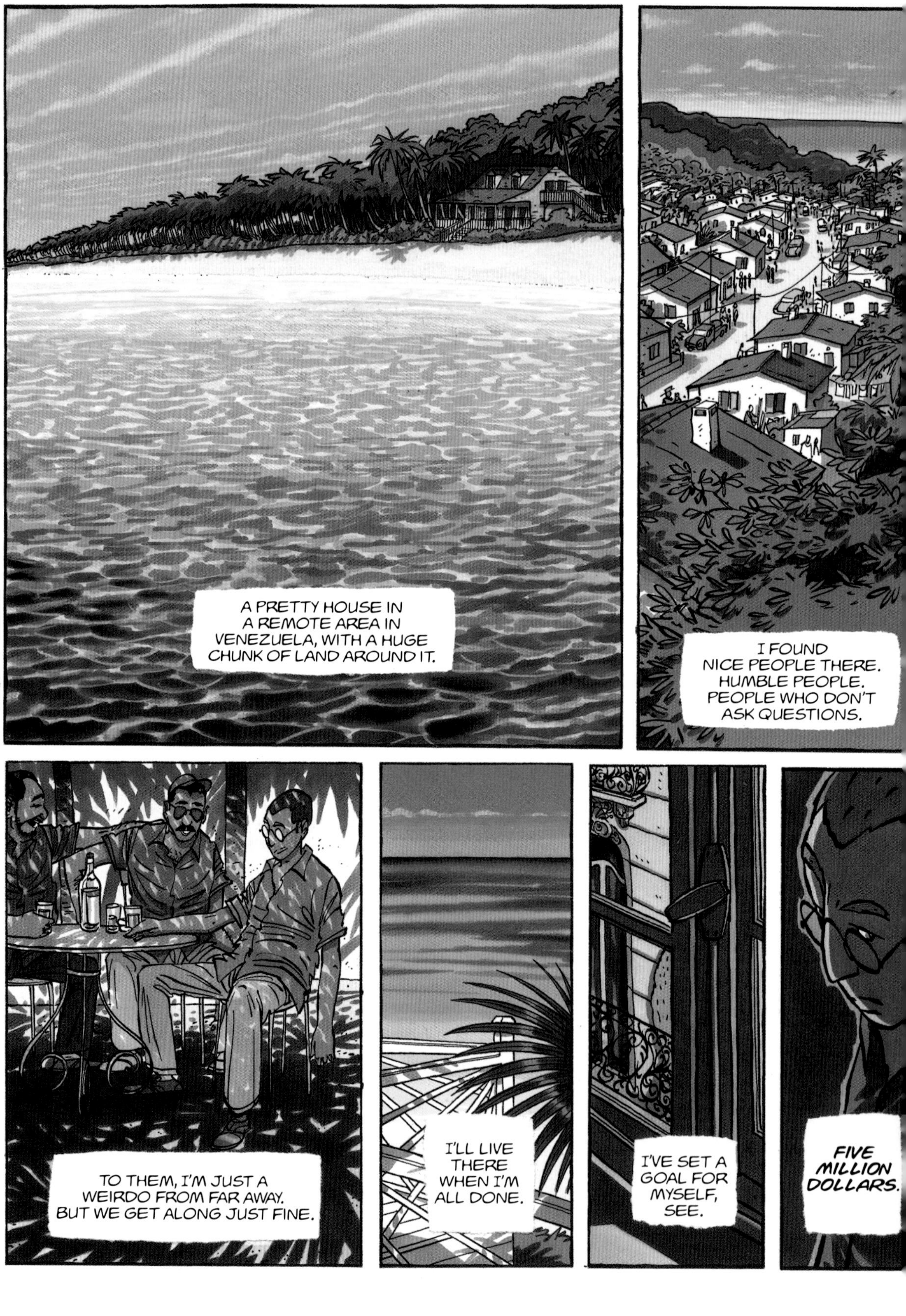
A PRETTY HOUSE IN A REMOTE AREA IN VENEZUELA, WITH A HUGE CHUNK OF LAND AROUND IT.
I FOUND NICE PEOPLE THERE. HUMBLE PEOPLE. PEOPLE WHO DON'T ASK QUESTIONS.
TO THEM, I'M JUST A WEIRDO FROM FAR AWAY. BUT WE GET ALONG JUST FINE.
I'LL LIVE THERE WHEN I'M ALL DONE.
I'VE SET A GOAL FOR MYSELF, SEE.
FIVE MILLION DOLLARS.

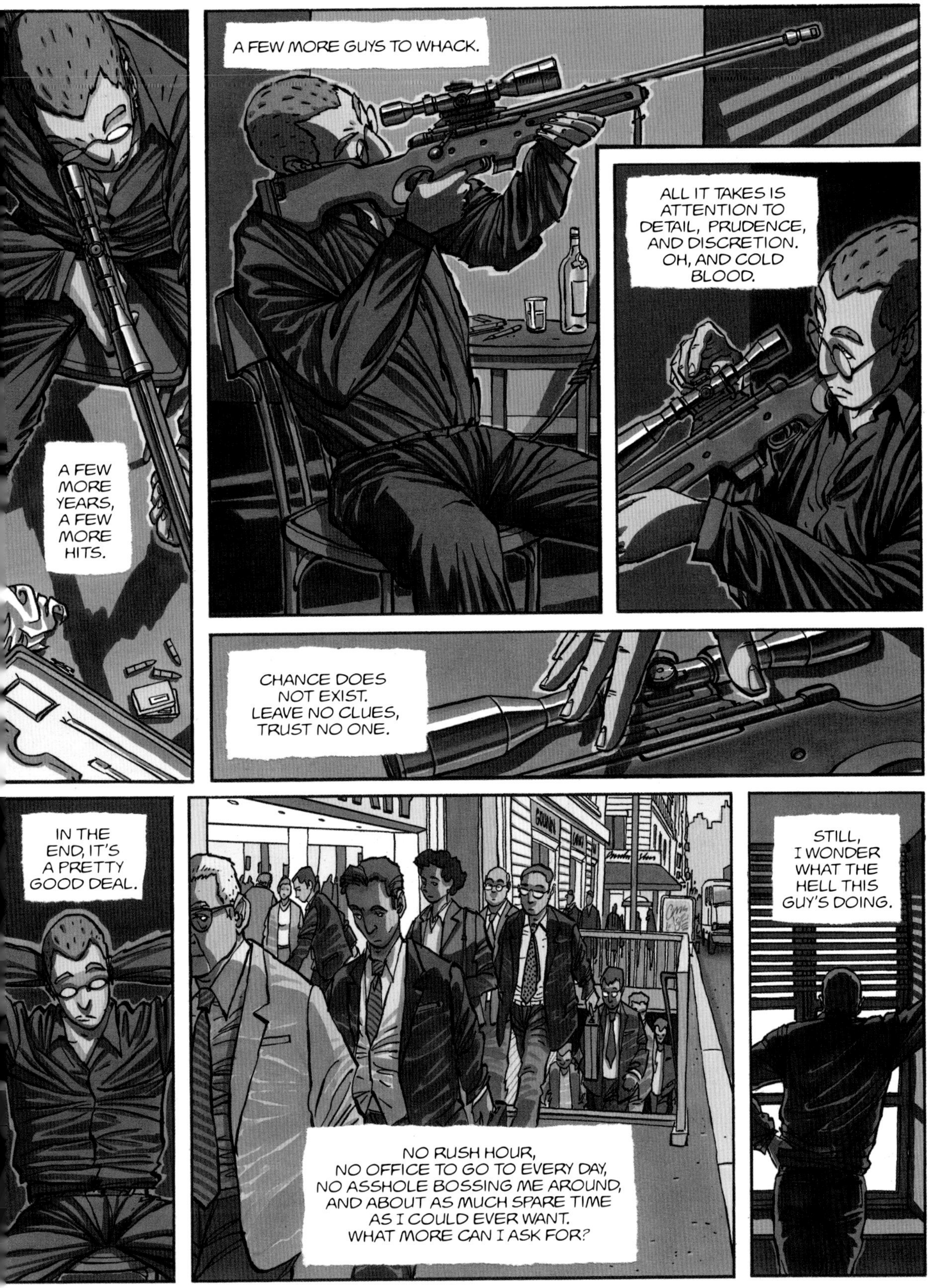
A FEW MORE GUYS TO WHACK.
A FEW MORE YEARS, A FEW MORE HITS.
ALL IT TAKES IS ATTENTION TO DETAIL, PRUDENCE, AND DISCRETION. OH, AND COLD BLOOD.
CHANCE DOES NOT EXIST. LEAVE NO CLUES, TRUST NO ONE.
IN THE END, IT'S A PRETTY GOOD DEAL.
NO RUSH HOUR, NO OFFICE TO GO TO EVERY DAY, NO ASSHOLE BOSSING ME AROUND, AND ABOUT AS MUCH SPARE TIME AS I COULD EVER WANT. WHAT MORE CAN I ASK FOR?
STILL, I WONDER WHAT THE HELL THIS GUY'S DOING.

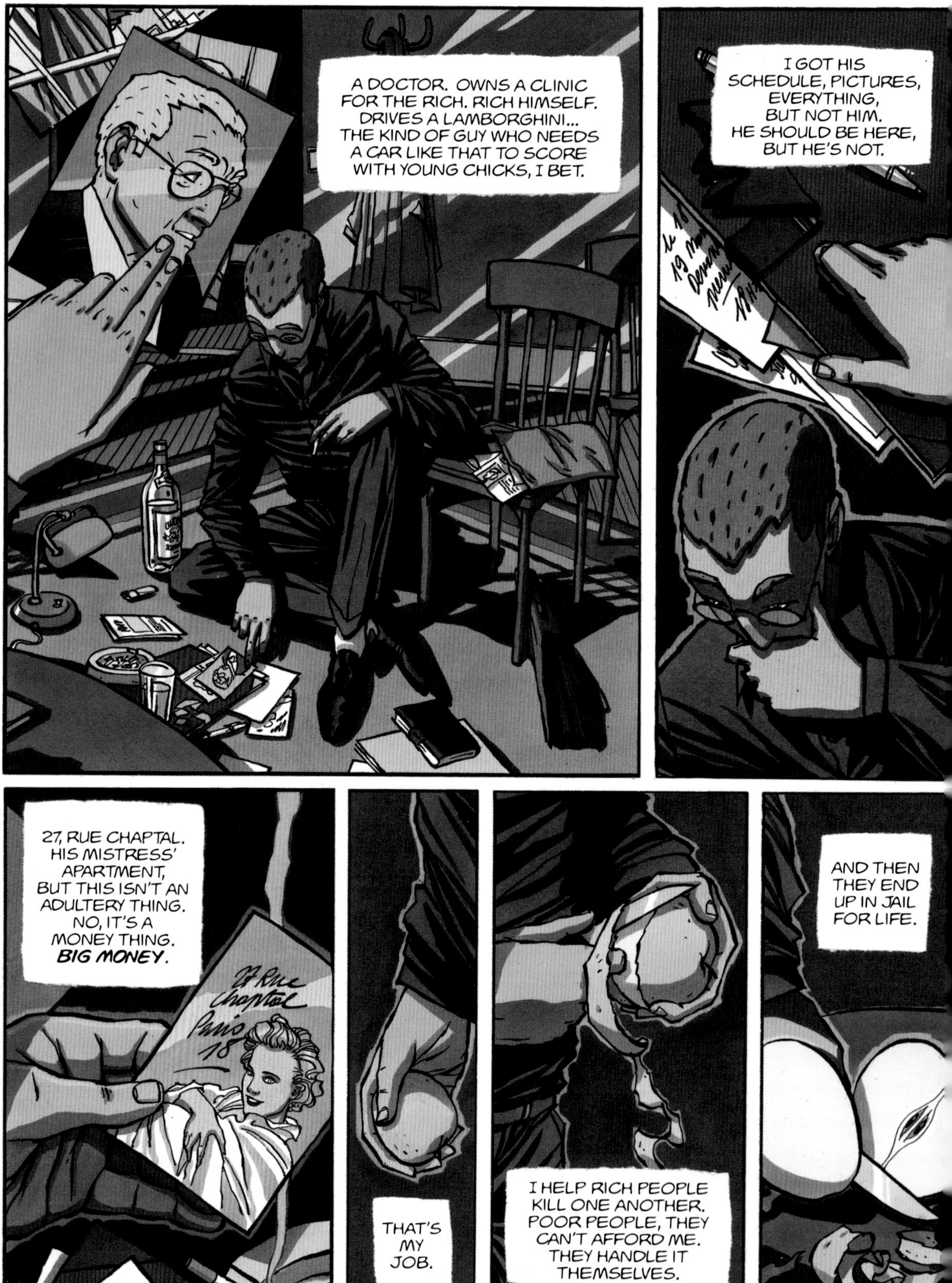
A DOCTOR. OWNS A CLINIC FOR THE RICH. RICH HIMSELF. DRIVES A LAMBORGHINI... THE KIND OF GUY WHO NEEDS A CAR LIKE THAT TO SCORE WITH YOUNG CHICKS, I BET.
I GOT HIS SCHEDULE, PICTURES, EVERYTHING, BUT NOT HIM. HE SHOULD BE HERE, BUT HE'S NOT.
27, RUE CHAPTAL. HIS MISTRESS' APARTMENT, BUT THIS ISN'T AN ADULTERY THING. NO, IT'S A MONEY THING. BIG MONEY.
27 Rue Chaptal Paris 18
THAT'S MY JOB.
I HELP RICH PEOPLE KILL ONE ANOTHER. POOR PEOPLE, THEY CAN'T AFFORD ME. THEY HANDLE IT THEMSELVES.
AND THEN THEY END UP IN JAIL FOR LIFE.

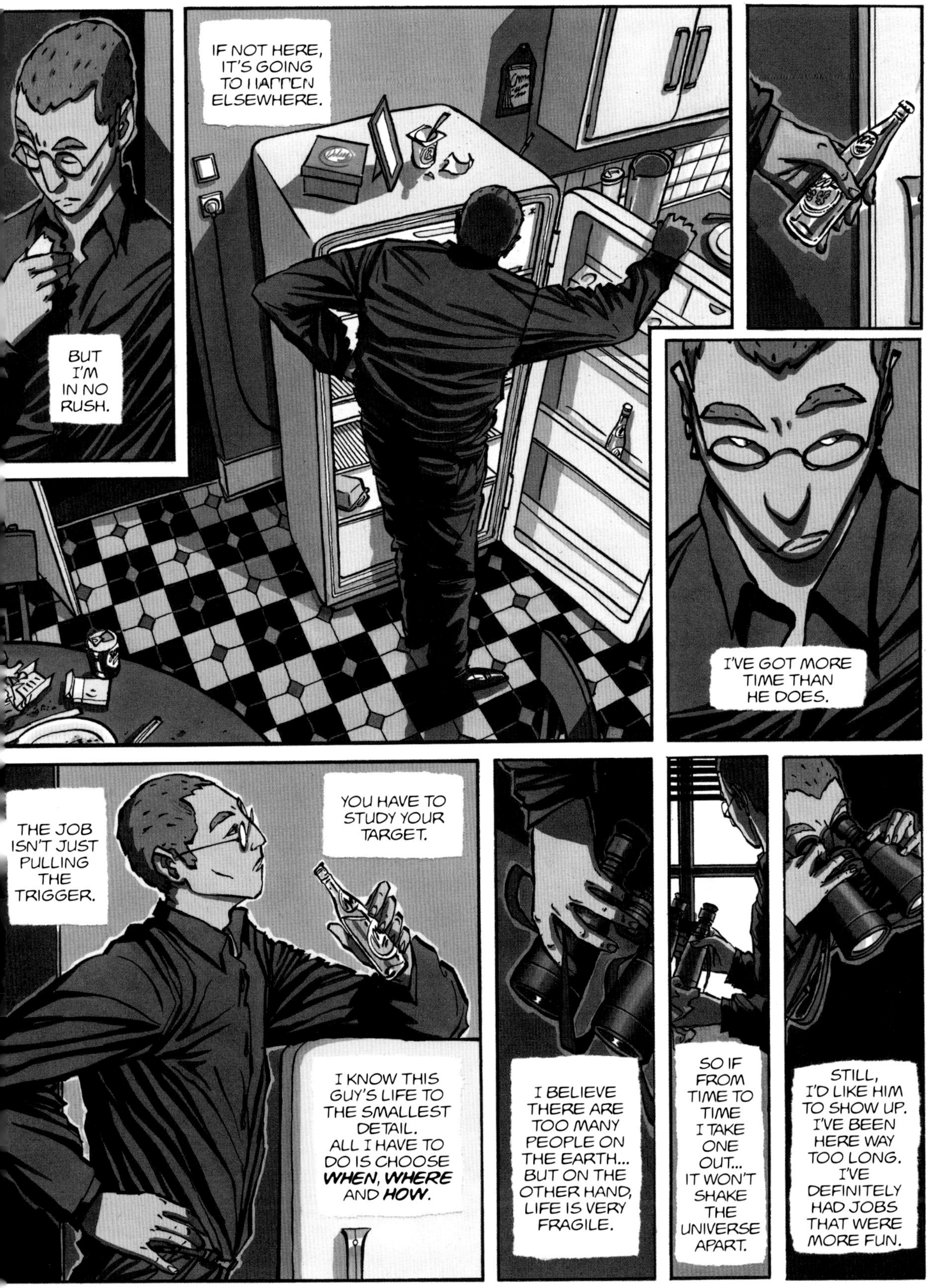

IF NOT HERE, IT'S GOING TO HAPPEN ELSEWHERE.
BUT I'M IN NO RUSH.
I'VE GOT MORE TIME THAN HE DOES.
THE JOB ISN'T JUST PULLING THE TRIGGER.
YOU HAVE TO STUDY YOUR TARGET.
I KNOW THIS GUY'S LIFE TO THE SMALLEST DETAIL. ALL I HAVE TO DO IS CHOOSE WHEN, WHERE AND HOW.
I BELIEVE THERE ARE TOO MANY PEOPLE ON THE EARTH... BUT ON THE OTHER HAND, LIFE IS VERY FRAGILE.
SO IF FROM TIME TO TIME I TAKE ONE OUT... IT WON'T SHAKE THE UNIVERSE APART.
STILL, I'D LIKE HIM TO SHOW UP. I'VE BEEN HERE WAY TOO LONG. I'VE DEFINITELY HAD JOBS THAT WERE MORE FUN.

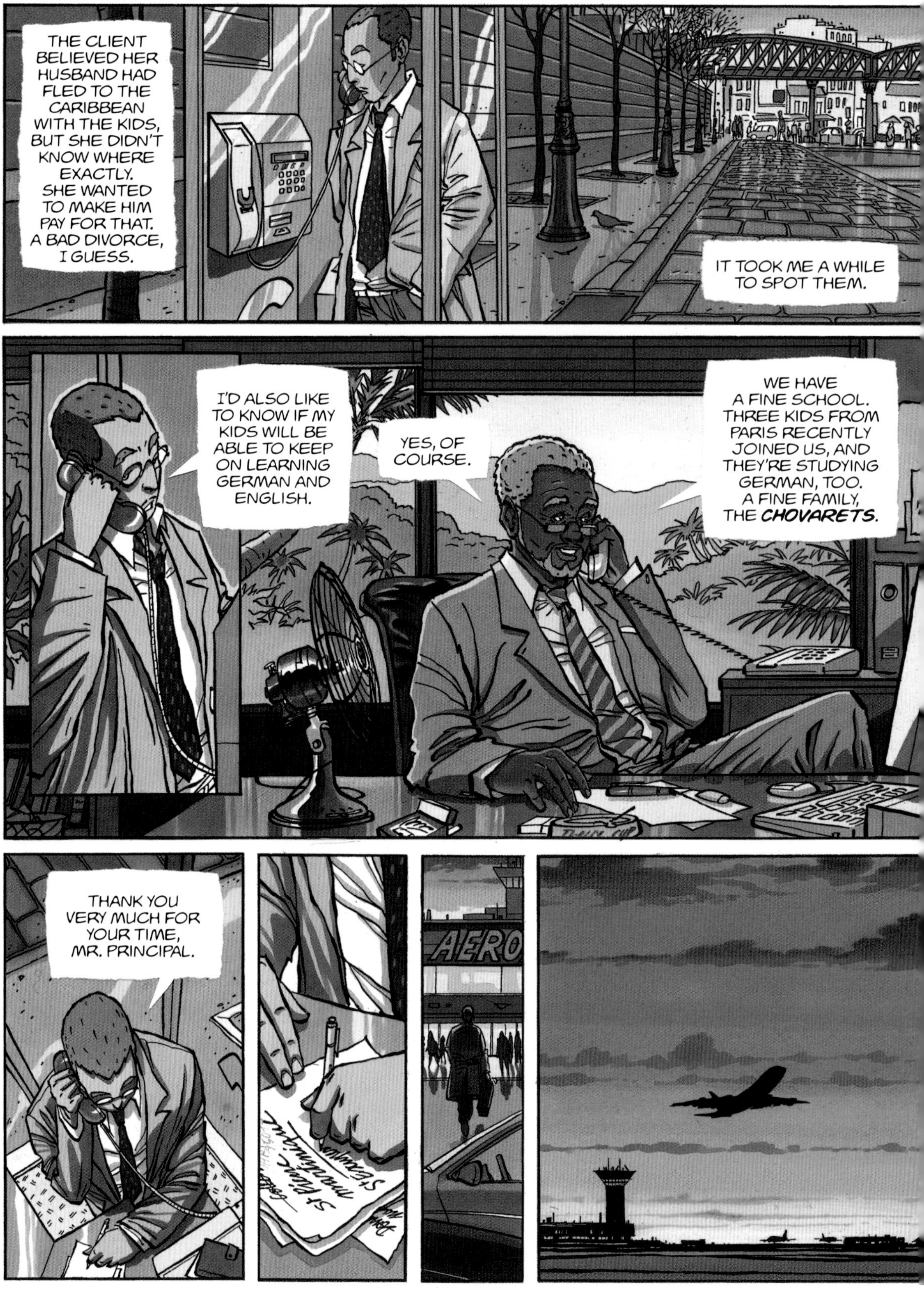
THE CLIENT BELIEVED HER HUSBAND HAD FLED TO THE CARIBBEAN WITH THE KIDS, BUT SHE DIDN'T KNOW WHERE EXACTLY. SHE WANTED TO MAKE HIM PAY FOR THAT. A BAD DIVORCE, I GUESS.
IT TOOK ME A WHILE TO SPOT THEM.
I'D ALSO LIKE TO KNOW IF MY KIDS WILL BE ABLE TO KEEP ON LEARNING GERMAN AND ENGLISH.
YES, OF COURSE.
WE HAVE A FINE SCHOOL. THREE KIDS FROM PARIS RECENTLY JOINED US, AND THEY'RE STUDYING GERMAN, TOO. A FINE FAMILY, THE ***CHOVARETS***.
THANK YOU VERY MUCH FOR YOUR TIME, MR. PRINCIPAL.
AERO

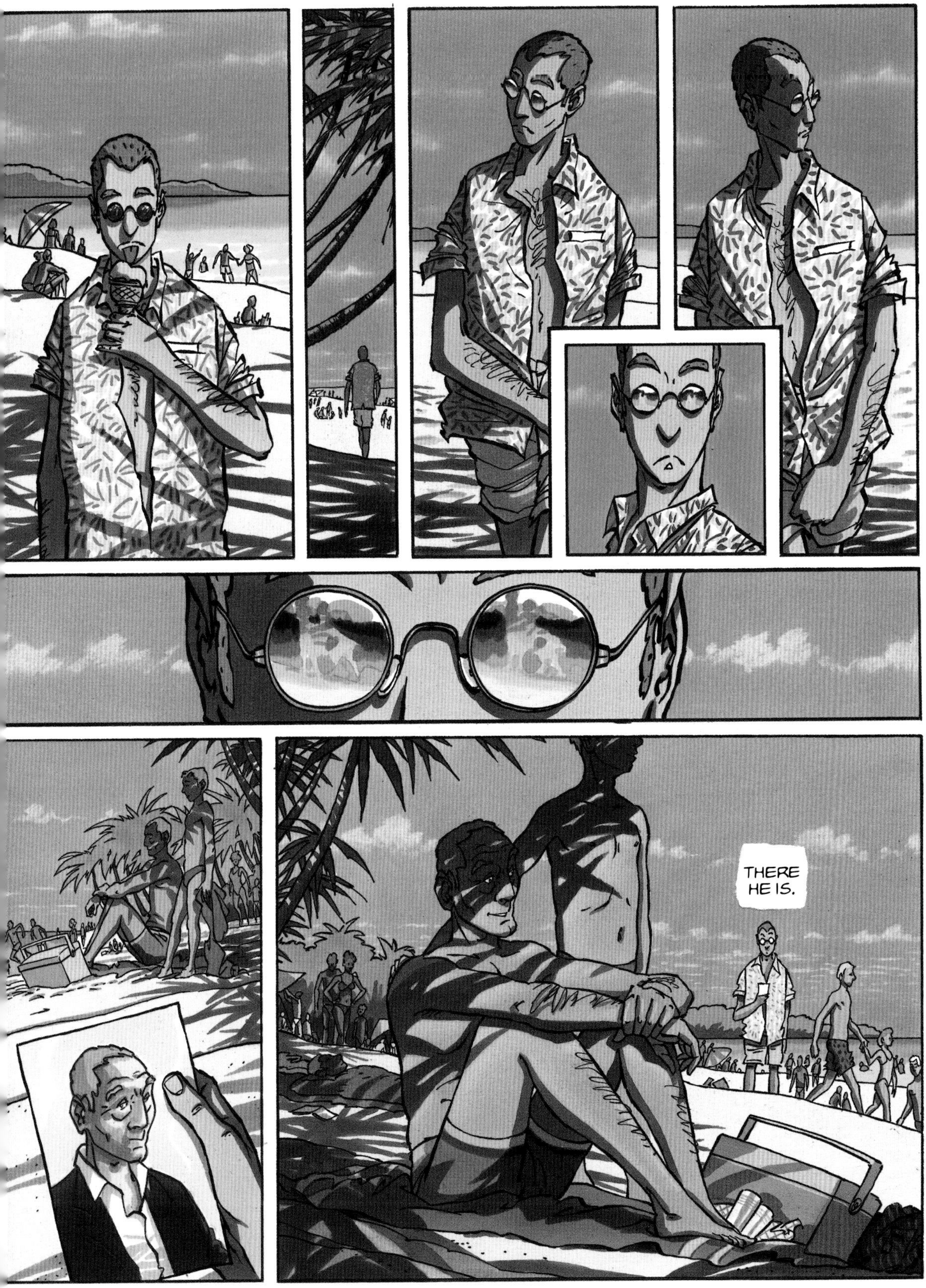
THERE HE IS.

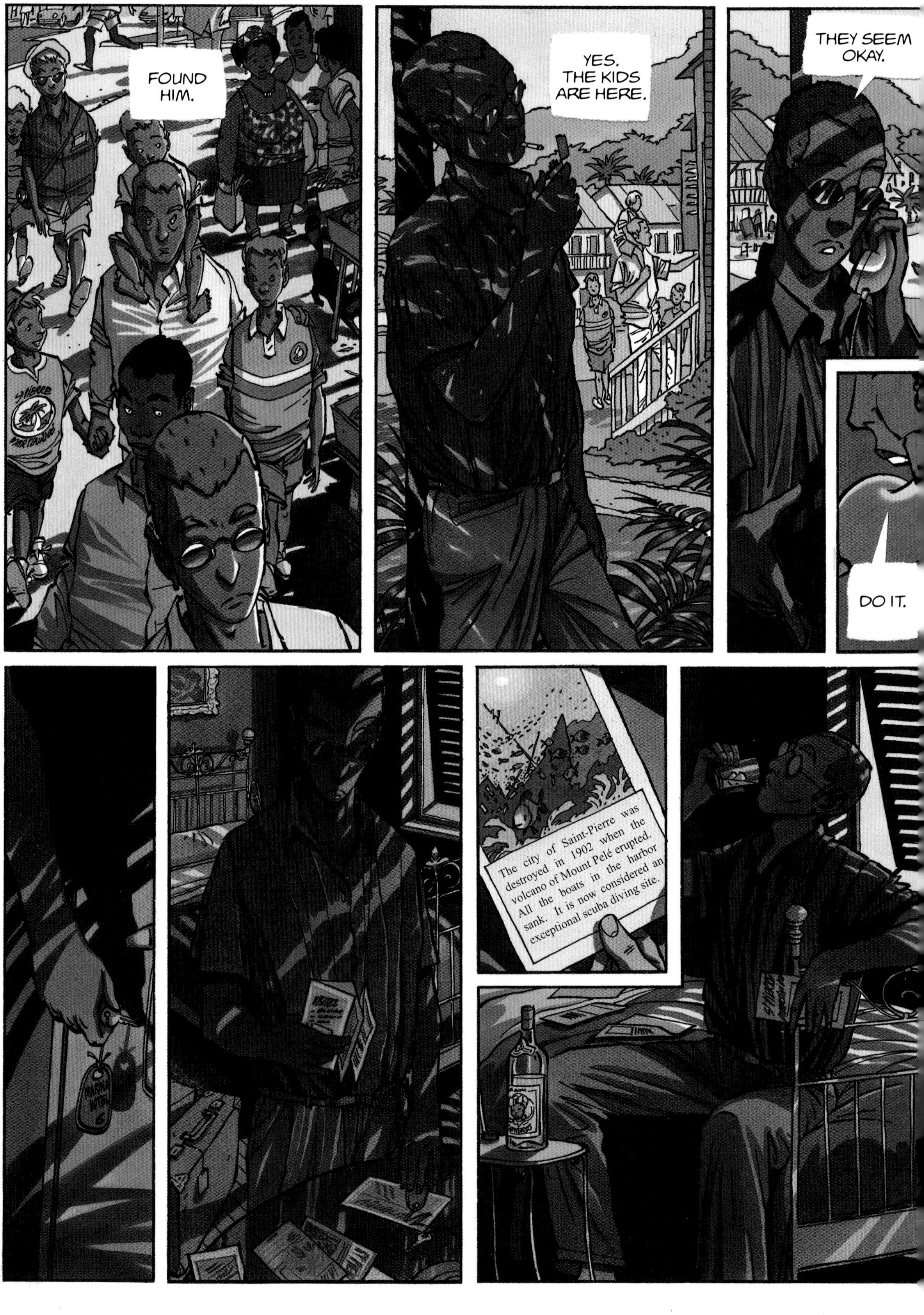
FOUND HIM.
YES. THE KIDS ARE HERE.
THEY SEEM OKAY.
DO IT.
The city of Saint-Pierre was destroyed in 1902 when the volcano of Mount Pelé erupted. All the boats in the harbor sank. It is now considered an exceptional scuba diving site.

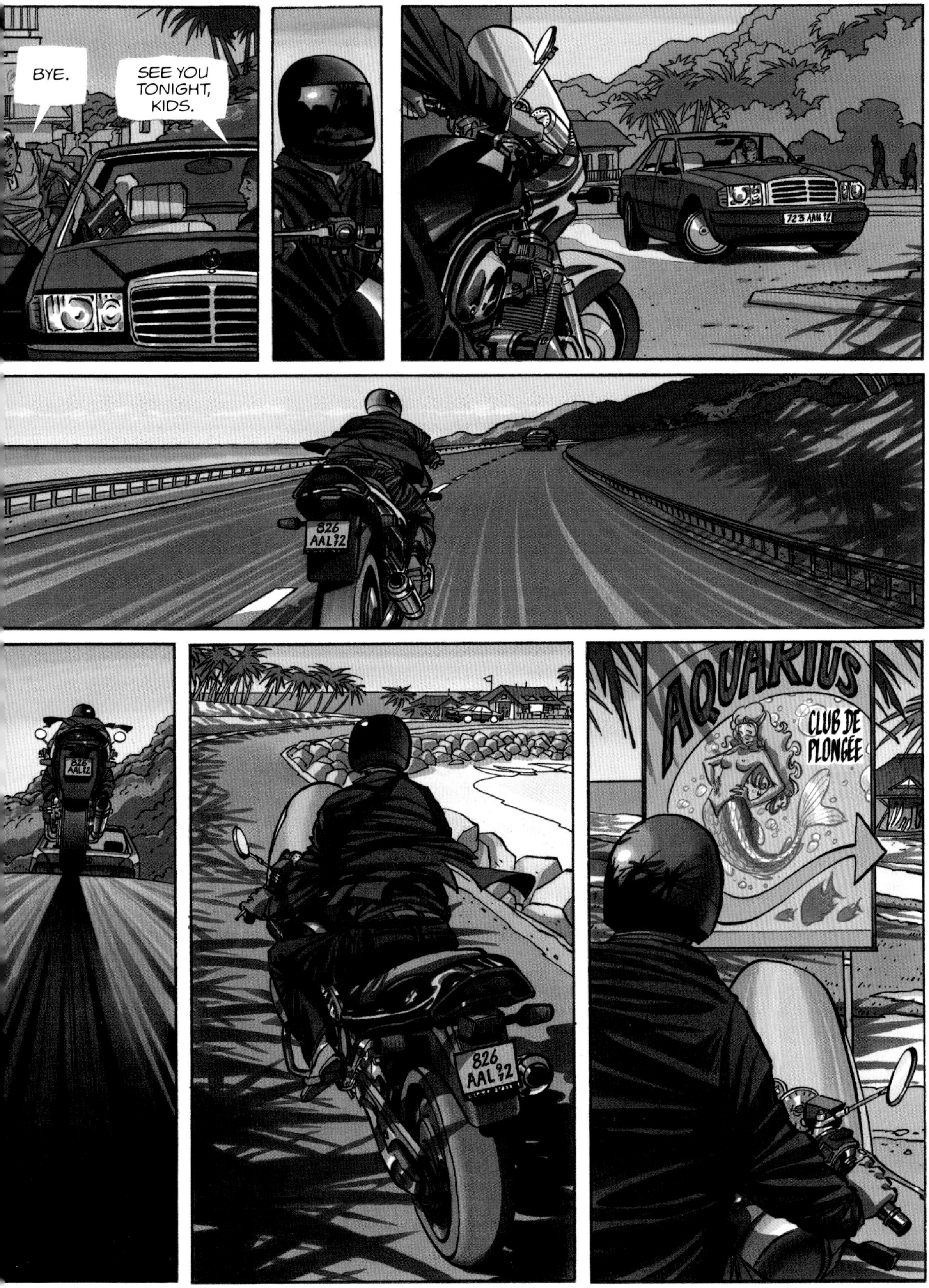
BYE.
SEE YOU TONIGHT, KIDS.
723 AAN 92
826 AAL 972
AQUARIUS
CLUB DE PLONGÉE

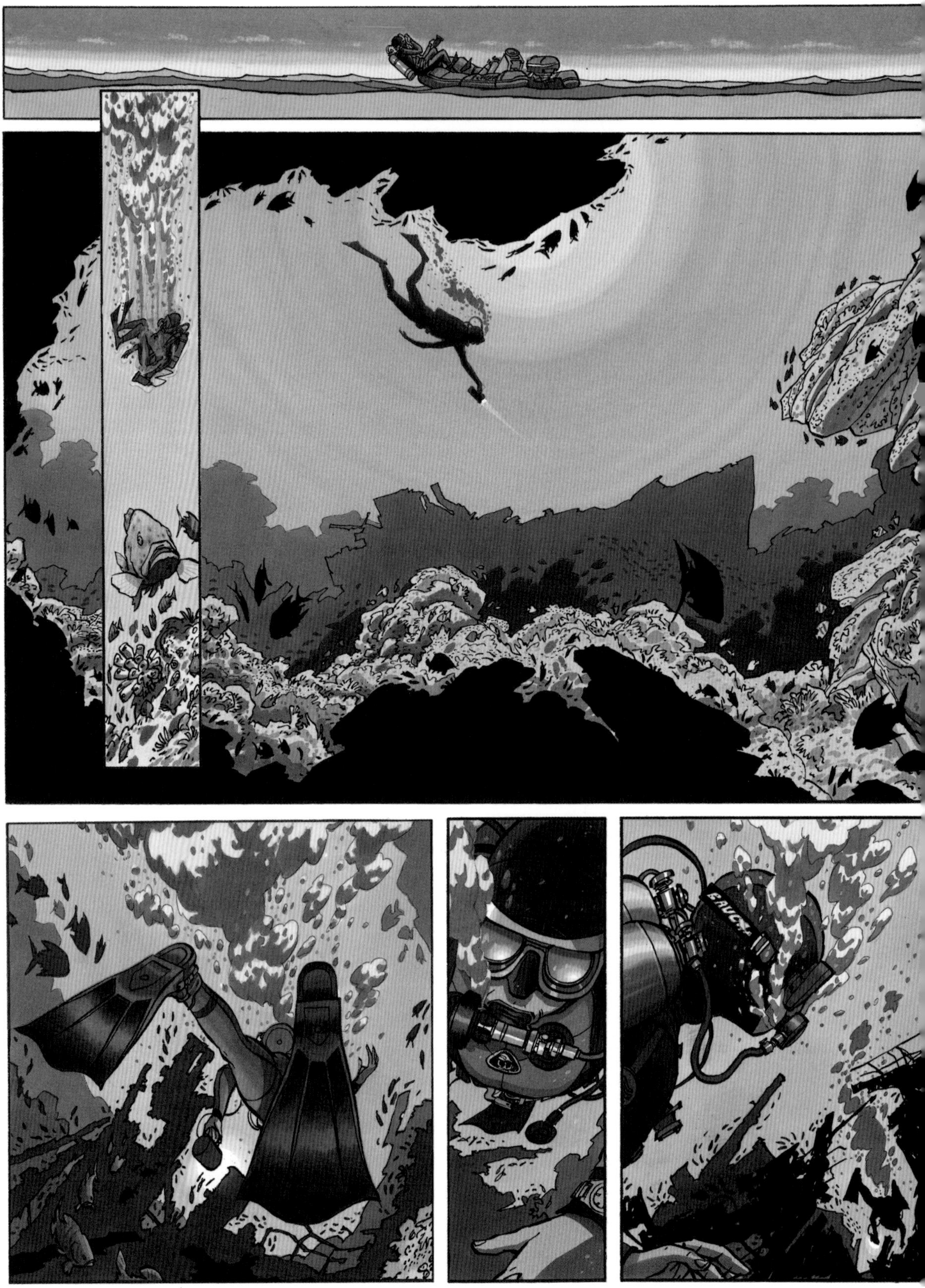

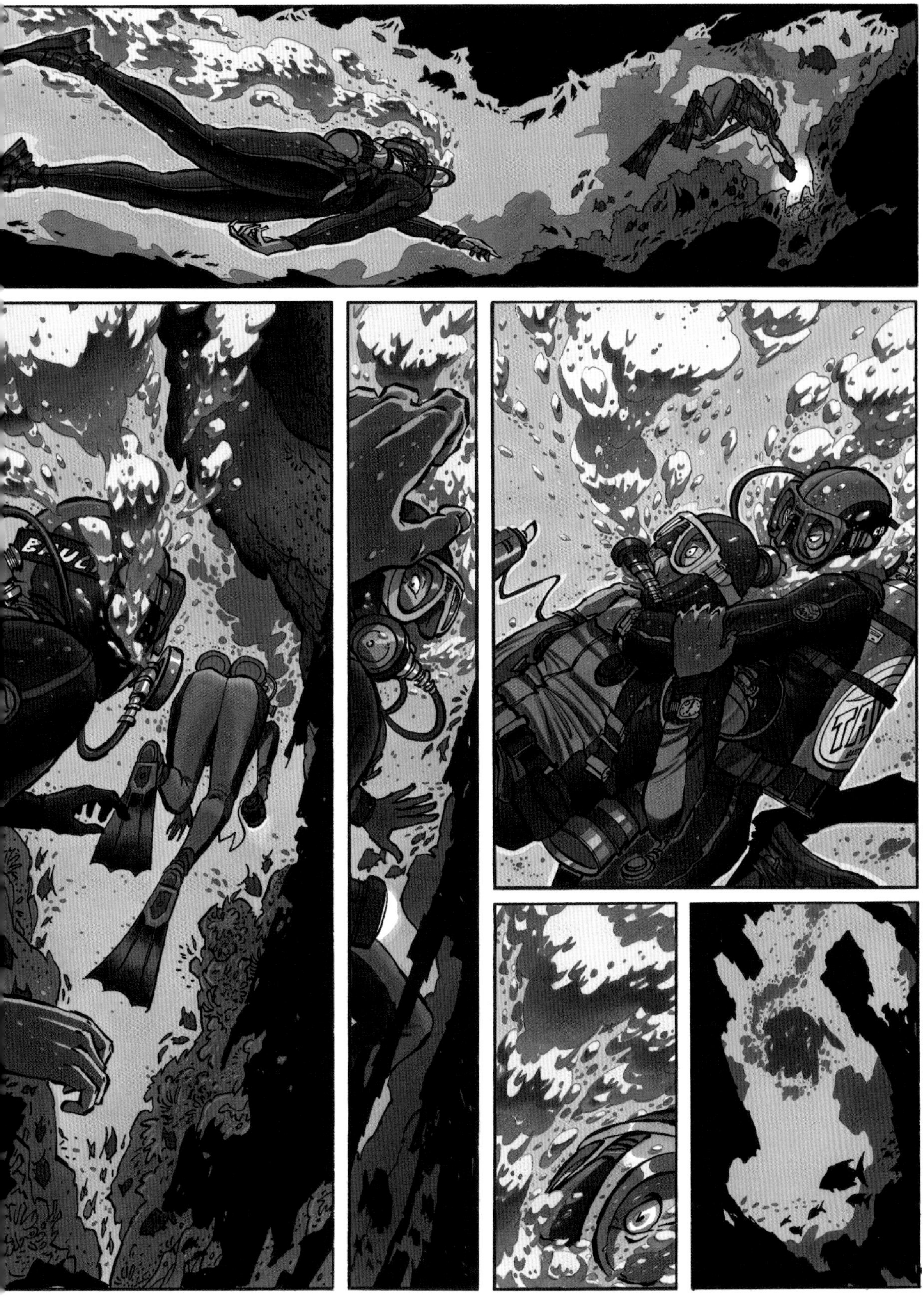

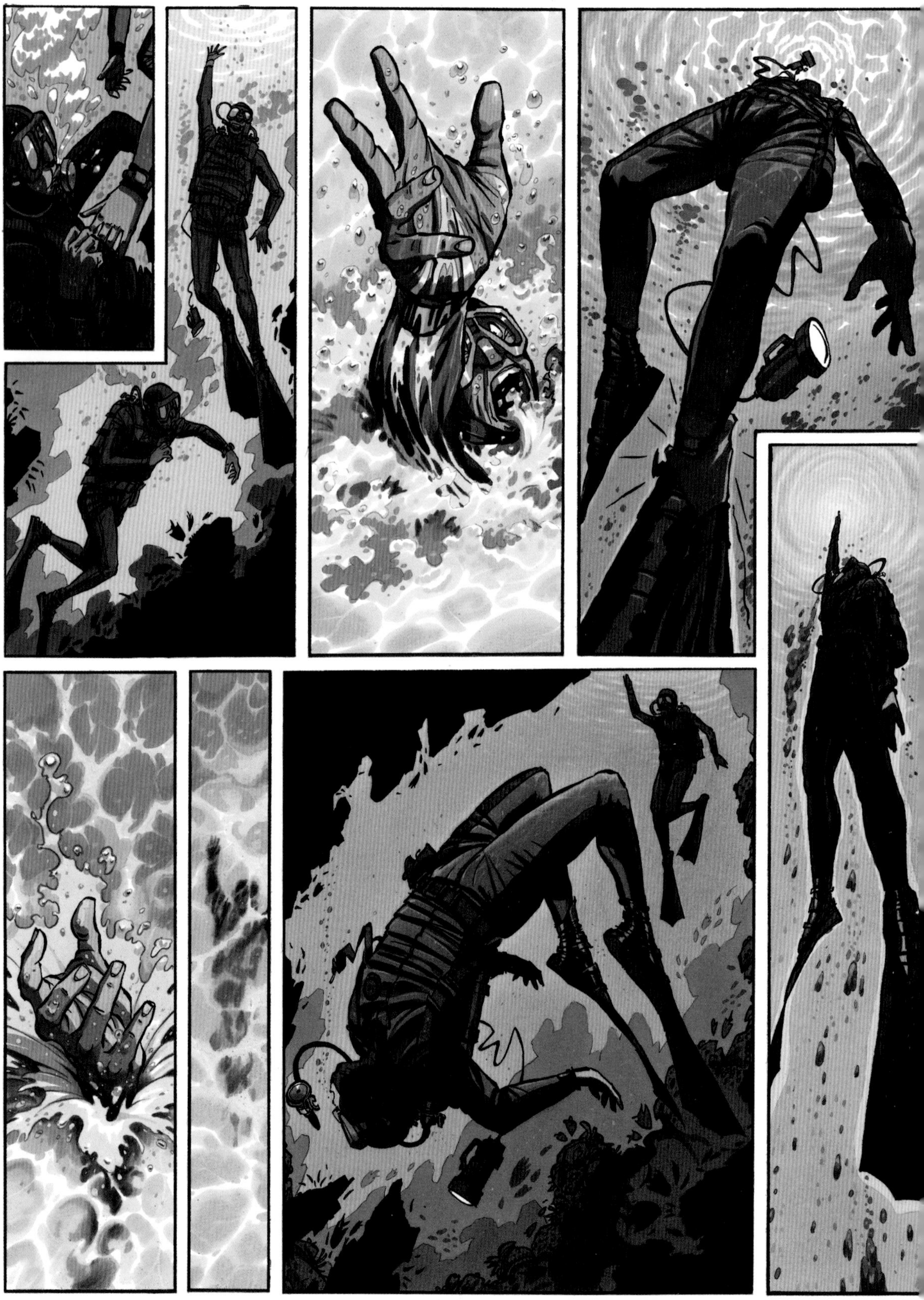

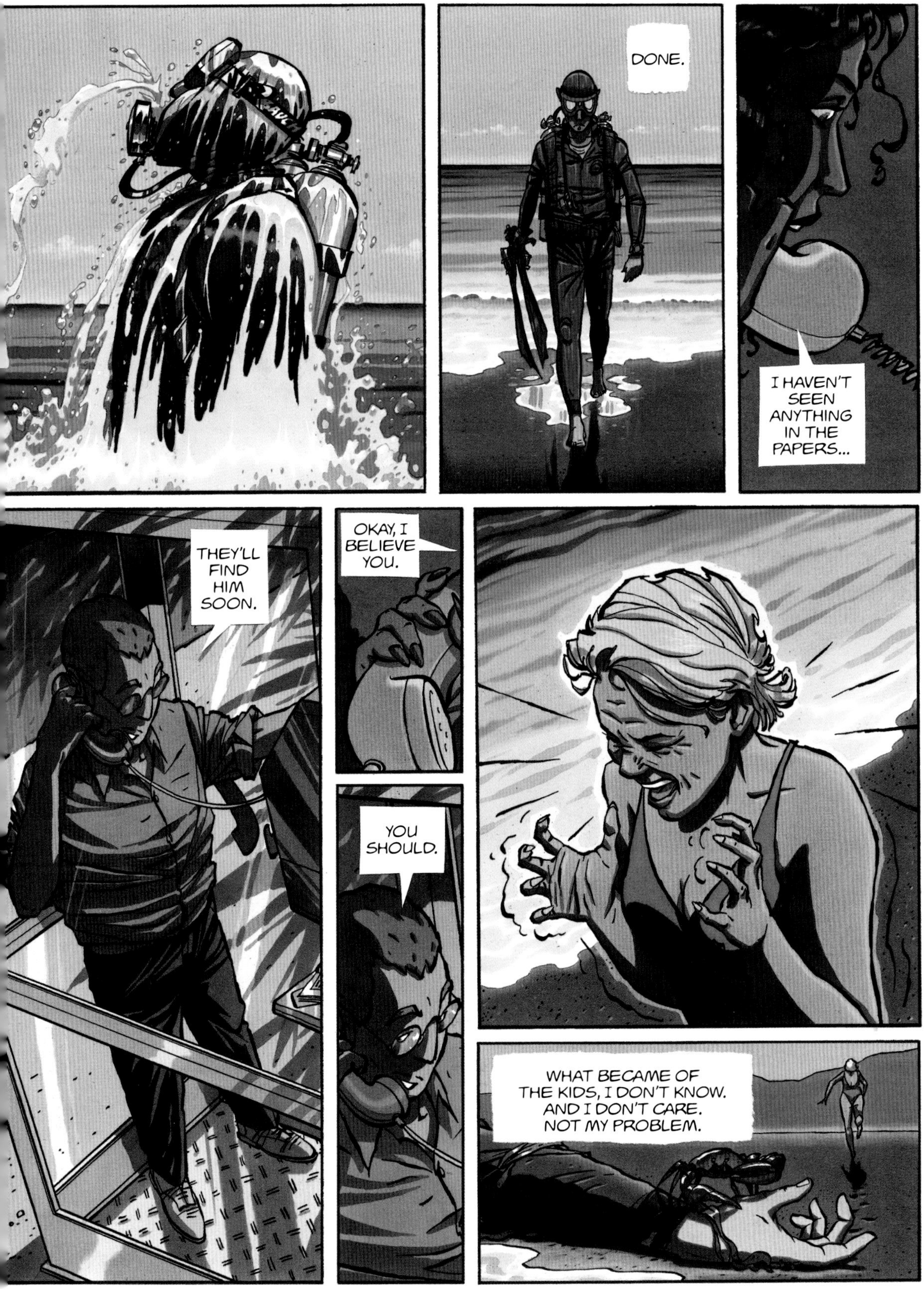
DONE.
I HAVEN'T SEEN ANYTHING IN THE PAPERS...
THEY'LL FIND HIM SOON.
OKAY, I BELIEVE YOU.
YOU SHOULD.
WHAT BECAME OF THE KIDS, I DON'T KNOW. AND I DON'T CARE. NOT MY PROBLEM.

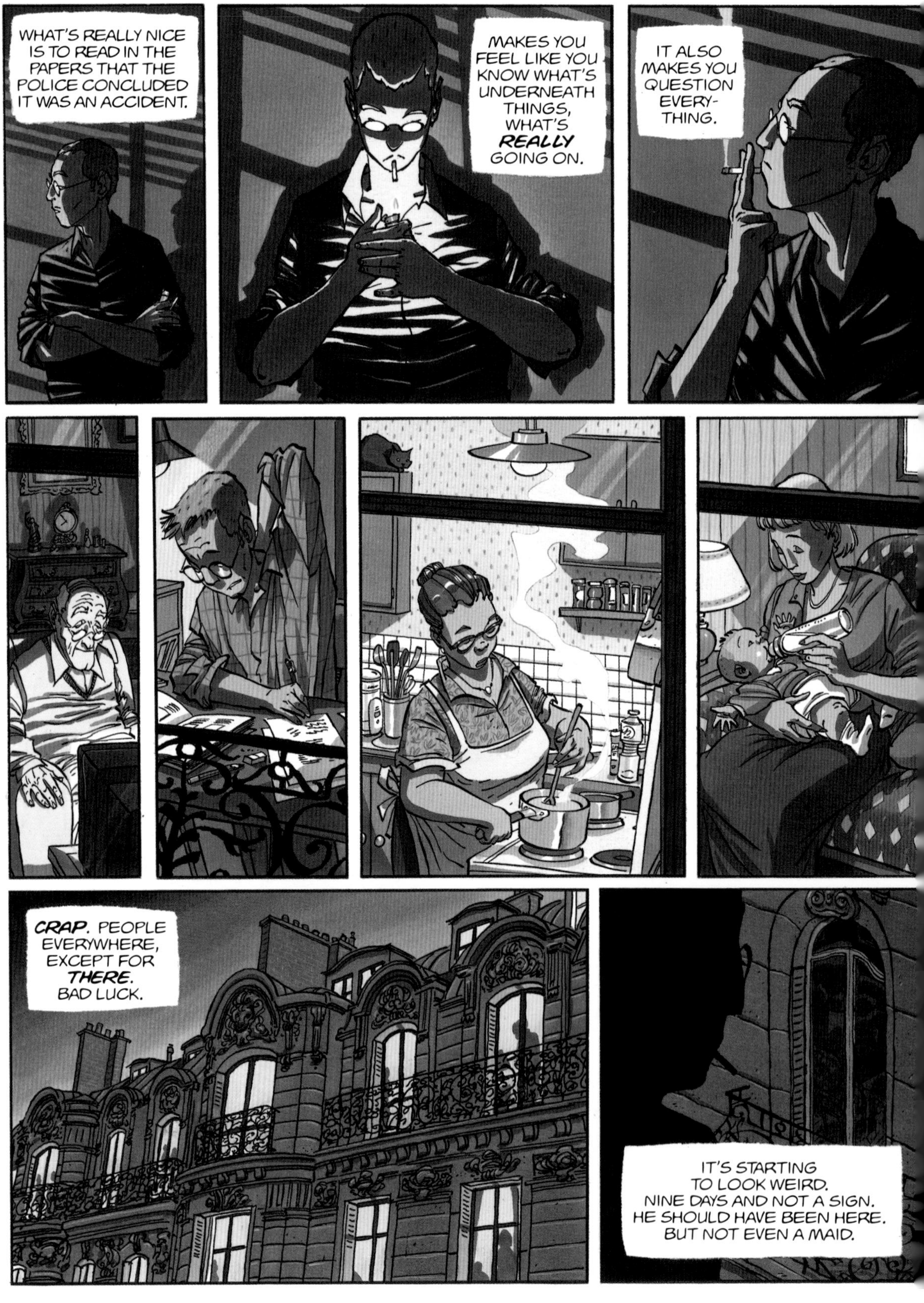
WHAT'S REALLY NICE IS TO READ IN THE PAPERS THAT THE POLICE CONCLUDED IT WAS AN ACCIDENT.
MAKES YOU FEEL LIKE YOU KNOW WHAT'S UNDERNEATH THINGS, WHAT'S ***REALLY*** GOING ON.
IT ALSO MAKES YOU QUESTION EVERY-THING.
CRAP. PEOPLE EVERYWHERE, EXCEPT FOR ***THERE***. BAD LUCK.
IT'S STARTING TO LOOK WEIRD. NINE DAYS AND NOT A SIGN. HE SHOULD HAVE BEEN HERE. BUT NOT EVEN A MAID.

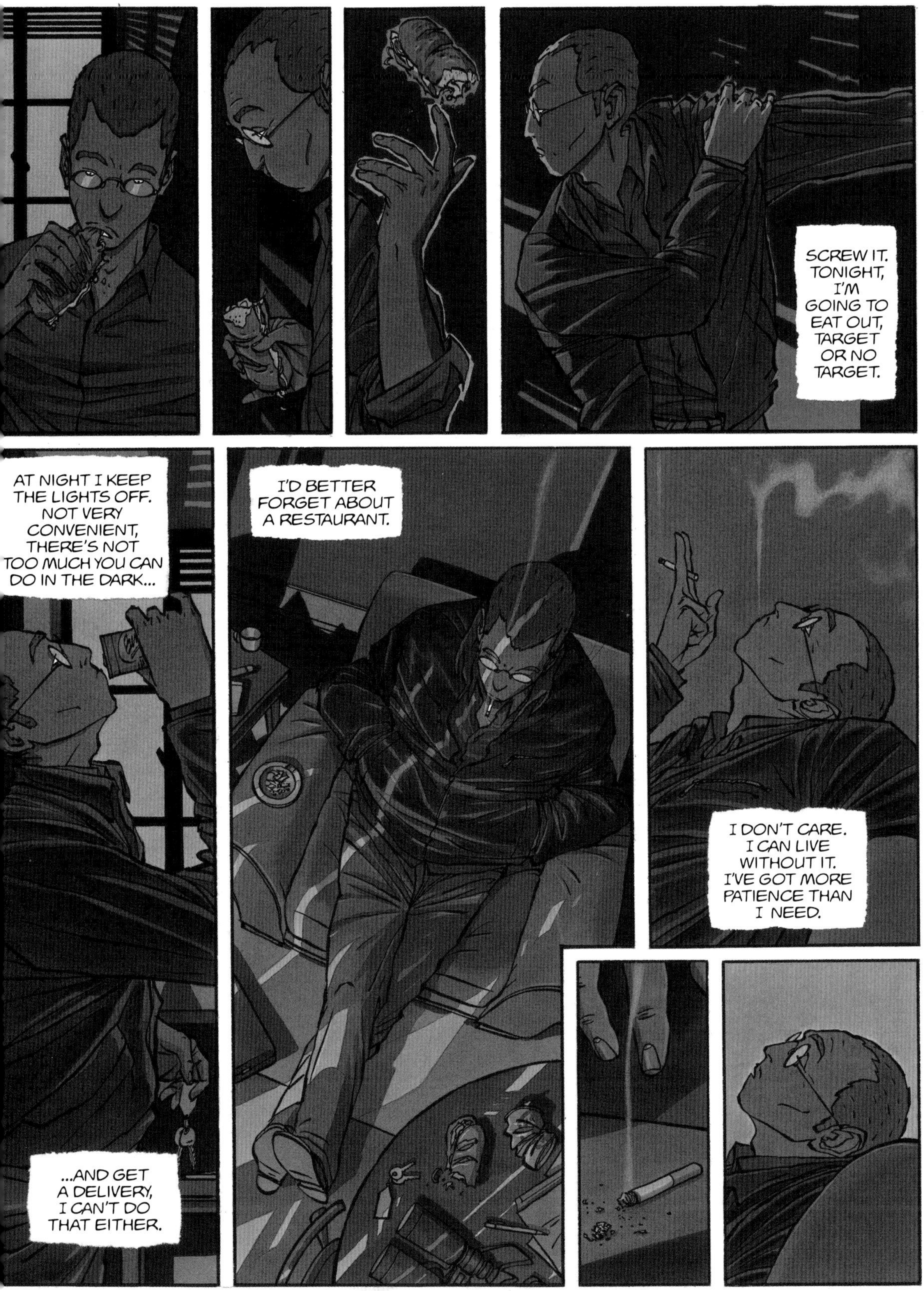
SCREW IT. TONIGHT, I'M GOING TO EAT OUT, TARGET OR NO TARGET.
AT NIGHT I KEEP THE LIGHTS OFF. NOT VERY CONVENIENT, THERE'S NOT TOO MUCH YOU CAN DO IN THE DARK...
...AND GET A DELIVERY, I CAN'T DO THAT EITHER.
I'D BETTER FORGET ABOUT A RESTAURANT.
I DON'T CARE. I CAN LIVE WITHOUT IT. I'VE GOT MORE PATIENCE THAN I NEED.

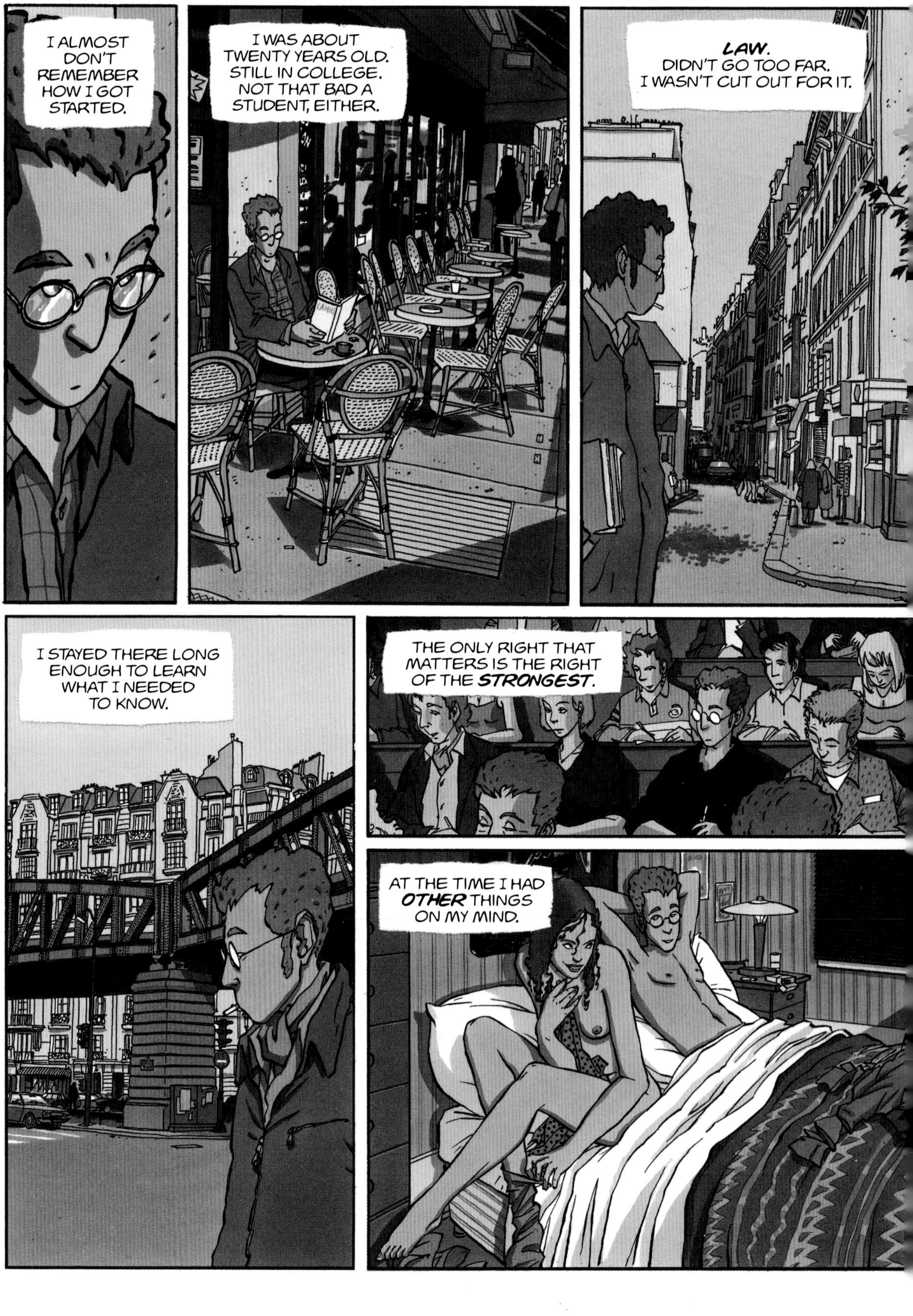
I ALMOST DON'T REMEMBER HOW I GOT STARTED.
I WAS ABOUT TWENTY YEARS OLD. STILL IN COLLEGE. NOT THAT BAD A STUDENT, EITHER.
CAMUS
LAW.
DIDN'T GO TOO FAR. I WASN'T CUT OUT FOR IT.
I STAYED THERE LONG ENOUGH TO LEARN WHAT I NEEDED TO KNOW.
THE ONLY RIGHT THAT MATTERS IS THE RIGHT OF THE STRONGEST.
AT THE TIME I HAD OTHER THINGS ON MY MIND.

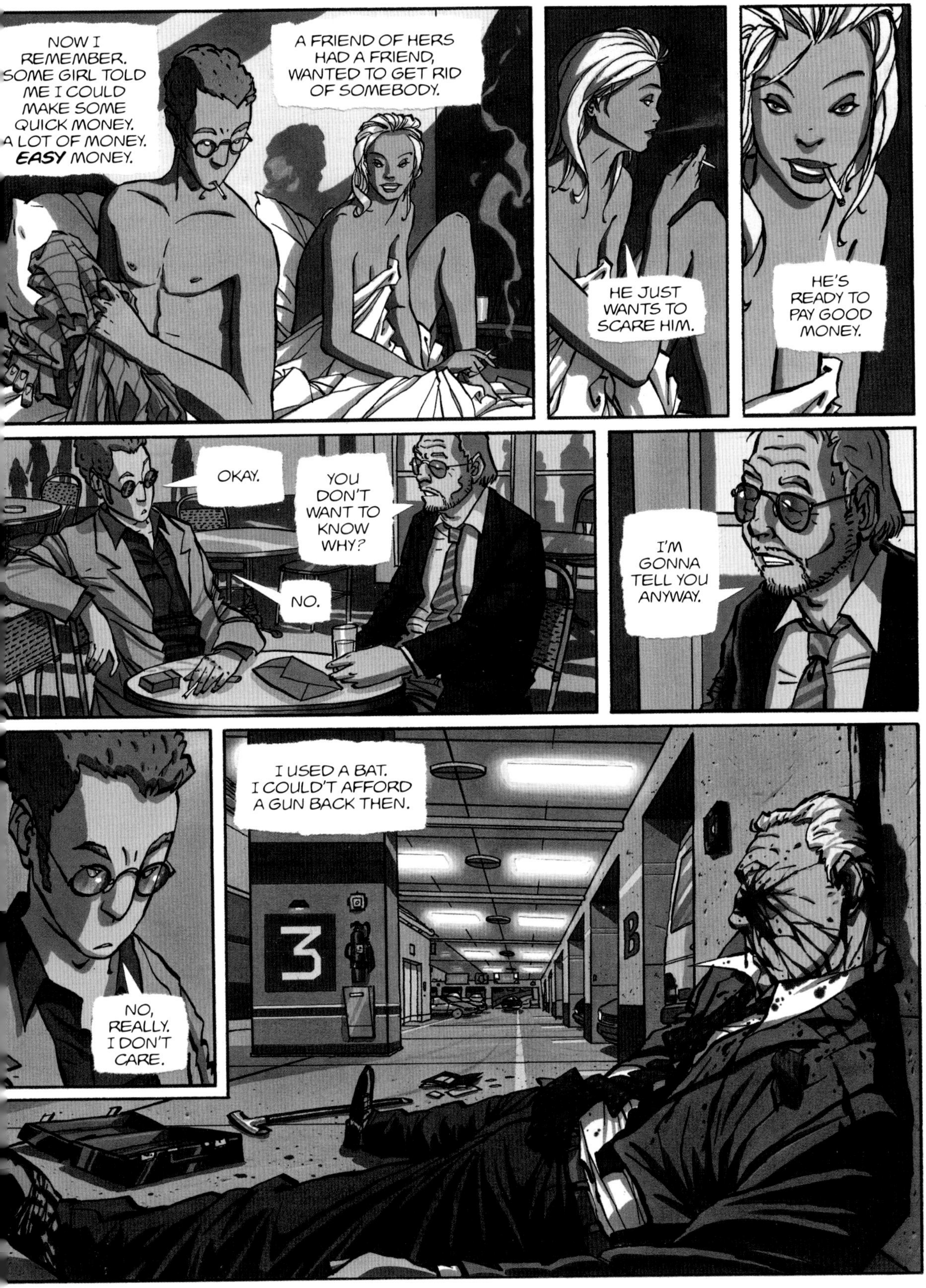
NOW I REMEMBER. SOME GIRL TOLD ME I COULD MAKE SOME QUICK MONEY. A LOT OF MONEY. EASY MONEY.
A FRIEND OF HERS HAD A FRIEND, WANTED TO GET RID OF SOMEBODY.
HE JUST WANTS TO SCARE HIM.
HE'S READY TO PAY GOOD MONEY.
OKAY.
YOU DON'T WANT TO KNOW WHY?
NO.
I'M GONNA TELL YOU ANYWAY.
NO, REALLY. I DON'T CARE.
I USED A BAT. I COULD'T AFFORD A GUN BACK THEN.
3
B

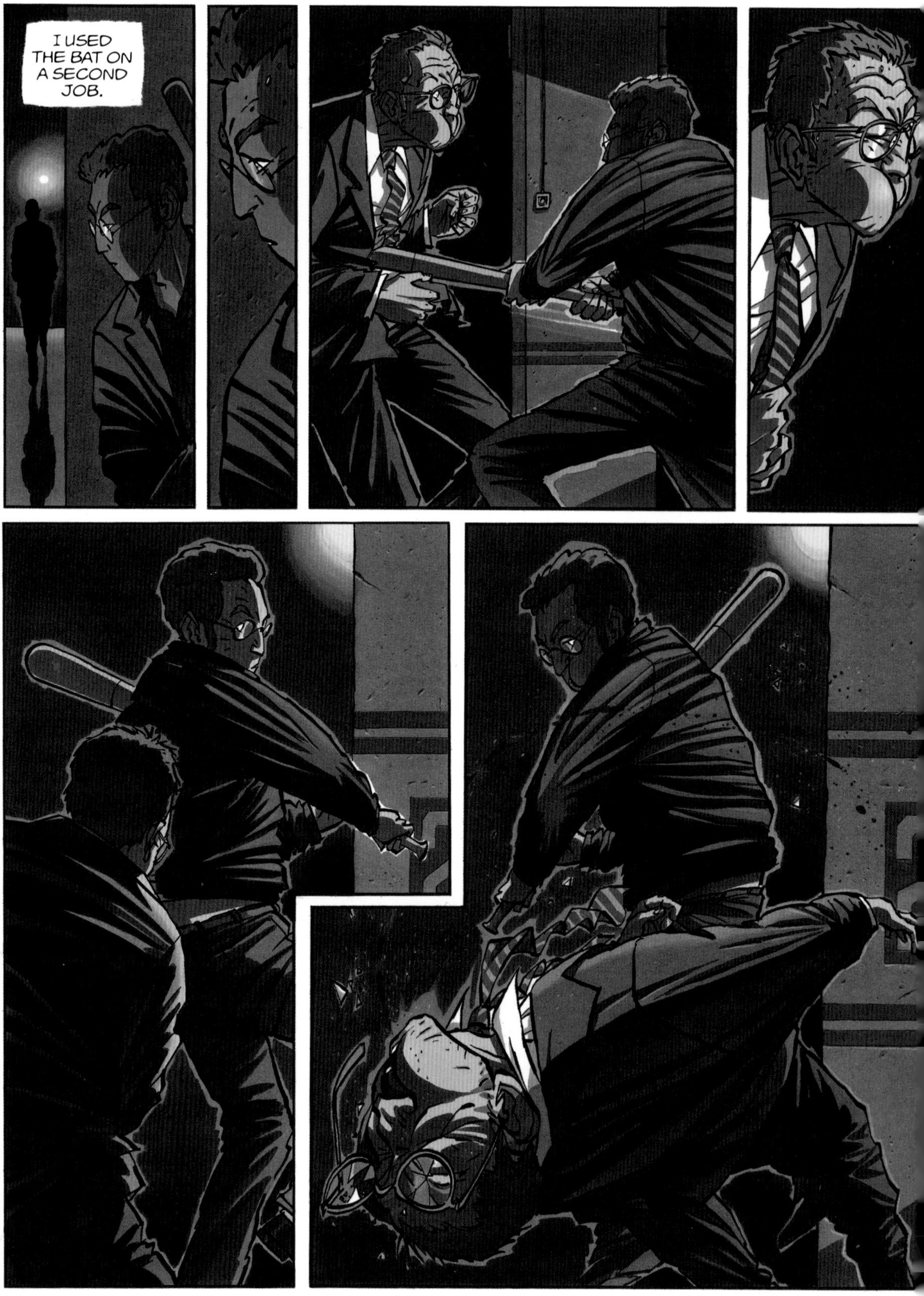
I USED THE BAT ON A SECOND JOB.

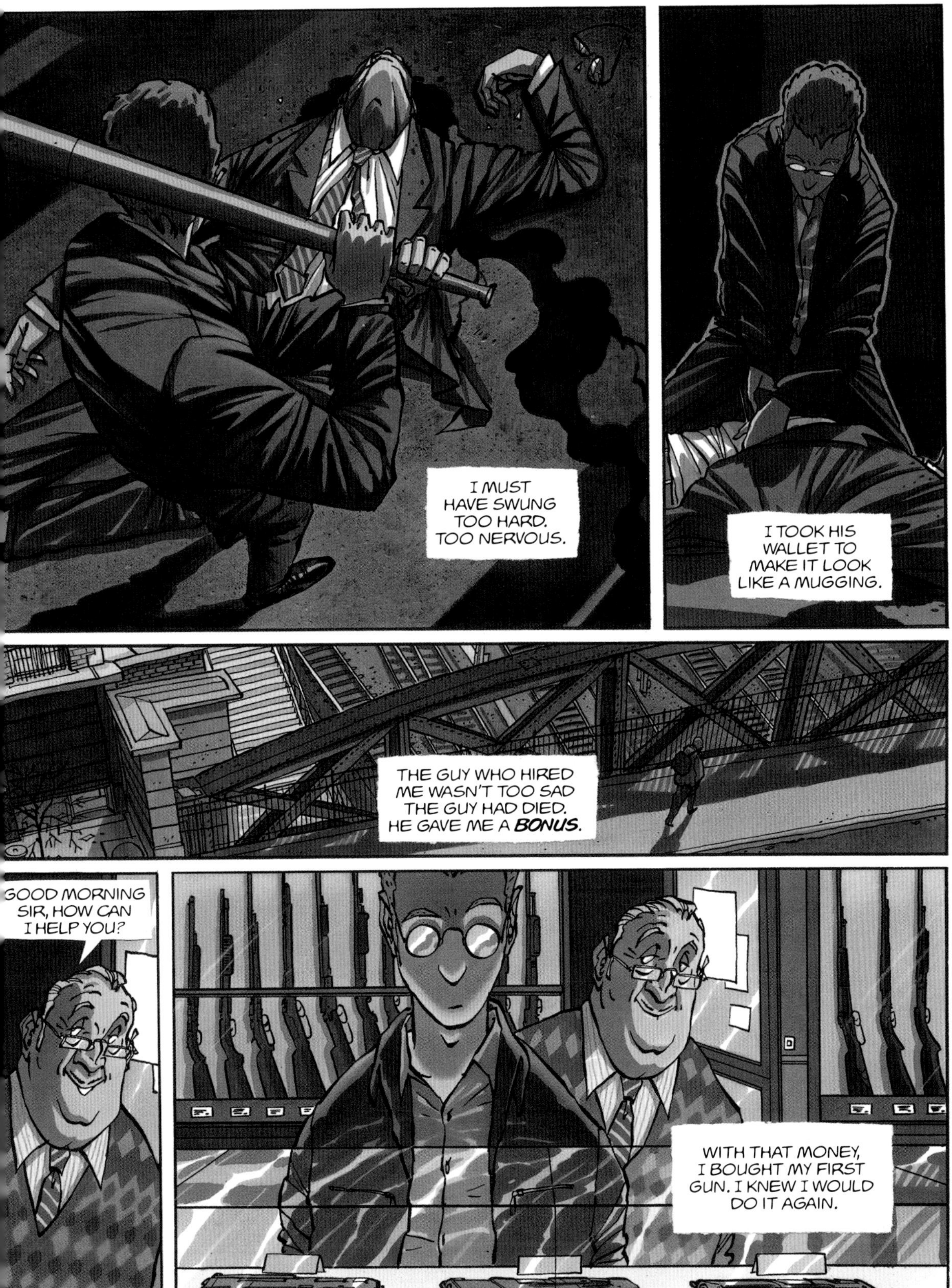
I MUST HAVE SWUNG TOO HARD. TOO NERVOUS.
I TOOK HIS WALLET TO MAKE IT LOOK LIKE A MUGGING.
THE GUY WHO HIRED ME WASN'T TOO SAD THE GUY HAD DIED. HE GAVE ME A **BONUS**.
GOOD MORNING SIR, HOW CAN I HELP YOU?
WITH THAT MONEY, I BOUGHT MY FIRST GUN. I KNEW I WOULD DO IT AGAIN.

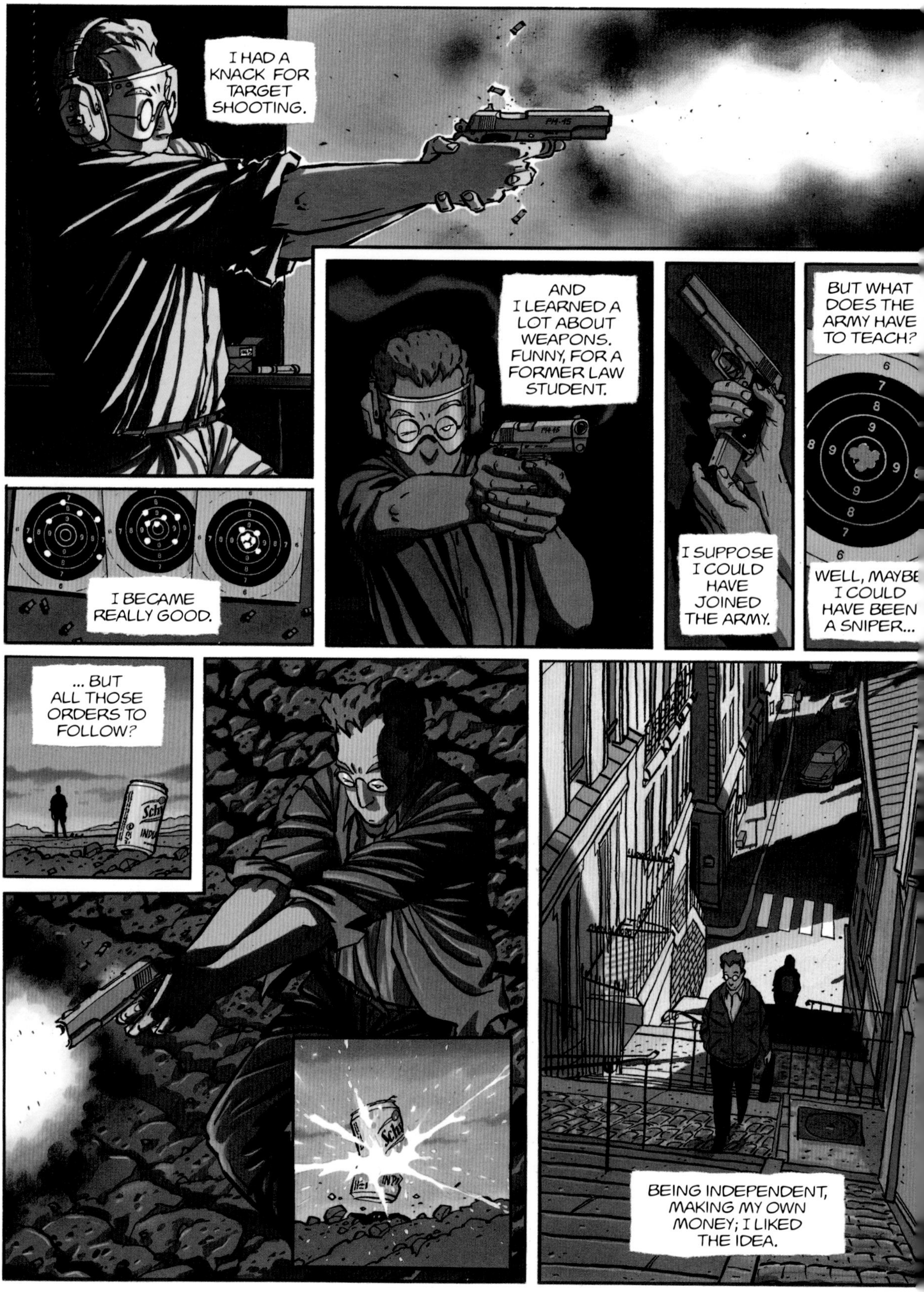
I HAD A KNACK FOR TARGET SHOOTING.
I BECAME REALLY GOOD.
AND I LEARNED A LOT ABOUT WEAPONS. FUNNY, FOR A FORMER LAW STUDENT.
I SUPPOSE I COULD HAVE JOINED THE ARMY.
BUT WHAT DOES THE ARMY HAVE TO TEACH?
WELL, MAYBE I COULD HAVE BEEN A SNIPER...
... BUT ALL THOSE ORDERS TO FOLLOW?
BEING INDEPENDENT, MAKING MY OWN MONEY; I LIKED THE IDEA.

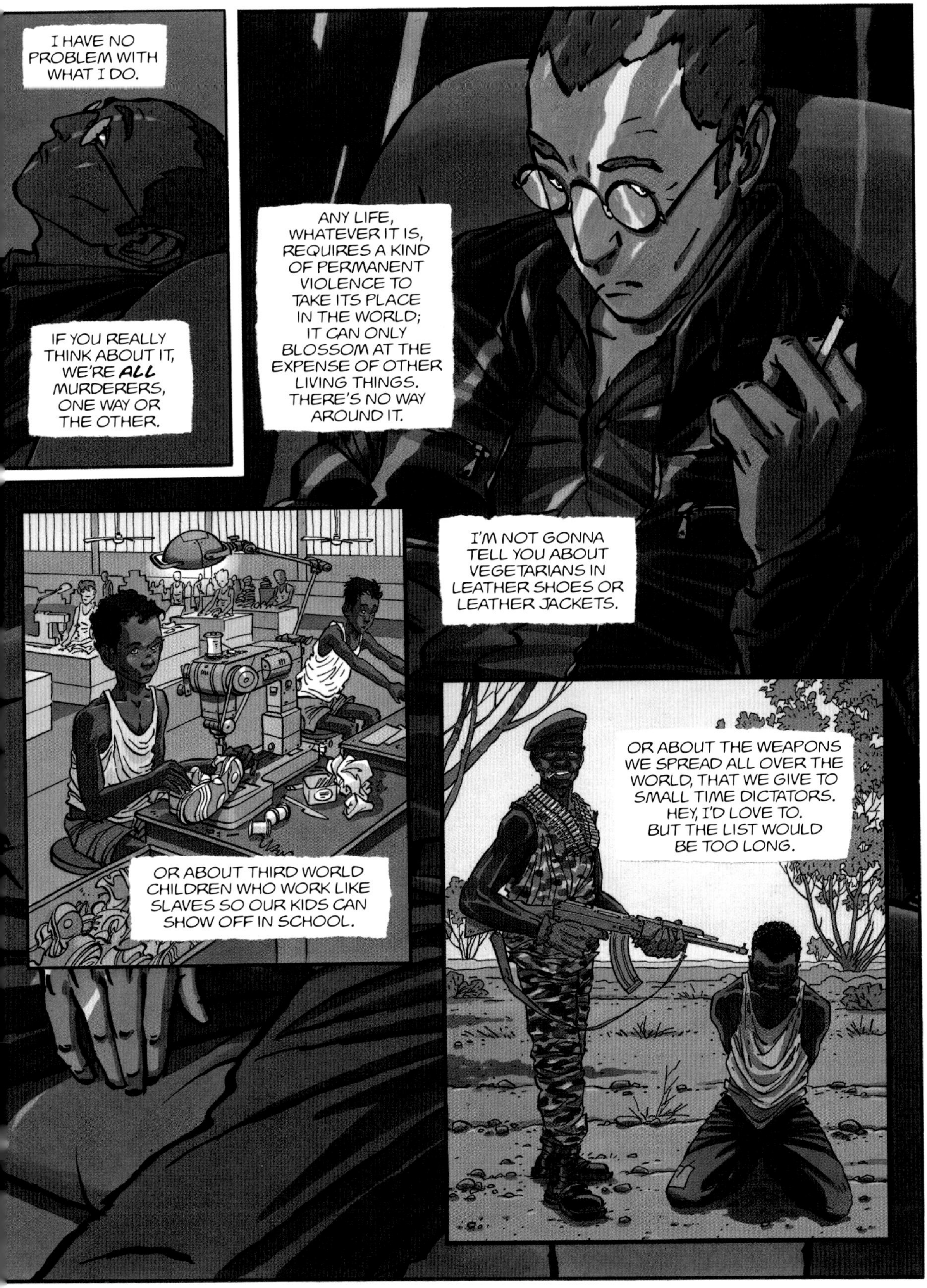
I HAVE NO PROBLEM WITH WHAT I DO.
IF YOU REALLY THINK ABOUT IT, WE'RE ALL MURDERERS, ONE WAY OR THE OTHER.
ANY LIFE, WHATEVER IT IS, REQUIRES A KIND OF PERMANENT VIOLENCE TO TAKE ITS PLACE IN THE WORLD; IT CAN ONLY BLOSSOM AT THE EXPENSE OF OTHER LIVING THINGS. THERE'S NO WAY AROUND IT.
I'M NOT GONNA TELL YOU ABOUT VEGETARIANS IN LEATHER SHOES OR LEATHER JACKETS.
OR ABOUT THIRD WORLD CHILDREN WHO WORK LIKE SLAVES SO OUR KIDS CAN SHOW OFF IN SCHOOL.
OR ABOUT THE WEAPONS WE SPREAD ALL OVER THE WORLD, THAT WE GIVE TO SMALL TIME DICTATORS. HEY, I'D LOVE TO. BUT THE LIST WOULD BE TOO LONG.

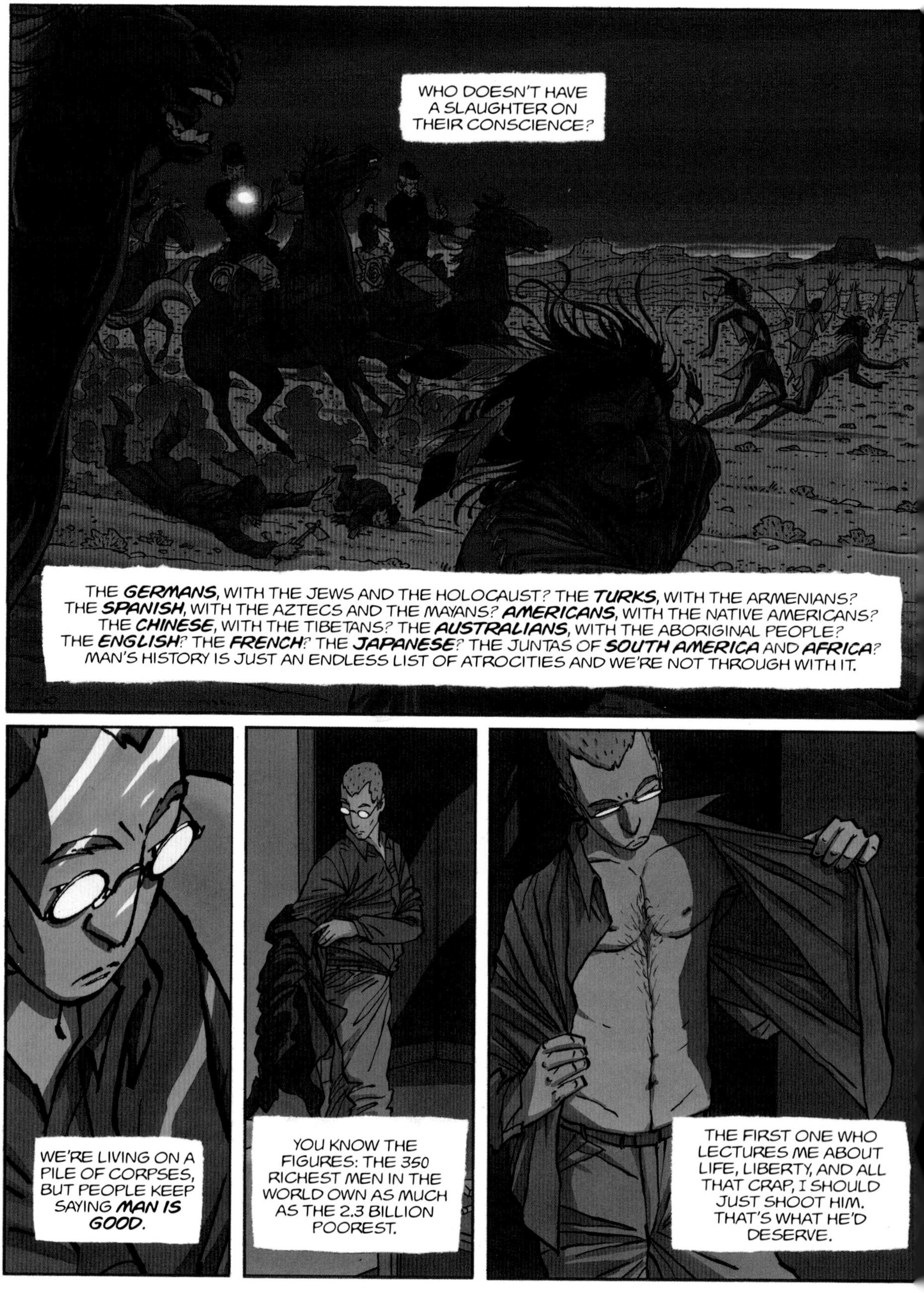
WHO DOESN'T HAVE A SLAUGHTER ON THEIR CONSCIENCE?
THE **GERMANS**, WITH THE JEWS AND THE HOLOCAUST? THE **TURKS**, WITH THE ARMENIANS? THE **SPANISH**, WITH THE AZTECS AND THE MAYANS? **AMERICANS**, WITH THE NATIVE AMERICANS? THE **CHINESE**, WITH THE TIBETANS? THE **AUSTRALIANS**, WITH THE ABORIGINAL PEOPLE? THE **ENGLISH**? THE **FRENCH**? THE **JAPANESE**? THE JUNTAS OF **SOUTH AMERICA** AND **AFRICA**? MAN'S HISTORY IS JUST AN ENDLESS LIST OF ATROCITIES AND WE'RE NOT THROUGH WITH IT.
WE'RE LIVING ON A PILE OF CORPSES, BUT PEOPLE KEEP SAYING **MAN IS GOOD**.
YOU KNOW THE FIGURES: THE 350 RICHEST MEN IN THE WORLD OWN AS MUCH AS THE 2.3 BILLION POOREST.
THE FIRST ONE WHO LECTURES ME ABOUT LIFE, LIBERTY, AND ALL THAT CRAP, I SHOULD JUST SHOOT HIM. THAT'S WHAT HE'D DESERVE.

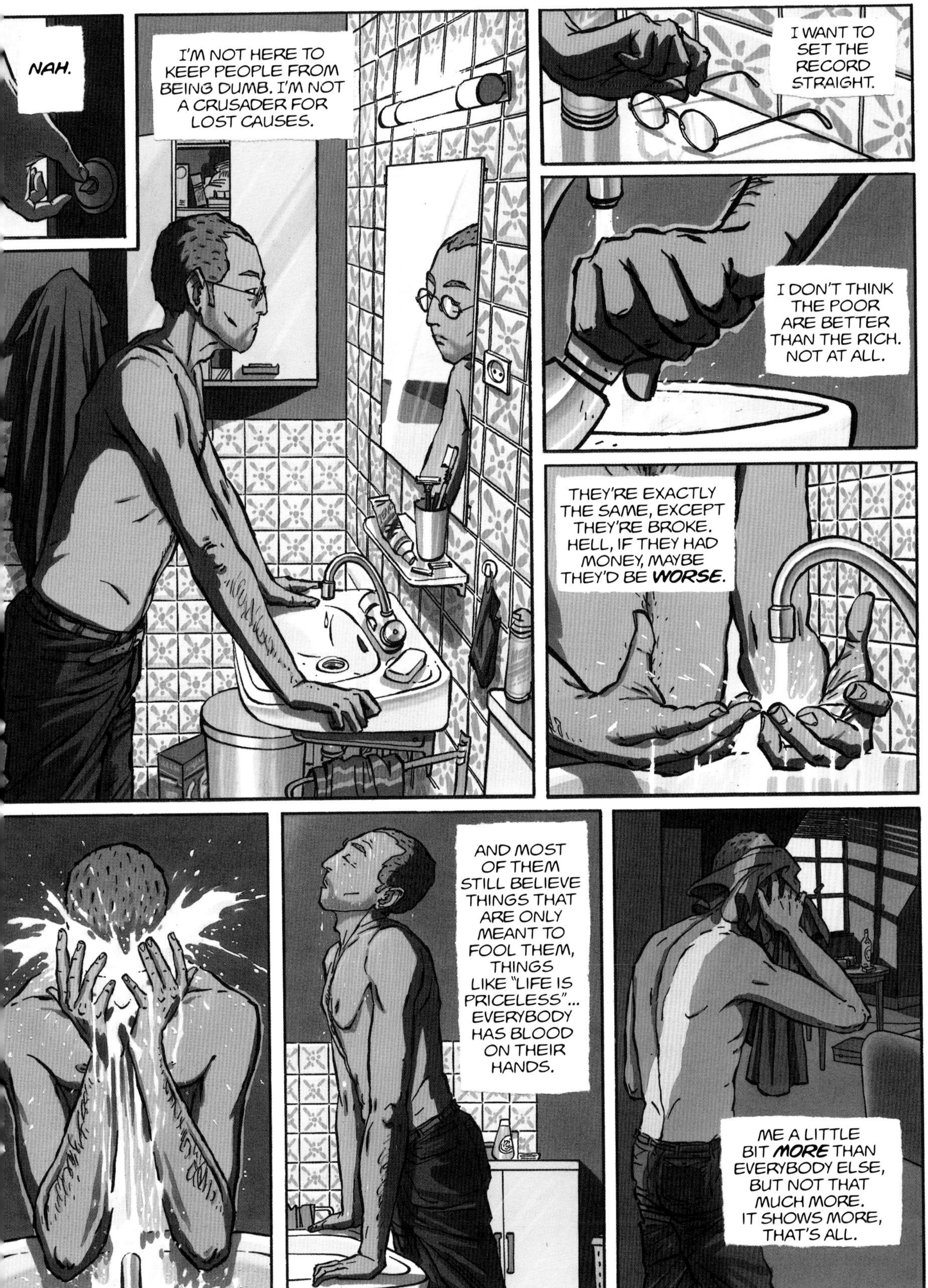
NAH.
I'M NOT HERE TO KEEP PEOPLE FROM BEING DUMB. I'M NOT A CRUSADER FOR LOST CAUSES.
I WANT TO SET THE RECORD STRAIGHT.
I DON'T THINK THE POOR ARE BETTER THAN THE RICH. NOT AT ALL.
THEY'RE EXACTLY THE SAME, EXCEPT THEY'RE BROKE. HELL, IF THEY HAD MONEY, MAYBE THEY'D BE **WORSE**.
AND MOST OF THEM STILL BELIEVE THINGS THAT ARE ONLY MEANT TO FOOL THEM, THINGS LIKE "LIFE IS PRICELESS"... EVERYBODY HAS BLOOD ON THEIR HANDS.
ME A LITTLE BIT **MORE** THAN EVERYBODY ELSE, BUT NOT THAT MUCH MORE. IT SHOWS MORE, THAT'S ALL.

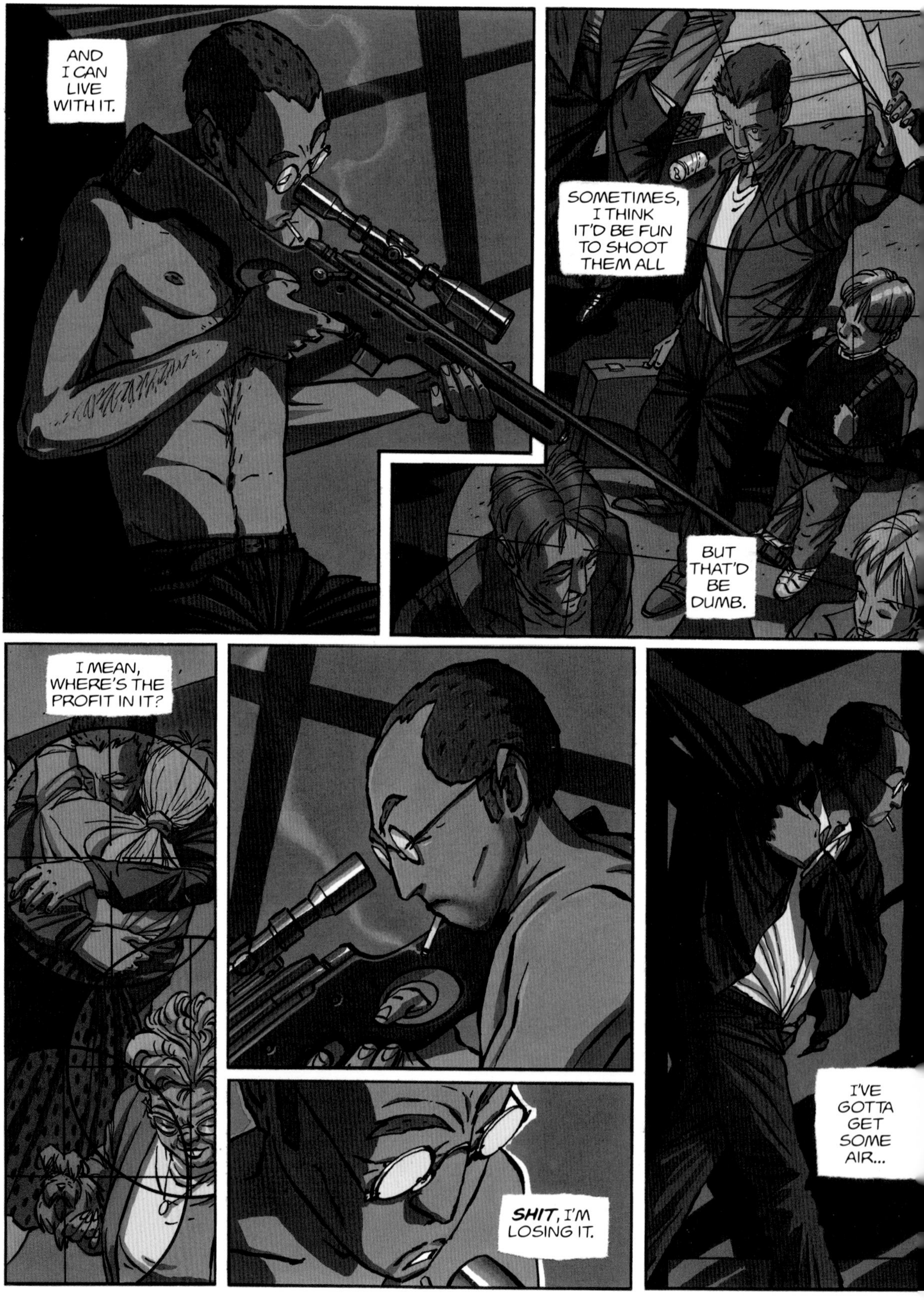
AND I CAN LIVE WITH IT.
SOMETIMES, I THINK IT'D BE FUN TO SHOOT THEM ALL
BUT THAT'D BE DUMB.
I MEAN, WHERE'S THE PROFIT IN IT?
SHIT, I'M LOSING IT.
I'VE GOTTA GET SOME AIR...

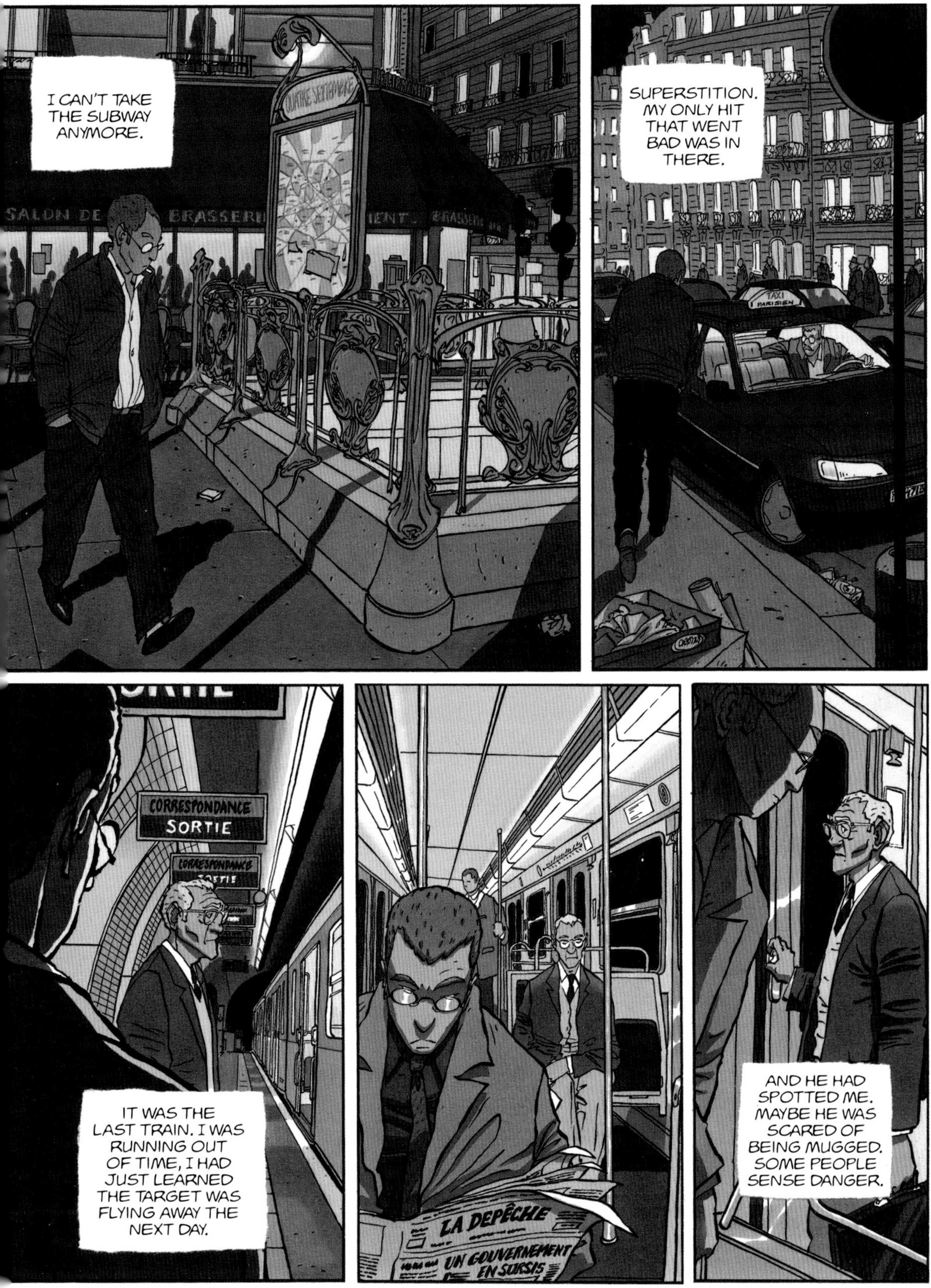
I CAN'T TAKE THE SUBWAY ANYMORE.
SUPERSTITION. MY ONLY HIT THAT WENT BAD WAS IN THERE.
TAXI PARISIEN
CORRESPONDANCE
SORTIE
IT WAS THE LAST TRAIN. I WAS RUNNING OUT OF TIME, I HAD JUST LEARNED THE TARGET WAS FLYING AWAY THE NEXT DAY.
LA DEPECHE
UN GOUVERNEMENT EN SURSIS
AND HE HAD SPOTTED ME. MAYBE HE WAS SCARED OF BEING MUGGED. SOME PEOPLE SENSE DANGER.

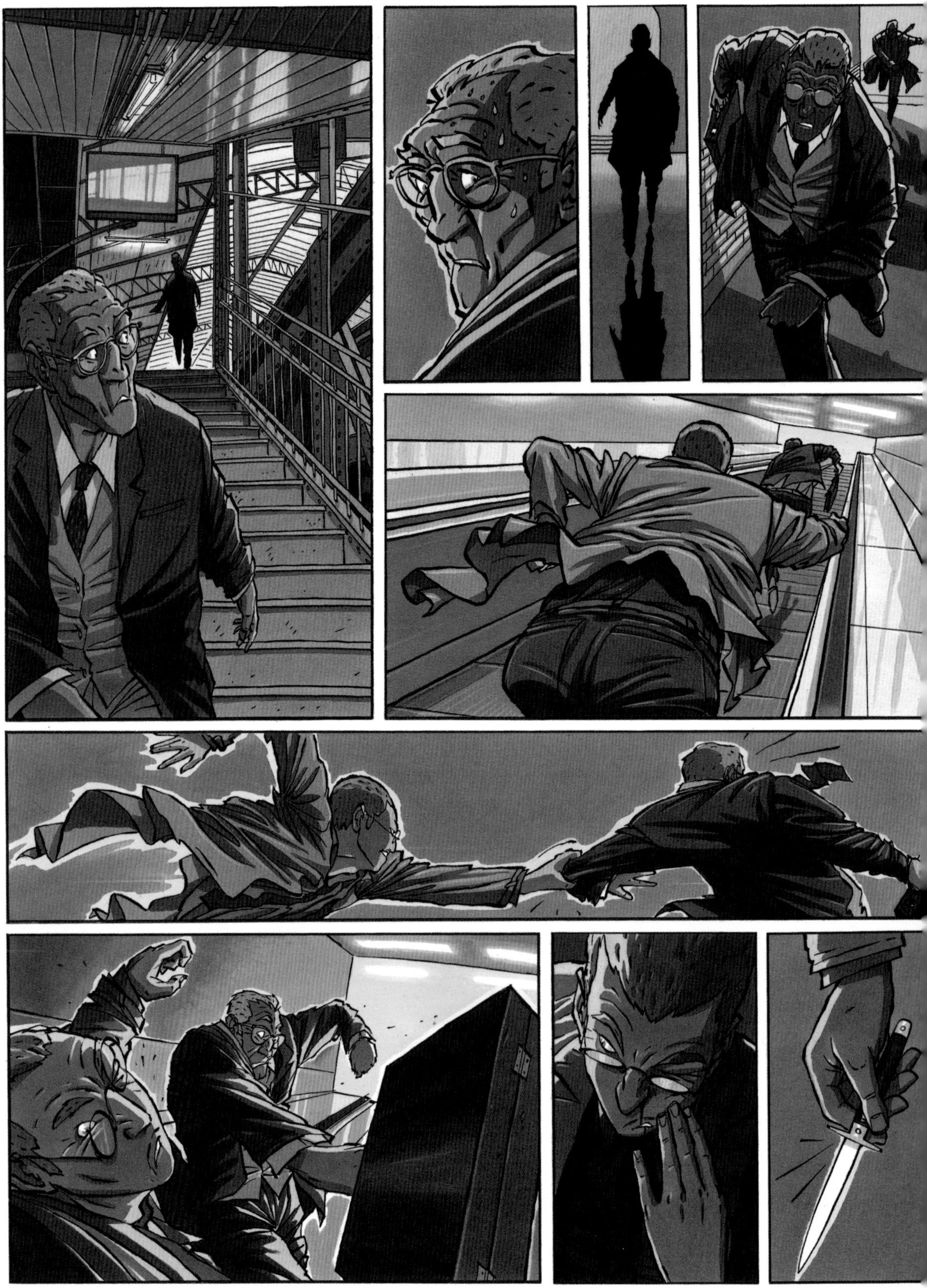

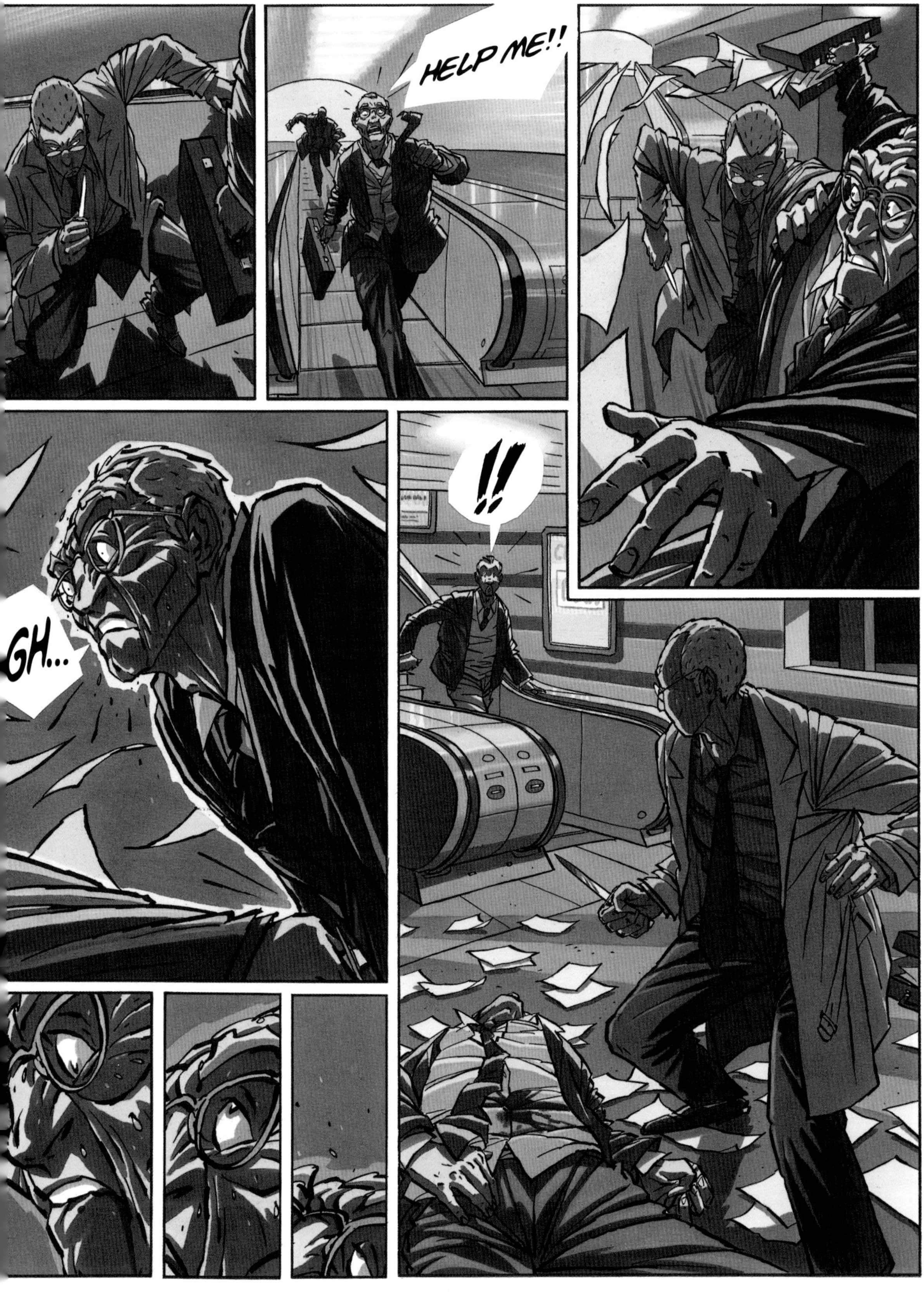
HELP ME!!
!!
GH...

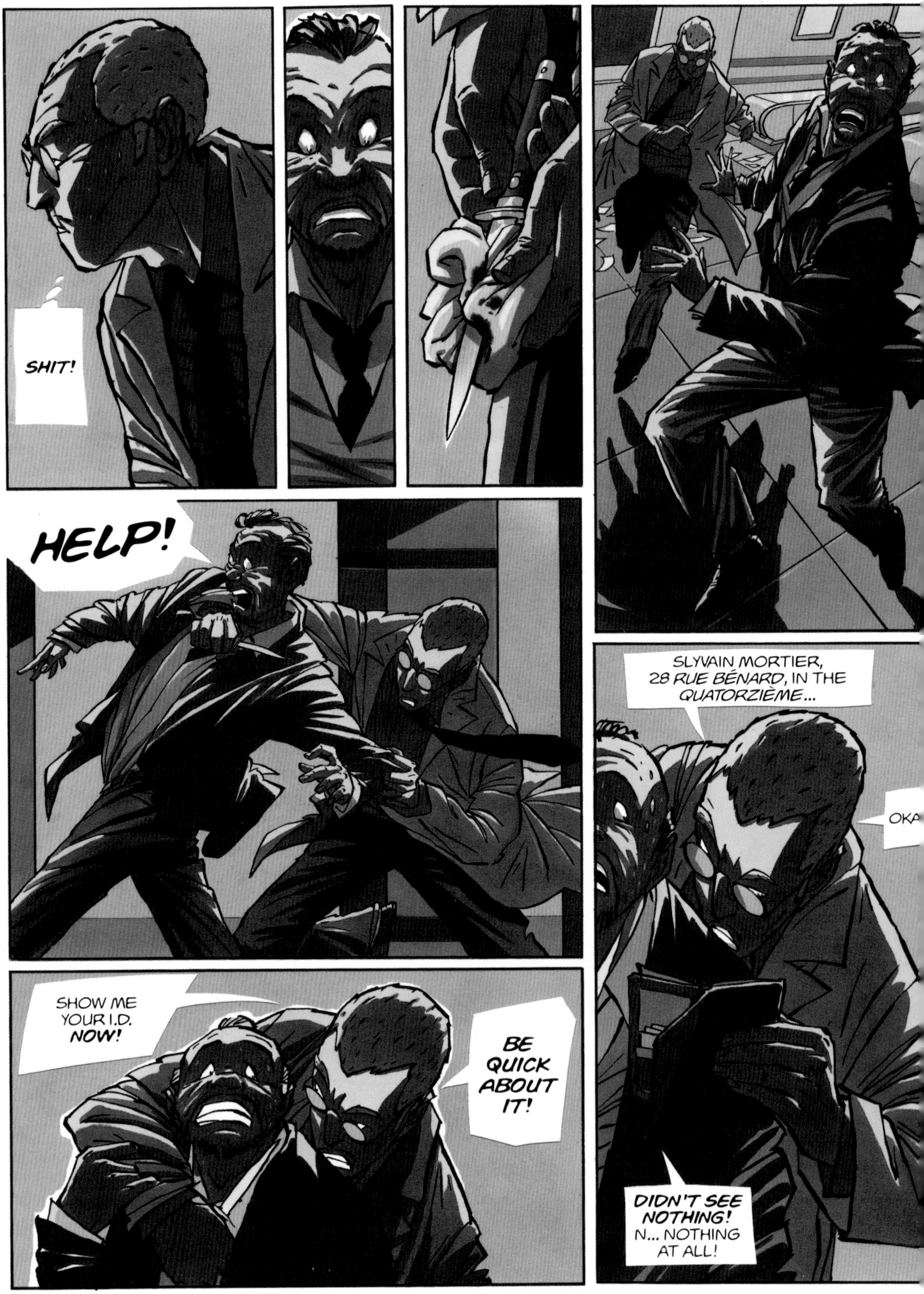
SHIT!
HELP!
SHOW ME YOUR I.D. NOW!
BE QUICK ABOUT IT!
SLYVAIN MORTIER, 28 RUE BÉNARD, IN THE QUATORZIÈME...
OKA
DIDN'T SEE NOTHING! N... NOTHING AT ALL!

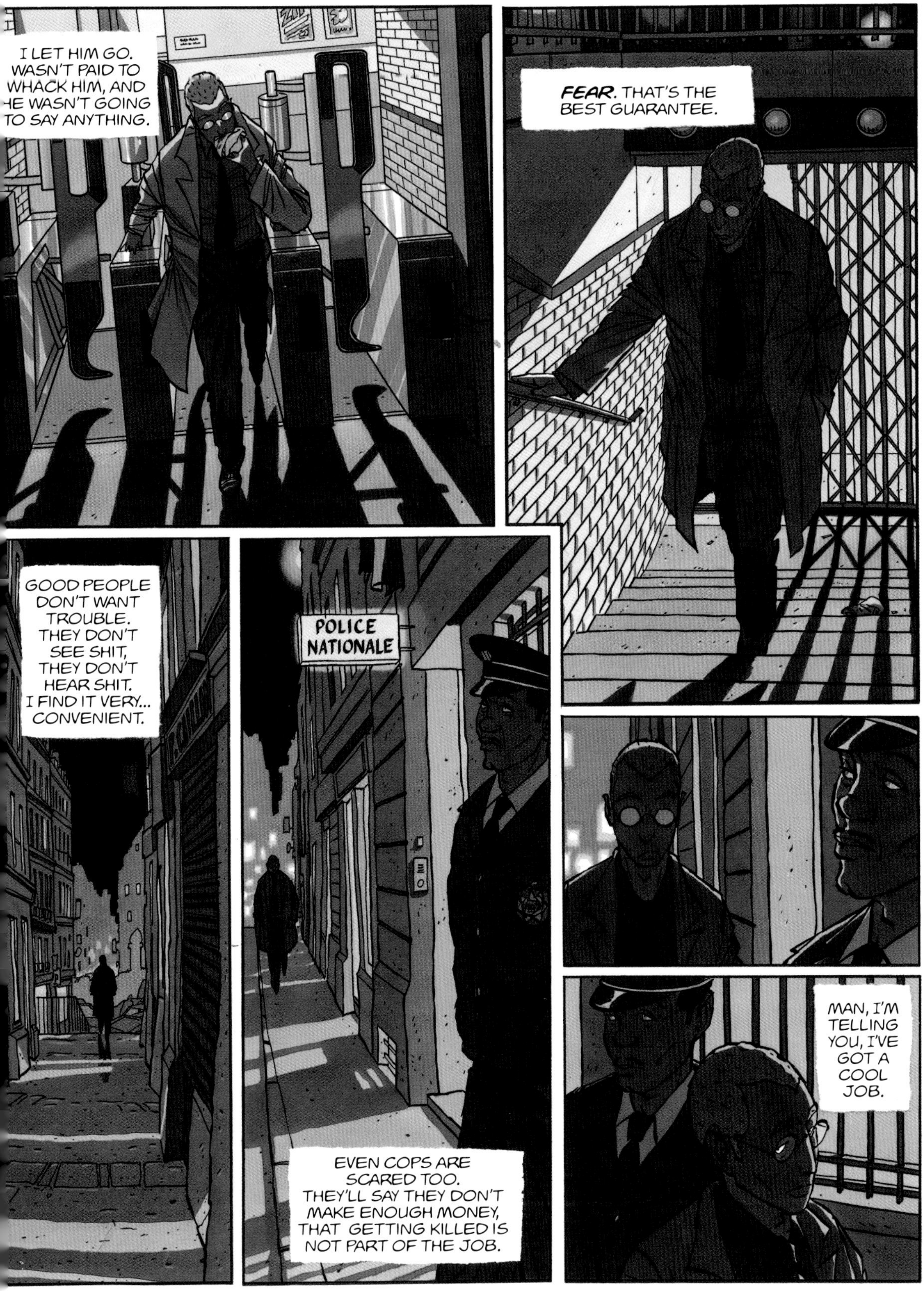
I LET HIM GO. WASN'T PAID TO WHACK HIM, AND HE WASN'T GOING TO SAY ANYTHING.
FEAR. THAT'S THE BEST GUARANTEE.
GOOD PEOPLE DON'T WANT TROUBLE. THEY DON'T SEE SHIT, THEY DON'T HEAR SHIT. I FIND IT VERY... CONVENIENT.
POLICE NATIONALE
EVEN COPS ARE SCARED TOO. THEY'LL SAY THEY DON'T MAKE ENOUGH MONEY, THAT GETTING KILLED IS NOT PART OF THE JOB.
MAN, I'M TELLING YOU, I'VE GOT A COOL JOB.

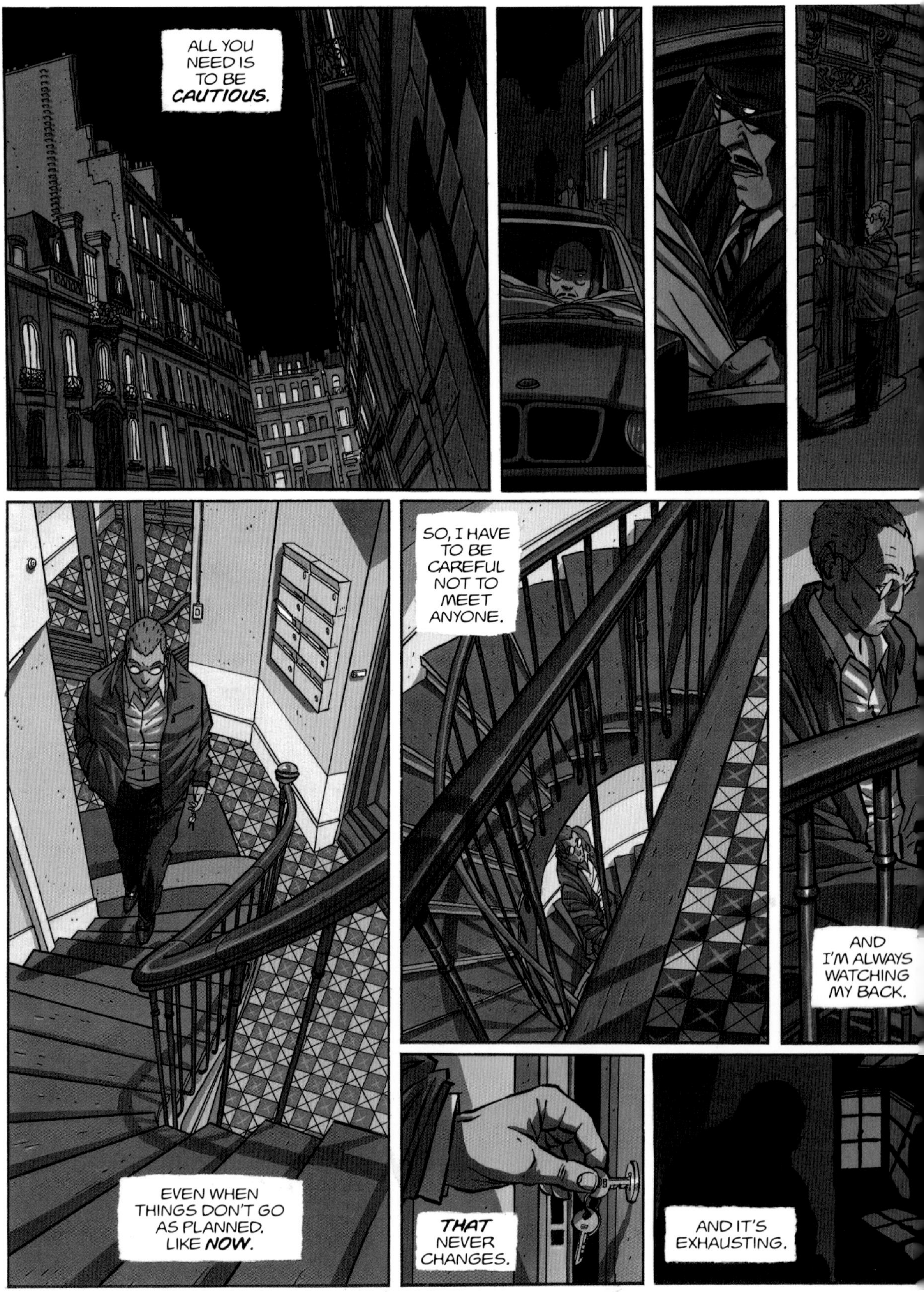
ALL YOU NEED IS TO BE CAUTIOUS.
EVEN WHEN THINGS DON'T GO AS PLANNED. LIKE NOW.
SO, I HAVE TO BE CAREFUL NOT TO MEET ANYONE.
AND I'M ALWAYS WATCHING MY BACK.
THAT NEVER CHANGES.
AND IT'S EXHAUSTING.

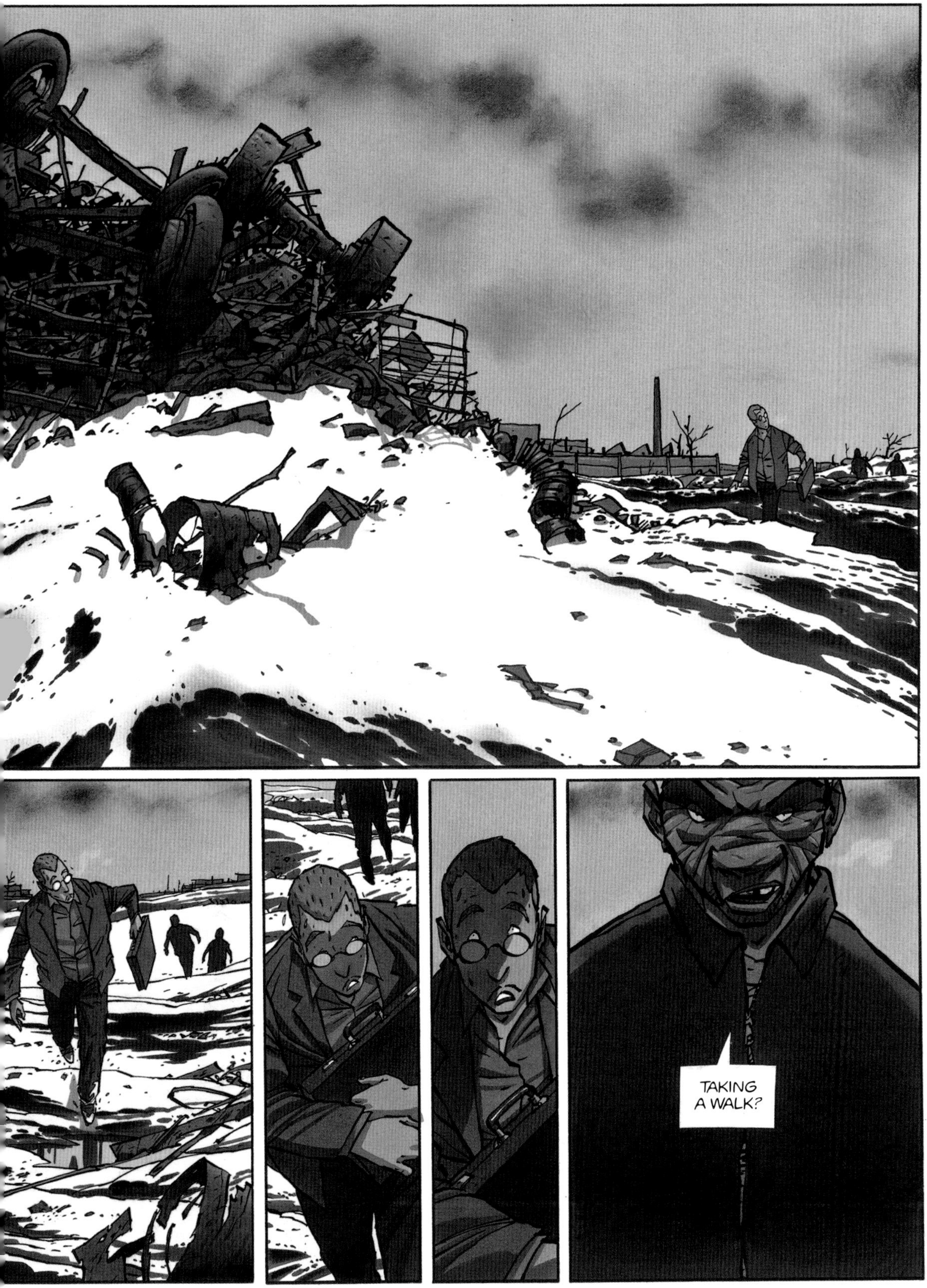
TAKING
A WALK?

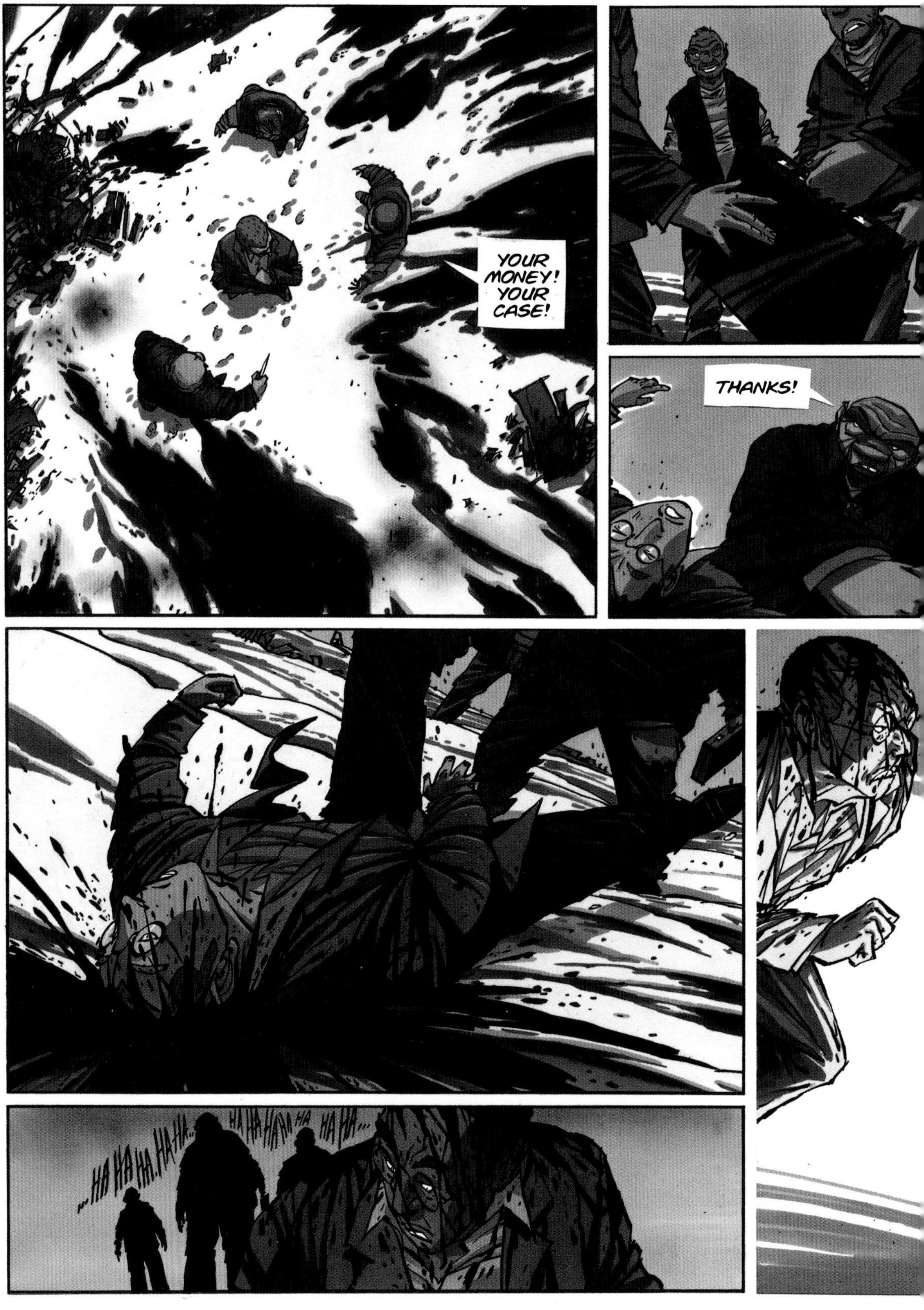
YOUR MONEY! YOUR CASE!
THANKS!
...HA HA HA...HA HA...
HA HA HA HA HA HA HA HA...

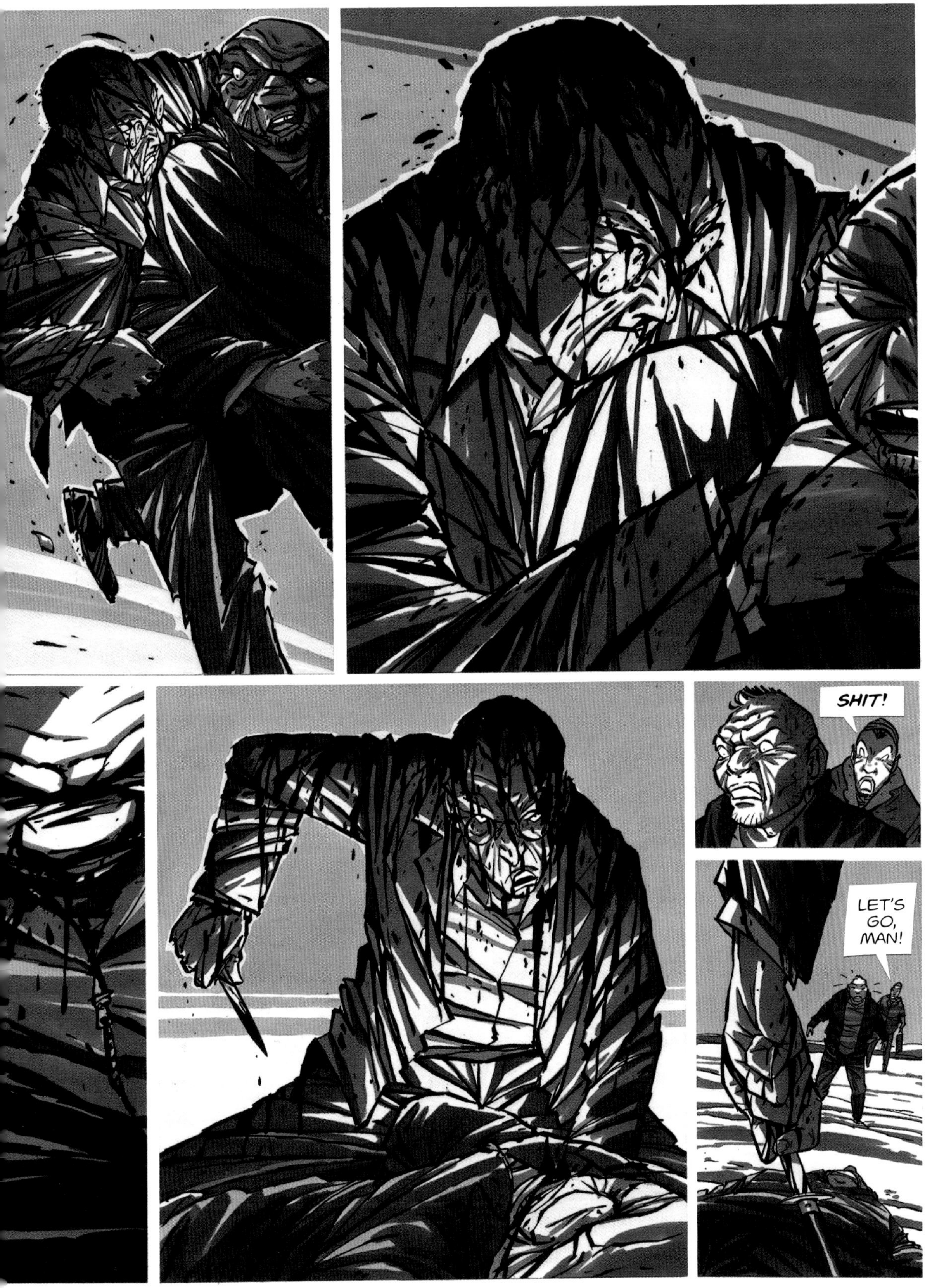
SHIT!
LET'S GO, MAN!

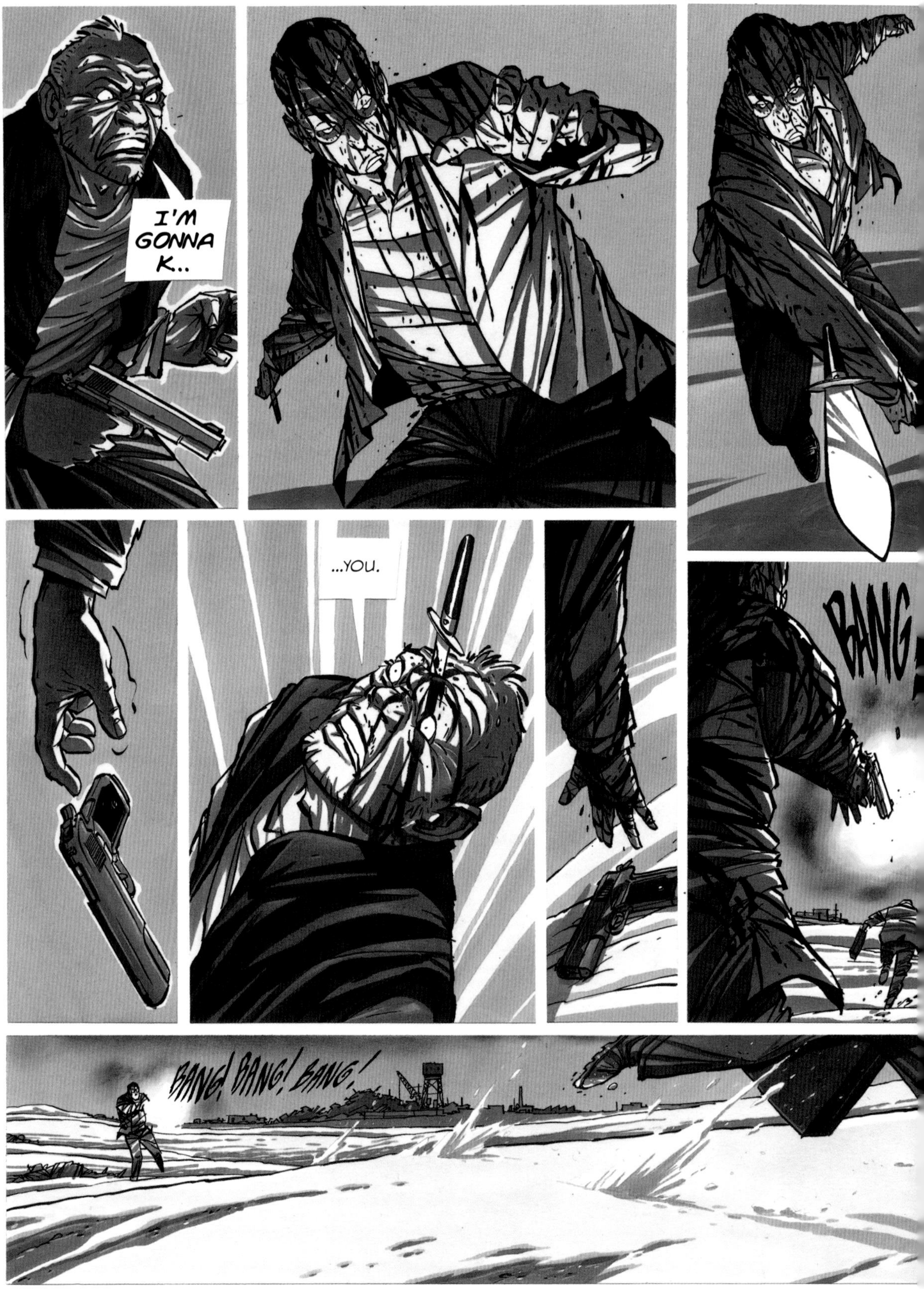
I'M GONNA K..
...YOU.
BANG
BANG! BANG! BANG!

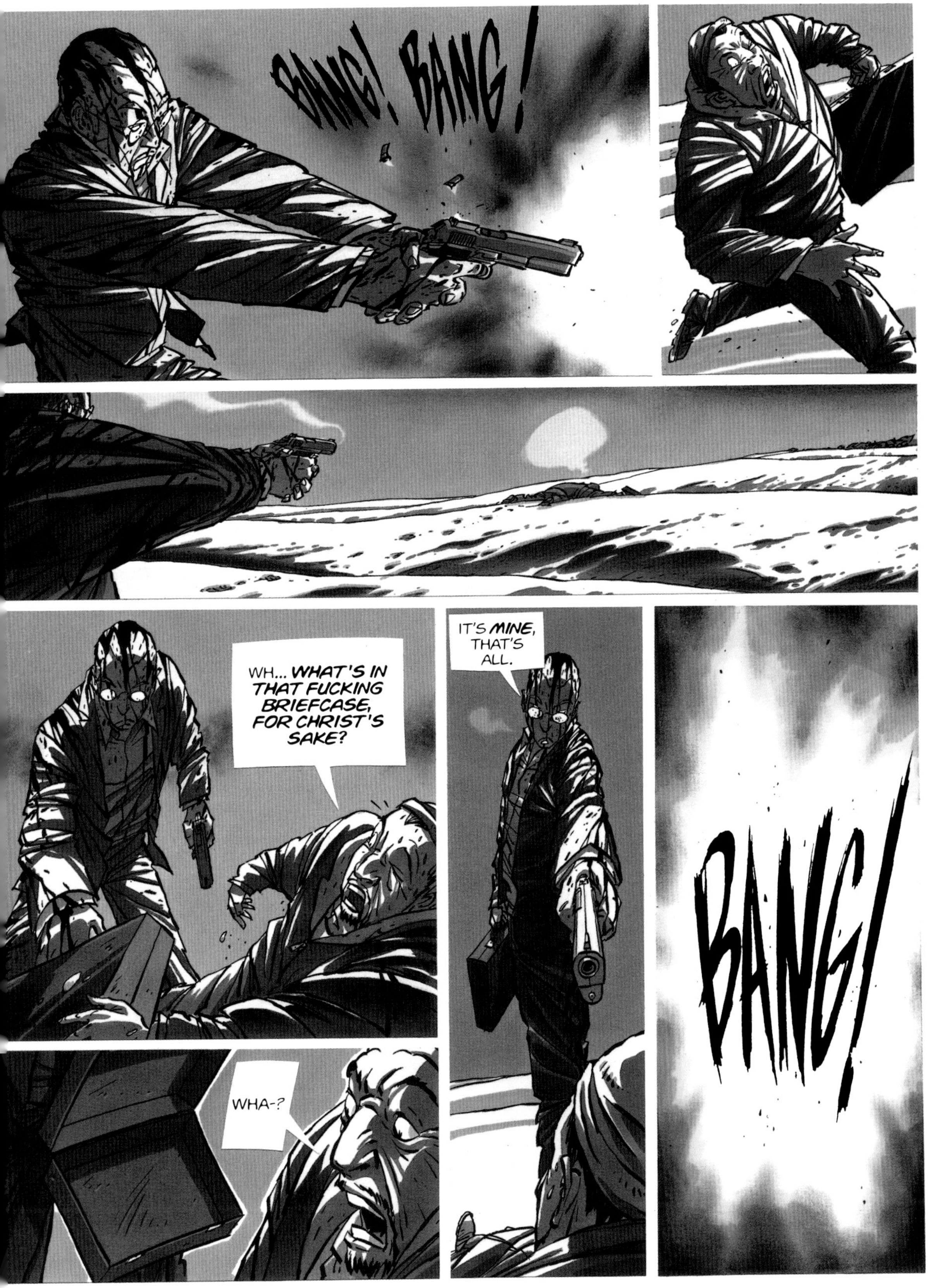
BANG! BANG!
WH... WHAT'S IN THAT FUCKING BRIEFCASE, FOR CHRIST'S SAKE?
WHA-?
IT'S MINE, THAT'S ALL.
BANG!

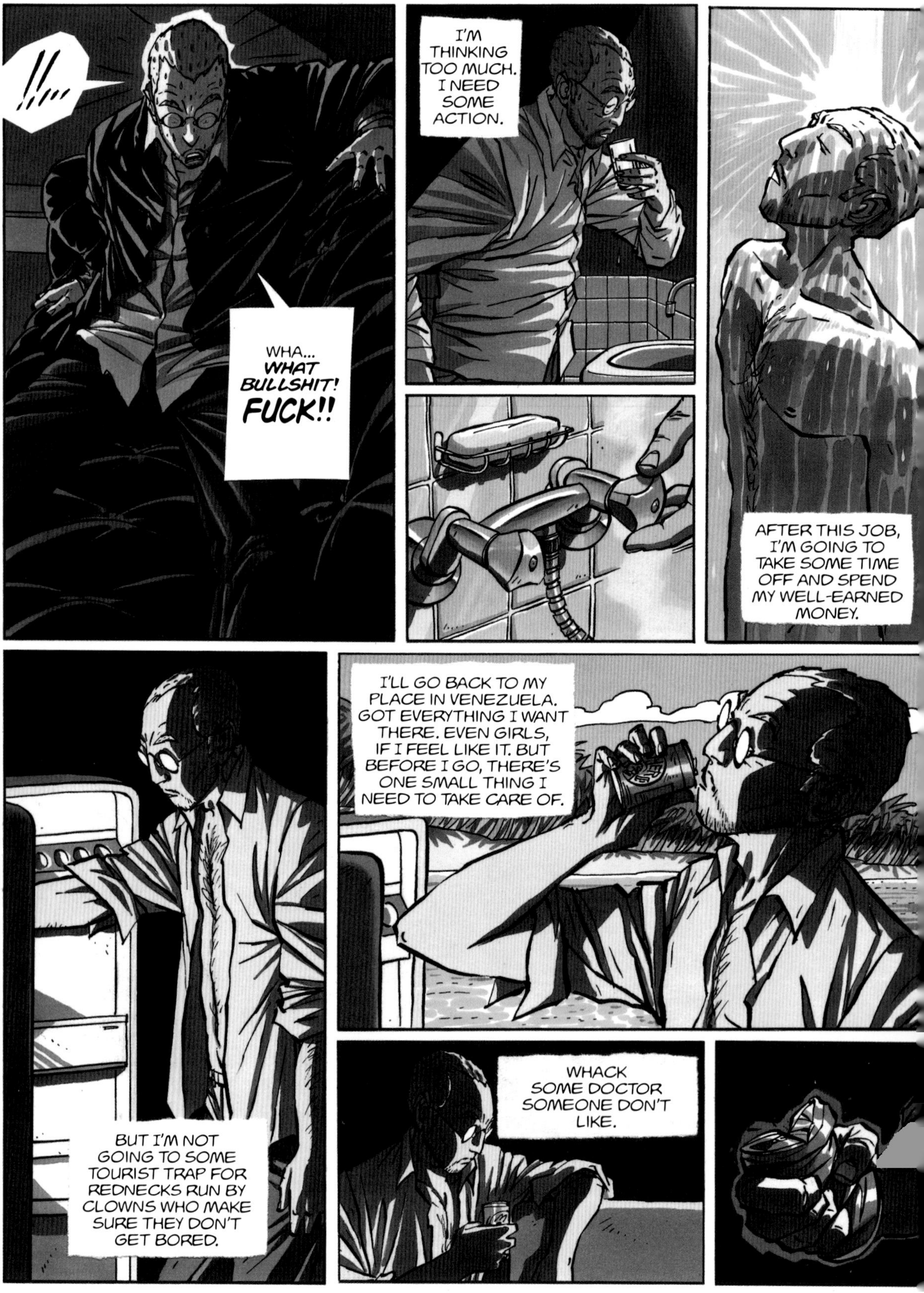
!!...
WHA... WHAT BULLSHIT! FUCK!!
I'M THINKING TOO MUCH. I NEED SOME ACTION.
AFTER THIS JOB, I'M GOING TO TAKE SOME TIME OFF AND SPEND MY WELL-EARNED MONEY.
BUT I'M NOT GOING TO SOME TOURIST TRAP FOR REDNECKS RUN BY CLOWNS WHO MAKE SURE THEY DON'T GET BORED.
I'LL GO BACK TO MY PLACE IN VENEZUELA. GOT EVERYTHING I WANT THERE. EVEN GIRLS, IF I FEEL LIKE IT. BUT BEFORE I GO, THERE'S ONE SMALL THING I NEED TO TAKE CARE OF.
WHACK SOME DOCTOR SOMEONE DON'T LIKE.

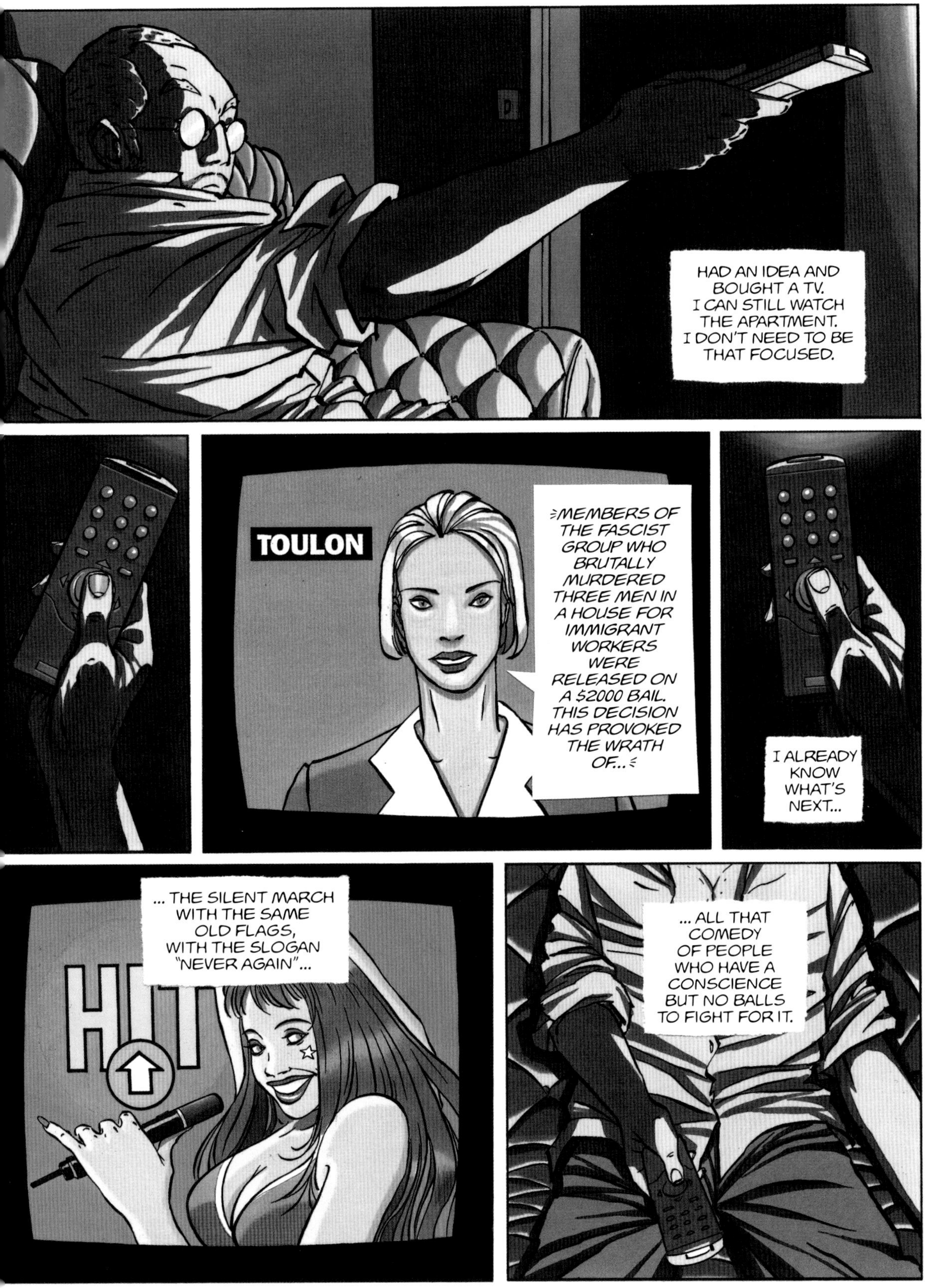
HAD AN IDEA AND BOUGHT A TV. I CAN STILL WATCH THE APARTMENT. I DON'T NEED TO BE THAT FOCUSED.
TOULON
MEMBERS OF THE FASCIST GROUP WHO BRUTALLY MURDERED THREE MEN IN A HOUSE FOR IMMIGRANT WORKERS WERE RELEASED ON A $2000 BAIL. THIS DECISION HAS PROVOKED THE WRATH OF...
I ALREADY KNOW WHAT'S NEXT...
... THE SILENT MARCH WITH THE SAME OLD FLAGS, WITH THE SLOGAN "NEVER AGAIN"...
HIT
... ALL THAT COMEDY OF PEOPLE WHO HAVE A CONSCIENCE BUT NO BALLS TO FIGHT FOR IT.

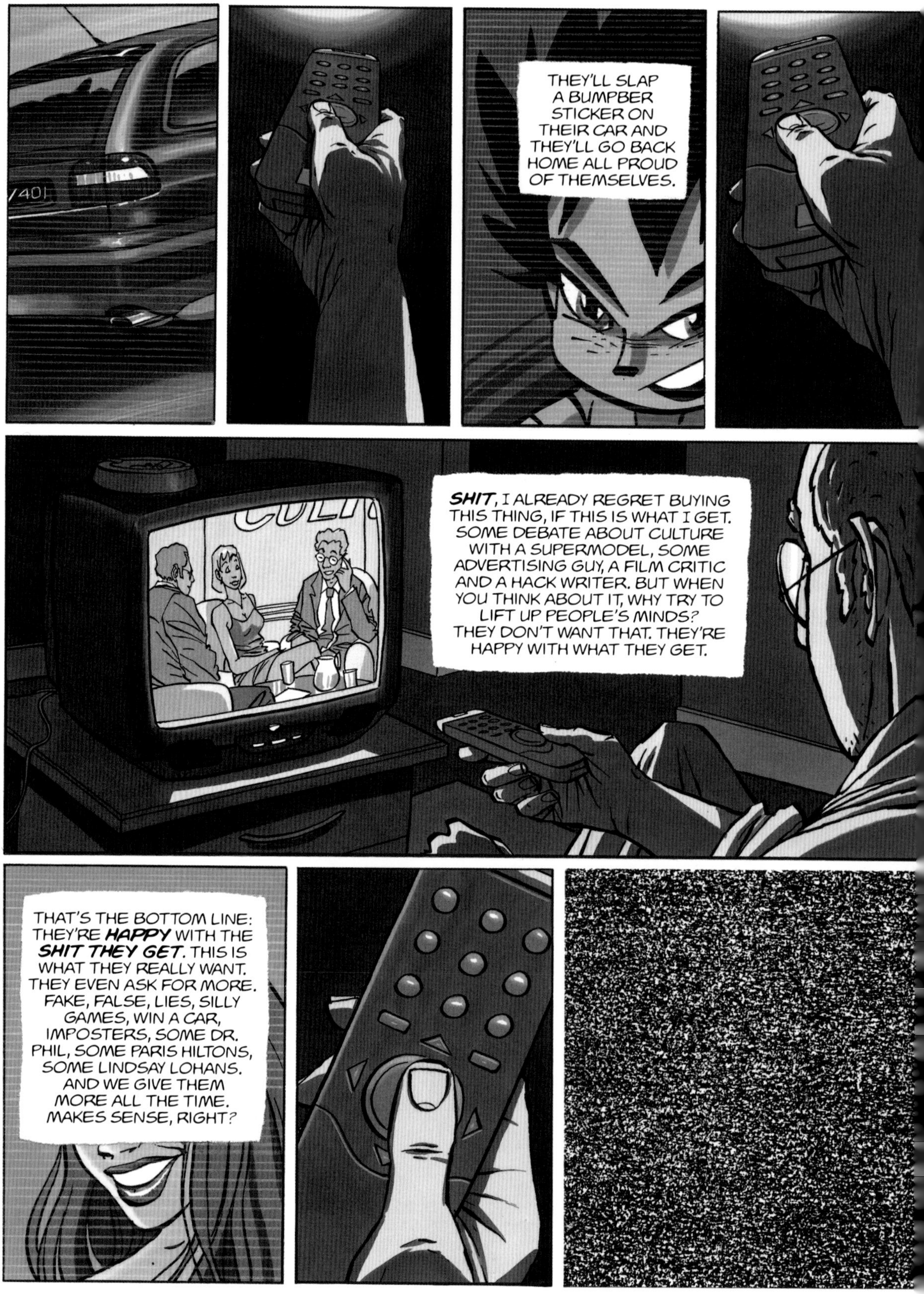
THEY'LL SLAP A BUMPBER STICKER ON THEIR CAR AND THEY'LL GO BACK HOME ALL PROUD OF THEMSELVES.
SHIT, I ALREADY REGRET BUYING THIS THING, IF THIS IS WHAT I GET. SOME DEBATE ABOUT CULTURE WITH A SUPERMODEL, SOME ADVERTISING GUY, A FILM CRITIC AND A HACK WRITER. BUT WHEN YOU THINK ABOUT IT, WHY TRY TO LIFT UP PEOPLE'S MINDS? THEY DON'T WANT THAT. THEY'RE HAPPY WITH WHAT THEY GET.
THAT'S THE BOTTOM LINE: THEY'RE HAPPY WITH THE SHIT THEY GET. THIS IS WHAT THEY REALLY WANT. THEY EVEN ASK FOR MORE. FAKE, FALSE, LIES, SILLY GAMES, WIN A CAR, IMPOSTERS, SOME DR. PHIL, SOME PARIS HILTONS, SOME LINDSAY LOHANS. AND WE GIVE THEM MORE ALL THE TIME. MAKES SENSE, RIGHT?

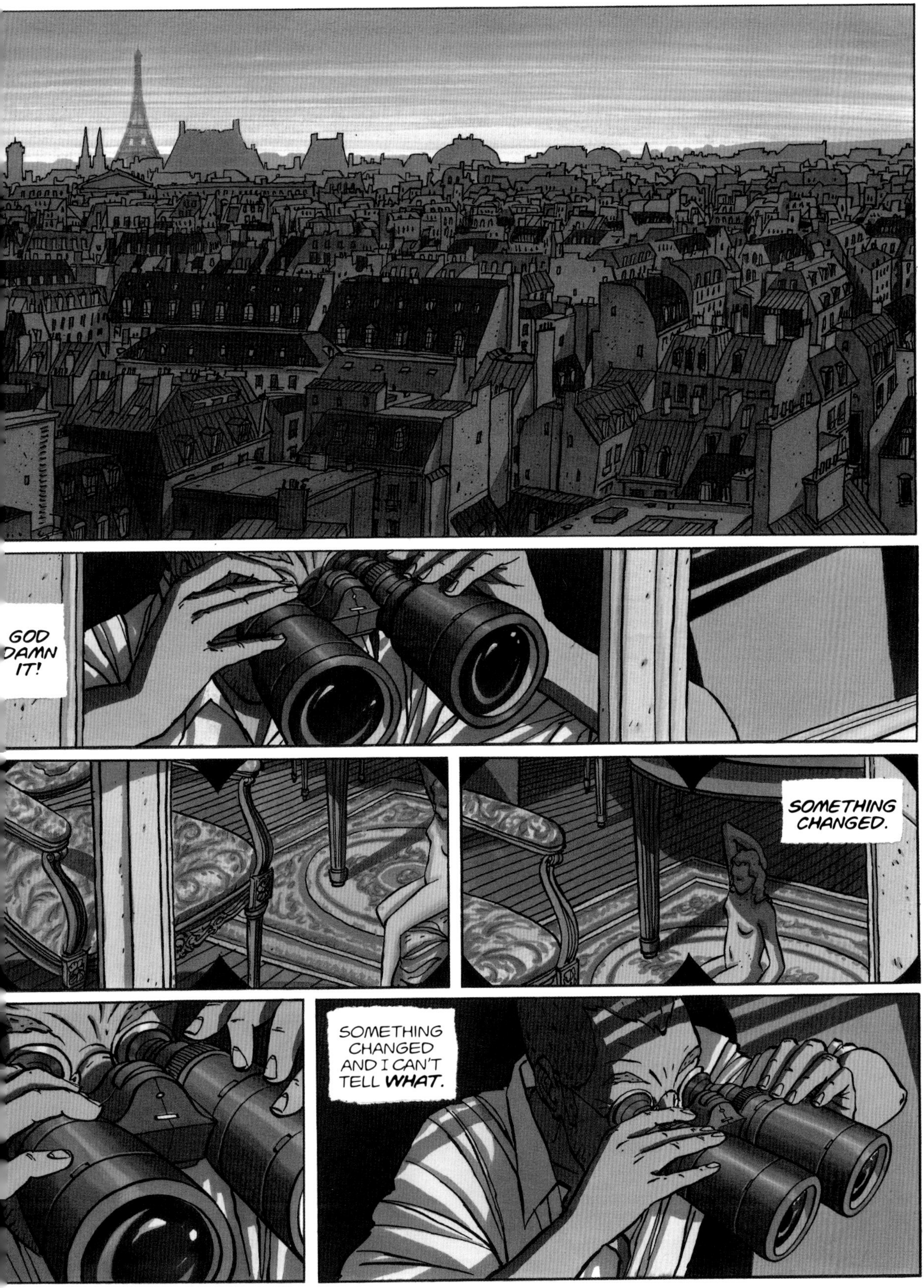
GOD DAMN IT!
SOMETHING CHANGED.
SOMETHING CHANGED AND I CAN'T TELL **WHAT**.

I SHOULD HAVE TAKEN PICTURES.

WHAT COULD IT BE?

I DON'T LIKE THIS ONE BIT. I GOTTA BE MORE CAREFUL.

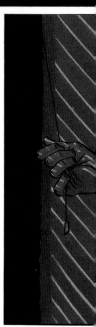

SOMETHING'S GONNA HAPPEN. I CAN *FEEL* IT.

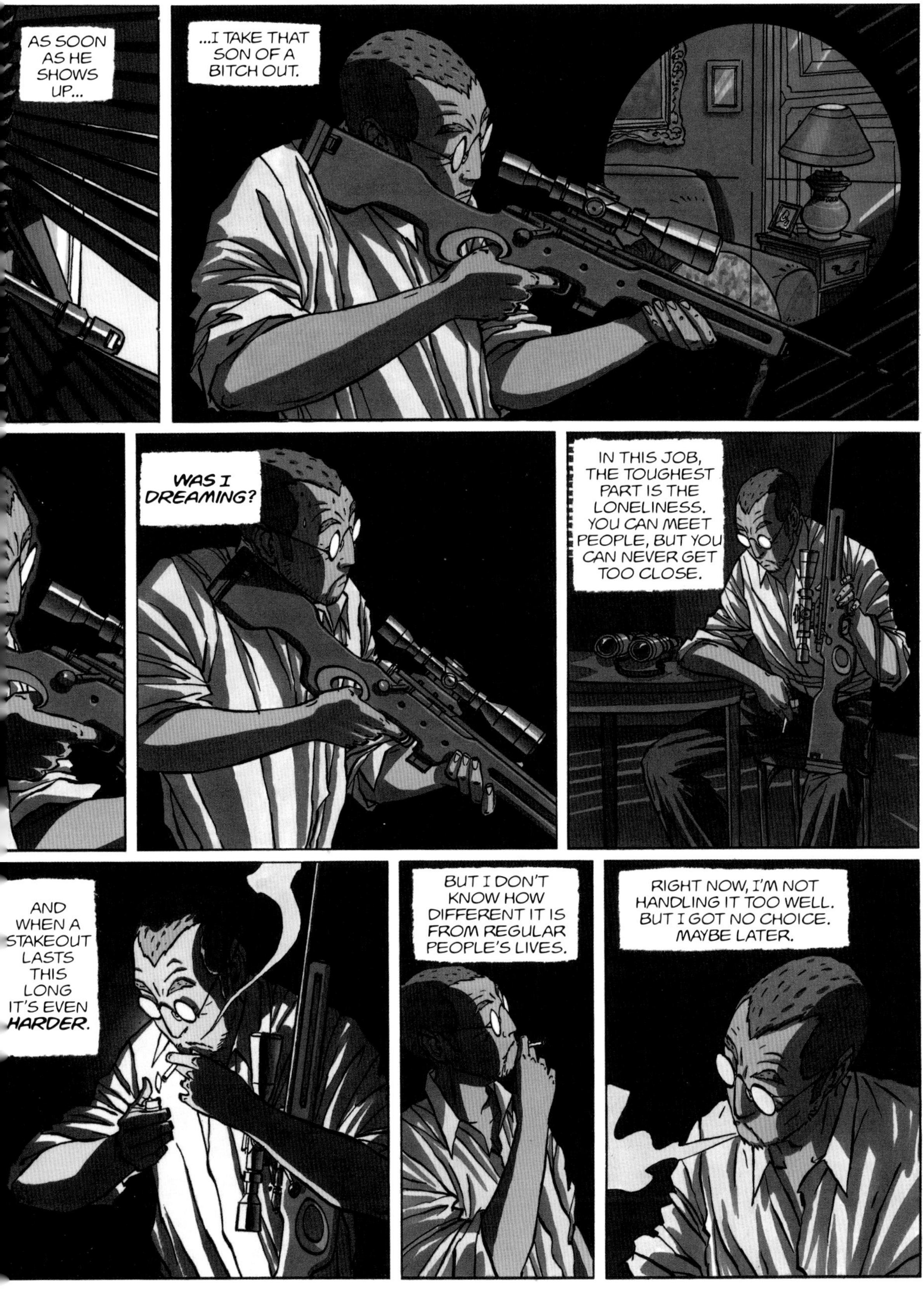
AS SOON AS HE SHOWS UP...
...I TAKE THAT SON OF A BITCH OUT.
WAS I DREAMING?
IN THIS JOB, THE TOUGHEST PART IS THE LONELINESS. YOU CAN MEET PEOPLE, BUT YOU CAN NEVER GET TOO CLOSE.
AND WHEN A STAKEOUT LASTS THIS LONG IT'S EVEN HARDER.
BUT I DON'T KNOW HOW DIFFERENT IT IS FROM REGULAR PEOPLE'S LIVES.
RIGHT NOW, I'M NOT HANDLING IT TOO WELL. BUT I GOT NO CHOICE. MAYBE LATER.

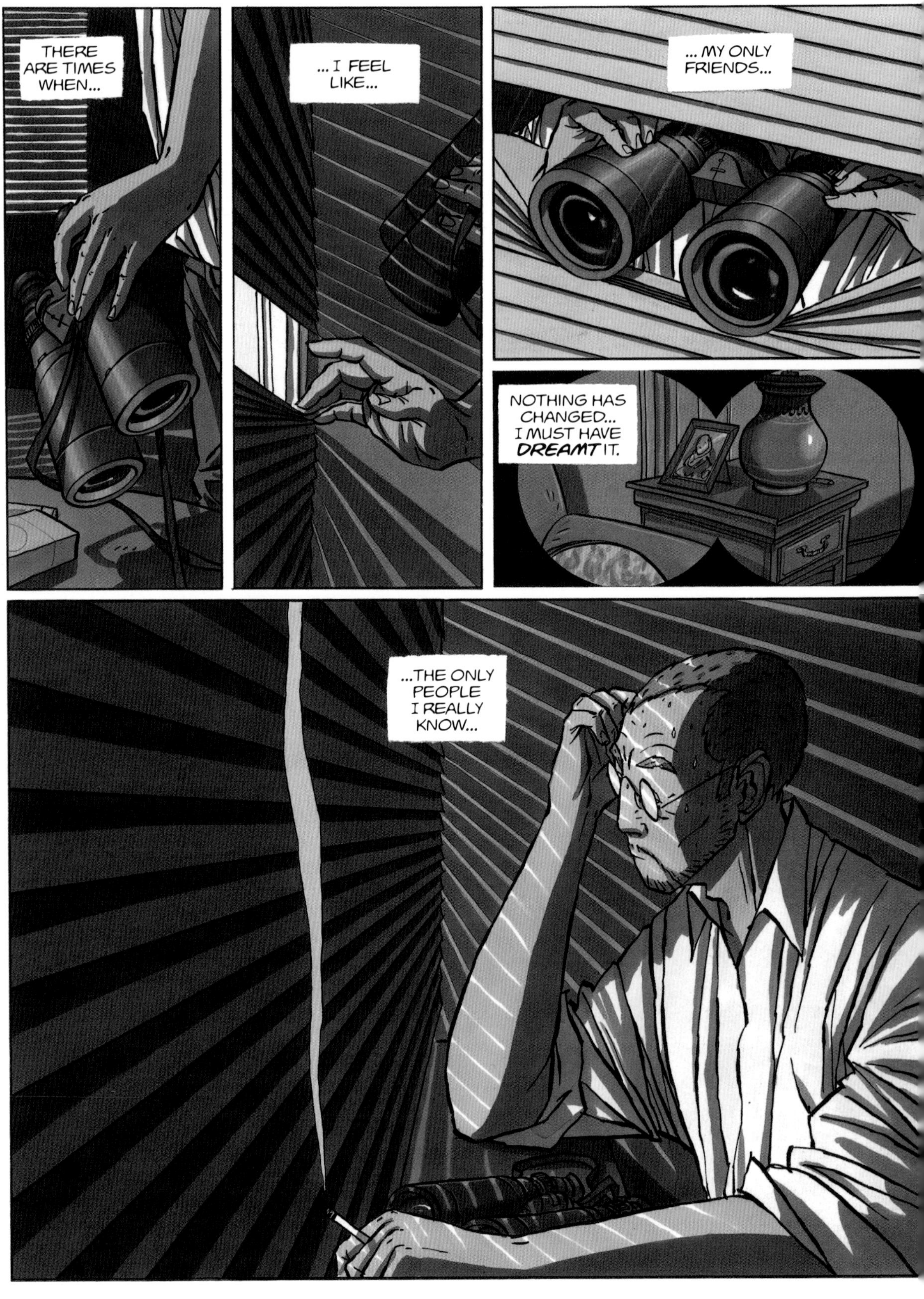
THERE ARE TIMES WHEN...
...I FEEL LIKE...
...MY ONLY FRIENDS...
NOTHING HAS CHANGED... I MUST HAVE DREAMT IT.
...THE ONLY PEOPLE I REALLY KNOW...

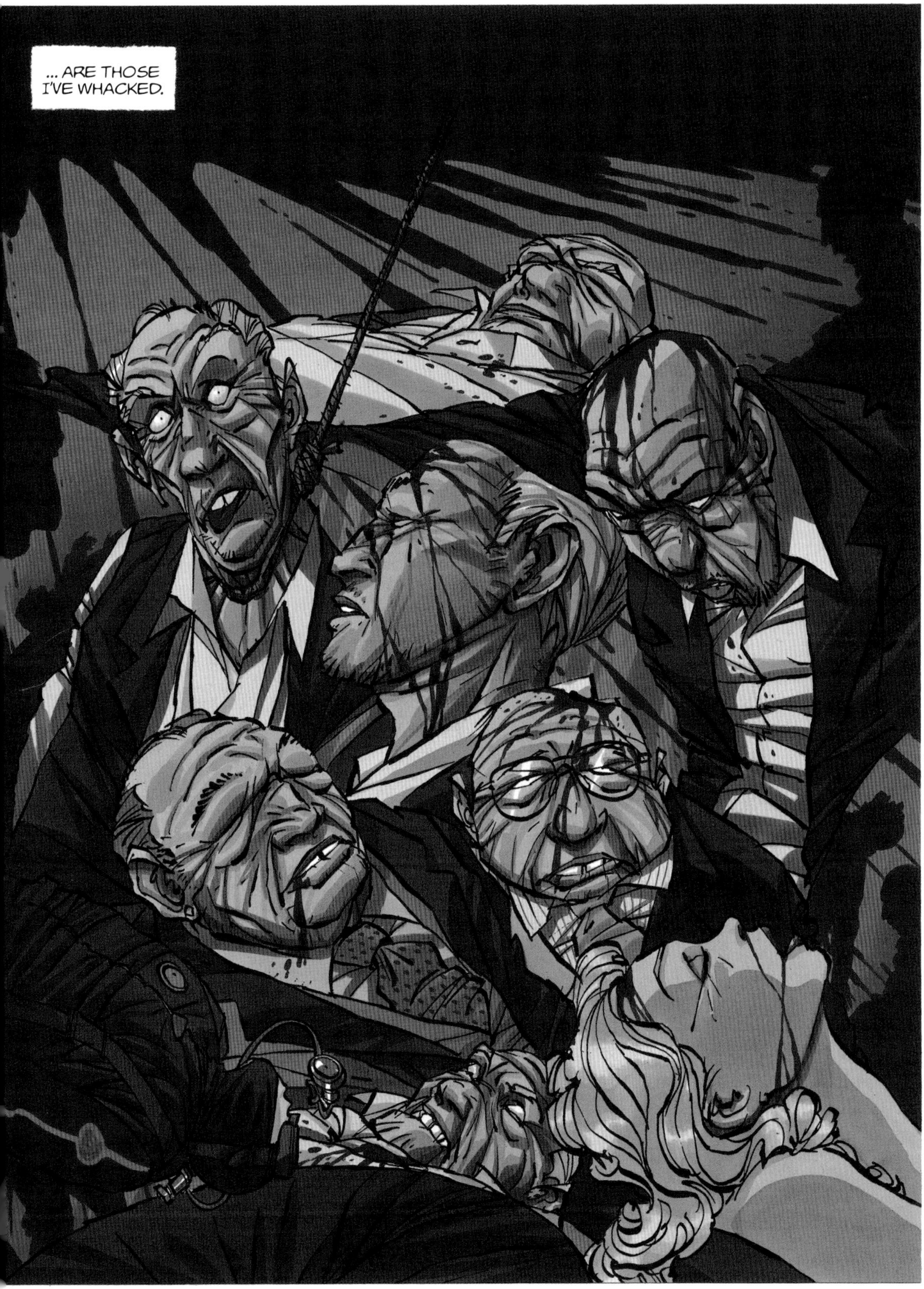
... ARE THOSE I'VE WHACKED.

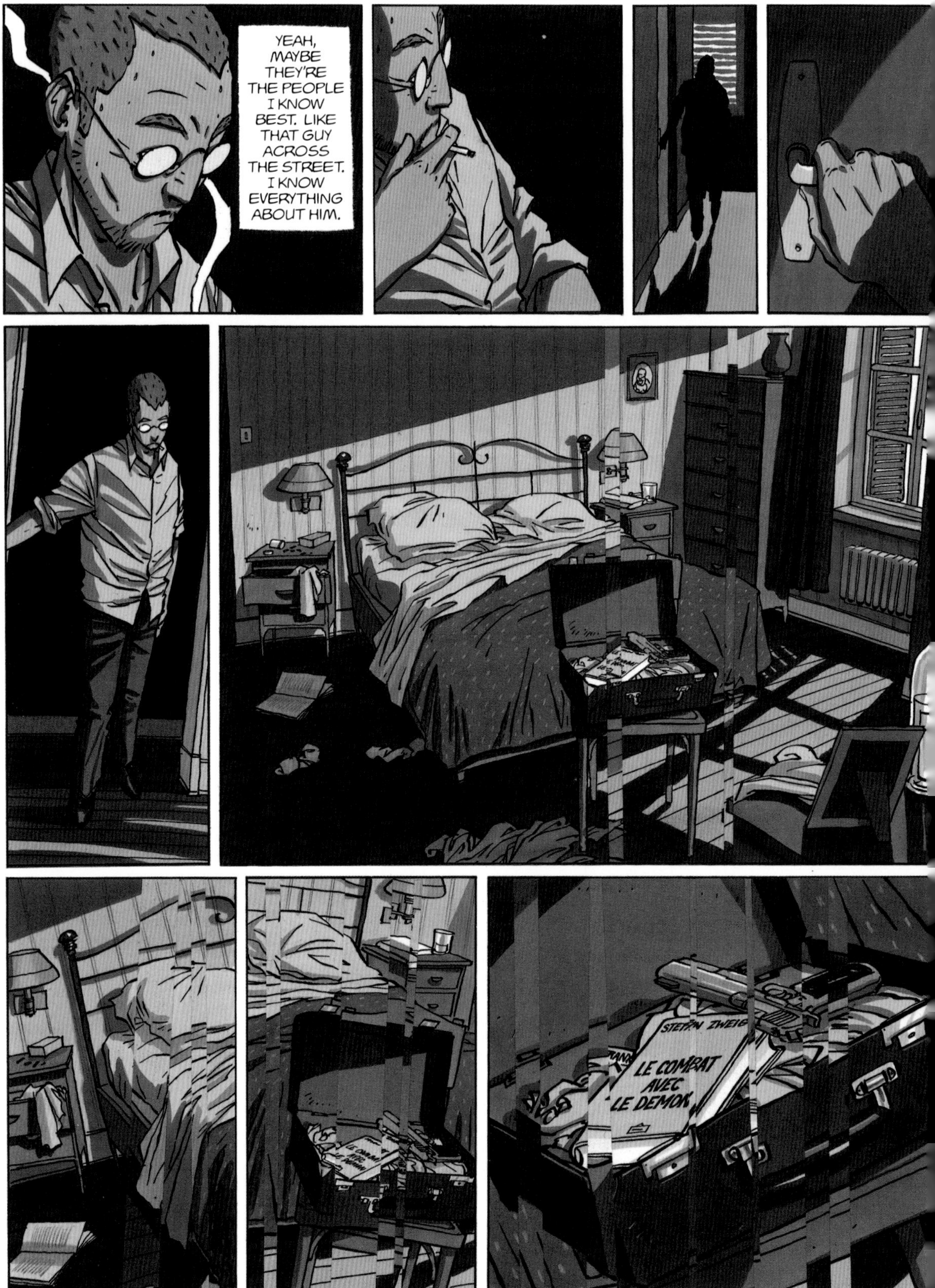
YEAH, MAYBE THEY'RE THE PEOPLE I KNOW BEST. LIKE THAT GUY ACROSS THE STREET. I KNOW EVERYTHING ABOUT HIM.
ZWEIG
LE COMBAT AVEC LE DEMON

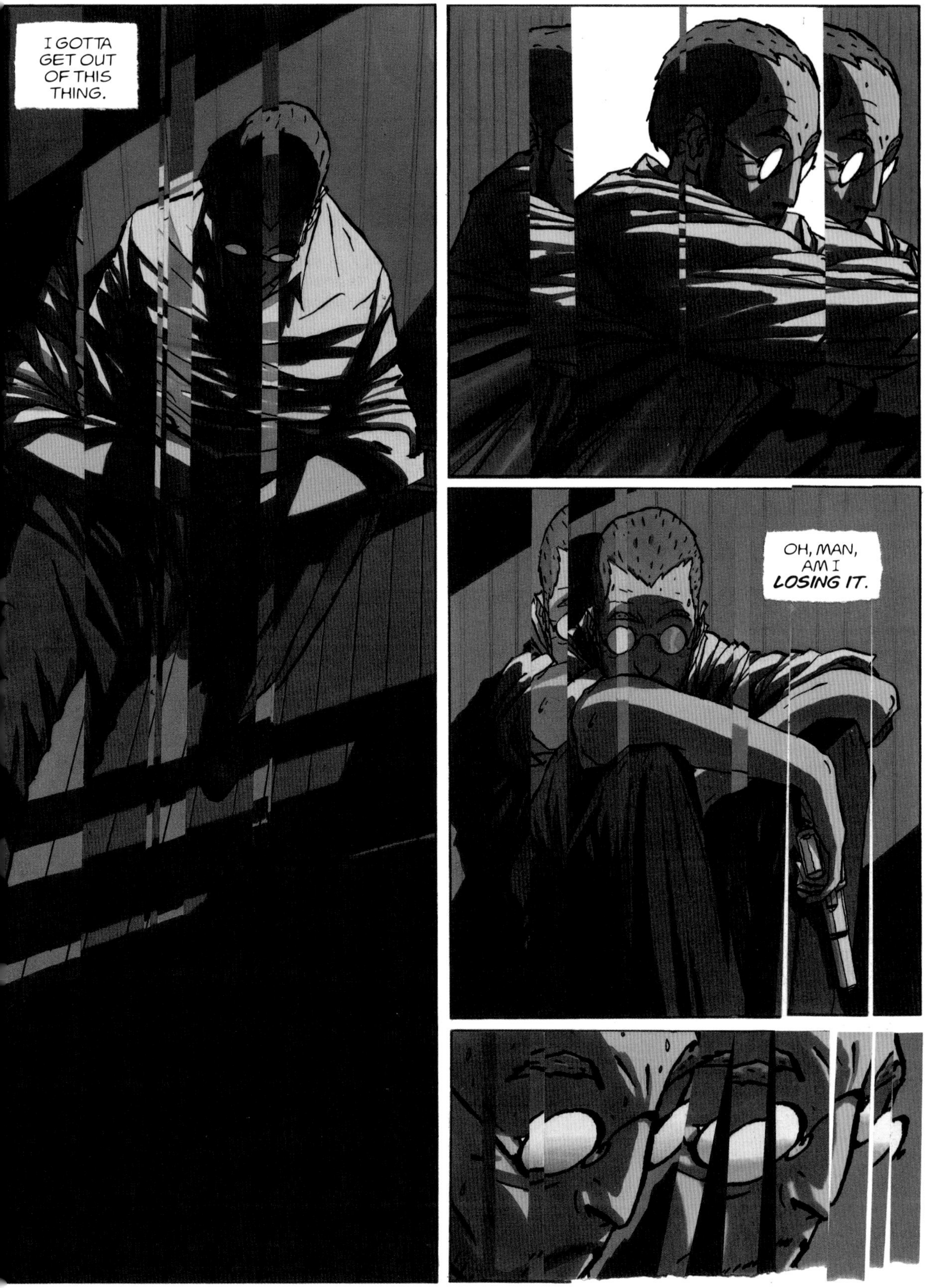
I GOTTA GET OUT OF THIS THING.
OH, MAN, AM I **LOSING IT**.

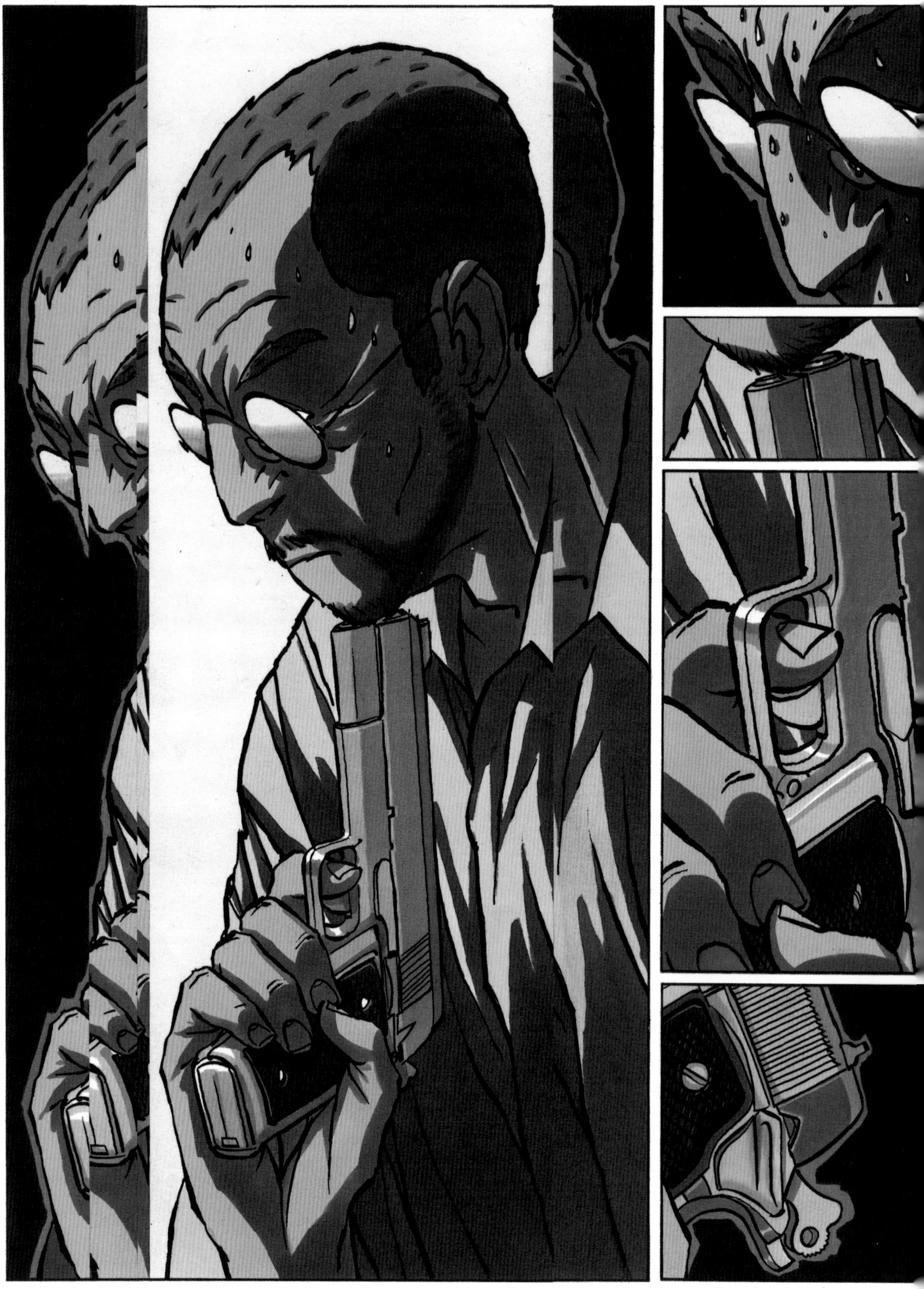

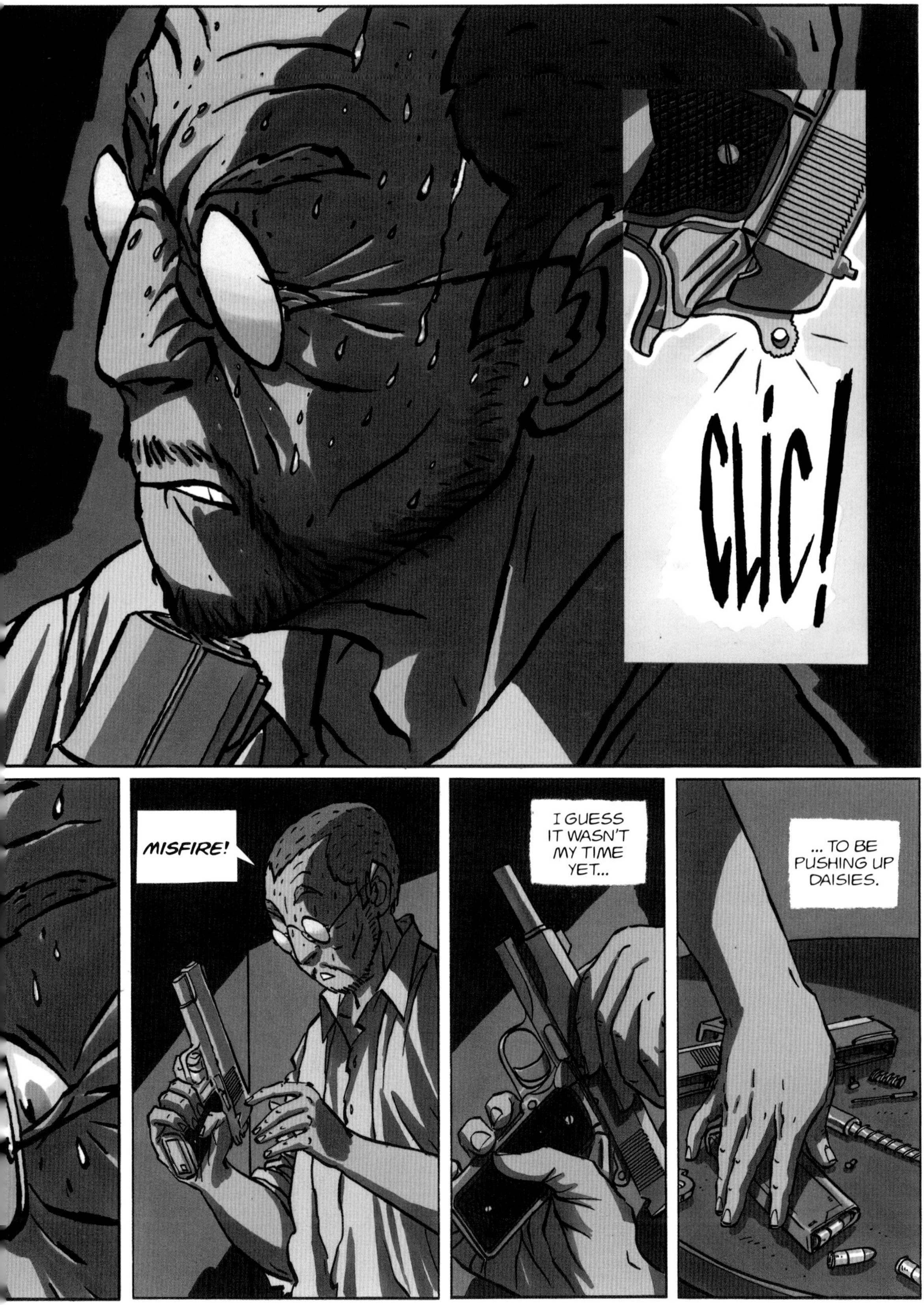
CLIC!
MISFIRE!
I GUESS IT WASN'T MY TIME YET...
... TO BE PUSHING UP DAISIES.

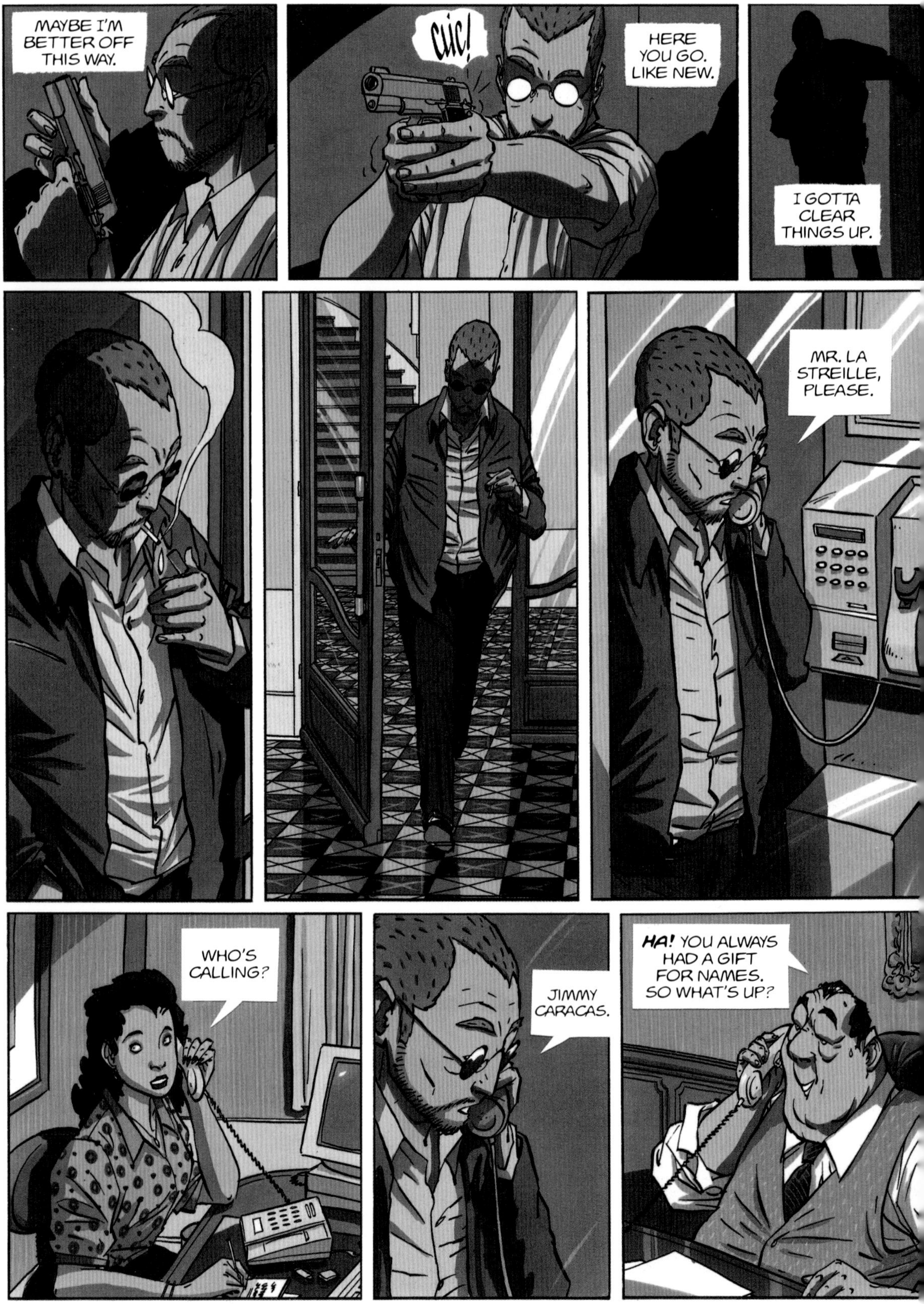
MAYBE I'M BETTER OFF THIS WAY.
CLIC!
HERE YOU GO. LIKE NEW.
I GOTTA CLEAR THINGS UP.
MR. LA STREILLE, PLEASE.
WHO'S CALLING?
JIMMY CARACAS.
HA! YOU ALWAYS HAD A GIFT FOR NAMES. SO WHAT'S UP?

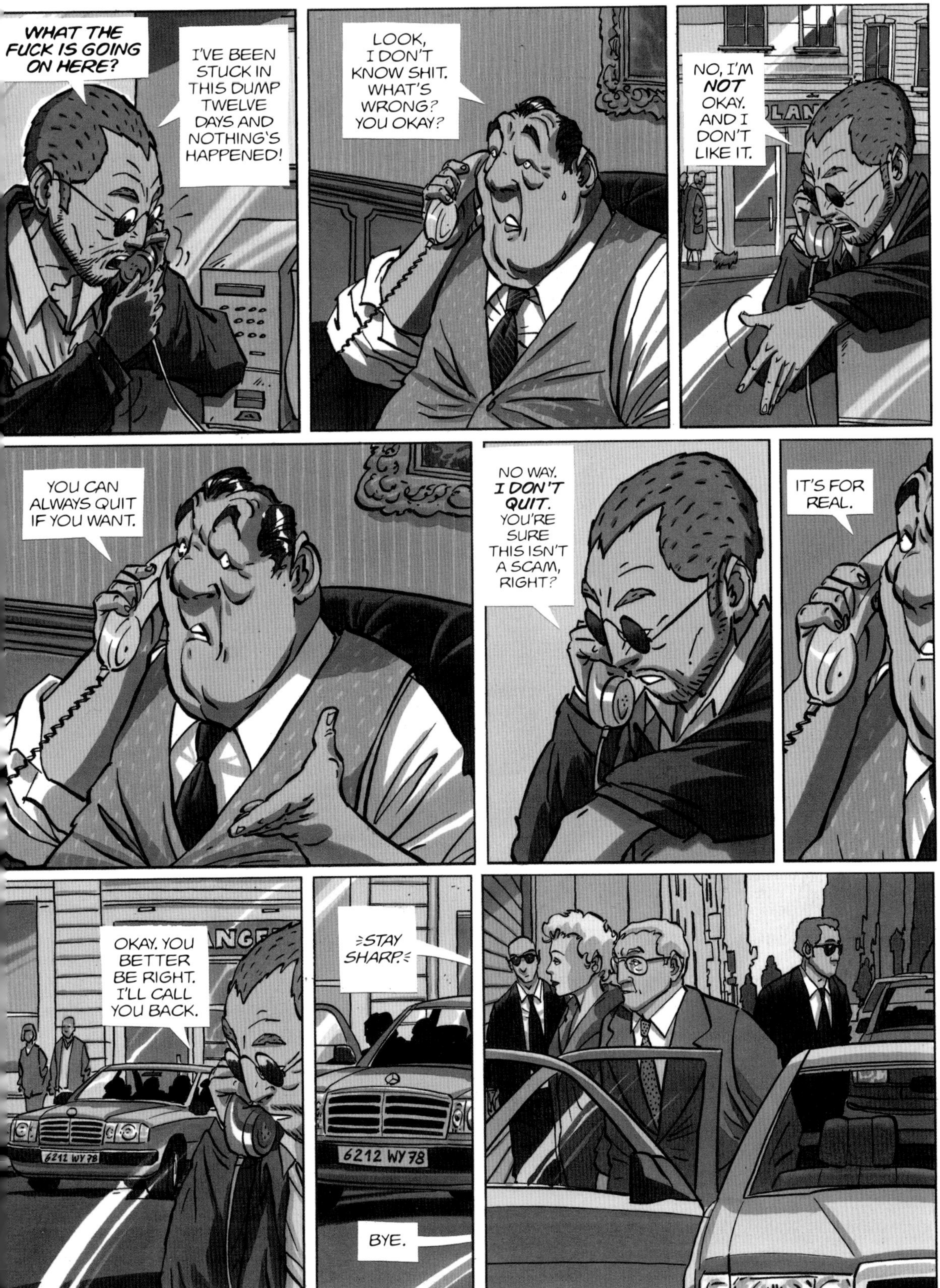
WHAT THE FUCK IS GOING ON HERE?
I'VE BEEN STUCK IN THIS DUMP TWELVE DAYS AND NOTHING'S HAPPENED!
LOOK, I DON'T KNOW SHIT. WHAT'S WRONG? YOU OKAY?
NO, I'M NOT OKAY. AND I DON'T LIKE IT.
YOU CAN ALWAYS QUIT IF YOU WANT.
NO WAY. I DON'T QUIT. YOU'RE SURE THIS ISN'T A SCAM, RIGHT?
IT'S FOR REAL.
OKAY. YOU BETTER BE RIGHT. I'LL CALL YOU BACK.
STAY SHARP.
BYE.

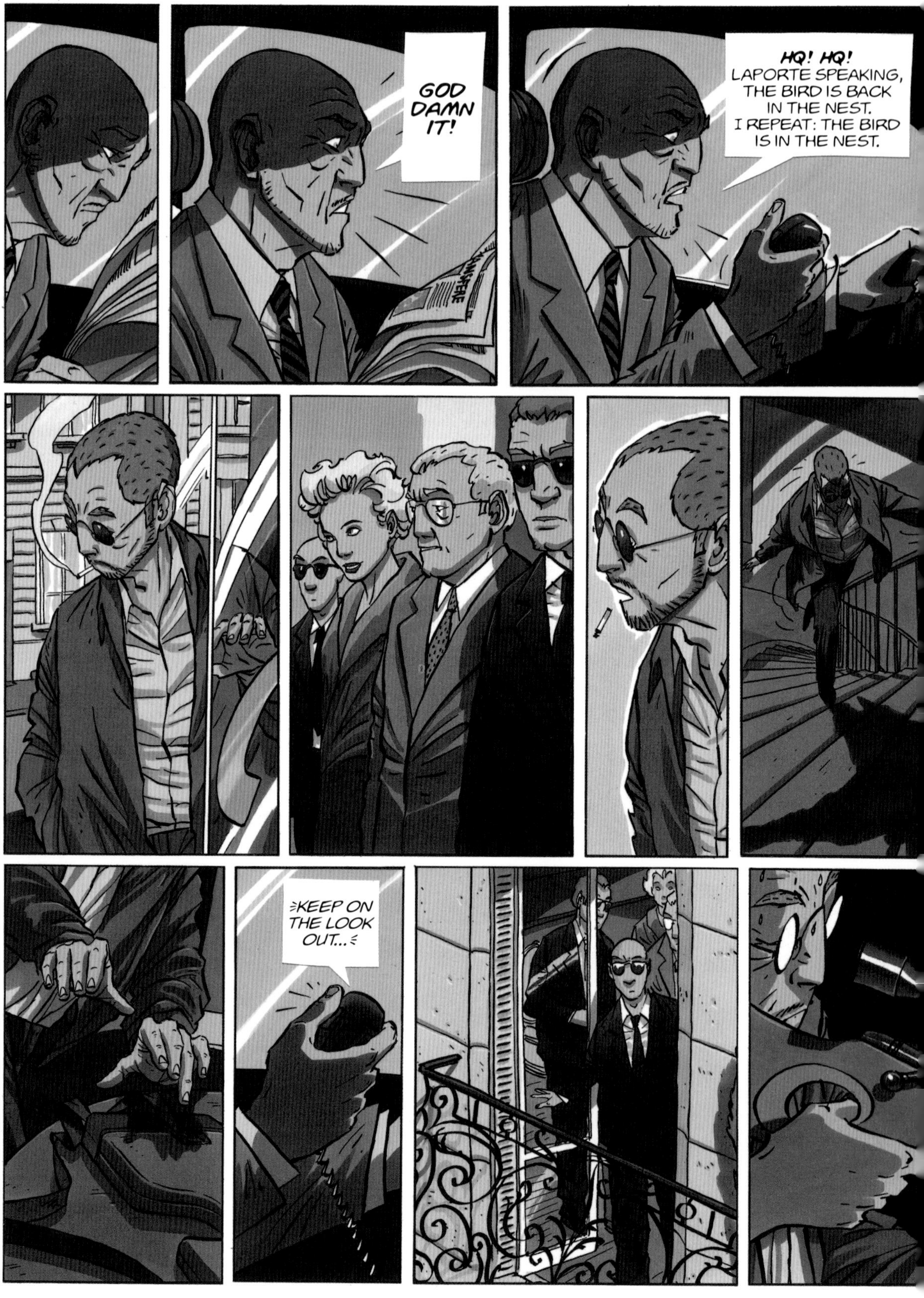
GOD DAMN IT!
HQ! HQ! LAPORTE SPEAKING, THE BIRD IS BACK IN THE NEST. I REPEAT: THE BIRD IS IN THE NEST.
KEEP ON THE LOOK OUT...

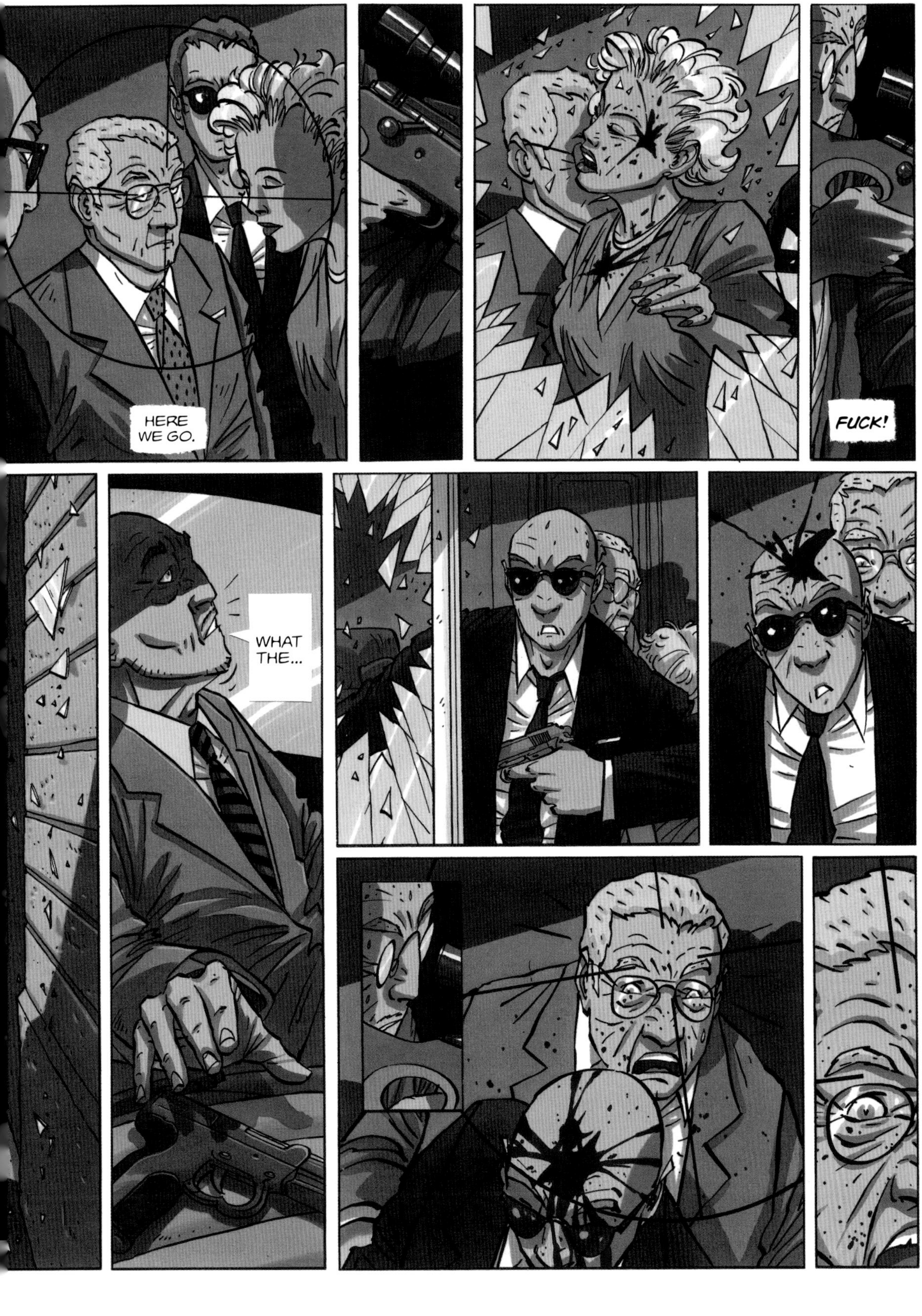
HERE WE GO.
FUCK!
WHAT THE...

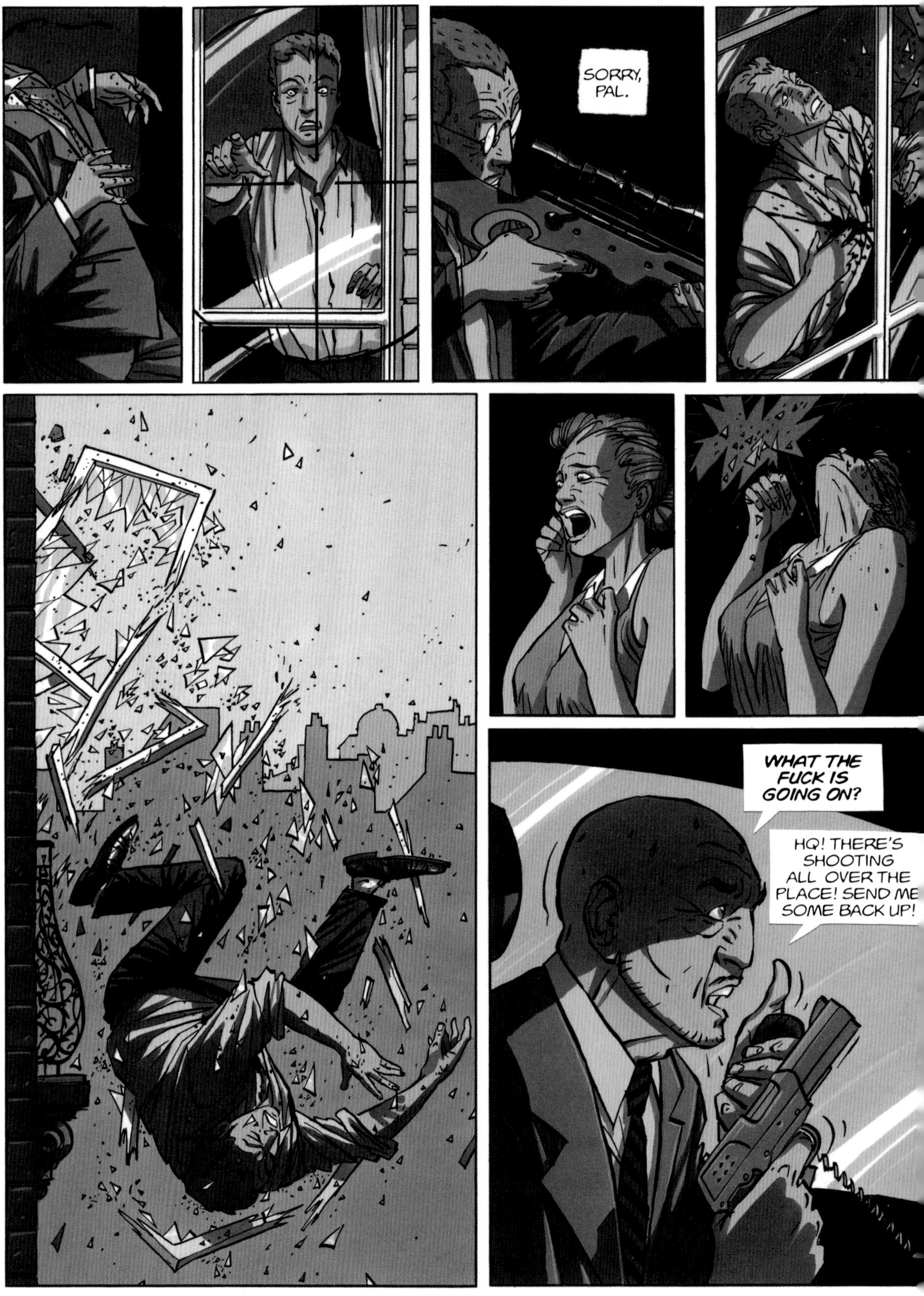
SORRY, PAL.
WHAT THE FUCK IS GOING ON?
HQ! THERE'S SHOOTING ALL OVER THE PLACE! SEND ME SOME BACK UP!

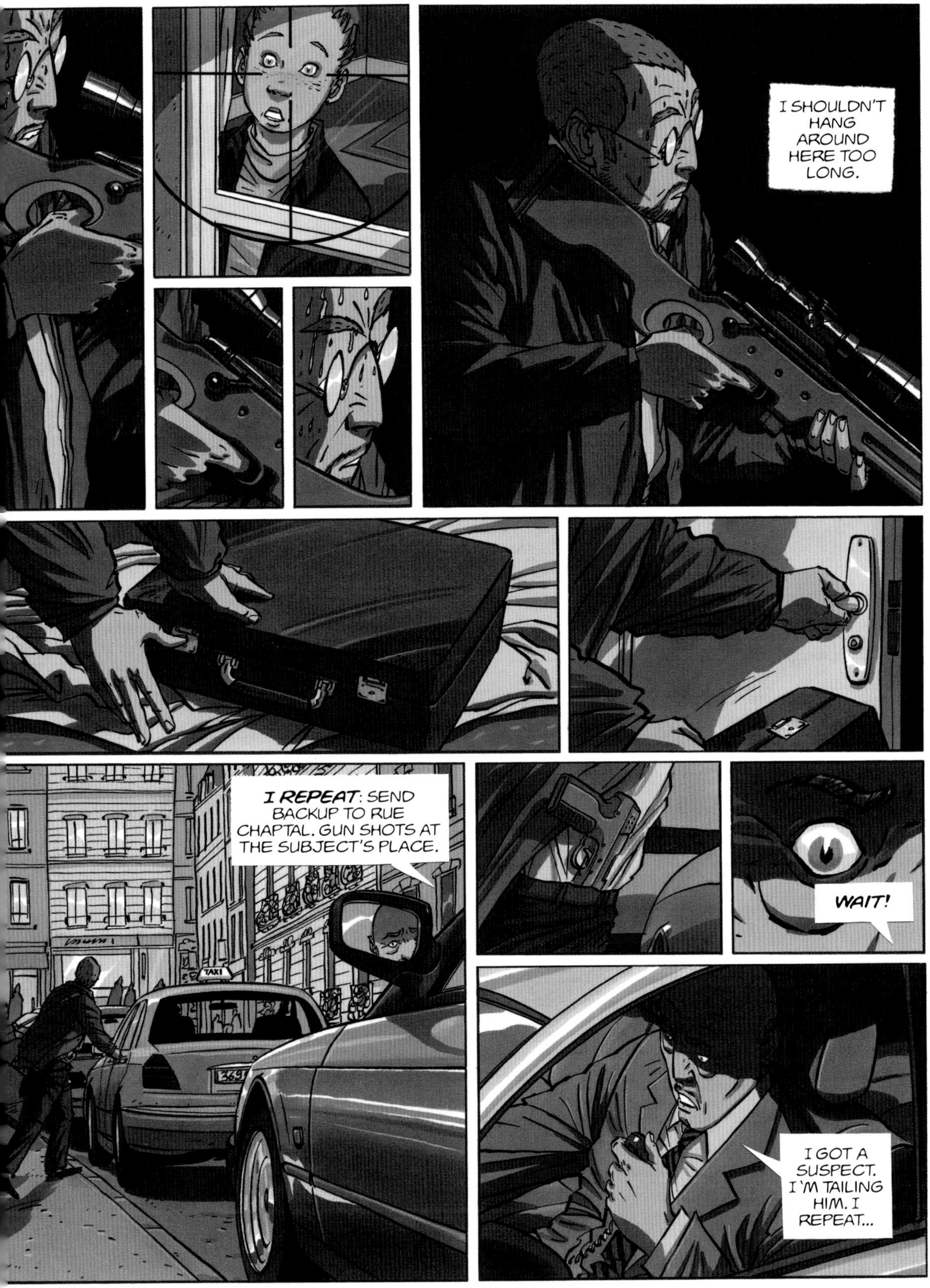
I SHOULDN'T HANG AROUND HERE TOO LONG.
I REPEAT: SEND BACKUP TO RUE CHAPTAL. GUN SHOTS AT THE SUBJECT'S PLACE.
WAIT!
I GOT A SUSPECT. I'M TAILING HIM. I REPEAT...

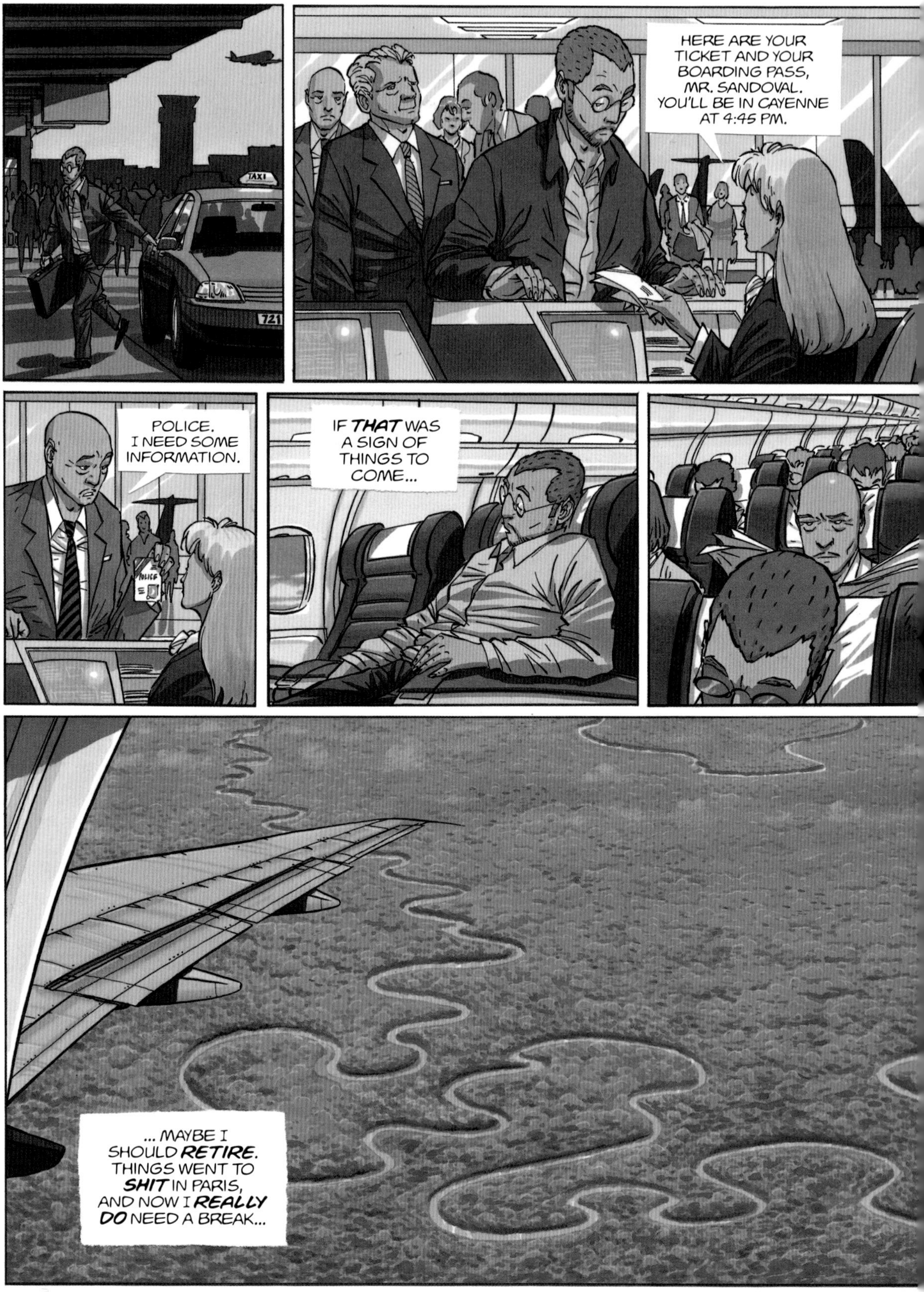
HERE ARE YOUR TICKET AND YOUR BOARDING PASS, MR. SANDOVAL. YOU'LL BE IN CAYENNE AT 4:45 PM.
POLICE. I NEED SOME INFORMATION.
IF THAT WAS A SIGN OF THINGS TO COME...
... MAYBE I SHOULD RETIRE. THINGS WENT TO SHIT IN PARIS, AND NOW I REALLY DO NEED A BREAK...

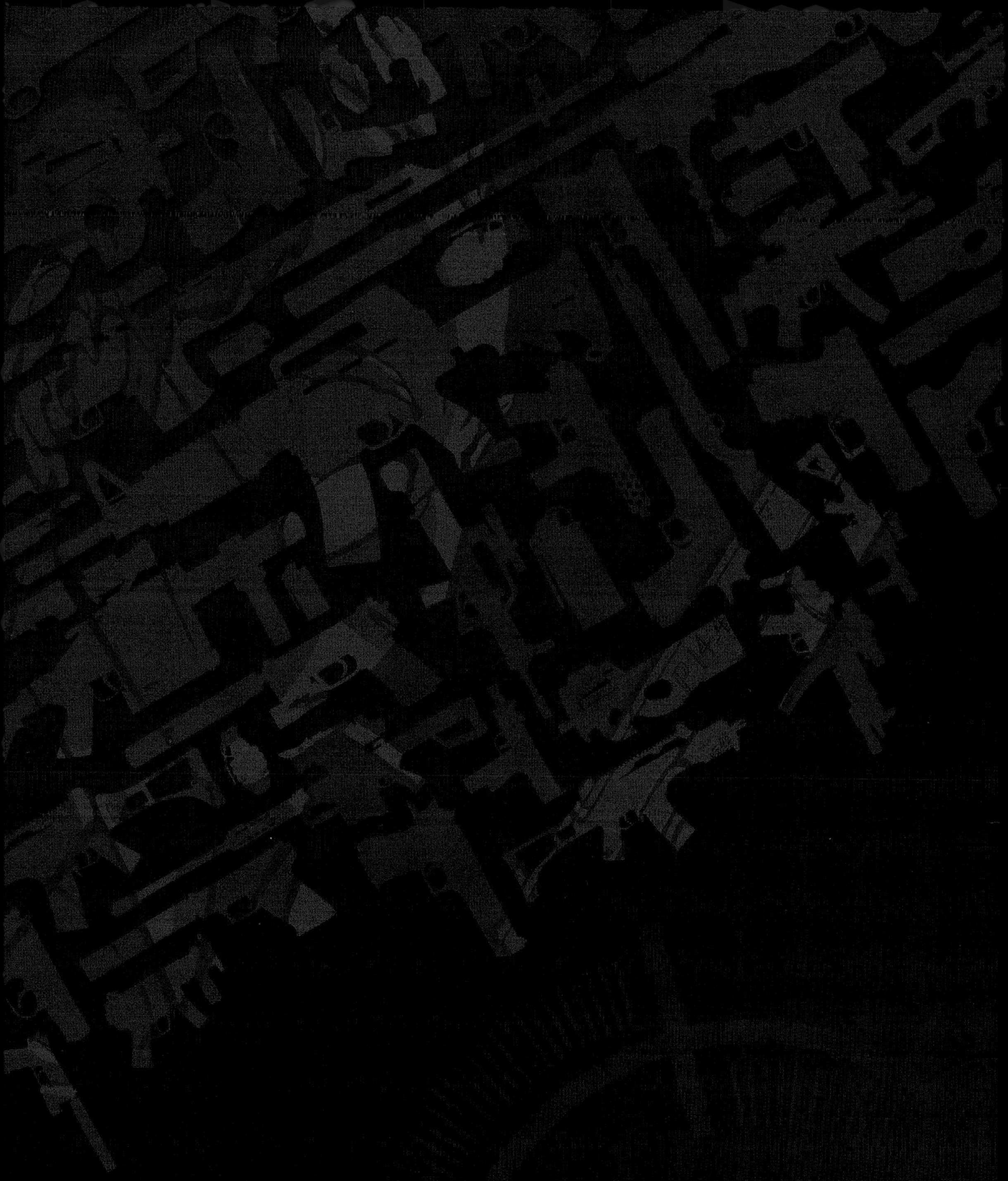

“ I have a **single** motive for what I’m doing: **money**. ”

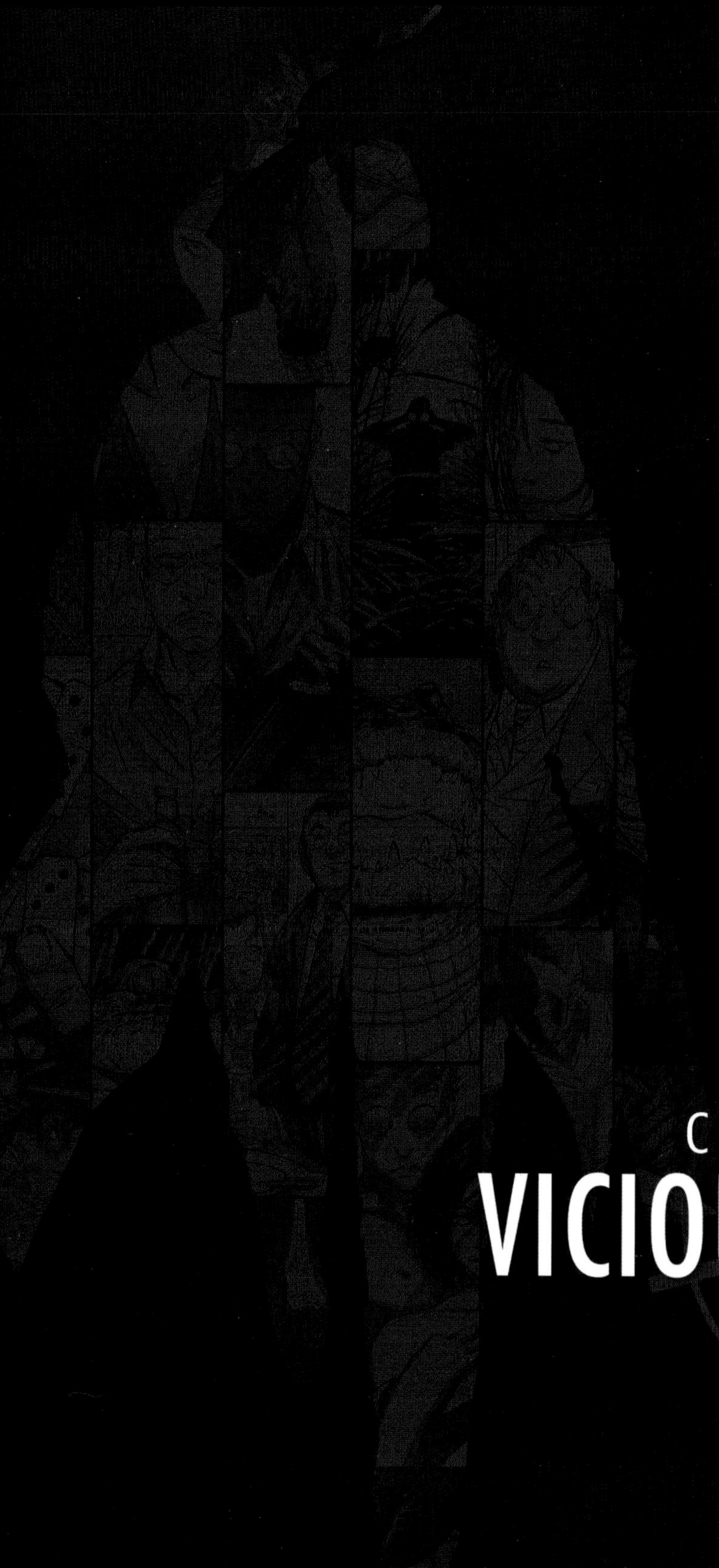

CHAPTER TWO
VICIOUS CYCLE

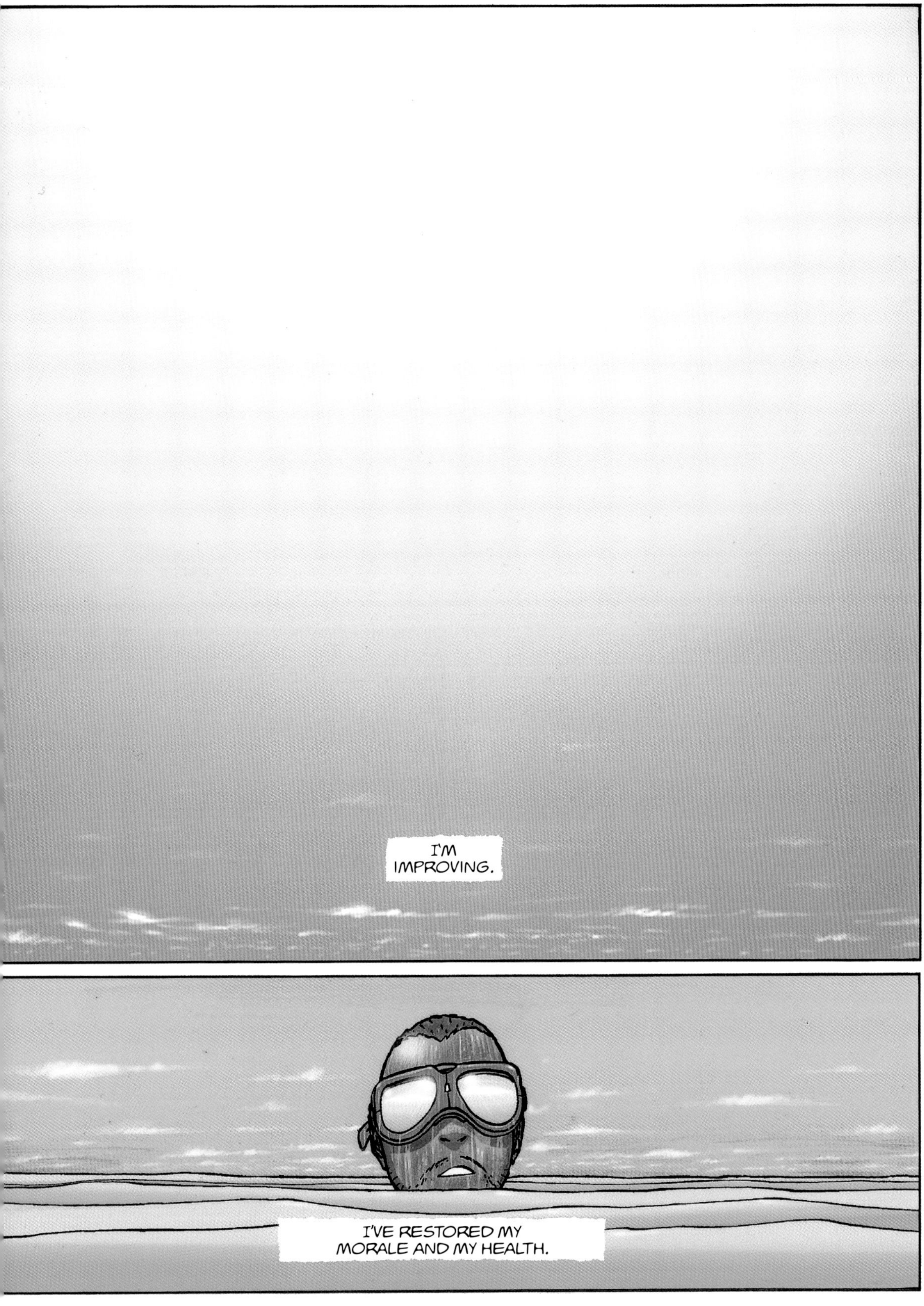
I'M IMPROVING.
I'VE RESTORED MY MORALE AND MY HEALTH.

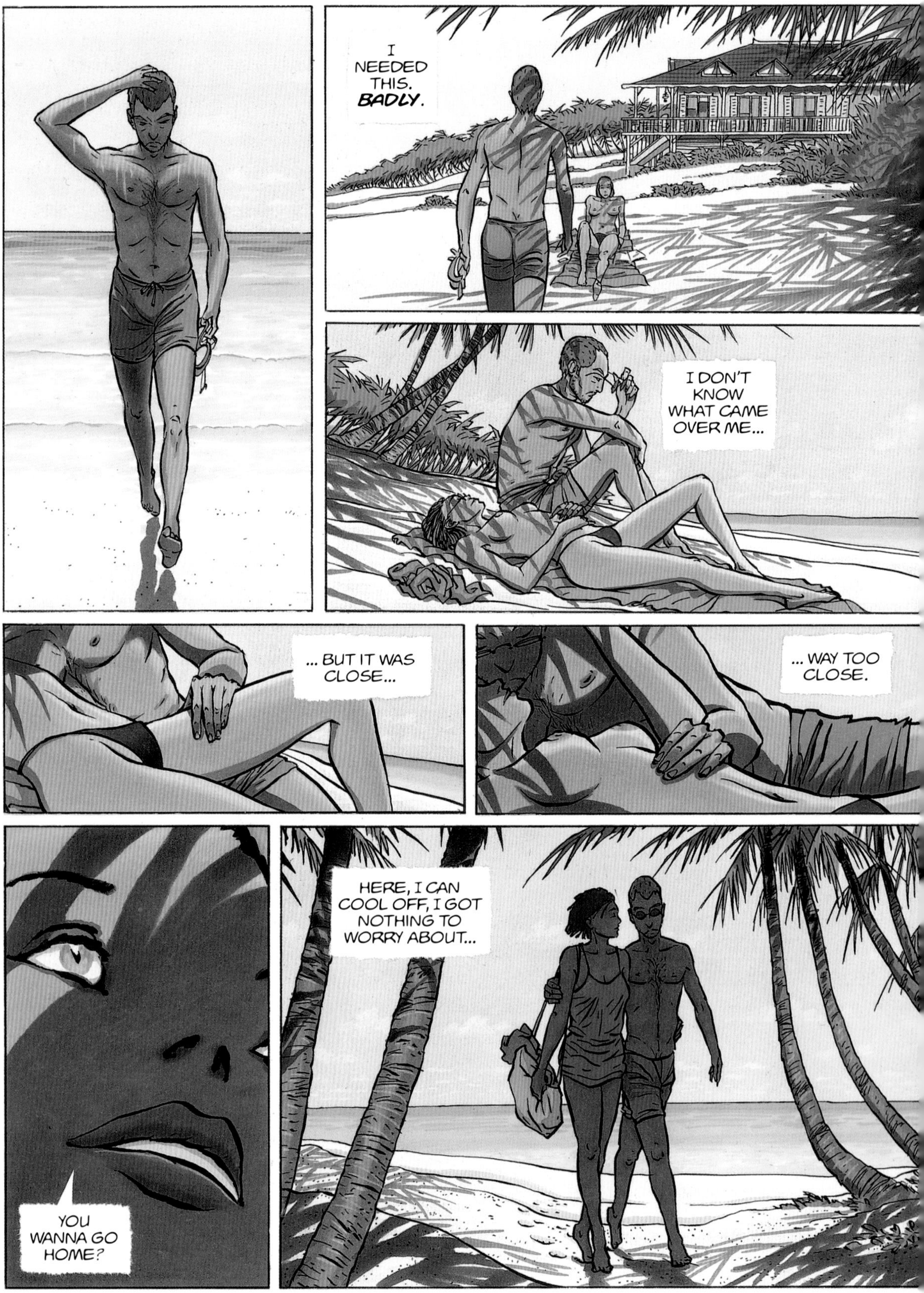
I NEEDED THIS. BADLY.
I DON'T KNOW WHAT CAME OVER ME...
... BUT IT WAS CLOSE...
... WAY TOO CLOSE.
YOU WANNA GO HOME?
HERE, I CAN COOL OFF, I GOT NOTHING TO WORRY ABOUT...

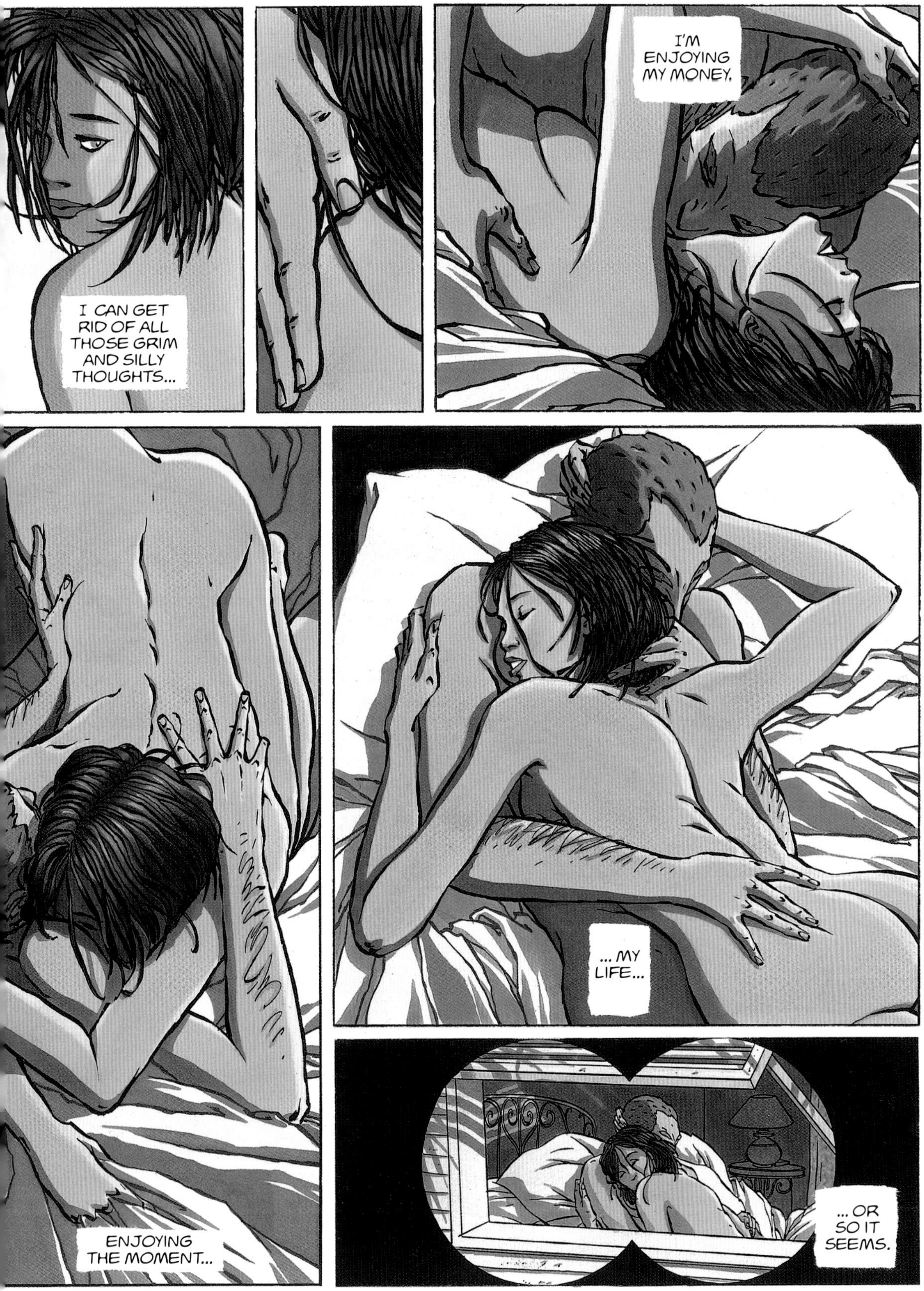
I CAN GET RID OF ALL THOSE GRIM AND SILLY THOUGHTS...
I'M ENJOYING MY MONEY.
ENJOYING THE MOMENT...
...MY LIFE...
...OR SO IT SEEMS.

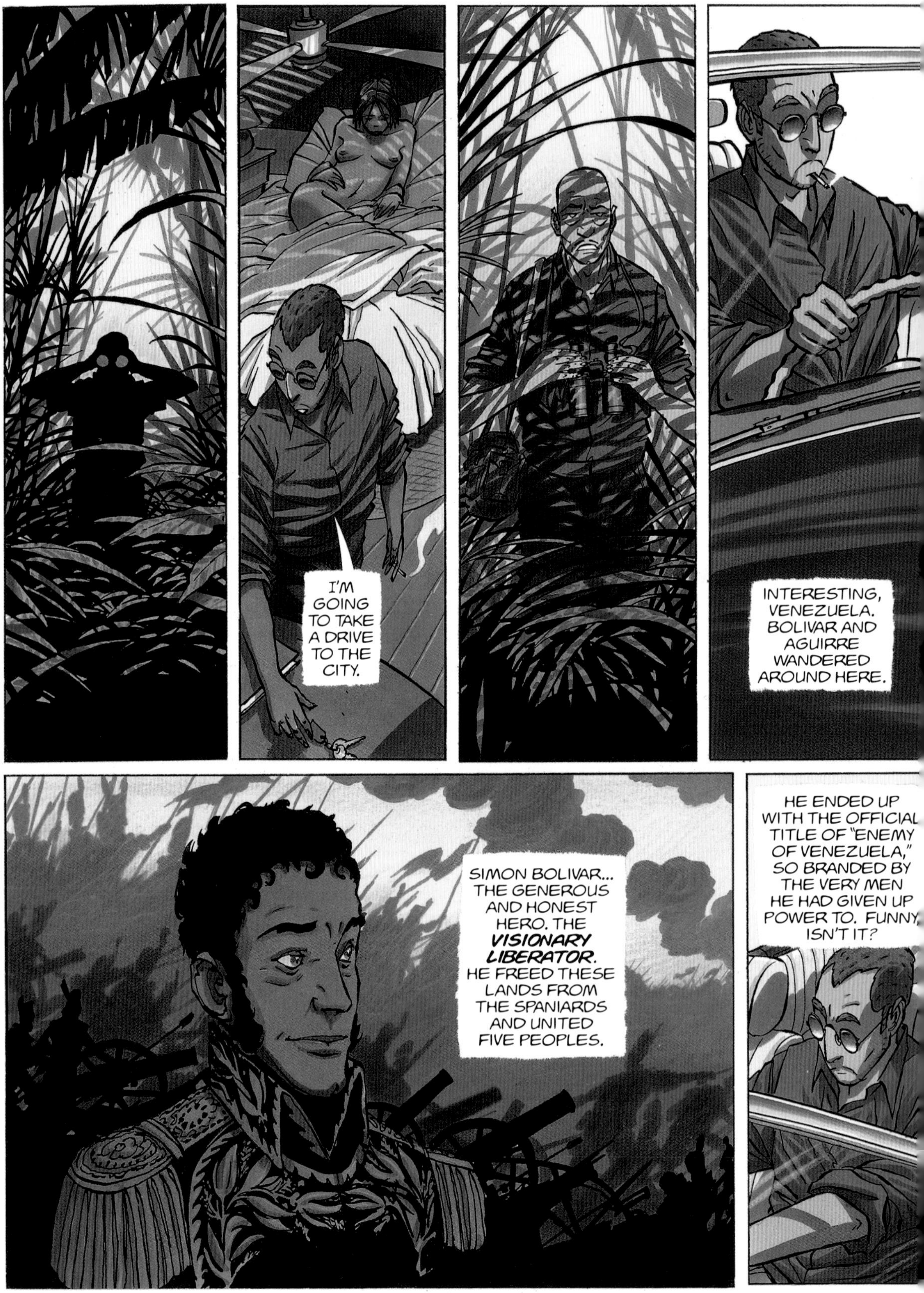
I'M GOING TO TAKE A DRIVE TO THE CITY.
INTERESTING, VENEZUELA. BOLIVAR AND AGUIRRE WANDERED AROUND HERE.
SIMON BOLIVAR... THE GENEROUS AND HONEST HERO. THE ***VISIONARY LIBERATOR***. HE FREED THESE LANDS FROM THE SPANIARDS AND UNITED FIVE PEOPLES.
HE ENDED UP WITH THE OFFICIAL TITLE OF "ENEMY OF VENEZUELA," SO BRANDED BY THE VERY MEN HE HAD GIVEN UP POWER TO. FUNNY, ISN'T IT?

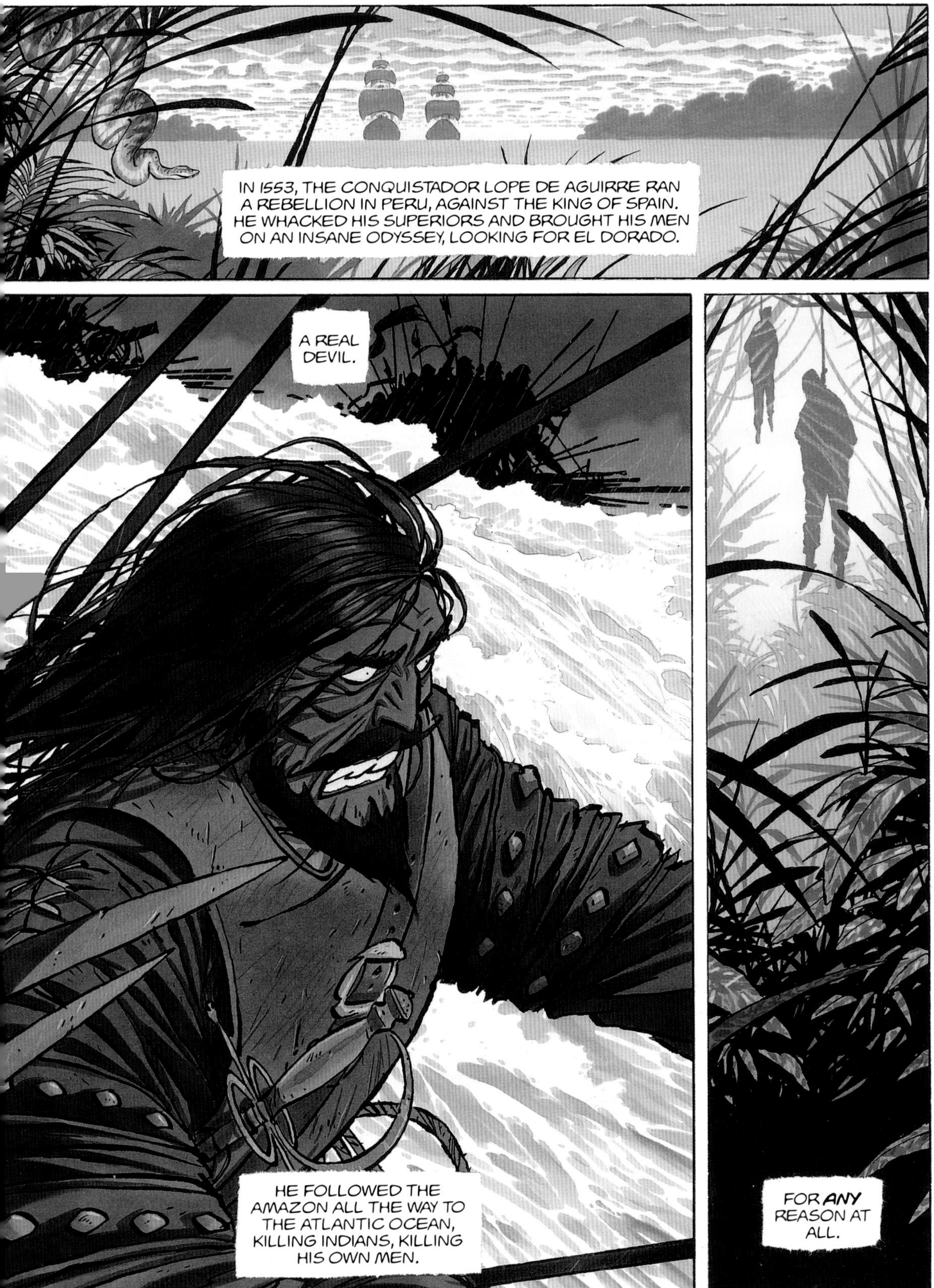

IN 1553, THE CONQUISTADOR LOPE DE AGUIRRE RAN A REBELLION IN PERU, AGAINST THE KING OF SPAIN. HE WHACKED HIS SUPERIORS AND BROUGHT HIS MEN ON AN INSANE ODYSSEY, LOOKING FOR EL DORADO.
A REAL DEVIL.
HE FOLLOWED THE AMAZON ALL THE WAY TO THE ATLANTIC OCEAN, KILLING INDIANS, KILLING HIS OWN MEN.
FOR **ANY** REASON AT ALL.

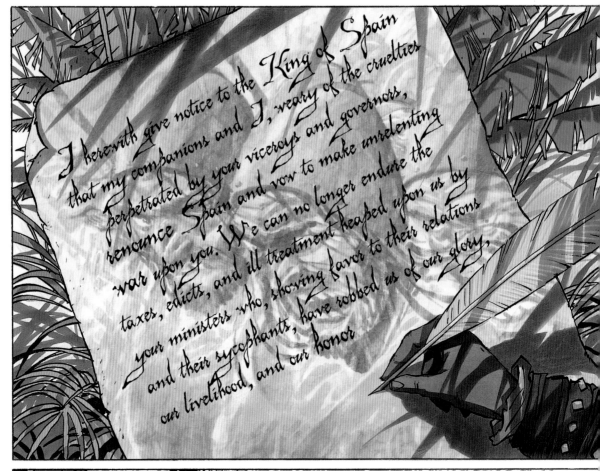

I herewith give notice to the *King of Spain* that my companions and I, weary of the cruelties perpetrated by your viceroys and governors, renounce Spain and vow to make unrelenting war upon you. We can no longer endure the taxes, edicts, and ill treatment heaped upon us by your ministers who, showing favor to their relations and their sycophants, have robbed us of our glory, our livelihood, and our honor

HE DIED VERY CLOSE TO HERE, BETRAYED AND ABANDONED. JUST LIKE BOLIVAR. THE EVIL AND THE GOOD, YET THE SAME FATE.

THERE IS A GOD FOR EVERYONE. THERE IS A FAIR REWARD AND THE SAME PUNISHMENT FOR ALL, PARADISE AND HELL.

BEFORE HE WAS MURDERED, AGUIRRE KILLED HIS OW DAUGHTER, "SO THAT SHE WOULD NOT BECOME A WHORE FOR SOLDIERS."

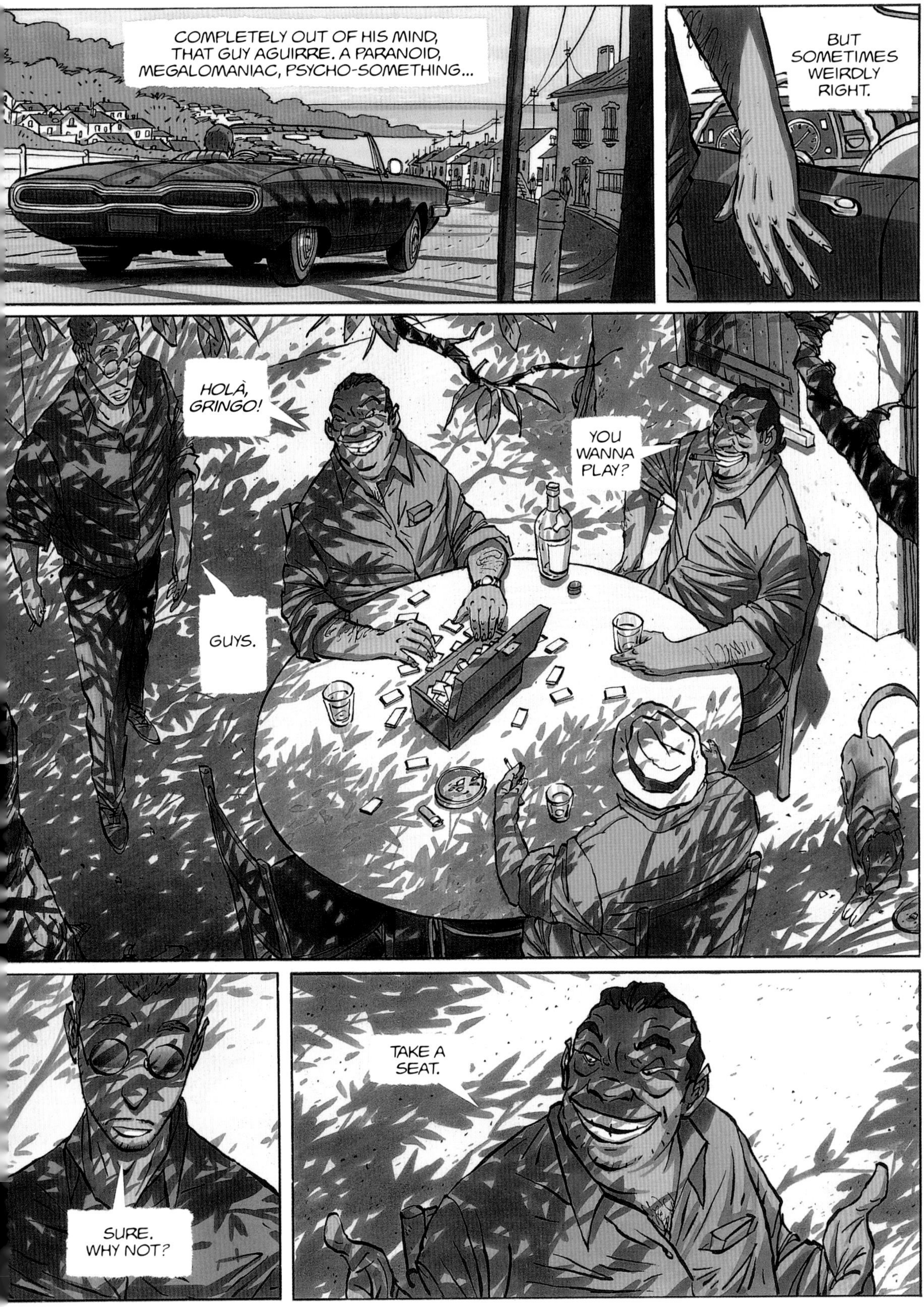
COMPLETELY OUT OF HIS MIND, THAT GUY AGUIRRE. A PARANOID, MEGALOMANIAC, PSYCHO-SOMETHING...
BUT SOMETIMES WEIRDLY RIGHT.
HOLÀ, GRINGO!
YOU WANNA PLAY?
GUYS.
SURE. WHY NOT?
TAKE A SEAT.

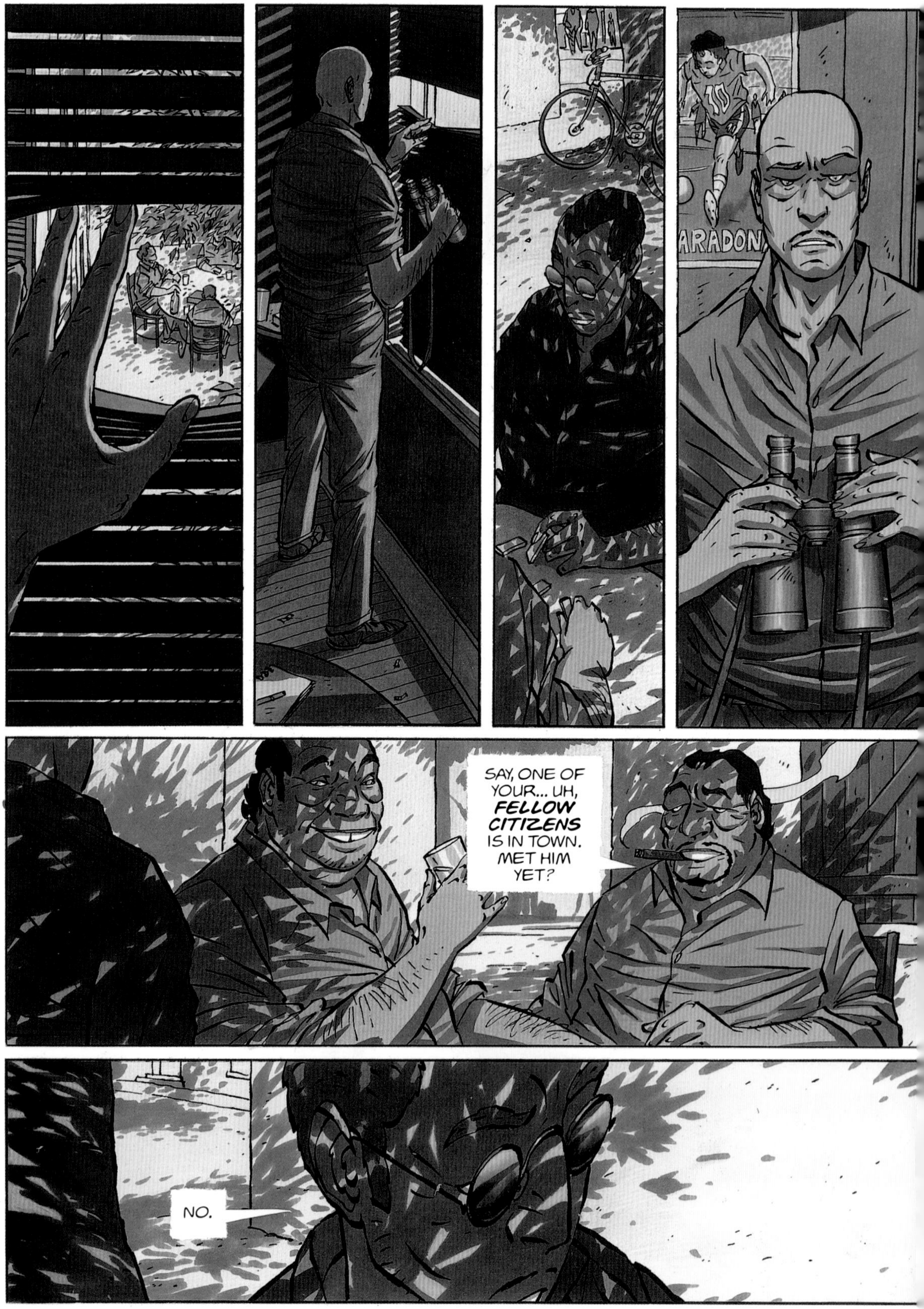
SAY, ONE OF YOUR... UH, **FELLOW CITIZENS** IS IN TOWN. MET HIM YET?
NO.

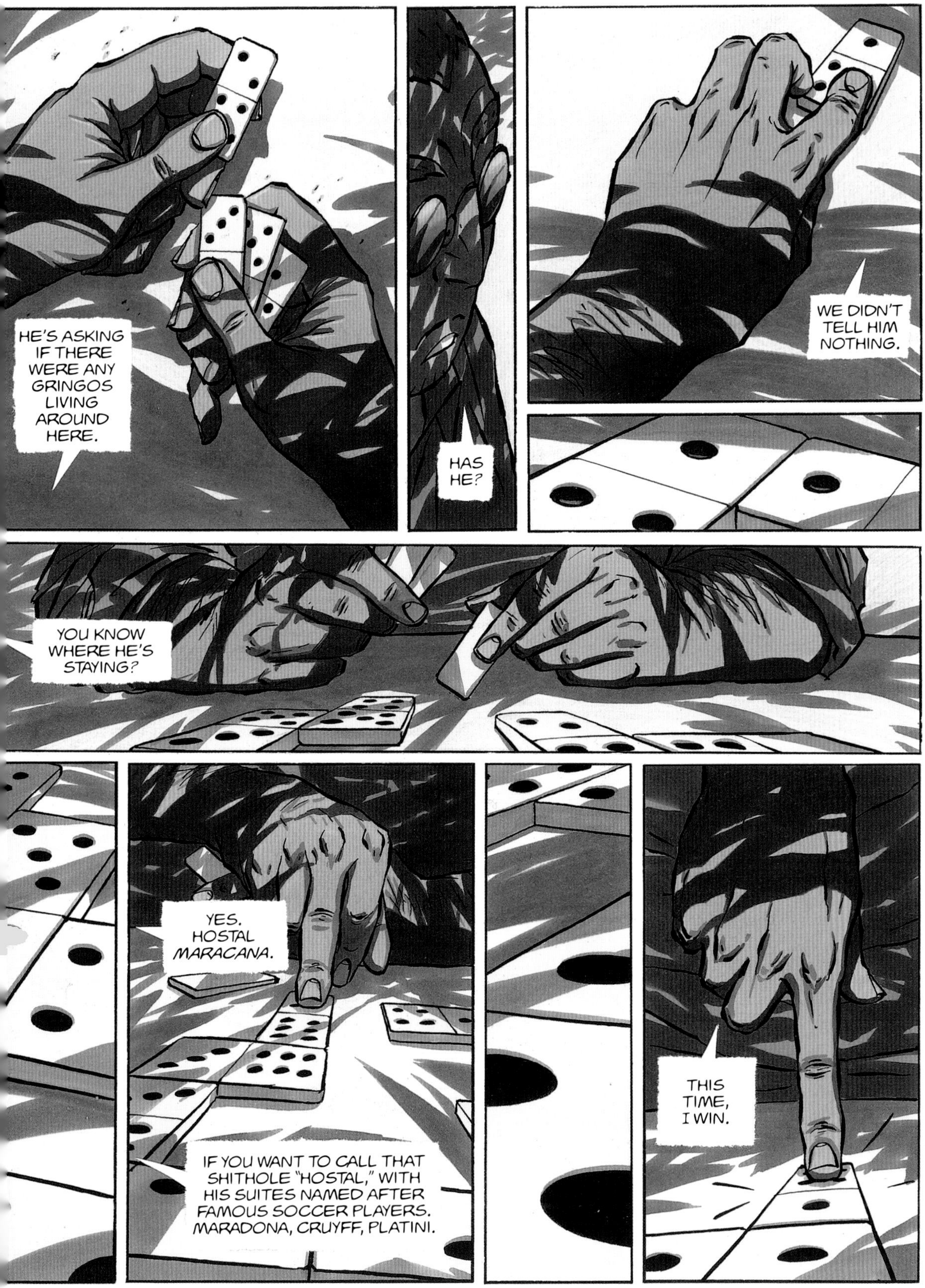
HE'S ASKING IF THERE WERE ANY GRINGOS LIVING AROUND HERE.
HAS HE?
WE DIDN'T TELL HIM NOTHING.
YOU KNOW WHERE HE'S STAYING?
YES. HOSTAL MARACANA.
IF YOU WANT TO CALL THAT SHITHOLE "HOSTAL," WITH HIS SUITES NAMED AFTER FAMOUS SOCCER PLAYERS. MARADONA, CRUYFF, PLATINI.
THIS TIME, I WIN.

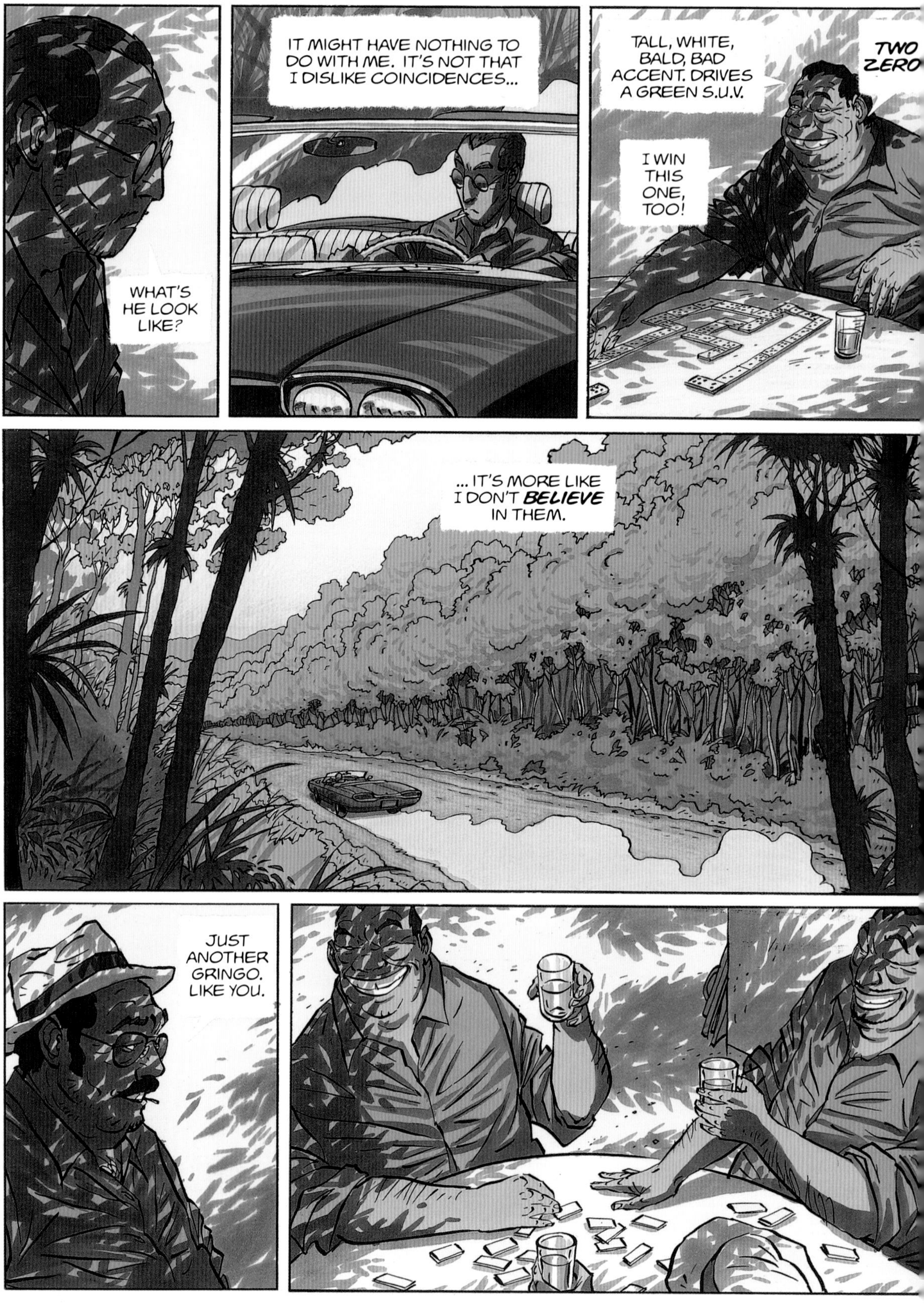
WHAT'S HE LOOK LIKE?
IT MIGHT HAVE NOTHING TO DO WITH ME. IT'S NOT THAT I DISLIKE COINCIDENCES...
TALL, WHITE, BALD, BAD ACCENT. DRIVES A GREEN S.U.V.
I WIN THIS ONE, TOO!
TWO ZERO
... IT'S MORE LIKE I DON'T BELIEVE IN THEM.
JUST ANOTHER GRINGO. LIKE YOU.

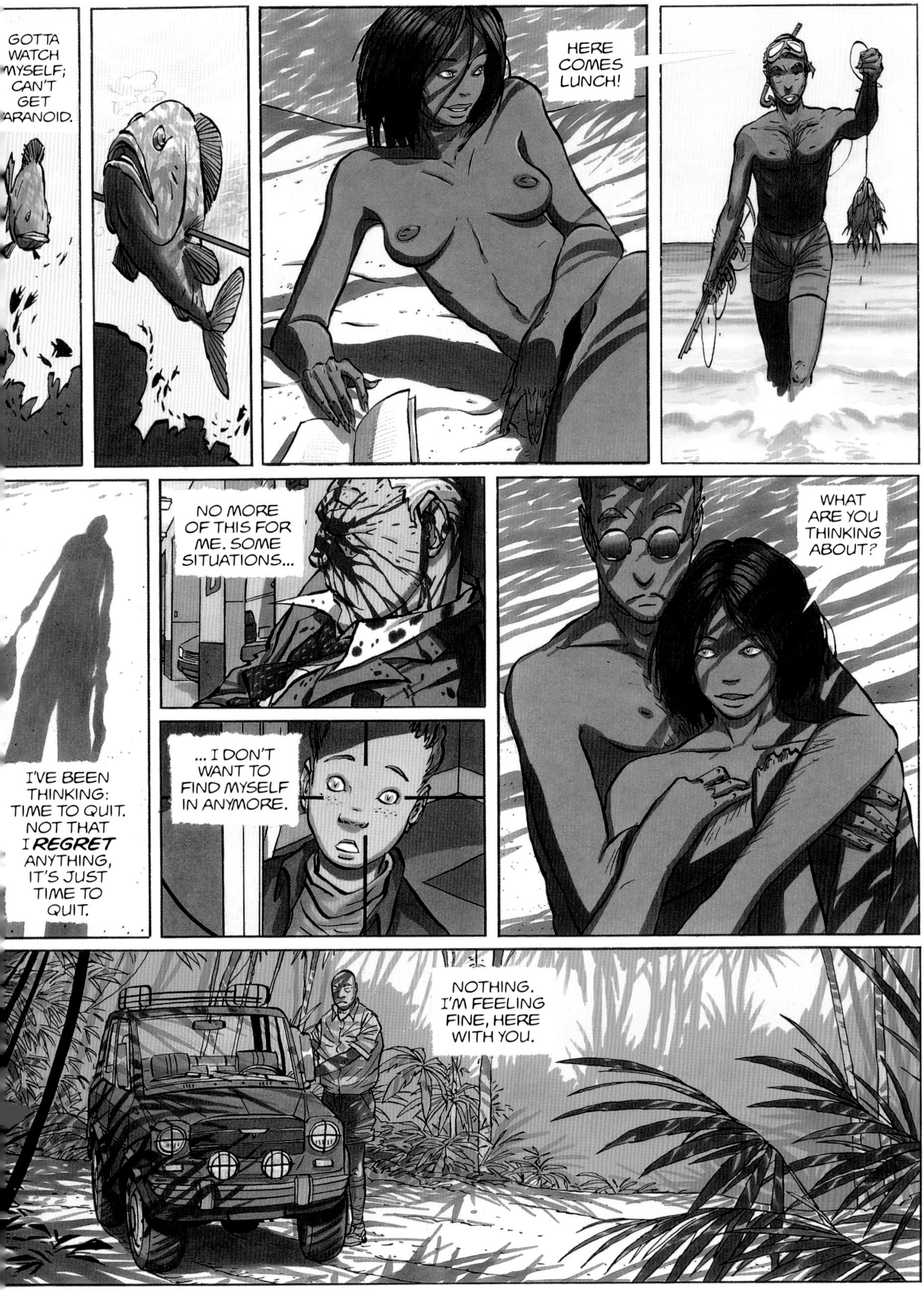
GOTTA WATCH MYSELF; CAN'T GET PARANOID.
HERE COMES LUNCH!
NO MORE OF THIS FOR ME. SOME SITUATIONS...
...I DON'T WANT TO FIND MYSELF IN ANYMORE.
I'VE BEEN THINKING: TIME TO QUIT. NOT THAT I REGRET ANYTHING, IT'S JUST TIME TO QUIT.
WHAT ARE YOU THINKING ABOUT?
NOTHING. I'M FEELING FINE, HERE WITH YOU.

AQUIRRE AND BOLIVAR WERE BETRAYED BY THOSE THEY'D TAKEN ALONG WITH THEM.

BUT ME, I HAVE NO LIEUTENANTS, NO BOSS, NO OBLIGATIONS. NO ONE CAN STAB *ME* IN THE BACK.

NO ONE EXCEPT MY *FIXER*.

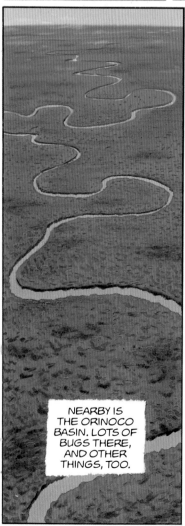

NEARBY IS THE ORINOCO BASIN. LOTS OF BUGS THERE, AND OTHER THINGS, TOO.

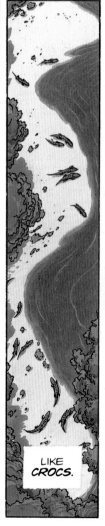

LIKE *CROCS*.

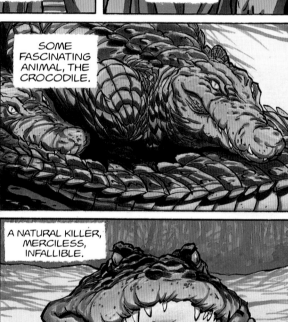

SOME FASCINATING ANIMAL, THE CROCODILE.

A NATURAL KILLER, MERCILESS, INFALLIBLE.

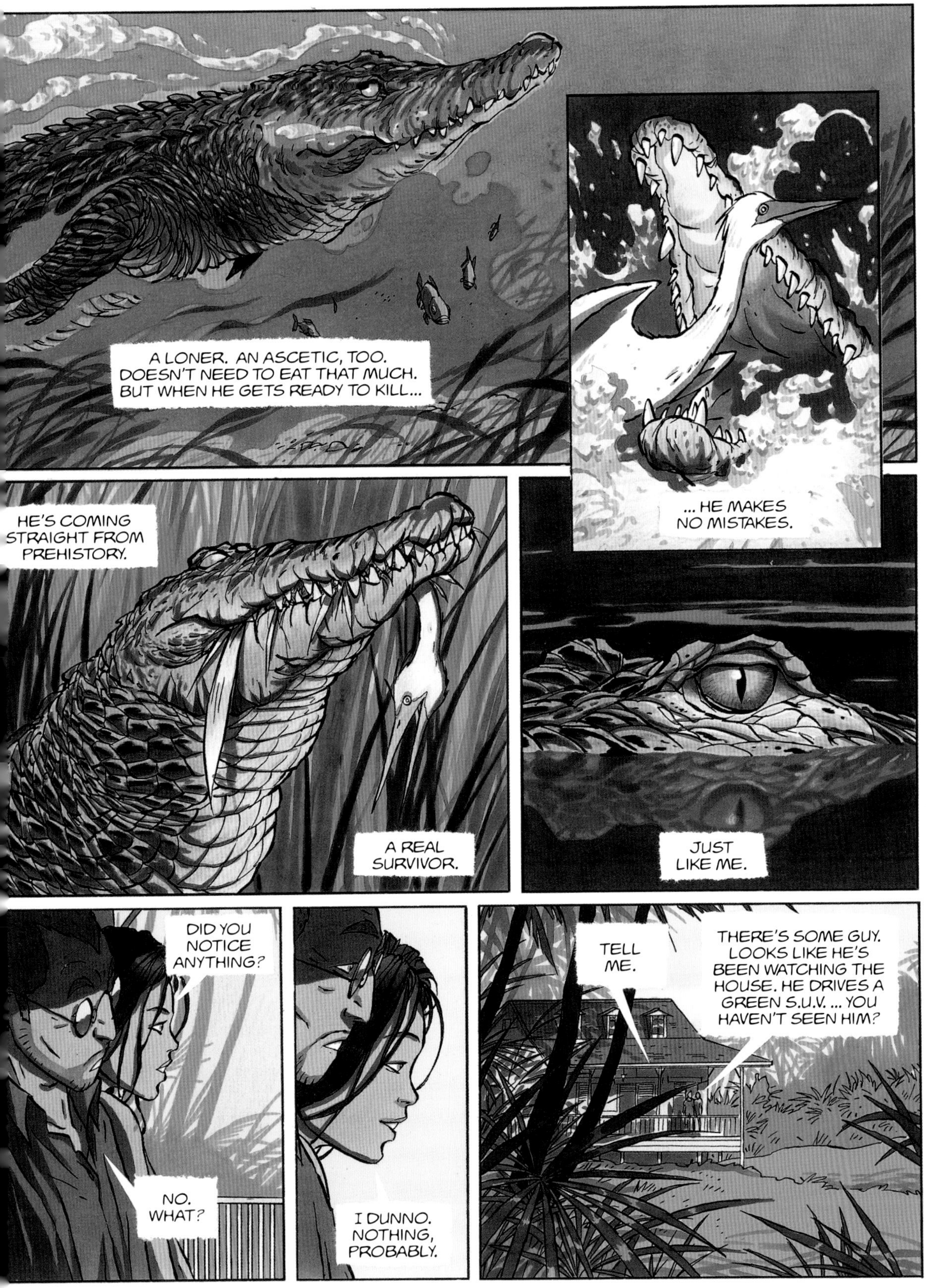
A LONER. AN ASCETIC, TOO. DOESN'T NEED TO EAT THAT MUCH. BUT WHEN HE GETS READY TO KILL...
... HE MAKES NO MISTAKES.
HE'S COMING STRAIGHT FROM PREHISTORY.
A REAL SURVIVOR.
JUST LIKE ME.
DID YOU NOTICE ANYTHING?
NO. WHAT?
I DUNNO. NOTHING, PROBABLY.
TELL ME.
THERE'S SOME GUY. LOOKS LIKE HE'S BEEN WATCHING THE HOUSE. HE DRIVES A GREEN S.U.V. ... YOU HAVEN'T SEEN HIM?

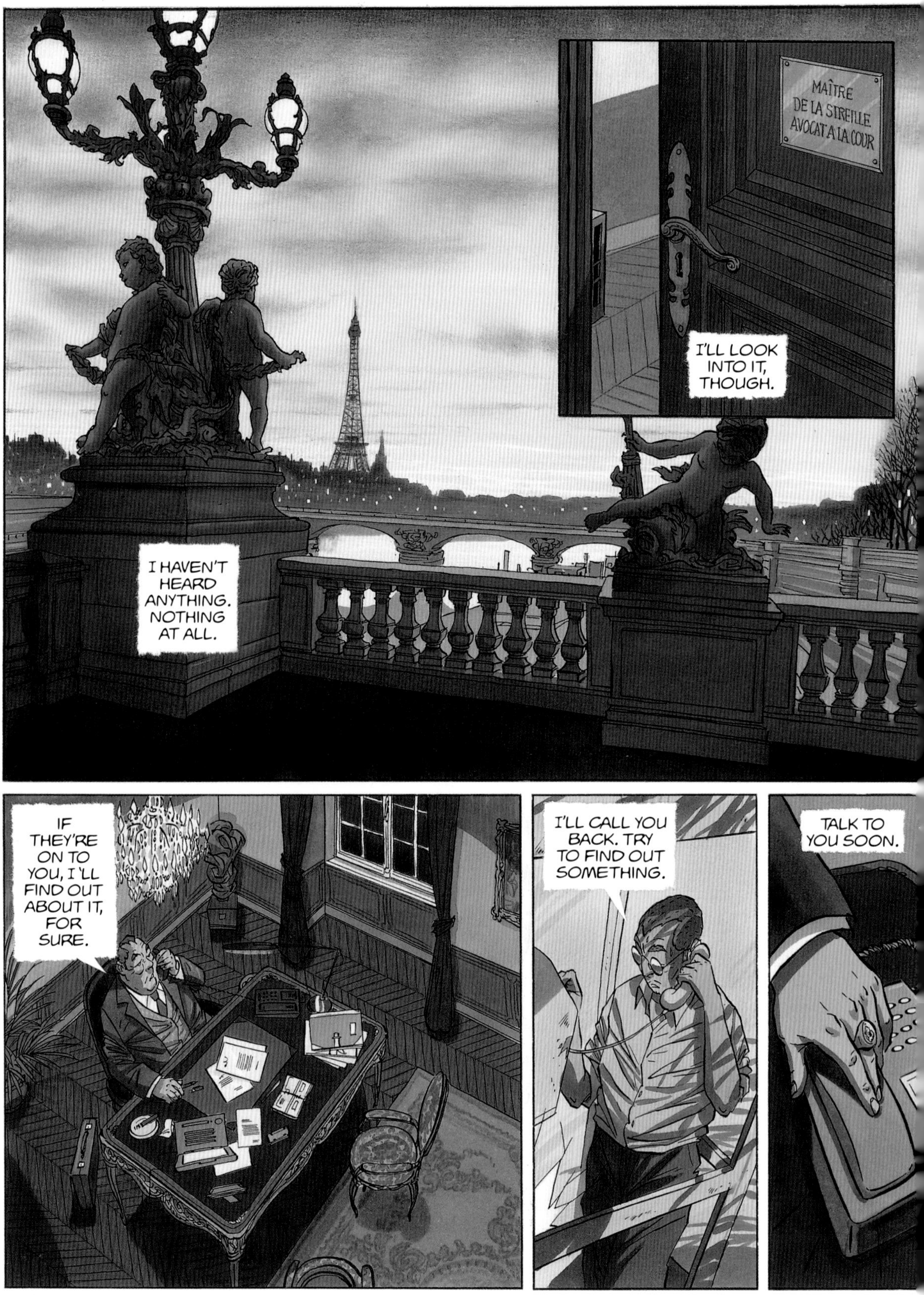
MAÎTRE
DE LA STREILLE
AVOCAT A LA COUR
I'LL LOOK INTO IT, THOUGH.
I HAVEN'T HEARD ANYTHING. NOTHING AT ALL.
IF THEY'RE ON TO YOU, I'LL FIND OUT ABOUT IT, FOR SURE.
I'LL CALL YOU BACK. TRY TO FIND OUT SOMETHING.
TALK TO YOU SOON.

WHEN YOU'VE LOOKED YOUR OWN DEATH IN THE FACE, THINGS ARE NEVER THE SAME.

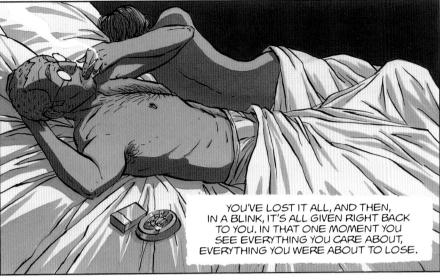

YOU'VE LOST IT ALL, AND THEN, IN A BLINK, IT'S ALL GIVEN RIGHT BACK TO YOU. IN THAT ONE MOMENT YOU SEE EVERYTHING YOU CARE ABOUT, EVERYTHING YOU WERE ABOUT TO LOSE.

AND THE NEXT SECOND YOU'RE THINKING YOUR WHOLE LIFE WASN'T WORTH *SHIT*.

THINKING LIKE THAT CAN DRIVE YOU NUTS.

THINKING LIKE THAT COULD MAKE YOU THINK NOTHING IS IMPORTANT...

...THAT YOU MIGHT AS WELL DESTROY EVERYTHING AROUND YOU.

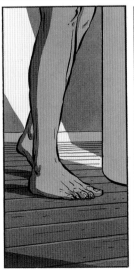

YEAH, THINKING LIKE THAT CAN REALLY DRIVE YOU *INSANE*.

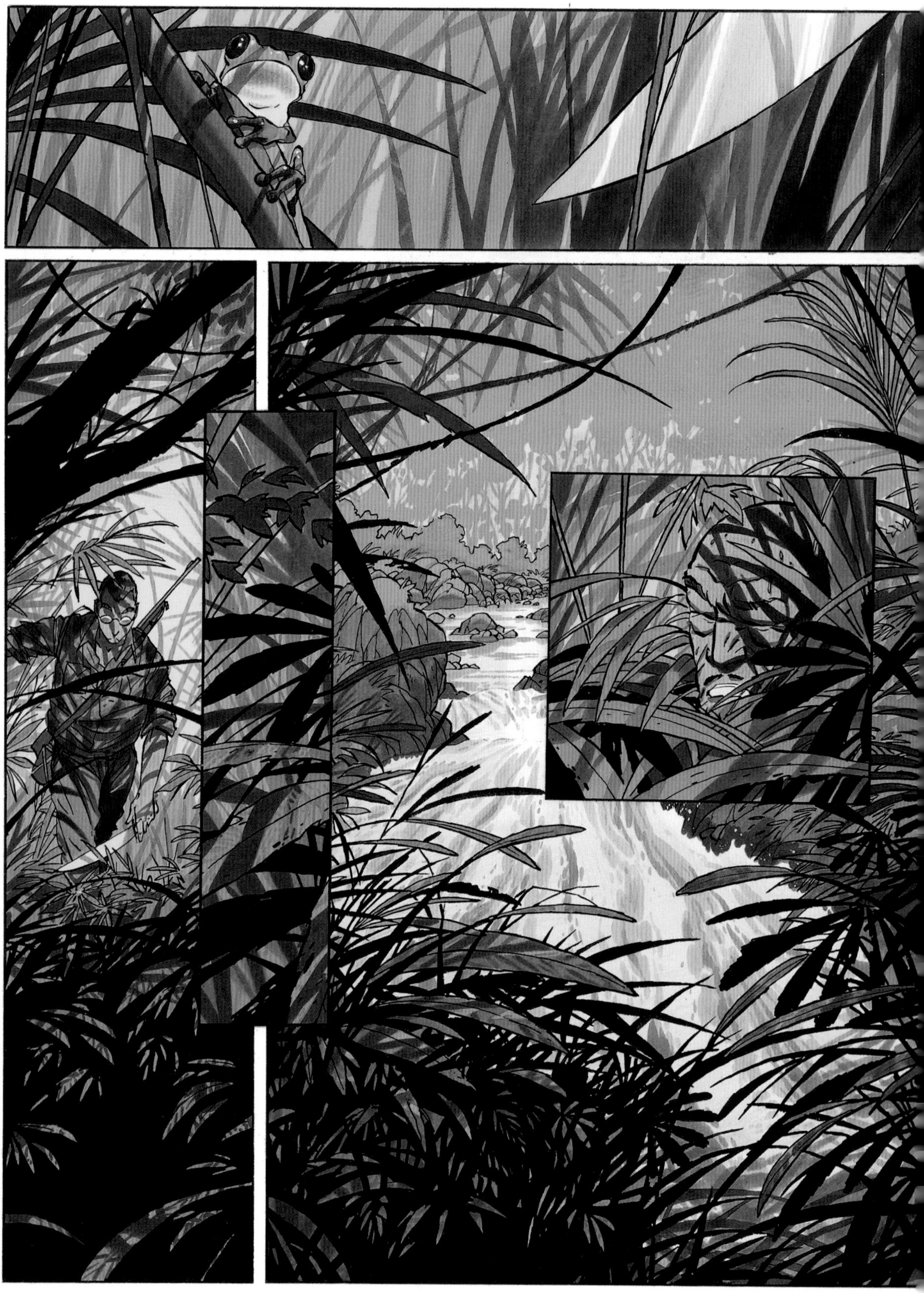

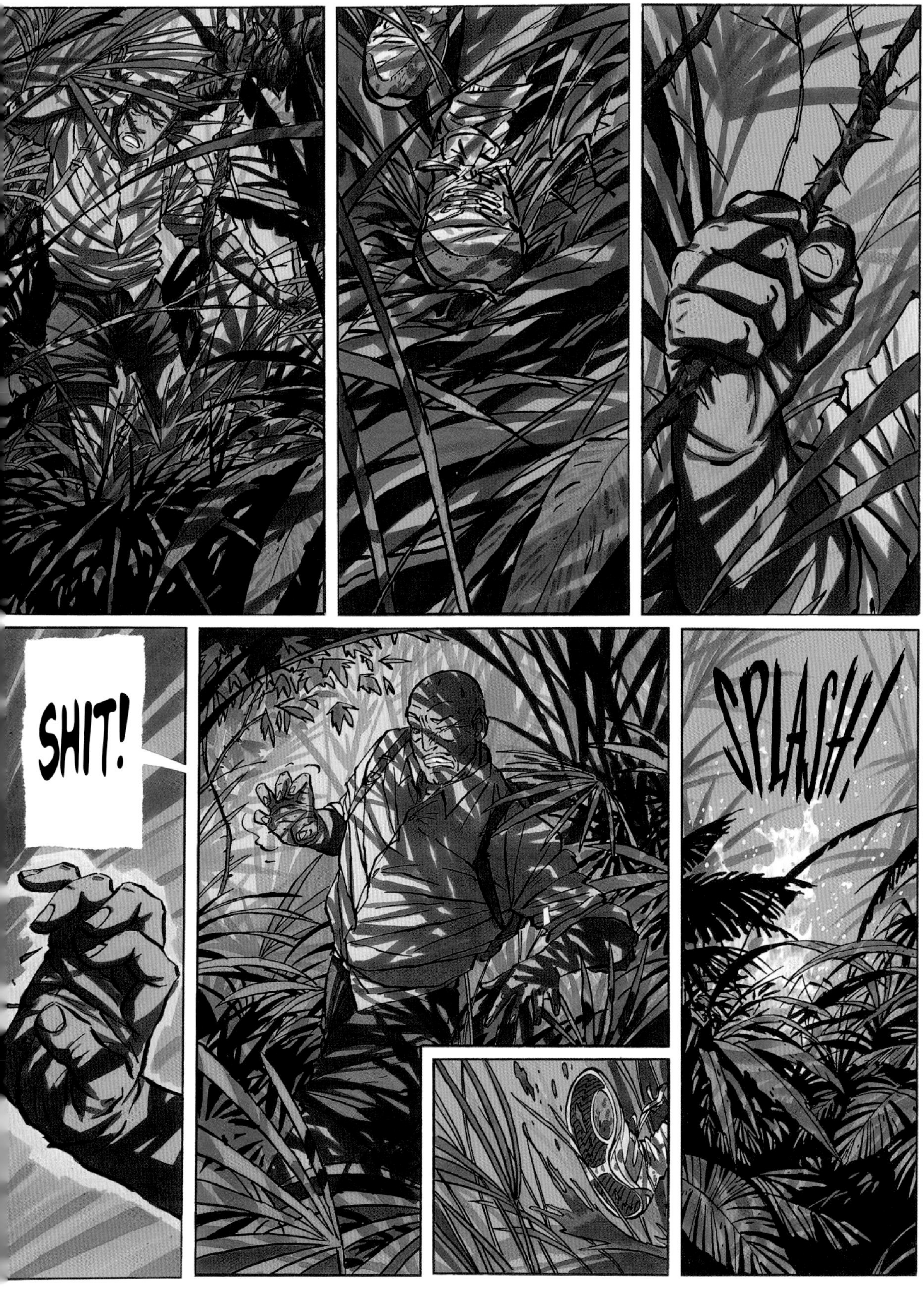
SHIT!
SPLASH!

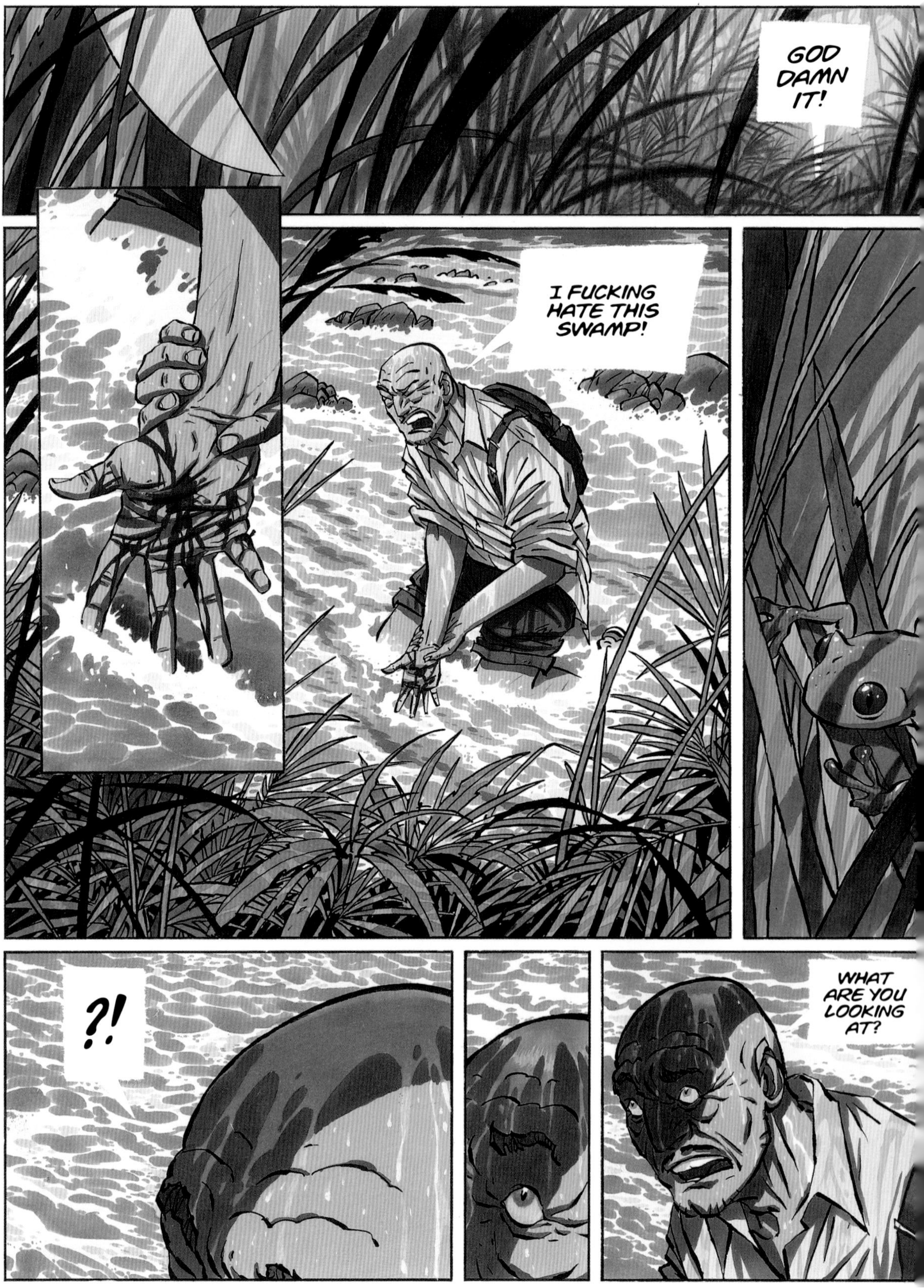
GOD DAMN IT!
I FUCKING HATE THIS SWAMP!
?!
WHAT ARE YOU LOOKING AT?

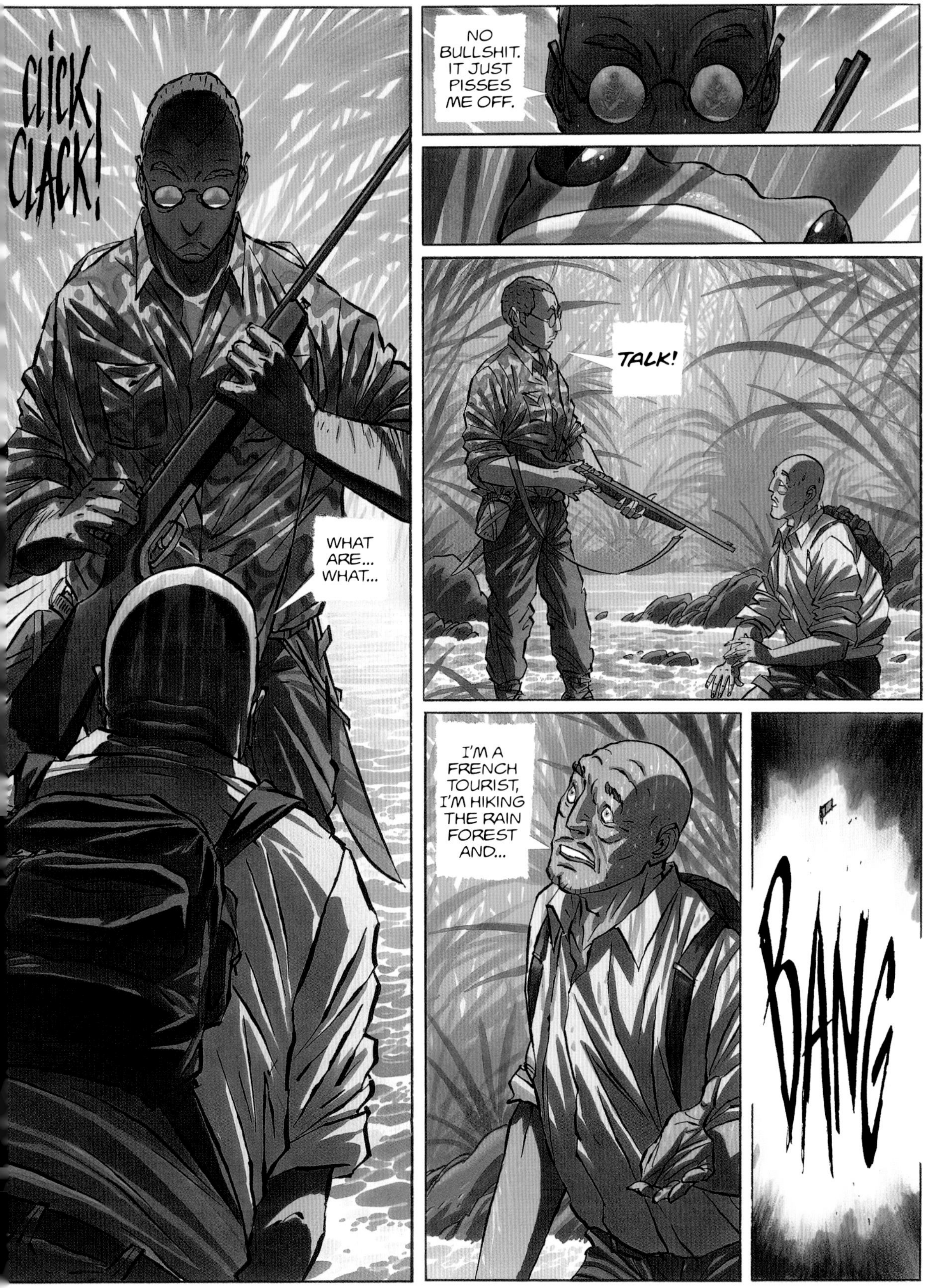
CLICK CLACK!
WHAT ARE... WHAT...
NO BULLSHIT. IT JUST PISSES ME OFF.
TALK!
I'M A FRENCH TOURIST, I'M HIKING THE RAIN FOREST AND...
BANG

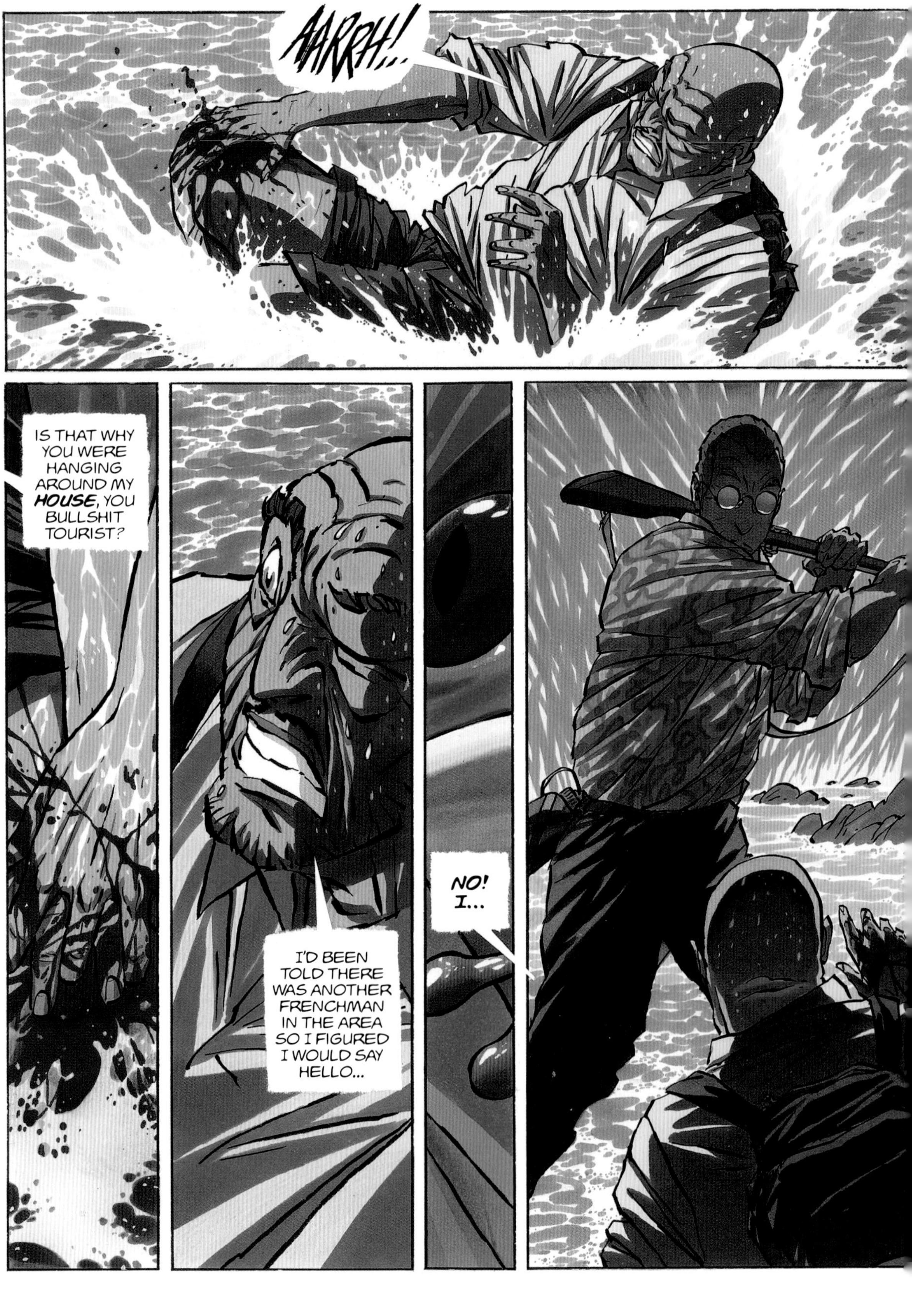
AARRH!..
IS THAT WHY YOU WERE HANGING AROUND MY **HOUSE**, YOU BULLSHIT TOURIST?
I'D BEEN TOLD THERE WAS ANOTHER FRENCHMAN IN THE AREA SO I FIGURED I WOULD SAY HELLO...
NO! I...

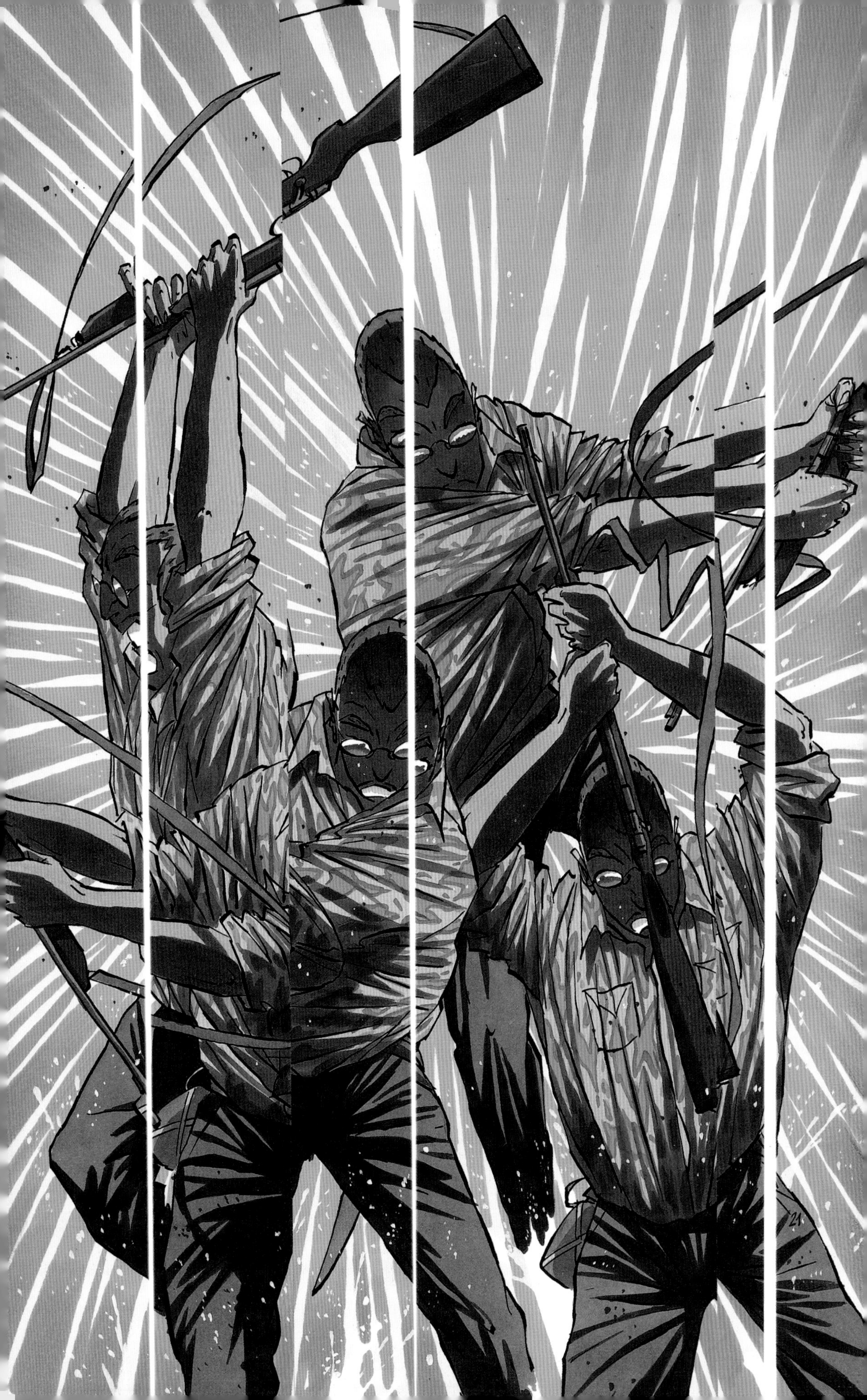

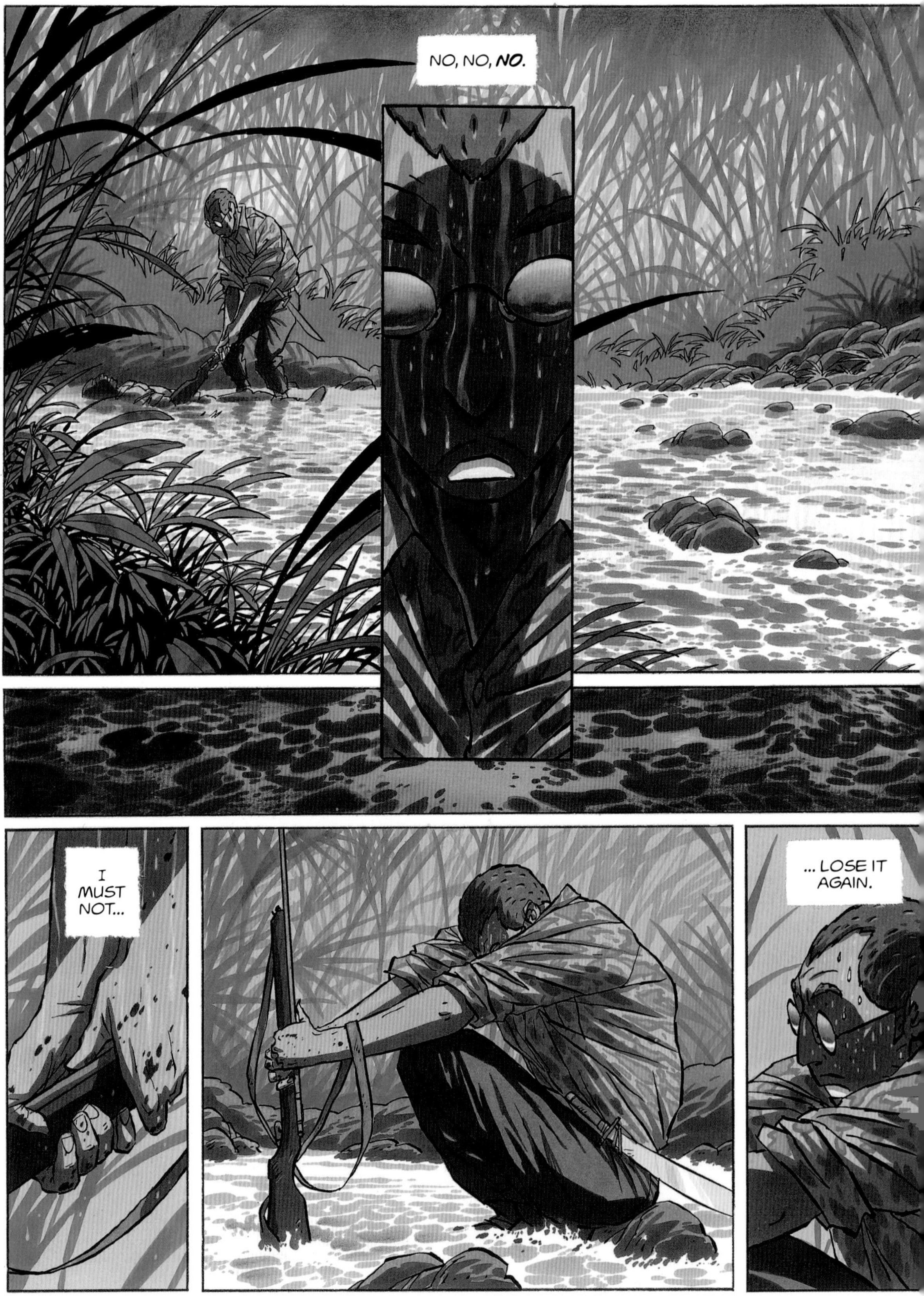
NO, NO, NO.
I MUST NOT...
... LOSE IT AGAIN.

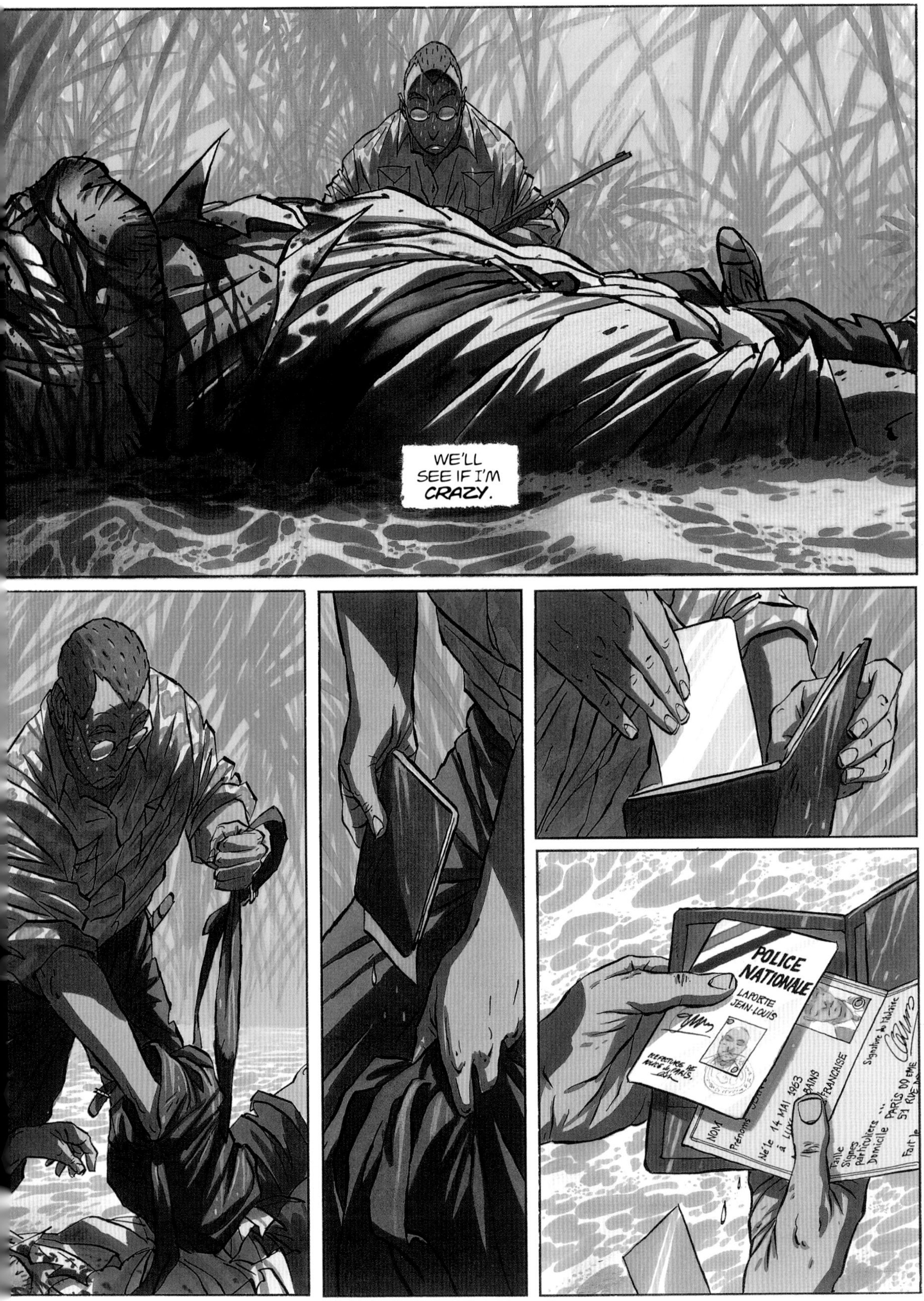
WE'LL SEE IF I'M CRAZY.
POLICE NATIONALE
LAPORTE
JEAN-LOUIS

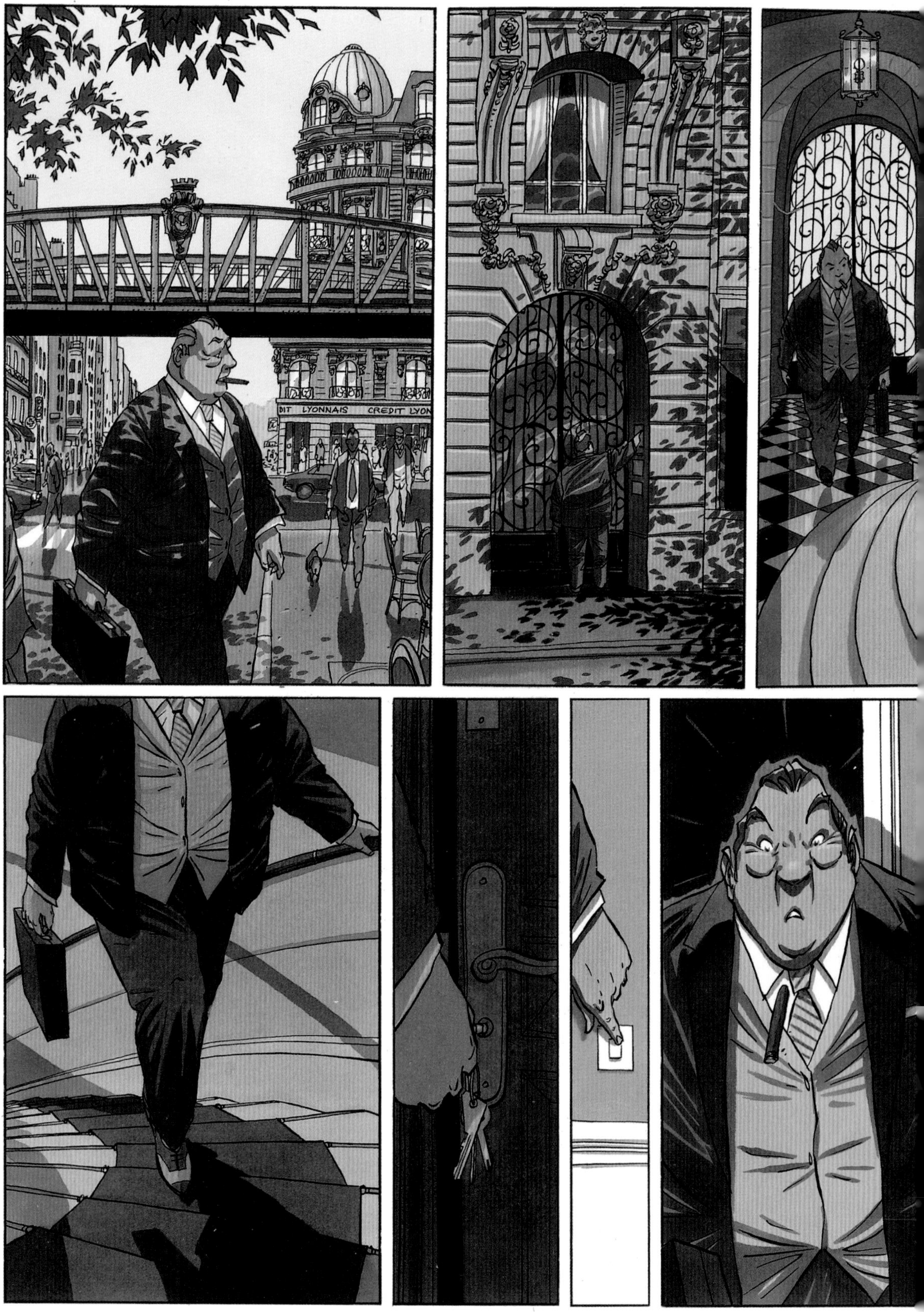
DIT LYONNAIS
CREDIT LYON

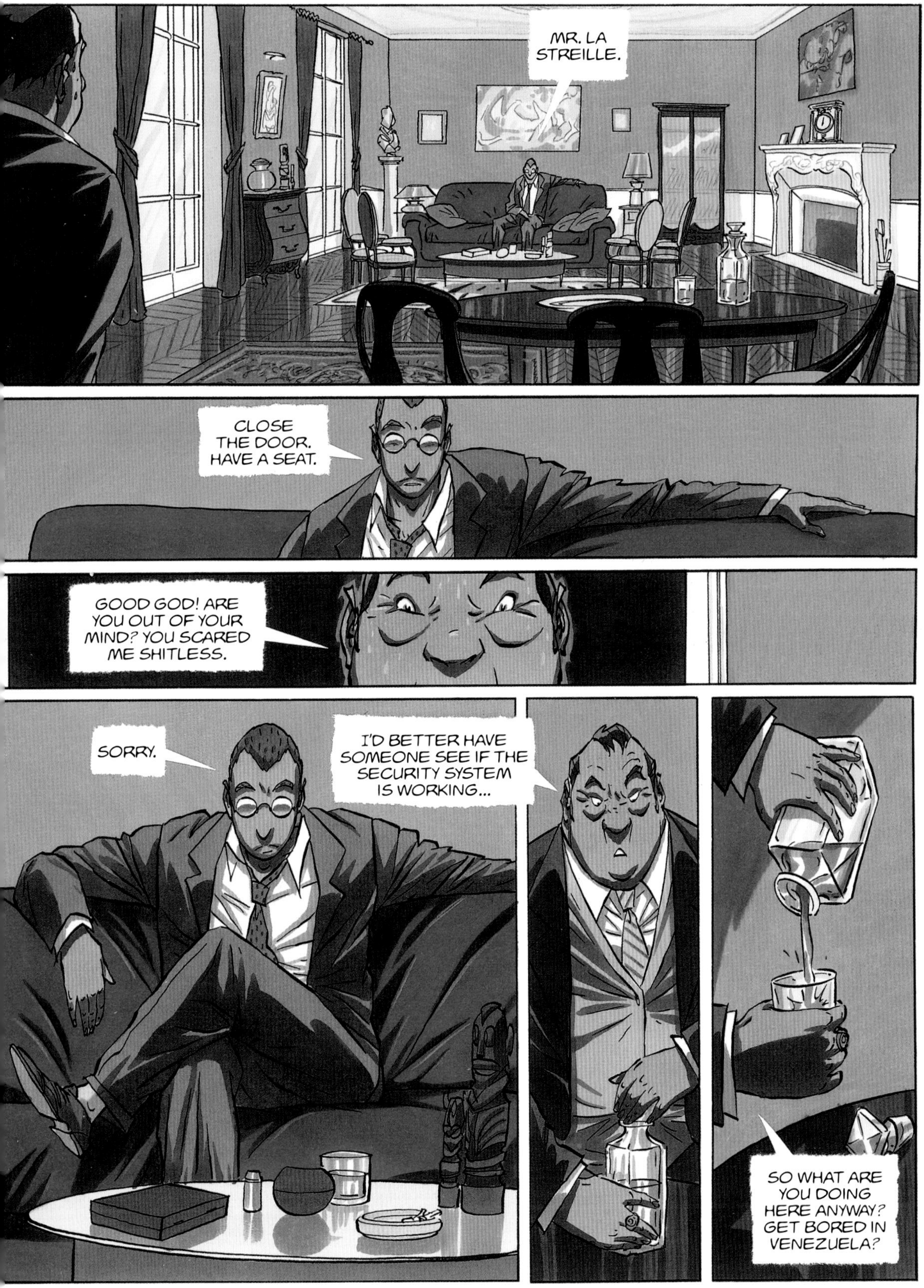
MR. LA STREILLE.
CLOSE THE DOOR. HAVE A SEAT.
GOOD GOD! ARE YOU OUT OF YOUR MIND? YOU SCARED ME SHITLESS.
SORRY.
I'D BETTER HAVE SOMEONE SEE IF THE SECURITY SYSTEM IS WORKING...
SO WHAT ARE YOU DOING HERE ANYWAY? GET BORED IN VENEZUELA?

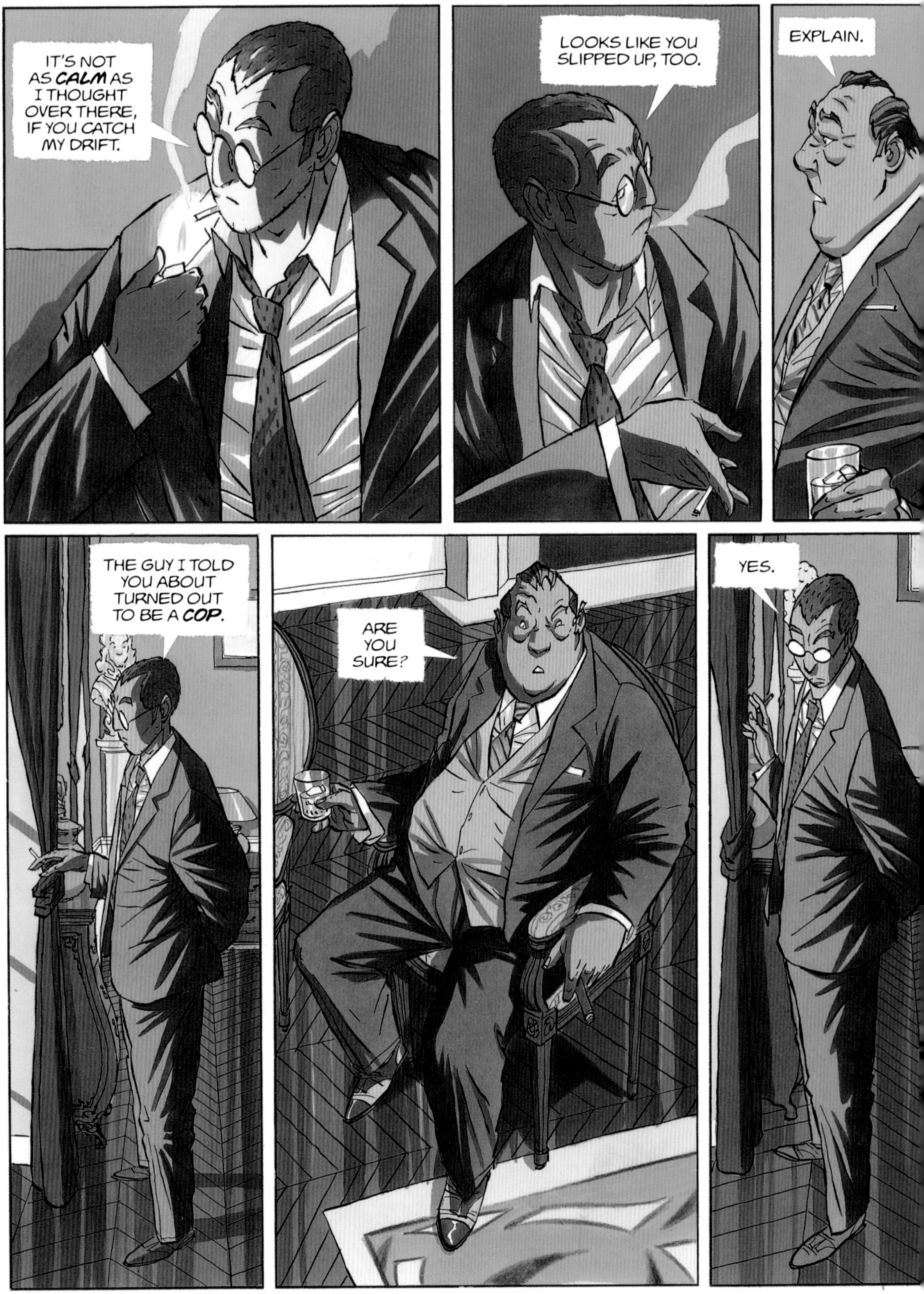
IT'S NOT AS **CALM** AS I THOUGHT OVER THERE, IF YOU CATCH MY DRIFT.
LOOKS LIKE YOU SLIPPED UP, TOO.
EXPLAIN.
THE GUY I TOLD YOU ABOUT TURNED OUT TO BE A **COP**.
ARE YOU SURE?
YES.

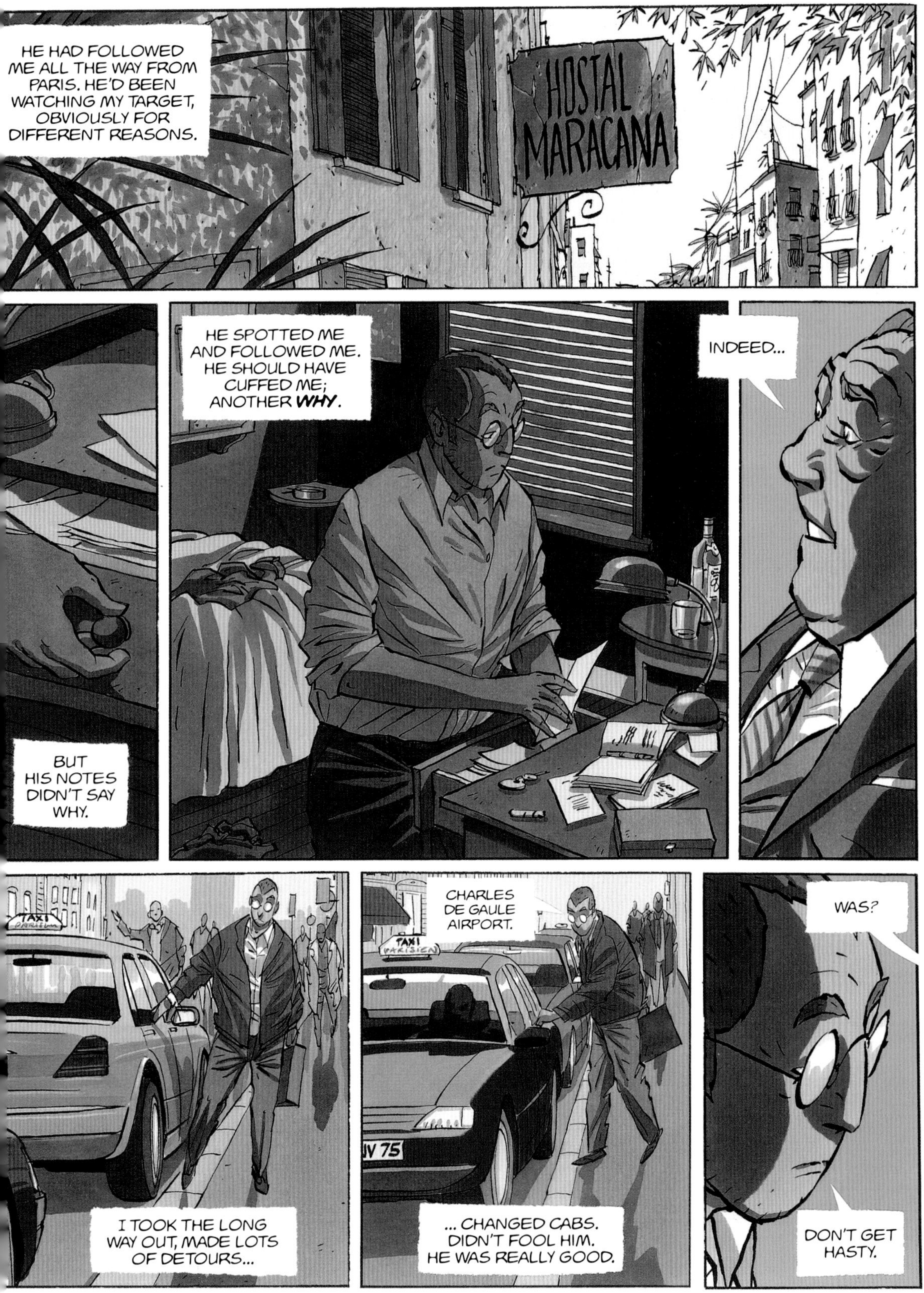
HE HAD FOLLOWED ME ALL THE WAY FROM PARIS. HE'D BEEN WATCHING MY TARGET, OBVIOUSLY FOR DIFFERENT REASONS.
HOSTAL MARACANA
BUT HIS NOTES DIDN'T SAY WHY.
HE SPOTTED ME AND FOLLOWED ME. HE SHOULD HAVE CUFFED ME; ANOTHER **WHY**.
INDEED...
TAXI
I TOOK THE LONG WAY OUT, MADE LOTS OF DETOURS...
CHARLES DE GAULE AIRPORT.
TAXI PARISIEN
... CHANGED CABS. DIDN'T FOOL HIM. HE WAS REALLY GOOD.
WAS?
DON'T GET HASTY.

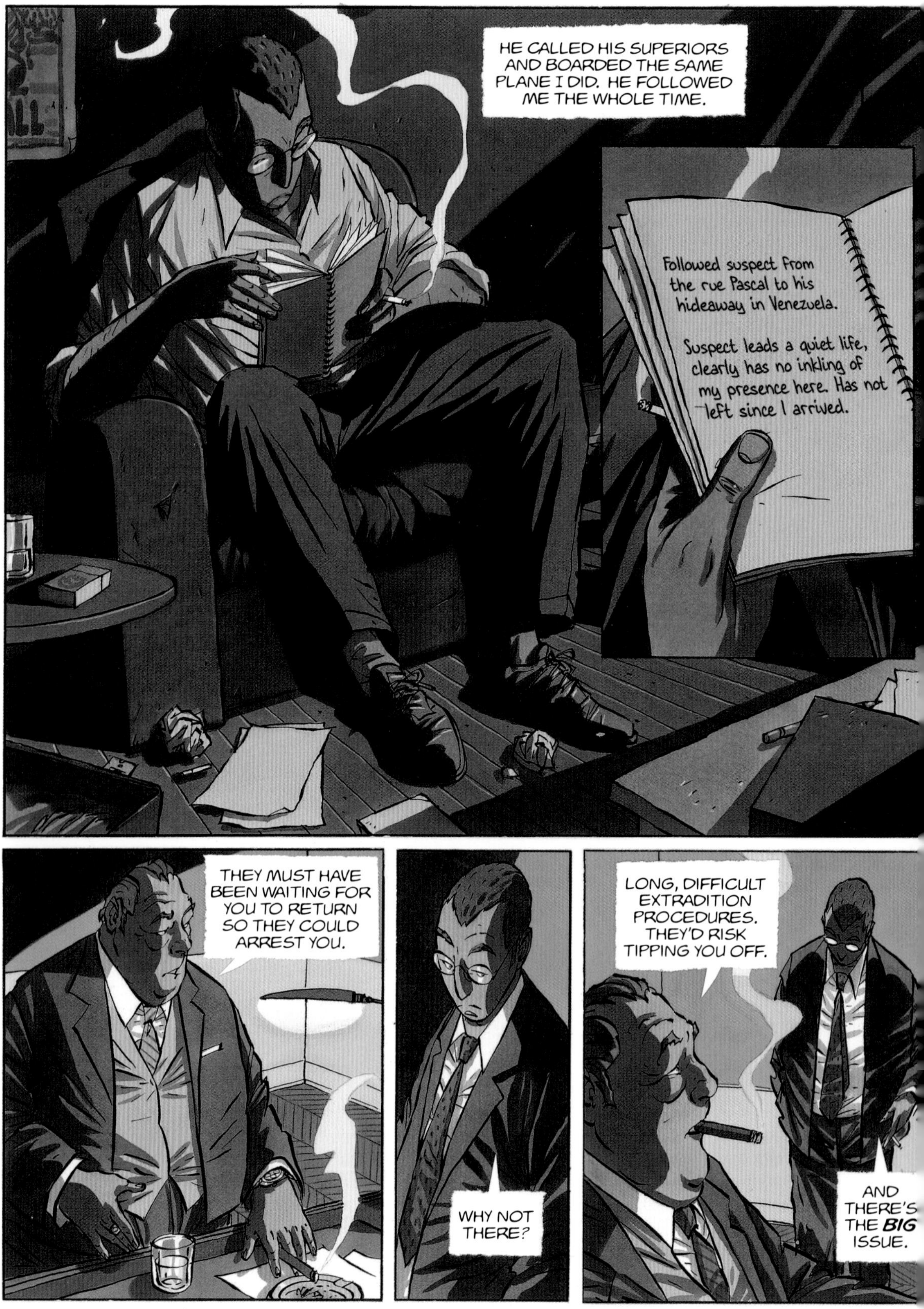
HE CALLED HIS SUPERIORS AND BOARDED THE SAME PLANE I DID. HE FOLLOWED ME THE WHOLE TIME.
Followed suspect from the rue Pascal to his hideaway in Venezuela.
Suspect leads a quiet life, clearly has no inkling of my presence here. Has not left since I arrived.
THEY MUST HAVE BEEN WAITING FOR YOU TO RETURN SO THEY COULD ARREST YOU.
WHY NOT THERE?
LONG, DIFFICULT EXTRADITION PROCEDURES. THEY'D RISK TIPPING YOU OFF.
AND THERE'S THE BIG ISSUE.

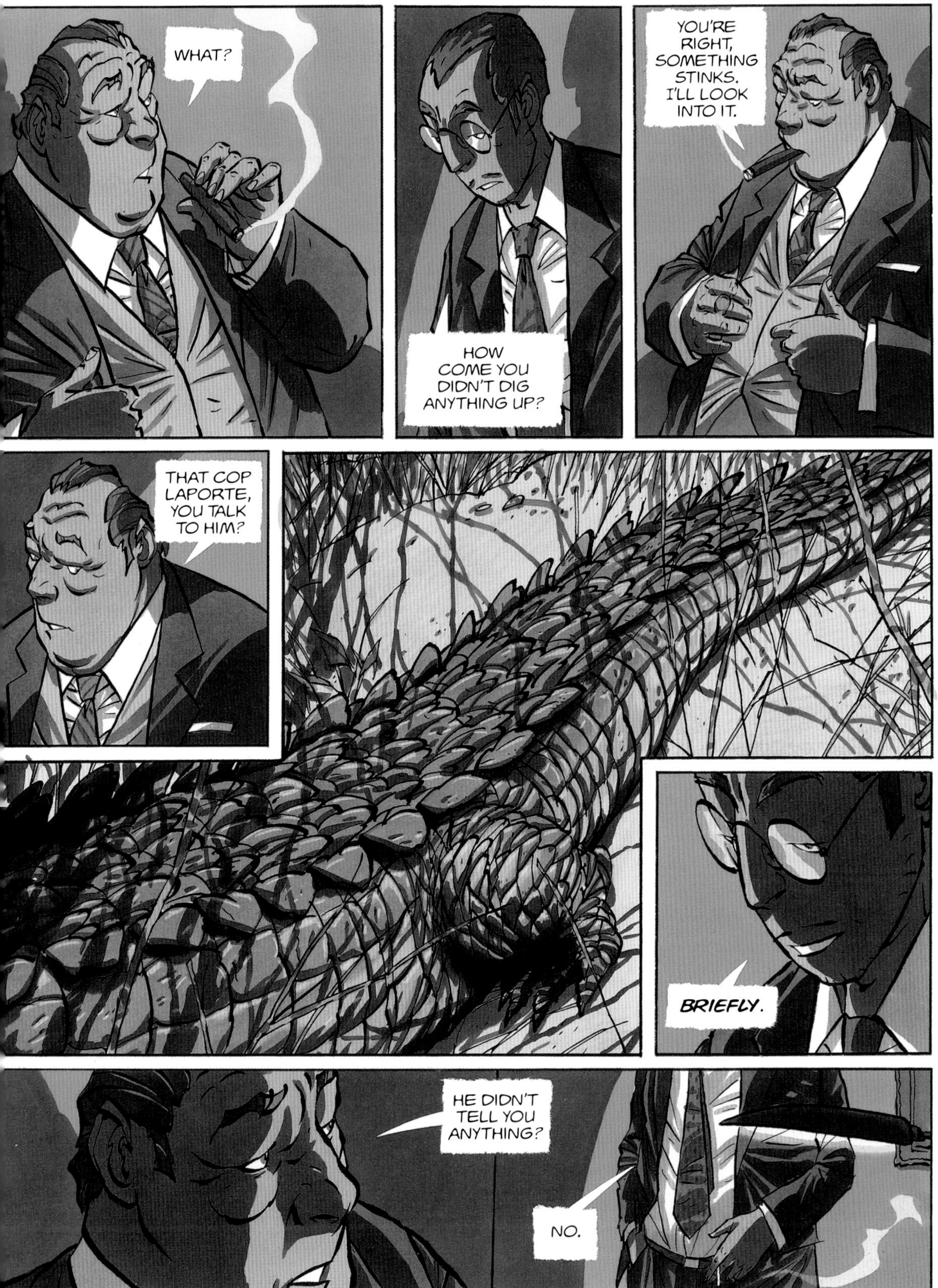
WHAT?
HOW COME YOU DIDN'T DIG ANYTHING UP?
YOU'RE RIGHT, SOMETHING STINKS. I'LL LOOK INTO IT.
THAT COP LAPORTE, YOU TALK TO HIM?
BRIEFLY.
HE DIDN'T TELL YOU ANYTHING?
NO.

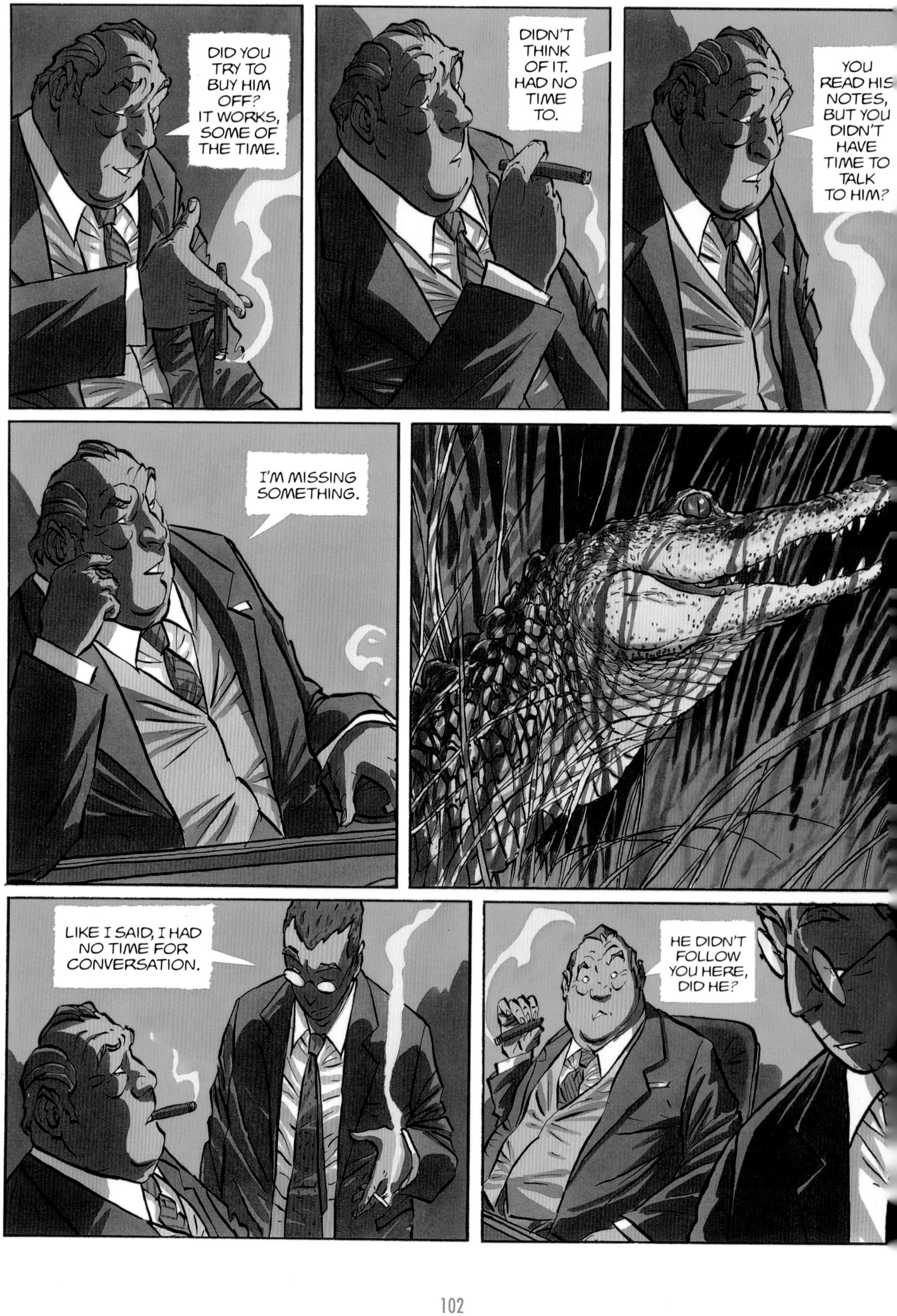
DID YOU TRY TO BUY HIM OFF? IT WORKS, SOME OF THE TIME.
DIDN'T THINK OF IT. HAD NO TIME TO.
YOU READ HIS NOTES, BUT YOU DIDN'T HAVE TIME TO TALK TO HIM?
I'M MISSING SOMETHING.
LIKE I SAID, I HAD NO TIME FOR CONVERSATION.
HE DIDN'T FOLLOW YOU HERE, DID HE?

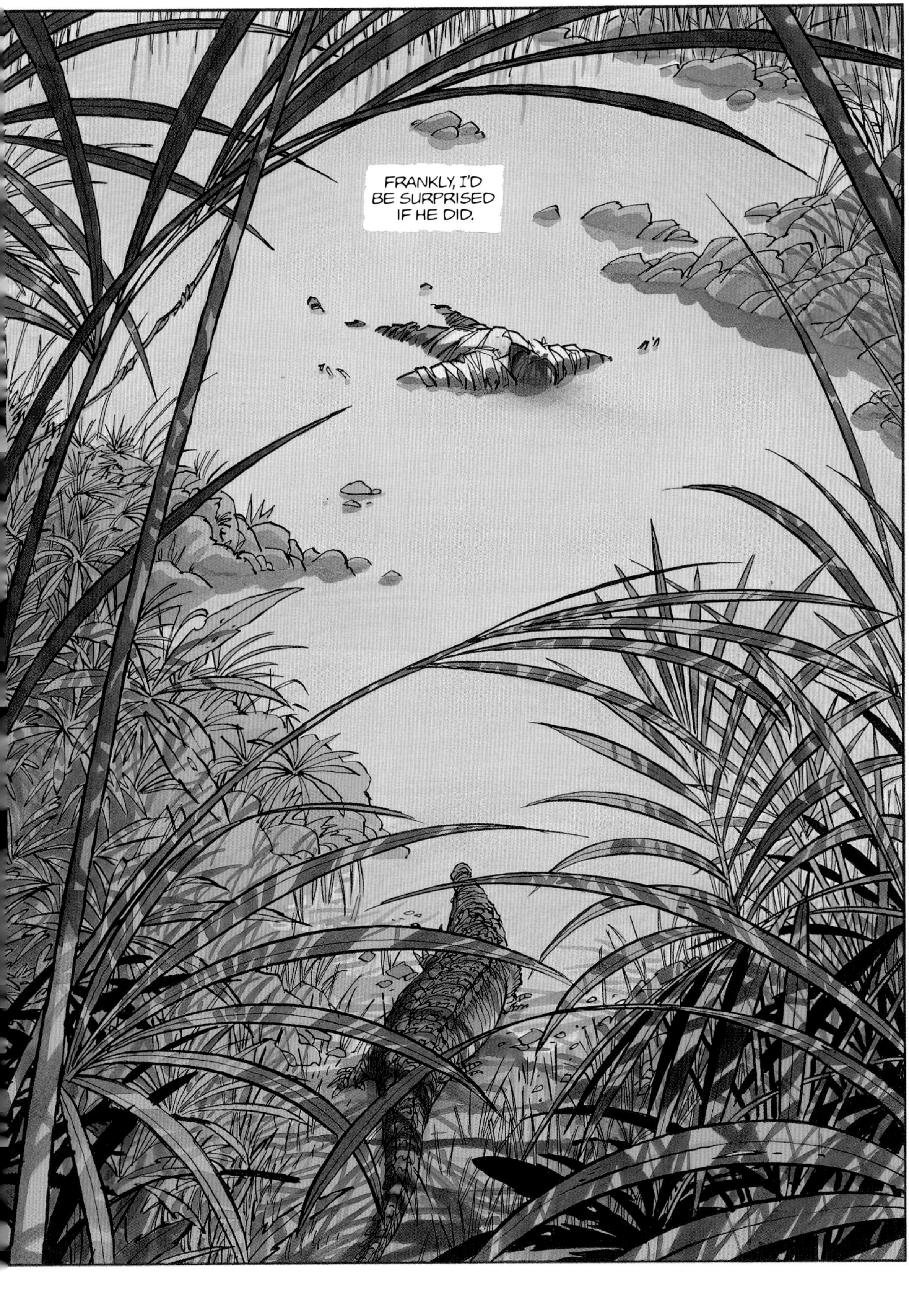
FRANKLY, I'D BE SURPRISED IF HE DID.

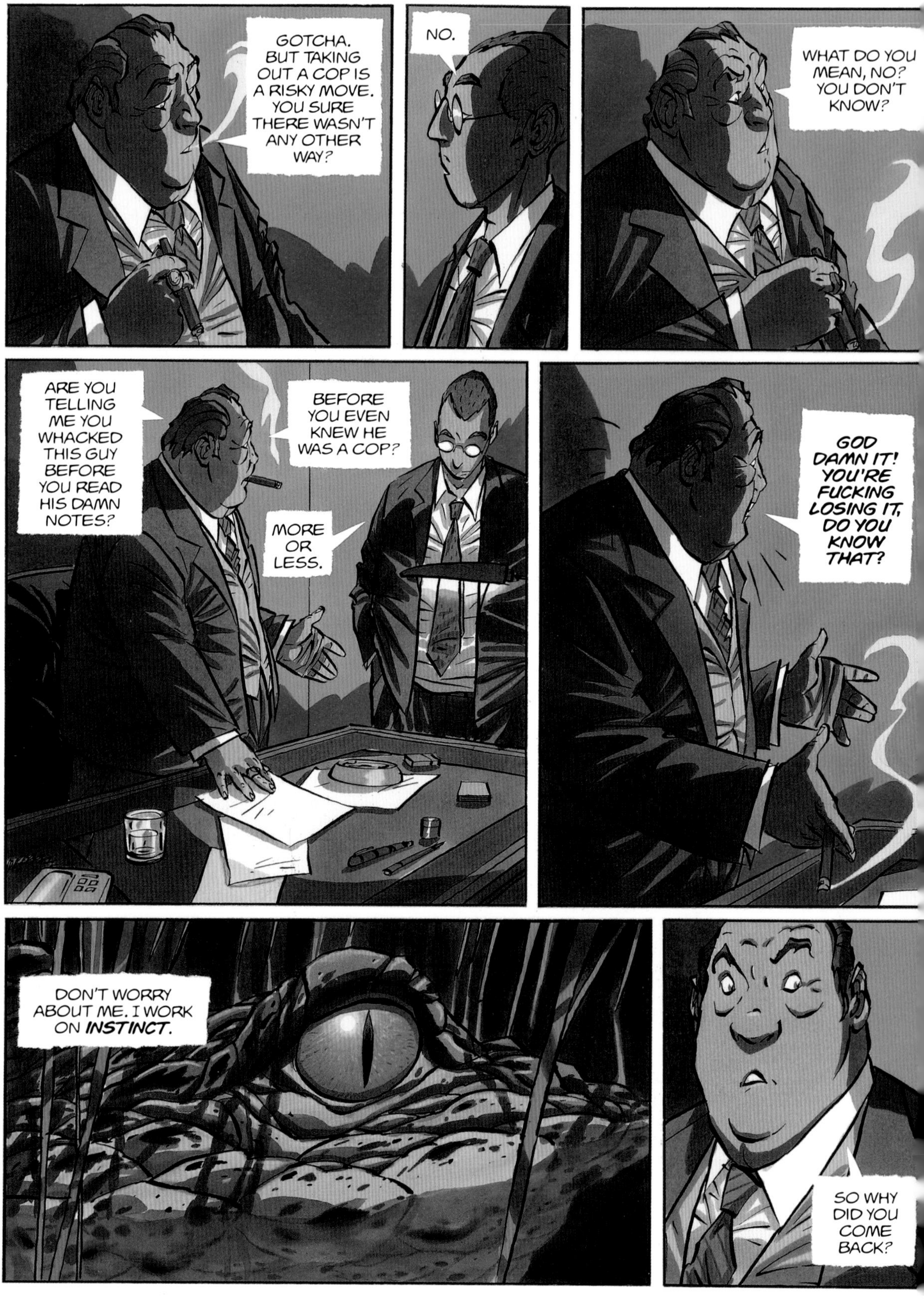
GOTCHA. BUT TAKING OUT A COP IS A RISKY MOVE. YOU SURE THERE WASN'T ANY OTHER WAY?
NO.
WHAT DO YOU MEAN, NO? YOU DON'T KNOW?
ARE YOU TELLING ME YOU WHACKED THIS GUY BEFORE YOU READ HIS DAMN NOTES?
BEFORE YOU EVEN KNEW HE WAS A COP?
MORE OR LESS.
GOD DAMN IT! YOU'RE FUCKING LOSING IT, DO YOU KNOW THAT?
DON'T WORRY ABOUT ME. I WORK ON INSTINCT.
SO WHY DID YOU COME BACK?

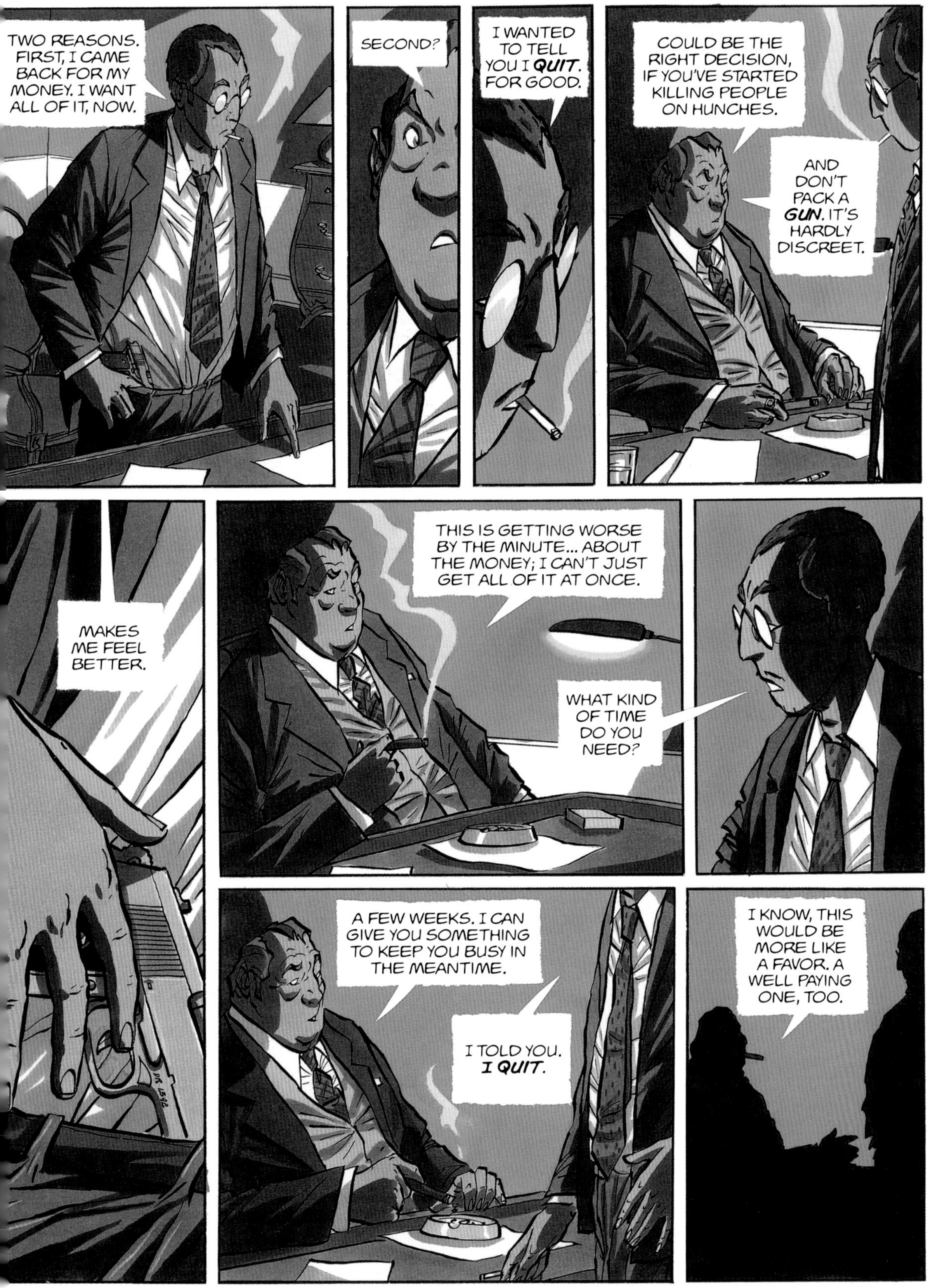
TWO REASONS. FIRST, I CAME BACK FOR MY MONEY. I WANT ALL OF IT, NOW.
SECOND?
I WANTED TO TELL YOU I **QUIT**. FOR GOOD.
COULD BE THE RIGHT DECISION, IF YOU'VE STARTED KILLING PEOPLE ON HUNCHES.
AND DON'T PACK A **GUN**. IT'S HARDLY DISCREET.
MAKES ME FEEL BETTER.
THIS IS GETTING WORSE BY THE MINUTE... ABOUT THE MONEY; I CAN'T JUST GET ALL OF IT AT ONCE.
WHAT KIND OF TIME DO YOU NEED?
A FEW WEEKS. I CAN GIVE YOU SOMETHING TO KEEP YOU BUSY IN THE MEANTIME.
I TOLD YOU. **I QUIT**.
I KNOW, THIS WOULD BE MORE LIKE A FAVOR. A WELL PAYING ONE, TOO.

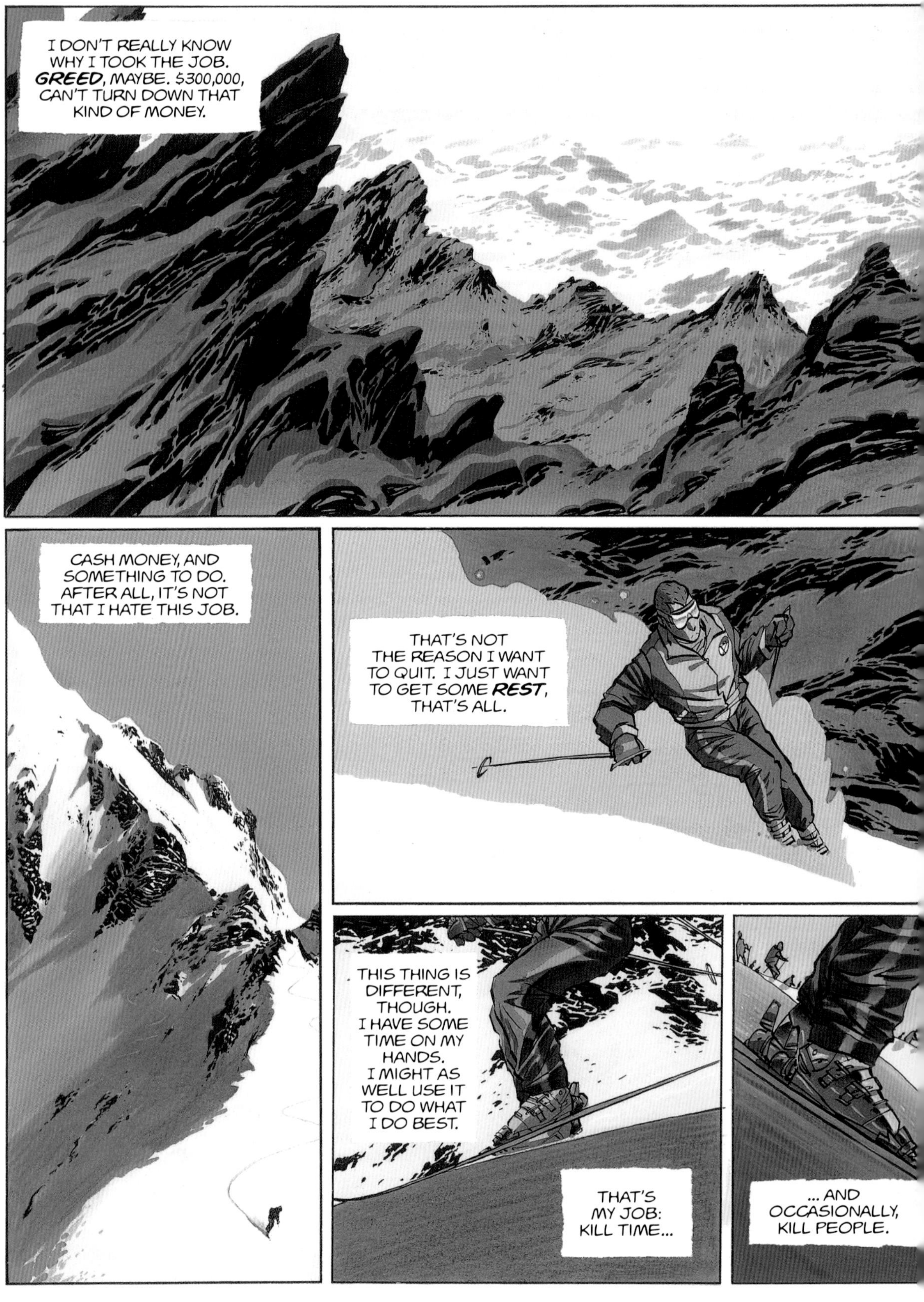
I DON'T REALLY KNOW WHY I TOOK THE JOB. **GREED**, MAYBE. $300,000, CAN'T TURN DOWN THAT KIND OF MONEY.
CASH MONEY, AND SOMETHING TO DO. AFTER ALL, IT'S NOT THAT I HATE THIS JOB.
THAT'S NOT THE REASON I WANT TO QUIT. I JUST WANT TO GET SOME **REST**, THAT'S ALL.
THIS THING IS DIFFERENT, THOUGH. I HAVE SOME TIME ON MY HANDS. I MIGHT AS WELL USE IT TO DO WHAT I DO BEST.
THAT'S MY JOB: KILL TIME...
...AND OCCASIONALLY, KILL PEOPLE.

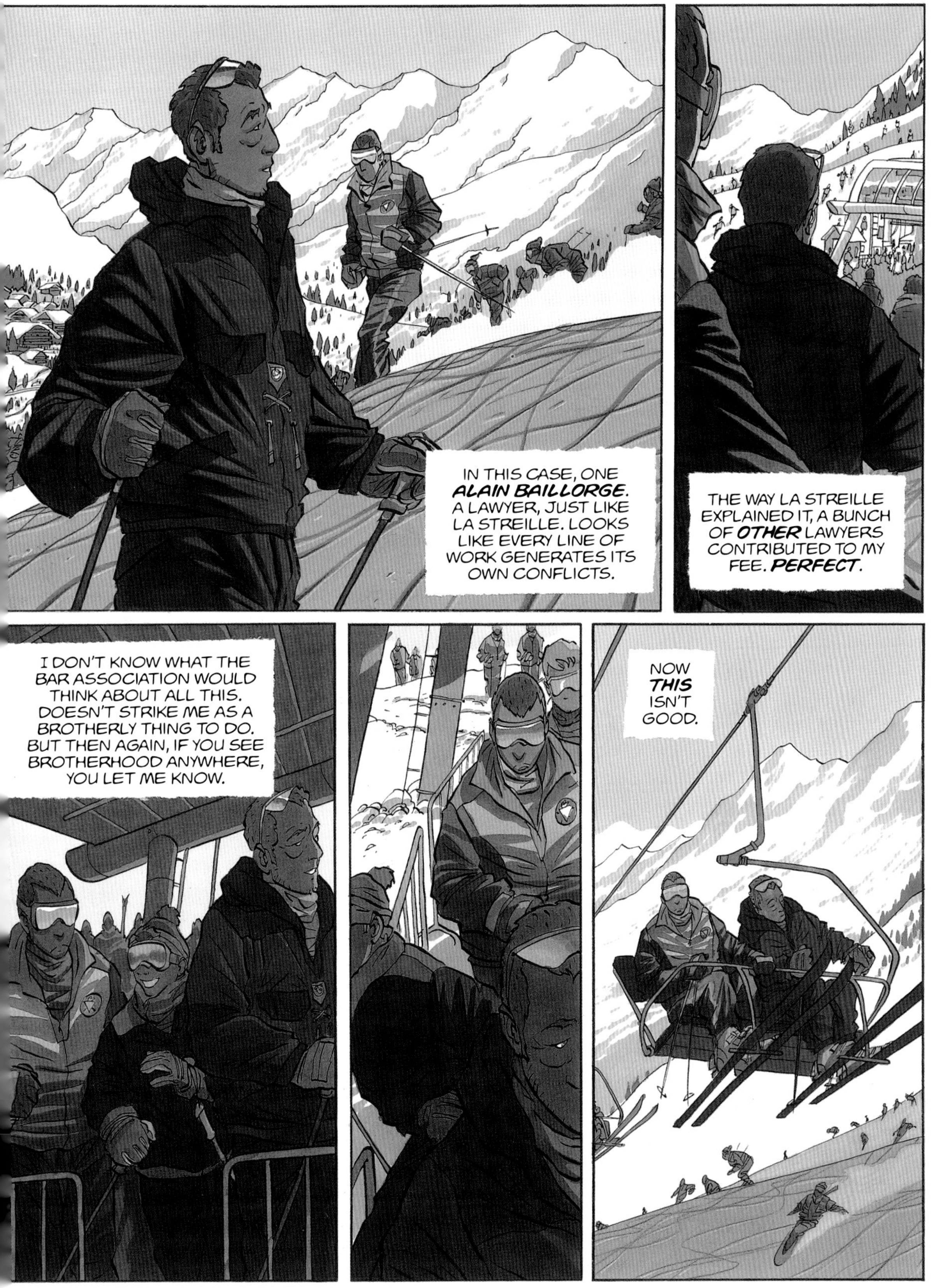
IN THIS CASE, ONE **ALAIN BAILLORGE**. A LAWYER, JUST LIKE LA STREILLE. LOOKS LIKE EVERY LINE OF WORK GENERATES ITS OWN CONFLICTS.
THE WAY LA STREILLE EXPLAINED IT, A BUNCH OF **OTHER** LAWYERS CONTRIBUTED TO MY FEE. **PERFECT**.
I DON'T KNOW WHAT THE BAR ASSOCIATION WOULD THINK ABOUT ALL THIS. DOESN'T STRIKE ME AS A BROTHERLY THING TO DO. BUT THEN AGAIN, IF YOU SEE BROTHERHOOD ANYWHERE, YOU LET ME KNOW.
NOW **THIS** ISN'T GOOD.

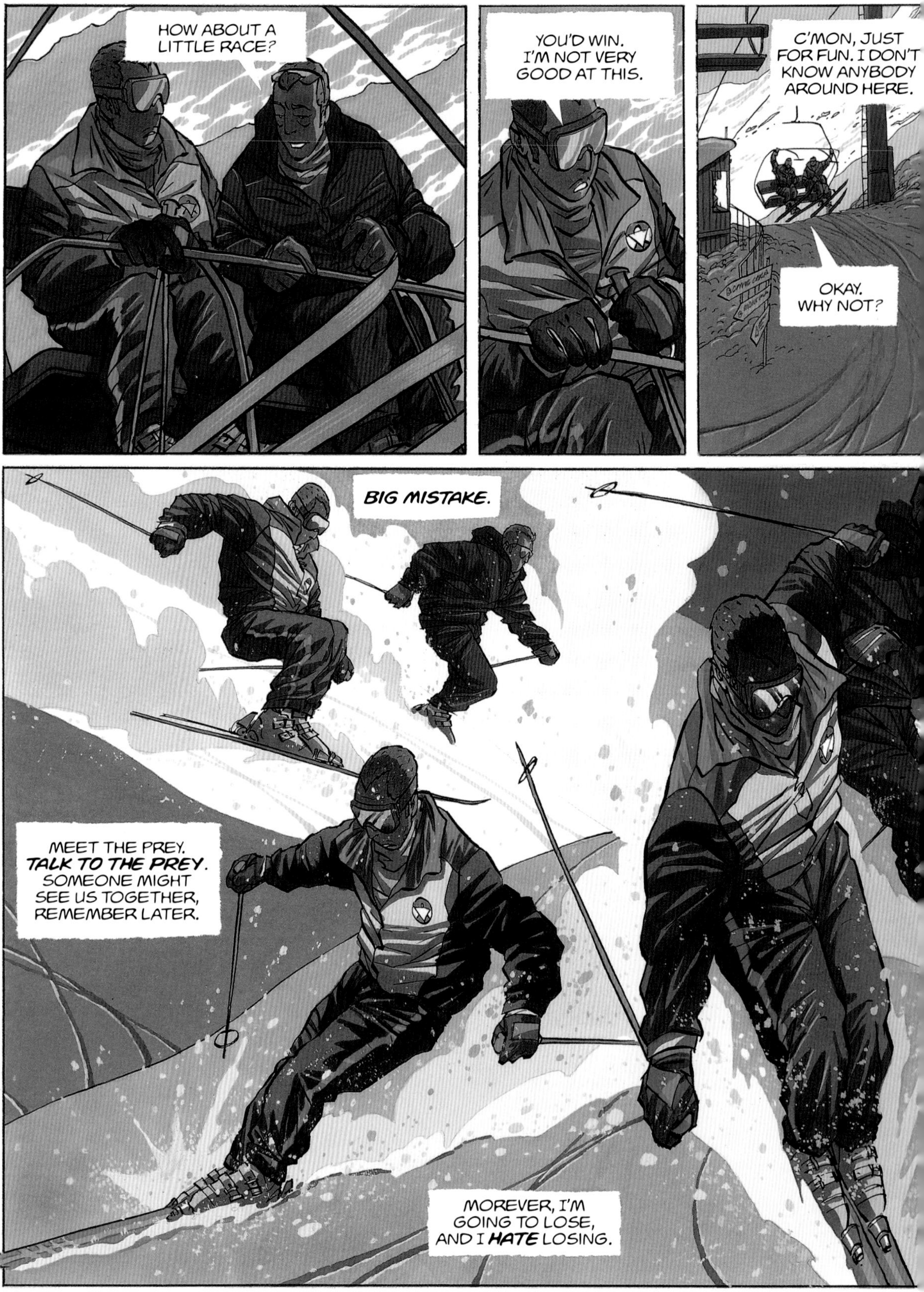
HOW ABOUT A LITTLE RACE?
YOU'D WIN. I'M NOT VERY GOOD AT THIS.
C'MON, JUST FOR FUN. I DON'T KNOW ANYBODY AROUND HERE.
OKAY. WHY NOT?
BIG MISTAKE.
MEET THE PREY. TALK TO THE PREY. SOMEONE MIGHT SEE US TOGETHER, REMEMBER LATER.
MOREVER, I'M GOING TO LOSE, AND I HATE LOSING.

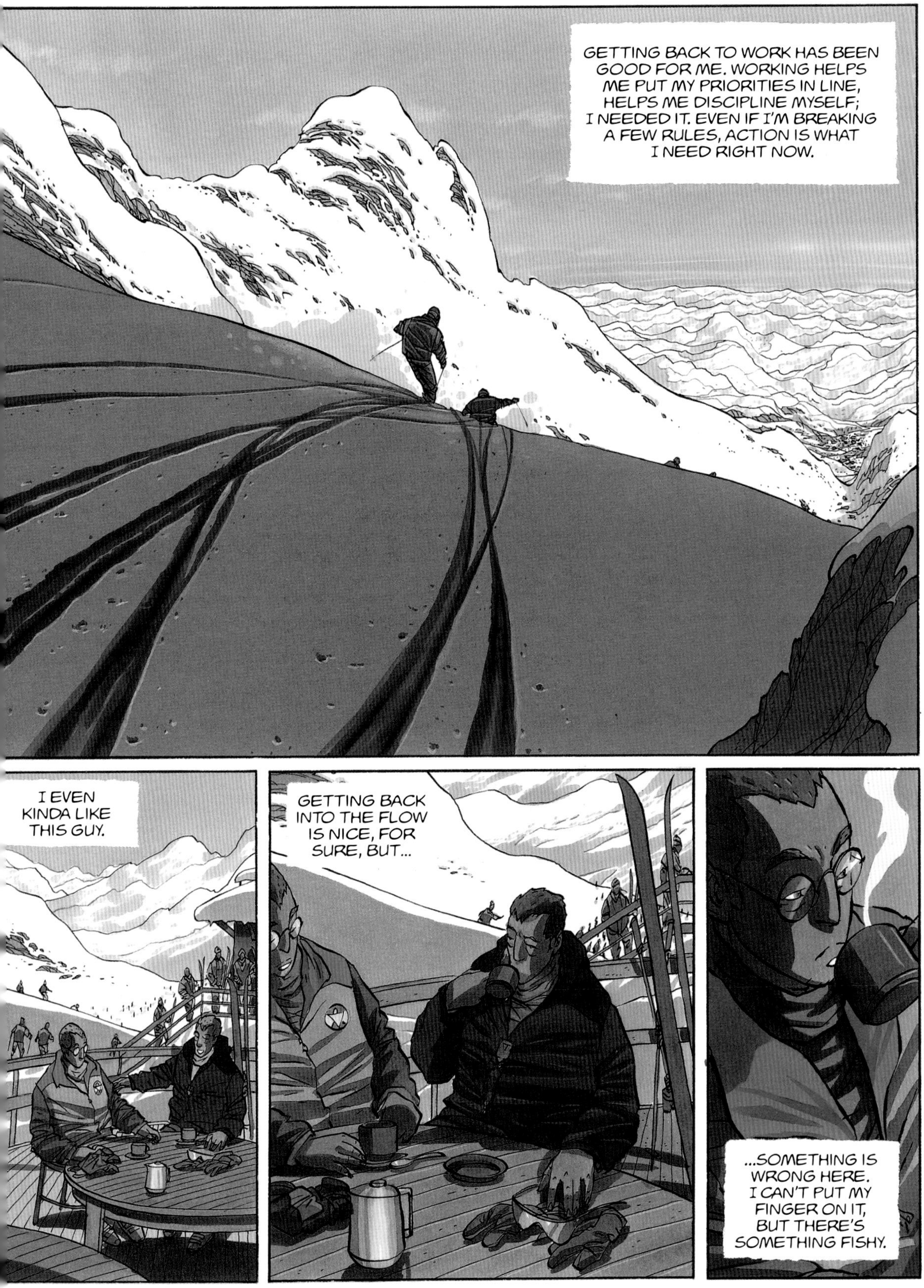
GETTING BACK TO WORK HAS BEEN GOOD FOR ME. WORKING HELPS ME PUT MY PRIORITIES IN LINE, HELPS ME DISCIPLINE MYSELF; I NEEDED IT. EVEN IF I'M BREAKING A FEW RULES, ACTION IS WHAT I NEED RIGHT NOW.
I EVEN KINDA LIKE THIS GUY.
GETTING BACK INTO THE FLOW IS NICE, FOR SURE, BUT...
...SOMETHING IS WRONG HERE. I CAN'T PUT MY FINGER ON IT, BUT THERE'S SOMETHING FISHY.

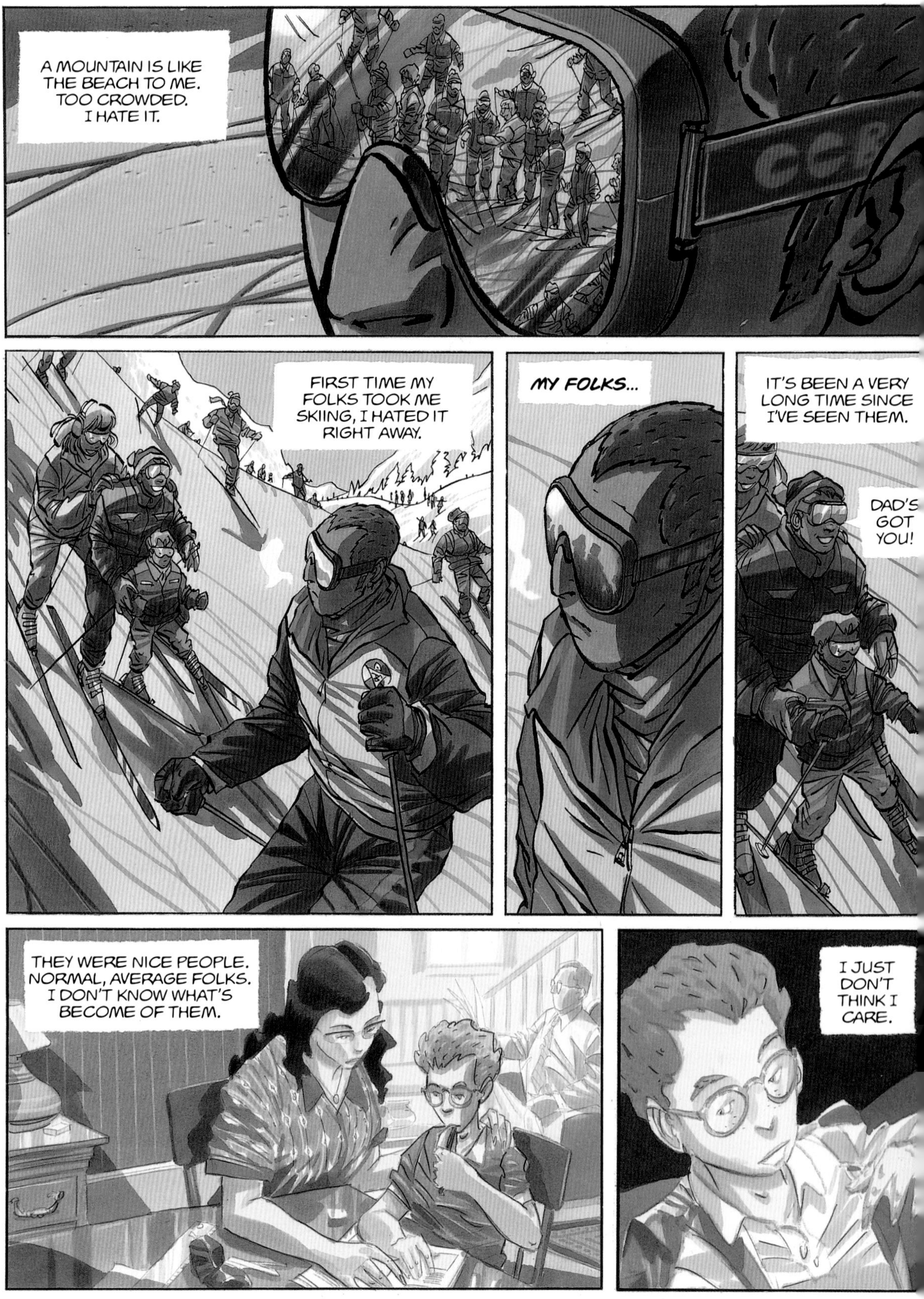
A MOUNTAIN IS LIKE THE BEACH TO ME. TOO CROWDED. I HATE IT.
FIRST TIME MY FOLKS TOOK ME SKIING, I HATED IT RIGHT AWAY.
MY FOLKS...
IT'S BEEN A VERY LONG TIME SINCE I'VE SEEN THEM.
DAD'S GOT YOU!
THEY WERE NICE PEOPLE. NORMAL, AVERAGE FOLKS. I DON'T KNOW WHAT'S BECOME OF THEM.
I JUST DON'T THINK I CARE.

WE MOVED FREQUENTLY, BECAUSE OF MY DAD'S JOB. I DON'T REMEMBER WHAT IT WAS EXACTLY. TOO LONG AGO; AND I THINK HE CHANGED IT A LOT.

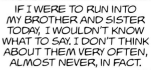

IF I WERE TO RUN INTO MY BROTHER AND SISTER TODAY, I WOULDN'T KNOW WHAT TO SAY. I DON'T THINK ABOUT THEM VERY OFTEN, ALMOST NEVER, IN FACT.

SEEMS LIKE ANOTHER LIFE.

AT SOME POINT, I FIGURED I'D BE BETTER OFF BY MYSELF.

THAT'S LIFE: YOU'RE ON YOUR OWN...

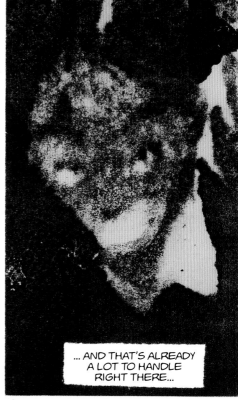

... AND THAT'S ALREADY A LOT TO HANDLE RIGHT THERE...

...MAYBE TOO MUCH.

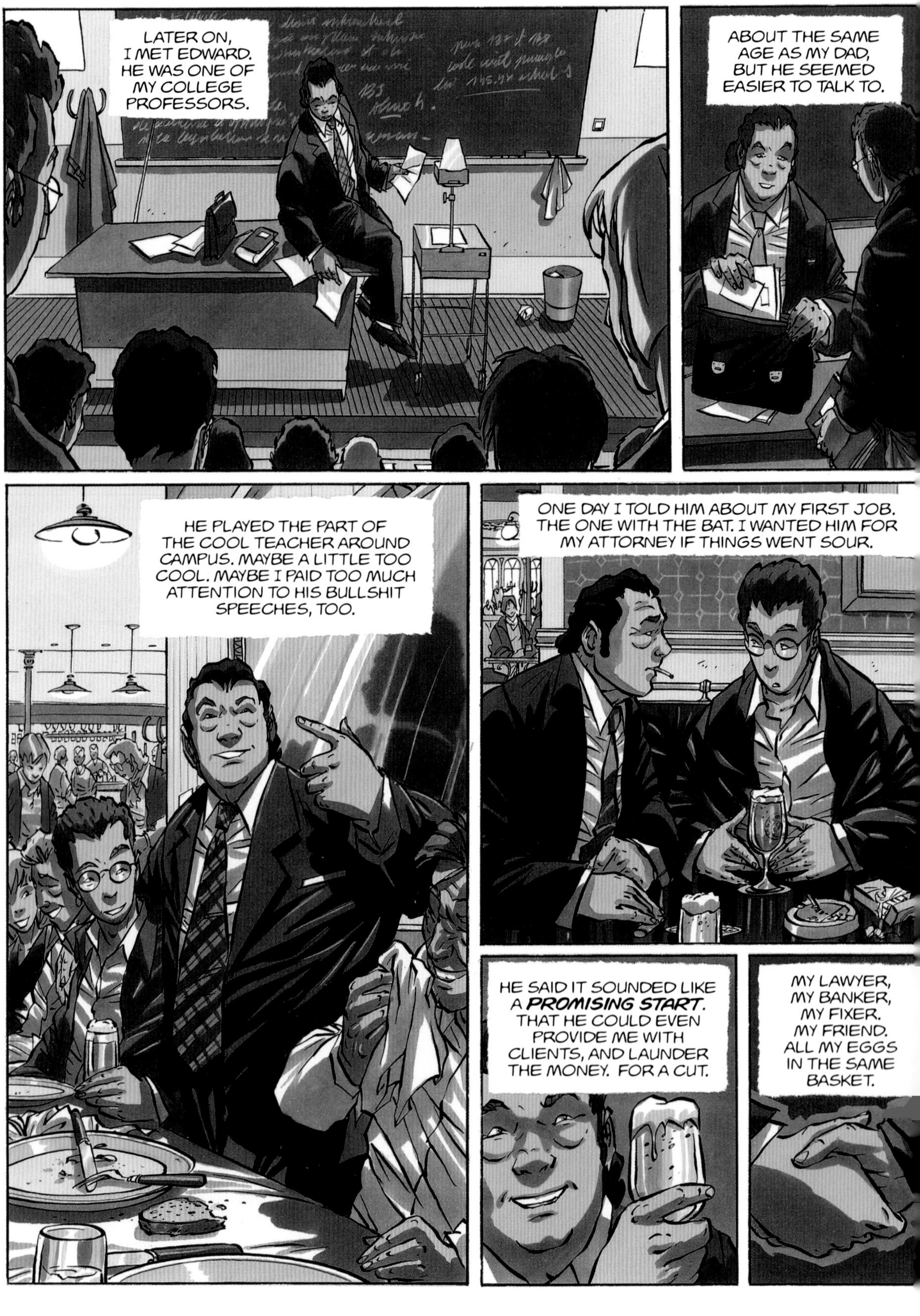
LATER ON, I MET EDWARD. HE WAS ONE OF MY COLLEGE PROFESSORS.
ABOUT THE SAME AGE AS MY DAD, BUT HE SEEMED EASIER TO TALK TO.
HE PLAYED THE PART OF THE COOL TEACHER AROUND CAMPUS. MAYBE A LITTLE TOO COOL. MAYBE I PAID TOO MUCH ATTENTION TO HIS BULLSHIT SPEECHES, TOO.
ONE DAY I TOLD HIM ABOUT MY FIRST JOB. THE ONE WITH THE BAT. I WANTED HIM FOR MY ATTORNEY IF THINGS WENT SOUR.
HE SAID IT SOUNDED LIKE A ***PROMISING START***. THAT HE COULD EVEN PROVIDE ME WITH CLIENTS, AND LAUNDER THE MONEY. FOR A CUT.
MY LAWYER, MY BANKER, MY FIXER. MY FRIEND. ALL MY EGGS IN THE SAME BASKET.

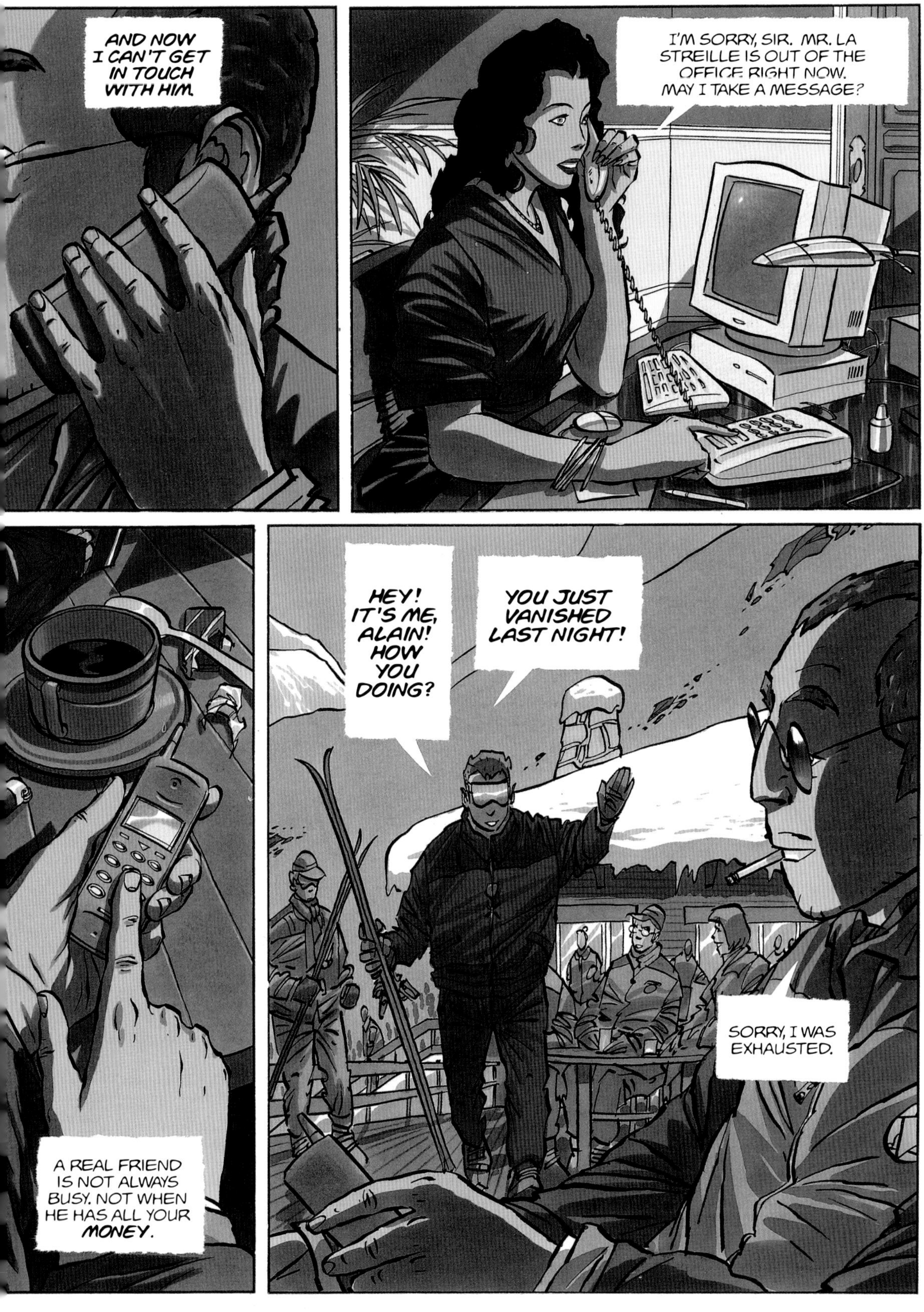
AND NOW I CAN'T GET IN TOUCH WITH HIM.
I'M SORRY, SIR. MR. LA STREILLE IS OUT OF THE OFFICE RIGHT NOW. MAY I TAKE A MESSAGE?
A REAL FRIEND IS NOT ALWAYS BUSY. NOT WHEN HE HAS ALL YOUR MONEY.
HEY! IT'S ME, ALAIN! HOW YOU DOING?
YOU JUST VANISHED LAST NIGHT!
SORRY, I WAS EXHAUSTED.

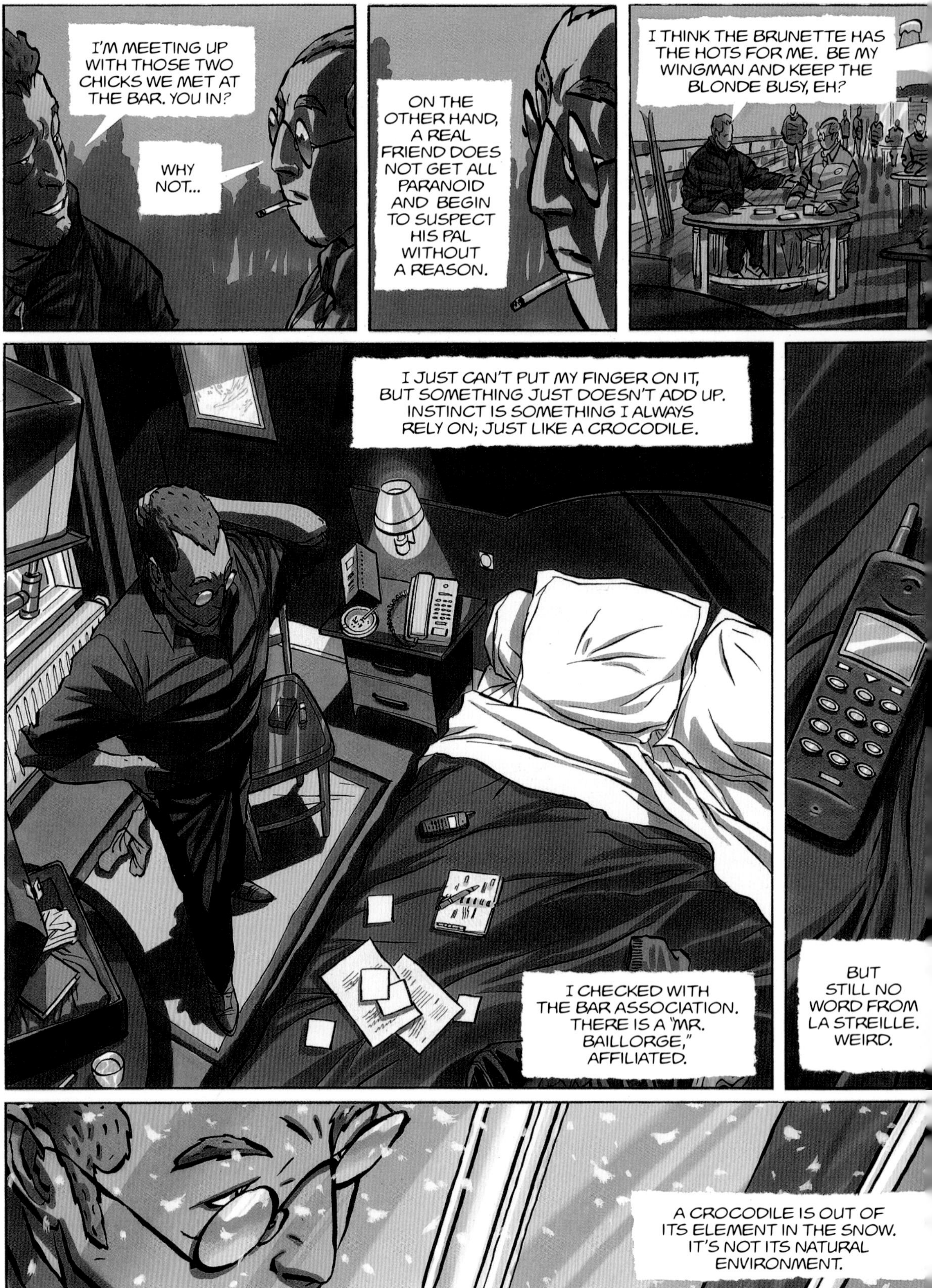
I'M MEETING UP WITH THOSE TWO CHICKS WE MET AT THE BAR. YOU IN?
WHY NOT...
ON THE OTHER HAND, A REAL FRIEND DOES NOT GET ALL PARANOID AND BEGIN TO SUSPECT HIS PAL WITHOUT A REASON.
I THINK THE BRUNETTE HAS THE HOTS FOR ME. BE MY WINGMAN AND KEEP THE BLONDE BUSY, EH?
I JUST CAN'T PUT MY FINGER ON IT, BUT SOMETHING JUST DOESN'T ADD UP. INSTINCT IS SOMETHING I ALWAYS RELY ON; JUST LIKE A CROCODILE.
I CHECKED WITH THE BAR ASSOCIATION. THERE IS A "MR. BAILLORGE," AFFILIATED.
BUT STILL NO WORD FROM LA STREILLE. WEIRD.
A CROCODILE IS OUT OF ITS ELEMENT IN THE SNOW. IT'S NOT ITS NATURAL ENVIRONMENT.

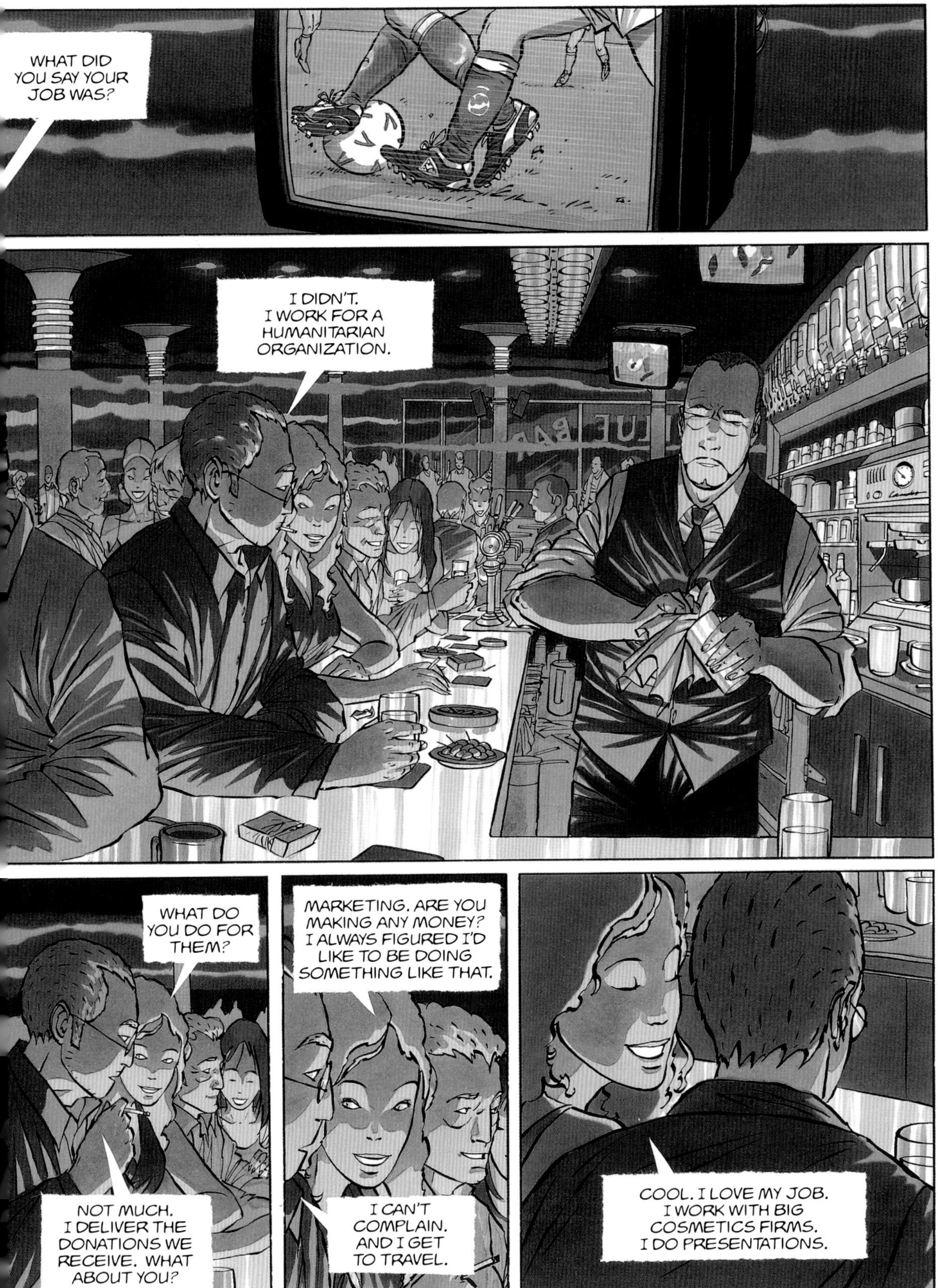
WHAT DID YOU SAY YOUR JOB WAS?
I DIDN'T. I WORK FOR A HUMANITARIAN ORGANIZATION.
WHAT DO YOU DO FOR THEM?
NOT MUCH. I DELIVER THE DONATIONS WE RECEIVE. WHAT ABOUT YOU?
MARKETING. ARE YOU MAKING ANY MONEY? I ALWAYS FIGURED I'D LIKE TO BE DOING SOMETHING LIKE THAT.
I CAN'T COMPLAIN. AND I GET TO TRAVEL.
COOL. I LOVE MY JOB. I WORK WITH BIG COSMETICS FIRMS. I DO PRESENTATIONS.

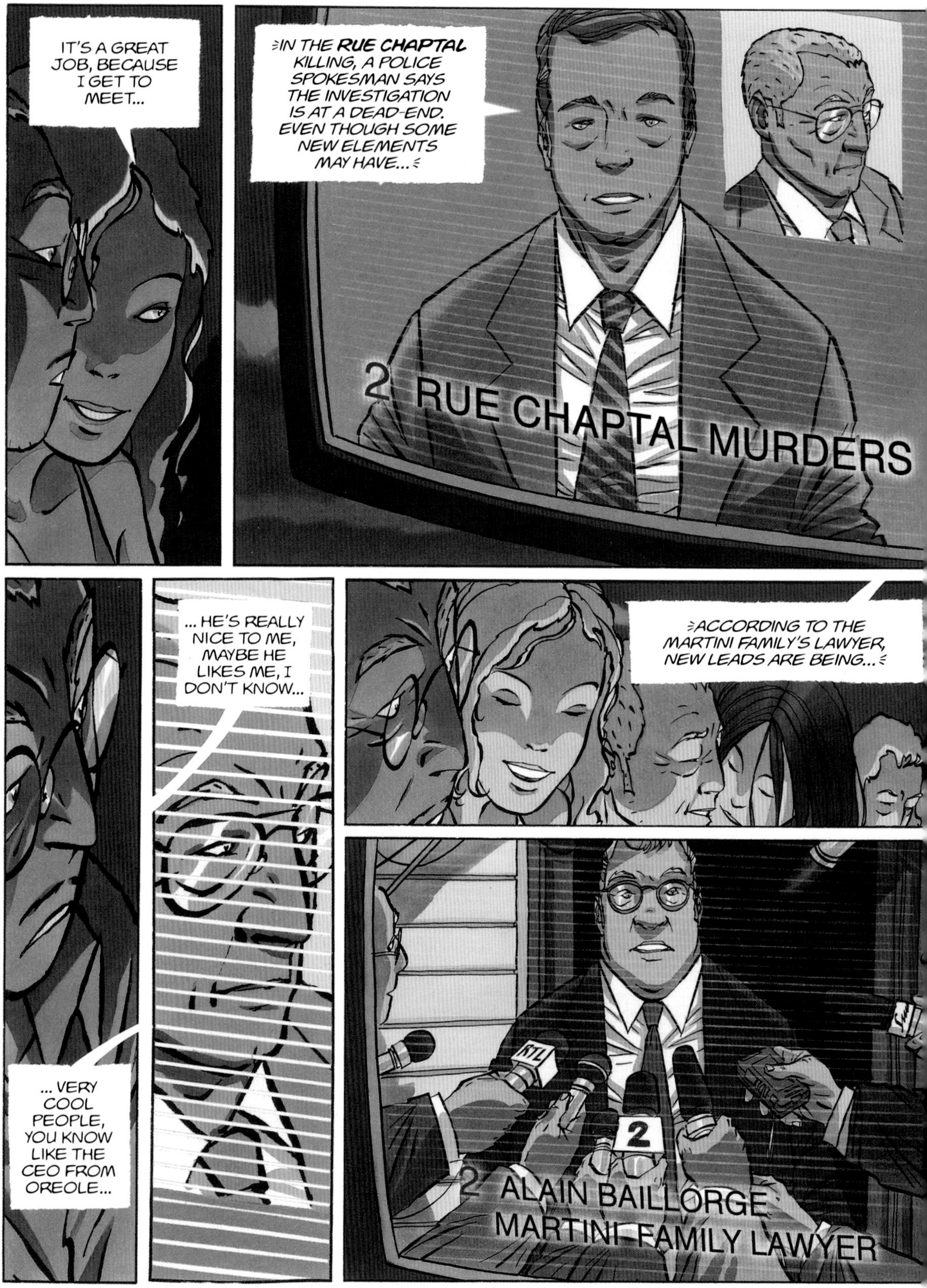
IT'S A GREAT JOB, BECAUSE I GET TO MEET...
IN THE RUE CHAPTAL KILLING, A POLICE SPOKESMAN SAYS THE INVESTIGATION IS AT A DEAD-END. EVEN THOUGH SOME NEW ELEMENTS MAY HAVE...
2 RUE CHAPTAL MURDERS
... HE'S REALLY NICE TO ME, MAYBE HE LIKES ME, I DON'T KNOW...
ACCORDING TO THE MARTINI FAMILY'S LAWYER, NEW LEADS ARE BEING...
... VERY COOL PEOPLE, YOU KNOW LIKE THE CEO FROM OREOLE...
RTL
2
2 ALAIN BAILLORGE
MARTINI FAMILY LAWYER

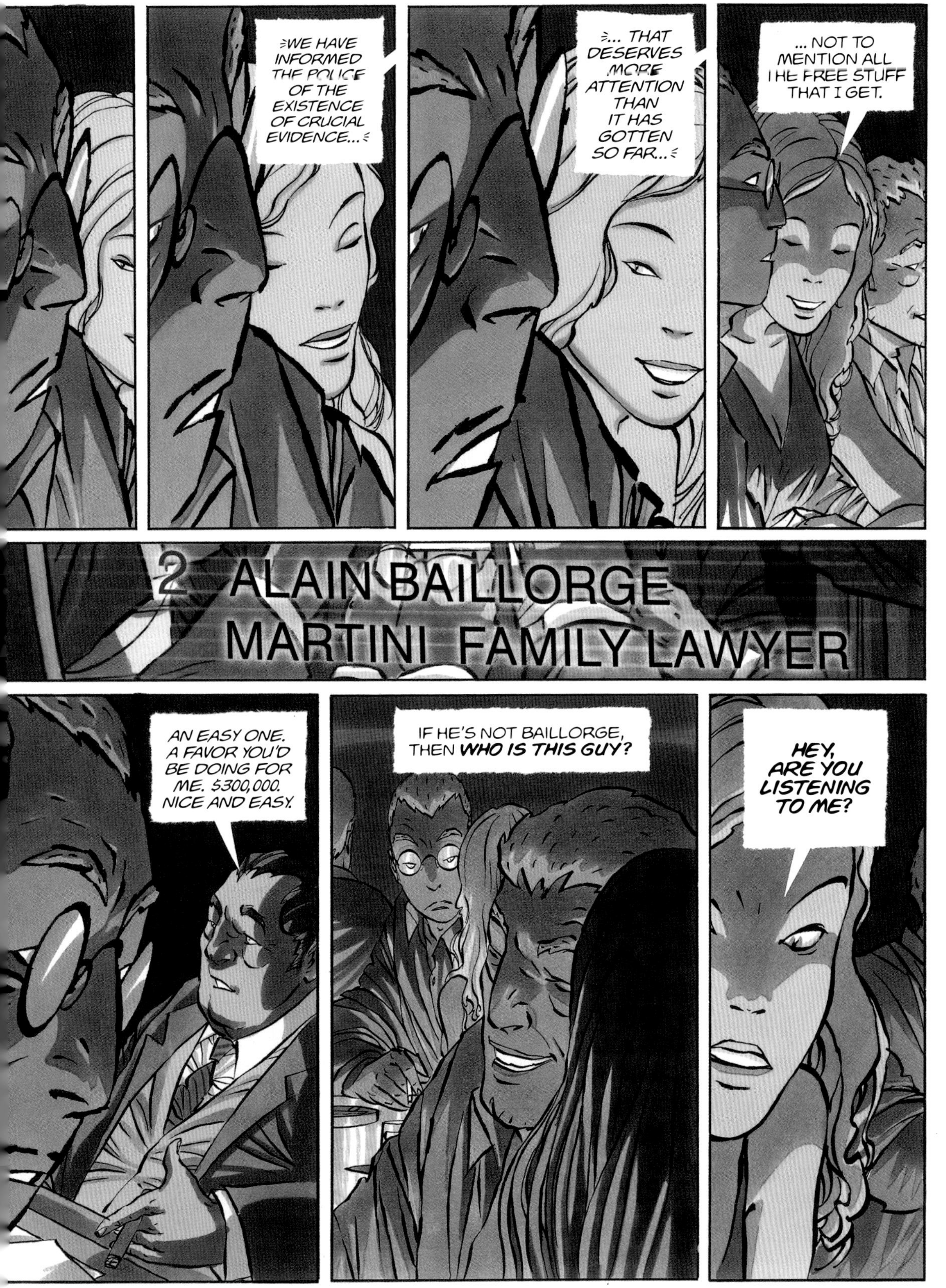
WE HAVE INFORMED THE POLICE OF THE EXISTENCE OF CRUCIAL EVIDENCE...
... THAT DESERVES MORE ATTENTION THAN IT HAS GOTTEN SO FAR...
... NOT TO MENTION ALL THE FREE STUFF THAT I GET.
2 ALAIN BAILLORGE
MARTINI FAMILY LAWYER
AN EASY ONE. A FAVOR YOU'D BE DOING FOR ME. $300,000. NICE AND EASY.
IF HE'S NOT BAILLORGE, THEN WHO IS THIS GUY?
HEY, ARE YOU LISTENING TO ME?

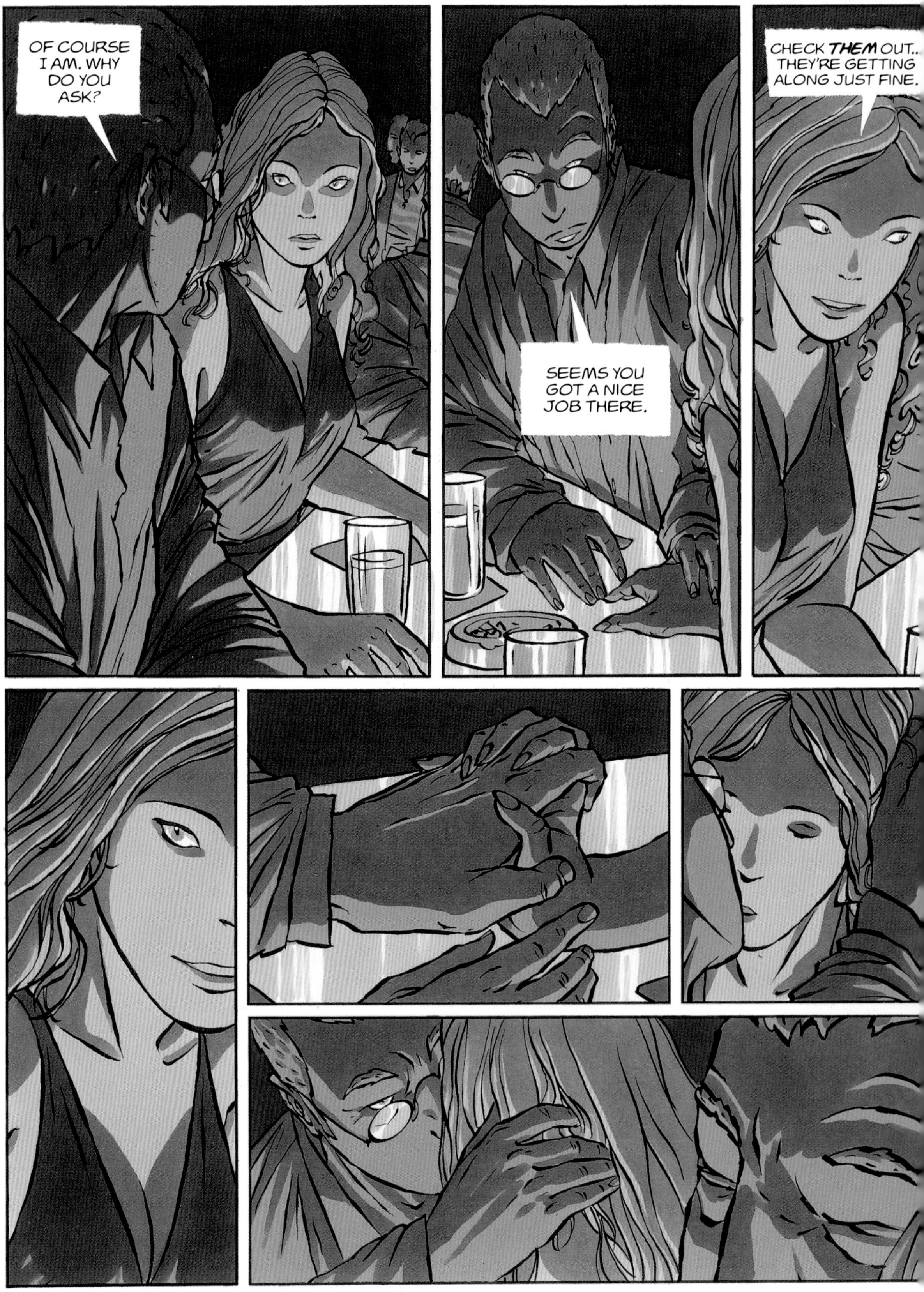
OF COURSE I AM. WHY DO YOU ASK?
SEEMS YOU GOT A NICE JOB THERE.
CHECK **THEM** OUT.. THEY'RE GETTING ALONG JUST FINE.

THINKING IS FINE, BUT WHEN YOU'RE DONE, YOU HAVE TO TAKE ACTION. OTHERWISE, IT'S POINTLESS.

A TRUE PRO DOES WHAT HE HAS TO DO, LIKE IT OR NOT.

AND I WANTED TO SOLVE EVERYTHING QUICK.

I COULDN'T WAIT ANY LONGER.

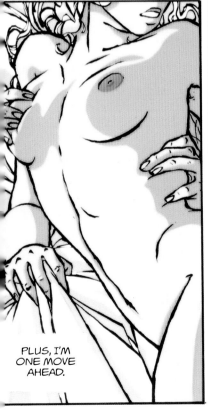

PLUS, I'M ONE MOVE AHEAD.

I KNOW, AND HE DOESN'T KNOW THAT I KNOW. TOO BAD FOR HIM.

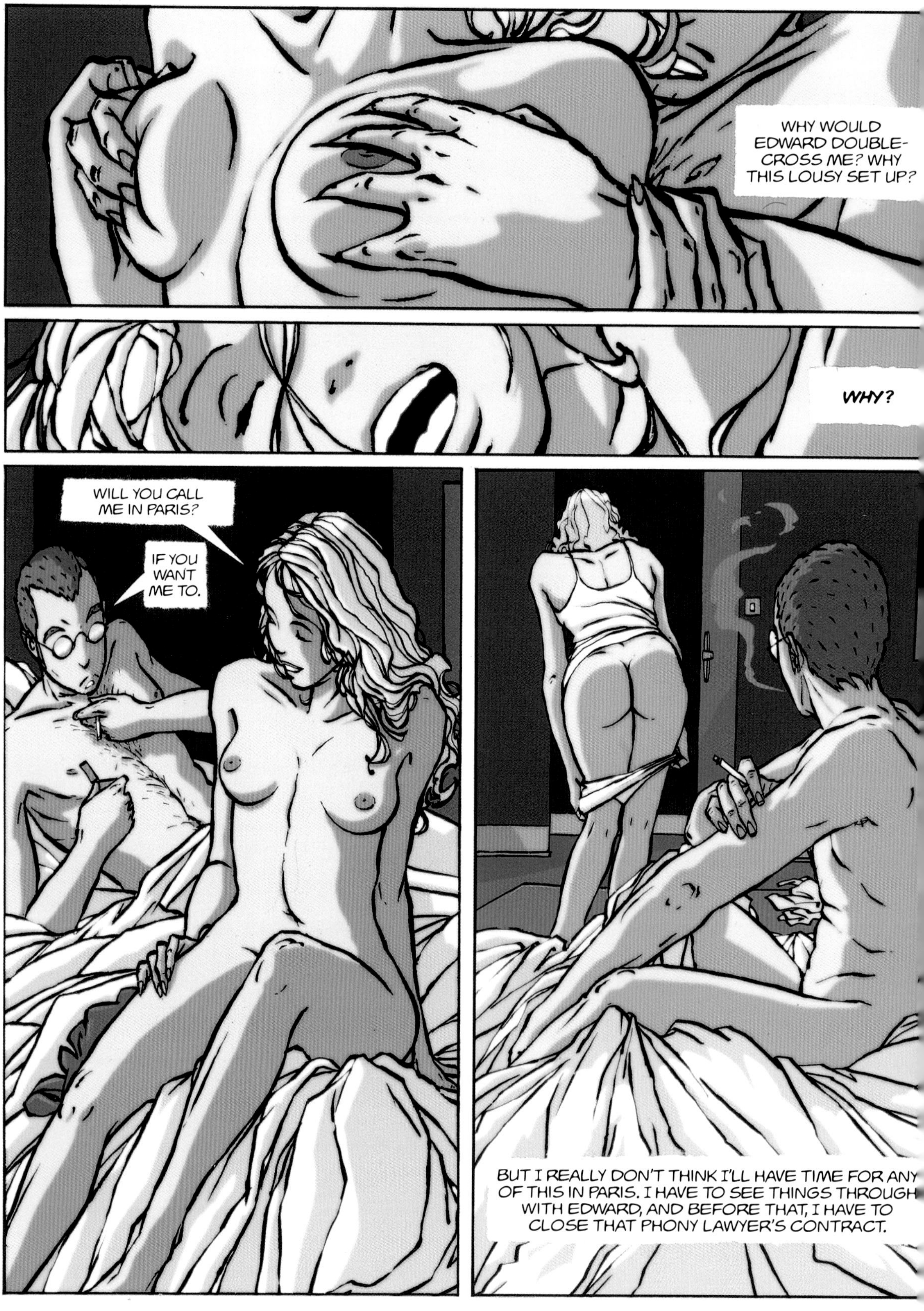
WHY WOULD EDWARD DOUBLE-CROSS ME? WHY THIS LOUSY SET UP?
WHY?
WILL YOU CALL ME IN PARIS?
IF YOU WANT ME TO.
BUT I REALLY DON'T THINK I'LL HAVE TIME FOR ANY OF THIS IN PARIS. I HAVE TO SEE THINGS THROUGH WITH EDWARD, AND BEFORE THAT, I HAVE TO CLOSE THAT PHONY LAWYER'S CONTRACT.

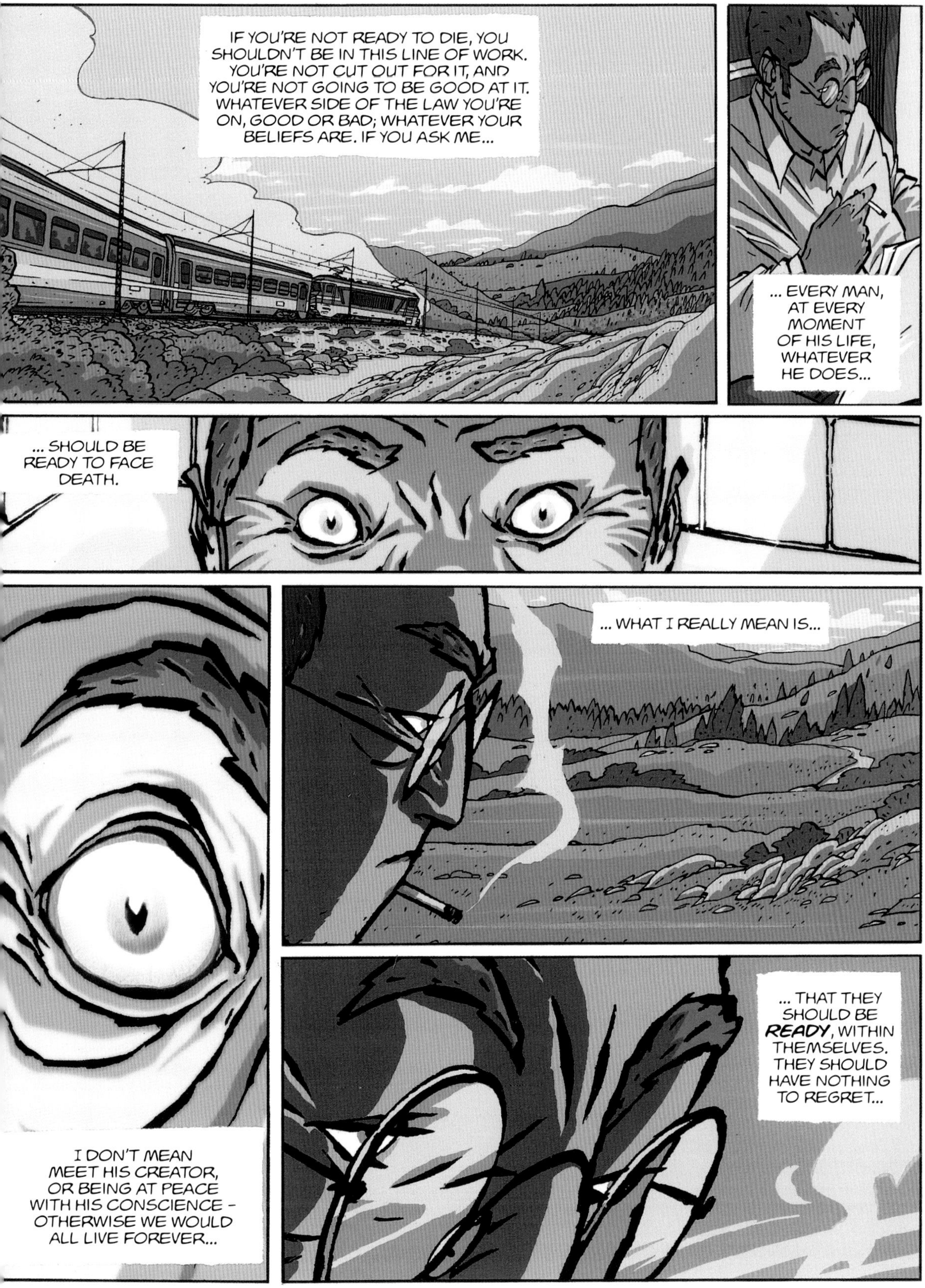
IF YOU'RE NOT READY TO DIE, YOU SHOULDN'T BE IN THIS LINE OF WORK. YOU'RE NOT CUT OUT FOR IT, AND YOU'RE NOT GOING TO BE GOOD AT IT. WHATEVER SIDE OF THE LAW YOU'RE ON, GOOD OR BAD; WHATEVER YOUR BELIEFS ARE. IF YOU ASK ME...
... EVERY MAN, AT EVERY MOMENT OF HIS LIFE, WHATEVER HE DOES...
... SHOULD BE READY TO FACE DEATH.
... WHAT I REALLY MEAN IS...
I DON'T MEAN MEET HIS CREATOR, OR BEING AT PEACE WITH HIS CONSCIENCE - OTHERWISE WE WOULD ALL LIVE FOREVER...
... THAT THEY SHOULD BE **READY**, WITHIN THEMSELVES. THEY SHOULD HAVE NOTHING TO REGRET...

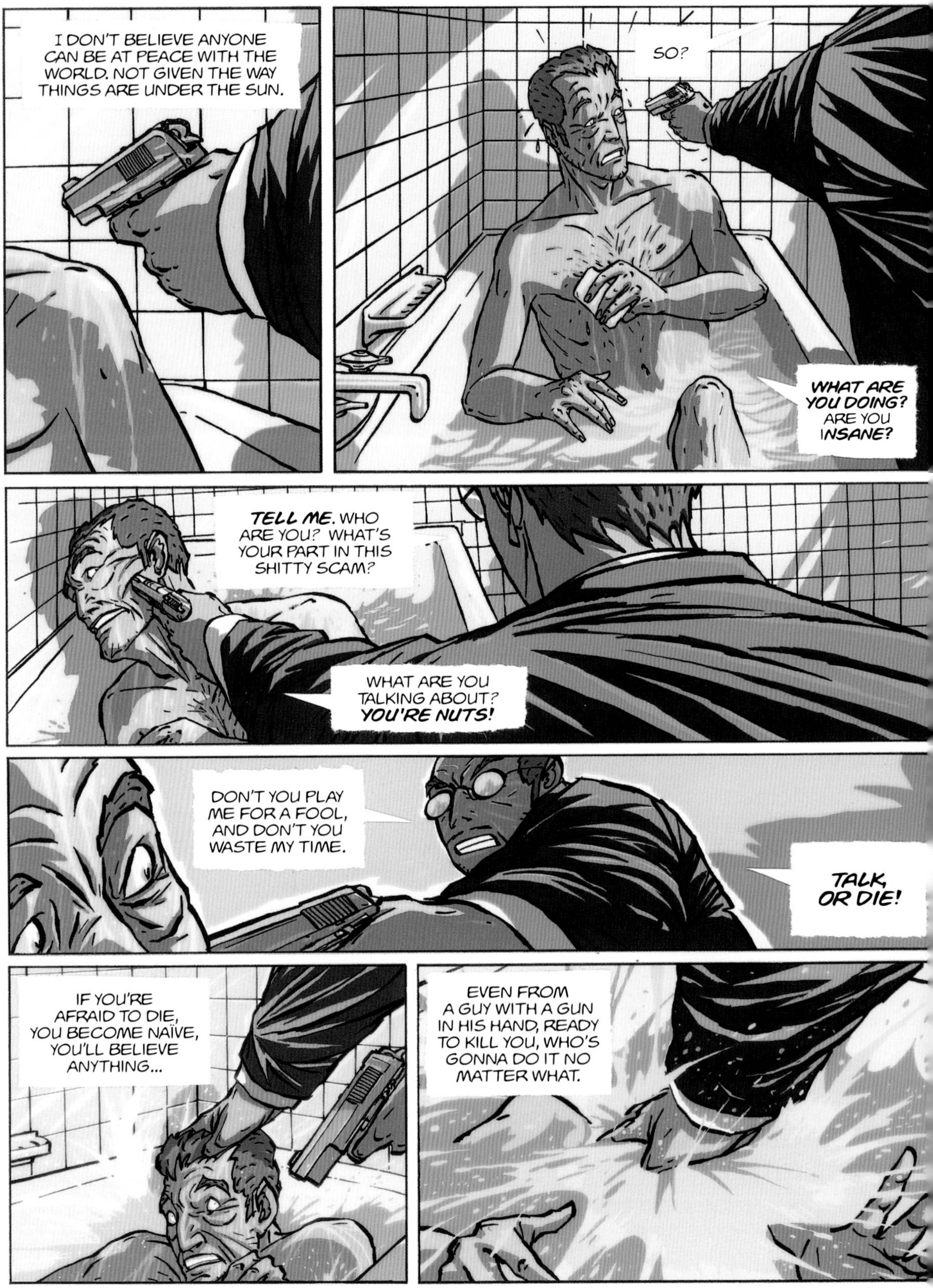
I DON'T BELIEVE ANYONE CAN BE AT PEACE WITH THE WORLD. NOT GIVEN THE WAY THINGS ARE UNDER THE SUN.
SO?
WHAT ARE YOU DOING? ARE YOU INSANE?
TELL ME. WHO ARE YOU? WHAT'S YOUR PART IN THIS SHITTY SCAM?
WHAT ARE YOU TALKING ABOUT? YOU'RE NUTS!
DON'T YOU PLAY ME FOR A FOOL, AND DON'T YOU WASTE MY TIME.
TALK, OR DIE!
IF YOU'RE AFRAID TO DIE, YOU BECOME NAÏVE, YOU'LL BELIEVE ANYTHING...
EVEN FROM A GUY WITH A GUN IN HIS HAND, READY TO KILL YOU, WHO'S GONNA DO IT NO MATTER WHAT.

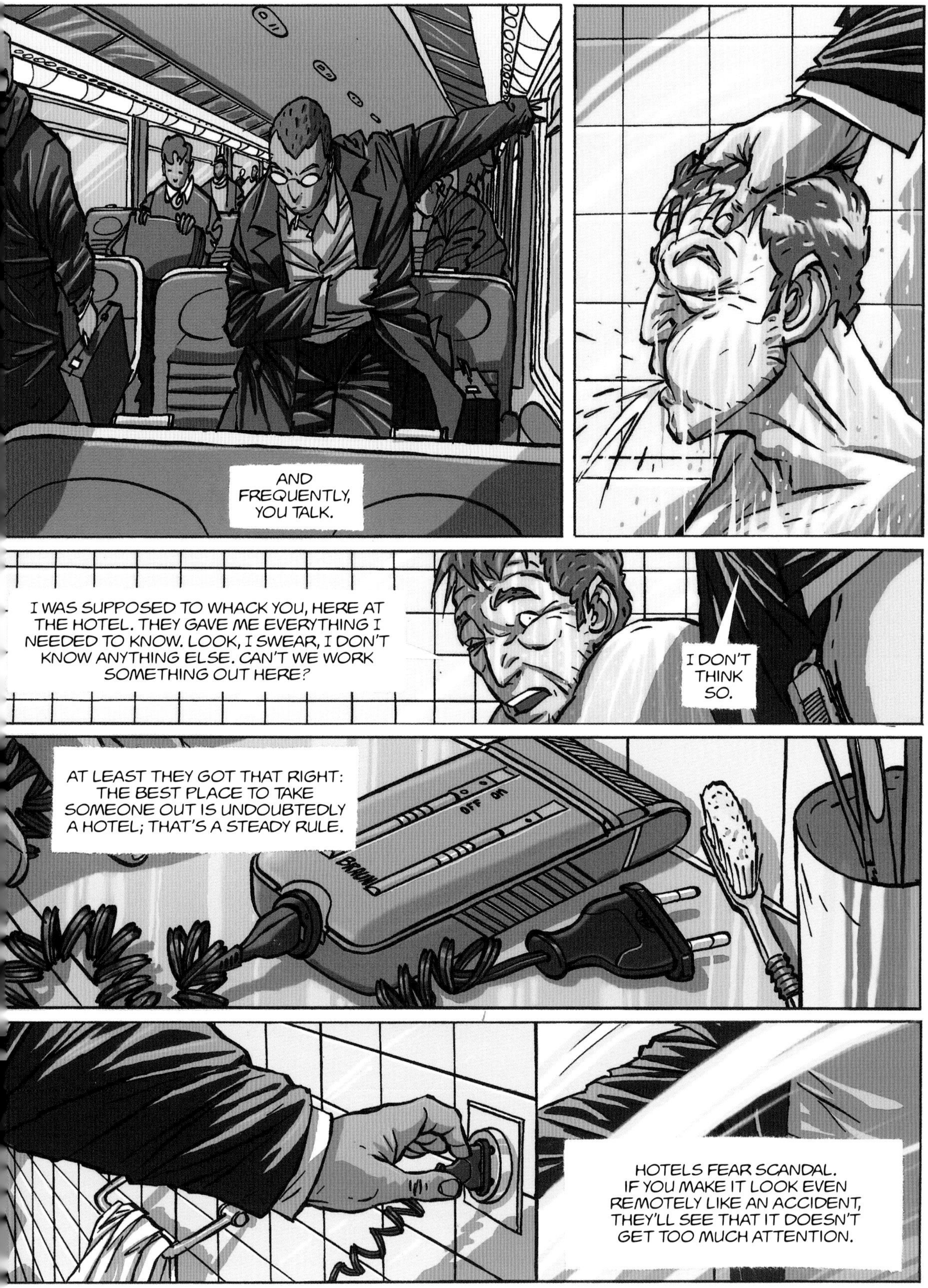
AND FREQUENTLY, YOU TALK.
I WAS SUPPOSED TO WHACK YOU, HERE AT THE HOTEL. THEY GAVE ME EVERYTHING I NEEDED TO KNOW. LOOK, I SWEAR, I DON'T KNOW ANYTHING ELSE. CAN'T WE WORK SOMETHING OUT HERE?
I DON'T THINK SO.
AT LEAST THEY GOT THAT RIGHT: THE BEST PLACE TO TAKE SOMEONE OUT IS UNDOUBTEDLY A HOTEL; THAT'S A STEADY RULE.
OFF ON
BRAUN
HOTELS FEAR SCANDAL. IF YOU MAKE IT LOOK EVEN REMOTELY LIKE AN ACCIDENT, THEY'LL SEE THAT IT DOESN'T GET TOO MUCH ATTENTION.

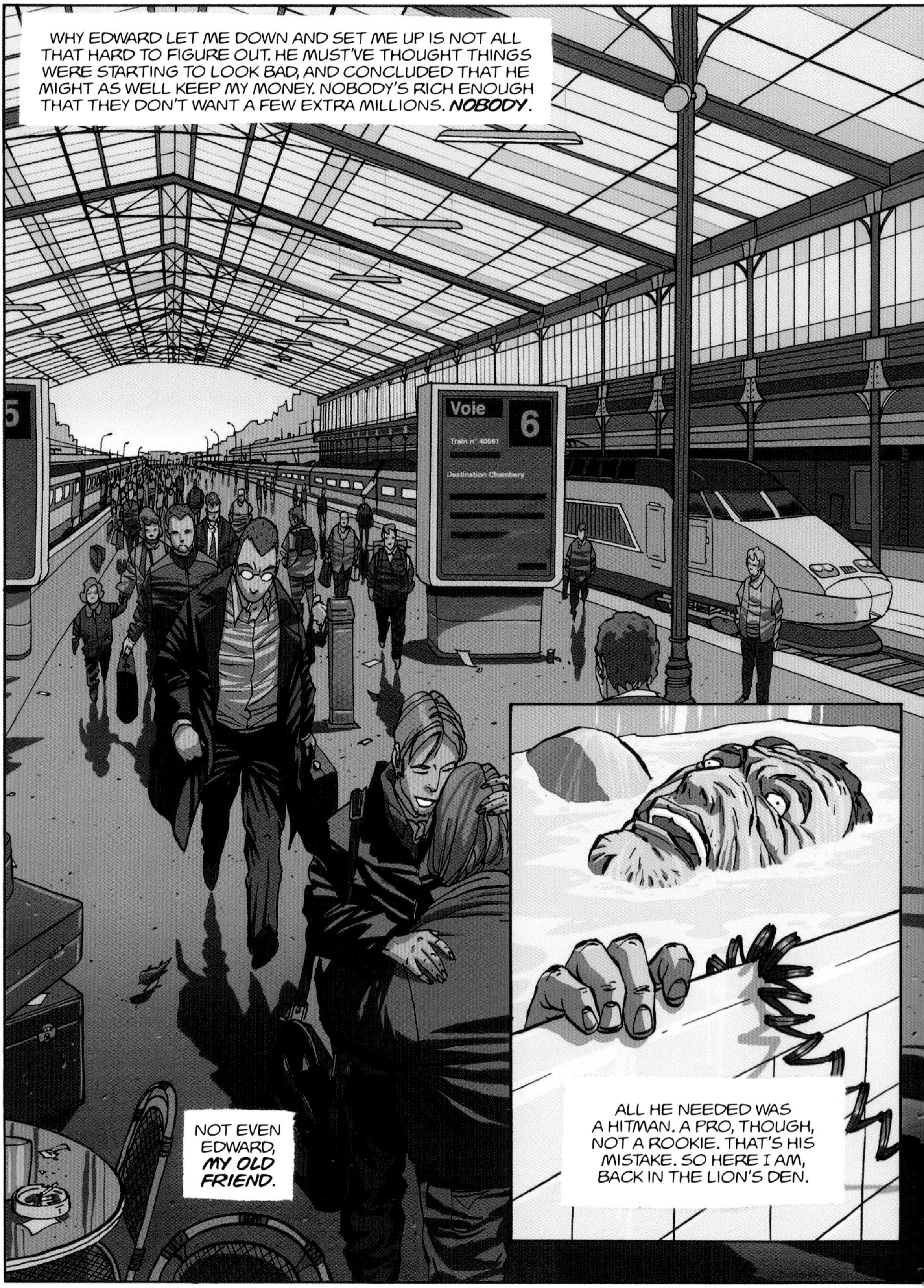
WHY EDWARD LET ME DOWN AND SET ME UP IS NOT ALL THAT HARD TO FIGURE OUT. HE MUST'VE THOUGHT THINGS WERE STARTING TO LOOK BAD, AND CONCLUDED THAT HE MIGHT AS WELL KEEP MY MONEY. NOBODY'S RICH ENOUGH THAT THEY DON'T WANT A FEW EXTRA MILLIONS. NOBODY.
Voie
6
Train n° 40561
Destination Chambery
NOT EVEN EDWARD, MY OLD FRIEND.
ALL HE NEEDED WAS A HITMAN. A PRO, THOUGH, NOT A ROOKIE. THAT'S HIS MISTAKE. SO HERE I AM, BACK IN THE LION'S DEN.

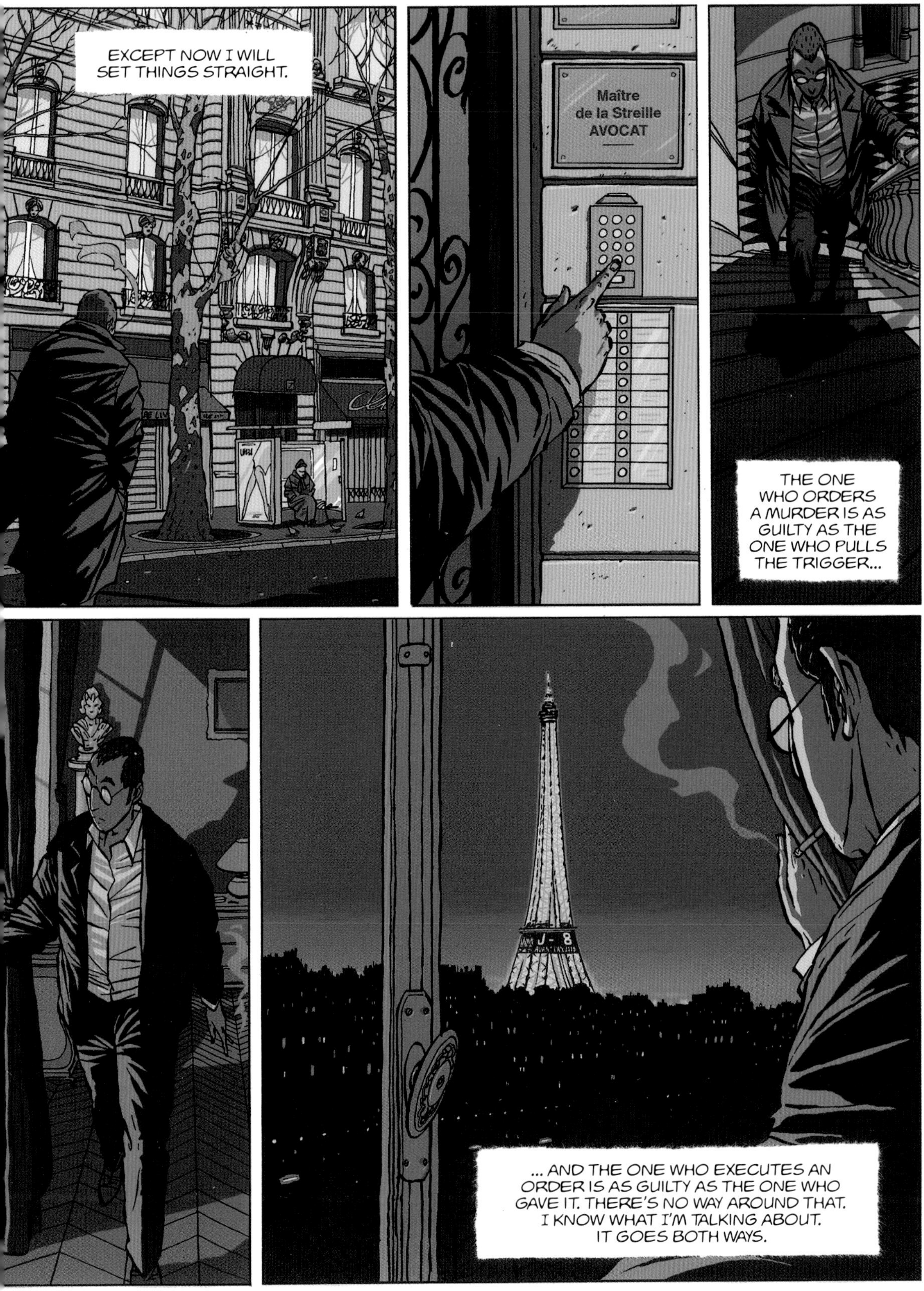
EXCEPT NOW I WILL SET THINGS STRAIGHT.
Maître de la Streille AVOCAT
THE ONE WHO ORDERS A MURDER IS AS GUILTY AS THE ONE WHO PULLS THE TRIGGER...
J-8
... AND THE ONE WHO EXECUTES AN ORDER IS AS GUILTY AS THE ONE WHO GAVE IT. THERE'S NO WAY AROUND THAT. I KNOW WHAT I'M TALKING ABOUT. IT GOES BOTH WAYS.

WHAT I MEAN IS: HITLER DIDN'T KILL ANYBODY. NEITHER DID GOERING. THEY FOUND THOUSANDS OF SCUMBAGS TO DO IT FOR THEM.

AND THEN THE SCUMBAGS SAID THEY WERE ONLY OBEYING ORDERS...

...THAT THEY HAD **NO CHOICE** ABOUT IT. THE SAME SCUMBAGS WE MEET EVERYWHERE, ALL THE TIME. ALL THEY'RE WAITING FOR IS A RISK-FREE OPPORTUNITY TO GIVE HELL TO THEIR FELLOW CITIZENS.

WITH THE SAME SICK REASONING, THE SAME LIES, THE SAME GOOD CONSCIENCE, AND THE SAME IMPUNITY.

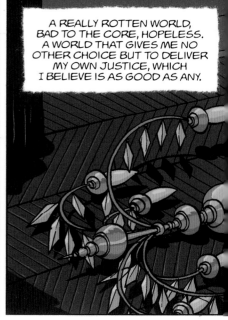

A REALLY ROTTEN WORLD, BAD TO THE CORE, HOPELESS. A WORLD THAT GIVES ME NO OTHER CHOICE BUT TO DELIVER MY OWN JUSTICE, WHICH I BELIEVE IS AS GOOD AS ANY.

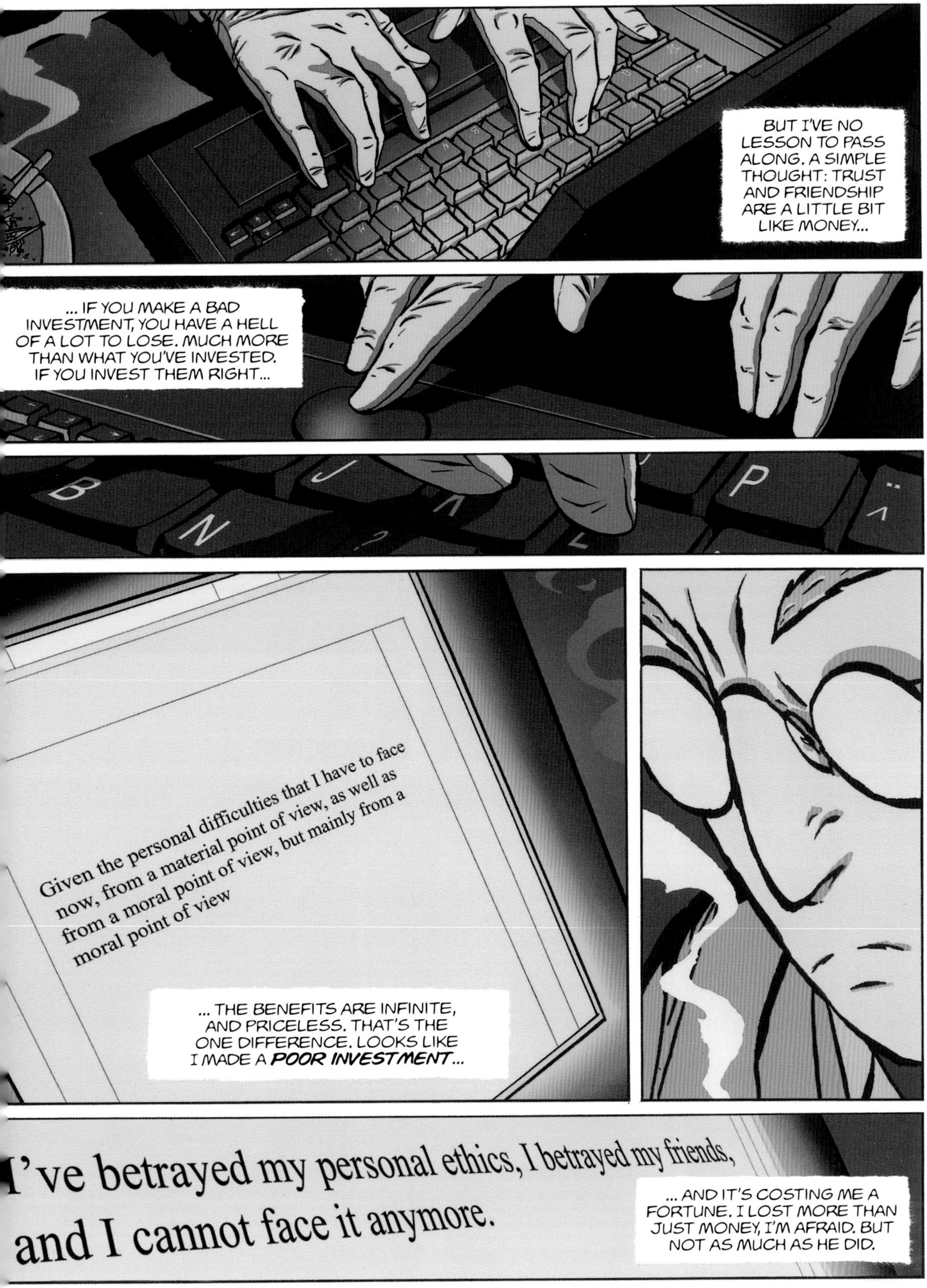
BUT I'VE NO LESSON TO PASS ALONG. A SIMPLE THOUGHT: TRUST AND FRIENDSHIP ARE A LITTLE BIT LIKE MONEY...
... IF YOU MAKE A BAD INVESTMENT, YOU HAVE A HELL OF A LOT TO LOSE. MUCH MORE THAN WHAT YOU'VE INVESTED. IF YOU INVEST THEM RIGHT...
Given the personal difficulties that I have to face now, from a material point of view, as well as from a moral point of view, but mainly from a from a moral point of view
... THE BENEFITS ARE INFINITE, AND PRICELESS. THAT'S THE ONE DIFFERENCE. LOOKS LIKE I MADE A POOR INVESTMENT...
I've betrayed my personal ethics, I betrayed my friends, and I cannot face it anymore.
... AND IT'S COSTING ME A FORTUNE. I LOST MORE THAN JUST MONEY, I'M AFRAID. BUT NOT AS MUCH AS HE DID.

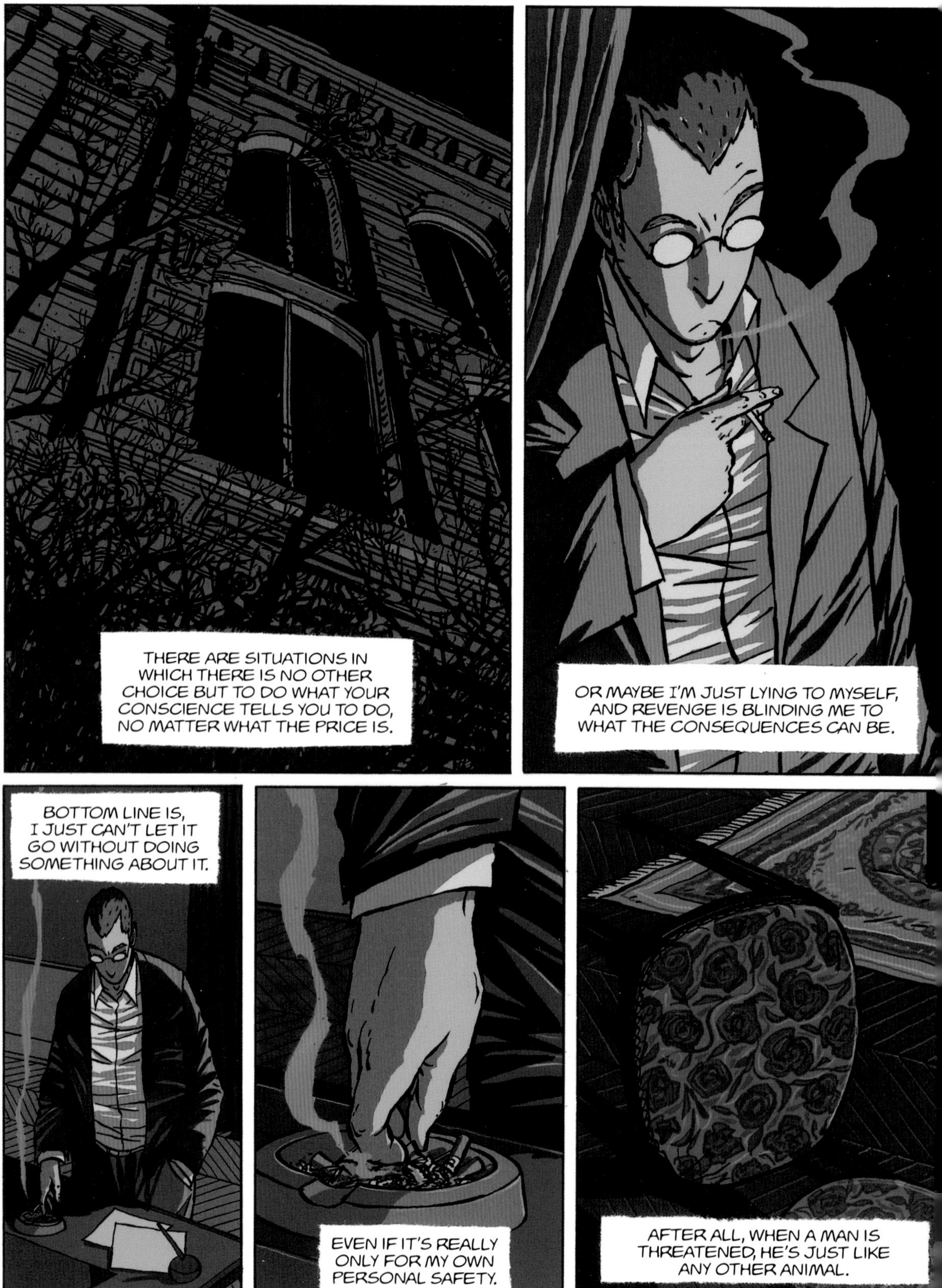
THERE ARE SITUATIONS IN WHICH THERE IS NO OTHER CHOICE BUT TO DO WHAT YOUR CONSCIENCE TELLS YOU TO DO, NO MATTER WHAT THE PRICE IS.
OR MAYBE I'M JUST LYING TO MYSELF, AND REVENGE IS BLINDING ME TO WHAT THE CONSEQUENCES CAN BE.
BOTTOM LINE IS, I JUST CAN'T LET IT GO WITHOUT DOING SOMETHING ABOUT IT.
EVEN IF IT'S REALLY ONLY FOR MY OWN PERSONAL SAFETY.
AFTER ALL, WHEN A MAN IS THREATENED, HE'S JUST LIKE ANY OTHER ANIMAL.

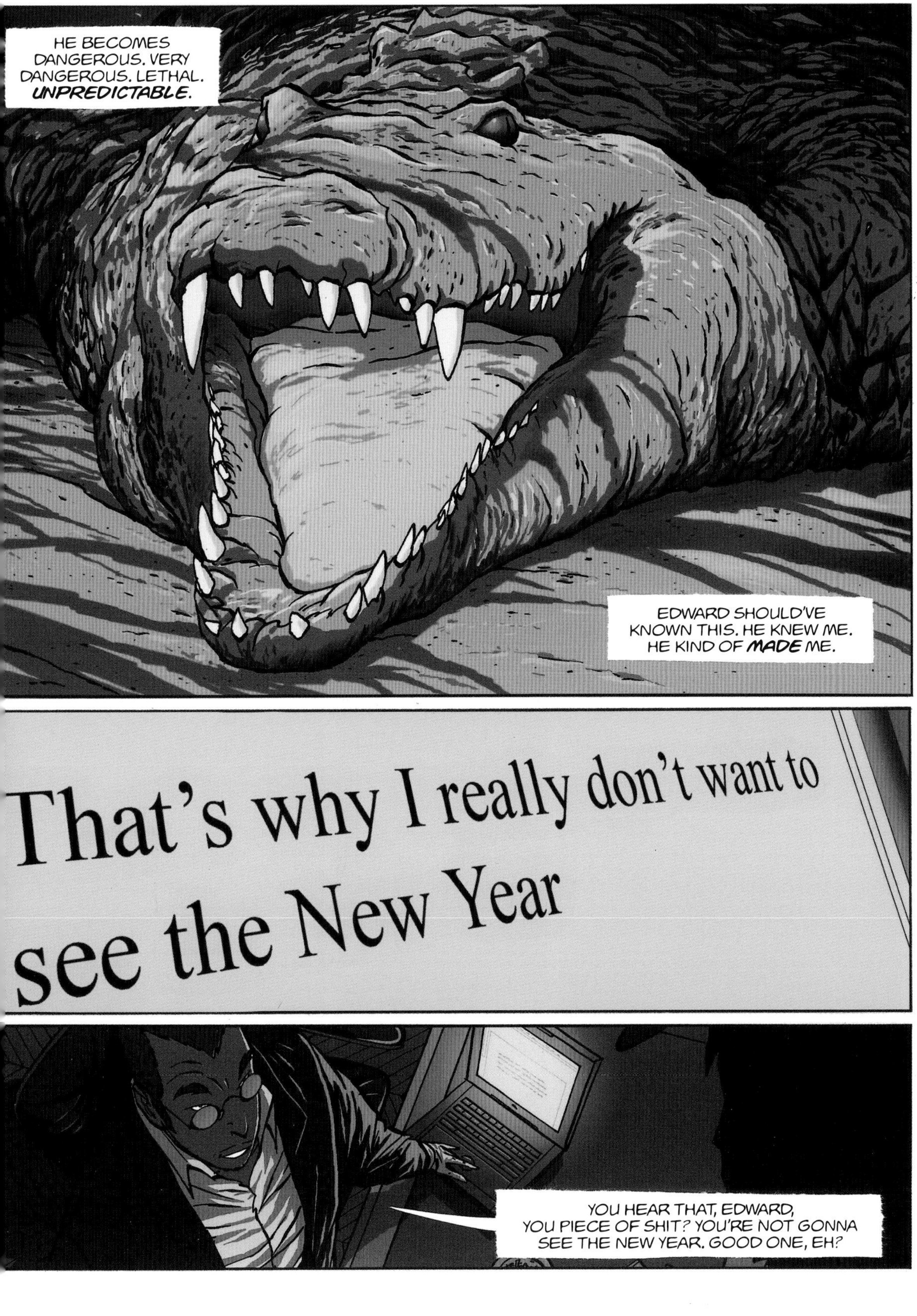
HE BECOMES DANGEROUS. VERY DANGEROUS. LETHAL. UNPREDICTABLE.
EDWARD SHOULD'VE KNOWN THIS. HE KNEW ME. HE KIND OF MADE ME.
That's why I really don't want to see the New Year
YOU HEAR THAT, EDWARD, YOU PIECE OF SHIT? YOU'RE NOT GONNA SEE THE NEW YEAR. GOOD ONE, EH?

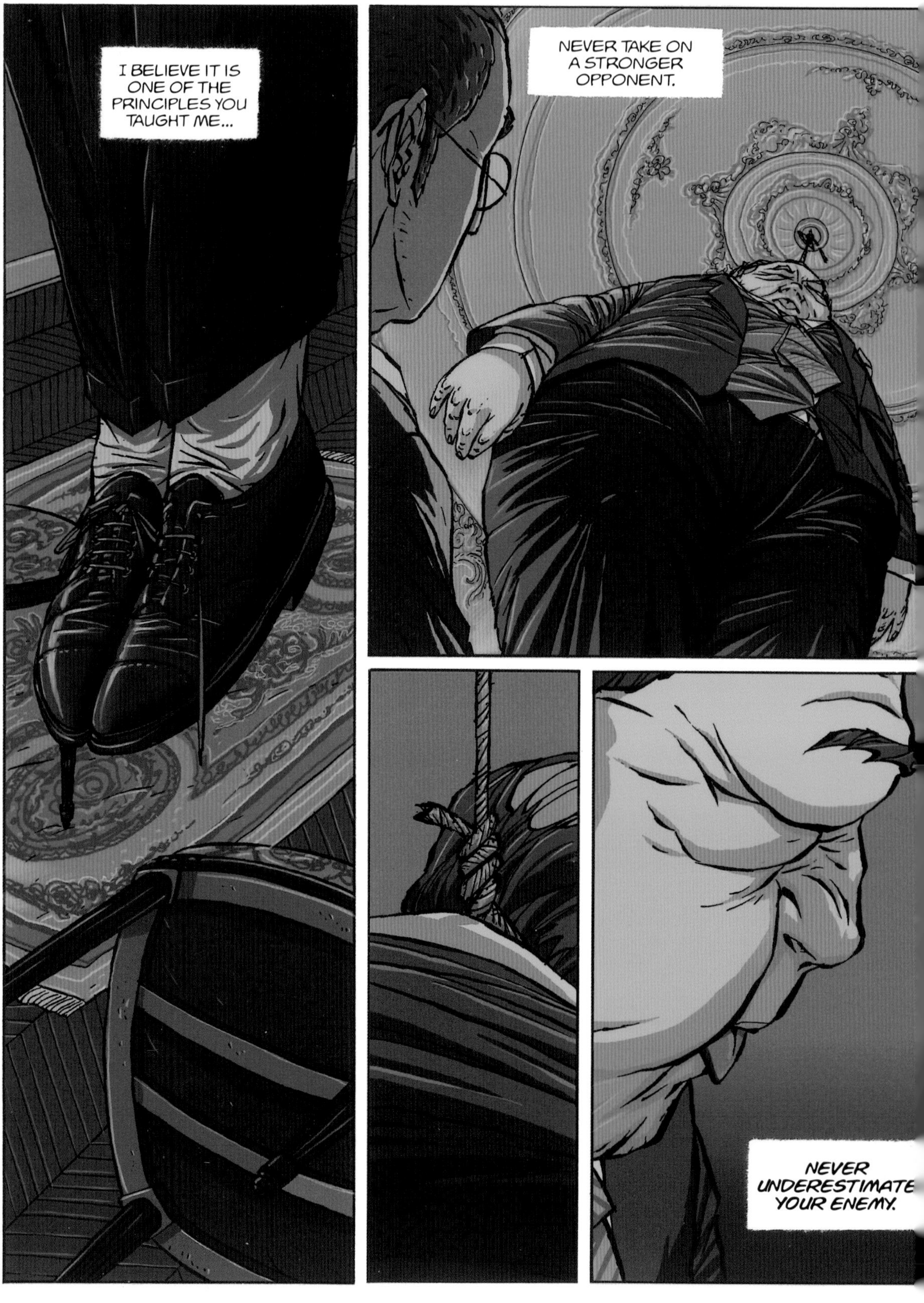
I BELIEVE IT IS ONE OF THE PRINCIPLES YOU TAUGHT ME...
NEVER TAKE ON A STRONGER OPPONENT.
NEVER UNDERESTIMATE YOUR ENEMY.

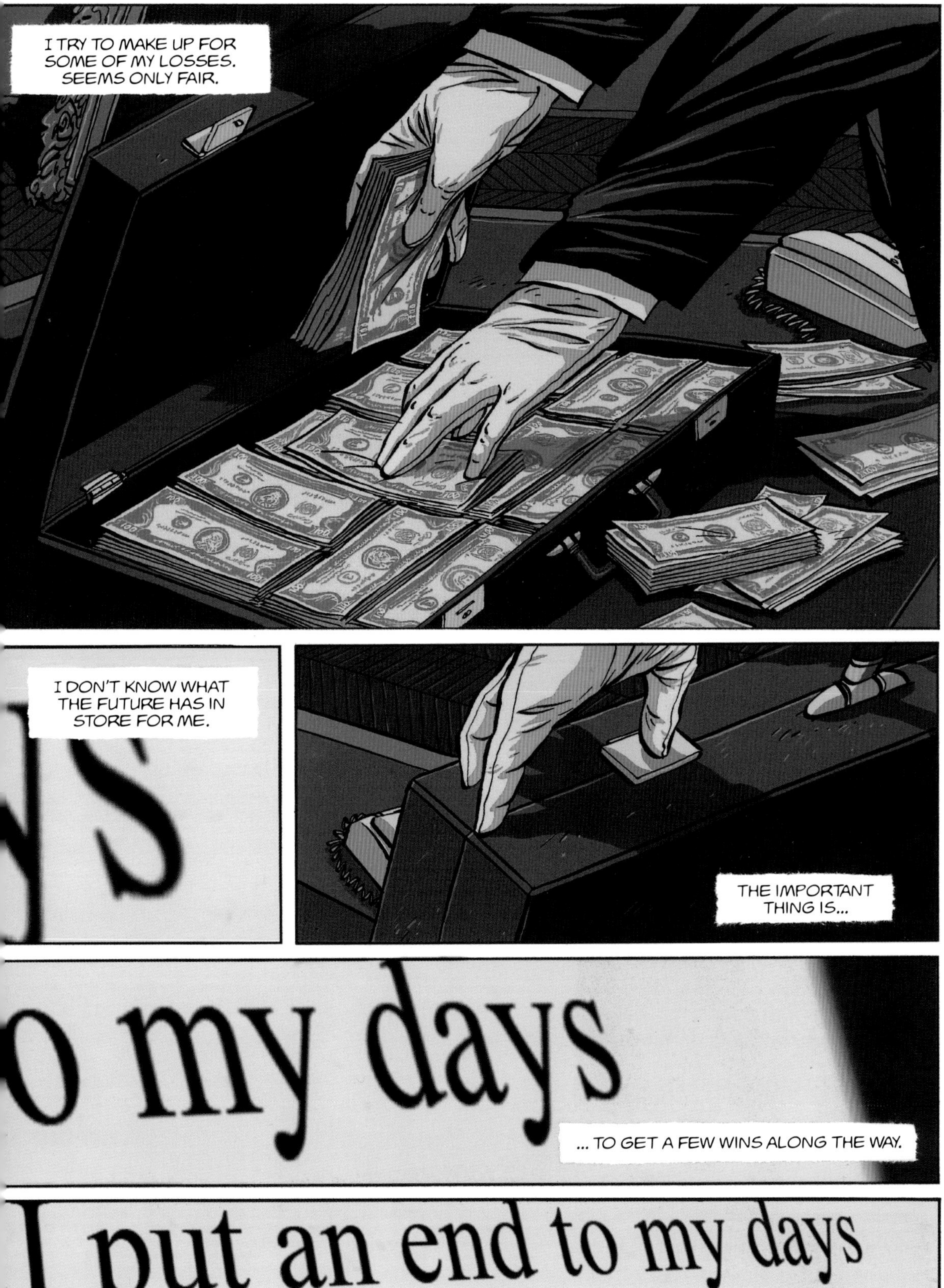
I TRY TO MAKE UP FOR SOME OF MY LOSSES. SEEMS ONLY FAIR.
I DON'T KNOW WHAT THE FUTURE HAS IN STORE FOR ME.
THE IMPORTANT THING IS...
o my days
... TO GET A FEW WINS ALONG THE WAY.
I put an end to my days

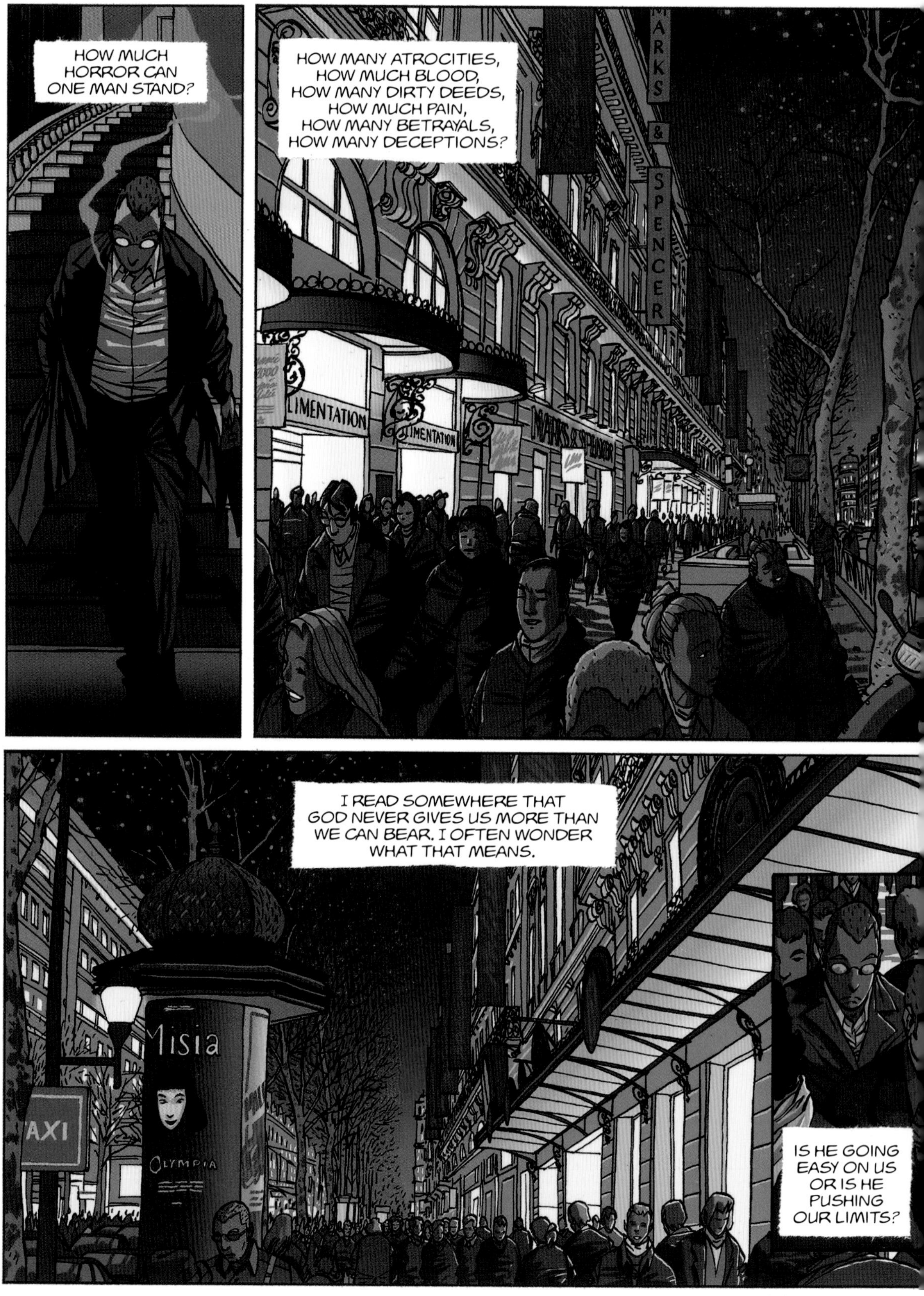
HOW MUCH HORROR CAN ONE MAN STAND?
HOW MANY ATROCITIES, HOW MUCH BLOOD, HOW MANY DIRTY DEEDS, HOW MUCH PAIN, HOW MANY BETRAYALS, HOW MANY DECEPTIONS?
MARKS & SPENCER
LIMENTATION
LIMENTATION
I READ SOMEWHERE THAT GOD NEVER GIVES US MORE THAN WE CAN BEAR. I OFTEN WONDER WHAT THAT MEANS.
Misia
OLYMPIA
AXI
IS HE GOING EASY ON US OR IS HE PUSHING OUR LIMITS?

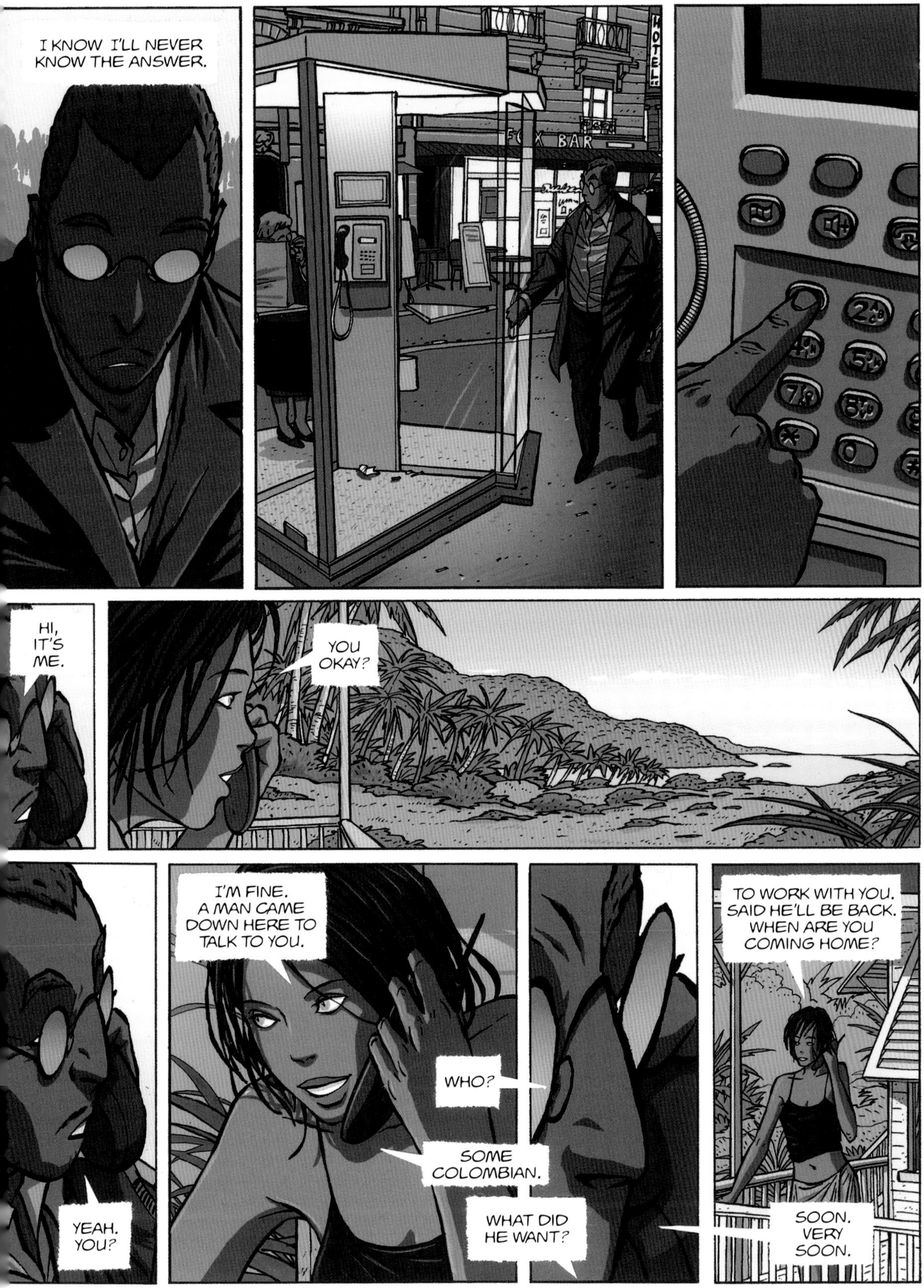
I KNOW I'LL NEVER KNOW THE ANSWER.
HOTEL
FOX BAR
HI, IT'S ME.
YOU OKAY?
YEAH. YOU?
I'M FINE. A MAN CAME DOWN HERE TO TALK TO YOU.
WHO?
SOME COLOMBIAN.
WHAT DID HE WANT?
TO WORK WITH YOU. SAID HE'LL BE BACK. WHEN ARE YOU COMING HOME?
SOON. VERY SOON.

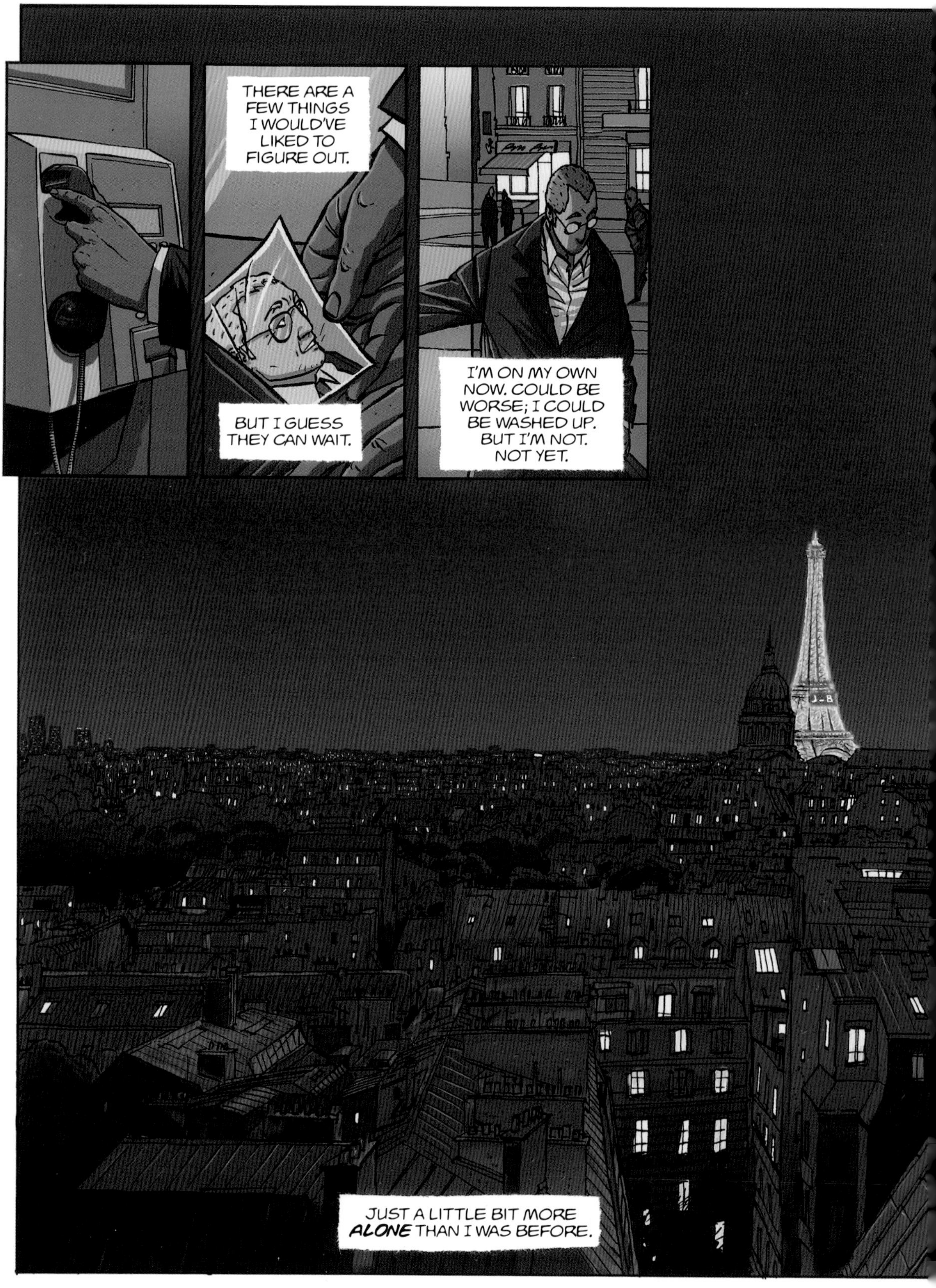
THERE ARE A FEW THINGS I WOULD'VE LIKED TO FIGURE OUT.
BUT I GUESS THEY CAN WAIT.
I'M ON MY OWN NOW. COULD BE WORSE; I COULD BE WASHED UP. BUT I'M NOT. NOT YET.
JUST A LITTLE BIT MORE *ALONE* THAN I WAS BEFORE.

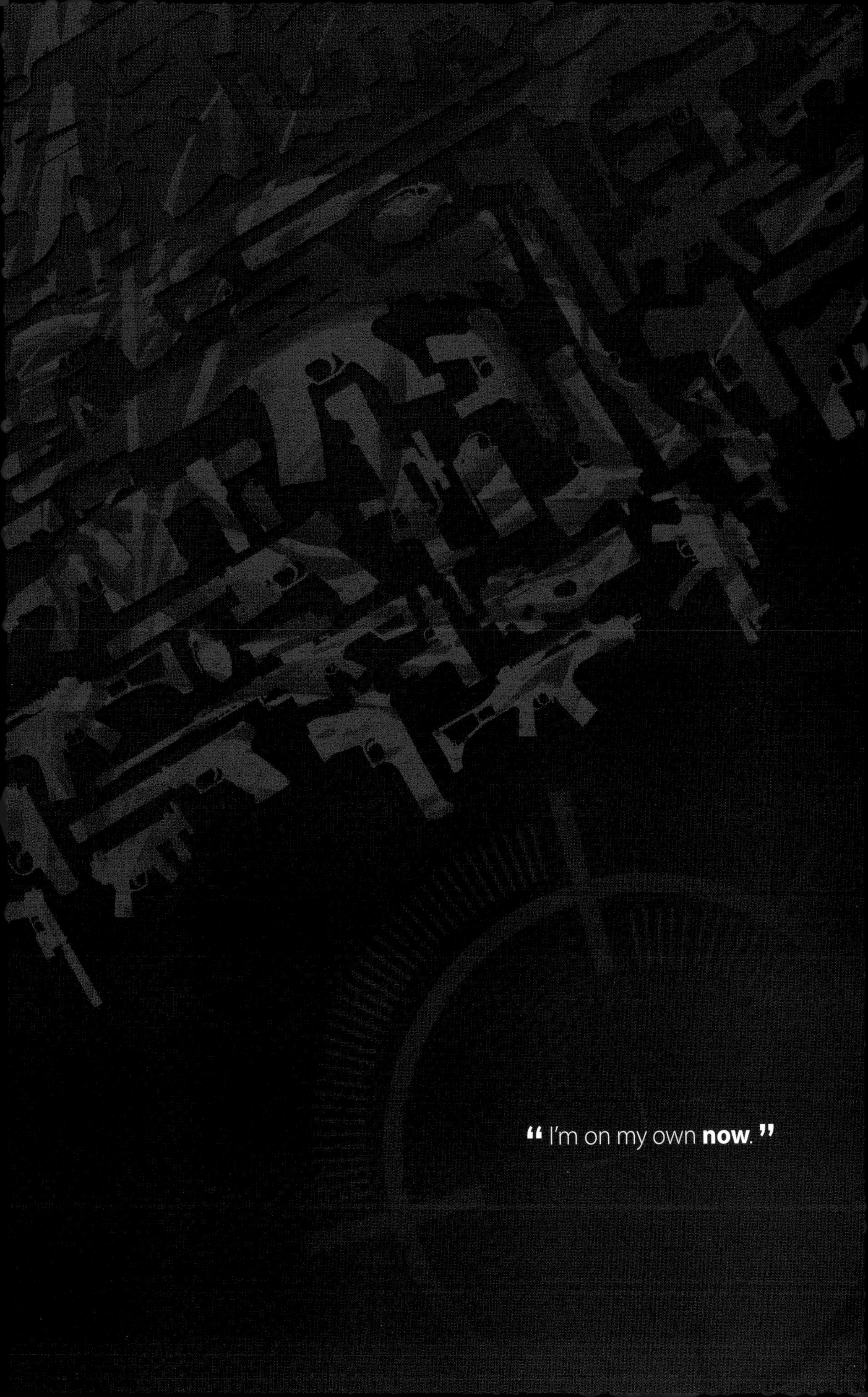
“ I’m on my own **now**. ”

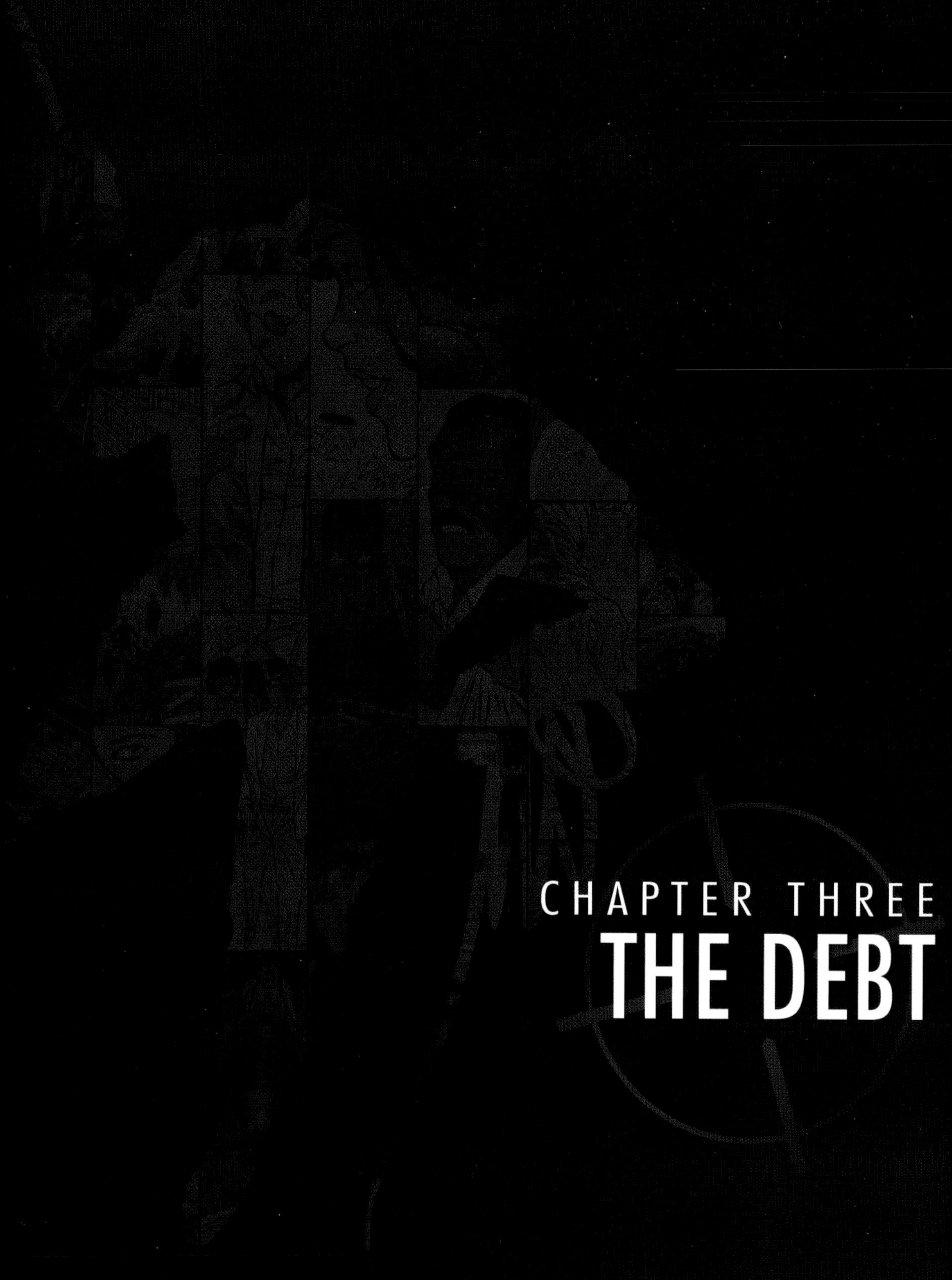

CHAPTER THREE
THE DEBT

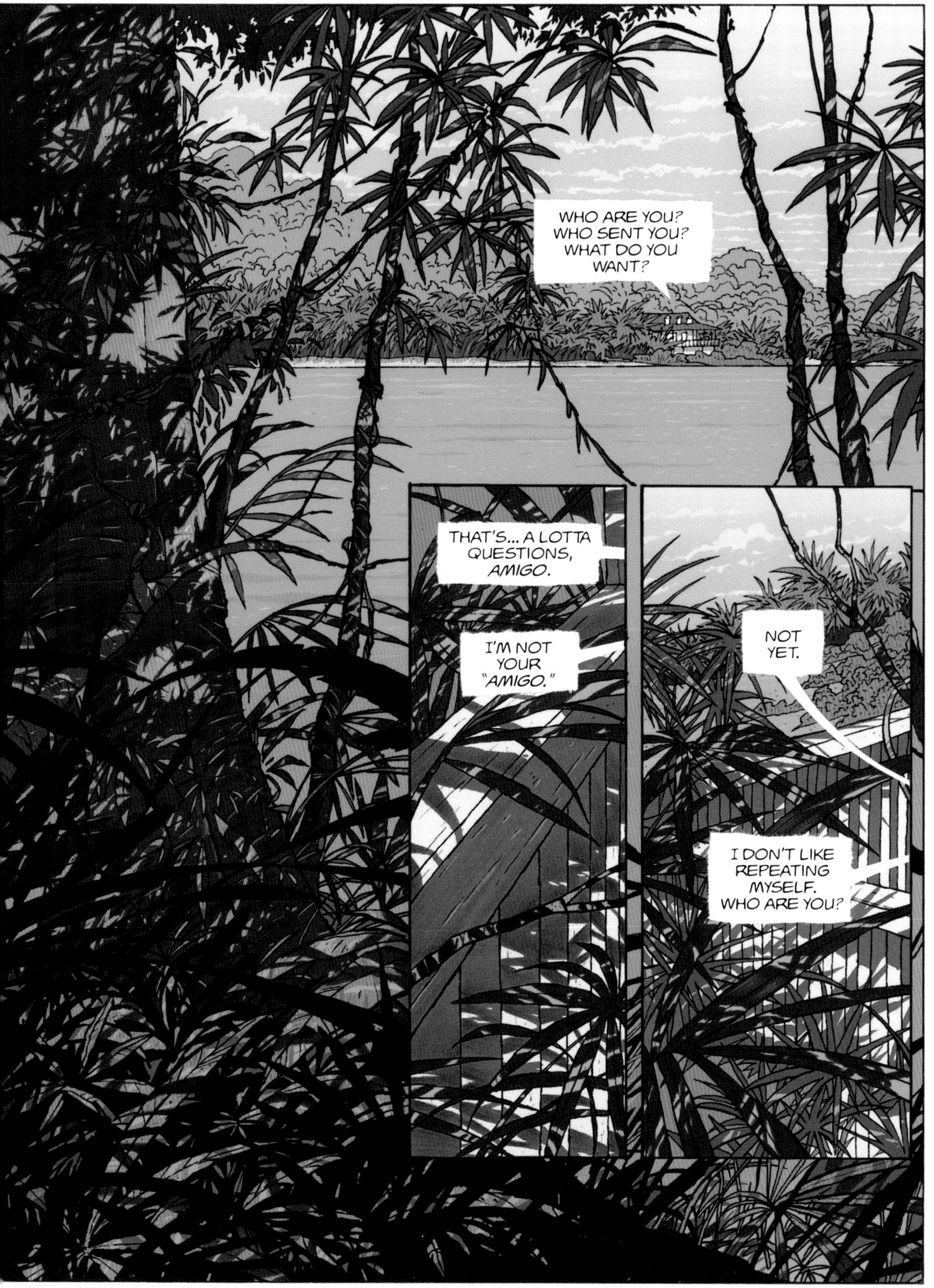
WHO ARE YOU? WHO SENT YOU? WHAT DO YOU WANT?
THAT'S... A LOTTA QUESTIONS, AMIGO.
I'M NOT YOUR "AMIGO."
NOT YET.
I DON'T LIKE REPEATING MYSELF. WHO ARE YOU?

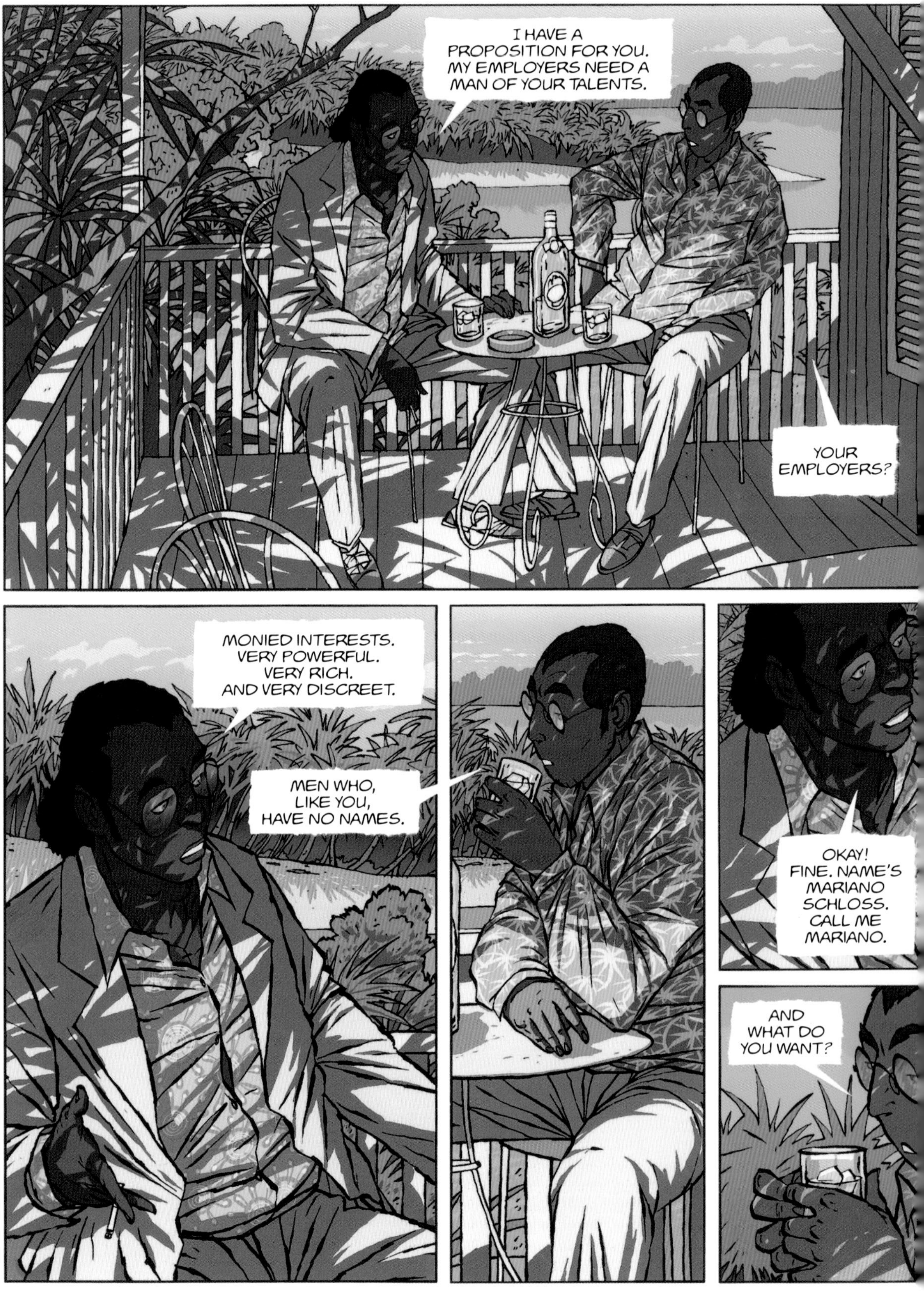
I HAVE A PROPOSITION FOR YOU. MY EMPLOYERS NEED A MAN OF YOUR TALENTS.
YOUR EMPLOYERS?
MONIED INTERESTS. VERY POWERFUL. VERY RICH. AND VERY DISCREET.
MEN WHO, LIKE YOU, HAVE NO NAMES.
OKAY! FINE. NAME'S MARIANO SCHLOSS. CALL ME MARIANO.
AND WHAT DO YOU WANT?

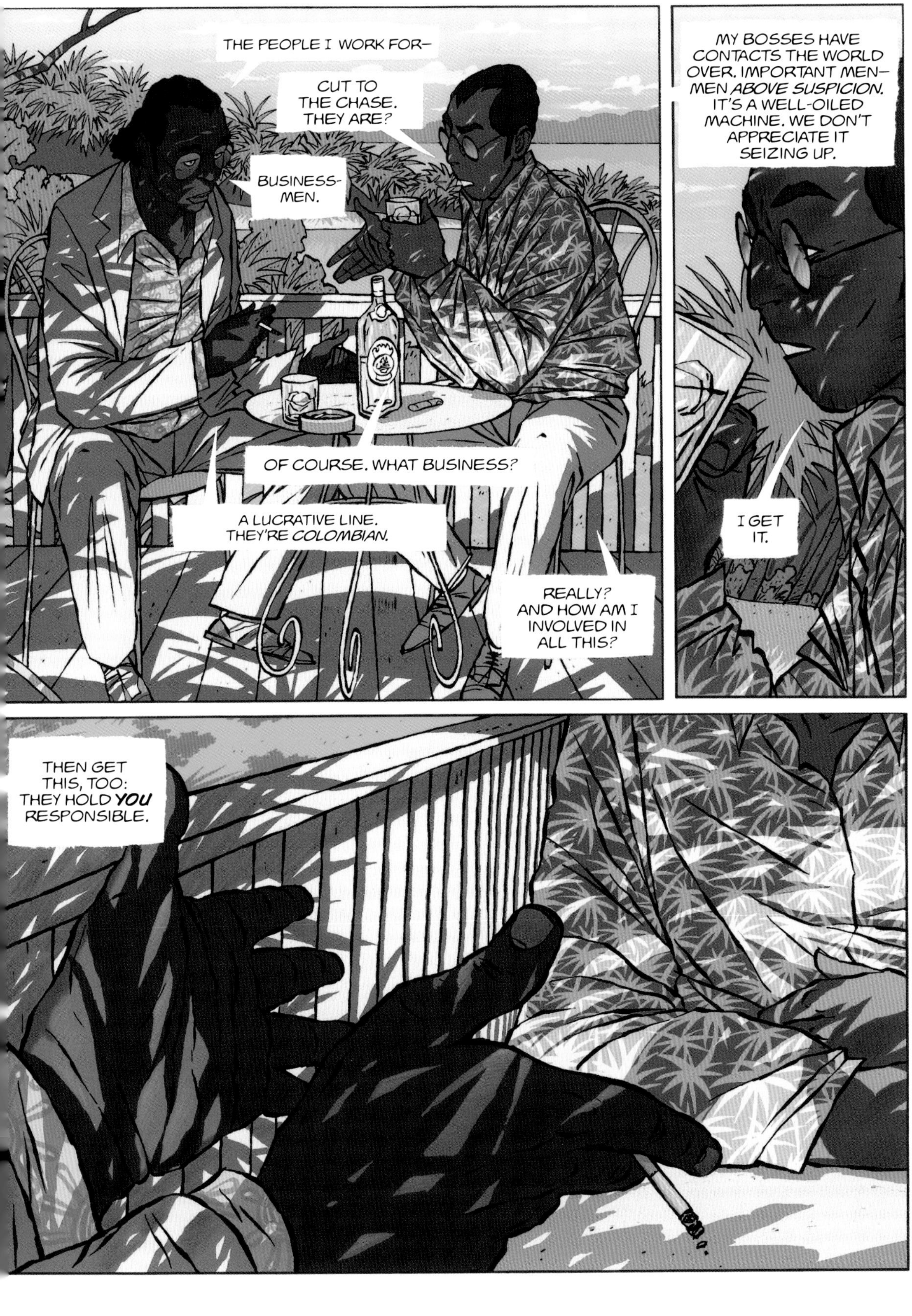
THE PEOPLE I WORK FOR—
CUT TO THE CHASE. THEY ARE?
BUSINESS-MEN.
OF COURSE. WHAT BUSINESS?
A LUCRATIVE LINE. THEY'RE *COLOMBIAN.*
REALLY? AND HOW AM I INVOLVED IN ALL THIS?
MY BOSSES HAVE CONTACTS THE WORLD OVER. IMPORTANT MEN—MEN *ABOVE SUSPICION.* IT'S A WELL-OILED MACHINE. WE DON'T APPRECIATE IT SEIZING UP.
I GET IT.
THEN GET THIS, TOO: THEY HOLD ***YOU*** RESPONSIBLE.

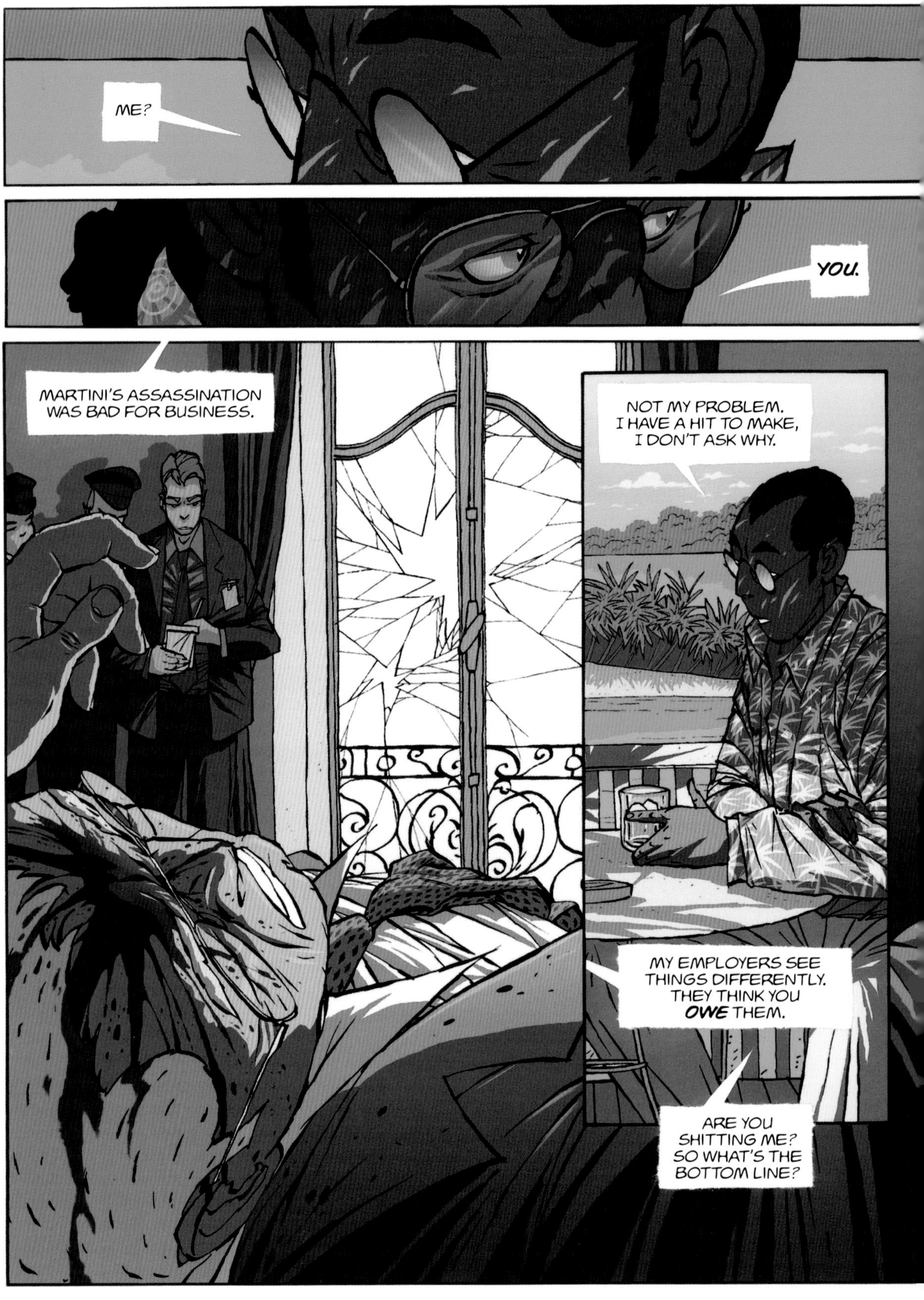
ME?
YOU.
MARTINI'S ASSASSINATION WAS BAD FOR BUSINESS.
NOT MY PROBLEM. I HAVE A HIT TO MAKE, I DON'T ASK WHY.
MY EMPLOYERS SEE THINGS DIFFERENTLY. THEY THINK YOU OWE THEM.
ARE YOU SHITTING ME? SO WHAT'S THE BOTTOM LINE?

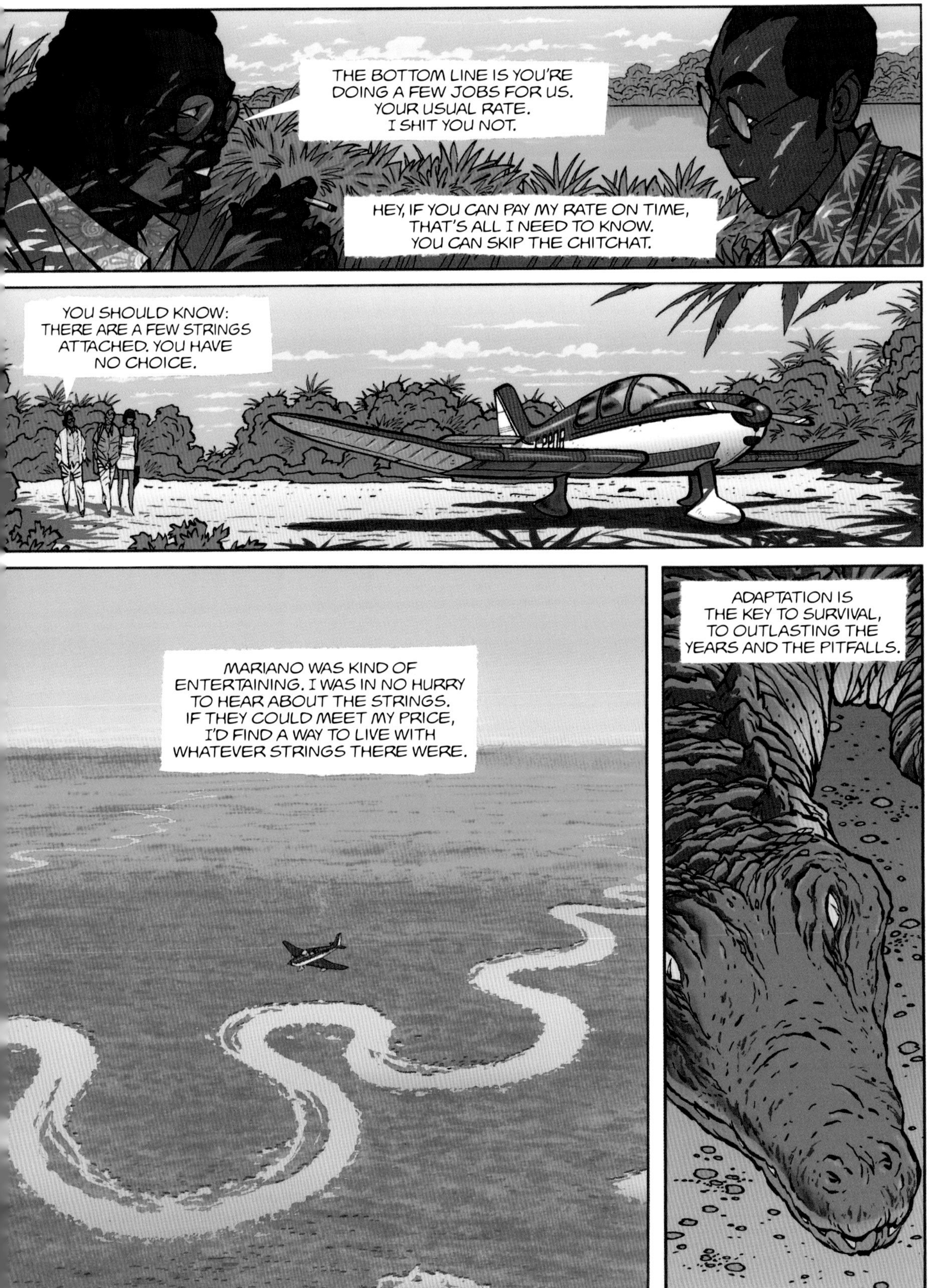
THE BOTTOM LINE IS YOU'RE DOING A FEW JOBS FOR US. YOUR USUAL RATE. I SHIT YOU NOT.
HEY, IF YOU CAN PAY MY RATE ON TIME, THAT'S ALL I NEED TO KNOW. YOU CAN SKIP THE CHITCHAT.
YOU SHOULD KNOW: THERE ARE A FEW STRINGS ATTACHED. YOU HAVE NO CHOICE.
MARIANO WAS KIND OF ENTERTAINING. I WAS IN NO HURRY TO HEAR ABOUT THE STRINGS. IF THEY COULD MEET MY PRICE, I'D FIND A WAY TO LIVE WITH WHATEVER STRINGS THERE WERE.
ADAPTATION IS THE KEY TO SURVIVAL, TO OUTLASTING THE YEARS AND THE PITFALLS.

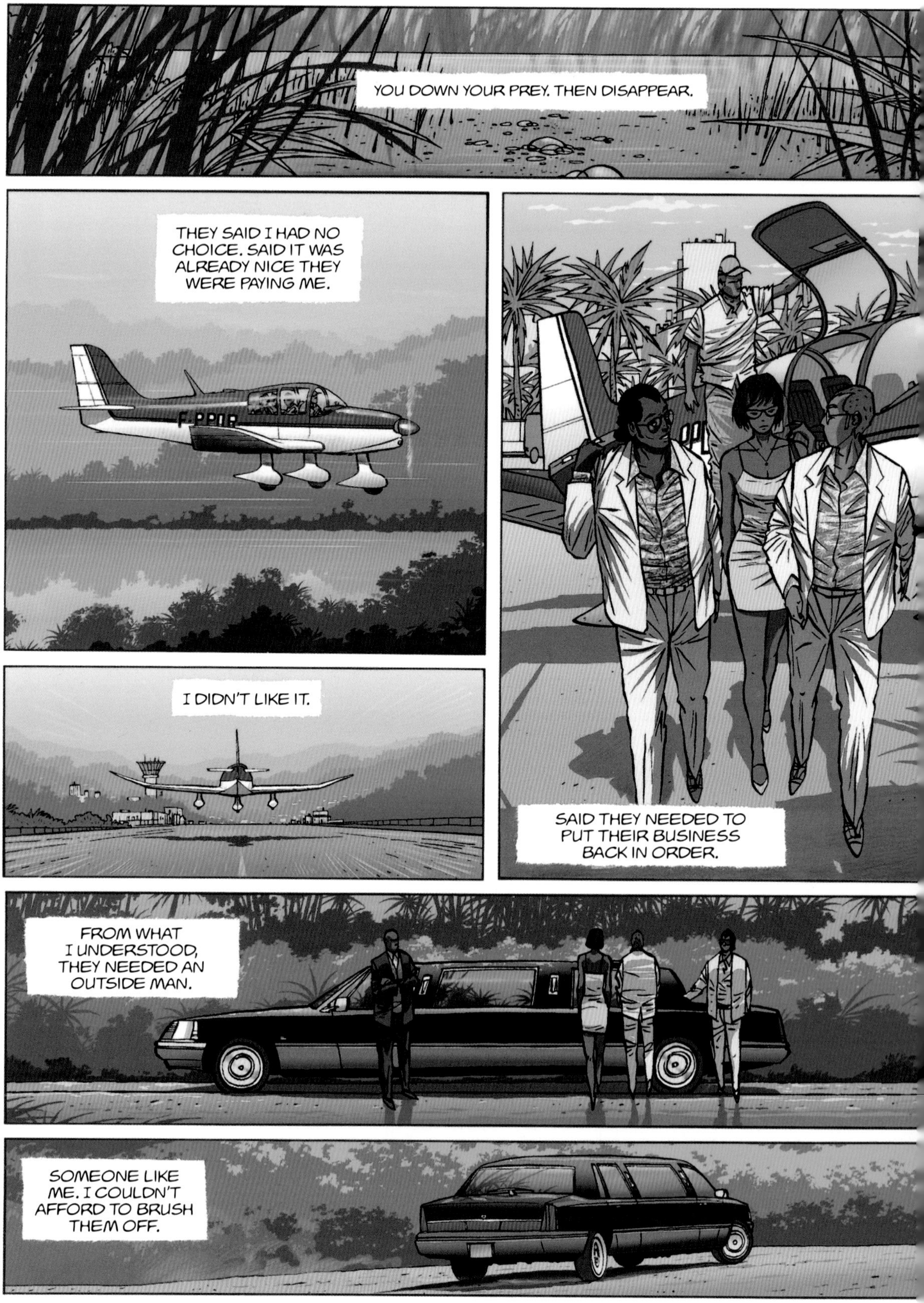

YOU DOWN YOUR PREY. THEN DISAPPEAR.
THEY SAID I HAD NO CHOICE. SAID IT WAS ALREADY NICE THEY WERE PAYING ME.
I DIDN'T LIKE IT.
SAID THEY NEEDED TO PUT THEIR BUSINESS BACK IN ORDER.
FROM WHAT I UNDERSTOOD, THEY NEEDED AN OUTSIDE MAN.
SOMEONE LIKE ME. I COULDN'T AFFORD TO BRUSH THEM OFF.

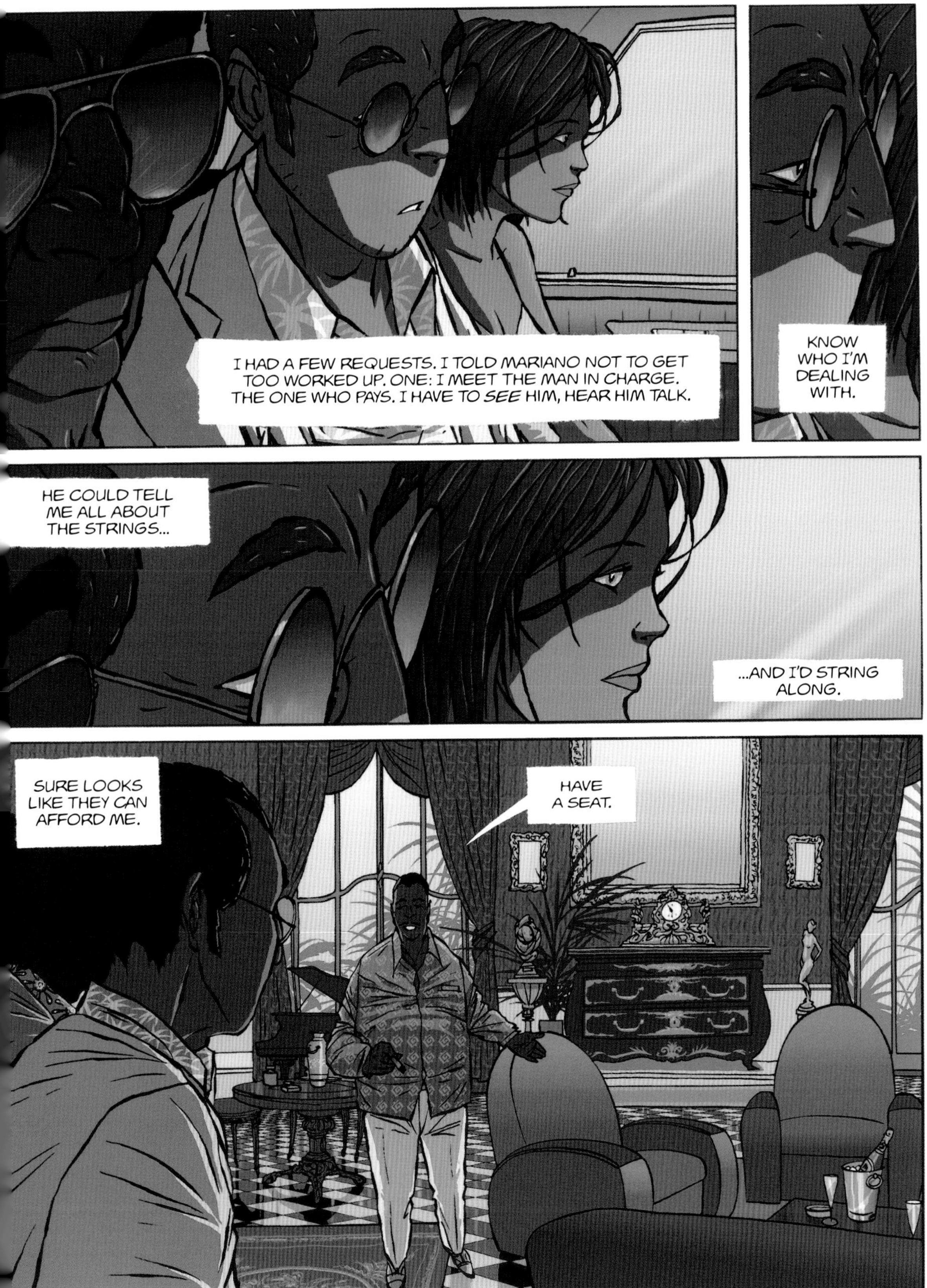
I HAD A FEW REQUESTS. I TOLD MARIANO NOT TO GET TOO WORKED UP. ONE: I MEET THE MAN IN CHARGE. THE ONE WHO PAYS. I HAVE TO *SEE* HIM, HEAR HIM TALK.
KNOW WHO I'M DEALING WITH.
HE COULD TELL ME ALL ABOUT THE STRINGS...
...AND I'D STRING ALONG.
SURE LOOKS LIKE THEY CAN AFFORD ME.
HAVE A SEAT.

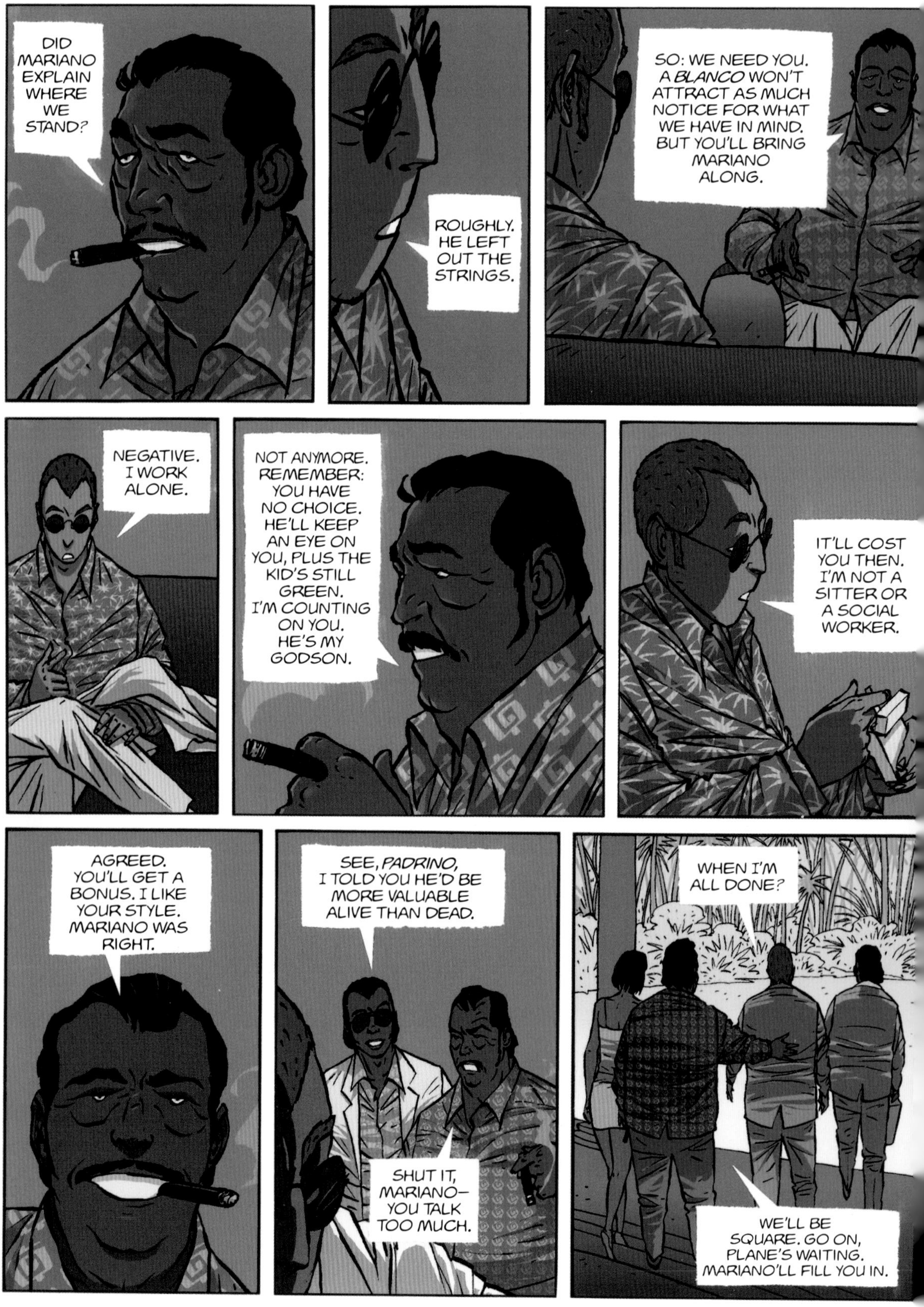
DID MARIANO EXPLAIN WHERE WE STAND?
ROUGHLY. HE LEFT OUT THE STRINGS.
SO: WE NEED YOU. A *BLANCO* WON'T ATTRACT AS MUCH NOTICE FOR WHAT WE HAVE IN MIND. BUT YOU'LL BRING MARIANO ALONG.
NEGATIVE. I WORK ALONE.
NOT ANYMORE. REMEMBER: YOU HAVE NO CHOICE. HE'LL KEEP AN EYE ON YOU, PLUS THE KID'S STILL GREEN. I'M COUNTING ON YOU. HE'S MY GODSON.
IT'LL COST YOU THEN. I'M NOT A SITTER OR A SOCIAL WORKER.
AGREED. YOU'LL GET A BONUS. I LIKE YOUR STYLE. MARIANO WAS RIGHT.
SEE, *PADRINO*, I TOLD YOU HE'D BE MORE VALUABLE ALIVE THAN DEAD.
SHUT IT, MARIANO— YOU TALK TOO MUCH.
WHEN I'M ALL DONE?
WE'LL BE SQUARE. GO ON, PLANE'S WAITING. MARIANO'LL FILL YOU IN.

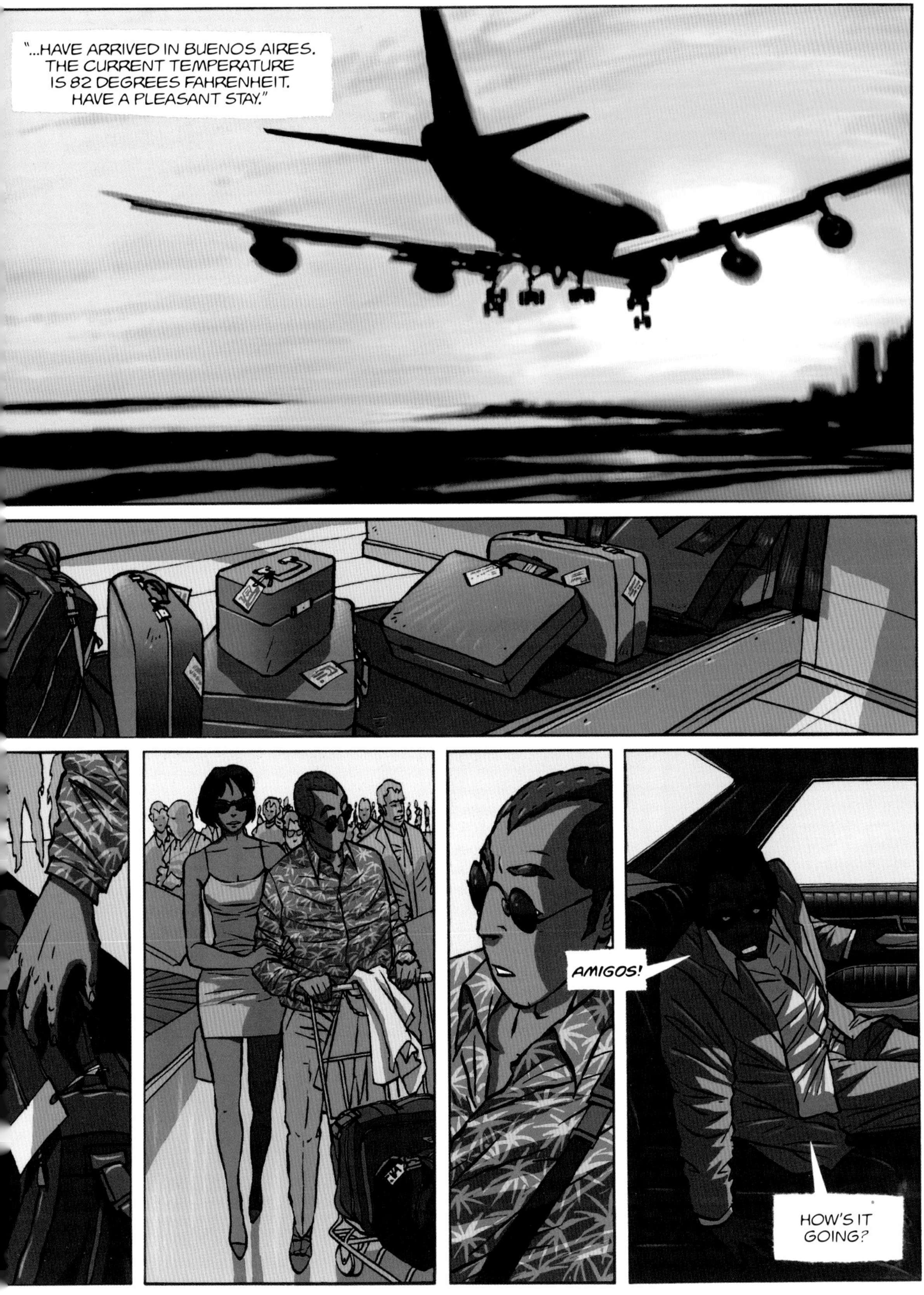
"...HAVE ARRIVED IN BUENOS AIRES. THE CURRENT TEMPERATURE IS 82 DEGREES FAHRENHEIT. HAVE A PLEASANT STAY."
AMIGOS!
HOW'S IT GOING?

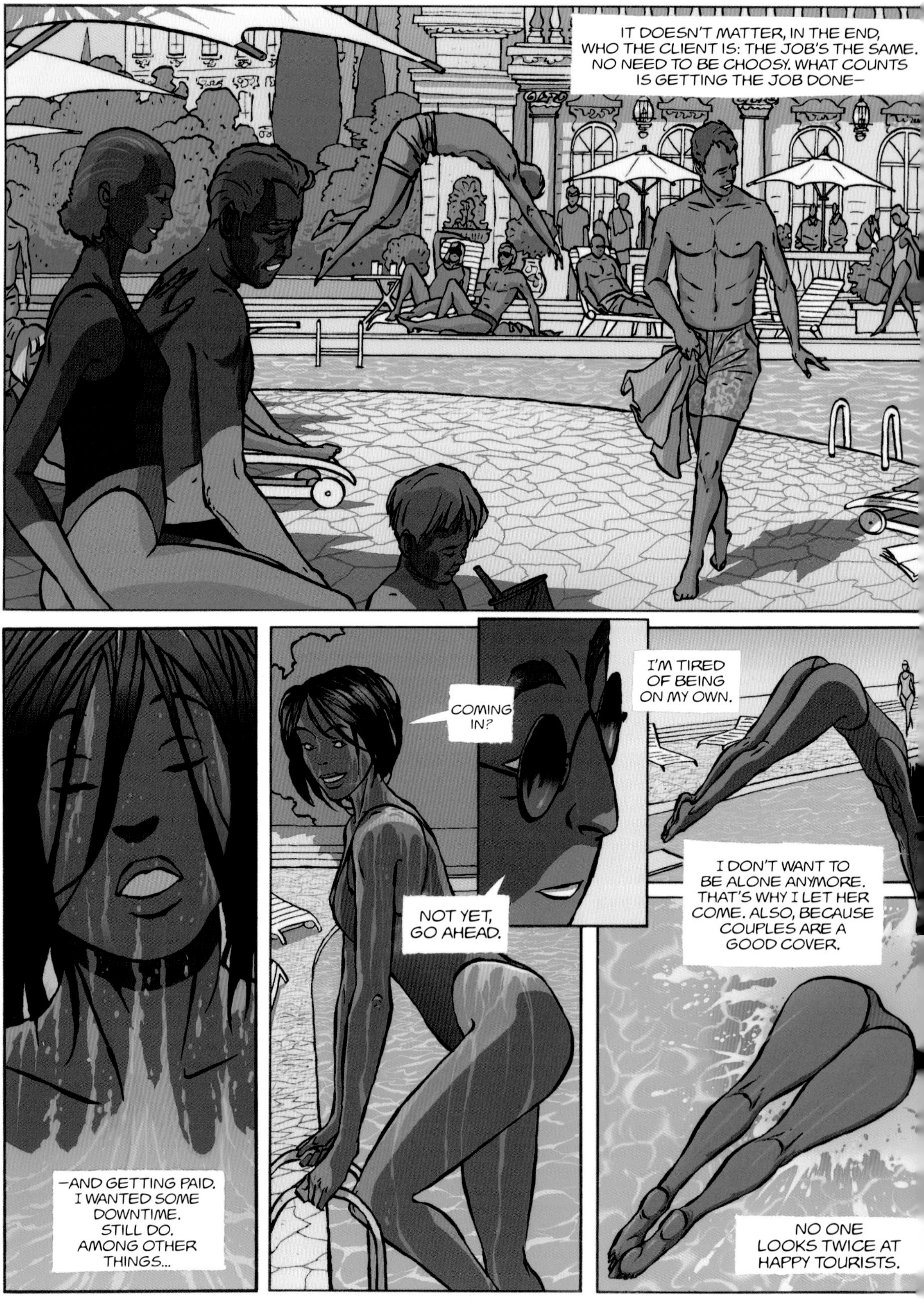
IT DOESN'T MATTER, IN THE END, WHO THE CLIENT IS: THE JOB'S THE SAME. NO NEED TO BE CHOOSY. WHAT COUNTS IS GETTING THE JOB DONE–
–AND GETTING PAID. I WANTED SOME DOWNTIME. STILL DO. AMONG OTHER THINGS...
COMING IN?
NOT YET, GO AHEAD.
I'M TIRED OF BEING ON MY OWN.
I DON'T WANT TO BE ALONE ANYMORE. THAT'S WHY I LET HER COME. ALSO, BECAUSE COUPLES ARE A GOOD COVER.
NO ONE LOOKS TWICE AT HAPPY TOURISTS.

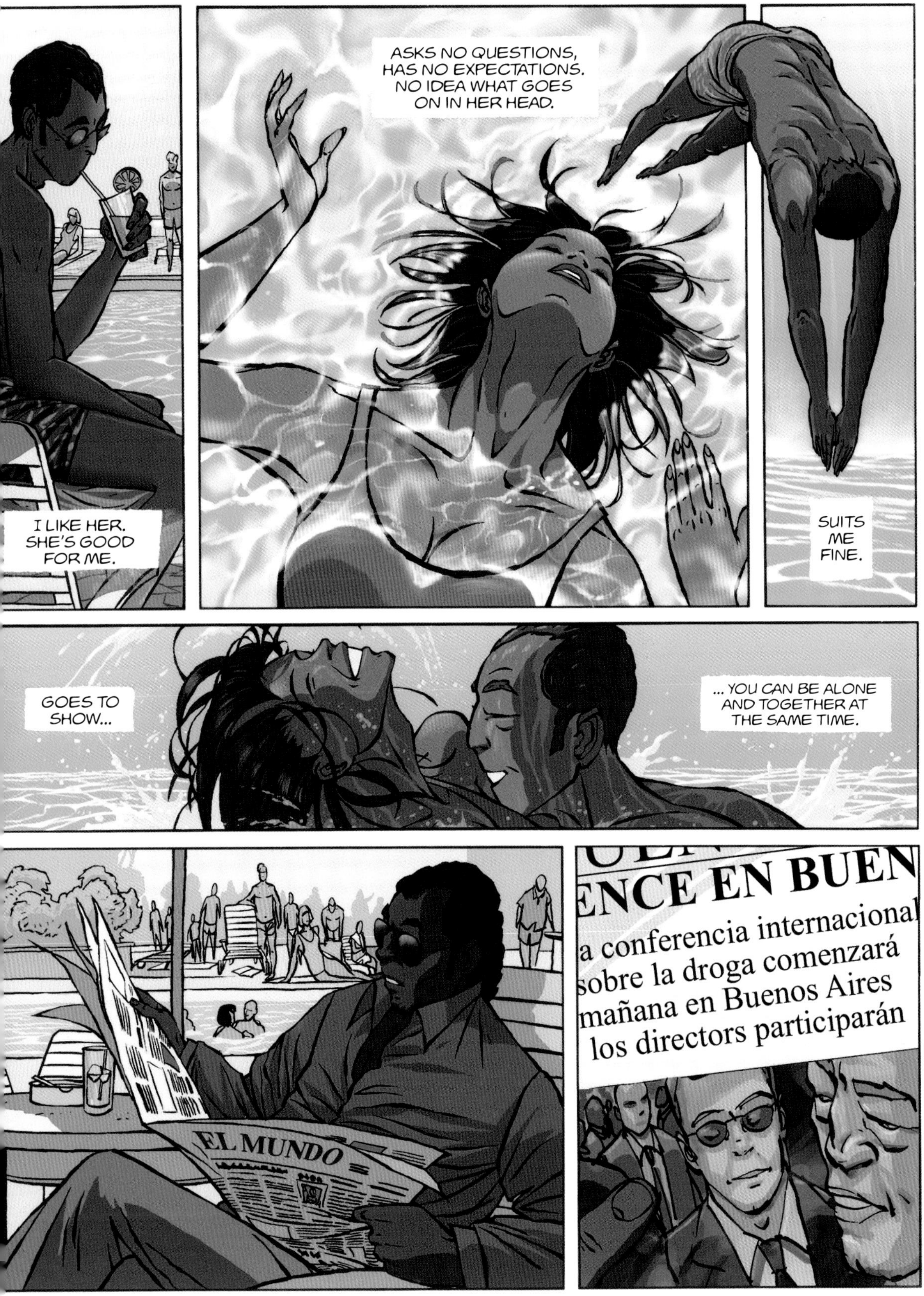
I LIKE HER.
SHE'S GOOD FOR ME.
ASKS NO QUESTIONS, HAS NO EXPECTATIONS. NO IDEA WHAT GOES ON IN HER HEAD.
SUITS ME FINE.
GOES TO SHOW...
...YOU CAN BE ALONE AND TOGETHER AT THE SAME TIME.
EL MUNDO
ENCE EN BUEN
a conferencia internacional
sobre la droga comenzará
mañana en Buenos Aires
los directors participarán

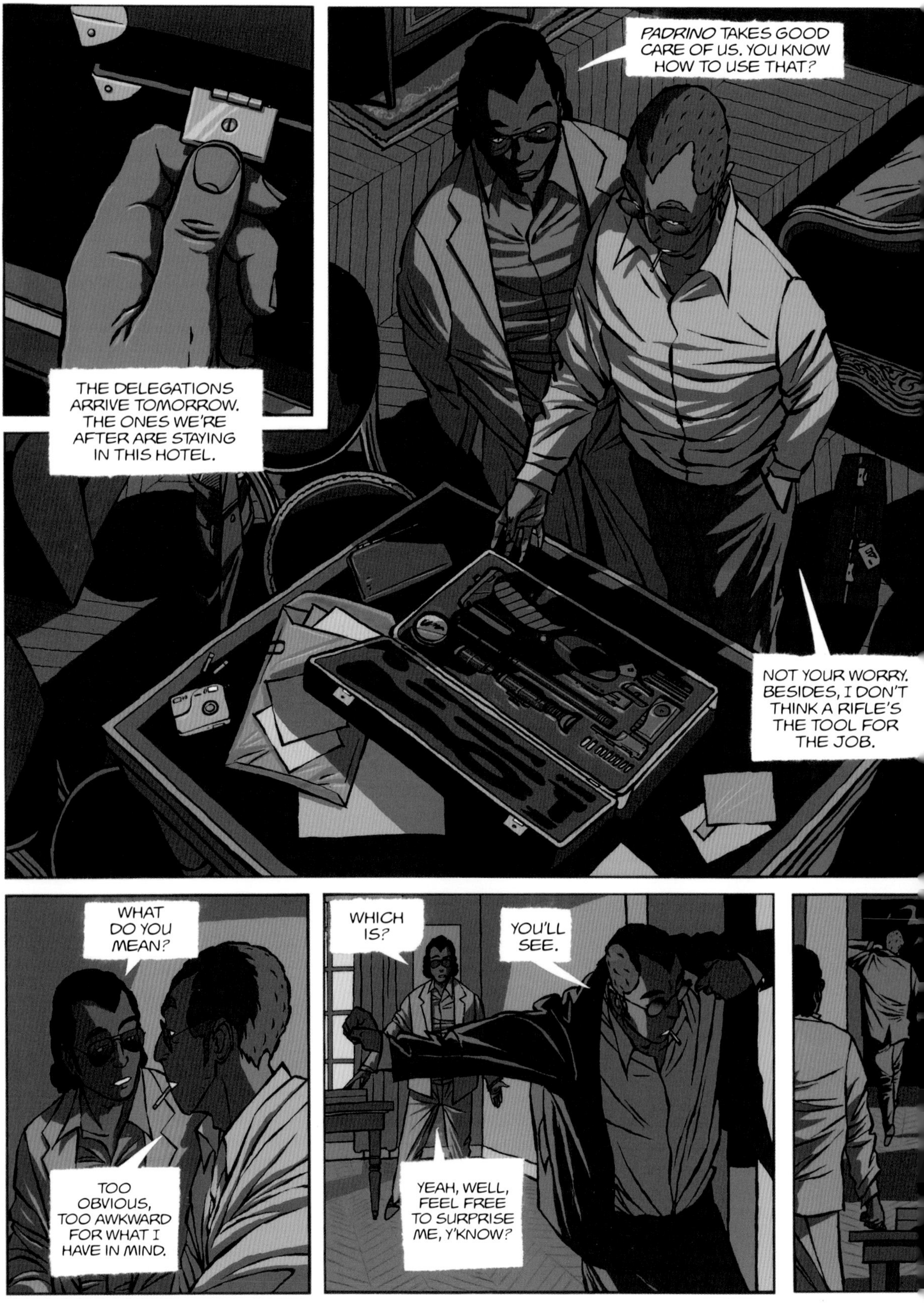
PADRINO TAKES GOOD CARE OF US. YOU KNOW HOW TO USE THAT?
THE DELEGATIONS ARRIVE TOMORROW. THE ONES WE'RE AFTER ARE STAYING IN THIS HOTEL.
NOT YOUR WORRY. BESIDES, I DON'T THINK A RIFLE'S THE TOOL FOR THE JOB.
WHAT DO YOU MEAN?
TOO OBVIOUS, TOO AWKWARD FOR WHAT I HAVE IN MIND.
WHICH IS?
YOU'LL SEE.
YEAH, WELL, FEEL FREE TO SURPRISE ME, Y'KNOW?

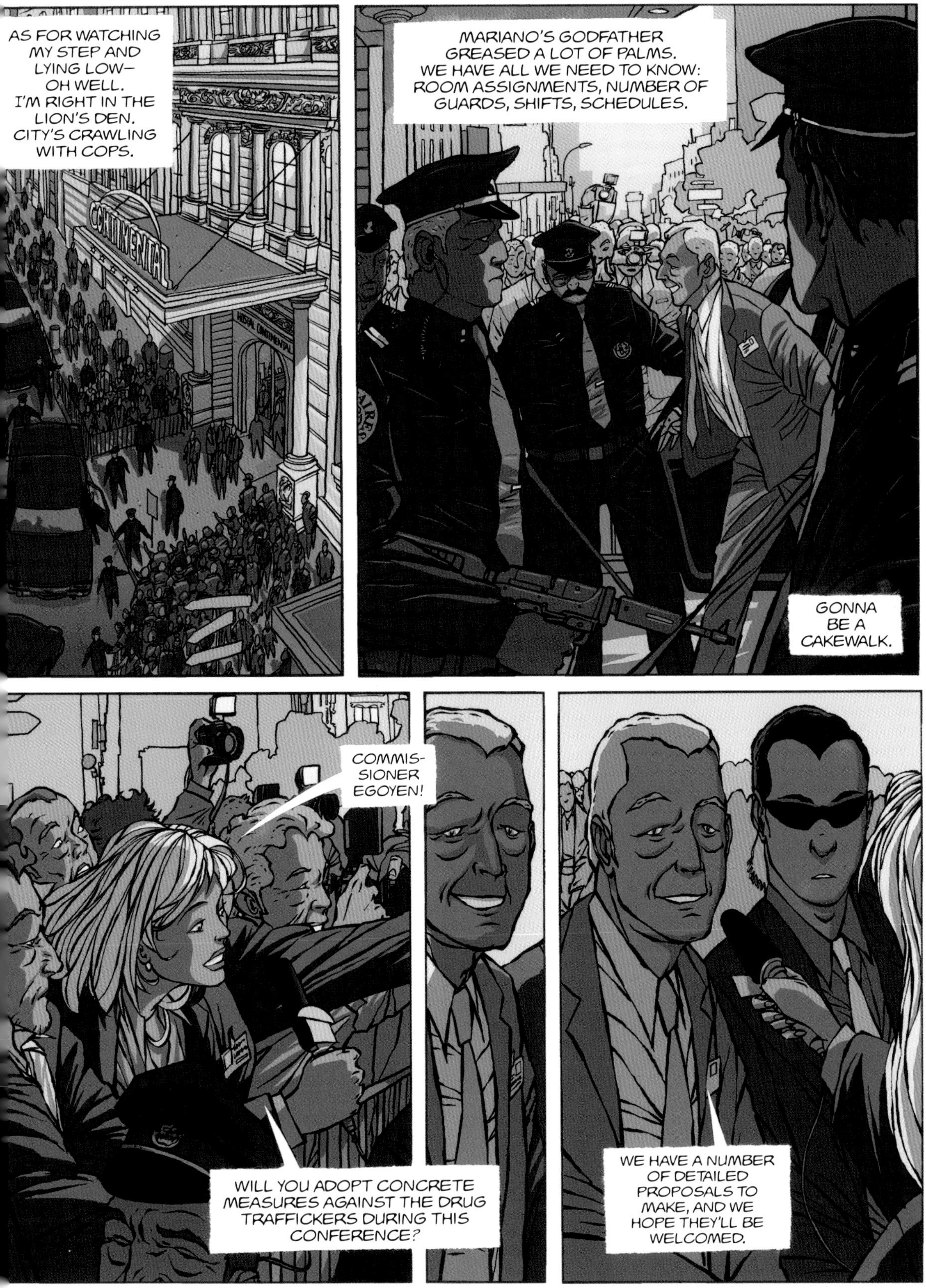
AS FOR WATCHING MY STEP AND LYING LOW— OH WELL. I'M RIGHT IN THE LION'S DEN. CITY'S CRAWLING WITH COPS.
CONTINENTAL
MARIANO'S GODFATHER GREASED A LOT OF PALMS. WE HAVE ALL WE NEED TO KNOW: ROOM ASSIGNMENTS, NUMBER OF GUARDS, SHIFTS, SCHEDULES.
GONNA BE A CAKEWALK.
COMMISSIONER EGOYEN!
WILL YOU ADOPT CONCRETE MEASURES AGAINST THE DRUG TRAFFICKERS DURING THIS CONFERENCE?
WE HAVE A NUMBER OF DETAILED PROPOSALS TO MAKE, AND WE HOPE THEY'LL BE WELCOMED.

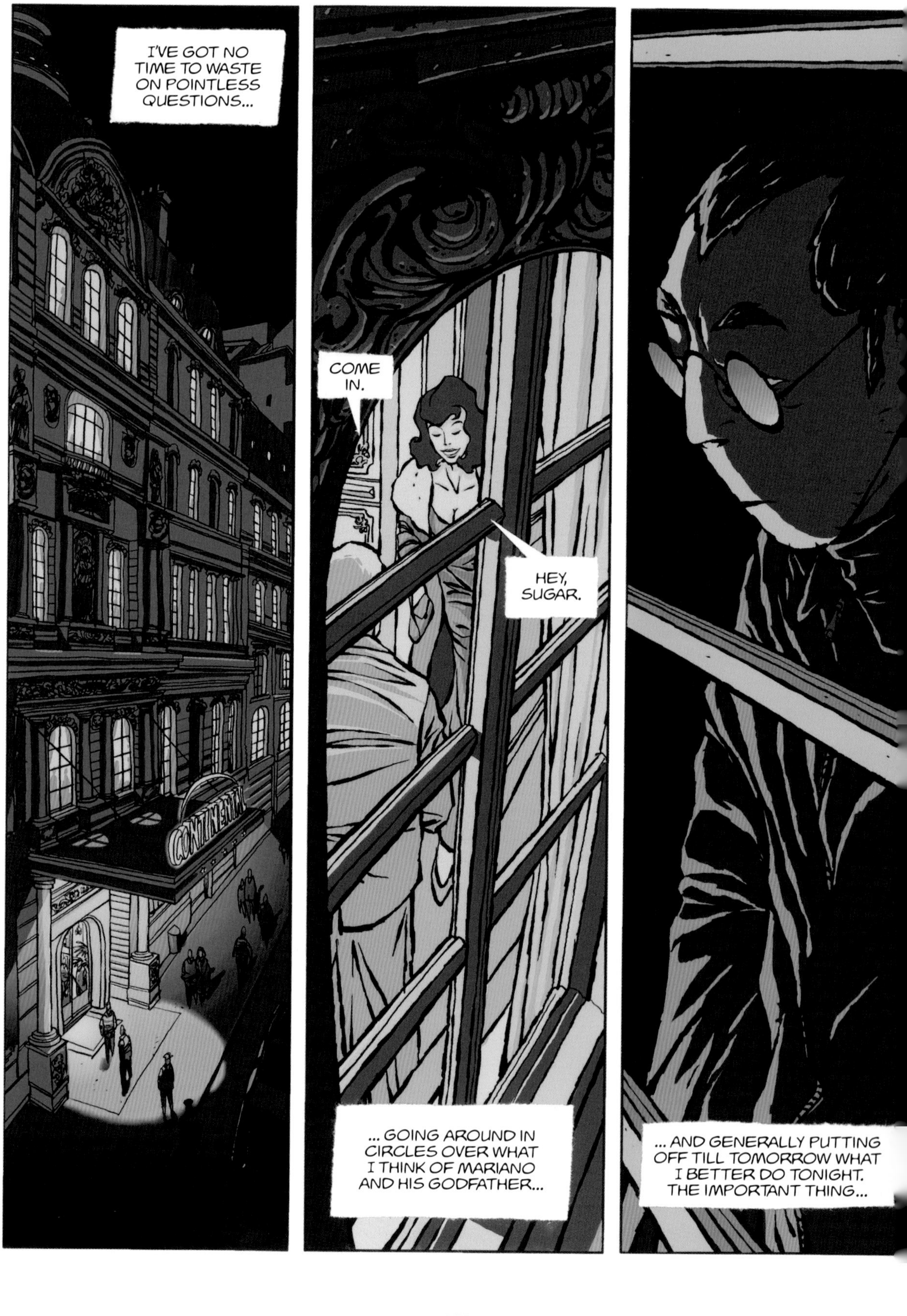
I'VE GOT NO TIME TO WASTE ON POINTLESS QUESTIONS...
CONTINENTAL
COME IN.
HEY, SUGAR.
... GOING AROUND IN CIRCLES OVER WHAT I THINK OF MARIANO AND HIS GODFATHER...
... AND GENERALLY PUTTING OFF TILL TOMORROW WHAT I BETTER DO TONIGHT. THE IMPORTANT THING...

... IS JUST TO WATCH MY BACK. AND MY MONEY.

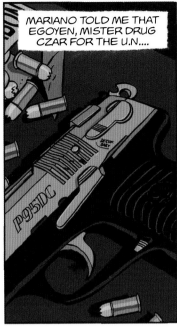

MARIANO TOLD ME THAT EGOYEN, MISTER DRUG CZAR FOR THE U.N....

... HAD A THING FOR CALL GIRLS.

AND THAT WHEN HE CALLED ON ONE: NO BODYGUARDS.

WHAT CAN I DO YOU FOR TONIGHT, SUGAR?

WHAT DID YOU HAVE IN MIND?

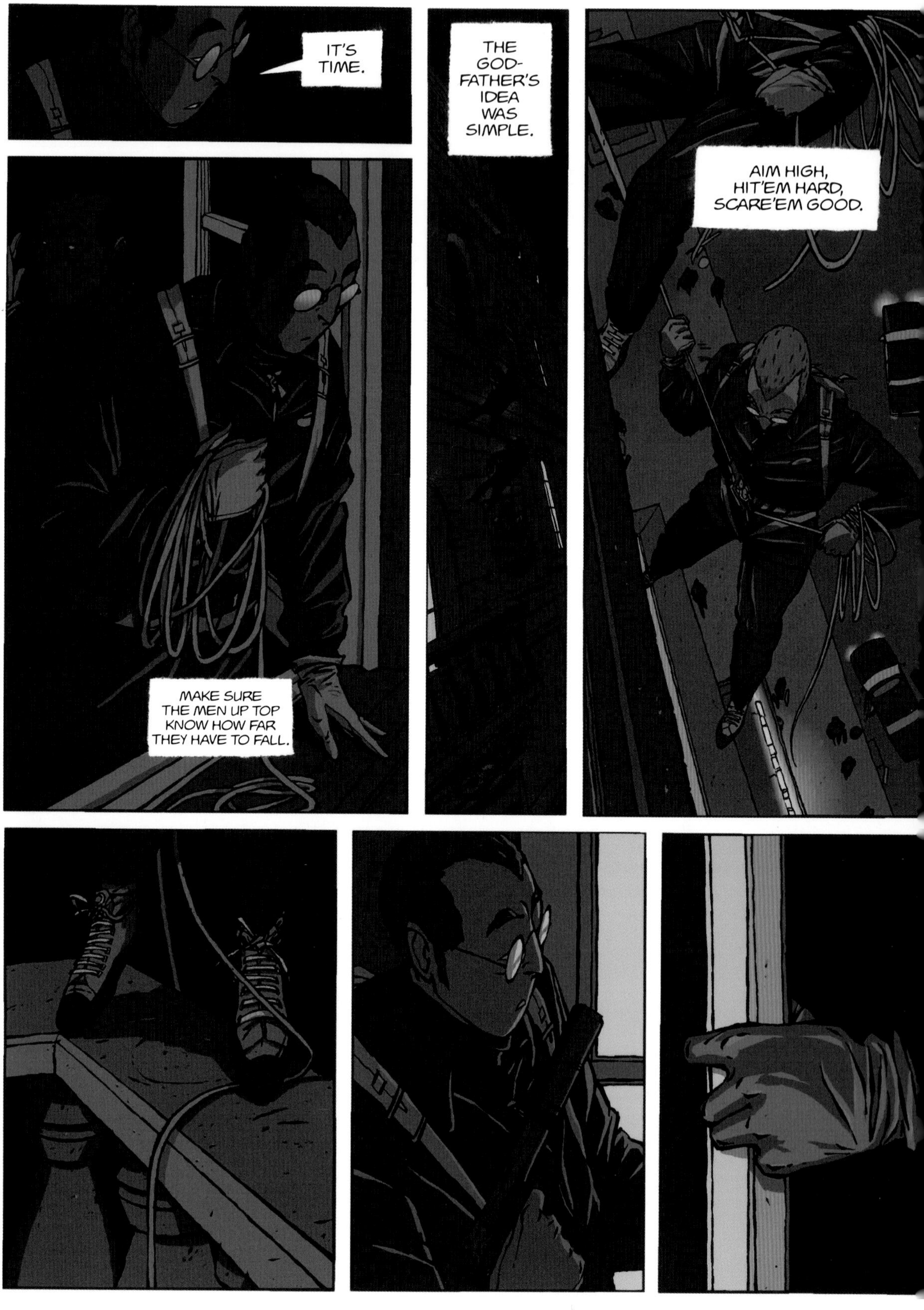
IT'S TIME.
THE GOD-FATHER'S IDEA WAS SIMPLE.
MAKE SURE THE MEN UP TOP KNOW HOW FAR THEY HAVE TO FALL.
AIM HIGH, HIT'EM HARD, SCARE'EM GOOD.

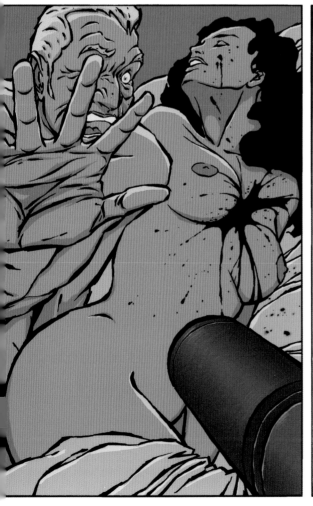

A CALCULATED RISK, BUT BETTING ON A MAN'S COWARDICE ISN'T A LONG SHOT.

IT USUALLY PAYS OFF WELL, AT LEAST IN THE SHORT TERM, AND THAT WAS ALL MARIANO'S GODFATHER CARED ABOUT.

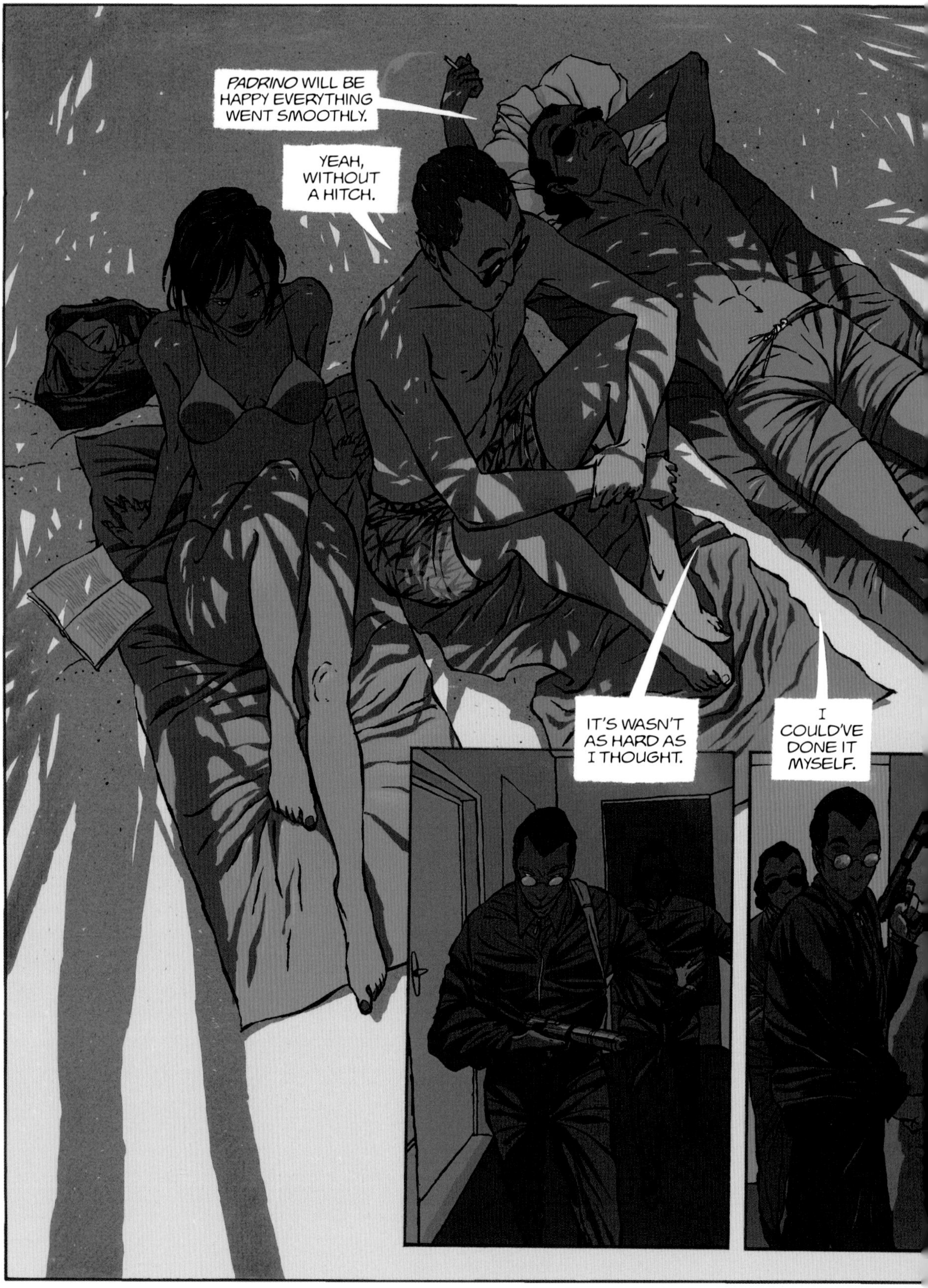
PADRINO WILL BE HAPPY EVERYTHING WENT SMOOTHLY.
YEAH, WITHOUT A HITCH.
IT'S WASN'T AS HARD AS I THOUGHT.
I COULD'VE DONE IT MYSELF.

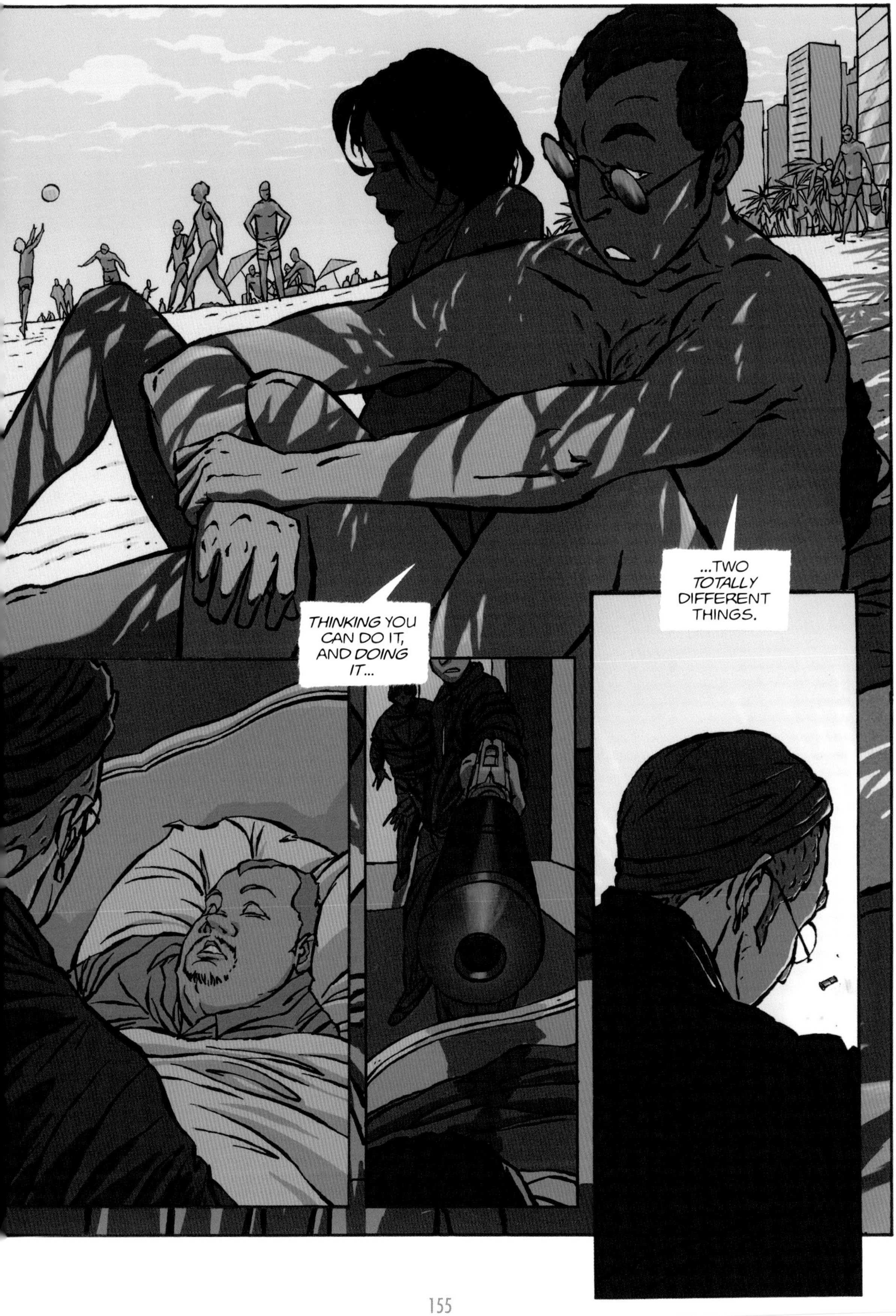
THINKING YOU CAN DO IT, AND DOING IT...
...TWO TOTALLY DIFFERENT THINGS.

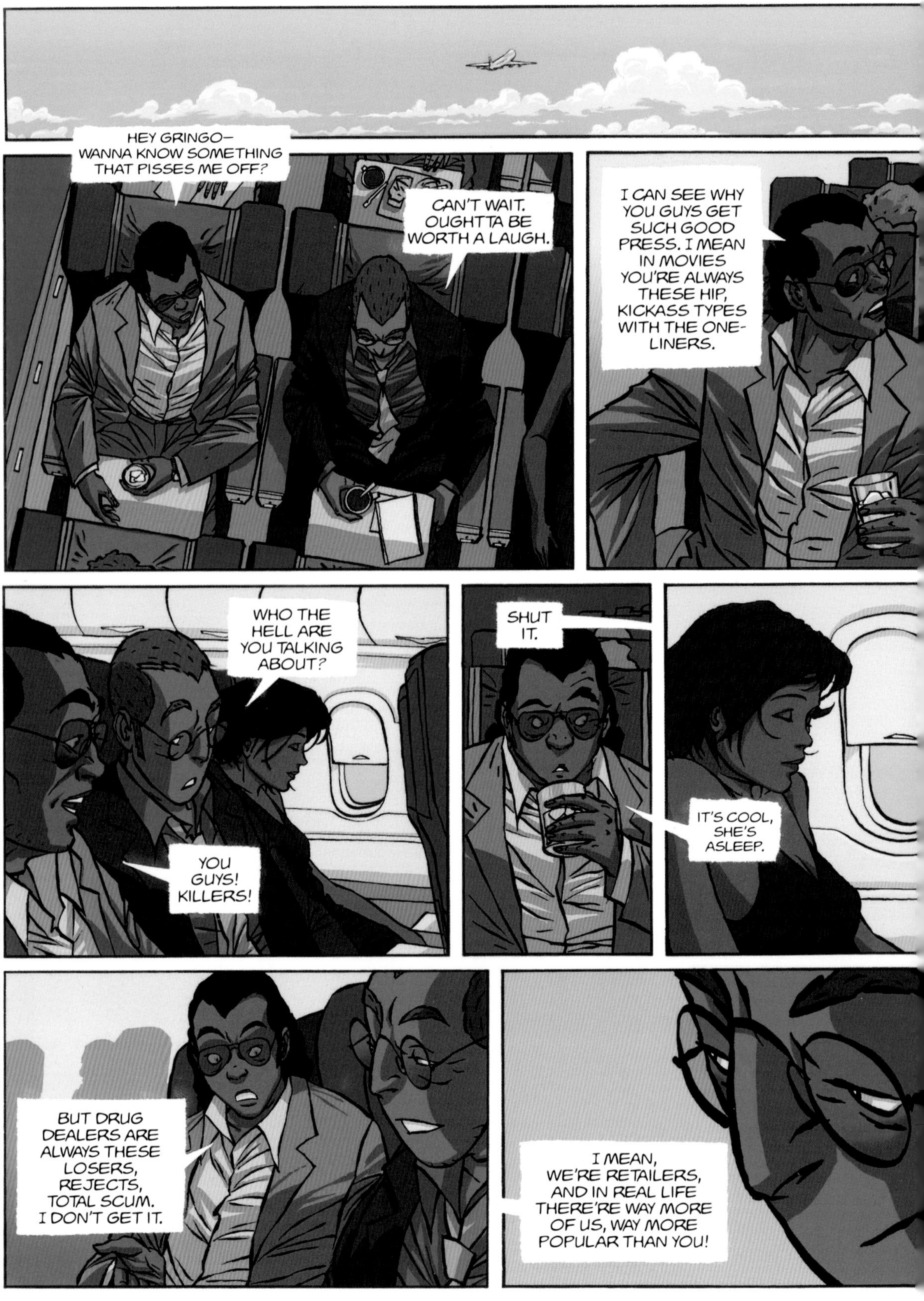
HEY GRINGO—
WANNA KNOW SOMETHING
THAT PISSES ME OFF?
CAN'T WAIT.
OUGHTTA BE
WORTH A LAUGH.
I CAN SEE WHY YOU GUYS GET SUCH GOOD PRESS. I MEAN IN MOVIES YOU'RE ALWAYS THESE HIP, KICKASS TYPES WITH THE ONE-LINERS.
WHO THE HELL ARE YOU TALKING ABOUT?
YOU GUYS! KILLERS!
SHUT IT.
IT'S COOL, SHE'S ASLEEP.
BUT DRUG DEALERS ARE ALWAYS THESE LOSERS, REJECTS, TOTAL SCUM. I DON'T GET IT.
I MEAN, WE'RE RETAILERS, AND IN REAL LIFE THERE'RE WAY MORE OF US, WAY MORE POPULAR THAN YOU!

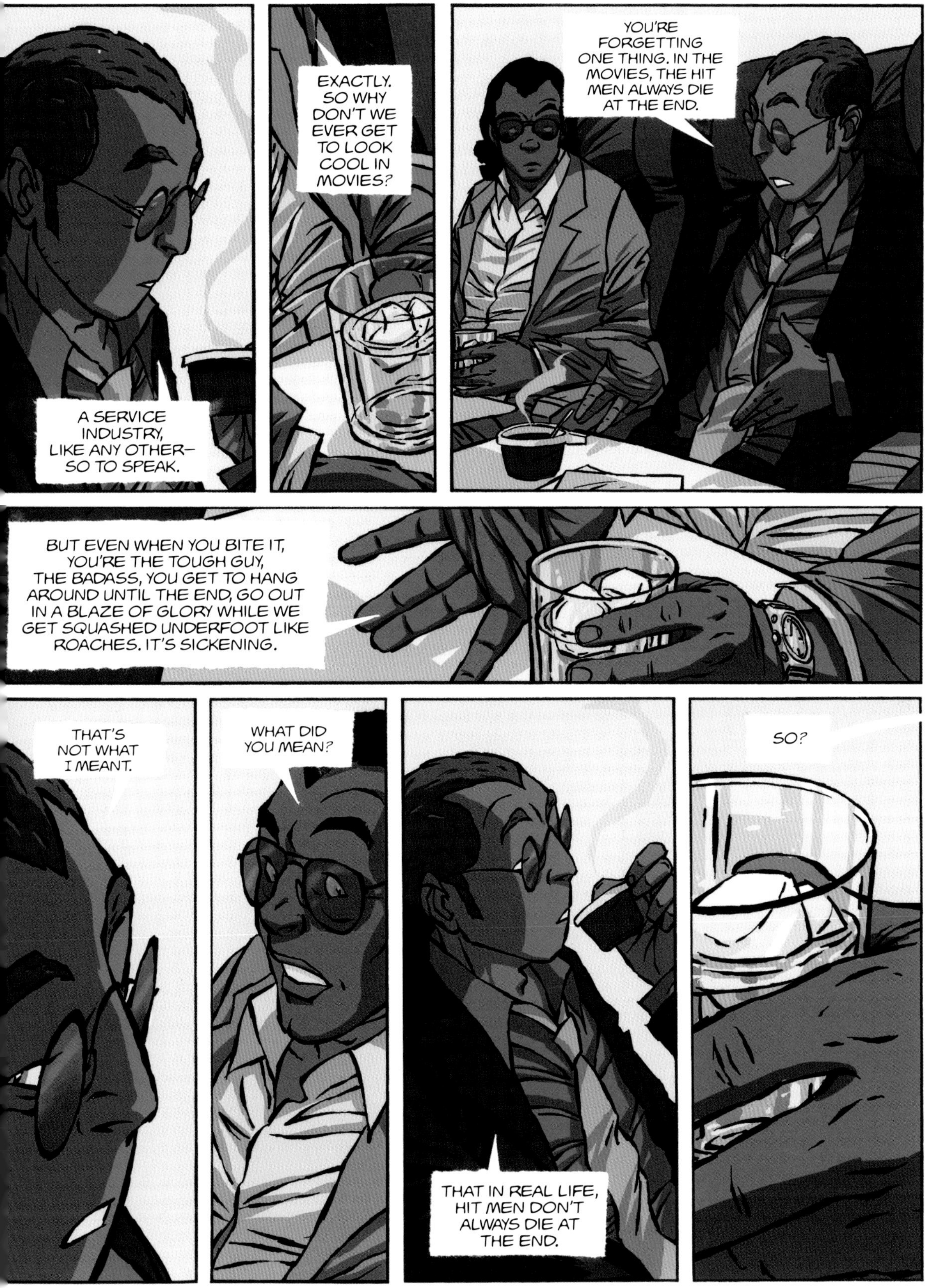
A SERVICE INDUSTRY, LIKE ANY OTHER– SO TO SPEAK.
EXACTLY. SO WHY DON'T WE EVER GET TO LOOK COOL IN MOVIES?
YOU'RE FORGETTING ONE THING. IN THE MOVIES, THE HIT MEN ALWAYS DIE AT THE END.
BUT EVEN WHEN YOU BITE IT, YOU'RE THE TOUGH GUY, THE BADASS, YOU GET TO HANG AROUND UNTIL THE END, GO OUT IN A BLAZE OF GLORY WHILE WE GET SQUASHED UNDERFOOT LIKE ROACHES. IT'S SICKENING.
THAT'S NOT WHAT I MEANT.
WHAT DID YOU MEAN?
THAT IN REAL LIFE, HIT MEN DON'T ALWAYS DIE AT THE END.
SO?

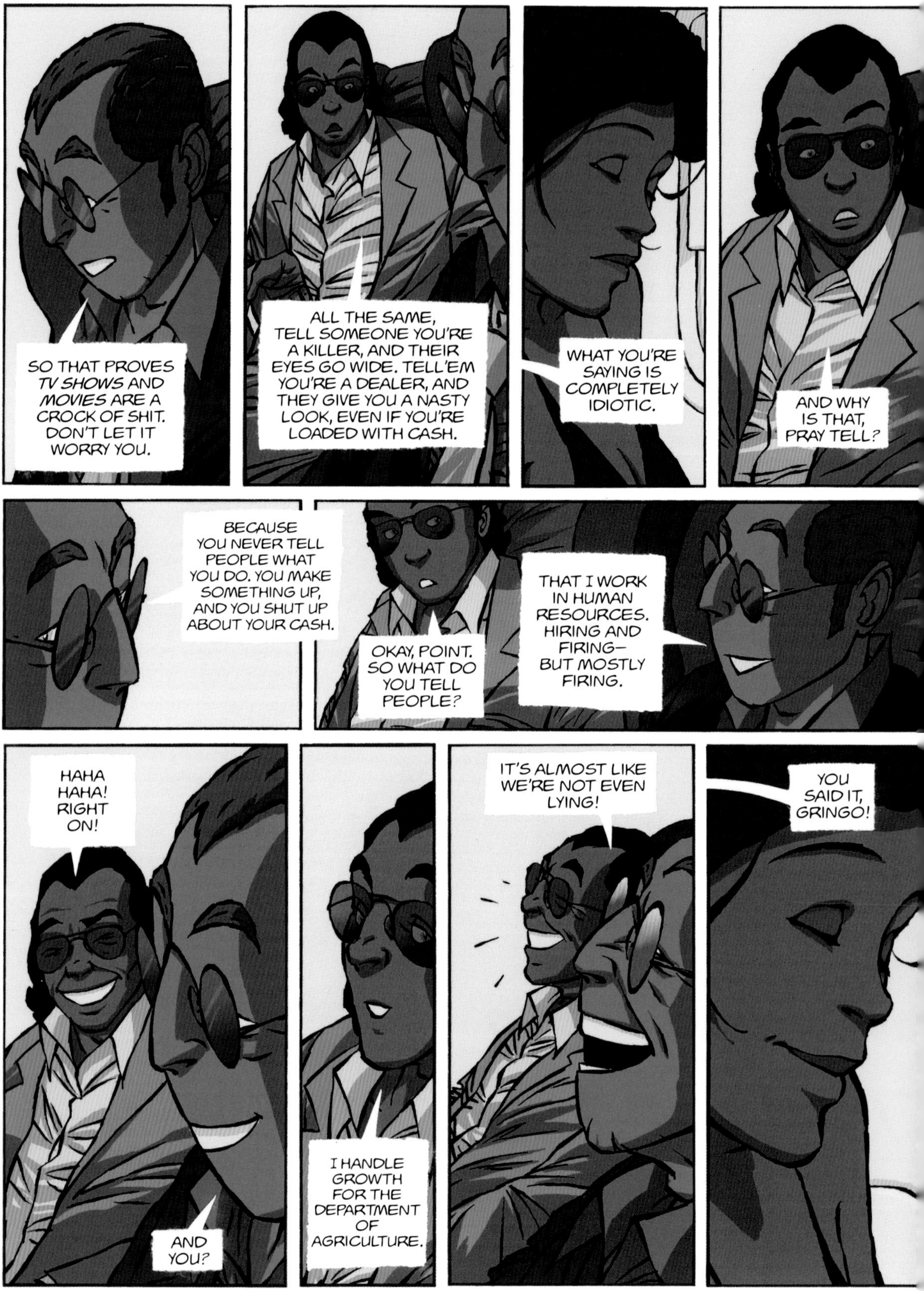
SO THAT PROVES *TV SHOWS* AND *MOVIES* ARE A CROCK OF SHIT. DON'T LET IT WORRY YOU.
ALL THE SAME, TELL SOMEONE YOU'RE A KILLER, AND THEIR EYES GO WIDE. TELL'EM YOU'RE A DEALER, AND THEY GIVE YOU A NASTY LOOK, EVEN IF YOU'RE LOADED WITH CASH.
WHAT YOU'RE SAYING IS COMPLETELY IDIOTIC.
AND WHY IS THAT, PRAY TELL?
BECAUSE YOU NEVER TELL PEOPLE WHAT YOU DO. YOU MAKE SOMETHING UP, AND YOU SHUT UP ABOUT YOUR CASH.
OKAY, POINT. SO WHAT DO YOU TELL PEOPLE?
THAT I WORK IN HUMAN RESOURCES. HIRING AND FIRING— BUT MOSTLY FIRING.
HAHA HAHA! RIGHT ON!
AND YOU?
I HANDLE GROWTH FOR THE DEPARTMENT OF AGRICULTURE.
IT'S ALMOST LIKE WE'RE NOT EVEN LYING!
YOU SAID IT, GRINGO!

THINGS WENT BETTER THAN I EXPECTED. I'D BEEN SURE MARIANO'S GODFATHER WAS PLANNING TO KILL ME.

I READ THE PAPERS. PANIC. SCANDAL. COULDN'T HAVE GONE BETTER. THE MEETINGS WERE CANCELLED AND NO RESOLUTIONS MADE. JUST YOUR USUAL SPEECHES AND HAND-WAVING.

AND YOUR END?

CANDY FROM A BABY, PADRINO.

THE INFORMATION YOU PROVIDED US WAS FIRST-RATE.

YOUR MONEY. WE'VE GOT ANOTHER JOB, TOO. INTERESTED?

WHY NOT?

GOOD! WE'RE GOING TO WORK WELL TOGETHER. KILLING THAT GIRL WAS GENIUS.

DID MARIANO BEHAVE HIMSELF?

HE TALKS TOO MUCH.

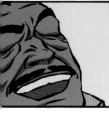

AND HE SAYS THE STUPIDEST THINGS.

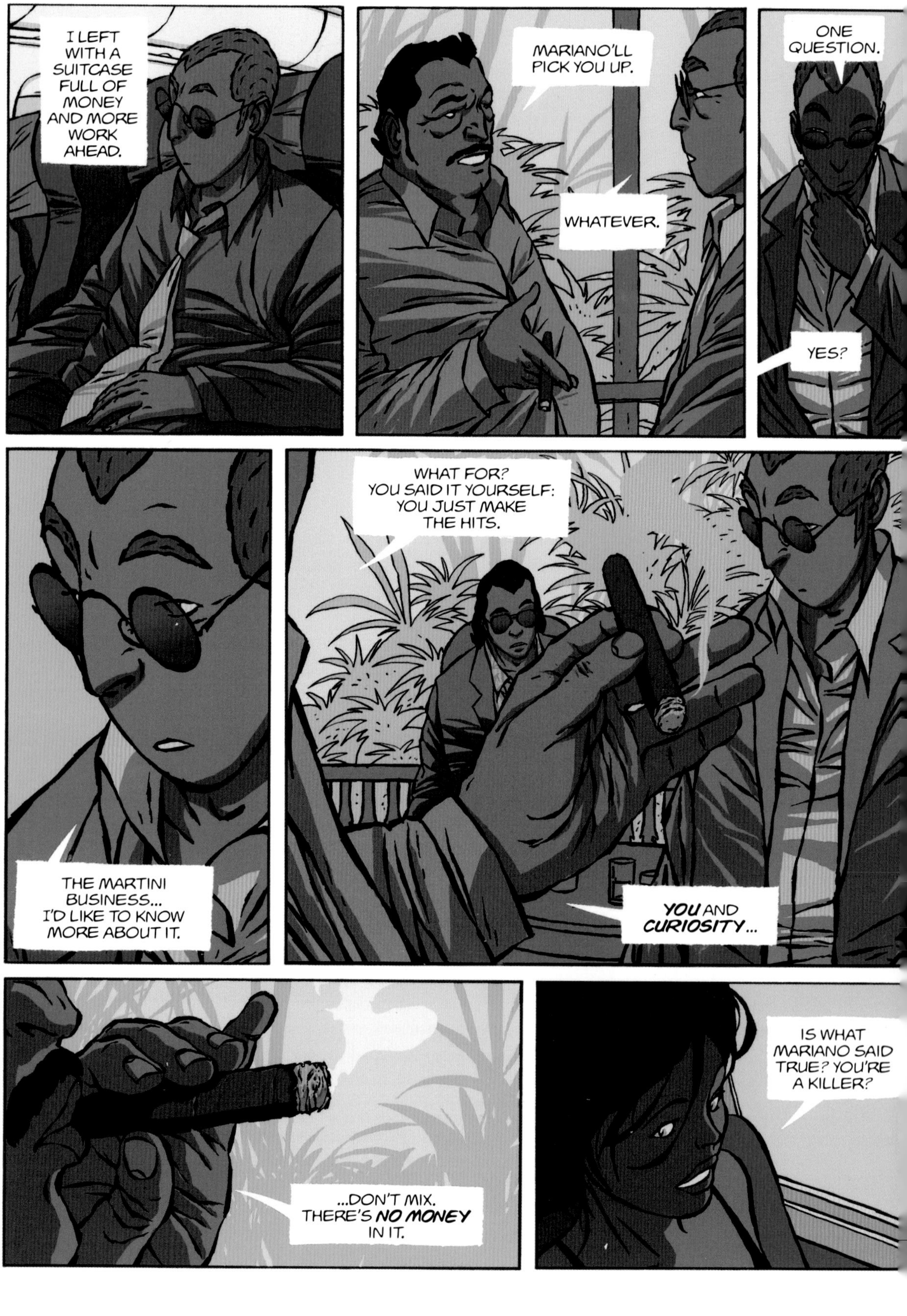
I LEFT WITH A SUITCASE FULL OF MONEY AND MORE WORK AHEAD.
MARIANO'LL PICK YOU UP.
WHATEVER.
ONE QUESTION.
YES?
THE MARTINI BUSINESS... I'D LIKE TO KNOW MORE ABOUT IT.
WHAT FOR? YOU SAID IT YOURSELF: YOU JUST MAKE THE HITS.
YOU AND CURIOSITY...
...DON'T MIX. THERE'S NO MONEY IN IT.
IS WHAT MARIANO SAID TRUE? YOU'RE A KILLER?

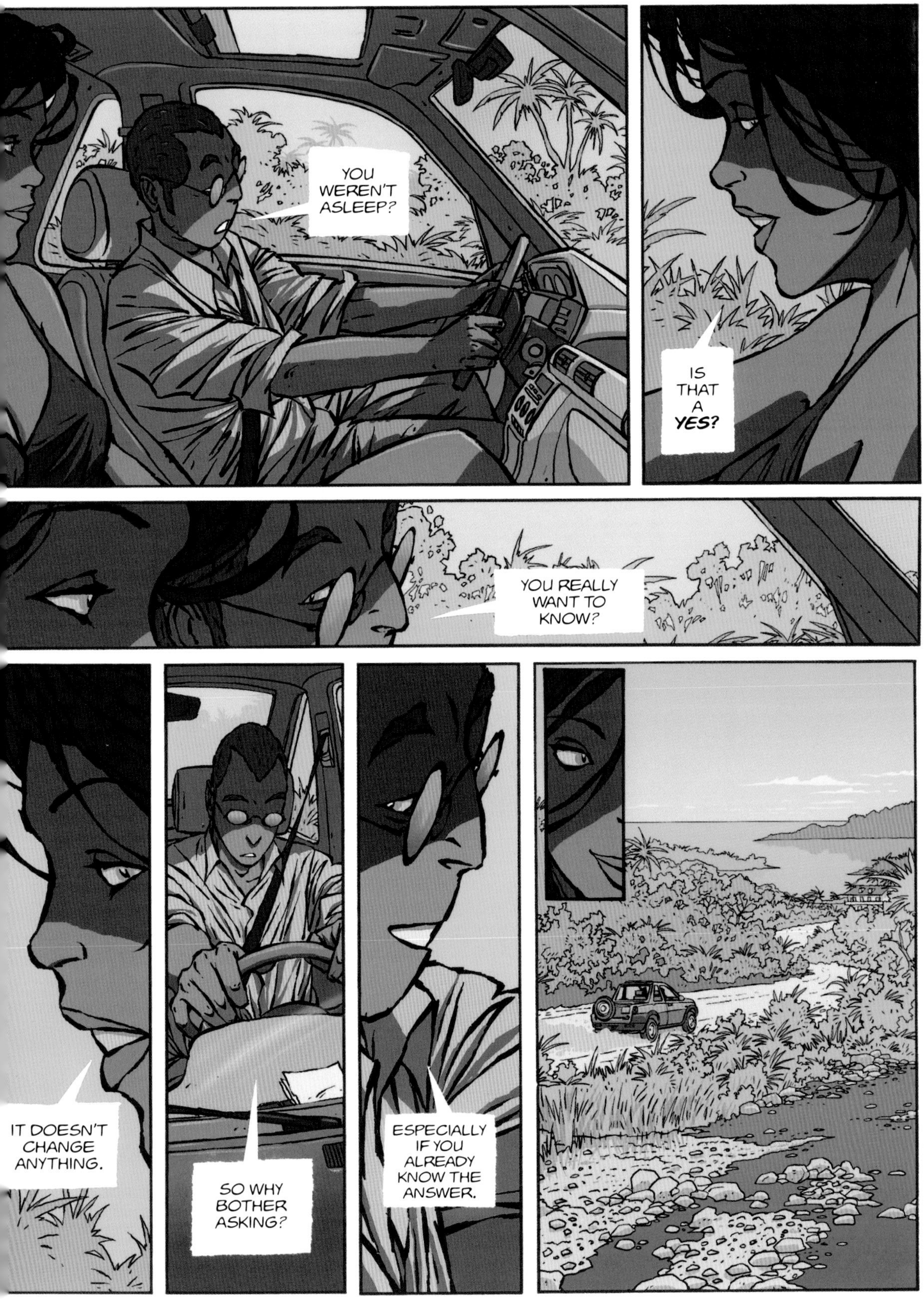
YOU WEREN'T ASLEEP?
IS THAT A *YES?*
YOU REALLY WANT TO KNOW?
IT DOESN'T CHANGE ANYTHING.
SO WHY BOTHER ASKING?
ESPECIALLY IF YOU ALREADY KNOW THE ANSWER.

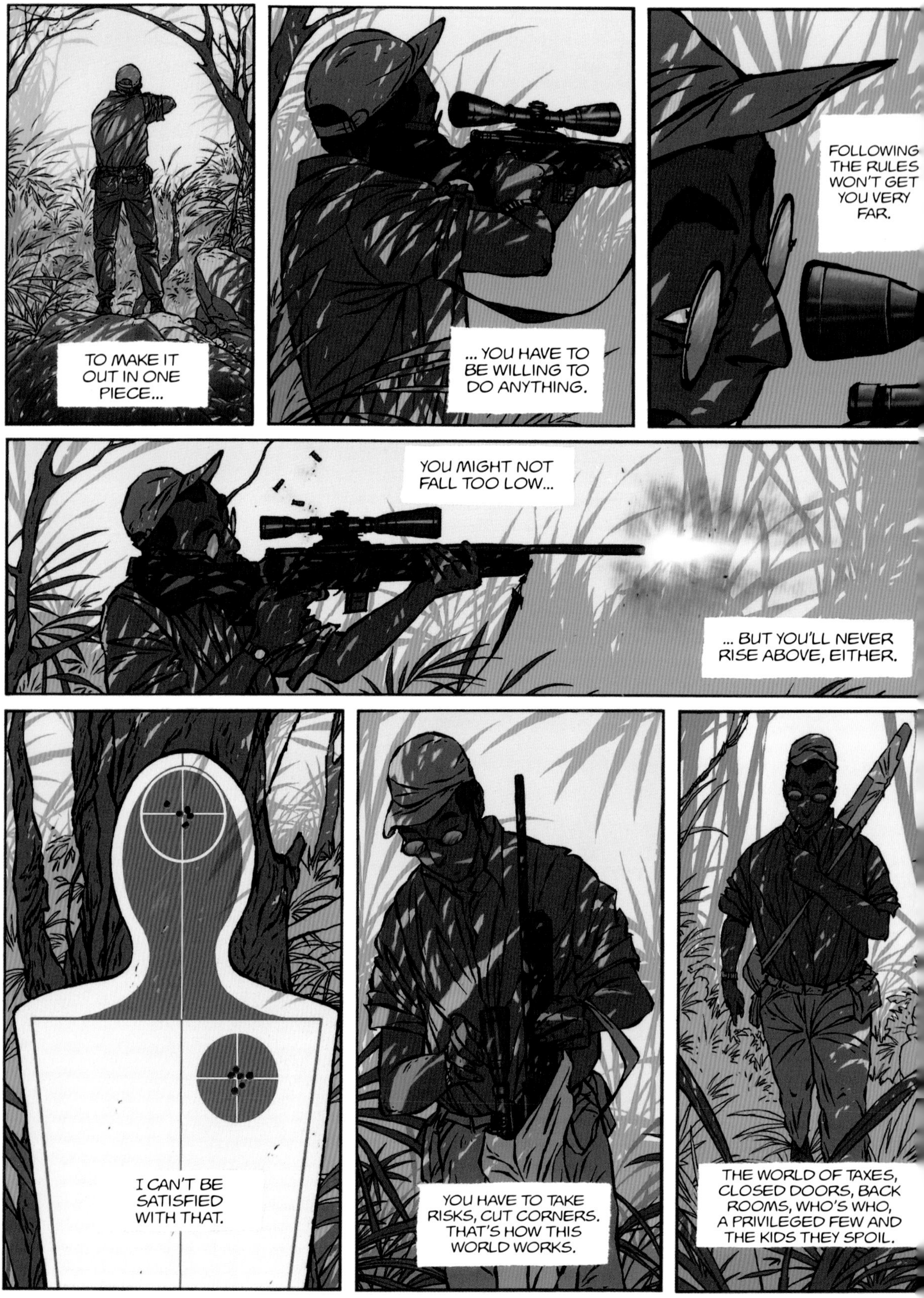
TO MAKE IT OUT IN ONE PIECE...
... YOU HAVE TO BE WILLING TO DO ANYTHING.
FOLLOWING THE RULES WON'T GET YOU VERY FAR.
YOU MIGHT NOT FALL TOO LOW...
... BUT YOU'LL NEVER RISE ABOVE, EITHER.
I CAN'T BE SATISFIED WITH THAT.
YOU HAVE TO TAKE RISKS, CUT CORNERS. THAT'S HOW THIS WORLD WORKS.
THE WORLD OF TAXES, CLOSED DOORS, BACK ROOMS, WHO'S WHO, A PRIVILEGED FEW AND THE KIDS THEY SPOIL.

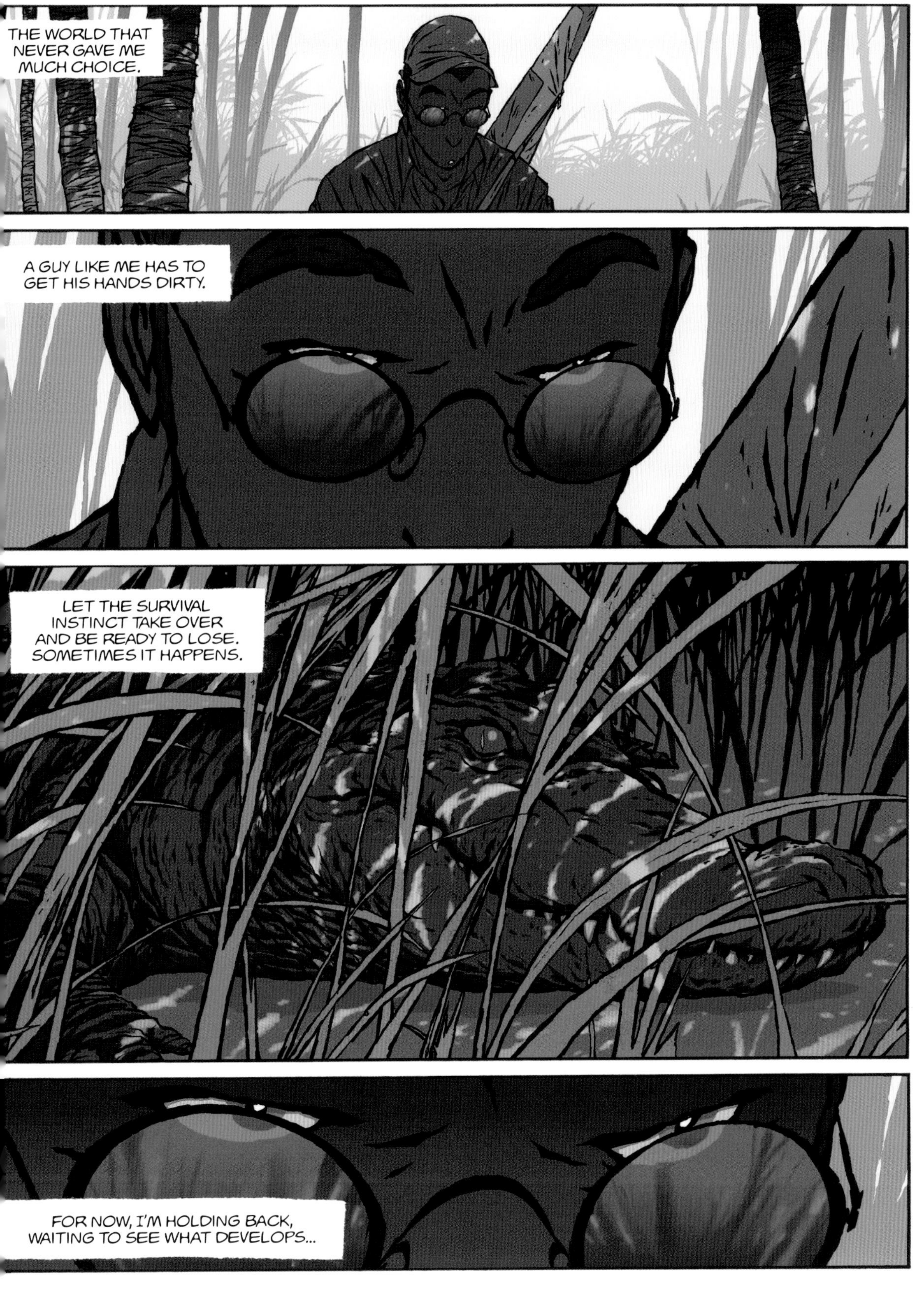
THE WORLD THAT NEVER GAVE ME MUCH CHOICE.
A GUY LIKE ME HAS TO GET HIS HANDS DIRTY.
LET THE SURVIVAL INSTINCT TAKE OVER AND BE READY TO LOSE. SOMETIMES IT HAPPENS.
FOR NOW, I'M HOLDING BACK, WAITING TO SEE WHAT DEVELOPS...

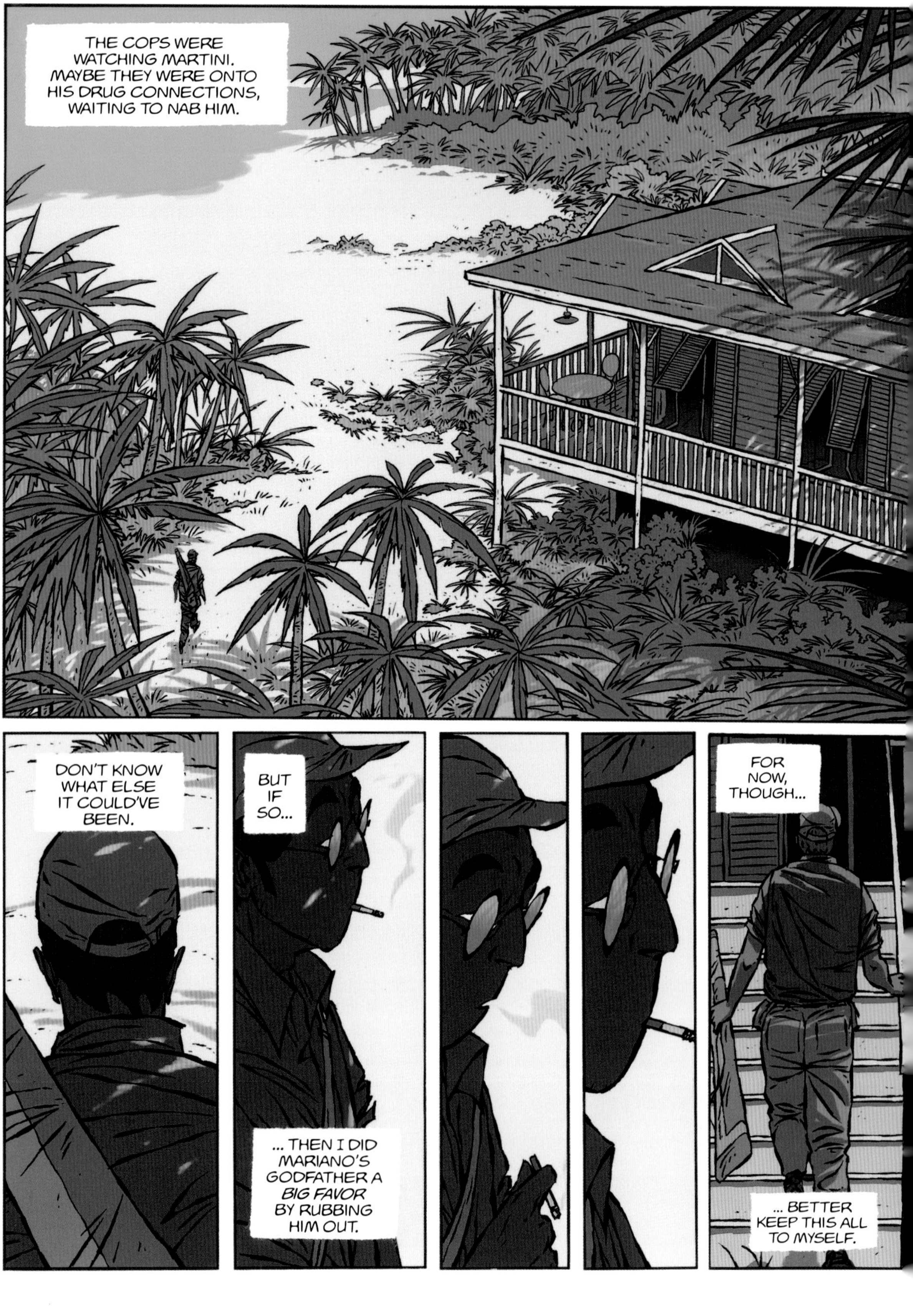
THE COPS WERE WATCHING MARTINI. MAYBE THEY WERE ONTO HIS DRUG CONNECTIONS, WAITING TO NAB HIM.
DON'T KNOW WHAT ELSE IT COULD'VE BEEN.
BUT IF SO...
... THEN I DID MARIANO'S GODFATHER A *BIG FAVOR* BY RUBBING HIM OUT.
FOR NOW, THOUGH...
... BETTER KEEP THIS ALL TO MYSELF.

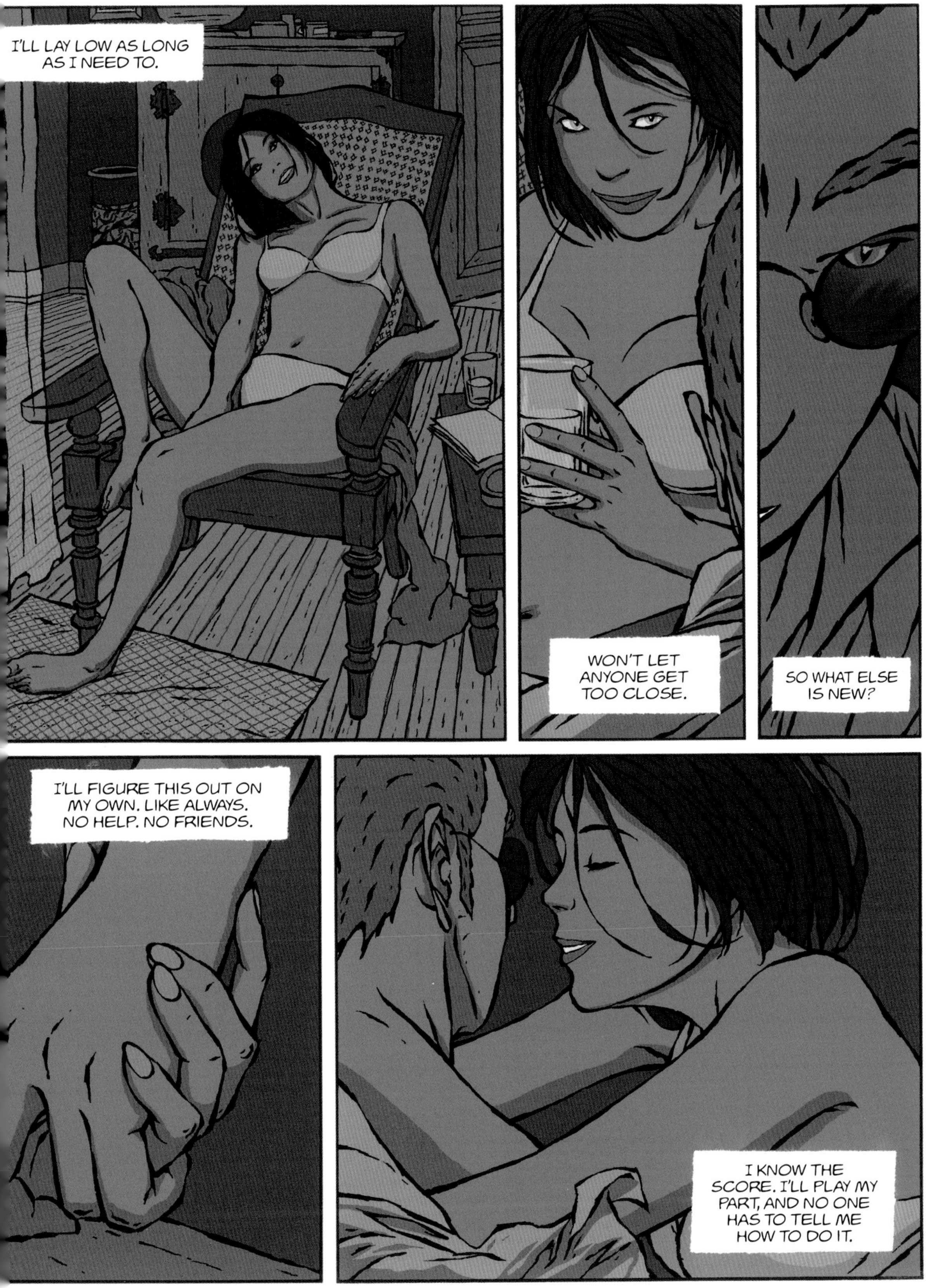
I'LL LAY LOW AS LONG AS I NEED TO.
WON'T LET ANYONE GET TOO CLOSE.
SO WHAT ELSE IS NEW?
I'LL FIGURE THIS OUT ON MY OWN. LIKE ALWAYS. NO HELP. NO FRIENDS.
I KNOW THE SCORE. I'LL PLAY MY PART, AND NO ONE HAS TO TELL ME HOW TO DO IT.

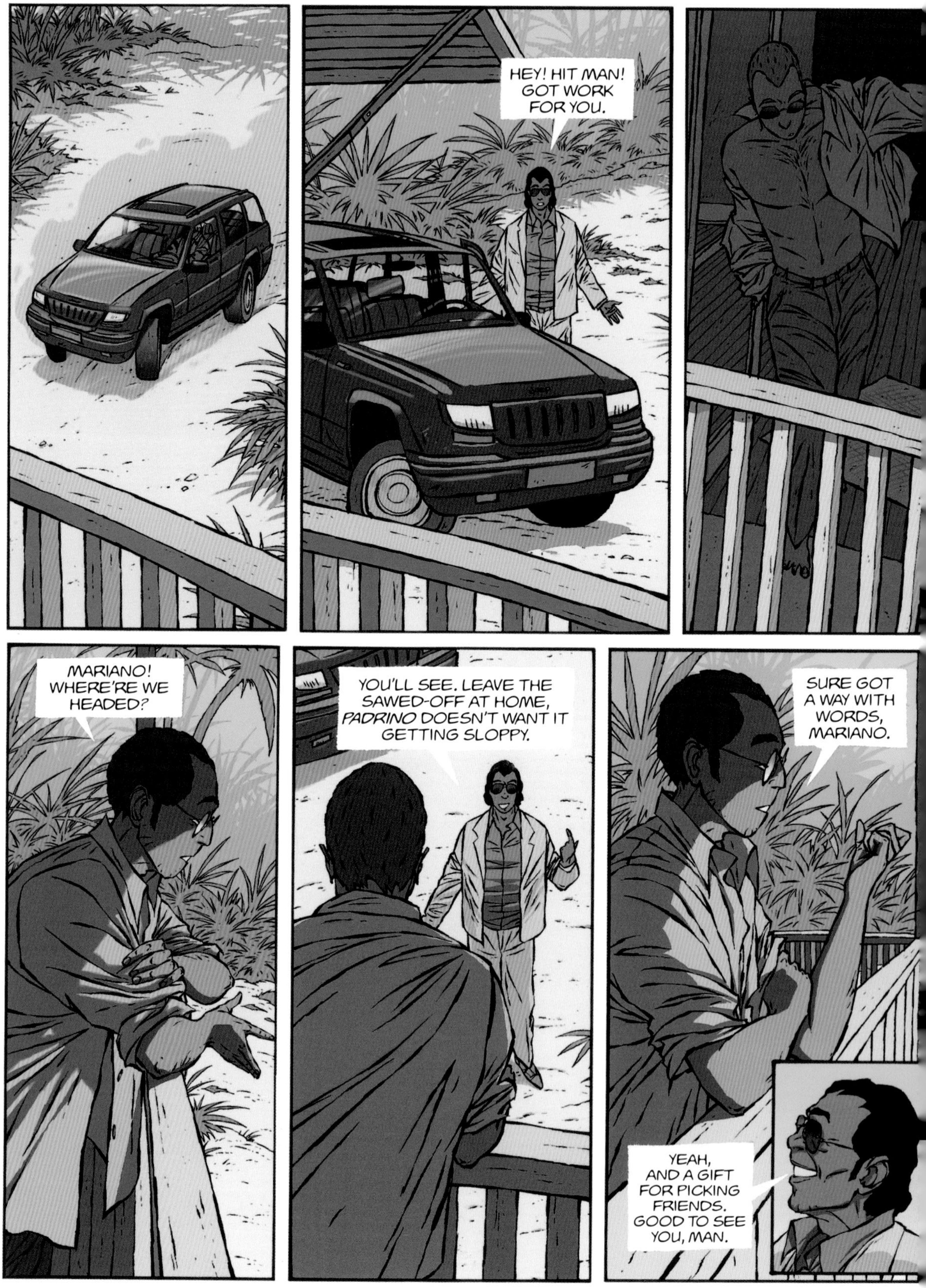
HEY! HIT MAN! GOT WORK FOR YOU.
MARIANO! WHERE'RE WE HEADED?
YOU'LL SEE. LEAVE THE SAWED-OFF AT HOME, PADRINO DOESN'T WANT IT GETTING SLOPPY.
SURE GOT A WAY WITH WORDS, MARIANO.
YEAH, AND A GIFT FOR PICKING FRIENDS. GOOD TO SEE YOU, MAN.

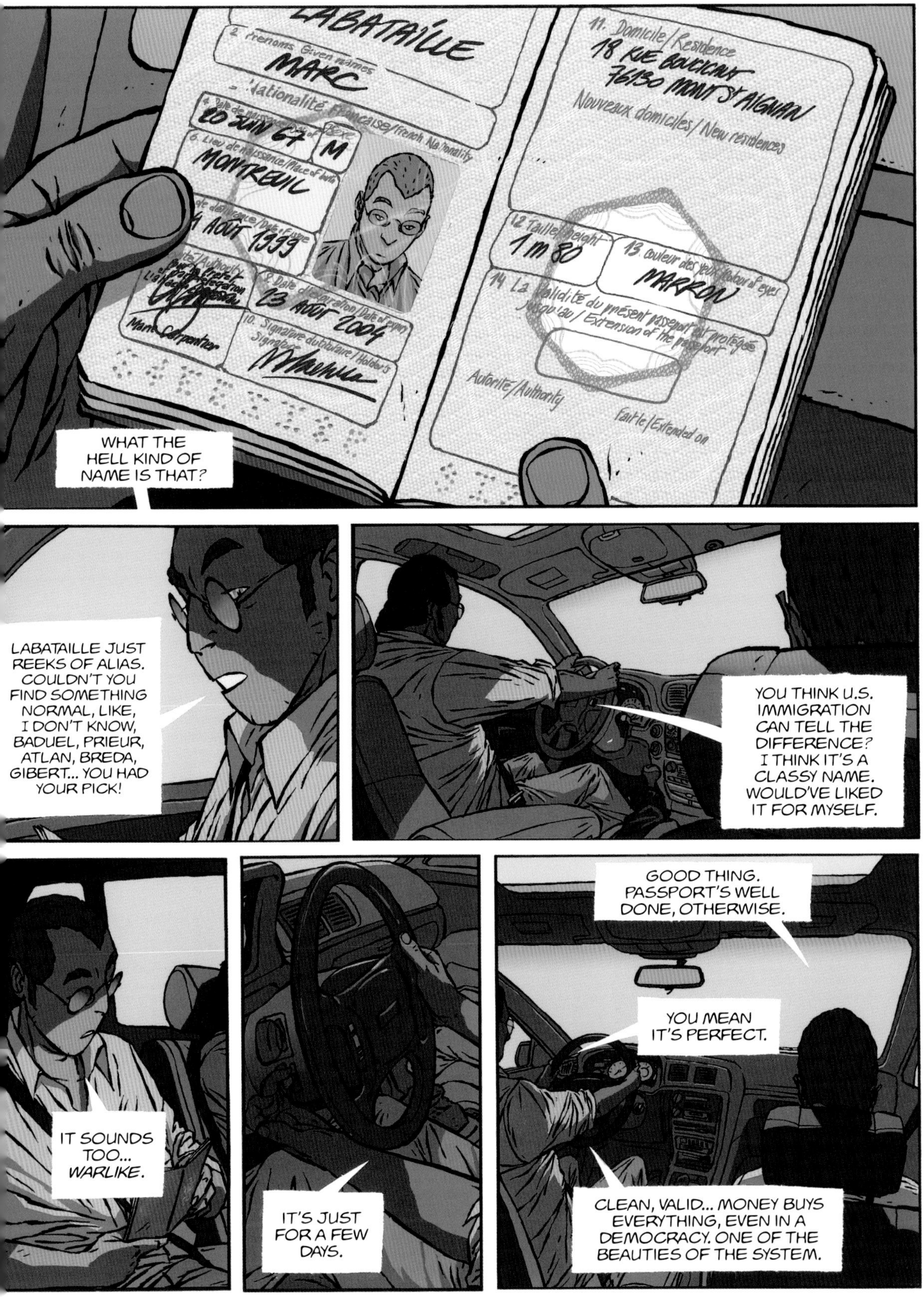
LABATAILLE
MARC
MONTREUIL
1 m 80
MARRON
WHAT THE HELL KIND OF NAME IS THAT?
LABATAILLE JUST REEKS OF ALIAS. COULDN'T YOU FIND SOMETHING NORMAL, LIKE, I DON'T KNOW, BADUEL, PRIEUR, ATLAN, BREDA, GIBERT... YOU HAD YOUR PICK!
YOU THINK U.S. IMMIGRATION CAN TELL THE DIFFERENCE? I THINK IT'S A CLASSY NAME. WOULD'VE LIKED IT FOR MYSELF.
IT SOUNDS TOO... *WARLIKE*.
IT'S JUST FOR A FEW DAYS.
GOOD THING. PASSPORT'S WELL DONE, OTHERWISE.
YOU MEAN IT'S PERFECT.
CLEAN, VALID... MONEY BUYS EVERYTHING, EVEN IN A DEMOCRACY. ONE OF THE BEAUTIES OF THE SYSTEM.

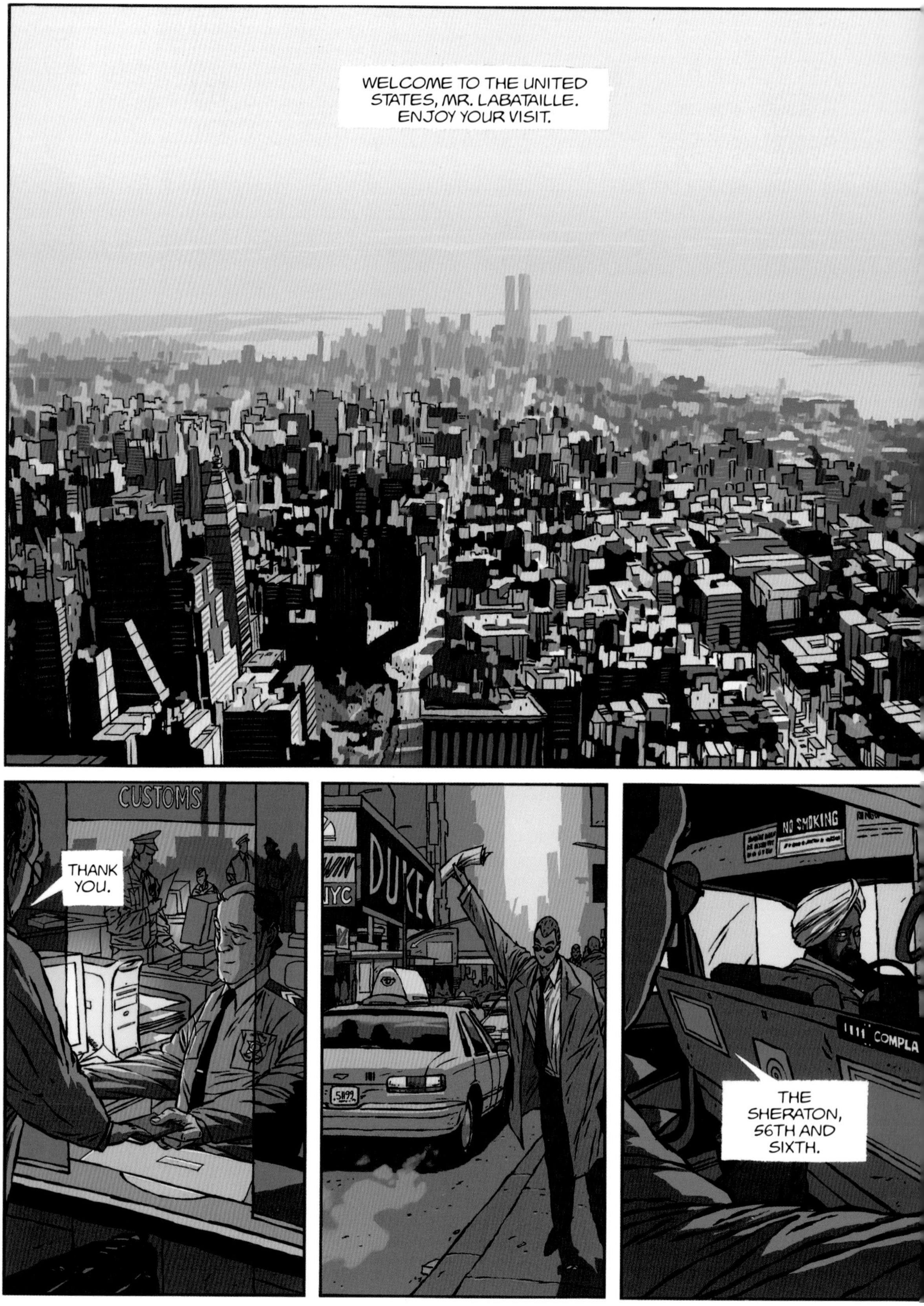
WELCOME TO THE UNITED STATES, MR. LABATAILLE. ENJOY YOUR VISIT.
CUSTOMS
THANK YOU.
DUKE
NYC
NO SMOKING
THE SHERATON, 56TH AND SIXTH.

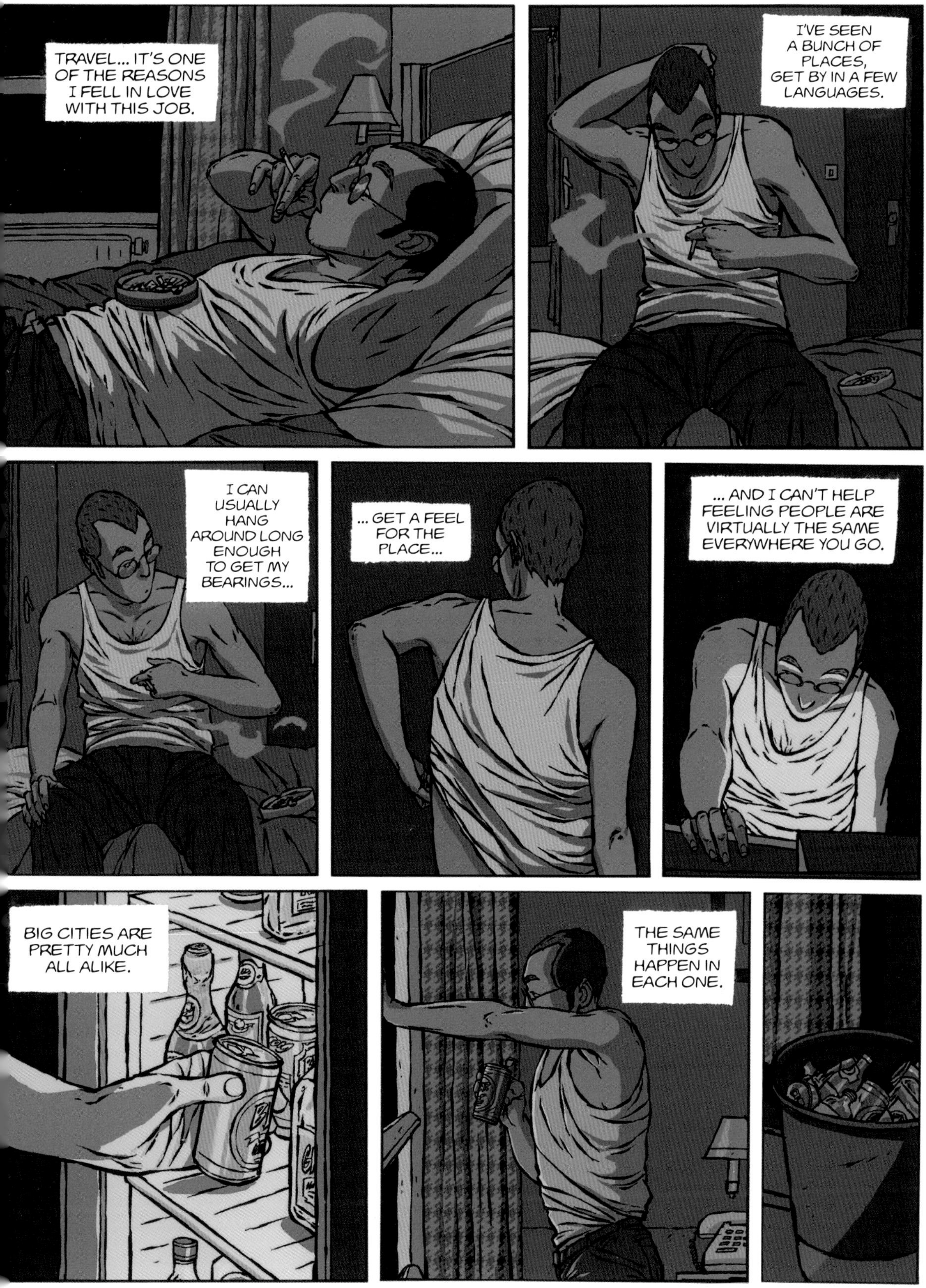
TRAVEL... IT'S ONE OF THE REASONS I FELL IN LOVE WITH THIS JOB.
I'VE SEEN A BUNCH OF PLACES, GET BY IN A FEW LANGUAGES.
I CAN USUALLY HANG AROUND LONG ENOUGH TO GET MY BEARINGS...
... GET A FEEL FOR THE PLACE...
... AND I CAN'T HELP FEELING PEOPLE ARE VIRTUALLY THE SAME EVERYWHERE YOU GO.
BIG CITIES ARE PRETTY MUCH ALL ALIKE.
THE SAME THINGS HAPPEN IN EACH ONE.

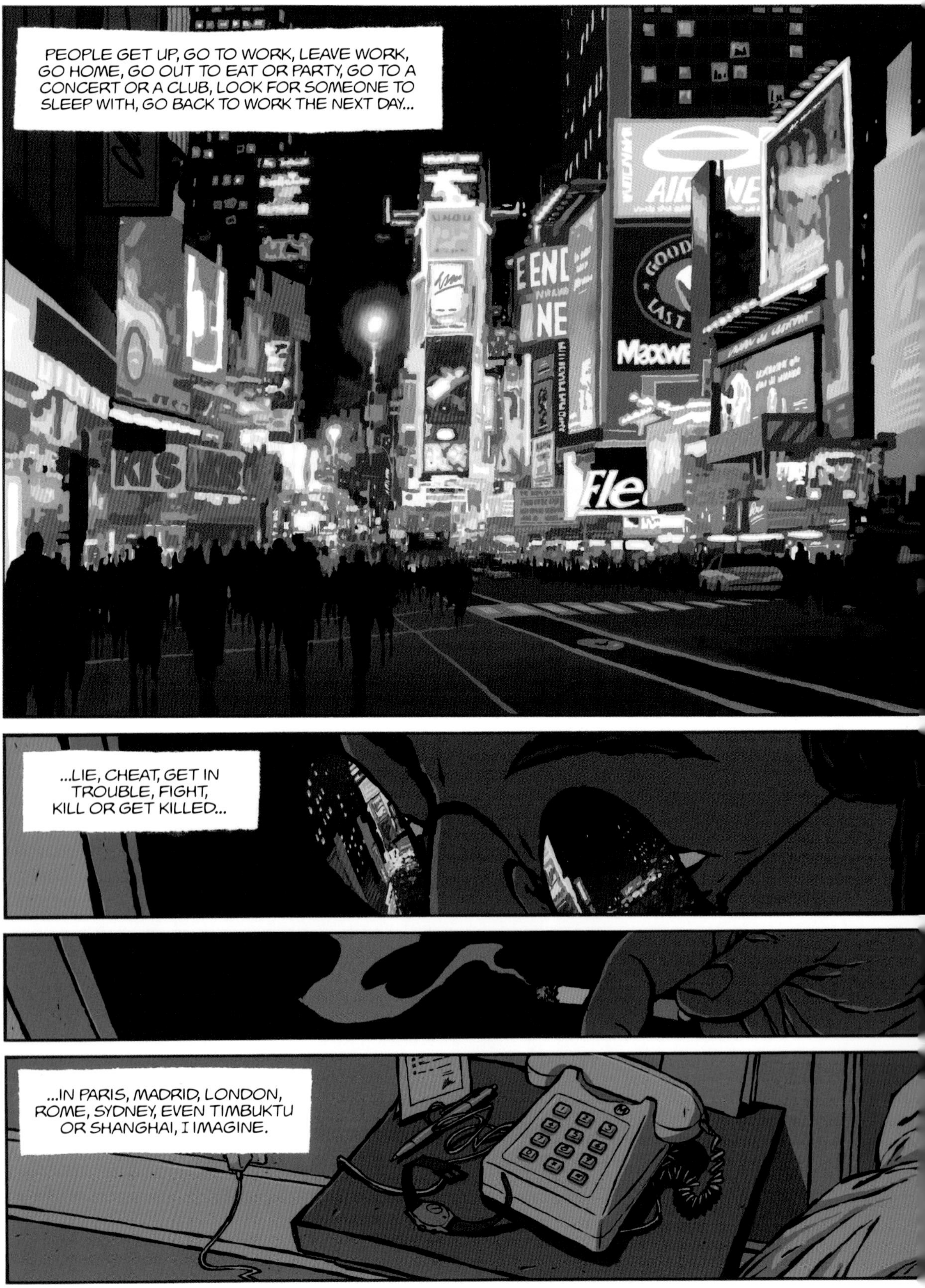
PEOPLE GET UP, GO TO WORK, LEAVE WORK, GO HOME, GO OUT TO EAT OR PARTY, GO TO A CONCERT OR A CLUB, LOOK FOR SOMEONE TO SLEEP WITH, GO BACK TO WORK THE NEXT DAY...
...LIE, CHEAT, GET IN TROUBLE, FIGHT, KILL OR GET KILLED...
...IN PARIS, MADRID, LONDON, ROME, SYDNEY, EVEN TIMBUKTU OR SHANGHAI, I IMAGINE.

EXCEPT THAT IN NEW YORK...

...IT'S ON A BIGGER SCALE.

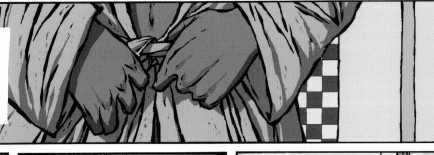

I'VE BEEN ROTTING IN THIS ROOM FOR THREE DAYS WAITING FOR A PHONE CALL. I'M GETTING FED UP, MAYBE EVEN CLAUSTROPHOBIC OR SOMETHING.

EVER SINCE PARIS, BEING COOPED UP...

... SITTING AROUND WAITING ...IS *NOT MY SCENE*.

SO, CALL OR NO CALL...

... MARIANO OR NO MARIANO, I'M GETTING SOME AIR.

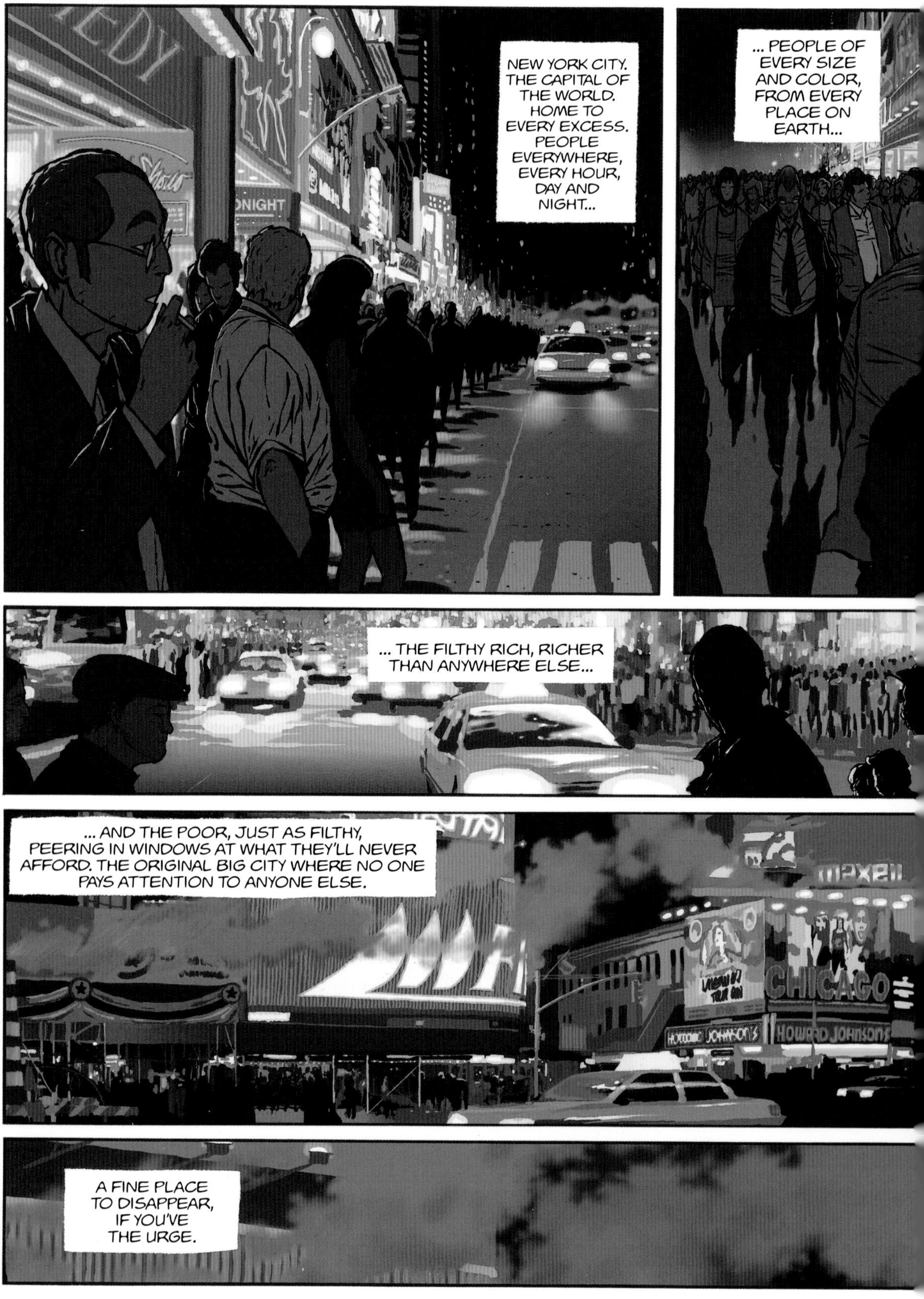
NEW YORK CITY. THE CAPITAL OF THE WORLD. HOME TO EVERY EXCESS. PEOPLE EVERYWHERE, EVERY HOUR, DAY AND NIGHT...
... PEOPLE OF EVERY SIZE AND COLOR, FROM EVERY PLACE ON EARTH...
... THE FILTHY RICH, RICHER THAN ANYWHERE ELSE...
... AND THE POOR, JUST AS FILTHY, PEERING IN WINDOWS AT WHAT THEY'LL NEVER AFFORD. THE ORIGINAL BIG CITY WHERE NO ONE PAYS ATTENTION TO ANYONE ELSE.
CHICAGO
HOWARD JOHNSON'S
A FINE PLACE TO DISAPPEAR, IF YOU'VE THE URGE.

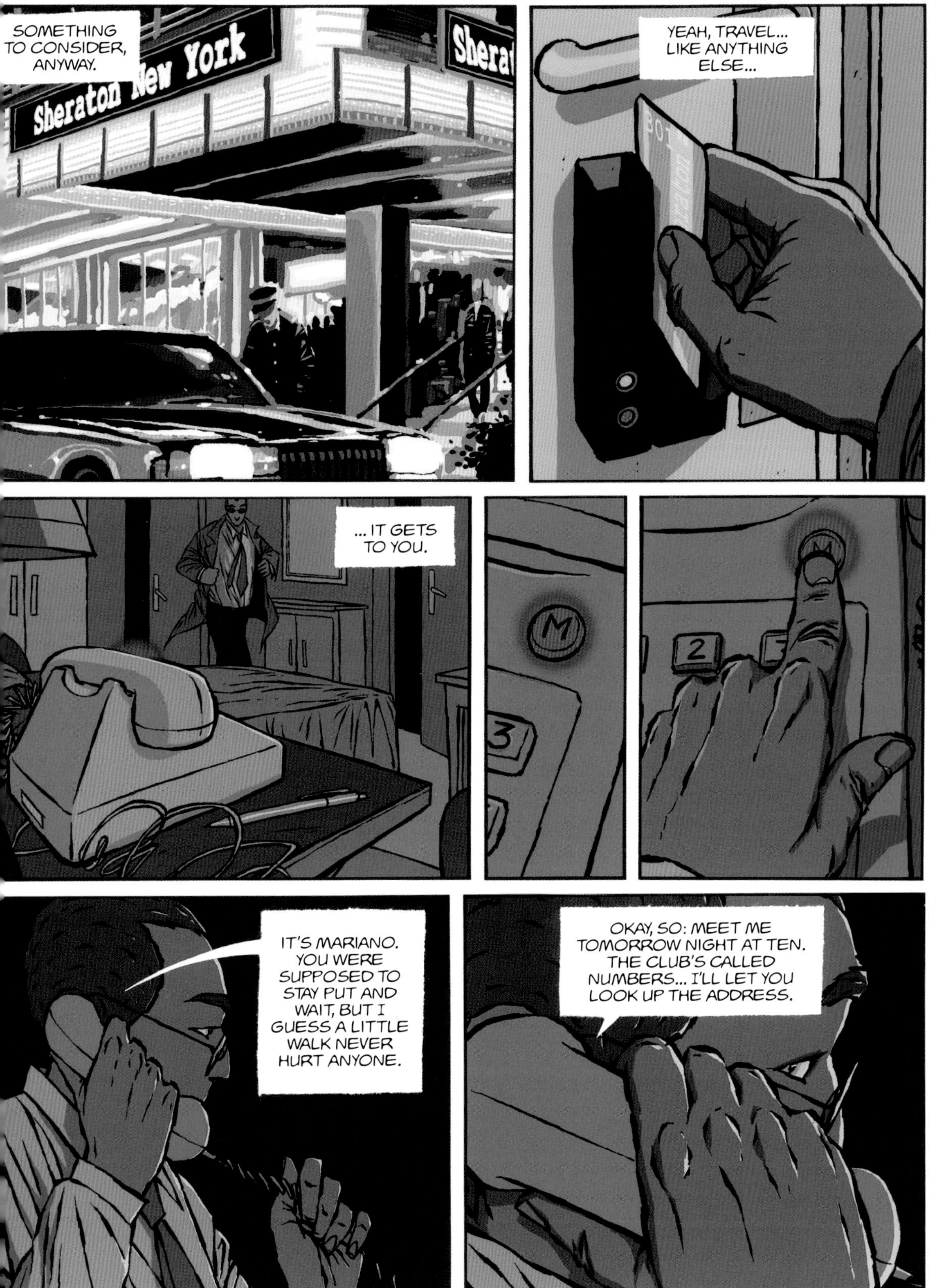
SOMETHING TO CONSIDER, ANYWAY.
Sheraton New York
YEAH, TRAVEL... LIKE ANYTHING ELSE...
...IT GETS TO YOU.
IT'S MARIANO. YOU WERE SUPPOSED TO STAY PUT AND WAIT, BUT I GUESS A LITTLE WALK NEVER HURT ANYONE.
OKAY, SO: MEET ME TOMORROW NIGHT AT TEN. THE CLUB'S CALLED NUMBERS... I'LL LET YOU LOOK UP THE ADDRESS.

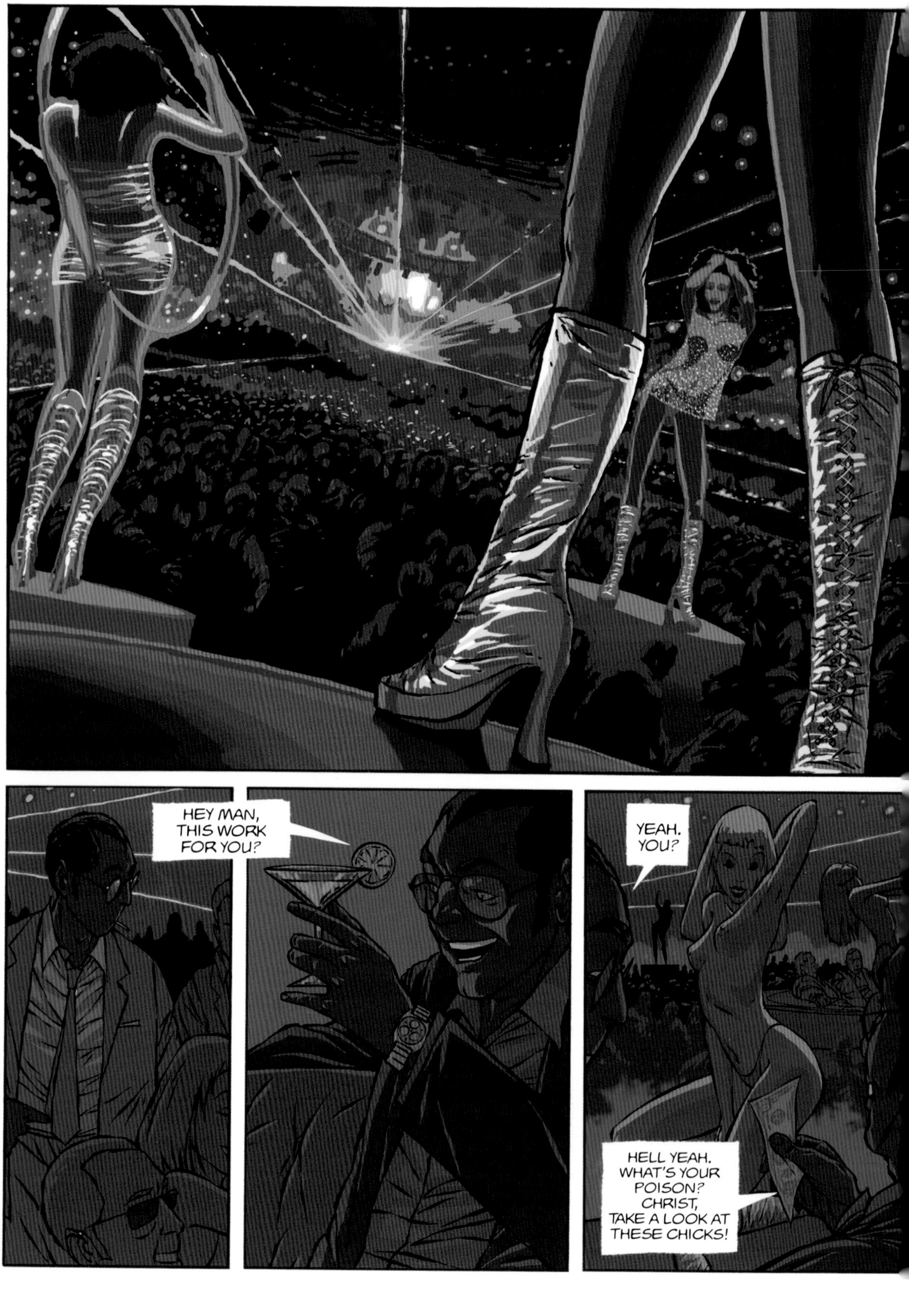
HEY MAN, THIS WORK FOR YOU?
YEAH. YOU?
HELL YEAH. WHAT'S YOUR POISON? CHRIST, TAKE A LOOK AT THESE CHICKS!

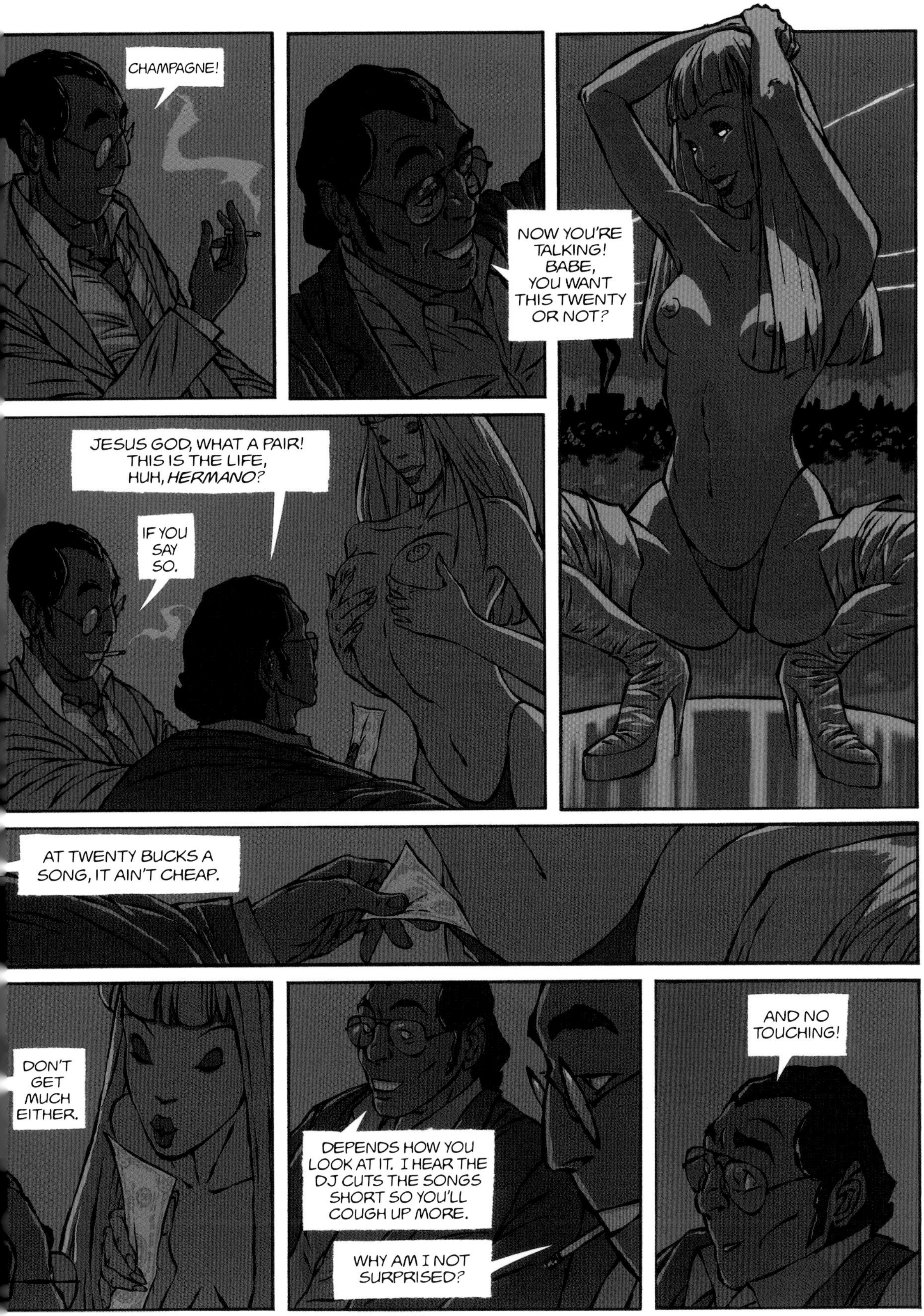
CHAMPAGNE!
NOW YOU'RE TALKING! BABE, YOU WANT THIS TWENTY OR NOT?
JESUS GOD, WHAT A PAIR! THIS IS THE LIFE, HUH, *HERMANO*?
IF YOU SAY SO.
AT TWENTY BUCKS A SONG, IT AIN'T CHEAP.
DON'T GET MUCH EITHER.
DEPENDS HOW YOU LOOK AT IT. I HEAR THE DJ CUTS THE SONGS SHORT SO YOU'LL COUGH UP MORE.
WHY AM I NOT SURPRISED?
AND NO TOUCHING!

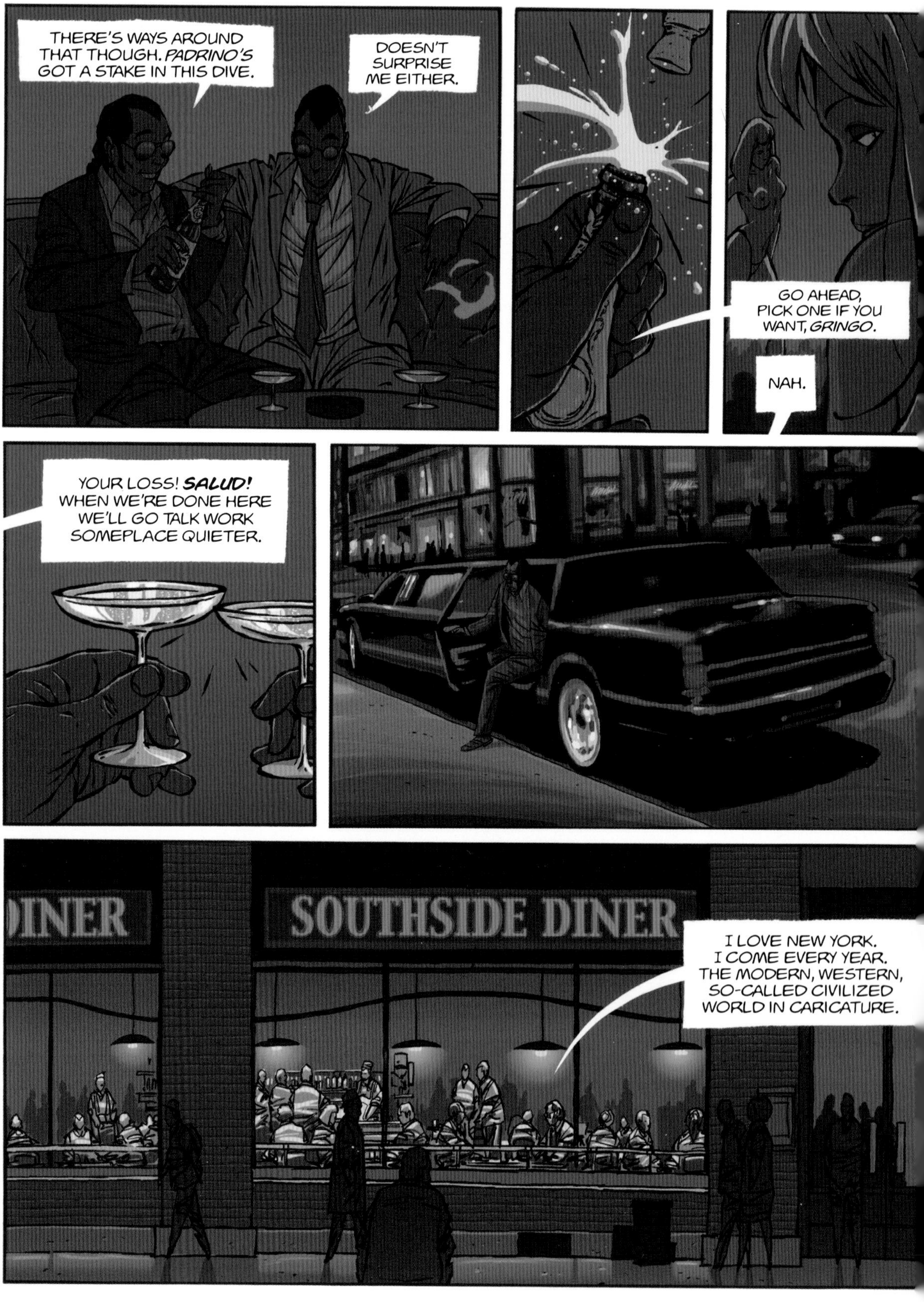
THERE'S WAYS AROUND THAT THOUGH. *PADRINO'S* GOT A STAKE IN THIS DIVE.
DOESN'T SURPRISE ME EITHER.
GO AHEAD, PICK ONE IF YOU WANT, *GRINGO*.
NAH.
YOUR LOSS! ***SALUD!*** WHEN WE'RE DONE HERE WE'LL GO TALK WORK SOMEPLACE QUIETER.
DINER
SOUTHSIDE DINER
I LOVE NEW YORK. I COME EVERY YEAR. THE MODERN, WESTERN, SO-CALLED CIVILIZED WORLD IN CARICATURE.

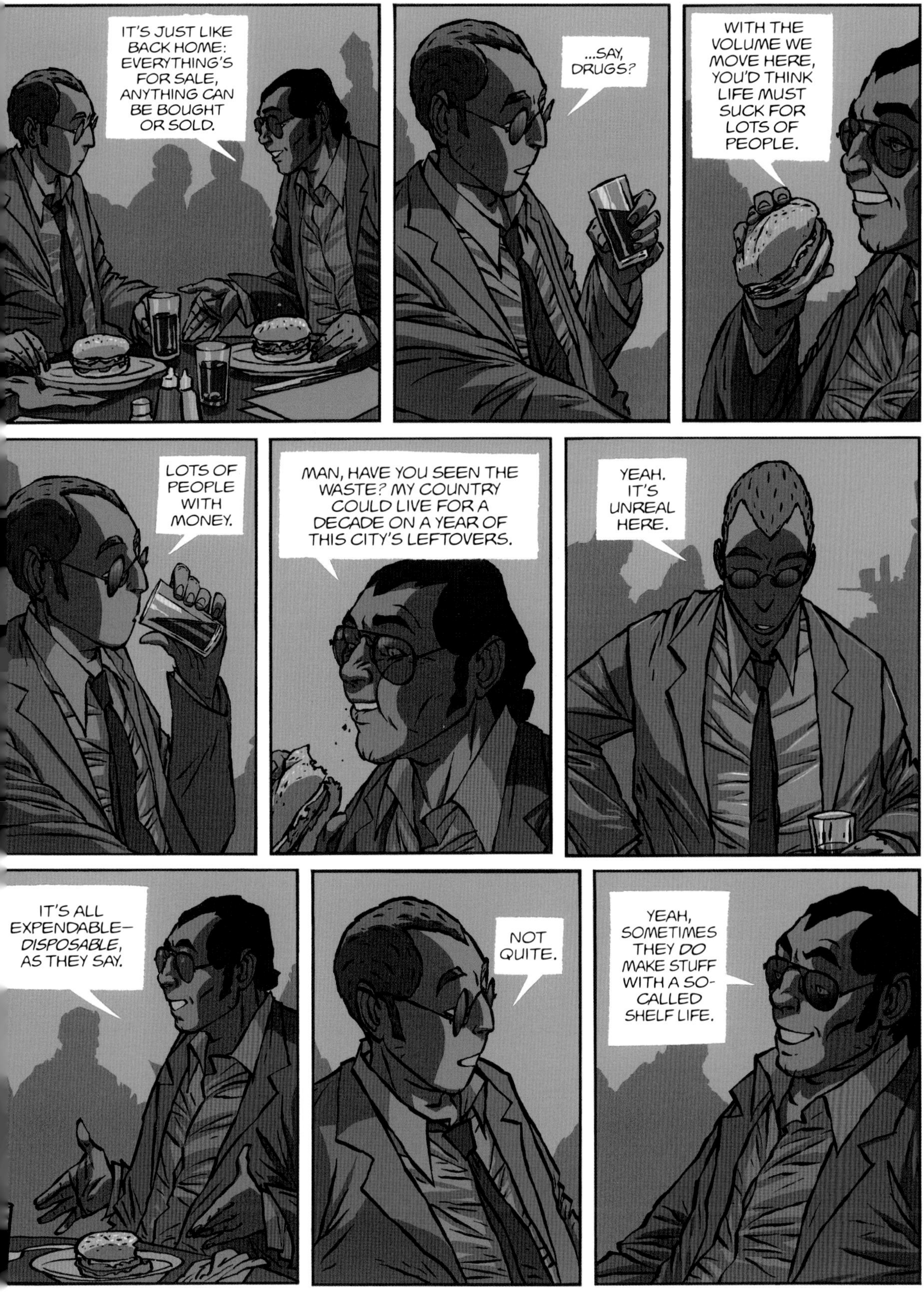
IT'S JUST LIKE BACK HOME: EVERYTHING'S FOR SALE, ANYTHING CAN BE BOUGHT OR SOLD.
...SAY, DRUGS?
WITH THE VOLUME WE MOVE HERE, YOU'D THINK LIFE MUST SUCK FOR LOTS OF PEOPLE.
LOTS OF PEOPLE WITH MONEY.
MAN, HAVE YOU SEEN THE WASTE? MY COUNTRY COULD LIVE FOR A DECADE ON A YEAR OF THIS CITY'S LEFTOVERS.
YEAH. IT'S UNREAL HERE.
IT'S ALL EXPENDABLE— *DISPOSABLE*, AS THEY SAY.
NOT QUITE.
YEAH, SOMETIMES THEY *DO* MAKE STUFF WITH A SO-CALLED SHELF LIFE.

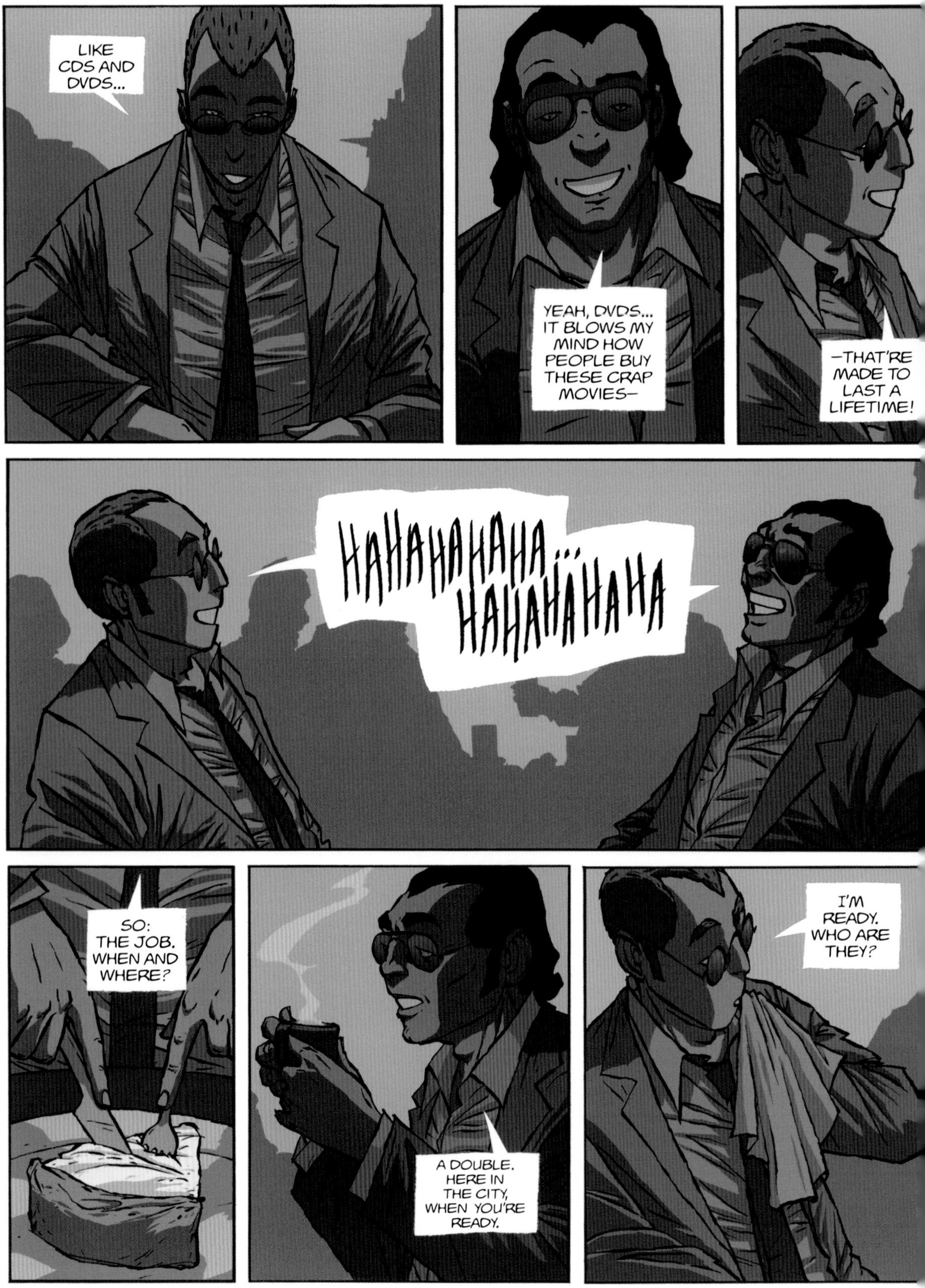
LIKE CDS AND DVDS...
YEAH, DVDS... IT BLOWS MY MIND HOW PEOPLE BUY THESE CRAP MOVIES—
—THAT'RE MADE TO LAST A LIFETIME!
HAHAHAHAHA... HAHAHAHAHA
SO: THE JOB. WHEN AND WHERE?
A DOUBLE. HERE IN THE CITY, WHEN YOU'RE READY.
I'M READY. WHO ARE THEY?

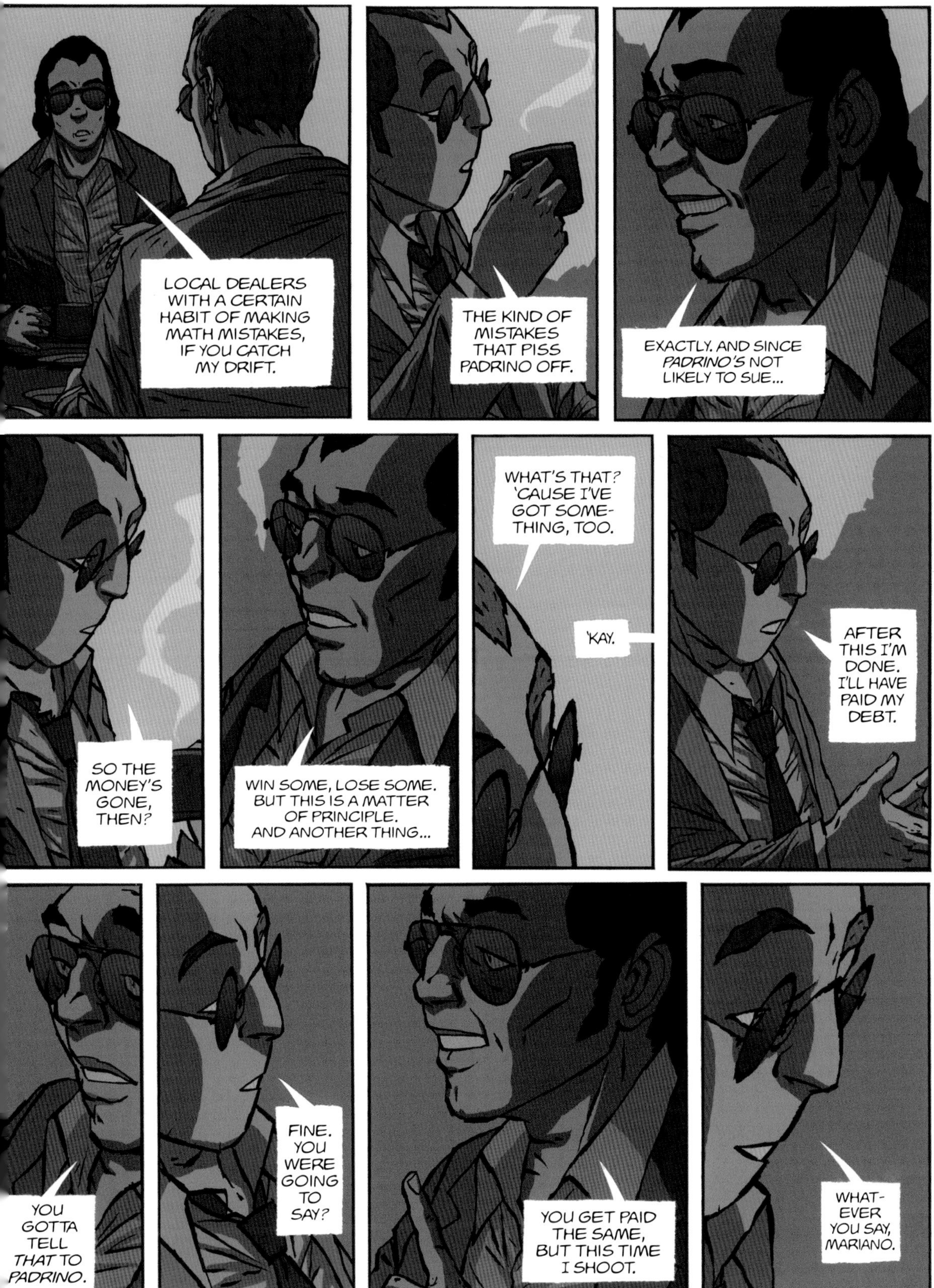
LOCAL DEALERS WITH A CERTAIN HABIT OF MAKING MATH MISTAKES, IF YOU CATCH MY DRIFT.
THE KIND OF MISTAKES THAT PISS PADRINO OFF.
EXACTLY. AND SINCE *PADRINO'S* NOT LIKELY TO SUE...
SO THE MONEY'S GONE, THEN?
WIN SOME, LOSE SOME. BUT THIS IS A MATTER OF PRINCIPLE. AND ANOTHER THING...
WHAT'S THAT? 'CAUSE I'VE GOT SOME-THING, TOO.
'KAY.
AFTER THIS I'M DONE. I'LL HAVE PAID MY DEBT.
YOU GOTTA TELL THAT TO *PADRINO.*
FINE. YOU WERE GOING TO SAY?
YOU GET PAID THE SAME, BUT THIS TIME I SHOOT.
WHAT-EVER YOU SAY, MARIANO.

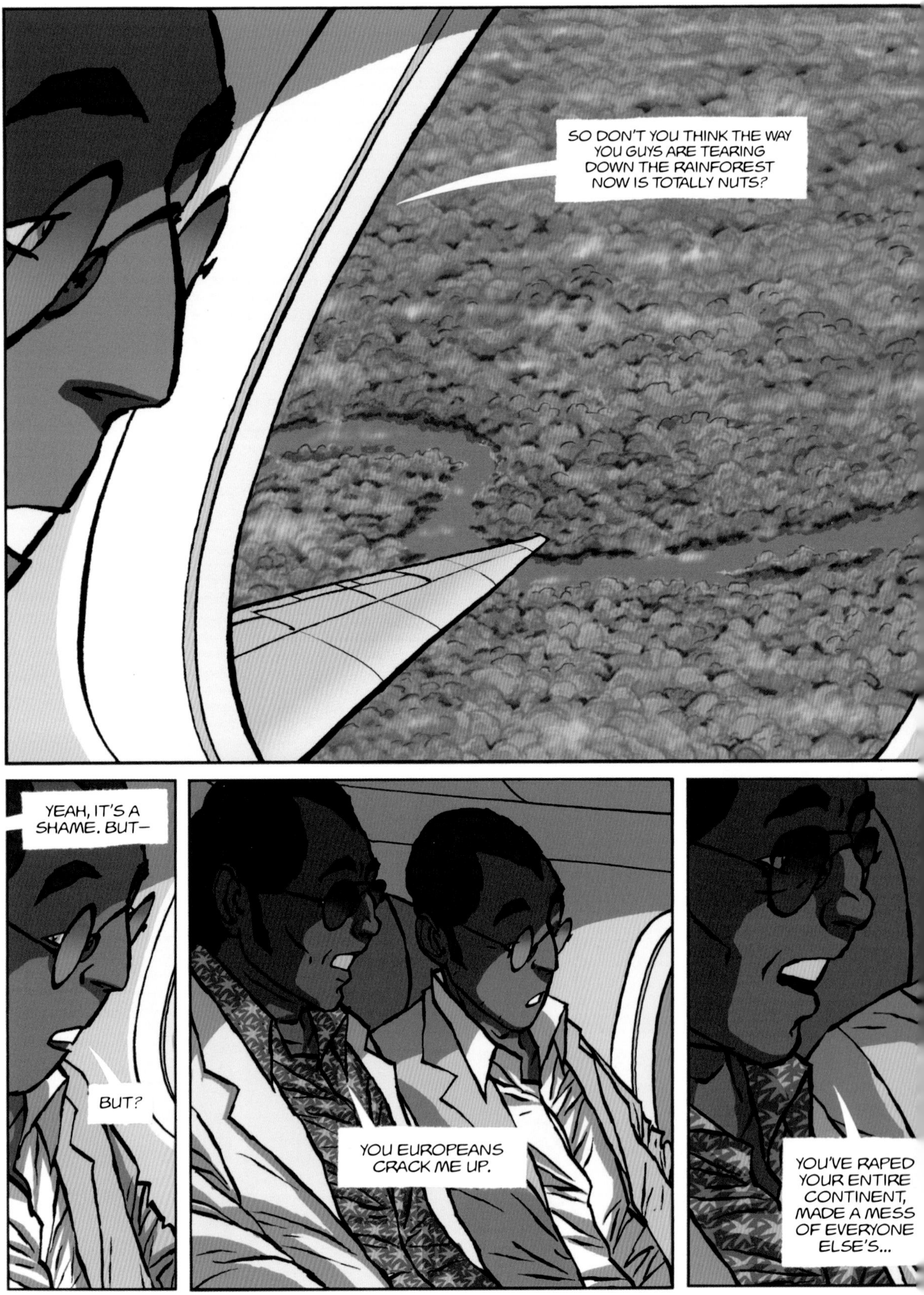
SO DON'T YOU THINK THE WAY YOU GUYS ARE TEARING DOWN THE RAINFOREST NOW IS TOTALLY NUTS?
YEAH, IT'S A SHAME. BUT—
BUT?
YOU EUROPEANS CRACK ME UP.
YOU'VE RAPED YOUR ENTIRE CONTINENT, MADE A MESS OF EVERYONE ELSE'S...

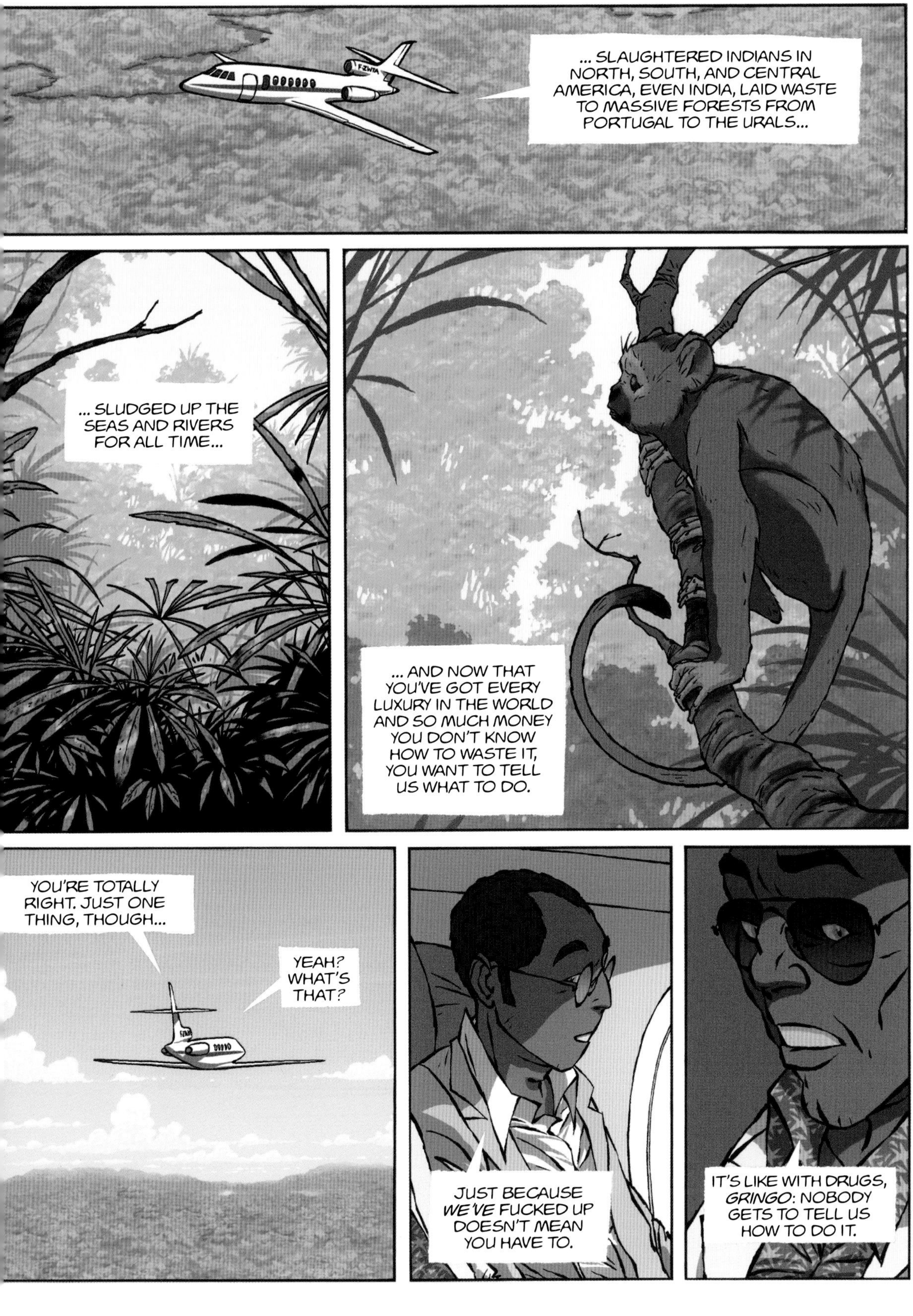
... SLAUGHTERED INDIANS IN NORTH, SOUTH, AND CENTRAL AMERICA, EVEN INDIA, LAID WASTE TO MASSIVE FORESTS FROM PORTUGAL TO THE URALS...
... SLUDGED UP THE SEAS AND RIVERS FOR ALL TIME...
... AND NOW THAT YOU'VE GOT EVERY LUXURY IN THE WORLD AND SO MUCH MONEY YOU DON'T KNOW HOW TO WASTE IT, YOU WANT TO TELL US WHAT TO DO.
YOU'RE TOTALLY RIGHT. JUST ONE THING, THOUGH...
YEAH? WHAT'S THAT?
JUST BECAUSE *WE'VE* FUCKED UP DOESN'T MEAN YOU HAVE TO.
IT'S LIKE WITH DRUGS, *GRINGO*: NOBODY GETS TO TELL US HOW TO DO IT.

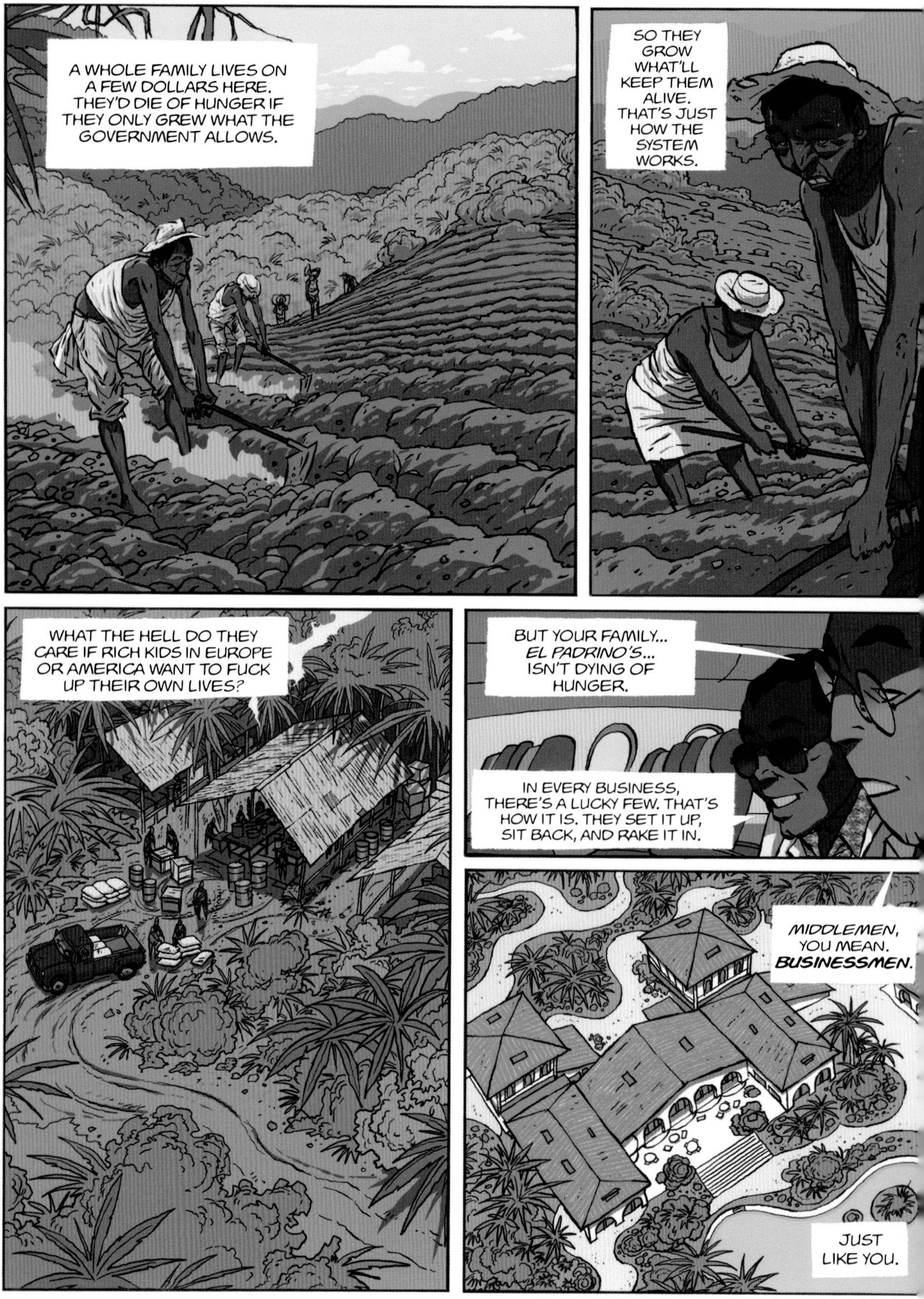
A WHOLE FAMILY LIVES ON A FEW DOLLARS HERE. THEY'D DIE OF HUNGER IF THEY ONLY GREW WHAT THE GOVERNMENT ALLOWS.
SO THEY GROW WHAT'LL KEEP THEM ALIVE. THAT'S JUST HOW THE SYSTEM WORKS.
WHAT THE HELL DO THEY CARE IF RICH KIDS IN EUROPE OR AMERICA WANT TO FUCK UP THEIR OWN LIVES?
BUT YOUR FAMILY... EL PADRINO'S... ISN'T DYING OF HUNGER.
IN EVERY BUSINESS, THERE'S A LUCKY FEW. THAT'S HOW IT IS. THEY SET IT UP, SIT BACK, AND RAKE IT IN.
MIDDLEMEN, YOU MEAN. BUSINESSMEN.
JUST LIKE YOU.

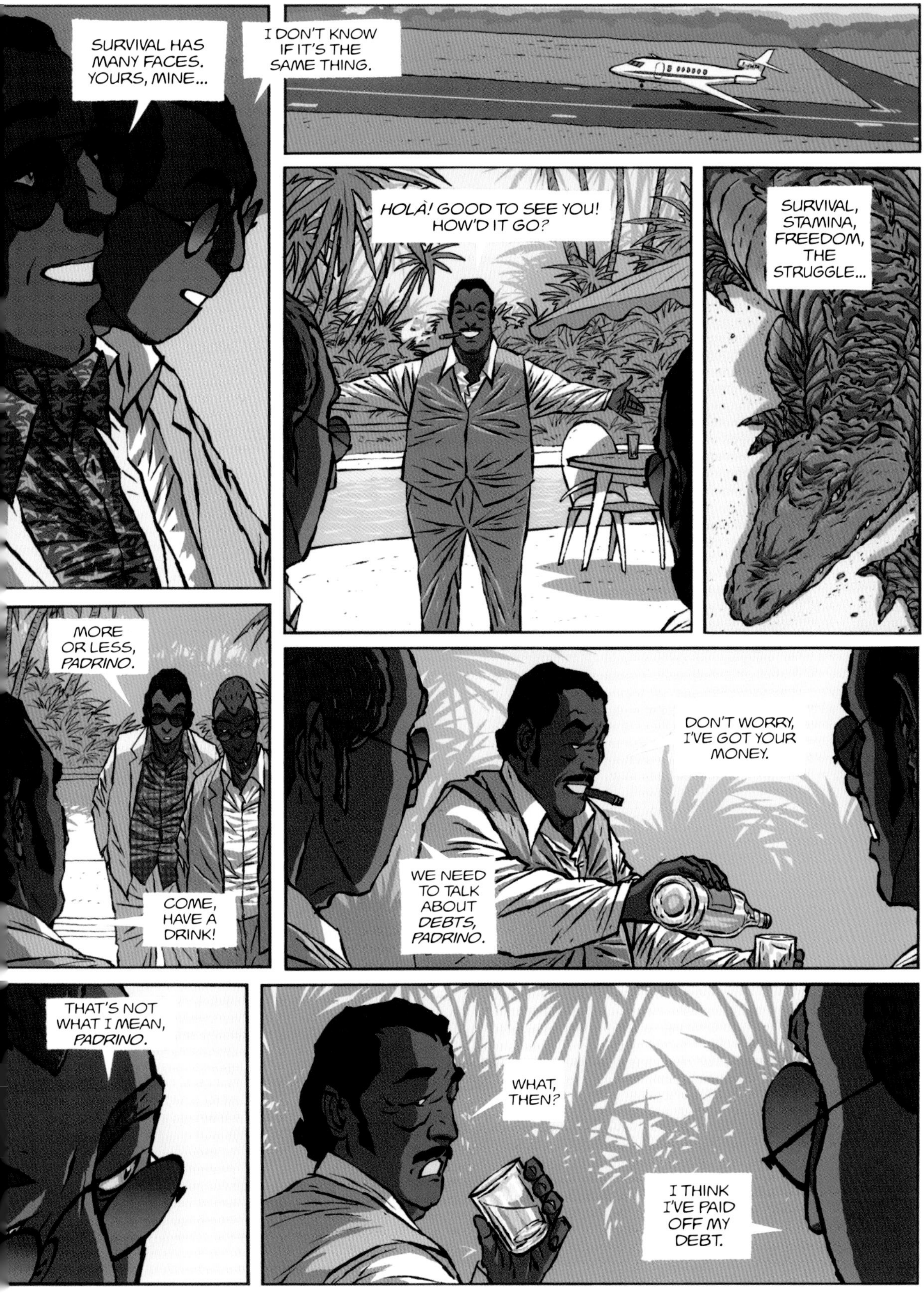
SURVIVAL HAS MANY FACES. YOURS, MINE...
I DON'T KNOW IF IT'S THE SAME THING.
HOLÀ! GOOD TO SEE YOU! HOW'D IT GO?
SURVIVAL, STAMINA, FREEDOM, THE STRUGGLE...
MORE OR LESS, PADRINO.
COME, HAVE A DRINK!
DON'T WORRY, I'VE GOT YOUR MONEY.
WE NEED TO TALK ABOUT DEBTS, PADRINO.
THAT'S NOT WHAT I MEAN, PADRINO.
WHAT, THEN?
I THINK I'VE PAID OFF MY DEBT.

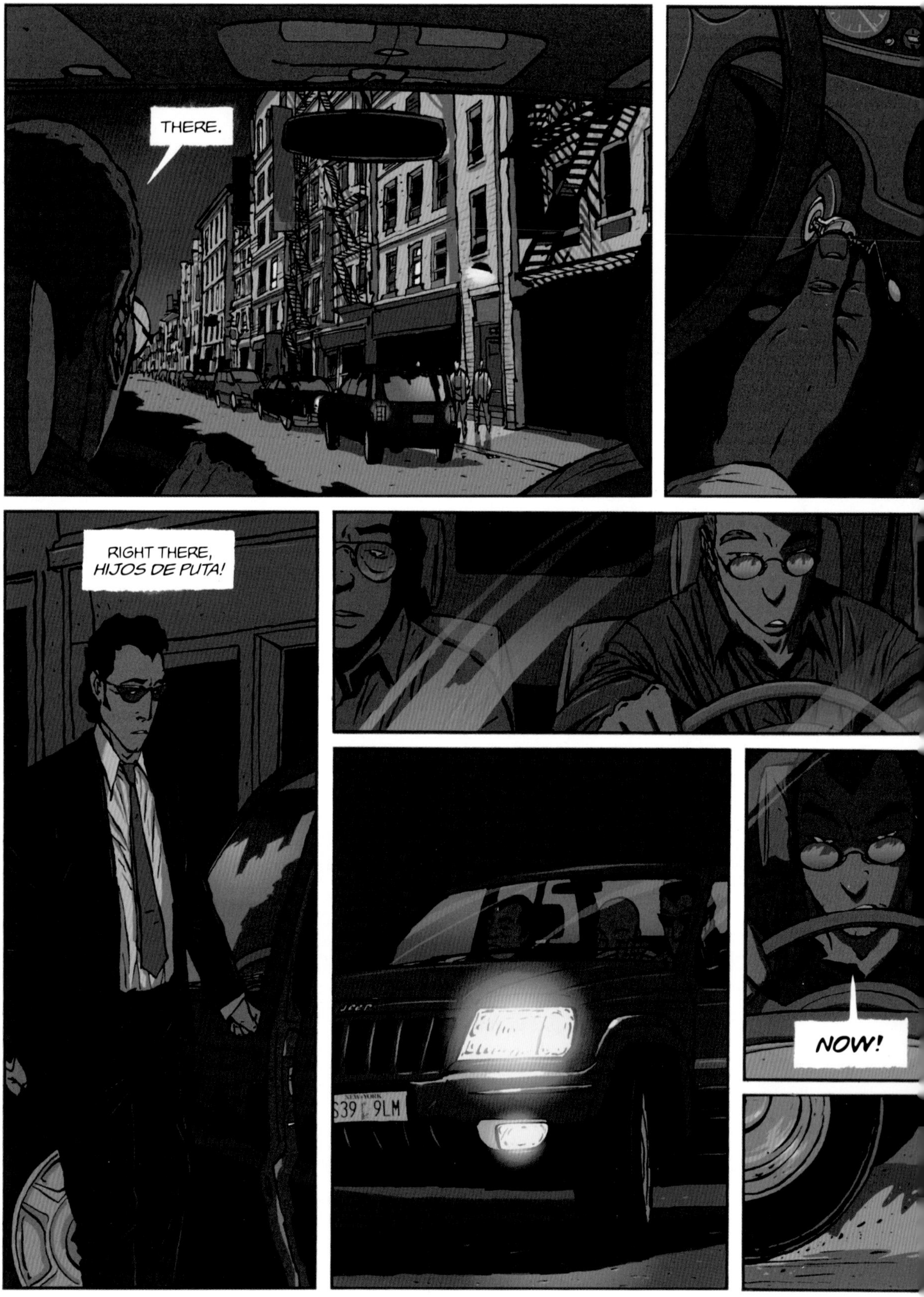
THERE.
RIGHT THERE, *HIJOS DE PUTA!*
NOW!

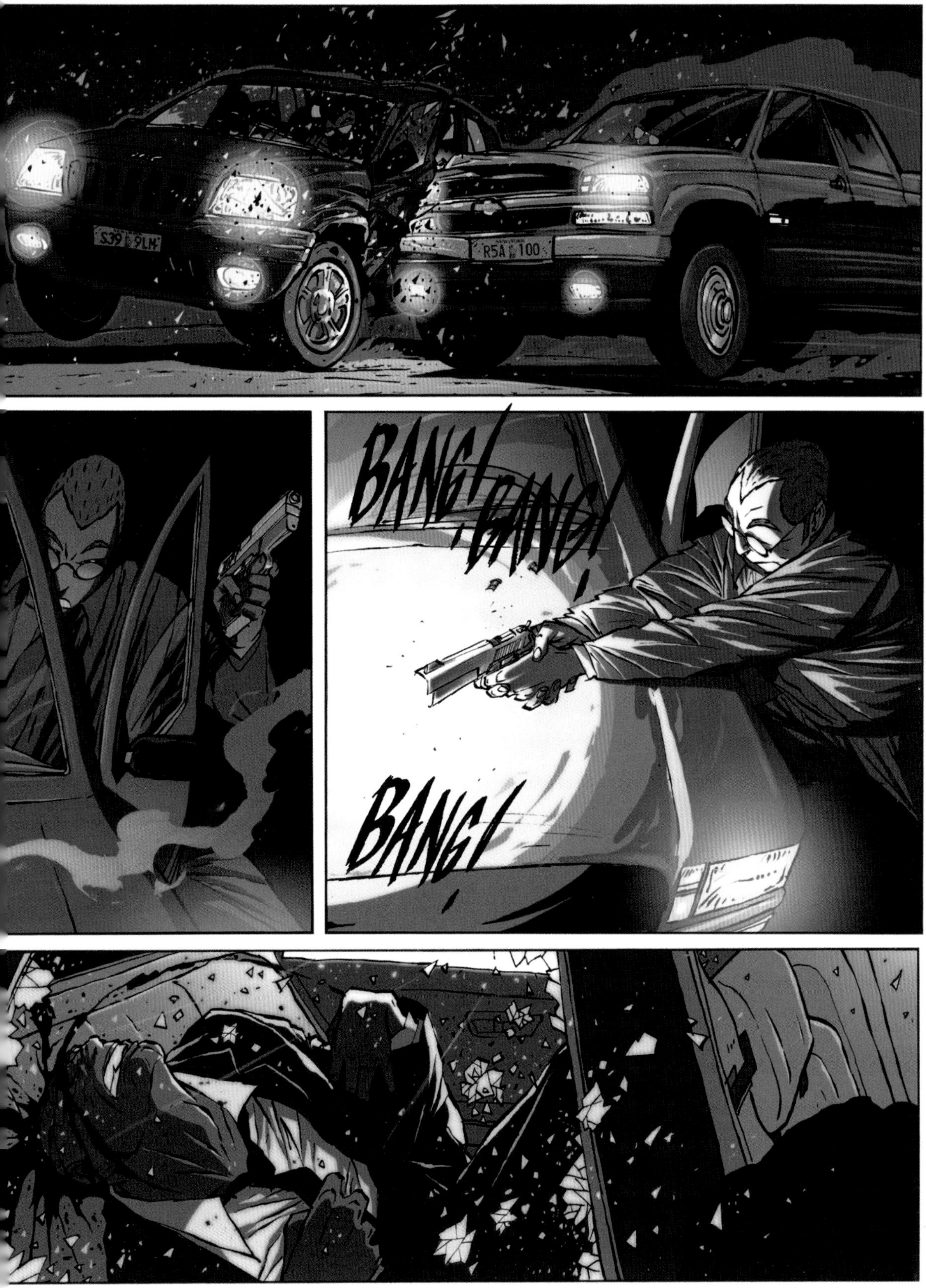
S39 9LM
R5A 100
BANG! BANG!
BANG!

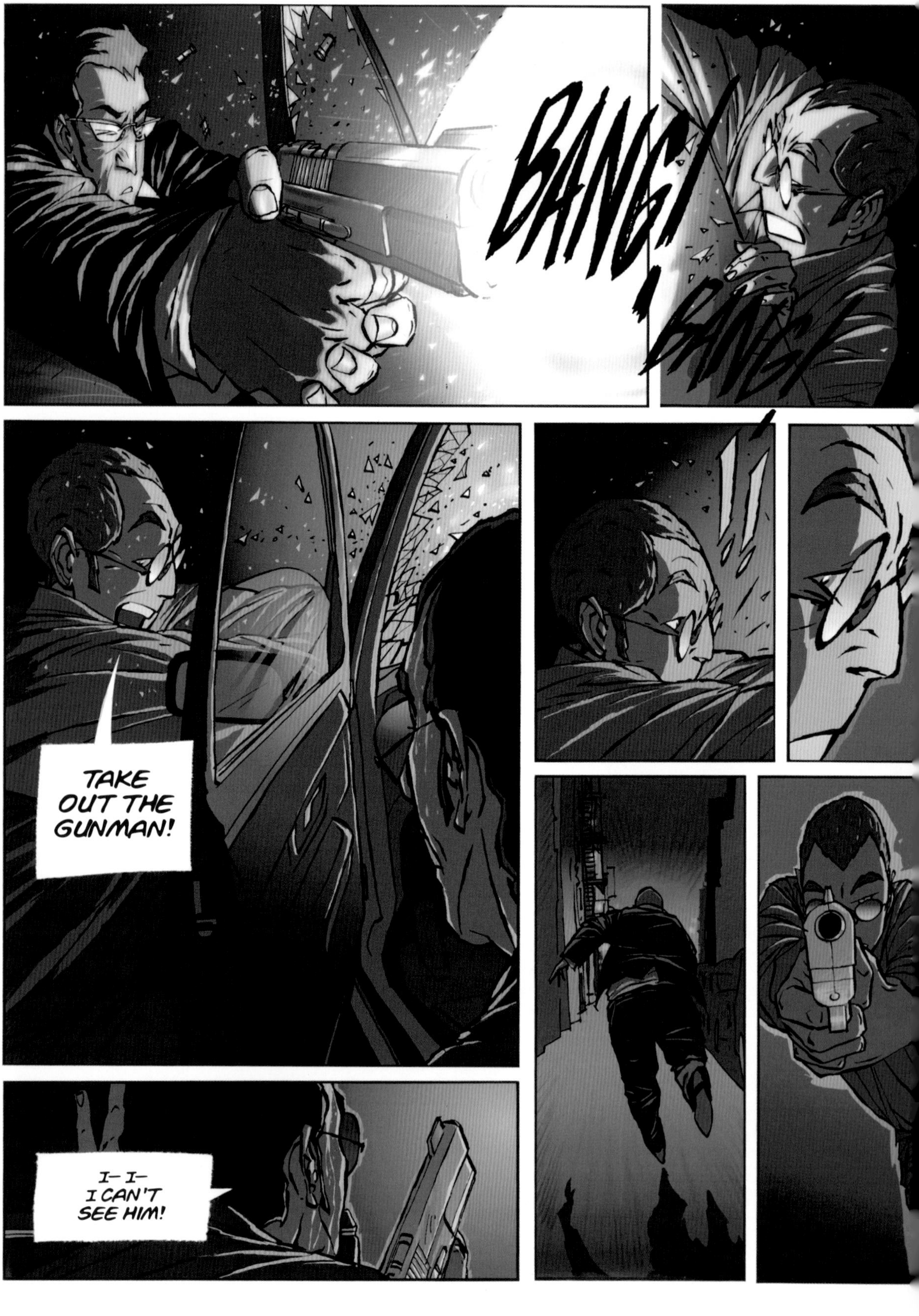
BANG!
BANG!
TAKE OUT THE GUNMAN!
I— I— I CAN'T SEE HIM!

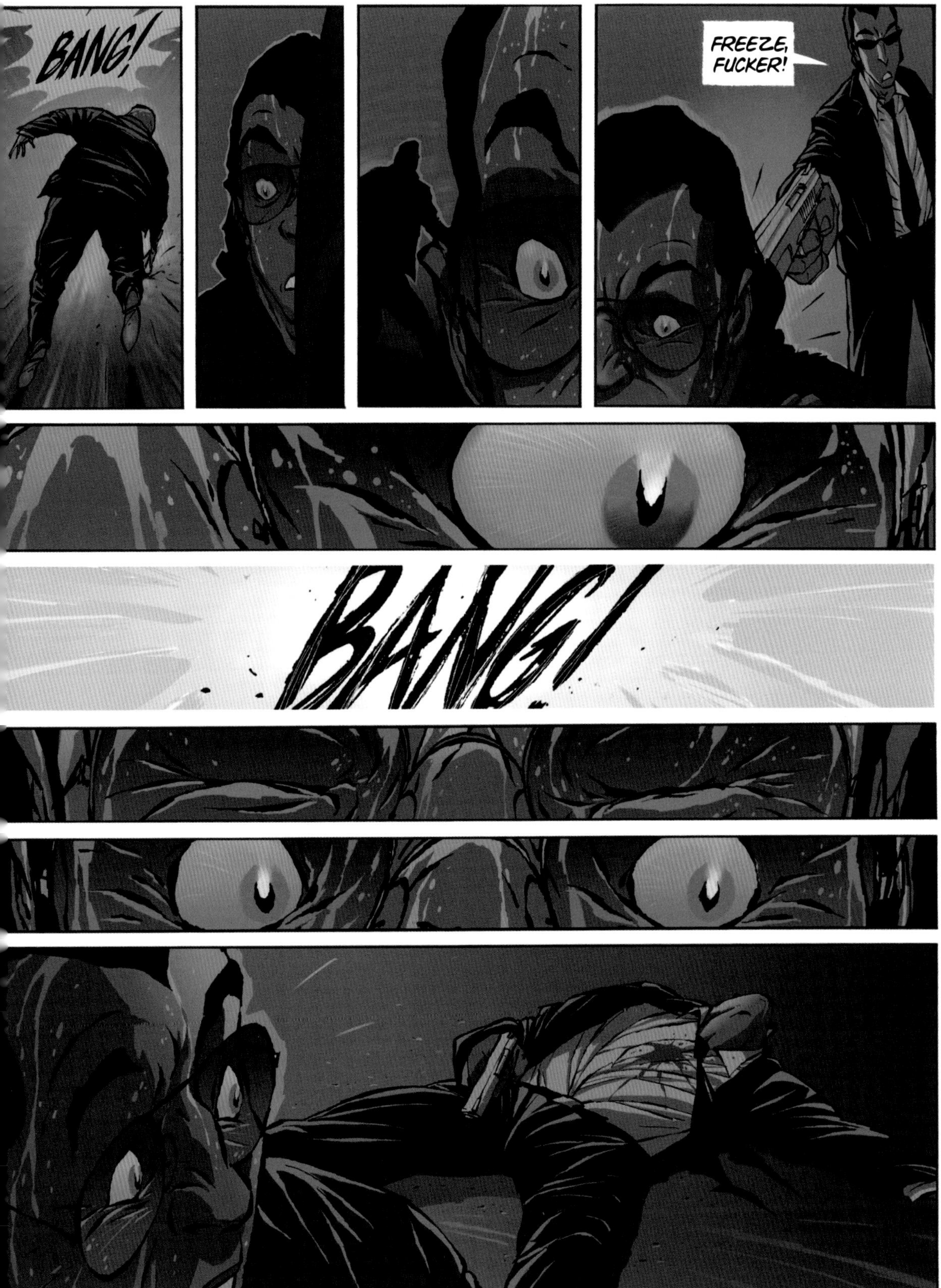
BANG!
FREEZE, FUCKER!
BANG!

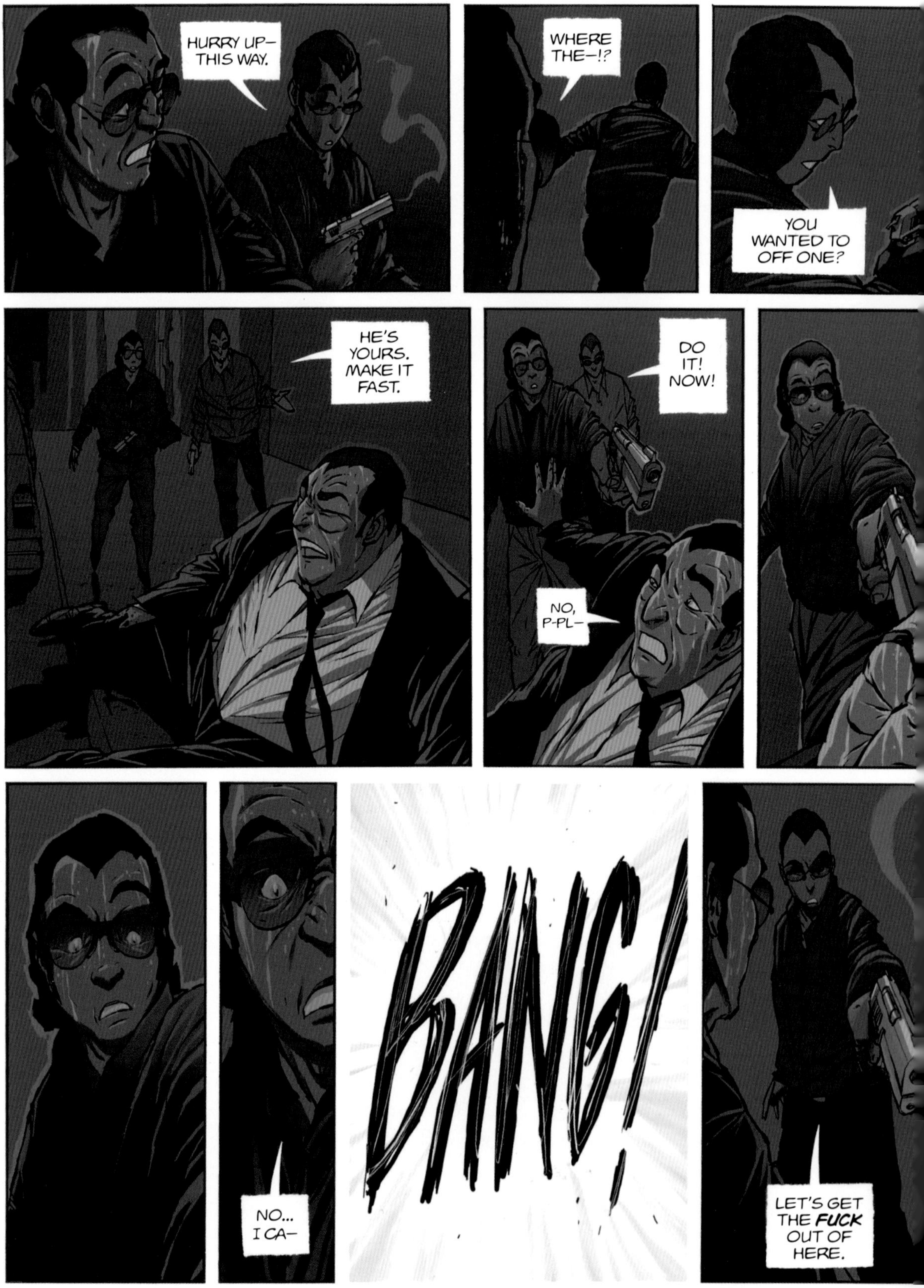
HURRY UP— THIS WAY.
WHERE THE—!?
YOU WANTED TO OFF ONE?
HE'S YOURS. MAKE IT FAST.
DO IT! NOW!
NO, P-PL—
NO... I CA—
BANG!
LET'S GET THE **FUCK** OUT OF HERE.

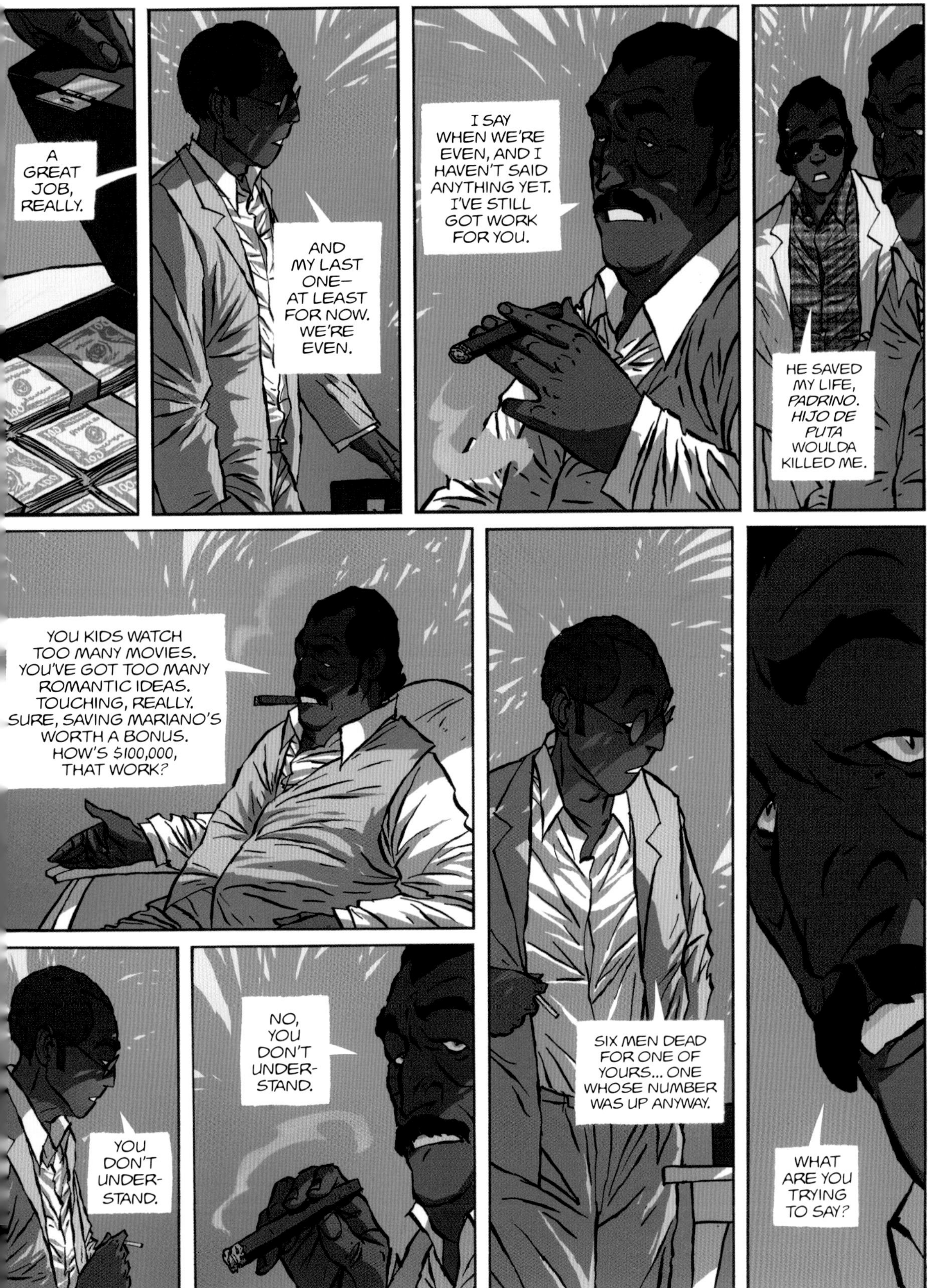
A GREAT JOB, REALLY.
AND MY LAST ONE— AT LEAST FOR NOW. WE'RE EVEN.
I SAY WHEN WE'RE EVEN, AND I HAVEN'T SAID ANYTHING YET. I'VE STILL GOT WORK FOR YOU.
HE SAVED MY LIFE, *PADRINO*. *HIJO DE PUTA* WOULDA KILLED ME.
YOU KIDS WATCH TOO MANY MOVIES. YOU'VE GOT TOO MANY ROMANTIC IDEAS. TOUCHING, REALLY. SURE, SAVING MARIANO'S WORTH A BONUS. HOW'S $100,000, THAT WORK?
SIX MEN DEAD FOR ONE OF YOURS... ONE WHOSE NUMBER WAS UP ANYWAY.
YOU DON'T UNDER-STAND.
NO, YOU DON'T UNDER-STAND.
WHAT ARE YOU TRYING TO SAY?

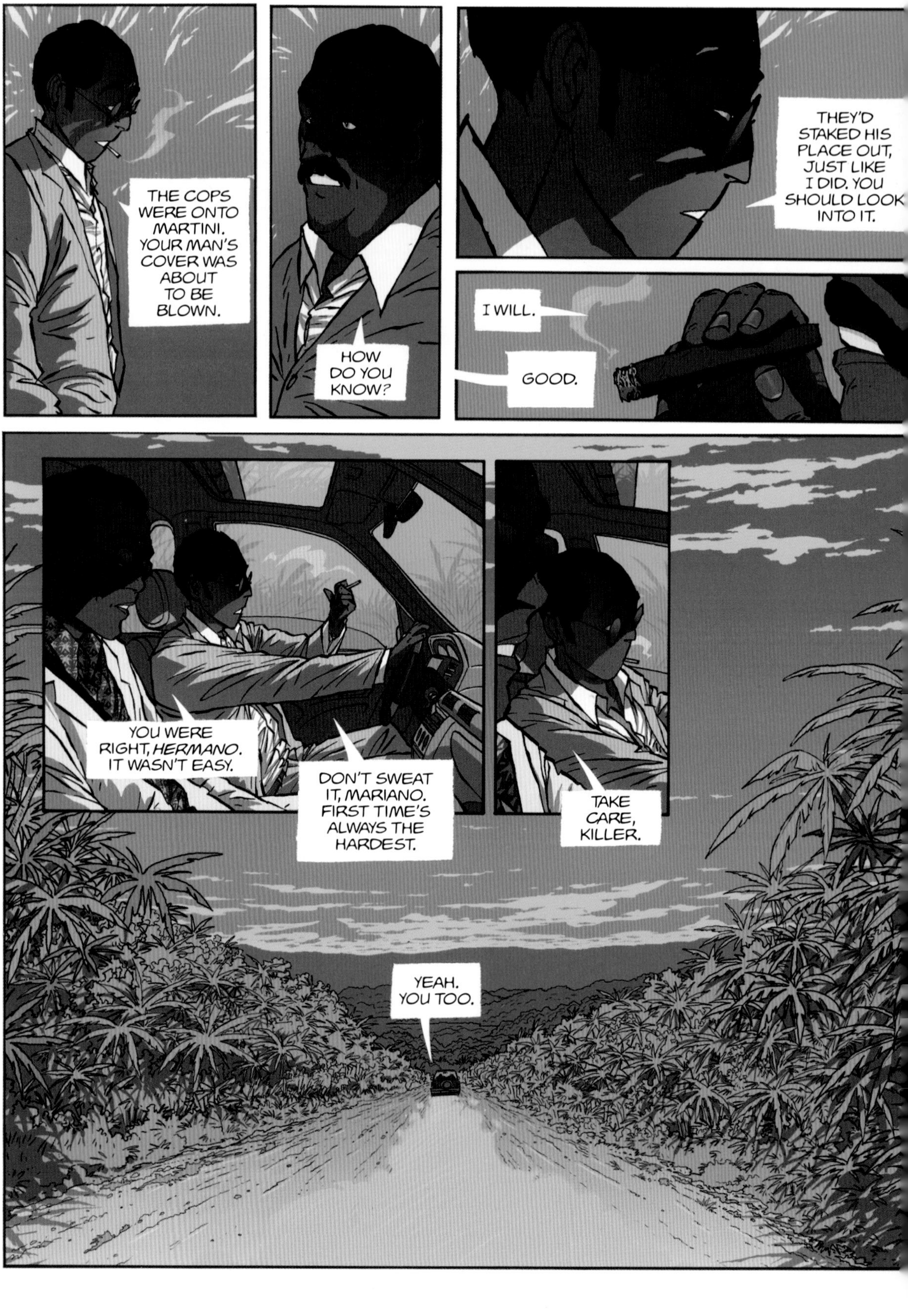
THE COPS WERE ONTO MARTINI. YOUR MAN'S COVER WAS ABOUT TO BE BLOWN.
HOW DO YOU KNOW?
THEY'D STAKED HIS PLACE OUT, JUST LIKE I DID. YOU SHOULD LOOK INTO IT.
I WILL.
GOOD.
YOU WERE RIGHT, *HERMANO*. IT WASN'T EASY.
DON'T SWEAT IT, MARIANO. FIRST TIME'S ALWAYS THE HARDEST.
TAKE CARE, KILLER.
YEAH. YOU TOO.

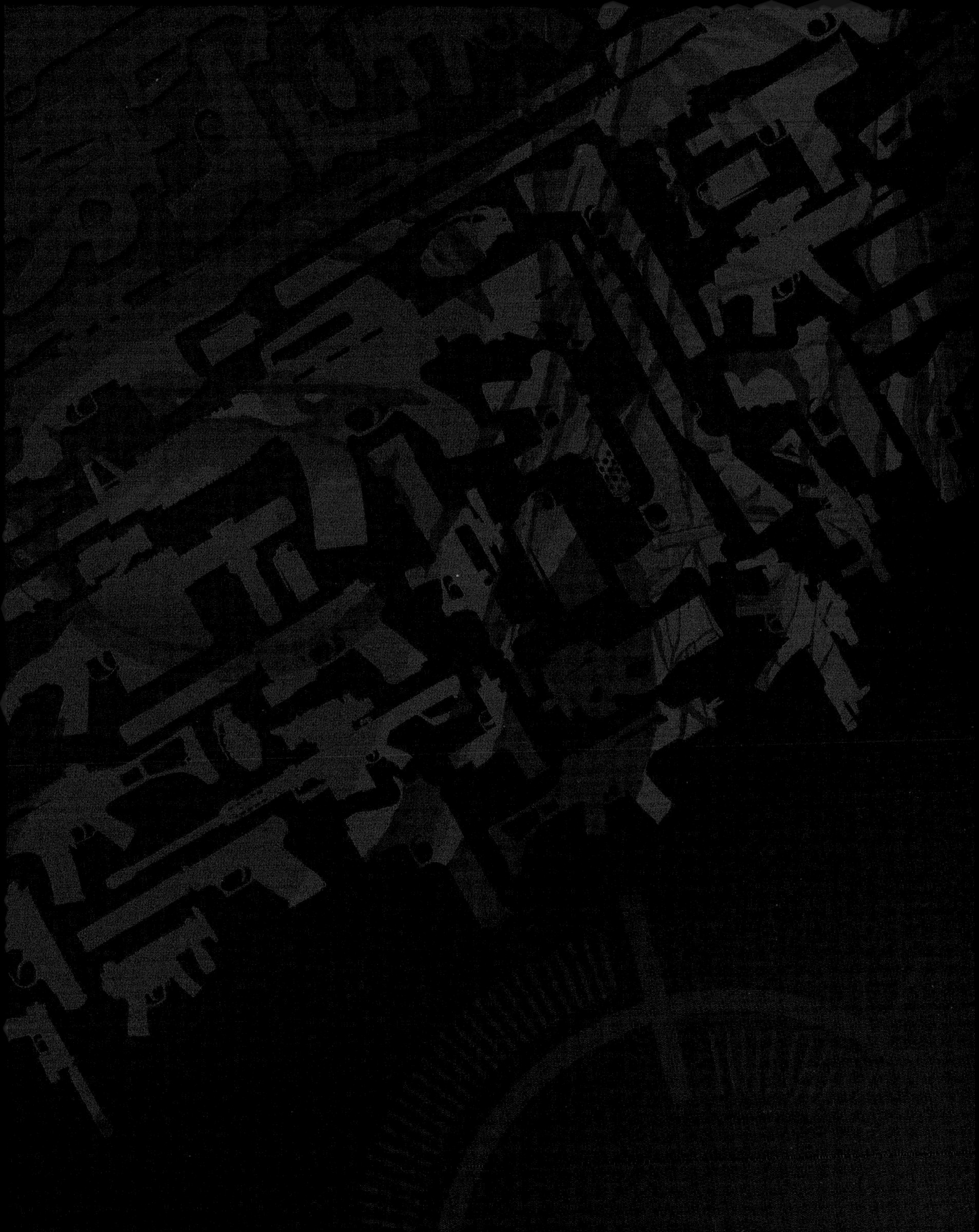

“I know the **score**. I’ll play my part, and **no one** has to tell me how to do it.”

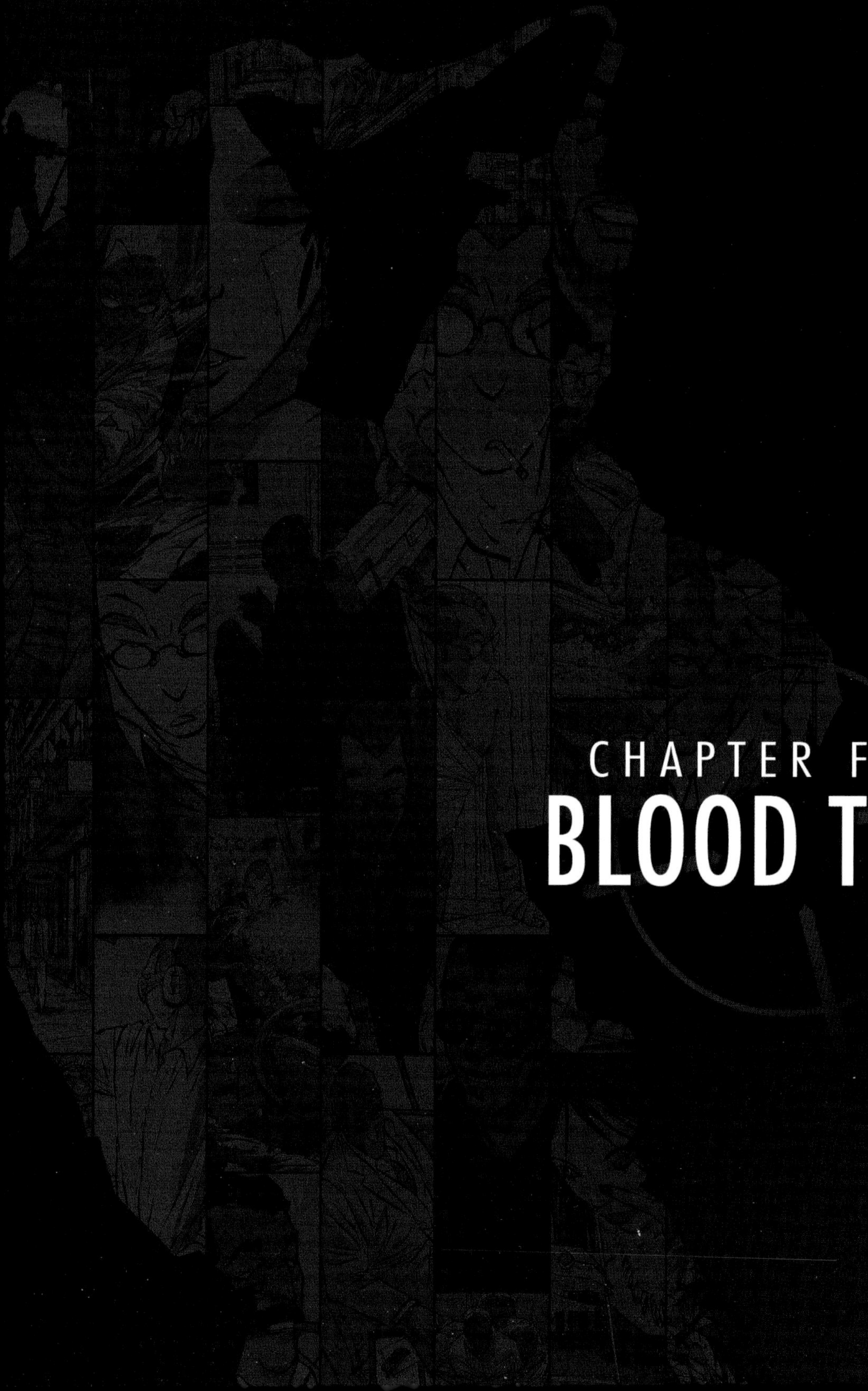

CHAPTER FOUR

BLOOD TIES

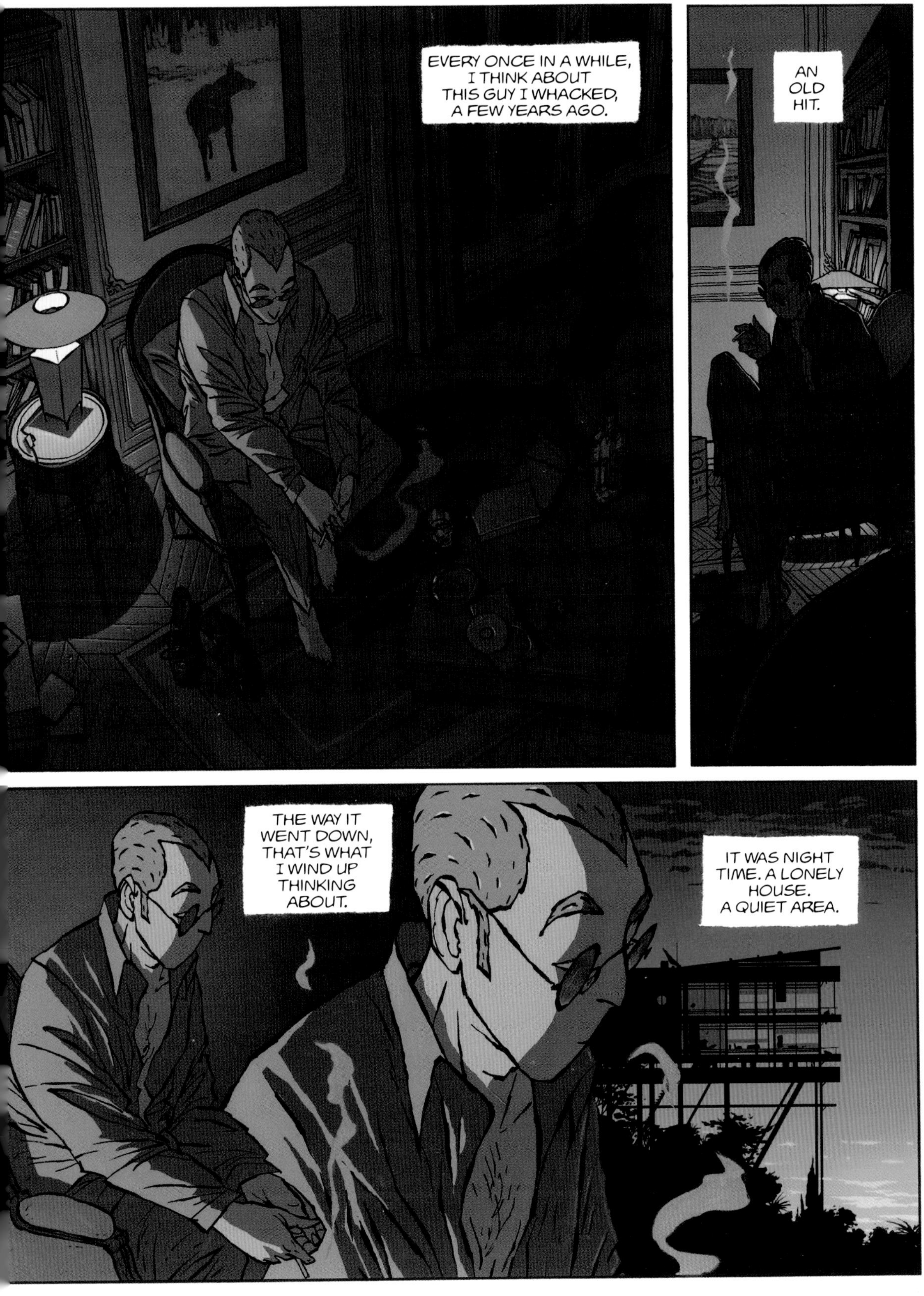
EVERY ONCE IN A WHILE, I THINK ABOUT THIS GUY I WHACKED, A FEW YEARS AGO.
AN OLD HIT.
THE WAY IT WENT DOWN, THAT'S WHAT I WIND UP THINKING ABOUT.
IT WAS NIGHT TIME. A LONELY HOUSE. A QUIET AREA.

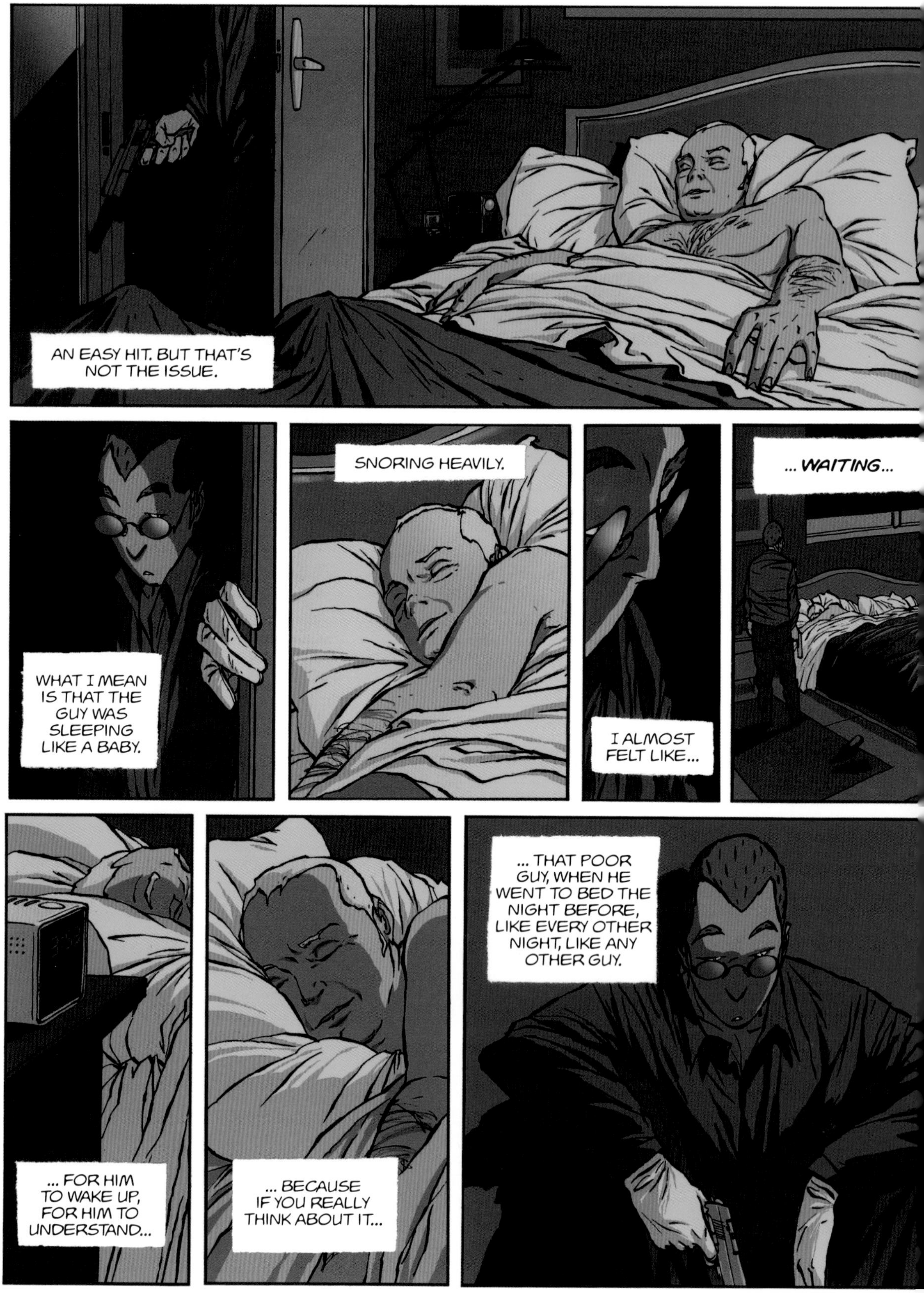
AN EASY HIT. BUT THAT'S NOT THE ISSUE.
WHAT I MEAN IS THAT THE GUY WAS SLEEPING LIKE A BABY.
SNORING HEAVILY.
I ALMOST FELT LIKE...
... *WAITING*...
... FOR HIM TO WAKE UP, FOR HIM TO UNDERSTAND...
... BECAUSE IF YOU REALLY THINK ABOUT IT...
... THAT POOR GUY, WHEN HE WENT TO BED THE NIGHT BEFORE, LIKE EVERY OTHER NIGHT, LIKE ANY OTHER GUY.

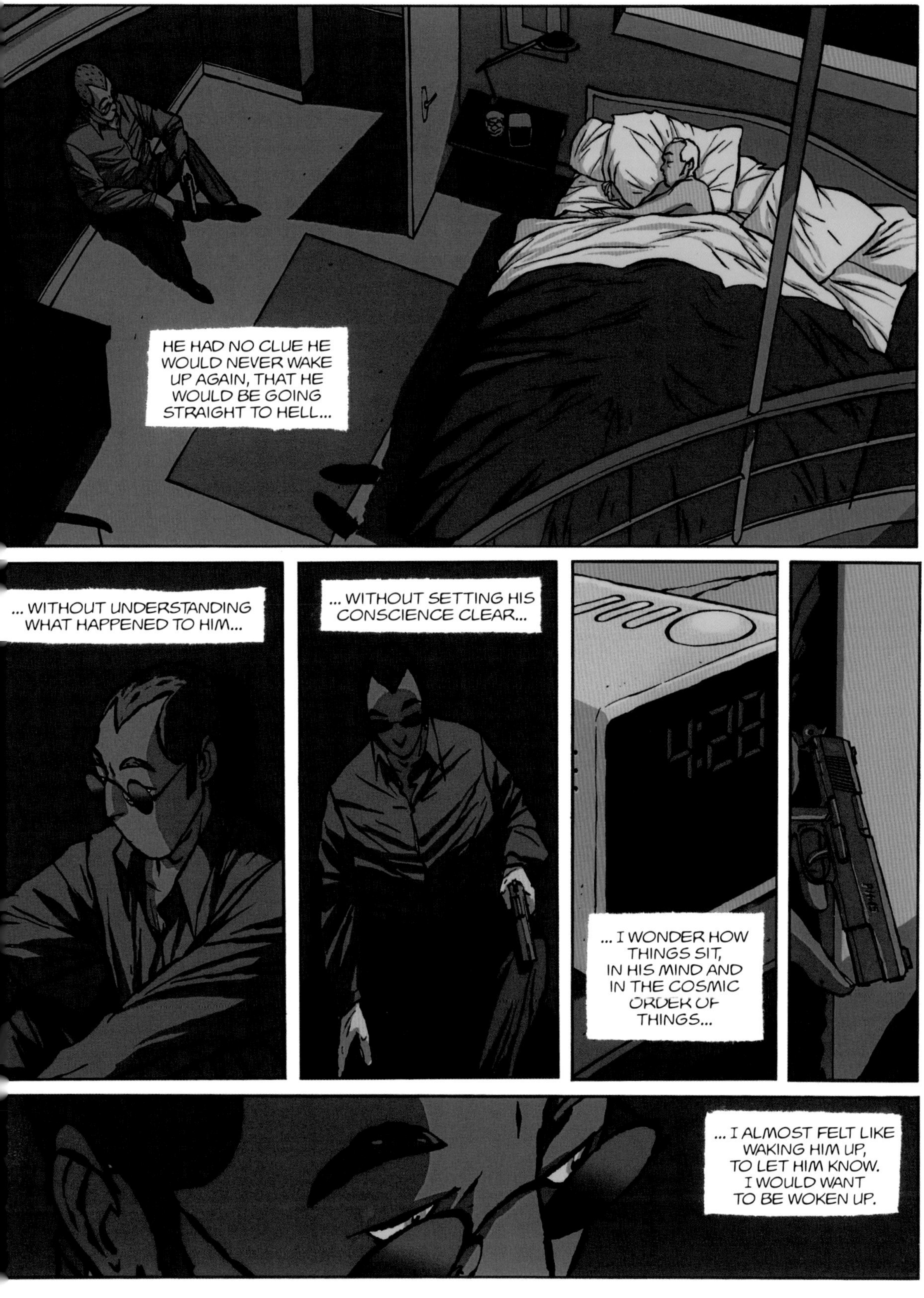
HE HAD NO CLUE HE WOULD NEVER WAKE UP AGAIN, THAT HE WOULD BE GOING STRAIGHT TO HELL...
... WITHOUT UNDERSTANDING WHAT HAPPENED TO HIM...
... WITHOUT SETTING HIS CONSCIENCE CLEAR...
4:29
... I WONDER HOW THINGS SIT, IN HIS MIND AND IN THE COSMIC ORDER OF THINGS...
... I ALMOST FELT LIKE WAKING HIM UP, TO LET HIM KNOW. I WOULD WANT TO BE WOKEN UP.

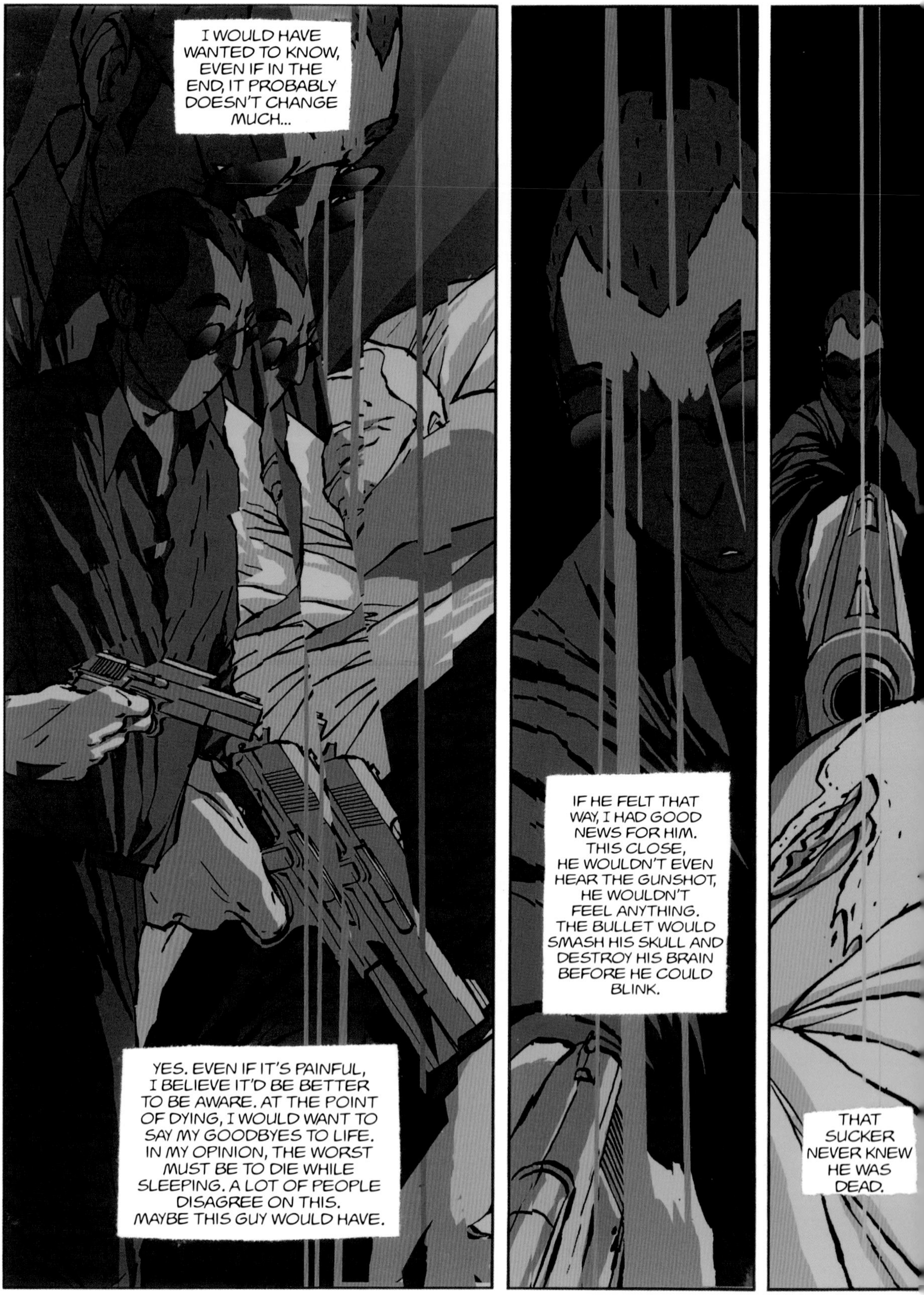
I WOULD HAVE WANTED TO KNOW, EVEN IF IN THE END, IT PROBABLY DOESN'T CHANGE MUCH...
YES. EVEN IF IT'S PAINFUL, I BELIEVE IT'D BE BETTER TO BE AWARE. AT THE POINT OF DYING, I WOULD WANT TO SAY MY GOODBYES TO LIFE. IN MY OPINION, THE WORST MUST BE TO DIE WHILE SLEEPING. A LOT OF PEOPLE DISAGREE ON THIS. MAYBE THIS GUY WOULD HAVE.
IF HE FELT THAT WAY, I HAD GOOD NEWS FOR HIM. THIS CLOSE, HE WOULDN'T EVEN HEAR THE GUNSHOT, HE WOULDN'T FEEL ANYTHING. THE BULLET WOULD SMASH HIS SKULL AND DESTROY HIS BRAIN BEFORE HE COULD BLINK.
THAT SUCKER NEVER KNEW HE WAS DEAD.

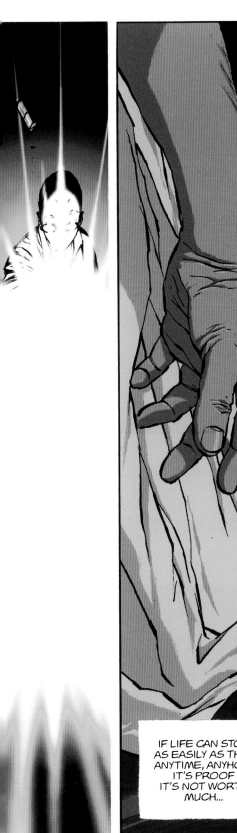

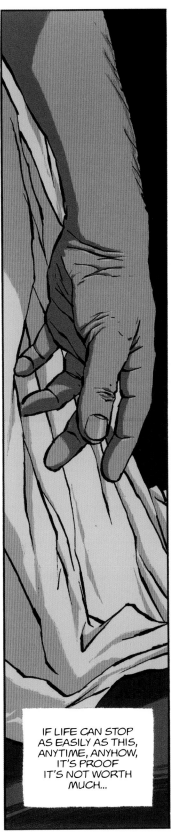

IF LIFE CAN STOP AS EASILY AS THIS, ANYTIME, ANYHOW, IT'S PROOF IT'S NOT WORTH MUCH...

...OR THAT IT'S *VERY, VERY VALUABLE.* EITHER WAY, YOU HAVE TO BE VERY CAREFUL WITH YOURSELF.

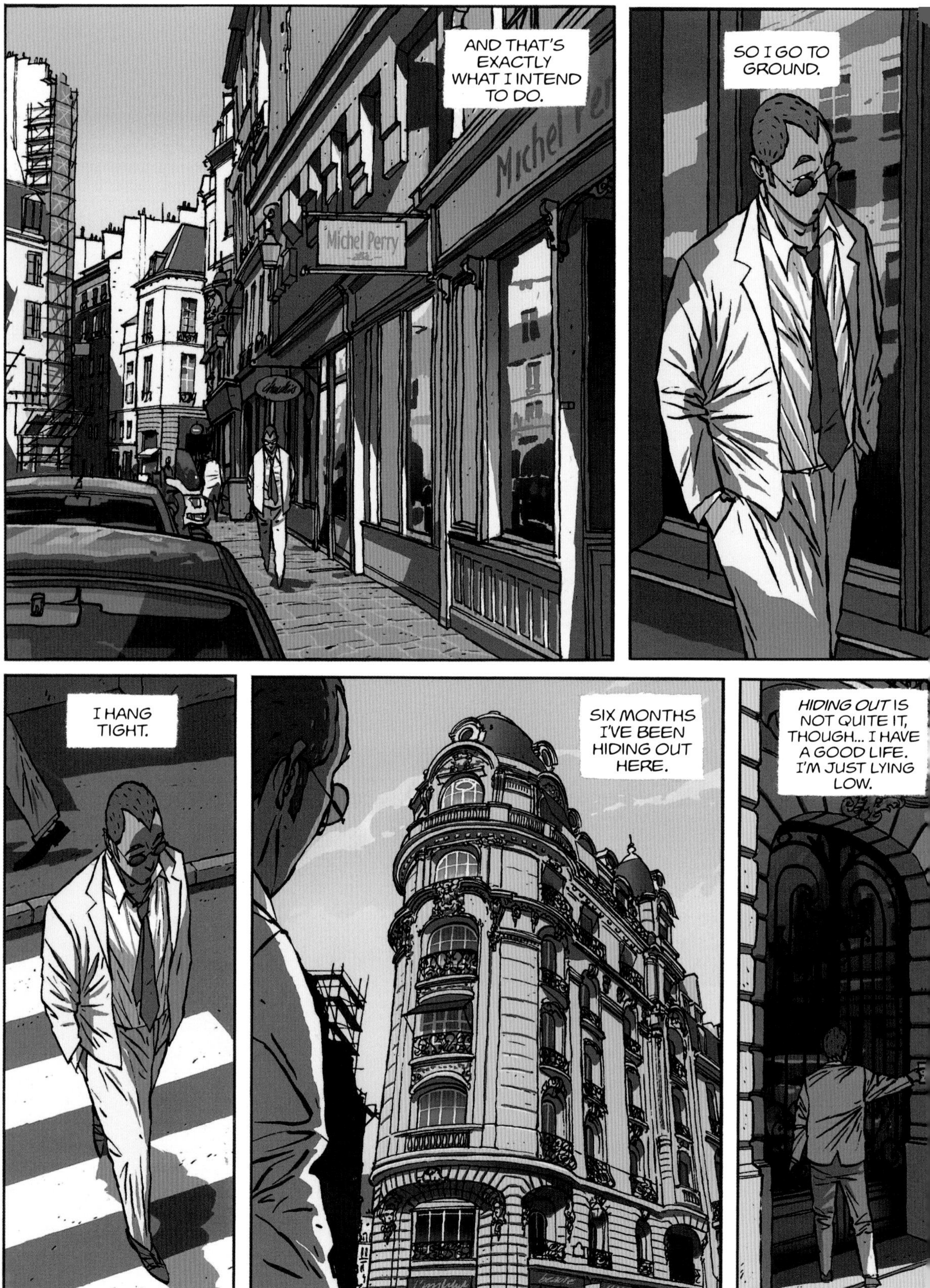
AND THAT'S EXACTLY WHAT I INTEND TO DO.
Michel Perry
SO I GO TO GROUND.
I HANG TIGHT.
SIX MONTHS I'VE BEEN HIDING OUT HERE.
HIDING OUT IS NOT QUITE IT, THOUGH... I HAVE A GOOD LIFE. I'M JUST LYING LOW.

IT'S A VERY SAFE PLACE...

AN APARTMENT I BOUGHT A LONG TIME AGO, ON MY OWN. NOBODY EVER KNEW ABOUT IT, NOT EVEN EDWARD.

UNDER A FALSE NAME.

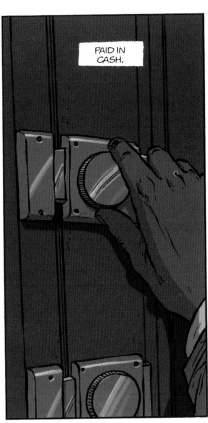

PAID IN CASH.

I ALWAYS LIKE TO SEE HOW THINGS WORK OUT WHEN THERE'S A BIG PILE OF CASH ON THE TABLE.

I'M USING THE NAME UNDER WHICH I BOUGHT THIS PLACE. I PUT THAT NAME ON THE MAILBOX, TOO.

I NEVER GET ANY MAIL, AND THAT'S FINE BY ME. ANY NAME IS AS GOOD AS THE OTHER. THEY MEAN NOTHING.

THEY CAN BE WIPED OUT AS QUICKLY AS A STAIN ON A PIECE OF CLOTHING.

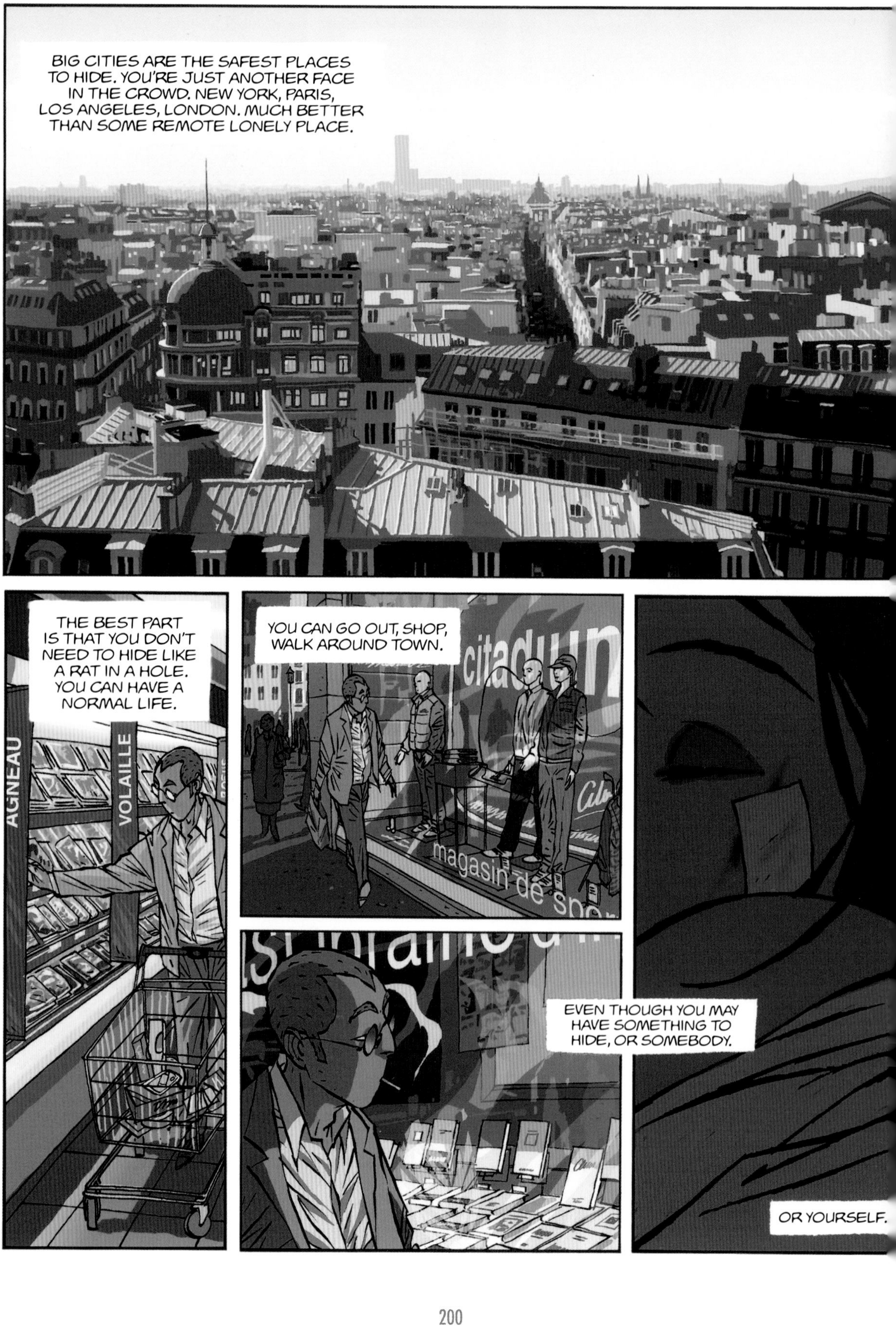
BIG CITIES ARE THE SAFEST PLACES TO HIDE. YOU'RE JUST ANOTHER FACE IN THE CROWD. NEW YORK, PARIS, LOS ANGELES, LONDON. MUCH BETTER THAN SOME REMOTE LONELY PLACE.
THE BEST PART IS THAT YOU DON'T NEED TO HIDE LIKE A RAT IN A HOLE. YOU CAN HAVE A NORMAL LIFE.
AGNEAU
VOLAILLE
YOU CAN GO OUT, SHOP, WALK AROUND TOWN.
magasin de spor
EVEN THOUGH YOU MAY HAVE SOMETHING TO HIDE, OR SOMEBODY.
OR YOURSELF.

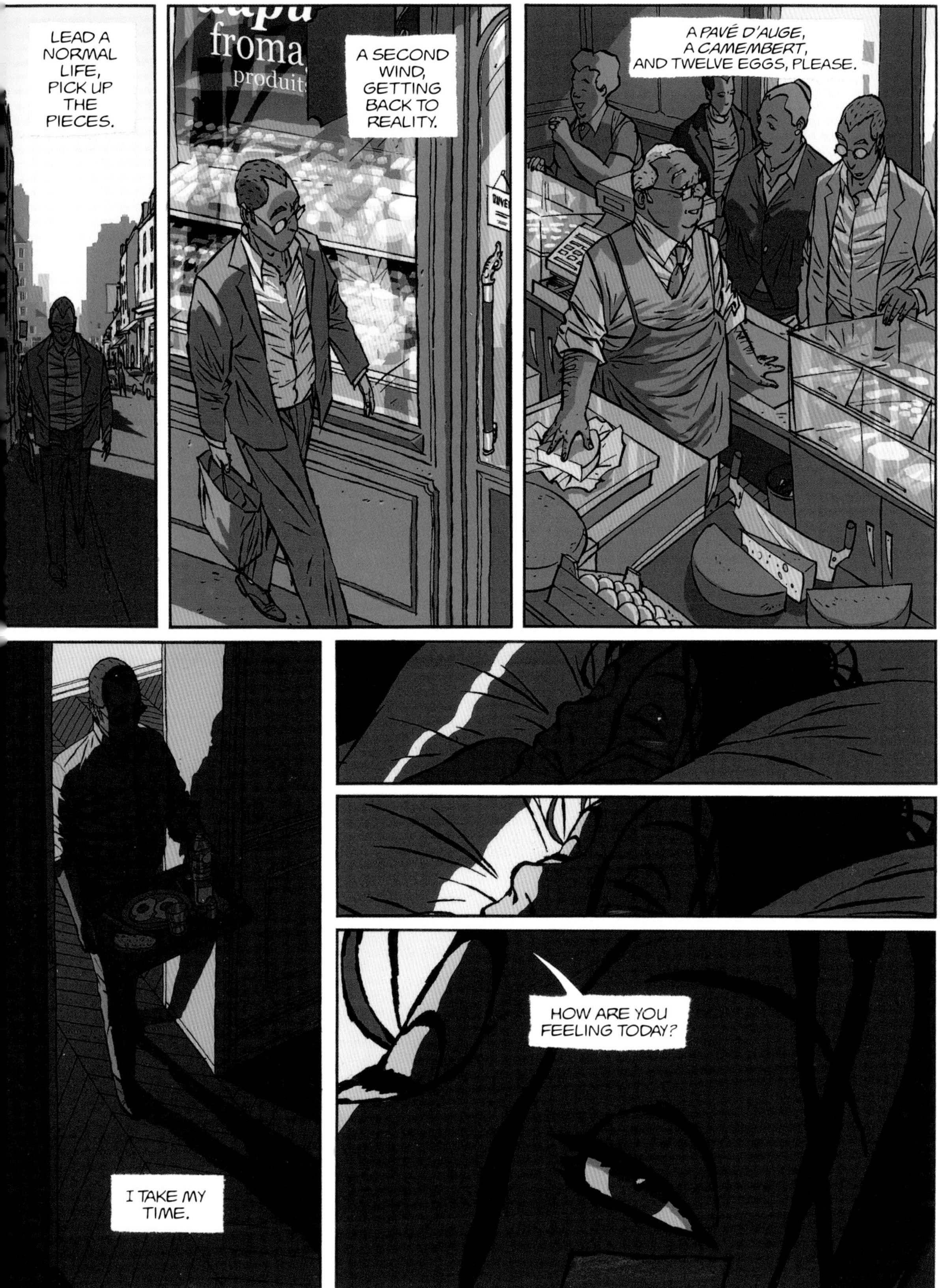
LEAD A NORMAL LIFE, PICK UP THE PIECES.
A SECOND WIND, GETTING BACK TO REALITY.
A *PAVÉ D'AUGE*, A *CAMEMBERT*, AND TWELVE EGGS, PLEASE.
I TAKE MY TIME.
HOW ARE YOU FEELING TODAY?

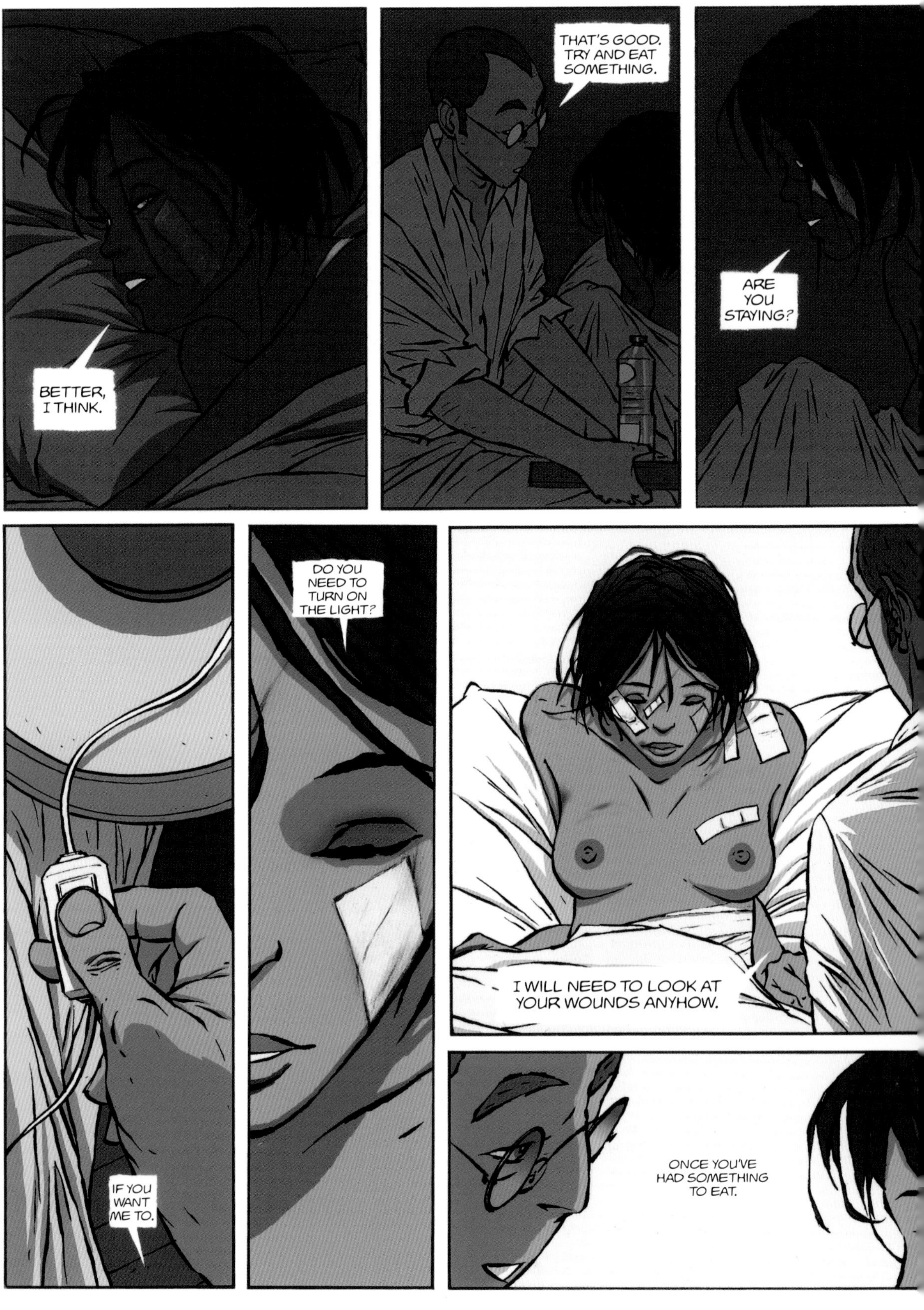
BETTER, I THINK.
THAT'S GOOD. TRY AND EAT SOMETHING.
ARE YOU STAYING?
IF YOU WANT ME TO.
DO YOU NEED TO TURN ON THE LIGHT?
I WILL NEED TO LOOK AT YOUR WOUNDS ANYHOW.
ONCE YOU'VE HAD SOMETHING TO EAT.

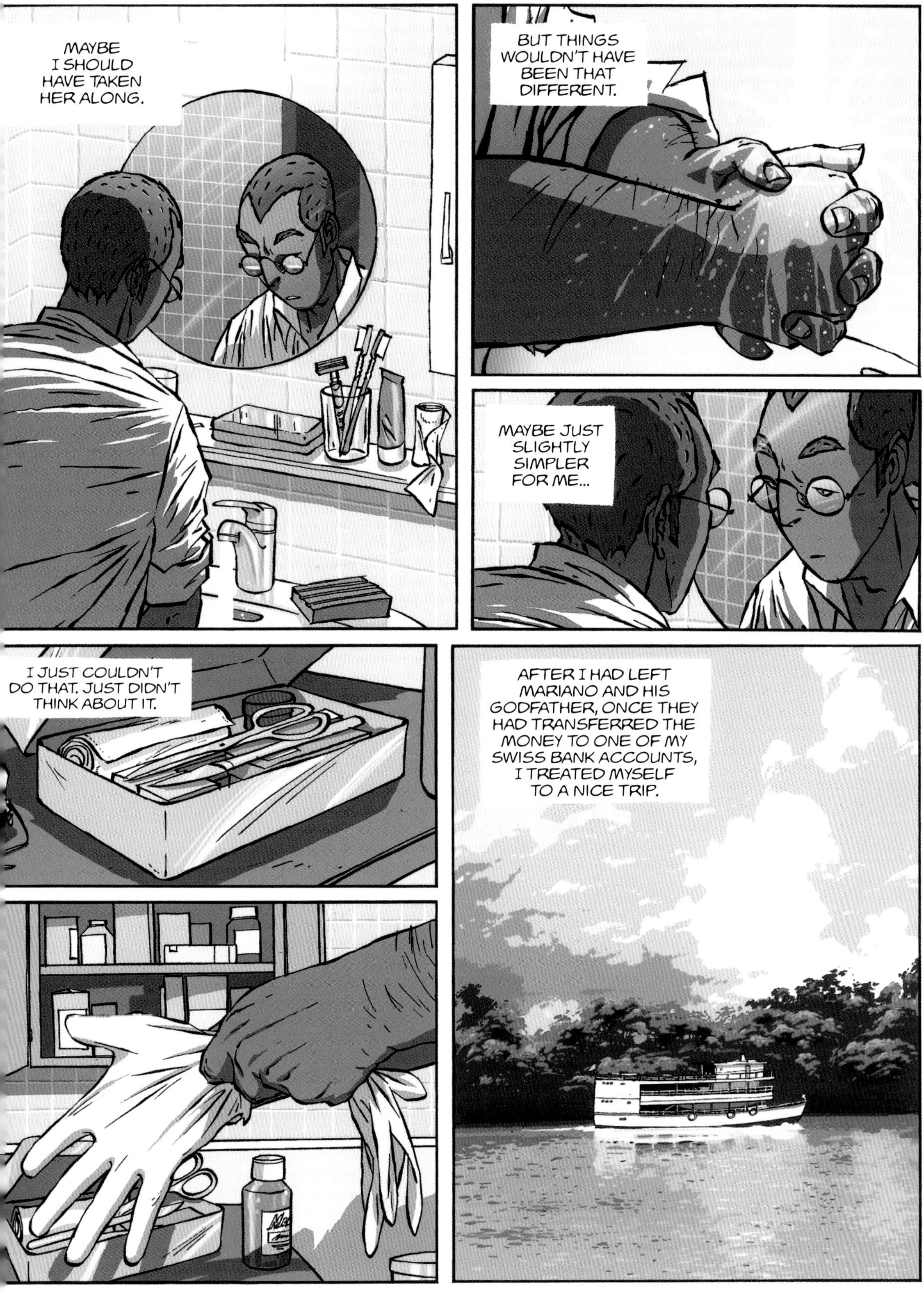
MAYBE I SHOULD HAVE TAKEN HER ALONG.
BUT THINGS WOULDN'T HAVE BEEN THAT DIFFERENT.
MAYBE JUST SLIGHTLY SIMPLER FOR ME...
I JUST COULDN'T DO THAT. JUST DIDN'T THINK ABOUT IT.
AFTER I HAD LEFT MARIANO AND HIS GODFATHER, ONCE THEY HAD TRANSFERRED THE MONEY TO ONE OF MY SWISS BANK ACCOUNTS, I TREATED MYSELF TO A NICE TRIP.

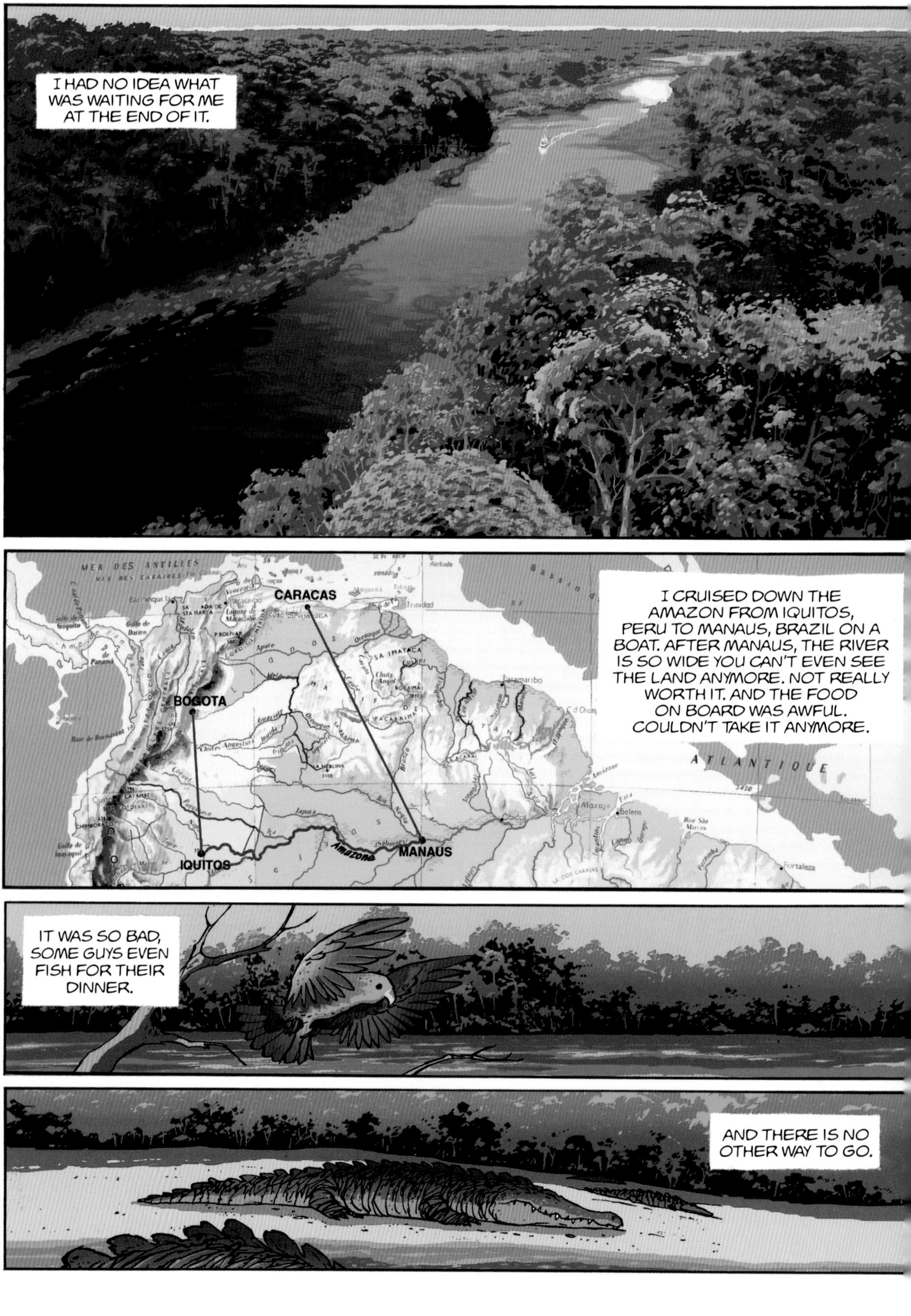
I HAD NO IDEA WHAT WAS WAITING FOR ME AT THE END OF IT.
MER DES ANTILLES
CARACAS
BOGOTA
IQUITOS
Amazone
MANAUS
ATLANTIQUE
I CRUISED DOWN THE AMAZON FROM IQUITOS, PERU TO MANAUS, BRAZIL ON A BOAT. AFTER MANAUS, THE RIVER IS SO WIDE YOU CAN'T EVEN SEE THE LAND ANYMORE. NOT REALLY WORTH IT. AND THE FOOD ON BOARD WAS AWFUL. COULDN'T TAKE IT ANYMORE.
IT WAS SO BAD, SOME GUYS EVEN FISH FOR THEIR DINNER.
AND THERE IS NO OTHER WAY TO GO.

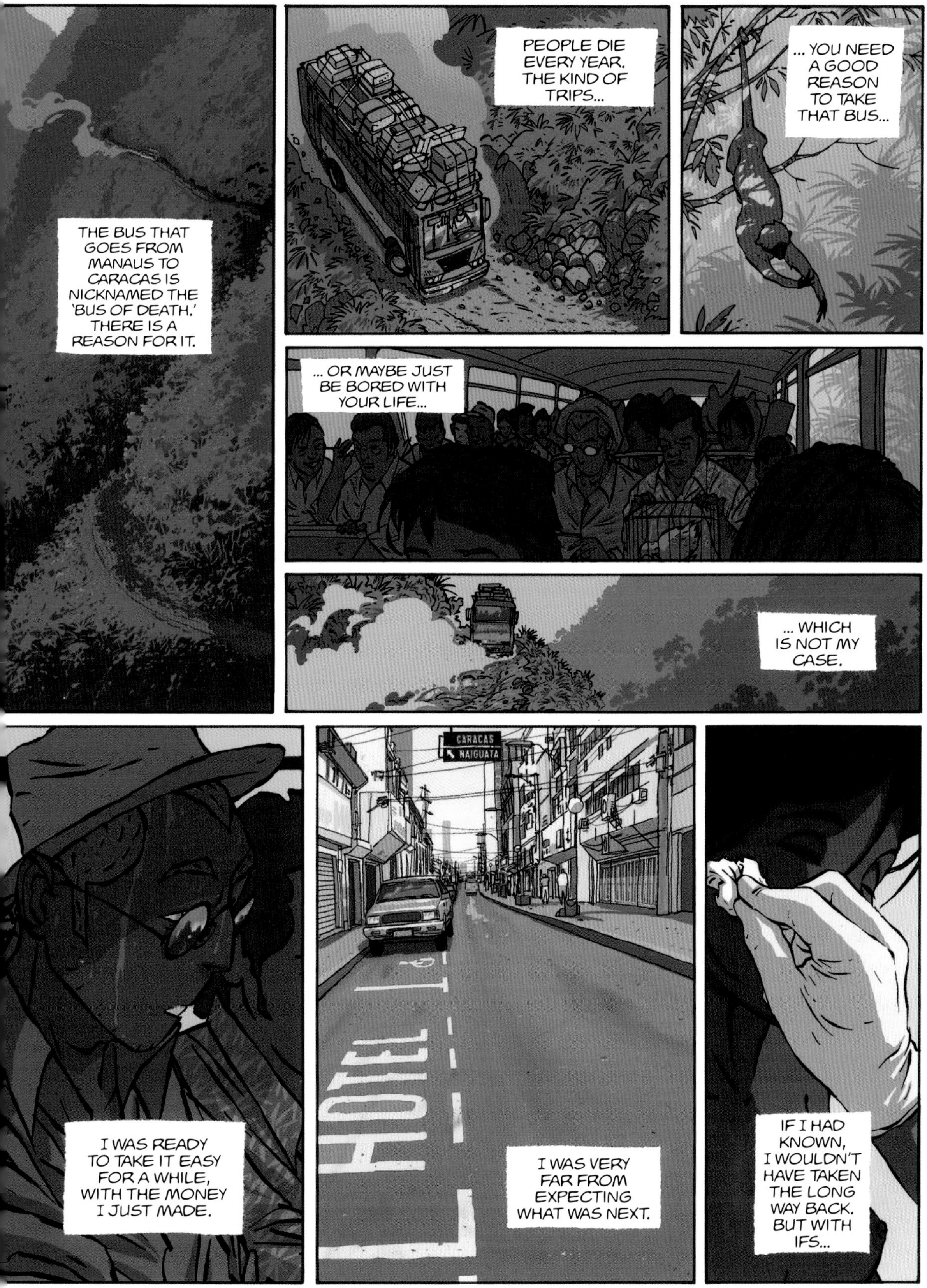
THE BUS THAT GOES FROM MANAUS TO CARACAS IS NICKNAMED THE 'BUS OF DEATH.' THERE IS A REASON FOR IT.
PEOPLE DIE EVERY YEAR. THE KIND OF TRIPS...
... YOU NEED A GOOD REASON TO TAKE THAT BUS...
... OR MAYBE JUST BE BORED WITH YOUR LIFE...
... WHICH IS NOT MY CASE.
I WAS READY TO TAKE IT EASY FOR A WHILE, WITH THE MONEY I JUST MADE.
CARACAS
NAIGUATA
HOTEL
I WAS VERY FAR FROM EXPECTING WHAT WAS NEXT.
IF I HAD KNOWN, I WOULDN'T HAVE TAKEN THE LONG WAY BACK. BUT WITH IFS...

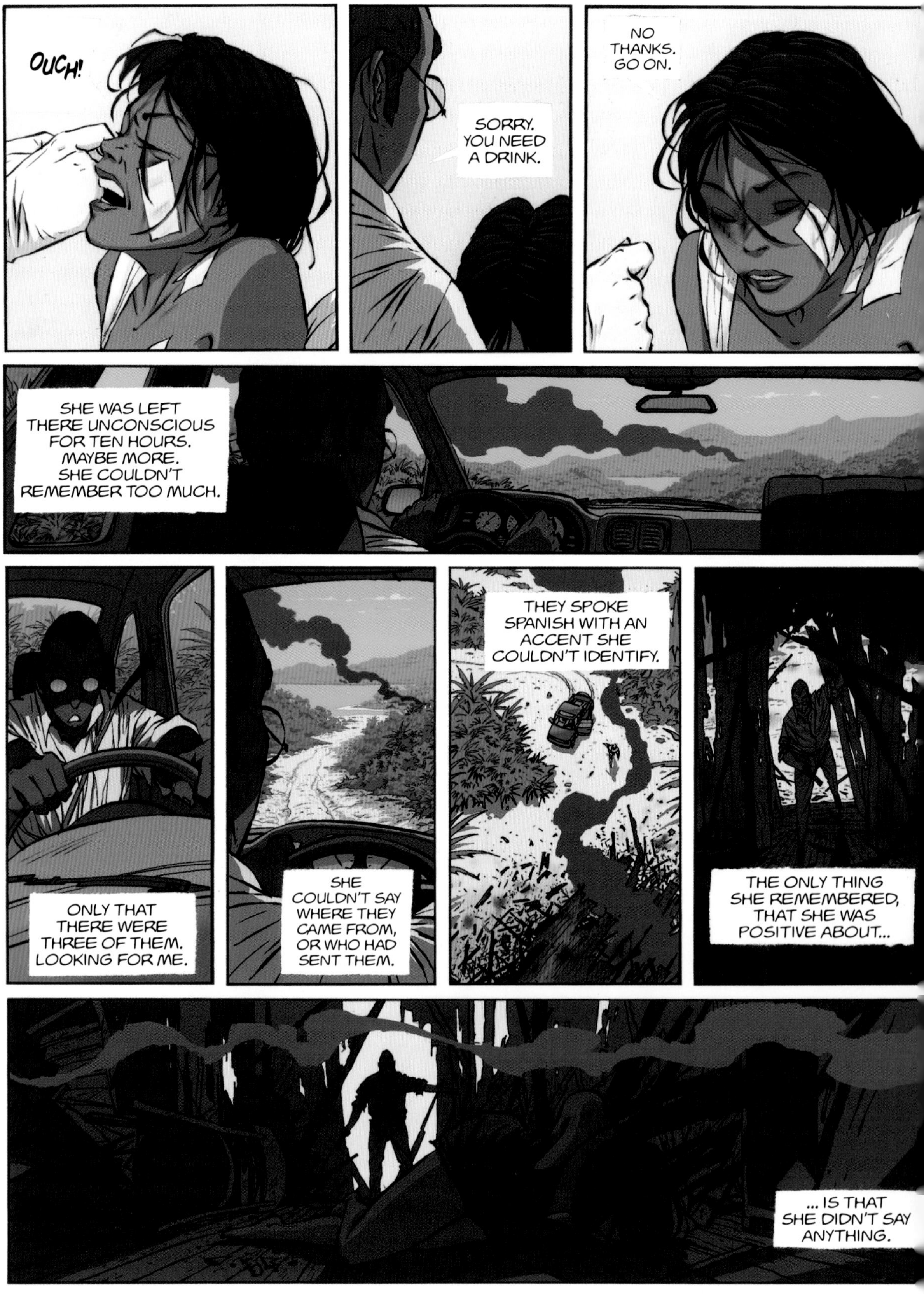
OUCH!
SORRY. YOU NEED A DRINK.
NO THANKS. GO ON.
SHE WAS LEFT THERE UNCONSCIOUS FOR TEN HOURS. MAYBE MORE. SHE COULDN'T REMEMBER TOO MUCH.
ONLY THAT THERE WERE THREE OF THEM. LOOKING FOR ME.
SHE COULDN'T SAY WHERE THEY CAME FROM, OR WHO HAD SENT THEM.
THEY SPOKE SPANISH WITH AN ACCENT SHE COULDN'T IDENTIFY.
THE ONLY THING SHE REMEMBERED, THAT SHE WAS POSITIVE ABOUT...
... IS THAT SHE DIDN'T SAY ANYTHING.

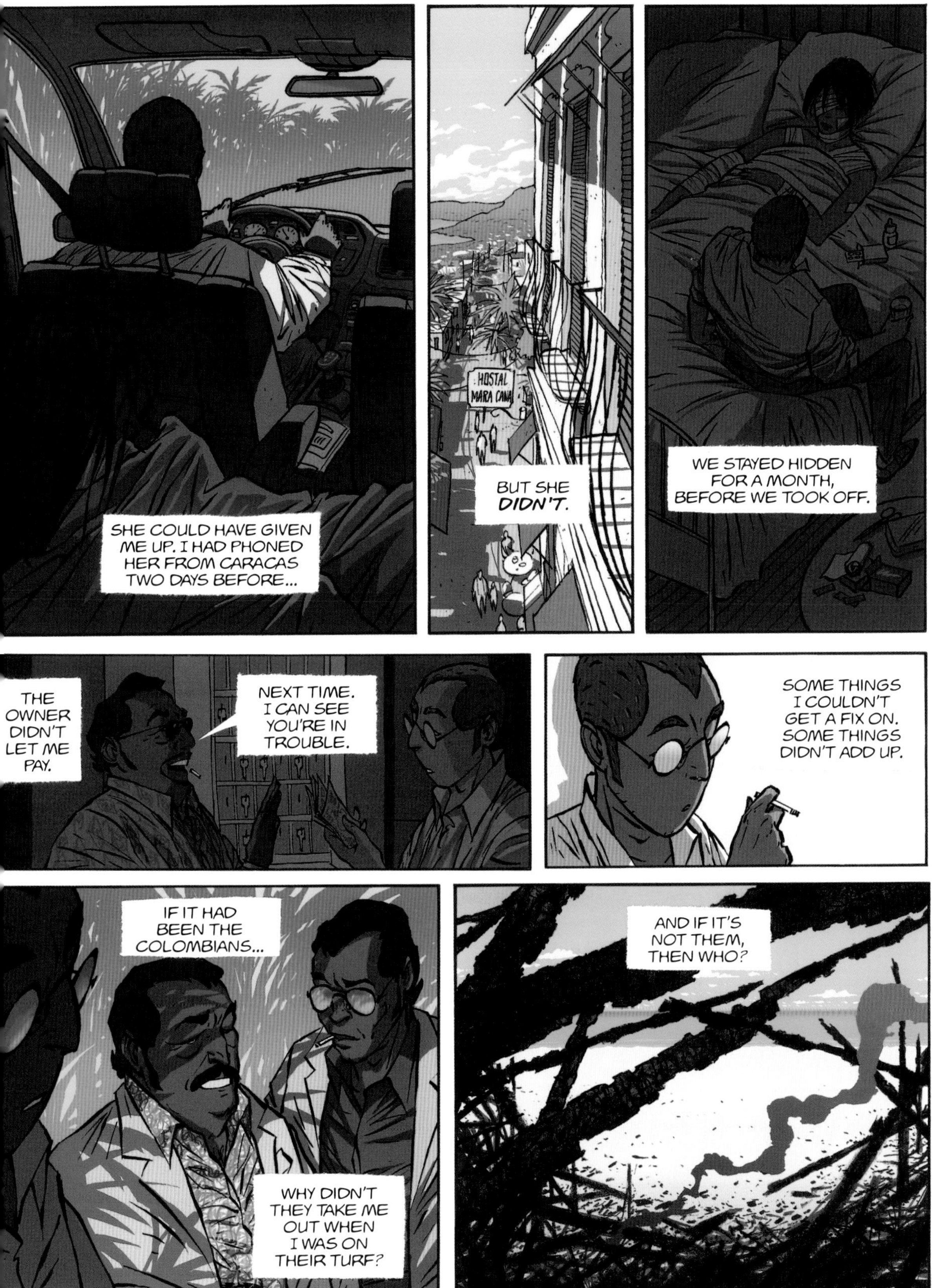
SHE COULD HAVE GIVEN ME UP. I HAD PHONED HER FROM CARACAS TWO DAYS BEFORE...
HOSTAL MARA CANA
BUT SHE ***DIDN'T***.
WE STAYED HIDDEN FOR A MONTH, BEFORE WE TOOK OFF.
THE OWNER DIDN'T LET ME PAY.
NEXT TIME. I CAN SEE YOU'RE IN TROUBLE.
SOME THINGS I COULDN'T GET A FIX ON. SOME THINGS DIDN'T ADD UP.
IF IT HAD BEEN THE COLOMBIANS...
WHY DIDN'T THEY TAKE ME OUT WHEN I WAS ON THEIR TURF?
AND IF IT'S NOT THEM, THEN WHO?

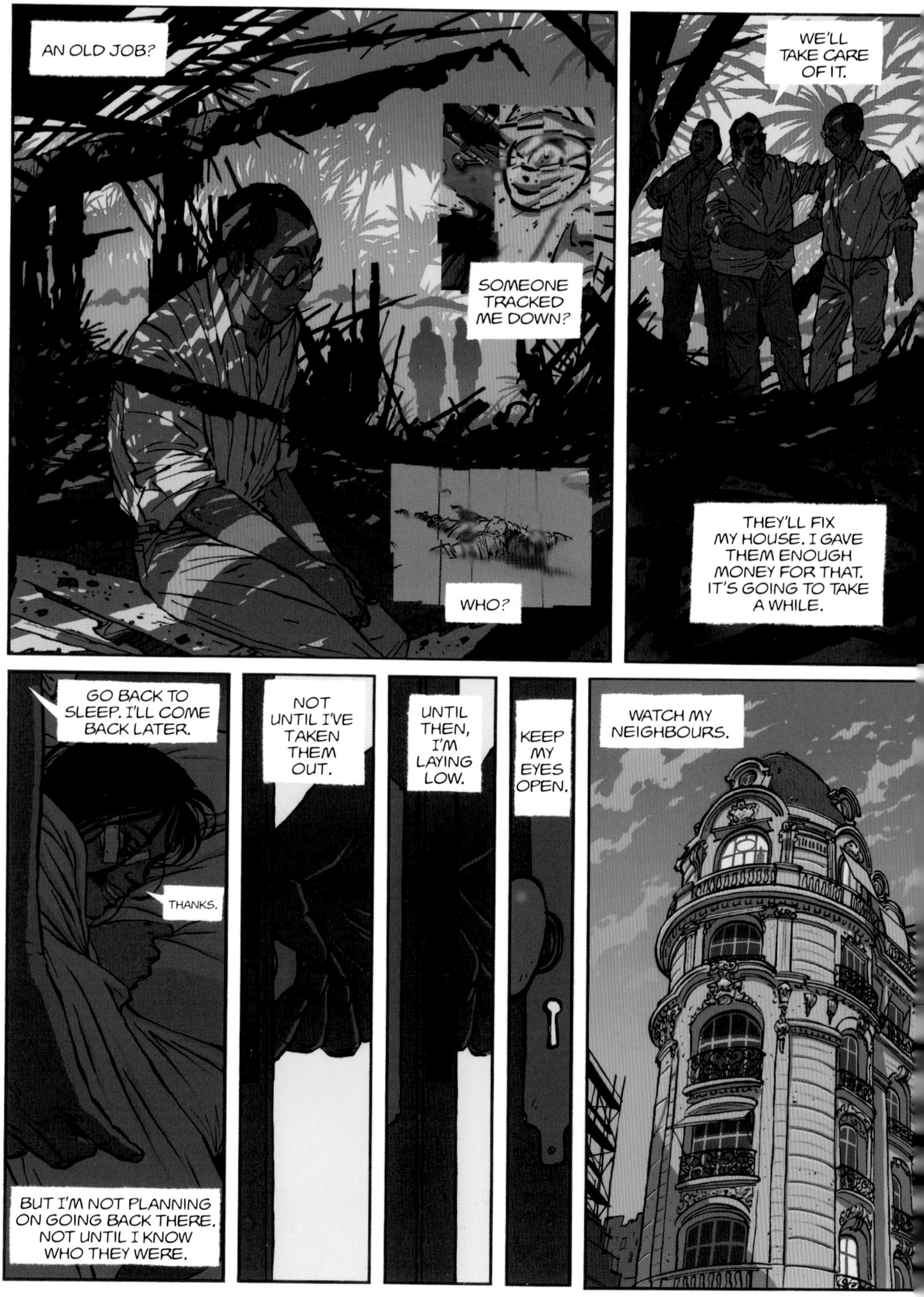
AN OLD JOB?
SOMEONE TRACKED ME DOWN?
WHO?
WE'LL TAKE CARE OF IT.
THEY'LL FIX MY HOUSE. I GAVE THEM ENOUGH MONEY FOR THAT. IT'S GOING TO TAKE A WHILE.
GO BACK TO SLEEP. I'LL COME BACK LATER.
THANKS.
BUT I'M NOT PLANNING ON GOING BACK THERE. NOT UNTIL I KNOW WHO THEY WERE.
NOT UNTIL I'VE TAKEN THEM OUT.
UNTIL THEN, I'M LAYING LOW.
KEEP MY EYES OPEN.
WATCH MY NEIGHBOURS.

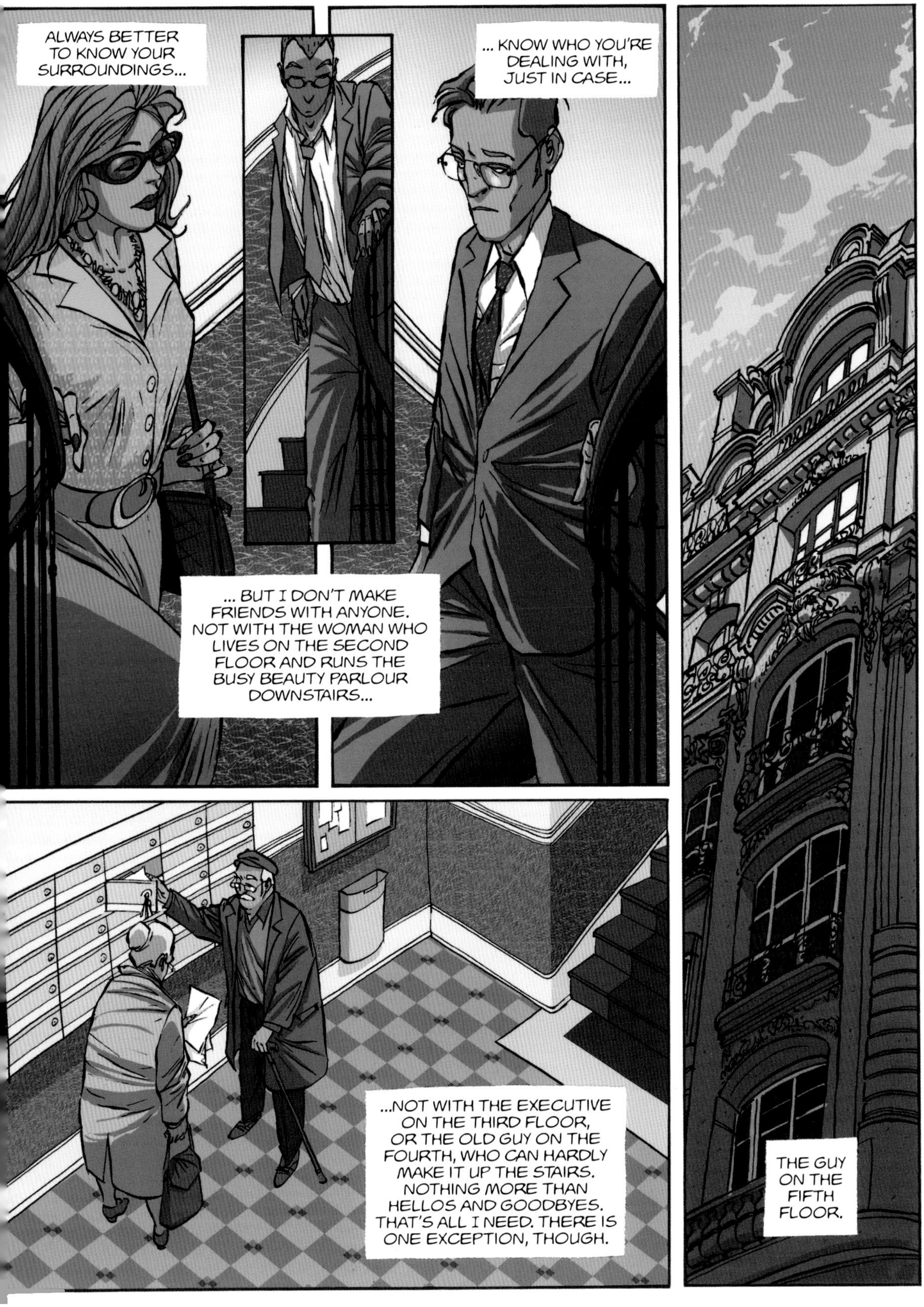
ALWAYS BETTER TO KNOW YOUR SURROUNDINGS...
... KNOW WHO YOU'RE DEALING WITH, JUST IN CASE...
... BUT I DON'T MAKE FRIENDS WITH ANYONE. NOT WITH THE WOMAN WHO LIVES ON THE SECOND FLOOR AND RUNS THE BUSY BEAUTY PARLOUR DOWNSTAIRS...
...NOT WITH THE EXECUTIVE ON THE THIRD FLOOR, OR THE OLD GUY ON THE FOURTH, WHO CAN HARDLY MAKE IT UP THE STAIRS. NOTHING MORE THAN HELLOS AND GOODBYES. THAT'S ALL I NEED. THERE IS ONE EXCEPTION, THOUGH.
THE GUY ON THE FIFTH FLOOR.

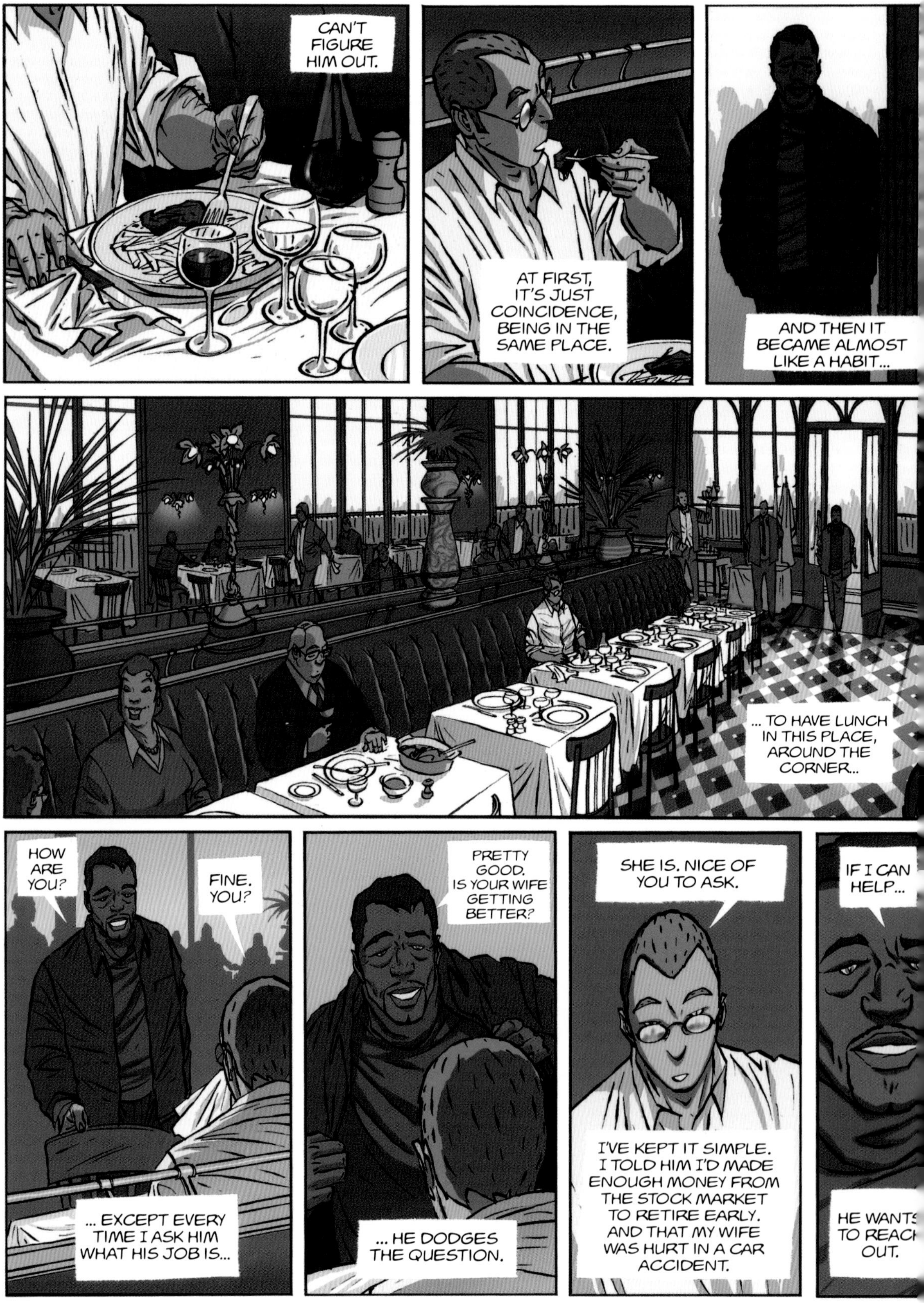
CAN'T FIGURE HIM OUT.
AT FIRST, IT'S JUST COINCIDENCE, BEING IN THE SAME PLACE.
AND THEN IT BECAME ALMOST LIKE A HABIT...
... TO HAVE LUNCH IN THIS PLACE, AROUND THE CORNER...
HOW ARE YOU?
FINE. YOU?
... EXCEPT EVERY TIME I ASK HIM WHAT HIS JOB IS...
PRETTY GOOD. IS YOUR WIFE GETTING BETTER?
... HE DODGES THE QUESTION.
SHE IS. NICE OF YOU TO ASK.
I'VE KEPT IT SIMPLE. I TOLD HIM I'D MADE ENOUGH MONEY FROM THE STOCK MARKET TO RETIRE EARLY. AND THAT MY WIFE WAS HURT IN A CAR ACCIDENT.
IF I CAN HELP...
HE WANTS TO REACH OUT.

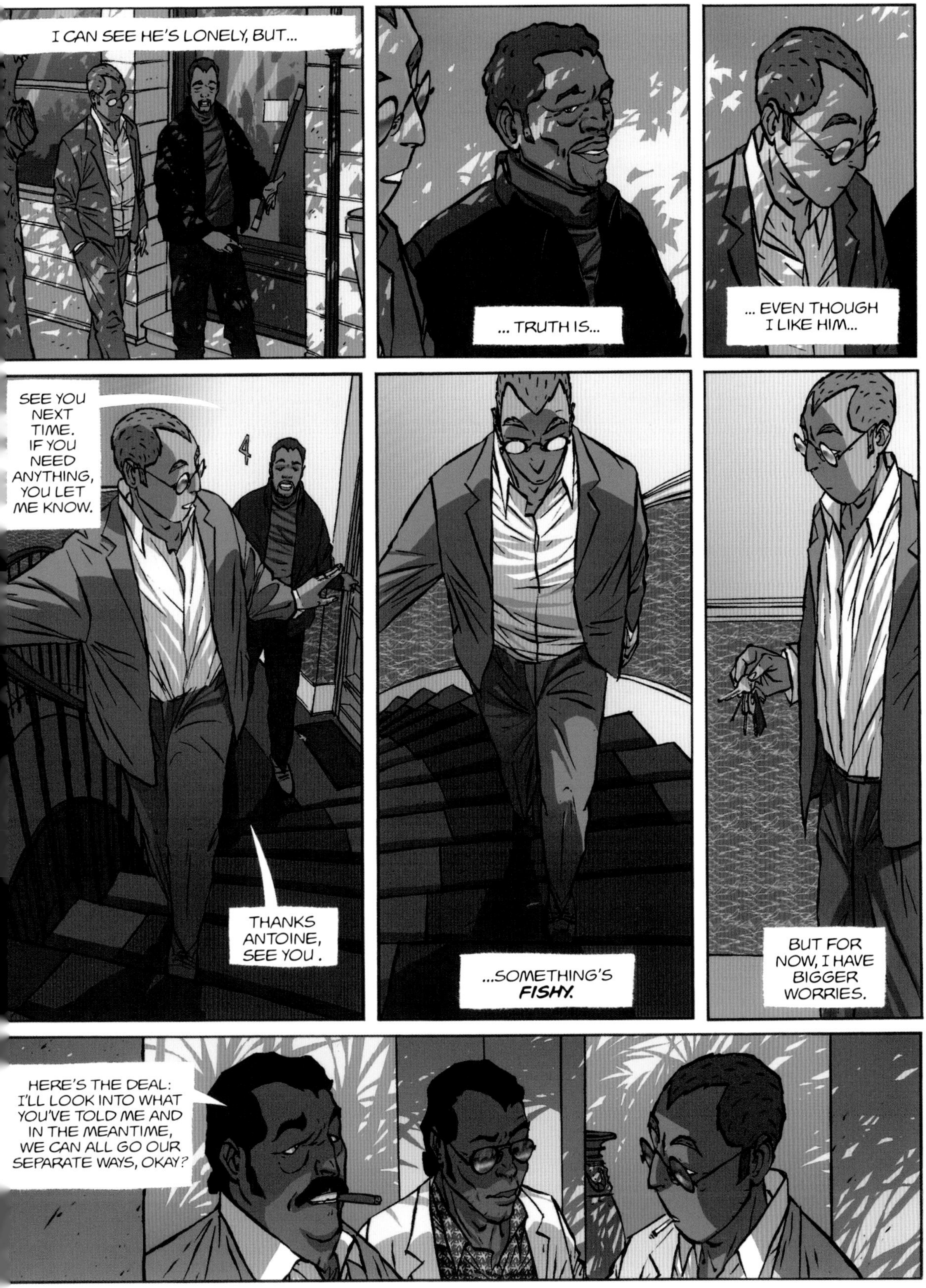
I CAN SEE HE'S LONELY, BUT...
... TRUTH IS...
... EVEN THOUGH I LIKE HIM...
SEE YOU NEXT TIME. IF YOU NEED ANYTHING, YOU LET ME KNOW.
THANKS ANTOINE, SEE YOU .
...SOMETHING'S *FISHY.*
BUT FOR NOW, I HAVE BIGGER WORRIES.
HERE'S THE DEAL: I'LL LOOK INTO WHAT YOU'VE TOLD ME AND IN THE MEANTIME, WE CAN ALL GO OUR SEPARATE WAYS, OKAY?

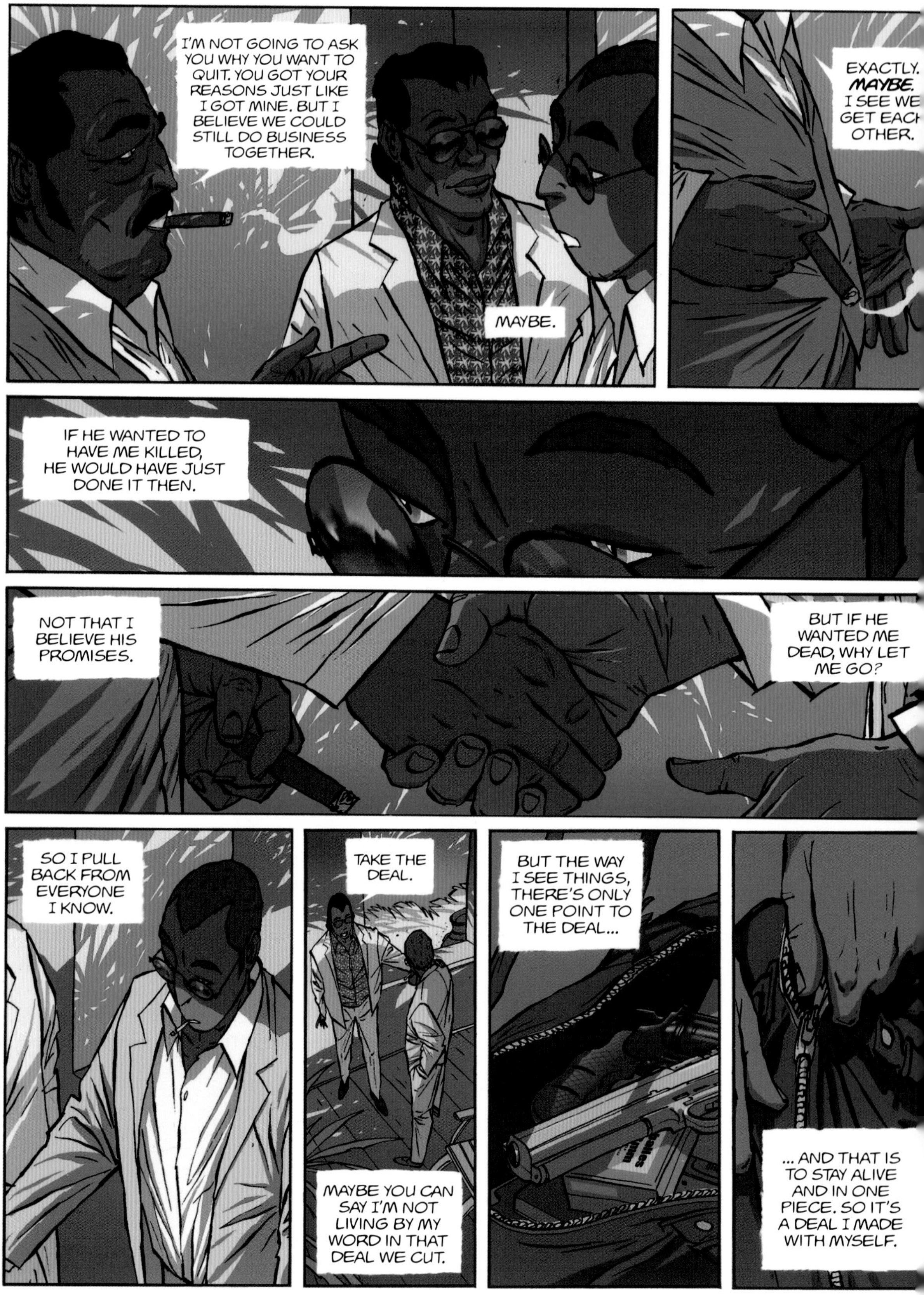
I'M NOT GOING TO ASK YOU WHY YOU WANT TO QUIT. YOU GOT YOUR REASONS JUST LIKE I GOT MINE. BUT I BELIEVE WE COULD STILL DO BUSINESS TOGETHER.
MAYBE.
EXACTLY. ***MAYBE.*** I SEE WE GET EACH OTHER.
IF HE WANTED TO HAVE ME KILLED, HE WOULD HAVE JUST DONE IT THEN.
NOT THAT I BELIEVE HIS PROMISES.
BUT IF HE WANTED ME DEAD, WHY LET ME GO?
SO I PULL BACK FROM EVERYONE I KNOW.
TAKE THE DEAL.
MAYBE YOU CAN SAY I'M NOT LIVING BY MY WORD IN THAT DEAL WE CUT.
BUT THE WAY I SEE THINGS, THERE'S ONLY ONE POINT TO THE DEAL...
...AND THAT IS TO STAY ALIVE AND IN ONE PIECE. SO IT'S A DEAL I MADE WITH MYSELF.

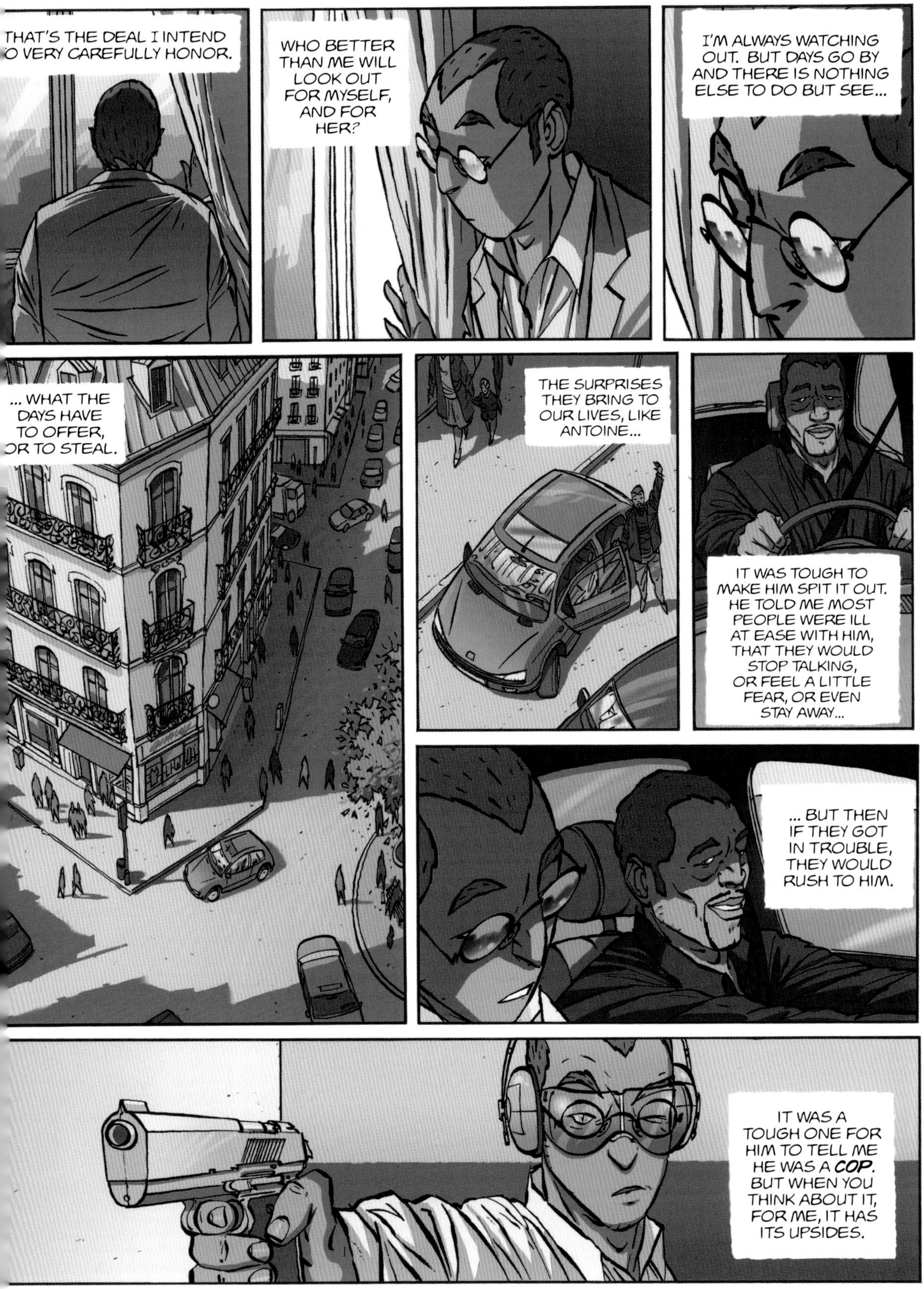
THAT'S THE DEAL I INTEND
O VERY CAREFULLY HONOR.
WHO BETTER THAN ME WILL LOOK OUT FOR MYSELF, AND FOR HER?
I'M ALWAYS WATCHING OUT. BUT DAYS GO BY AND THERE IS NOTHING ELSE TO DO BUT SEE...
... WHAT THE DAYS HAVE TO OFFER, OR TO STEAL.
THE SURPRISES THEY BRING TO OUR LIVES, LIKE ANTOINE...
IT WAS TOUGH TO MAKE HIM SPIT IT OUT. HE TOLD ME MOST PEOPLE WERE ILL AT EASE WITH HIM, THAT THEY WOULD STOP TALKING, OR FEEL A LITTLE FEAR, OR EVEN STAY AWAY...
... BUT THEN IF THEY GOT IN TROUBLE, THEY WOULD RUSH TO HIM.
IT WAS A TOUGH ONE FOR HIM TO TELL ME HE WAS A **COP**. BUT WHEN YOU THINK ABOUT IT, FOR ME, IT HAS ITS UPSIDES.

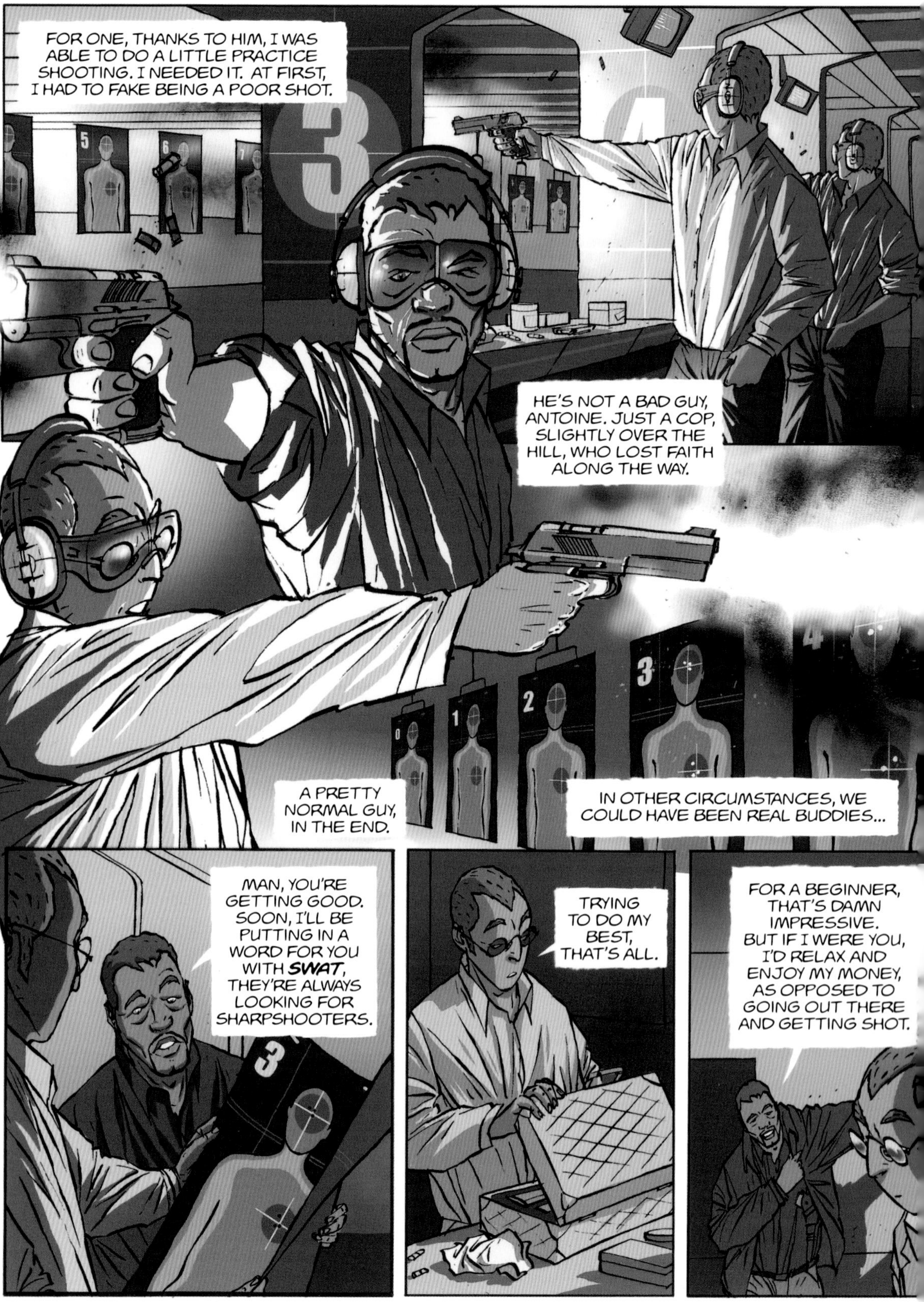
FOR ONE, THANKS TO HIM, I WAS ABLE TO DO A LITTLE PRACTICE SHOOTING. I NEEDED IT. AT FIRST, I HAD TO FAKE BEING A POOR SHOT.
HE'S NOT A BAD GUY, ANTOINE. JUST A COP, SLIGHTLY OVER THE HILL, WHO LOST FAITH ALONG THE WAY.
A PRETTY NORMAL GUY, IN THE END.
IN OTHER CIRCUMSTANCES, WE COULD HAVE BEEN REAL BUDDIES...
MAN, YOU'RE GETTING GOOD. SOON, I'LL BE PUTTING IN A WORD FOR YOU WITH SWAT, THEY'RE ALWAYS LOOKING FOR SHARPSHOOTERS.
TRYING TO DO MY BEST, THAT'S ALL.
FOR A BEGINNER, THAT'S DAMN IMPRESSIVE. BUT IF I WERE YOU, I'D RELAX AND ENJOY MY MONEY, AS OPPOSED TO GOING OUT THERE AND GETTING SHOT.

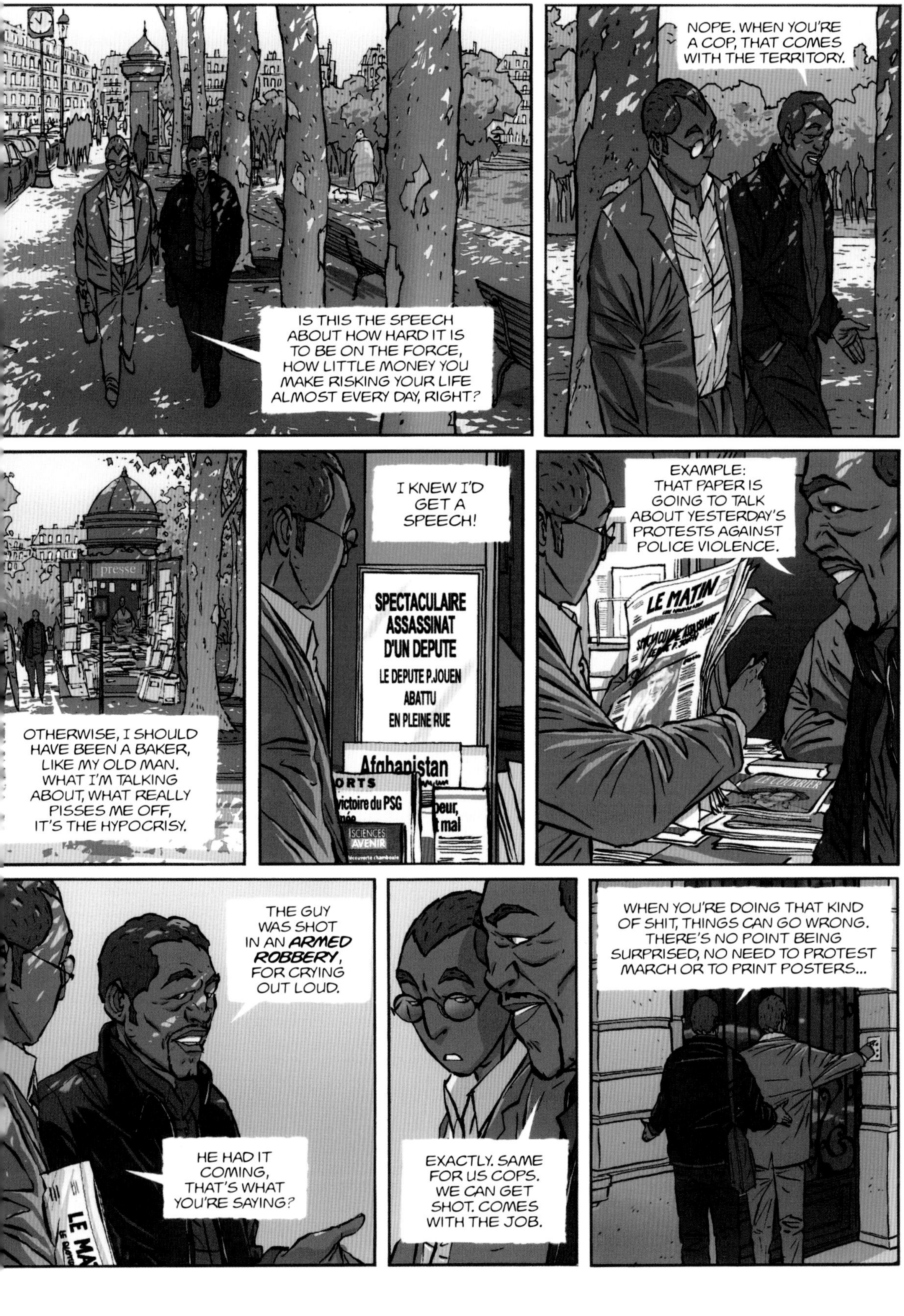
IS THIS THE SPEECH ABOUT HOW HARD IT IS TO BE ON THE FORCE, HOW LITTLE MONEY YOU MAKE RISKING YOUR LIFE ALMOST EVERY DAY, RIGHT?
NOPE. WHEN YOU'RE A COP, THAT COMES WITH THE TERRITORY.
presse
OTHERWISE, I SHOULD HAVE BEEN A BAKER, LIKE MY OLD MAN. WHAT I'M TALKING ABOUT, WHAT REALLY PISSES ME OFF, IT'S THE HYPOCRISY.
I KNEW I'D GET A SPEECH!
SPECTACULAIRE ASSASSINAT D'UN DEPUTE
LE DEPUTE P.JOUEN ABATTU EN PLEINE RUE
Afghanistan
victoire du PSG
SCIENCES AVENIR
EXAMPLE: THAT PAPER IS GOING TO TALK ABOUT YESTERDAY'S PROTESTS AGAINST POLICE VIOLENCE.
LE MATIN
LE COURRIER
THE GUY WAS SHOT IN AN ***ARMED ROBBERY***, FOR CRYING OUT LOUD.
HE HAD IT COMING, THAT'S WHAT YOU'RE SAYING?
EXACTLY. SAME FOR US COPS. WE CAN GET SHOT. COMES WITH THE JOB.
WHEN YOU'RE DOING THAT KIND OF SHIT, THINGS CAN GO WRONG. THERE'S NO POINT BEING SURPRISED, NO NEED TO PROTEST MARCH OR TO PRINT POSTERS...

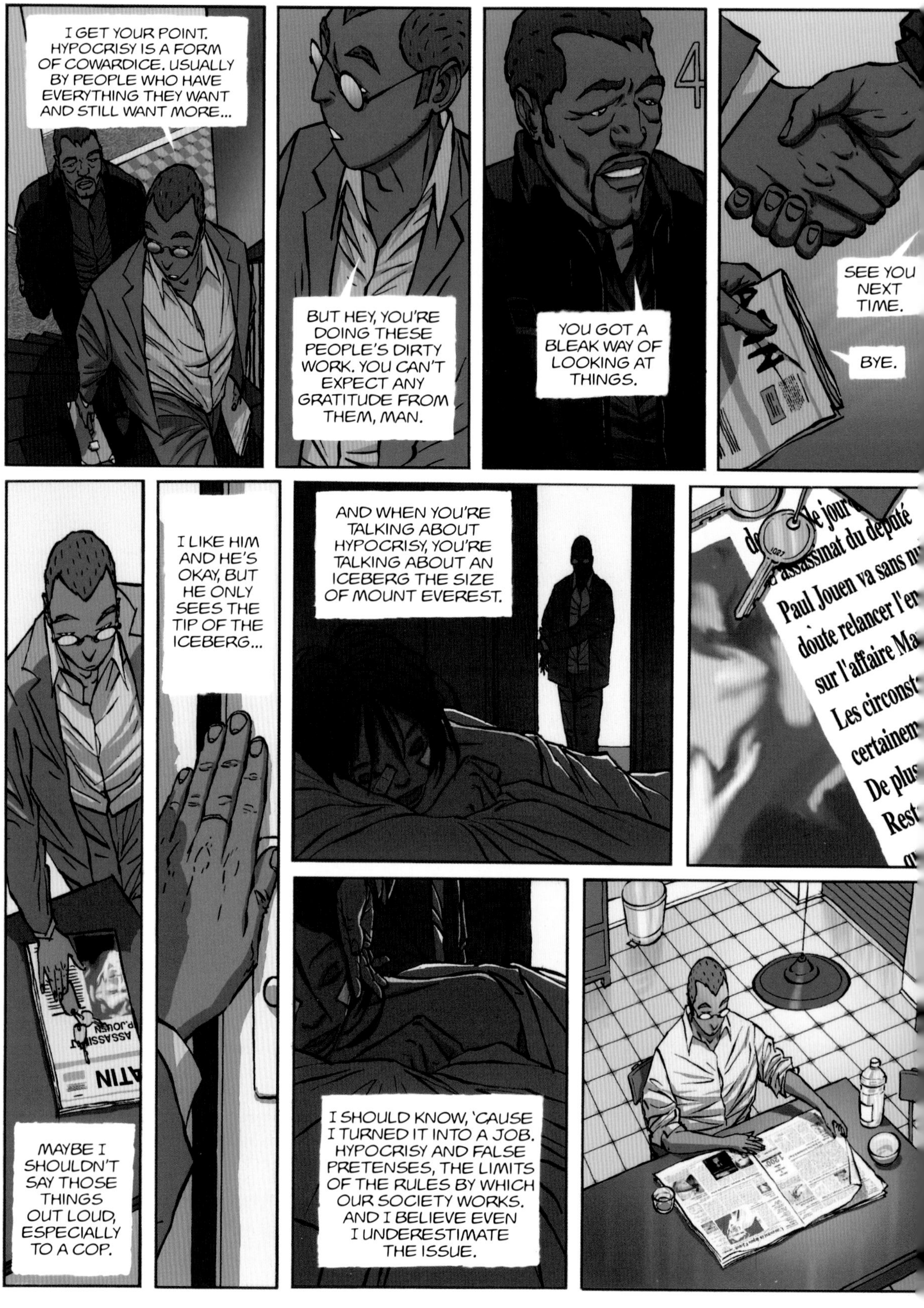
I GET YOUR POINT. HYPOCRISY IS A FORM OF COWARDICE. USUALLY BY PEOPLE WHO HAVE EVERYTHING THEY WANT AND STILL WANT MORE...
BUT HEY, YOU'RE DOING THESE PEOPLE'S DIRTY WORK. YOU CAN'T EXPECT ANY GRATITUDE FROM THEM, MAN.
4
YOU GOT A BLEAK WAY OF LOOKING AT THINGS.
SEE YOU NEXT TIME.
BYE.
I LIKE HIM AND HE'S OKAY, BUT HE ONLY SEES THE TIP OF THE ICEBERG...
MAYBE I SHOULDN'T SAY THOSE THINGS OUT LOUD, ESPECIALLY TO A COP.
AND WHEN YOU'RE TALKING ABOUT HYPOCRISY, YOU'RE TALKING ABOUT AN ICEBERG THE SIZE OF MOUNT EVEREST.
assassinat du député
Paul Jouen va sans
doute relancer
sur l'affaire
Les circonst
De plus
I SHOULD KNOW, 'CAUSE I TURNED IT INTO A JOB. HYPOCRISY AND FALSE PRETENSES, THE LIMITS OF THE RULES BY WHICH OUR SOCIETY WORKS. AND I BELIEVE EVEN I UNDERESTIMATE THE ISSUE.

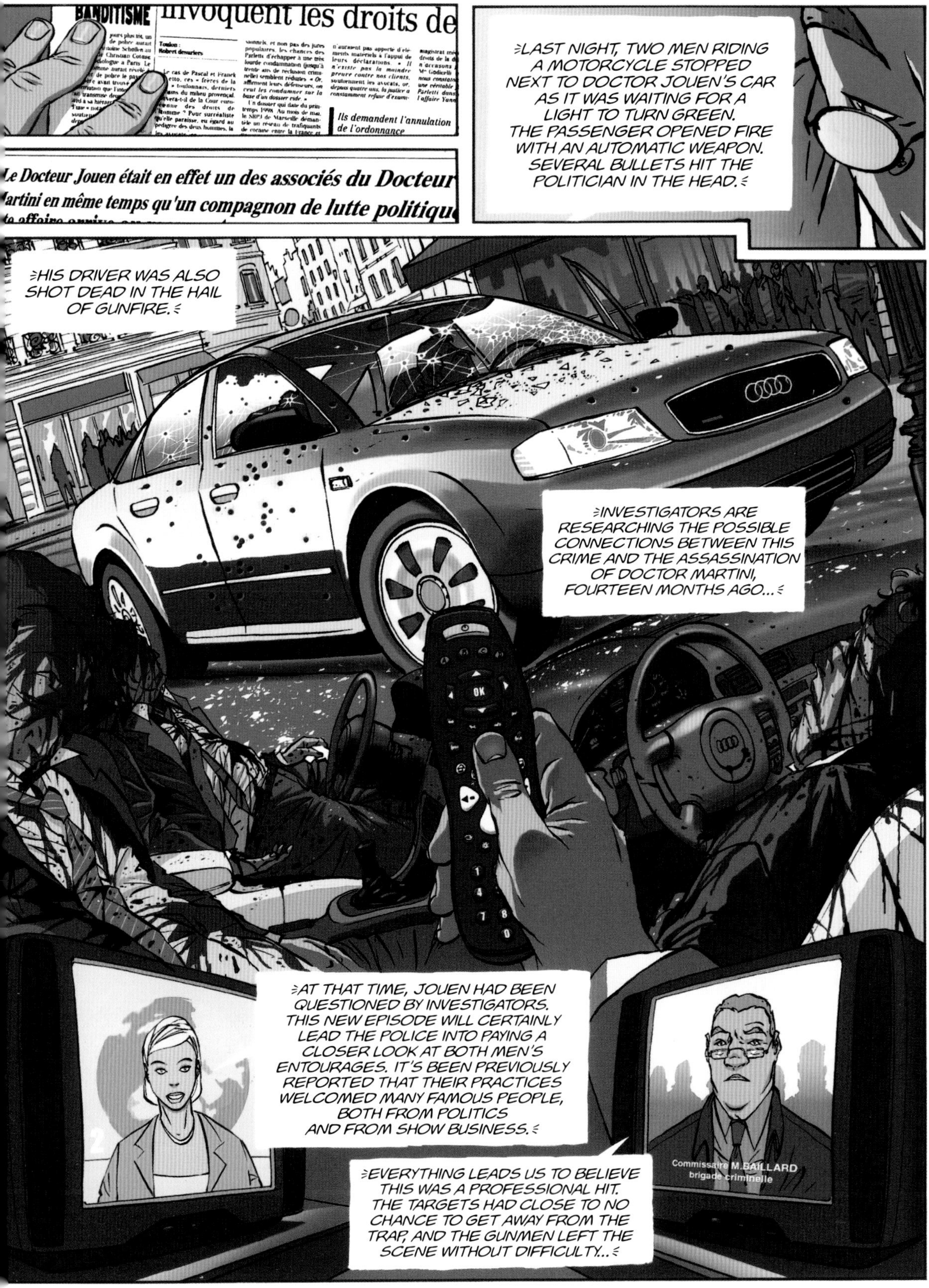
BANDITISME
invoquent les droits de
Ils demandent l'annulation de l'ordonnance
Le Docteur Jouen était en effet un des associés du Docteur
artini en même temps qu'un compagnon de lutte politiqu
LAST NIGHT, TWO MEN RIDING A MOTORCYCLE STOPPED NEXT TO DOCTOR JOUEN'S CAR AS IT WAS WAITING FOR A LIGHT TO TURN GREEN. THE PASSENGER OPENED FIRE WITH AN AUTOMATIC WEAPON. SEVERAL BULLETS HIT THE POLITICIAN IN THE HEAD.
HIS DRIVER WAS ALSO SHOT DEAD IN THE HAIL OF GUNFIRE.
INVESTIGATORS ARE RESEARCHING THE POSSIBLE CONNECTIONS BETWEEN THIS CRIME AND THE ASSASSINATION OF DOCTOR MARTINI, FOURTEEN MONTHS AGO...
AT THAT TIME, JOUEN HAD BEEN QUESTIONED BY INVESTIGATORS. THIS NEW EPISODE WILL CERTAINLY LEAD THE POLICE INTO PAYING A CLOSER LOOK AT BOTH MEN'S ENTOURAGES. IT'S BEEN PREVIOUSLY REPORTED THAT THEIR PRACTICES WELCOMED MANY FAMOUS PEOPLE, BOTH FROM POLITICS AND FROM SHOW BUSINESS.
Commissaire M.BAILLARD
brigade criminelle
EVERYTHING LEADS US TO BELIEVE THIS WAS A PROFESSIONAL HIT. THE TARGETS HAD CLOSE TO NO CHANCE TO GET AWAY FROM THE TRAP, AND THE GUNMEN LEFT THE SCENE WITHOUT DIFFICULTY...

=THE PRESIDENT OF THE PARLIAMENT DECLARED THAT "THE ENTIRE COUNTRY WAS TARGETED BY THIS CRIME," AND ASKED THE DECEASED'S COLLEAGUES TO OBSERVE A MINUTE OF SILENCE.=

= SEVERAL POLITICIANS NOTED THAT THIS WAS ONLY THE THIRD TIME SINCE WORLD WAR TWO THAT ONE OF THEM...=

A KEY THING THAT I'VE LEARNED DOING THIS JOB...

... NEVER BELIEVE IN COINCID- ENCES.

NEVER.

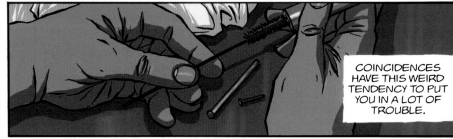

COINCIDENCES HAVE THIS WEIRD TENDENCY TO PUT YOU IN A LOT OF TROUBLE.

SO IF YOU FIND ONE, YOU EITHER HAVE TO RUN AWAY FROM IT, OR TAKE IT OUT.

BAD NEWS?

I DON'T KNOW. YOU SHOULD GO BACK TO BED.

COME WITH ME.

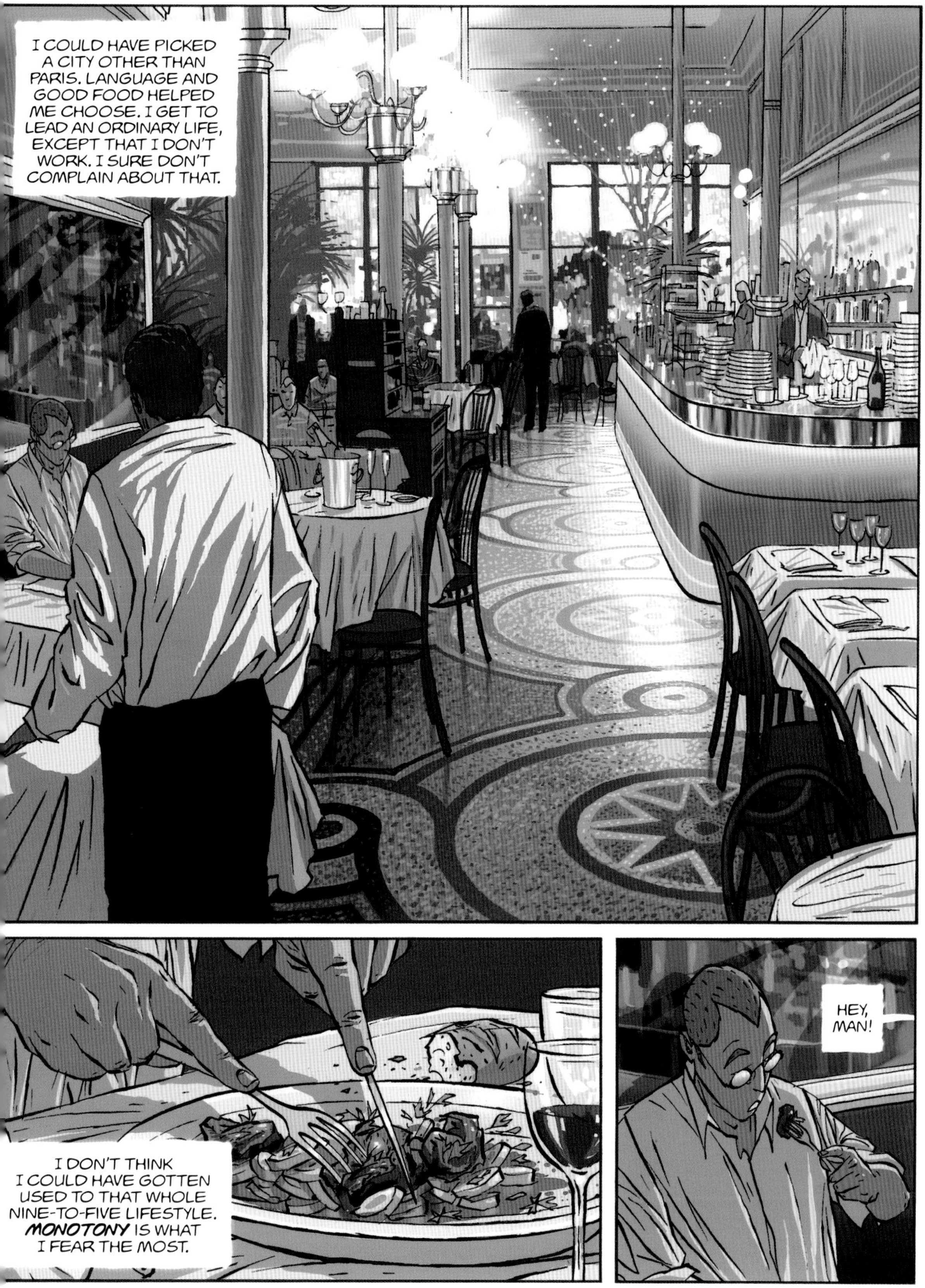
I COULD HAVE PICKED A CITY OTHER THAN PARIS. LANGUAGE AND GOOD FOOD HELPED ME CHOOSE. I GET TO LEAD AN ORDINARY LIFE, EXCEPT THAT I DON'T WORK. I SURE DON'T COMPLAIN ABOUT THAT.
I DON'T THINK I COULD HAVE GOTTEN USED TO THAT WHOLE NINE-TO-FIVE LIFESTYLE. **MONOTONY** IS WHAT I FEAR THE MOST.
HEY, MAN!

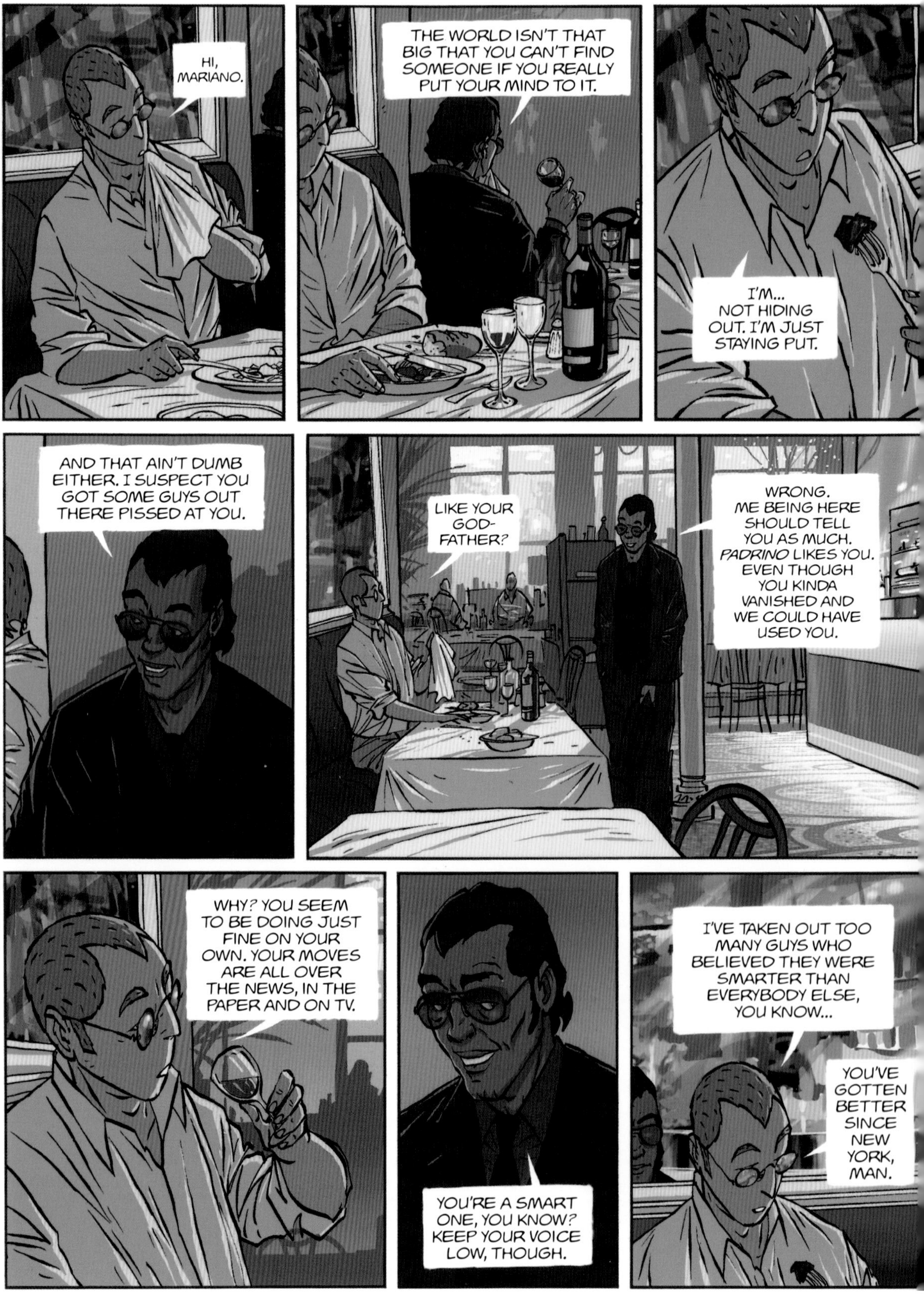
HI, MARIANO.
THE WORLD ISN'T THAT BIG THAT YOU CAN'T FIND SOMEONE IF YOU REALLY PUT YOUR MIND TO IT.
I'M... NOT HIDING OUT. I'M JUST STAYING PUT.
AND THAT AIN'T DUMB EITHER. I SUSPECT YOU GOT SOME GUYS OUT THERE PISSED AT YOU.
LIKE YOUR GOD-FATHER?
WRONG. ME BEING HERE SHOULD TELL YOU AS MUCH. *PADRINO* LIKES YOU. EVEN THOUGH YOU KINDA VANISHED AND WE COULD HAVE USED YOU.
WHY? YOU SEEM TO BE DOING JUST FINE ON YOUR OWN. YOUR MOVES ARE ALL OVER THE NEWS, IN THE PAPER AND ON TV.
YOU'RE A SMART ONE, YOU KNOW? KEEP YOUR VOICE LOW, THOUGH.
I'VE TAKEN OUT TOO MANY GUYS WHO BELIEVED THEY WERE SMARTER THAN EVERYBODY ELSE, YOU KNOW...
YOU'VE GOTTEN BETTER SINCE NEW YORK, MAN.

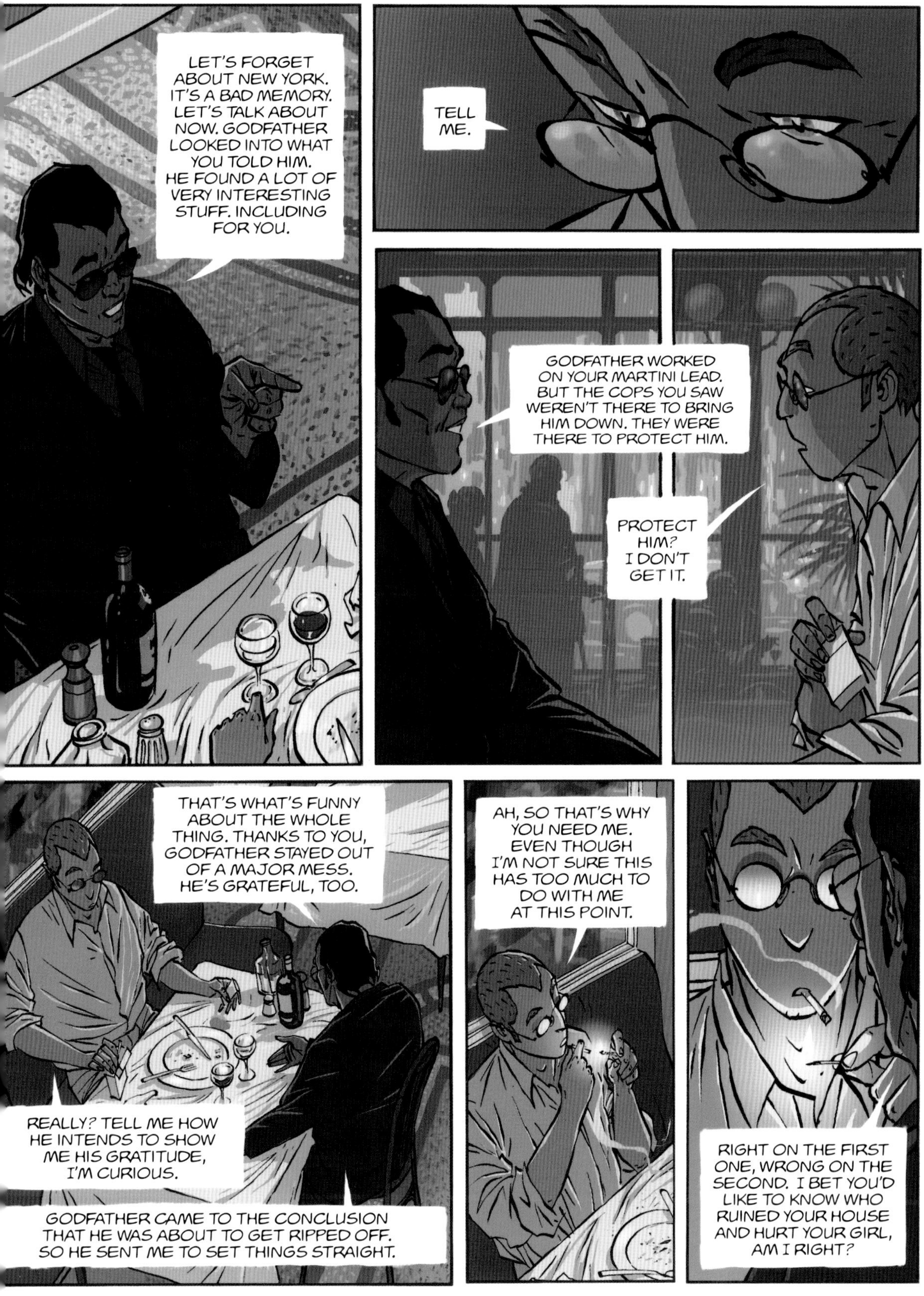
LET'S FORGET ABOUT NEW YORK. IT'S A BAD MEMORY. LET'S TALK ABOUT NOW. GODFATHER LOOKED INTO WHAT YOU TOLD HIM. HE FOUND A LOT OF VERY INTERESTING STUFF. INCLUDING FOR YOU.
TELL ME.
GODFATHER WORKED ON YOUR MARTINI LEAD. BUT THE COPS YOU SAW WEREN'T THERE TO BRING HIM DOWN. THEY WERE THERE TO PROTECT HIM.
PROTECT HIM? I DON'T GET IT.
THAT'S WHAT'S FUNNY ABOUT THE WHOLE THING. THANKS TO YOU, GODFATHER STAYED OUT OF A MAJOR MESS. HE'S GRATEFUL, TOO.
REALLY? TELL ME HOW HE INTENDS TO SHOW ME HIS GRATITUDE, I'M CURIOUS.
GODFATHER CAME TO THE CONCLUSION THAT HE WAS ABOUT TO GET RIPPED OFF. SO HE SENT ME TO SET THINGS STRAIGHT.
AH, SO THAT'S WHY YOU NEED ME. EVEN THOUGH I'M NOT SURE THIS HAS TOO MUCH TO DO WITH ME AT THIS POINT.
RIGHT ON THE FIRST ONE, WRONG ON THE SECOND. I BET YOU'D LIKE TO KNOW WHO RUINED YOUR HOUSE AND HURT YOUR GIRL, AM I RIGHT?

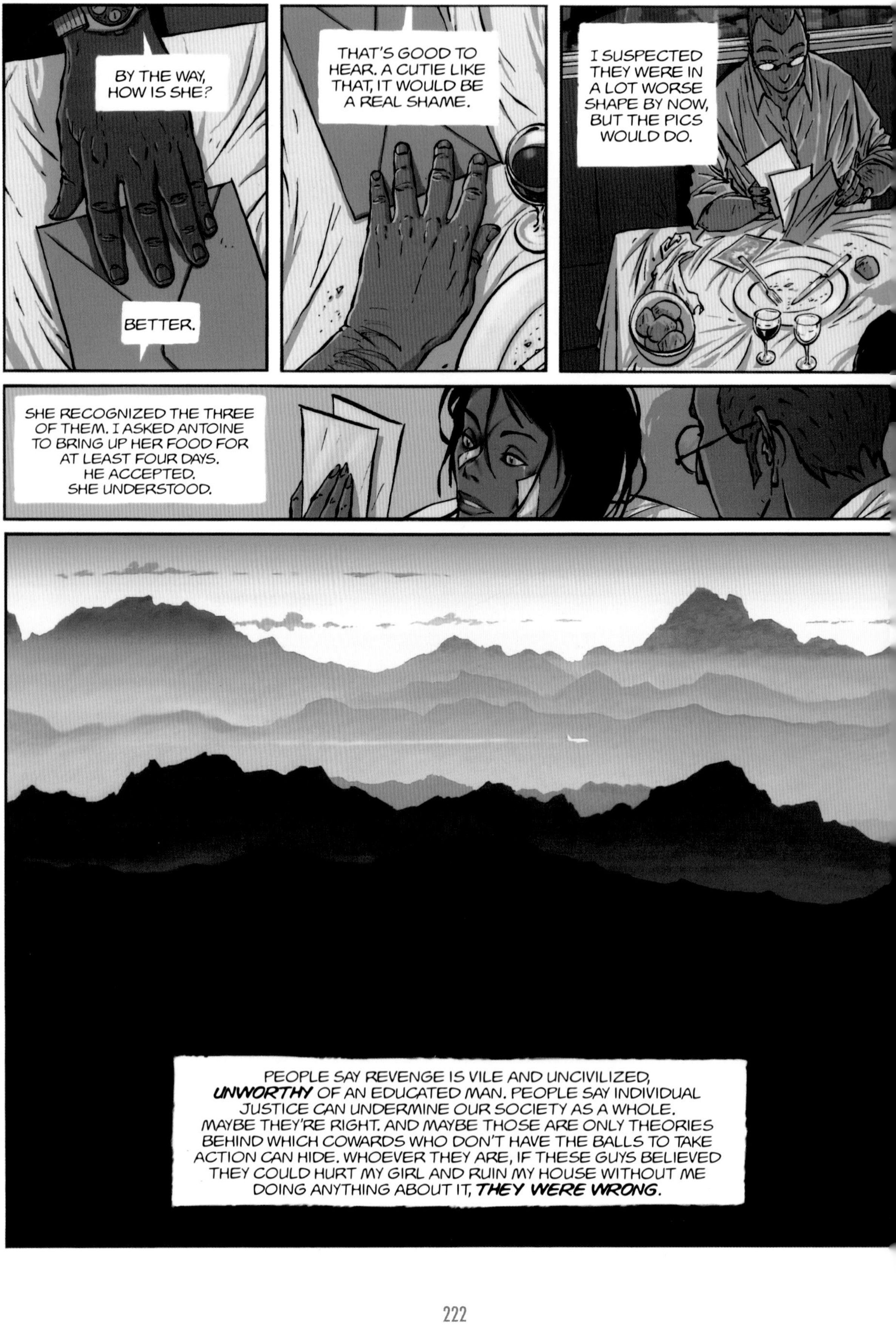
BY THE WAY, HOW IS SHE?
BETTER.
THAT'S GOOD TO HEAR. A CUTIE LIKE THAT, IT WOULD BE A REAL SHAME.
I SUSPECTED THEY WERE IN A LOT WORSE SHAPE BY NOW, BUT THE PICS WOULD DO.
SHE RECOGNIZED THE THREE OF THEM. I ASKED ANTOINE TO BRING UP HER FOOD FOR AT LEAST FOUR DAYS. HE ACCEPTED. SHE UNDERSTOOD.
PEOPLE SAY REVENGE IS VILE AND UNCIVILIZED, UNWORTHY OF AN EDUCATED MAN. PEOPLE SAY INDIVIDUAL JUSTICE CAN UNDERMINE OUR SOCIETY AS A WHOLE. MAYBE THEY'RE RIGHT. AND MAYBE THOSE ARE ONLY THEORIES BEHIND WHICH COWARDS WHO DON'T HAVE THE BALLS TO TAKE ACTION CAN HIDE. WHOEVER THEY ARE, IF THESE GUYS BELIEVED THEY COULD HURT MY GIRL AND RUIN MY HOUSE WITHOUT ME DOING ANYTHING ABOUT IT, THEY WERE WRONG.

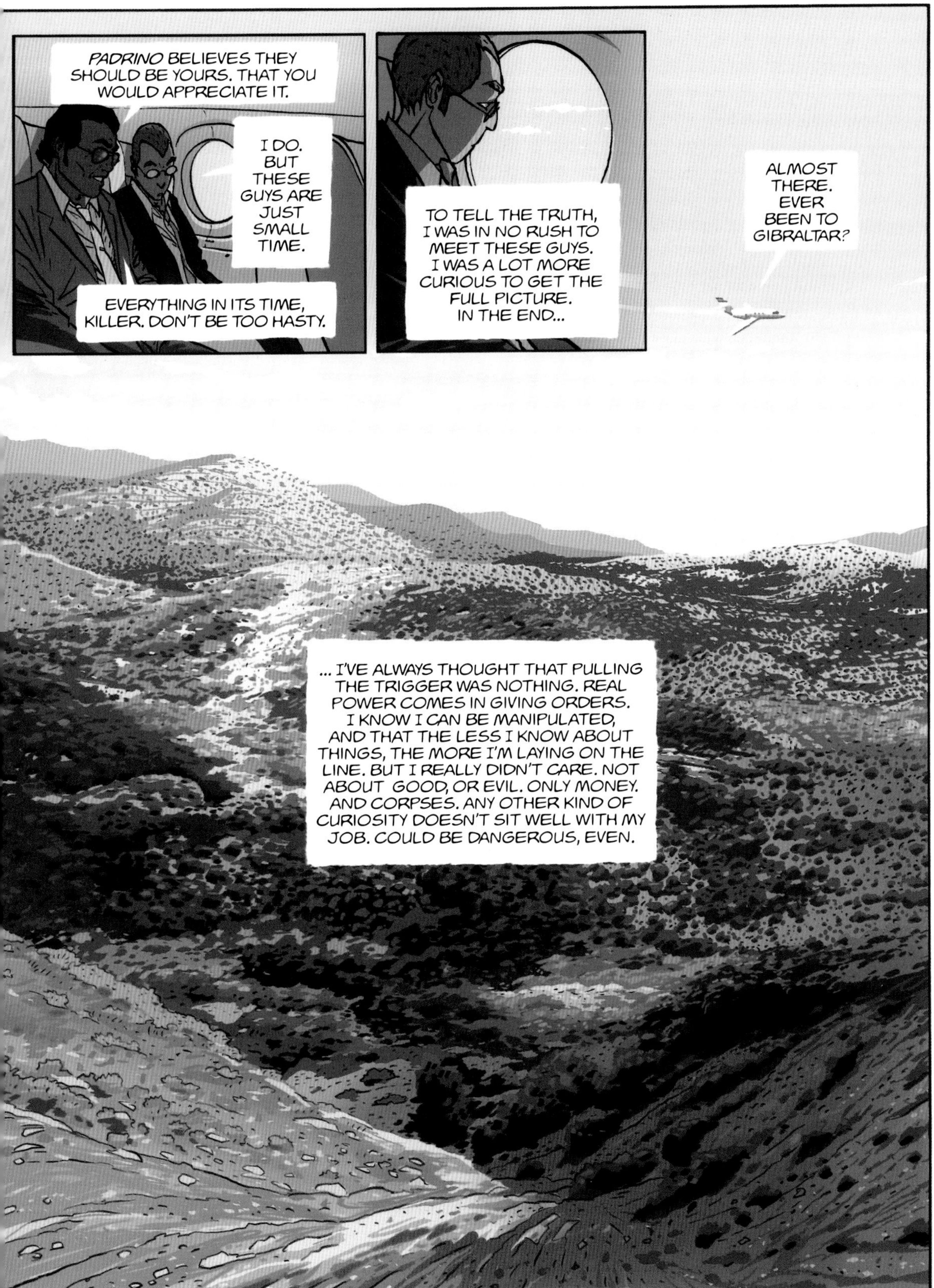
PADRINO BELIEVES THEY SHOULD BE YOURS. THAT YOU WOULD APPRECIATE IT.
I DO. BUT THESE GUYS ARE JUST SMALL TIME.
EVERYTHING IN ITS TIME, KILLER. DON'T BE TOO HASTY.
TO TELL THE TRUTH, I WAS IN NO RUSH TO MEET THESE GUYS. I WAS A LOT MORE CURIOUS TO GET THE FULL PICTURE. IN THE END...
ALMOST THERE. EVER BEEN TO GIBRALTAR?
... I'VE ALWAYS THOUGHT THAT PULLING THE TRIGGER WAS NOTHING. REAL POWER COMES IN GIVING ORDERS. I KNOW I CAN BE MANIPULATED, AND THAT THE LESS I KNOW ABOUT THINGS, THE MORE I'M LAYING ON THE LINE. BUT I REALLY DIDN'T CARE. NOT ABOUT GOOD, OR EVIL. ONLY MONEY. AND CORPSES. ANY OTHER KIND OF CURIOSITY DOESN'T SIT WELL WITH MY JOB. COULD BE DANGEROUS, EVEN.

DURING THE MIDDLE AGES AND RENAISSANCE, MEN FEARED TO DIE WHILE SLEEPING, BECAUSE THEN THEY HAD NO TIME TO CONFESS, AND THEY BELIEVED THEY WOULD GO STRAIGHT TO HELL.

S'ALL COOL?

SI.

DID WE GET SOFT, OR JUST LOSE OUR ILLUSIONS? WAS IT BRAVERY OR FOOLISHNESS?

DEPENDS ON WHAT YOU BELIEVE IN.

YOU DIDN'T HURT THEM TOO MUCH, DID YOU?

NAH...

HA! HA! HA!

THEY HAVEN'T BEEN VERY TALKATIVE. MAYBE THEY DIDN'T KNOW TOO MUCH IN THE FIRST PLACE.

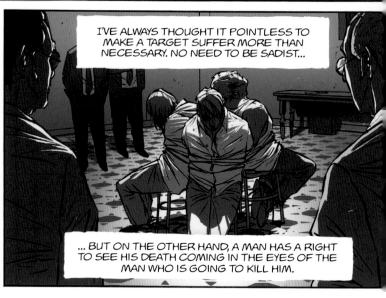

I'VE ALWAYS THOUGHT IT POINTLESS TO MAKE A TARGET SUFFER MORE THAN NECESSARY. NO NEED TO BE SADIST...

... BUT ON THE OTHER HAND, A MAN HAS A RIGHT TO SEE HIS DEATH COMING IN THE EYES OF THE MAN WHO IS GOING TO KILL HIM.

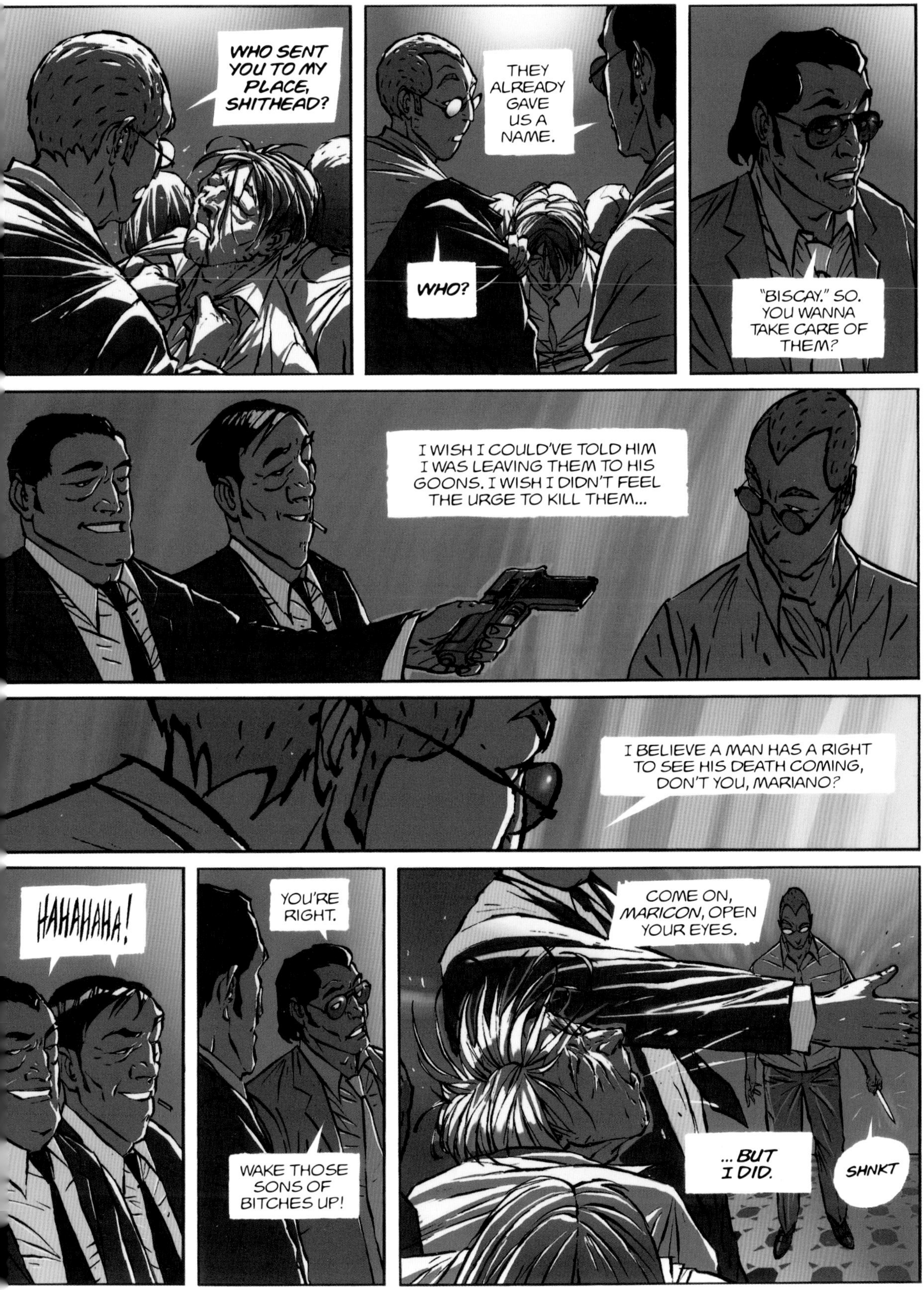
WHO SENT YOU TO MY PLACE, SHITHEAD?
THEY ALREADY GAVE US A NAME.
WHO?
"BISCAY." SO. YOU WANNA TAKE CARE OF THEM?
I WISH I COULD'VE TOLD HIM I WAS LEAVING THEM TO HIS GOONS. I WISH I DIDN'T FEEL THE URGE TO KILL THEM...
I BELIEVE A MAN HAS A RIGHT TO SEE HIS DEATH COMING, DON'T YOU, MARIANO?
HAHAHAHA!
YOU'RE RIGHT.
WAKE THOSE SONS OF BITCHES UP!
COME ON, MARICON, OPEN YOUR EYES.
...BUT I DID.
SHNKT

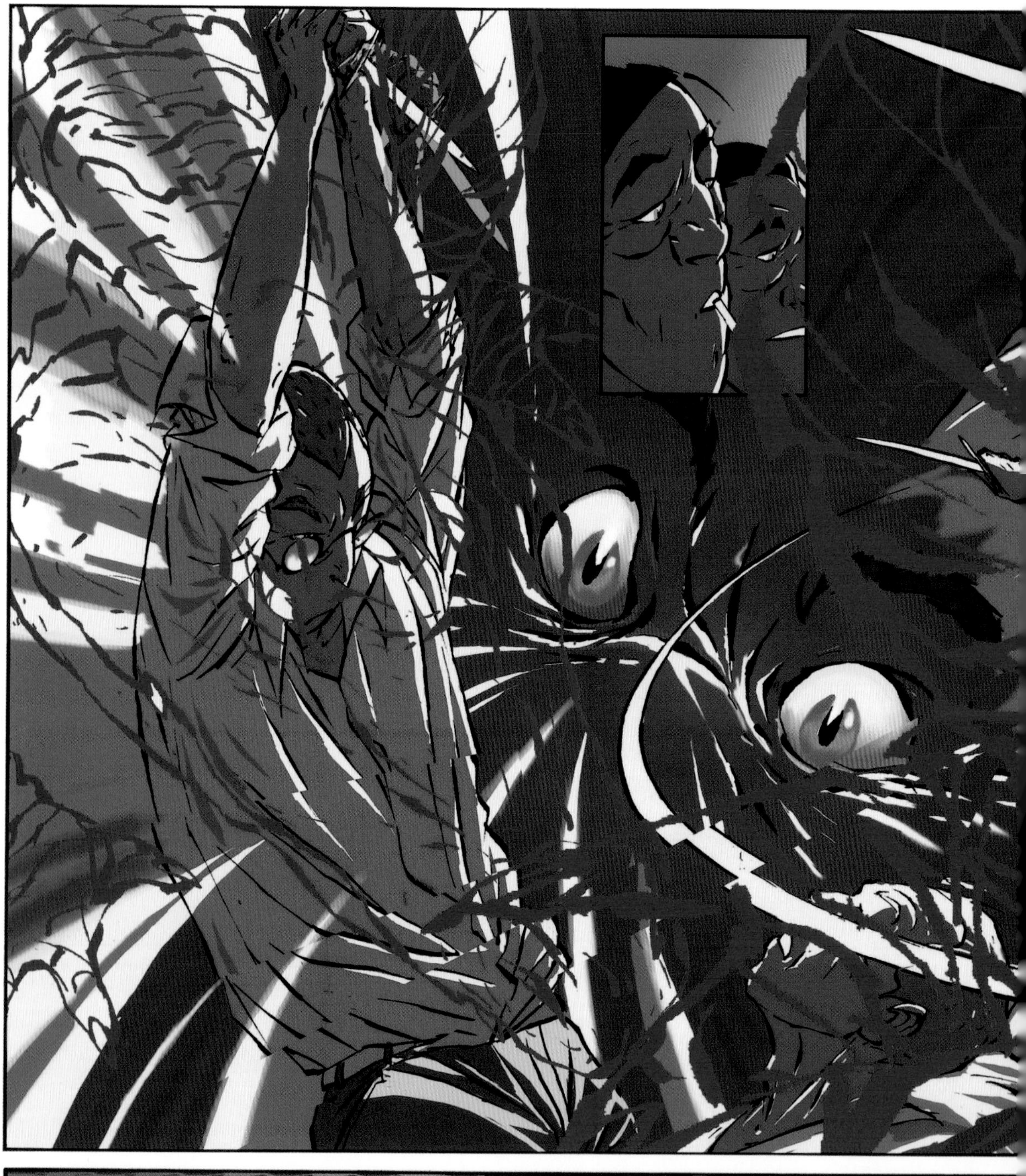

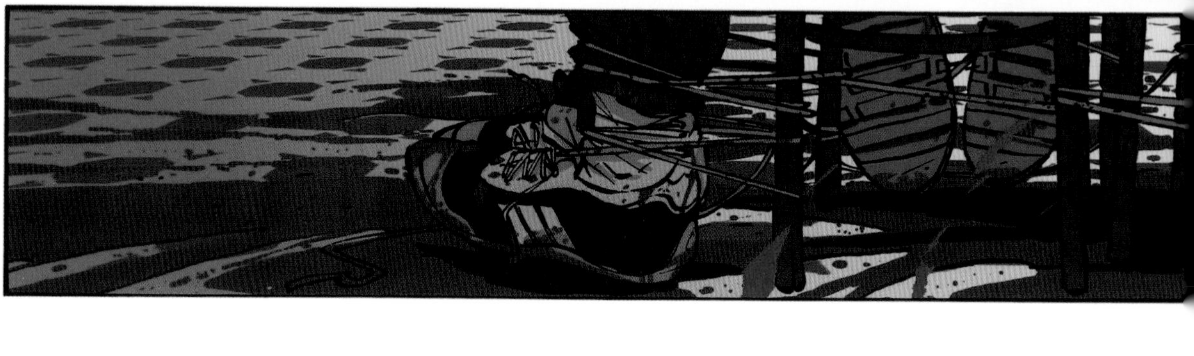

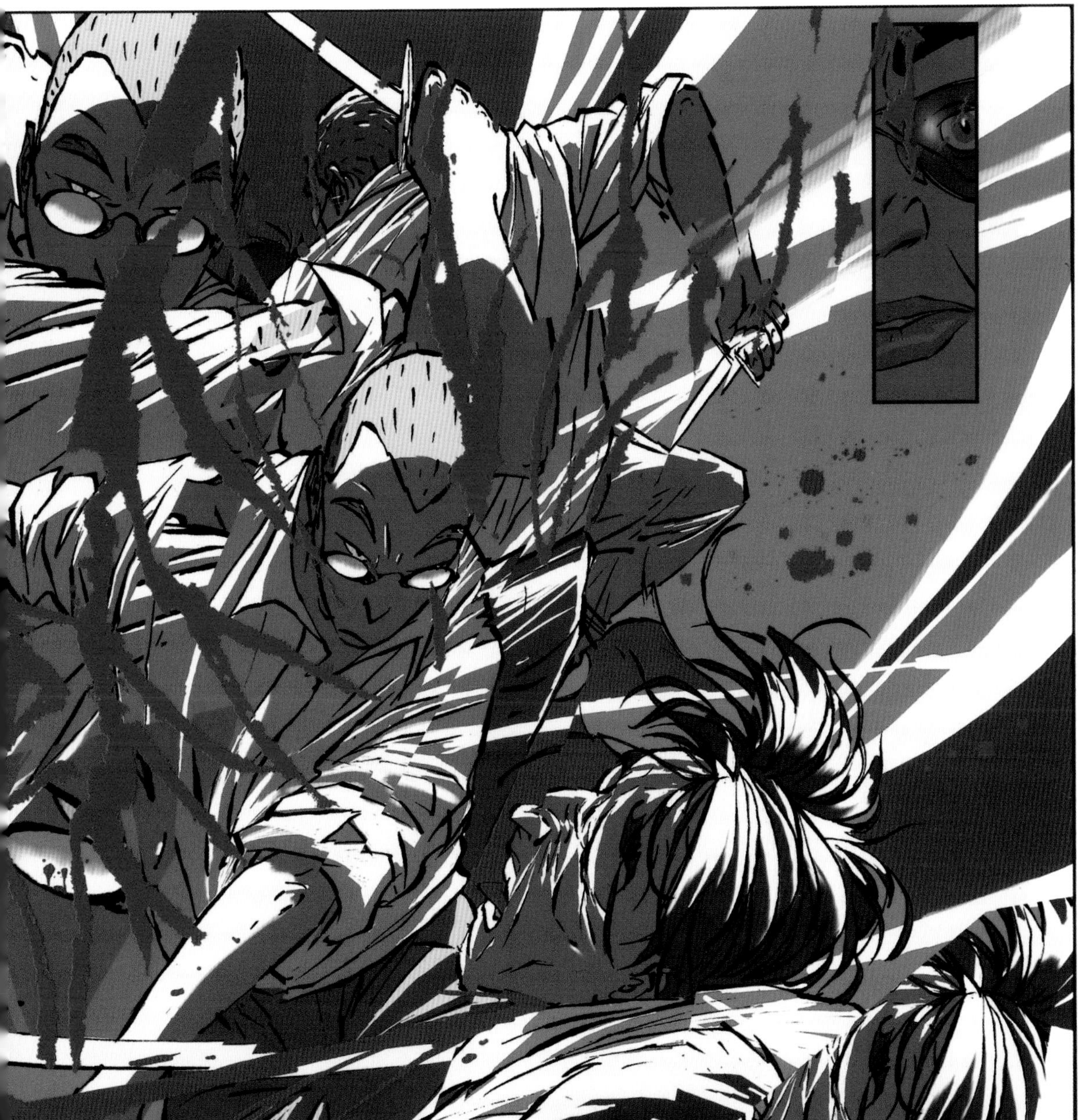

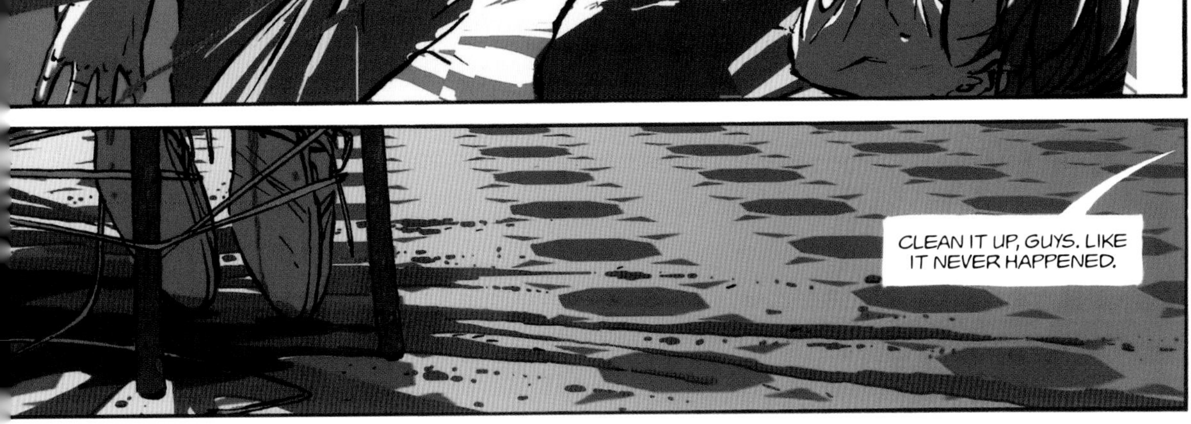
CLEAN IT UP, GUYS. LIKE IT NEVER HAPPENED.

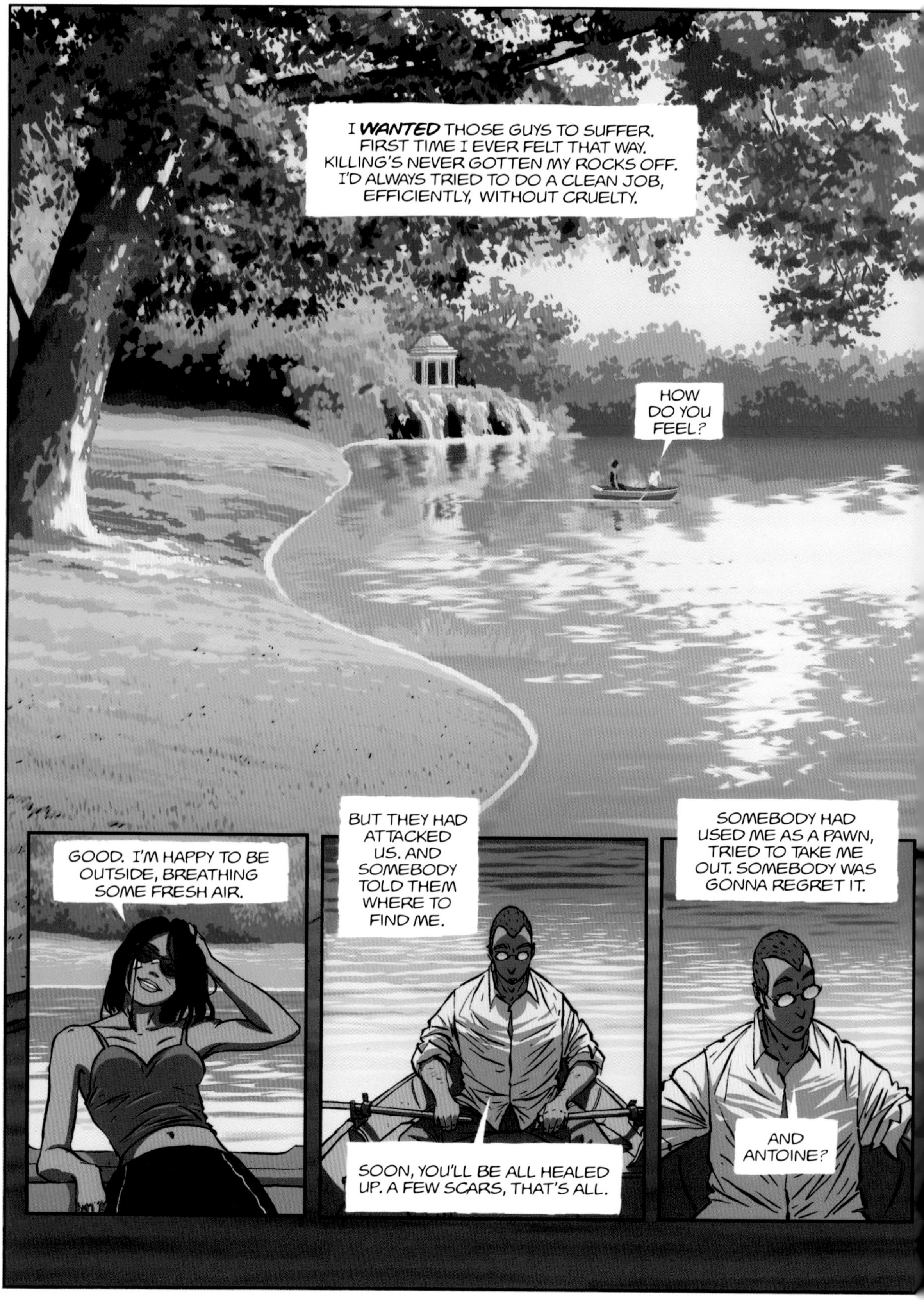
I WANTED THOSE GUYS TO SUFFER. FIRST TIME I EVER FELT THAT WAY. KILLING'S NEVER GOTTEN MY ROCKS OFF. I'D ALWAYS TRIED TO DO A CLEAN JOB, EFFICIENTLY, WITHOUT CRUELTY.
HOW DO YOU FEEL?
GOOD. I'M HAPPY TO BE OUTSIDE, BREATHING SOME FRESH AIR.
BUT THEY HAD ATTACKED US. AND SOMEBODY TOLD THEM WHERE TO FIND ME.
SOON, YOU'LL BE ALL HEALED UP. A FEW SCARS, THAT'S ALL.
SOMEBODY HAD USED ME AS A PAWN, TRIED TO TAKE ME OUT. SOMEBODY WAS GONNA REGRET IT.
AND ANTOINE?

HE'S BEEN REALLY GOOD. I DIDN'T SEE HIM YESTERDAY, THOUGH.

I HEARD FOOTSTEPS IN HIS APARTMENT. I MEANT TO ASK SOMETHING...

OH?

... WHY DID MARIANO COME BACK WITH YOU?

WE'VE A FEW THINGS TO TAKE CARE OF. I MAY HAVE TO GO AWAY AGAIN FOR A WHILE.

DO WHAT YOU NEED TO DO, BUT BE CAREFUL.

NOT A BAD PIECE OF ADVICE. THE WAY THINGS LOOKED, I WASN'T GOING TO SEE ANY PEACE ANYTIME SOON.

ANTOINE?

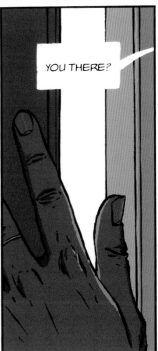

YOU THERE?

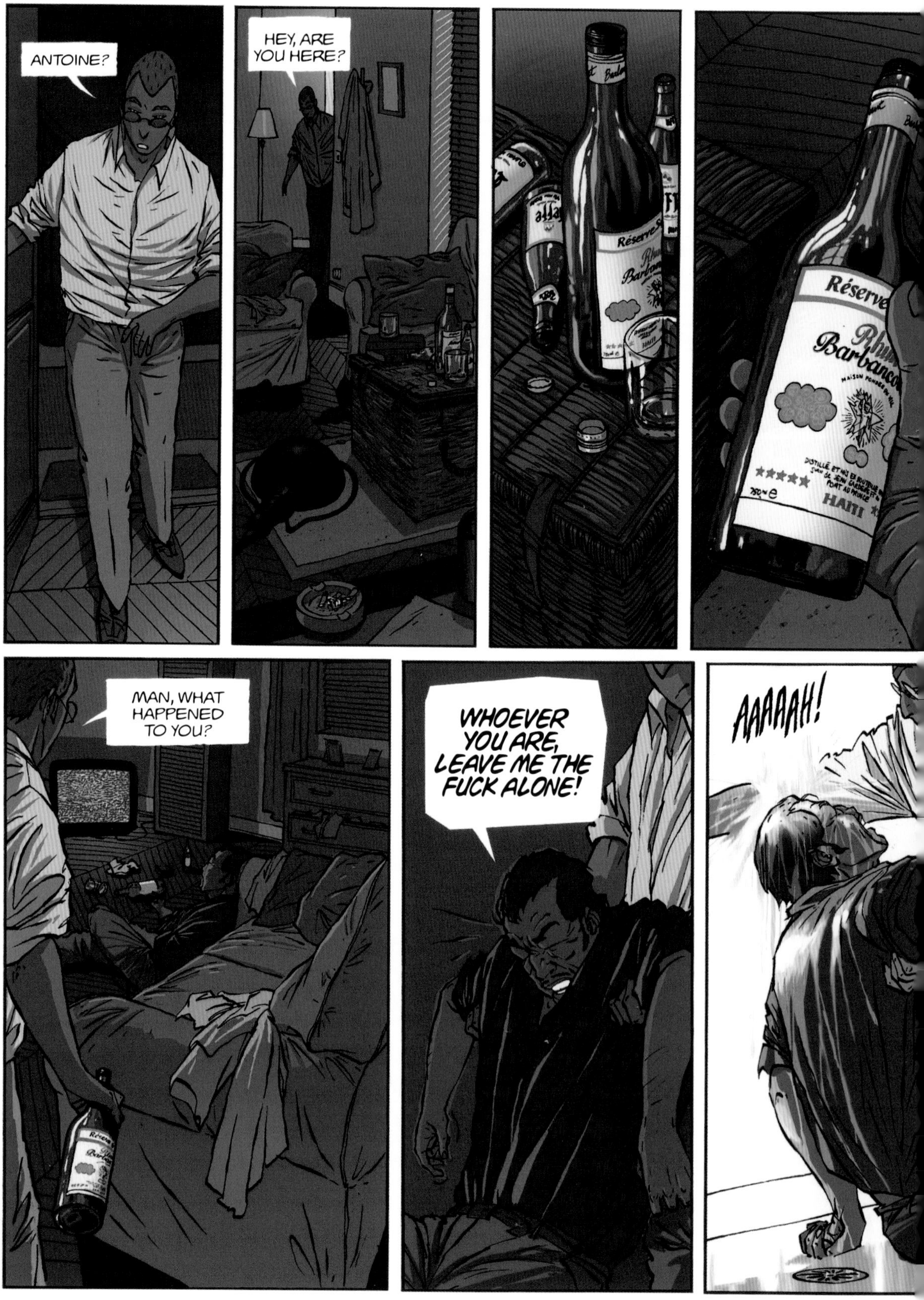
ANTOINE?
HEY, ARE YOU HERE?
Réserve
Rhum Barbancourt
HAITI
MAN, WHAT HAPPENED TO YOU?
WHOEVER YOU ARE, LEAVE ME THE FUCK ALONE!
AAAAAH!

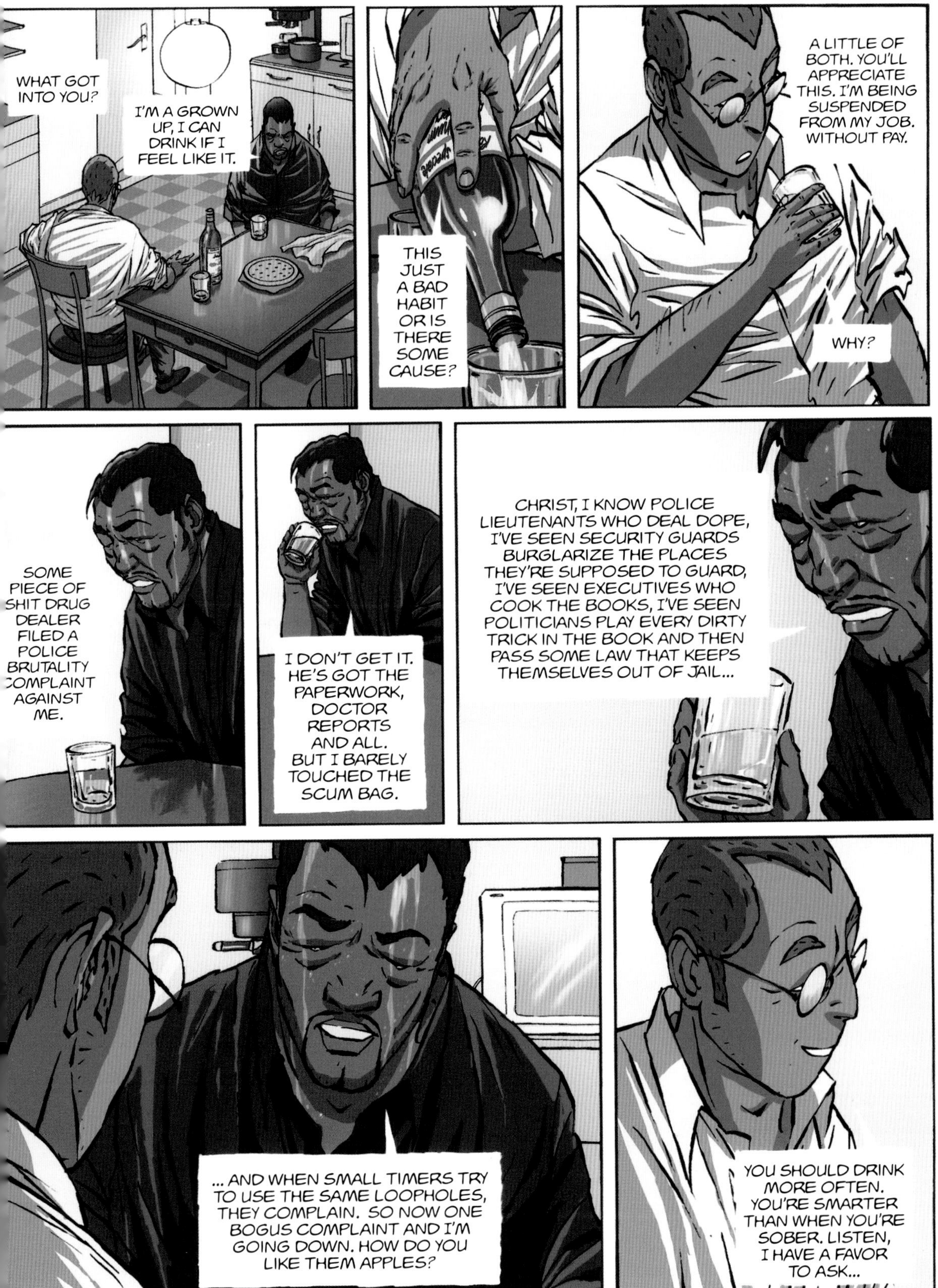
WHAT GOT INTO YOU?
I'M A GROWN UP, I CAN DRINK IF I FEEL LIKE IT.
THIS JUST A BAD HABIT OR IS THERE SOME CAUSE?
A LITTLE OF BOTH. YOU'LL APPRECIATE THIS. I'M BEING SUSPENDED FROM MY JOB. WITHOUT PAY.
WHY?
SOME PIECE OF SHIT DRUG DEALER FILED A POLICE BRUTALITY COMPLAINT AGAINST ME.
I DON'T GET IT. HE'S GOT THE PAPERWORK, DOCTOR REPORTS AND ALL. BUT I BARELY TOUCHED THE SCUM BAG.
CHRIST, I KNOW POLICE LIEUTENANTS WHO DEAL DOPE, I'VE SEEN SECURITY GUARDS BURGLARIZE THE PLACES THEY'RE SUPPOSED TO GUARD, I'VE SEEN EXECUTIVES WHO COOK THE BOOKS, I'VE SEEN POLITICIANS PLAY EVERY DIRTY TRICK IN THE BOOK AND THEN PASS SOME LAW THAT KEEPS THEMSELVES OUT OF JAIL...
... AND WHEN SMALL TIMERS TRY TO USE THE SAME LOOPHOLES, THEY COMPLAIN. SO NOW ONE BOGUS COMPLAINT AND I'M GOING DOWN. HOW DO YOU LIKE THEM APPLES?
YOU SHOULD DRINK MORE OFTEN. YOU'RE SMARTER THAN WHEN YOU'RE SOBER. LISTEN, I HAVE A FAVOR TO ASK...

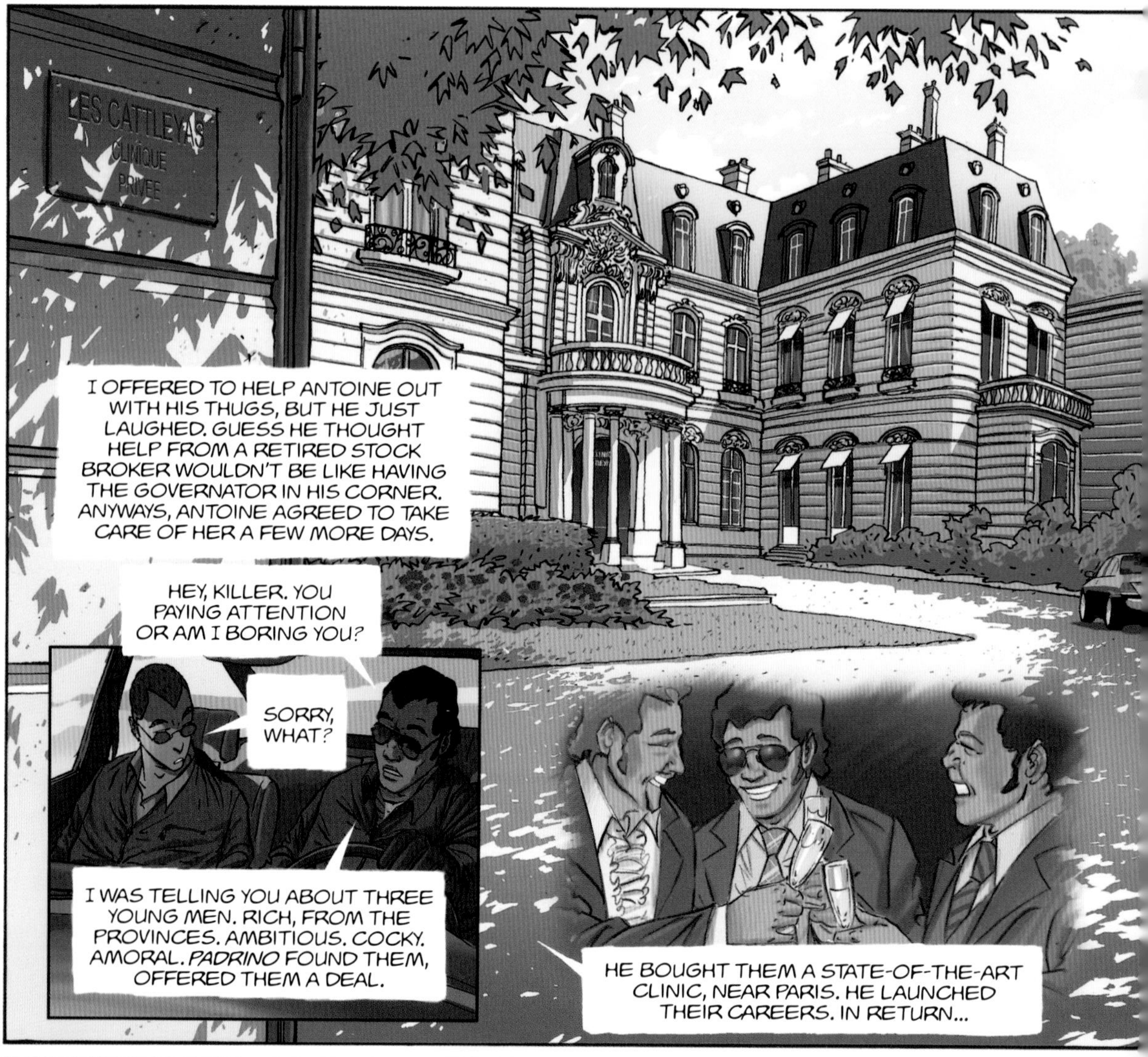
LES CATTLEYAS
CLINIQUE
PRIVEE
I OFFERED TO HELP ANTOINE OUT WITH HIS THUGS, BUT HE JUST LAUGHED. GUESS HE THOUGHT HELP FROM A RETIRED STOCK BROKER WOULDN'T BE LIKE HAVING THE GOVERNATOR IN HIS CORNER. ANYWAYS, ANTOINE AGREED TO TAKE CARE OF HER A FEW MORE DAYS.
HEY, KILLER. YOU PAYING ATTENTION OR AM I BORING YOU?
SORRY, WHAT?
I WAS TELLING YOU ABOUT THREE YOUNG MEN. RICH, FROM THE PROVINCES. AMBITIOUS. COCKY. AMORAL. *PADRINO* FOUND THEM, OFFERED THEM A DEAL.
HE BOUGHT THEM A STATE-OF-THE-ART CLINIC, NEAR PARIS. HE LAUNCHED THEIR CAREERS. IN RETURN...

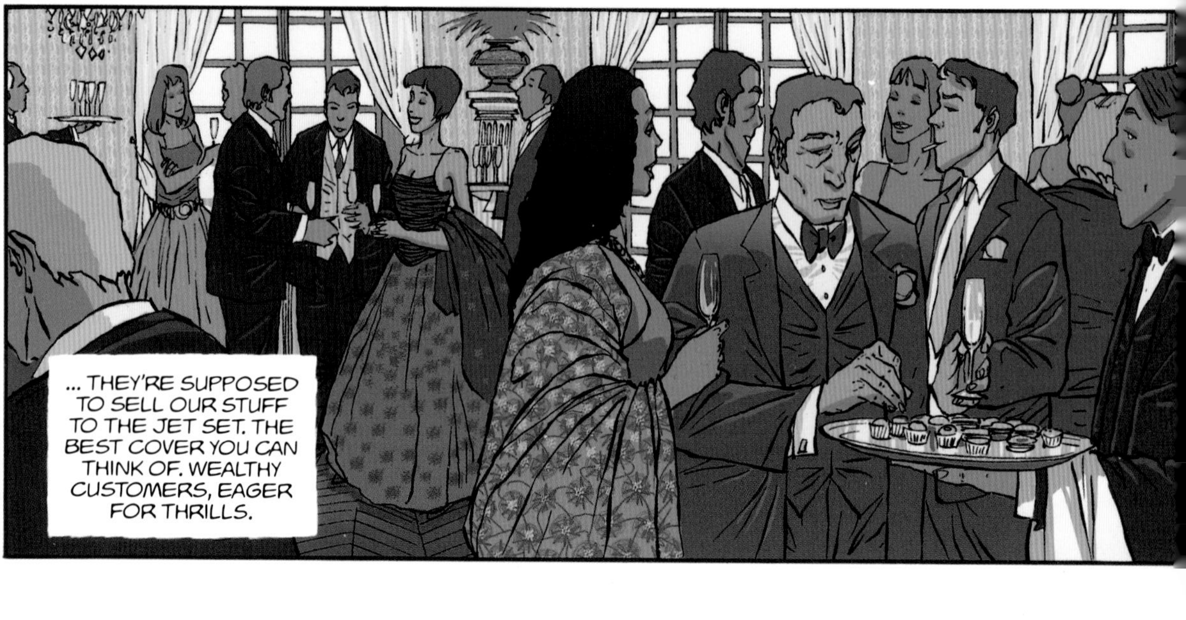
... THEY'RE SUPPOSED TO SELL OUR STUFF TO THE JET SET. THE BEST COVER YOU CAN THINK OF. WEALTHY CUSTOMERS, EAGER FOR THRILLS.

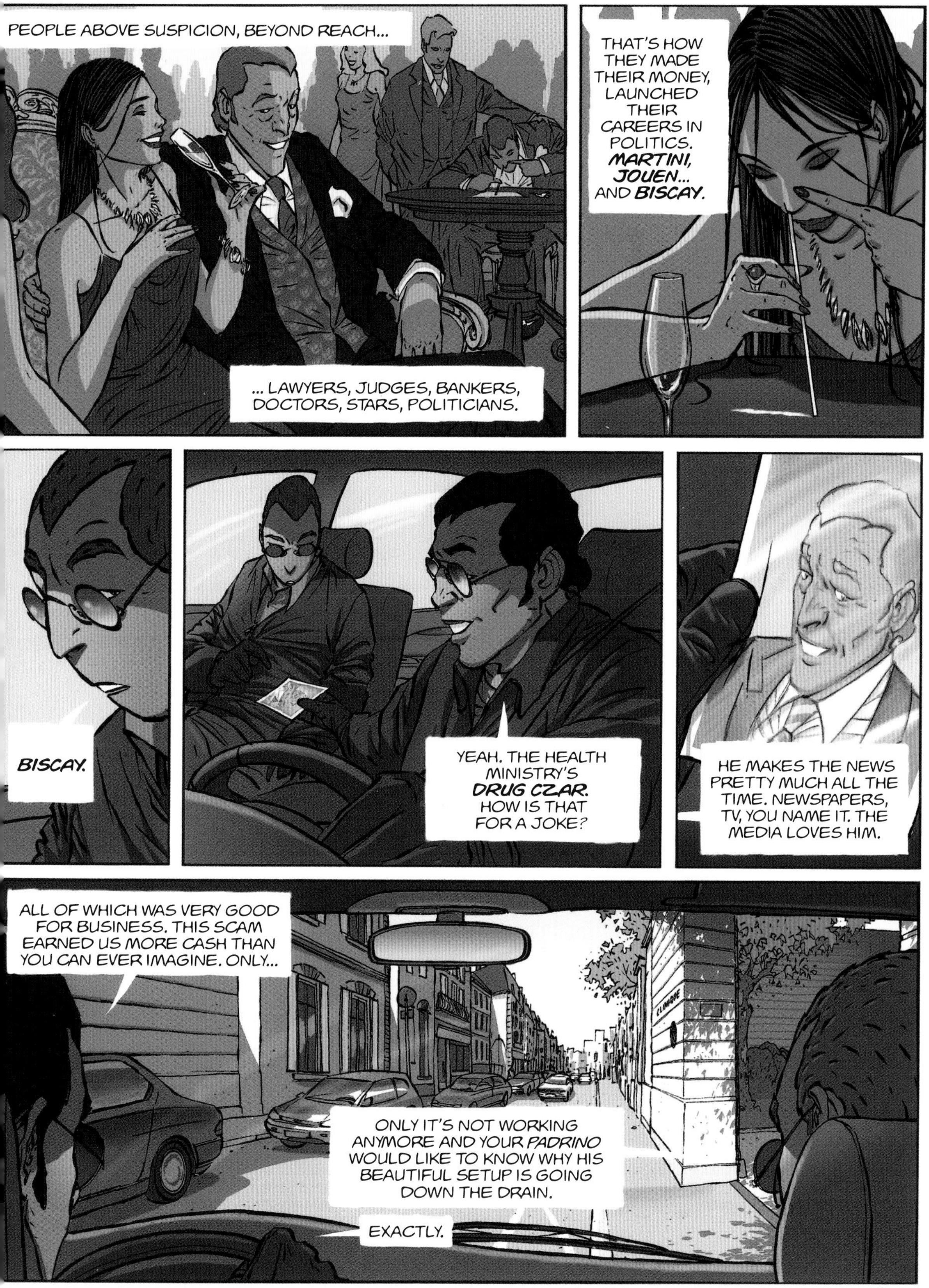
PEOPLE ABOVE SUSPICION, BEYOND REACH...
... LAWYERS, JUDGES, BANKERS, DOCTORS, STARS, POLITICIANS.
THAT'S HOW THEY MADE THEIR MONEY, LAUNCHED THEIR CAREERS IN POLITICS. MARTINI, JOUEN... AND BISCAY.
BISCAY.
YEAH. THE HEALTH MINISTRY'S DRUG CZAR. HOW IS THAT FOR A JOKE?
HE MAKES THE NEWS PRETTY MUCH ALL THE TIME. NEWSPAPERS, TV, YOU NAME IT. THE MEDIA LOVES HIM.
ALL OF WHICH WAS VERY GOOD FOR BUSINESS. THIS SCAM EARNED US MORE CASH THAN YOU CAN EVER IMAGINE. ONLY...
ONLY IT'S NOT WORKING ANYMORE AND YOUR PADRINO WOULD LIKE TO KNOW WHY HIS BEAUTIFUL SETUP IS GOING DOWN THE DRAIN.
EXACTLY.

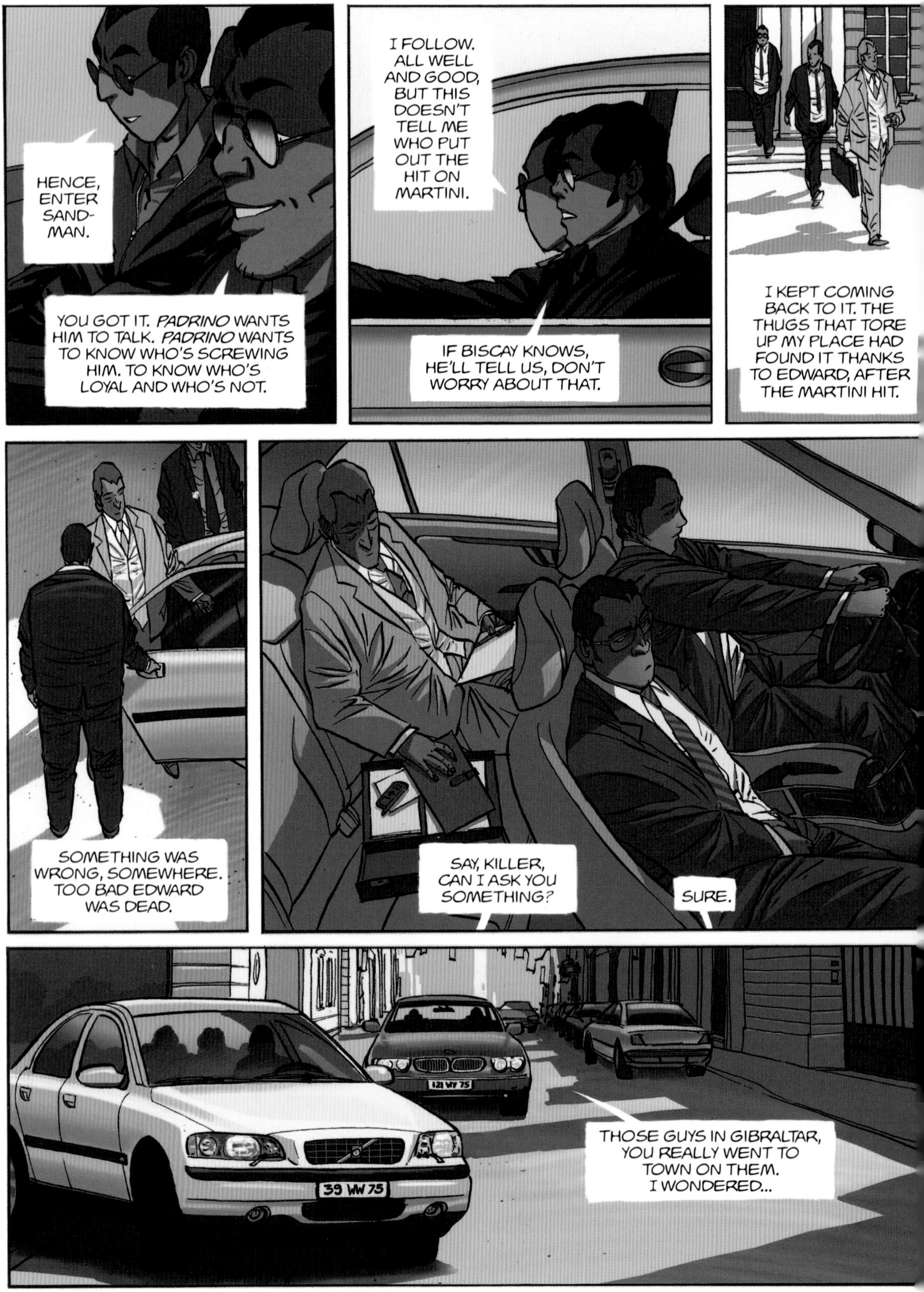
HENCE, ENTER SANDMAN.
YOU GOT IT. *PADRINO* WANTS HIM TO TALK. *PADRINO* WANTS TO KNOW WHO'S SCREWING HIM. TO KNOW WHO'S LOYAL AND WHO'S NOT.
I FOLLOW. ALL WELL AND GOOD, BUT THIS DOESN'T TELL ME WHO PUT OUT THE HIT ON MARTINI.
IF BISCAY KNOWS, HE'LL TELL US, DON'T WORRY ABOUT THAT.
I KEPT COMING BACK TO IT. THE THUGS THAT TORE UP MY PLACE HAD FOUND IT THANKS TO EDWARD, AFTER THE MARTINI HIT.
SOMETHING WAS WRONG, SOMEWHERE. TOO BAD EDWARD WAS DEAD.
SAY, KILLER, CAN I ASK YOU SOMETHING?
SURE.
121 WY 75
39 WW 75
THOSE GUYS IN GIBRALTAR, YOU REALLY WENT TO TOWN ON THEM. I WONDERED...

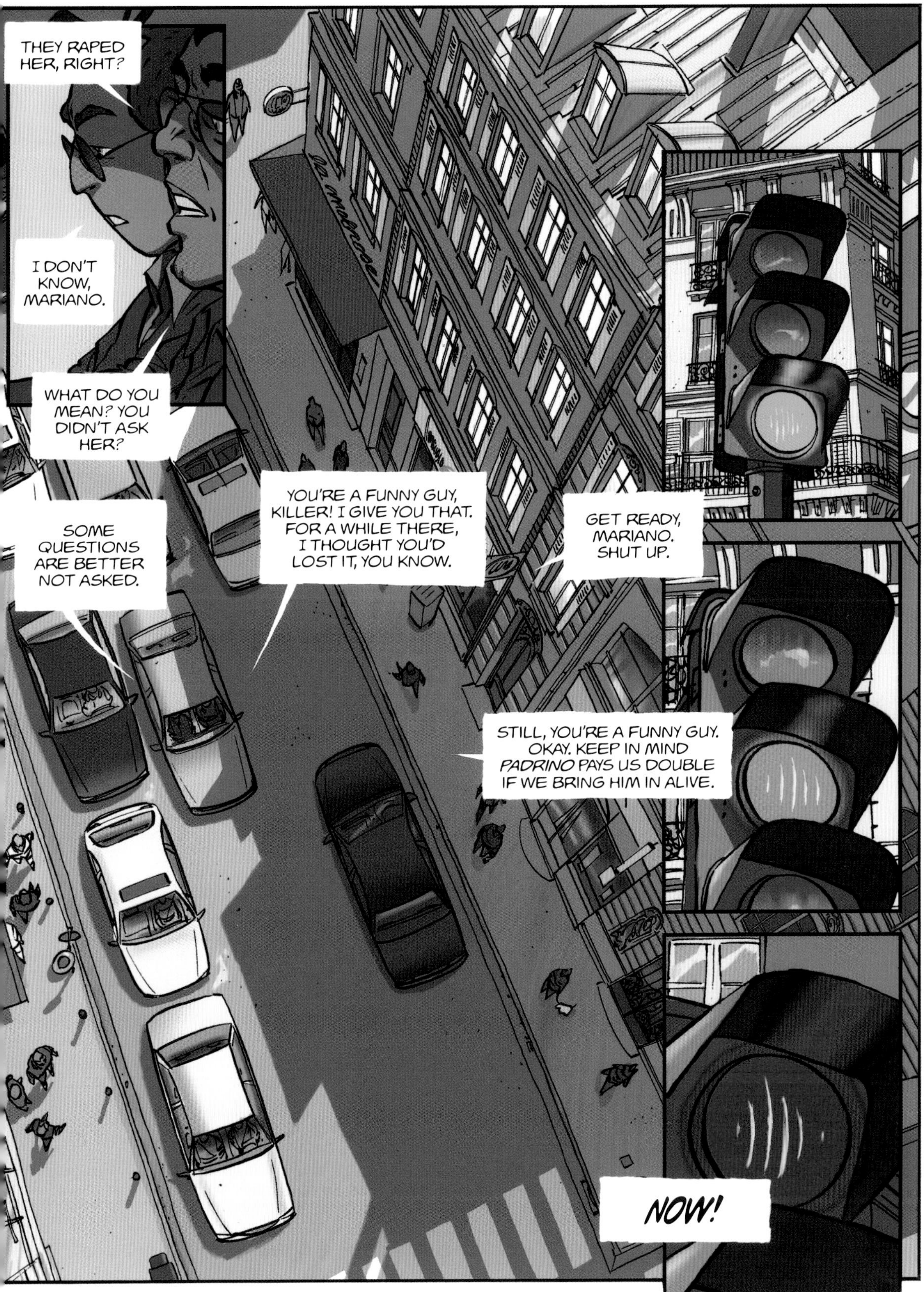
THEY RAPED HER, RIGHT?
I DON'T KNOW, MARIANO.
WHAT DO YOU MEAN? YOU DIDN'T ASK HER?
SOME QUESTIONS ARE BETTER NOT ASKED.
YOU'RE A FUNNY GUY, KILLER! I GIVE YOU THAT. FOR A WHILE THERE, I THOUGHT YOU'D LOST IT, YOU KNOW.
GET READY, MARIANO. SHUT UP.
STILL, YOU'RE A FUNNY GUY. OKAY. KEEP IN MIND *PADRINO* PAYS US DOUBLE IF WE BRING HIM IN ALIVE.
NOW!

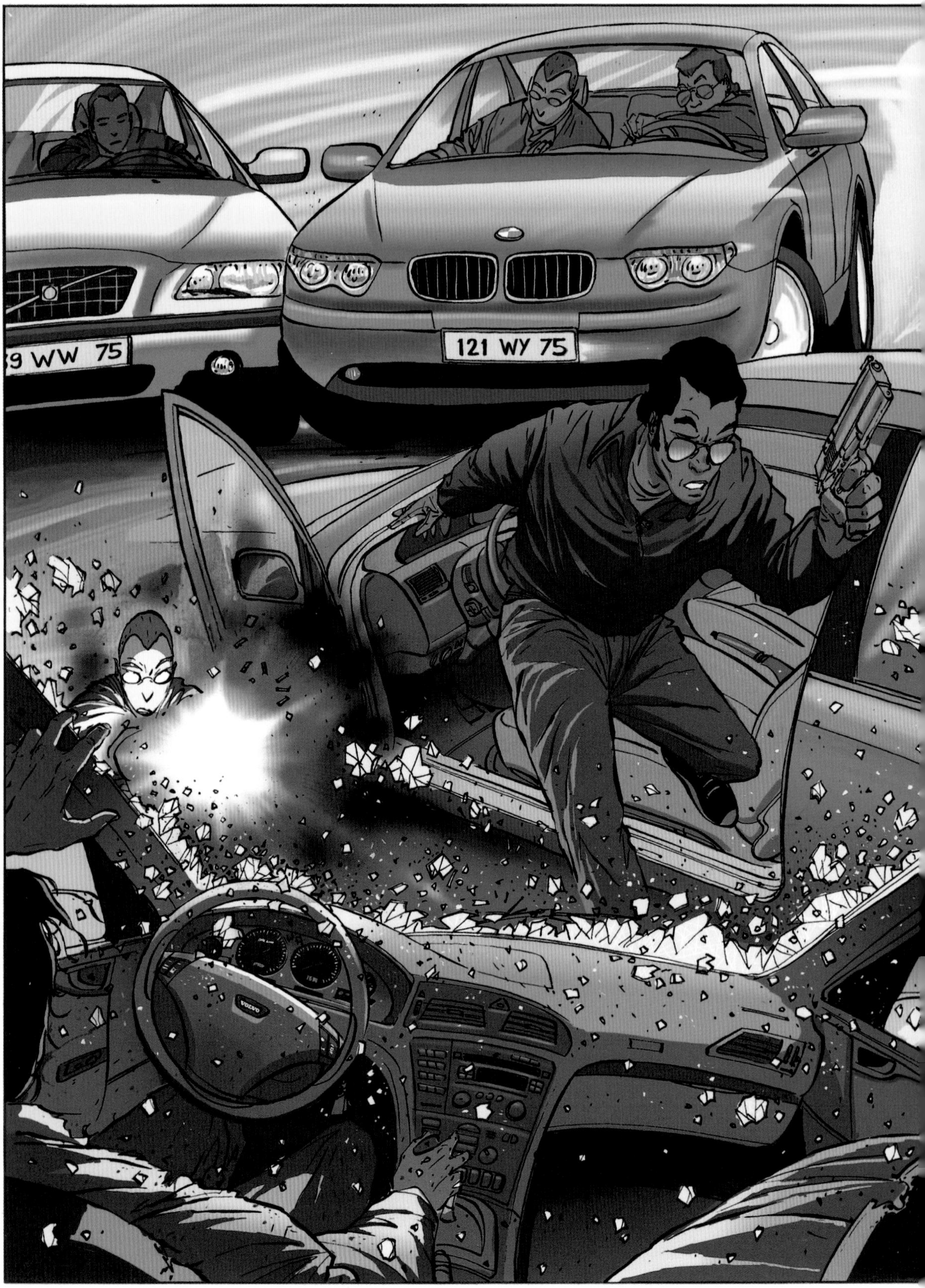
9 WW 75
121 WY 75

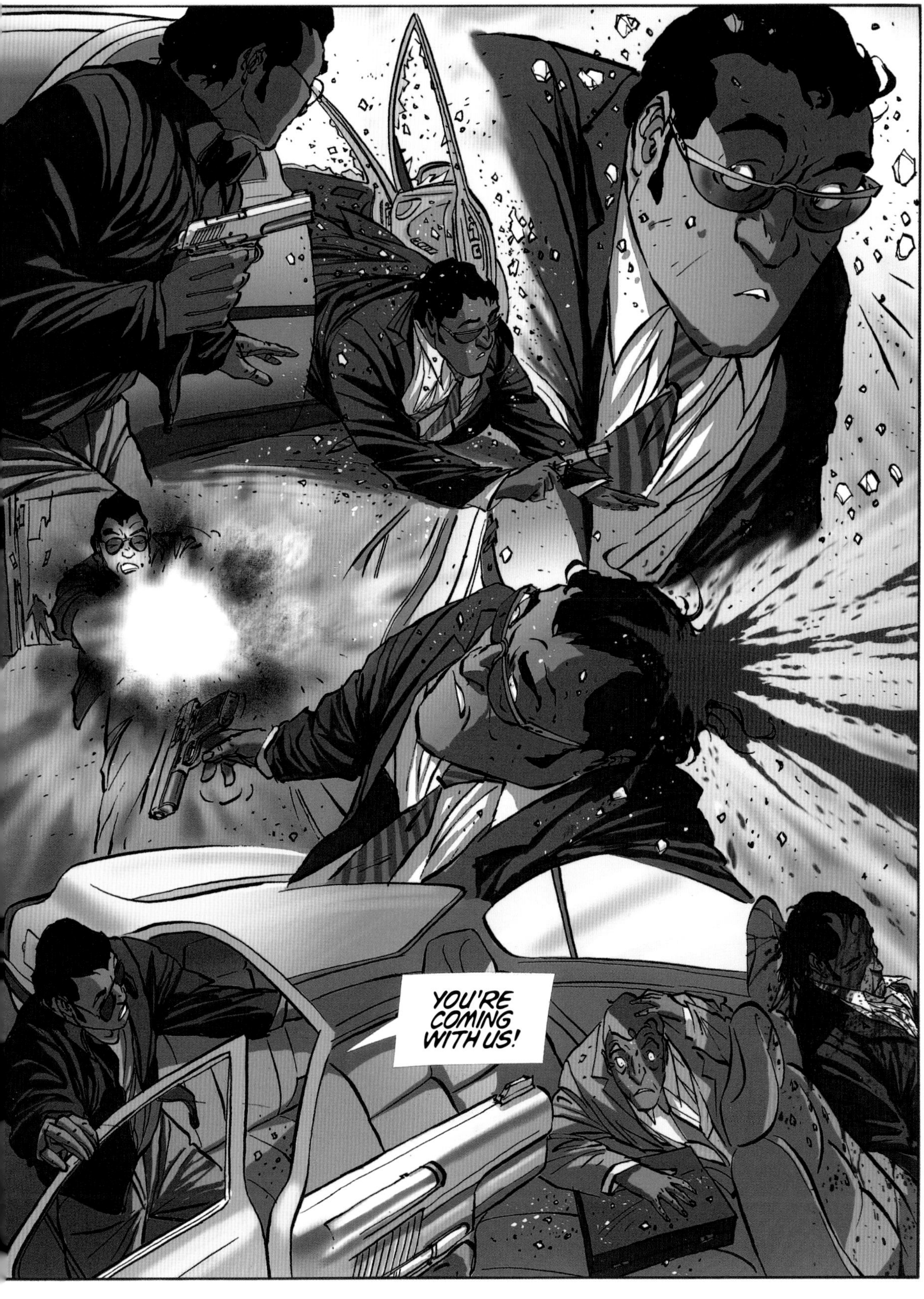
YOU'RE COMING WITH US!

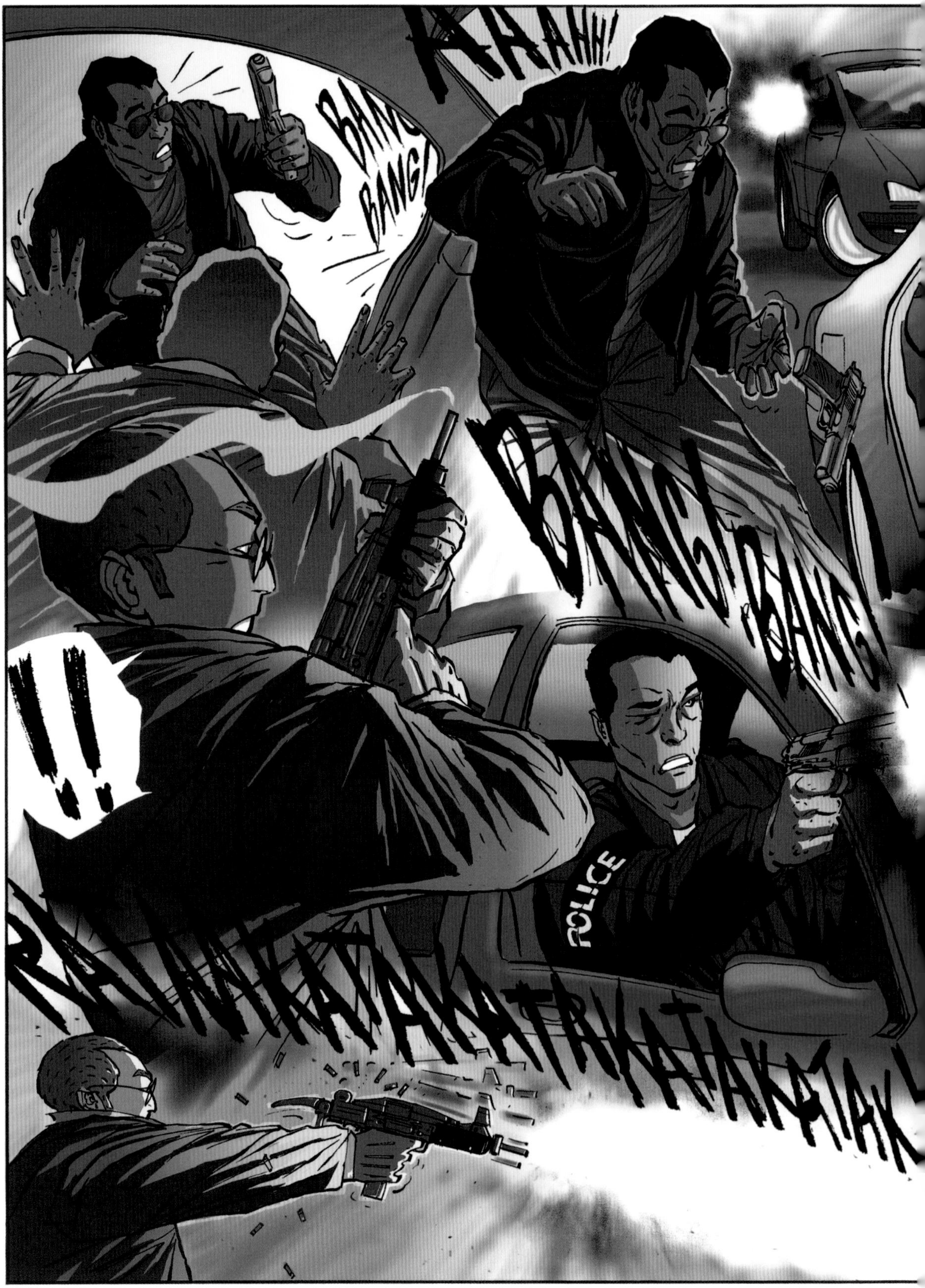
BANG! BANG!
KRAHH!
BANG! BANG!
!!
KATAKATAKATAKATAKATAK

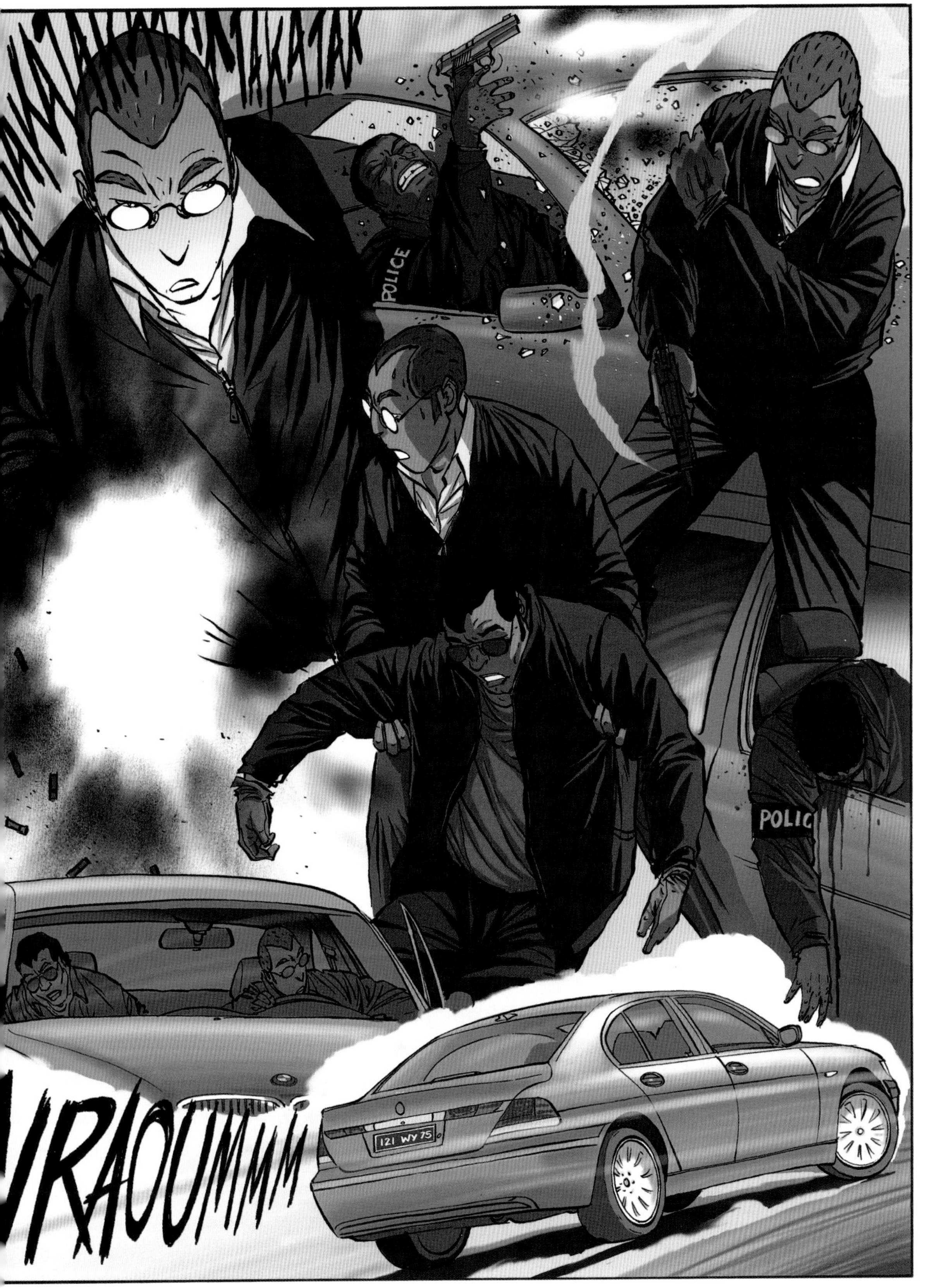
TAKATAK
POLICE
POLIC
VRAOUMMM
121 WY 75

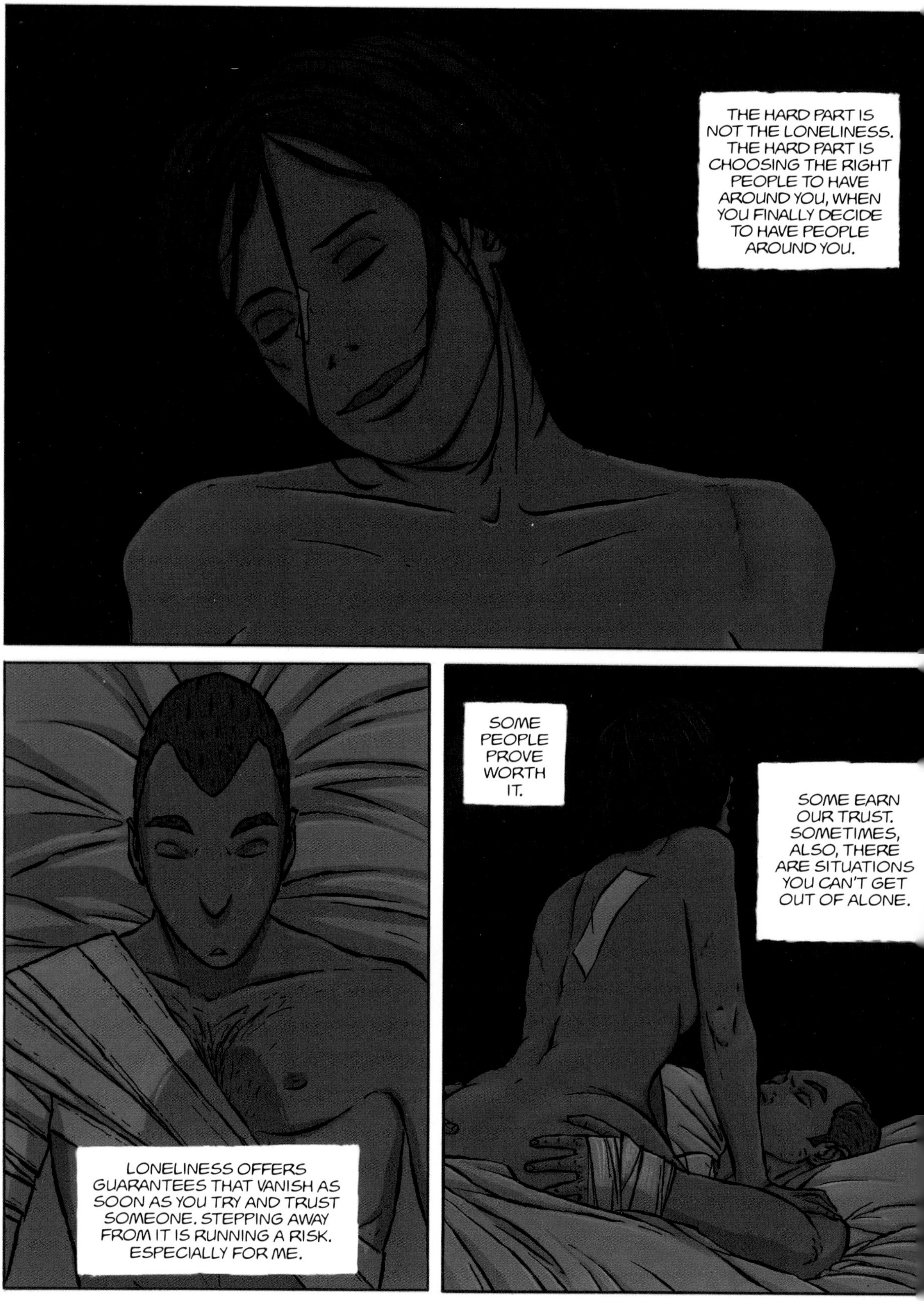
THE HARD PART IS NOT THE LONELINESS. THE HARD PART IS CHOOSING THE RIGHT PEOPLE TO HAVE AROUND YOU, WHEN YOU FINALLY DECIDE TO HAVE PEOPLE AROUND YOU.
LONELINESS OFFERS GUARANTEES THAT VANISH AS SOON AS YOU TRY AND TRUST SOMEONE. STEPPING AWAY FROM IT IS RUNNING A RISK. ESPECIALLY FOR ME.
SOME PEOPLE PROVE WORTH IT.
SOME EARN OUR TRUST. SOMETIMES, ALSO, THERE ARE SITUATIONS YOU CAN'T GET OUT OF ALONE.

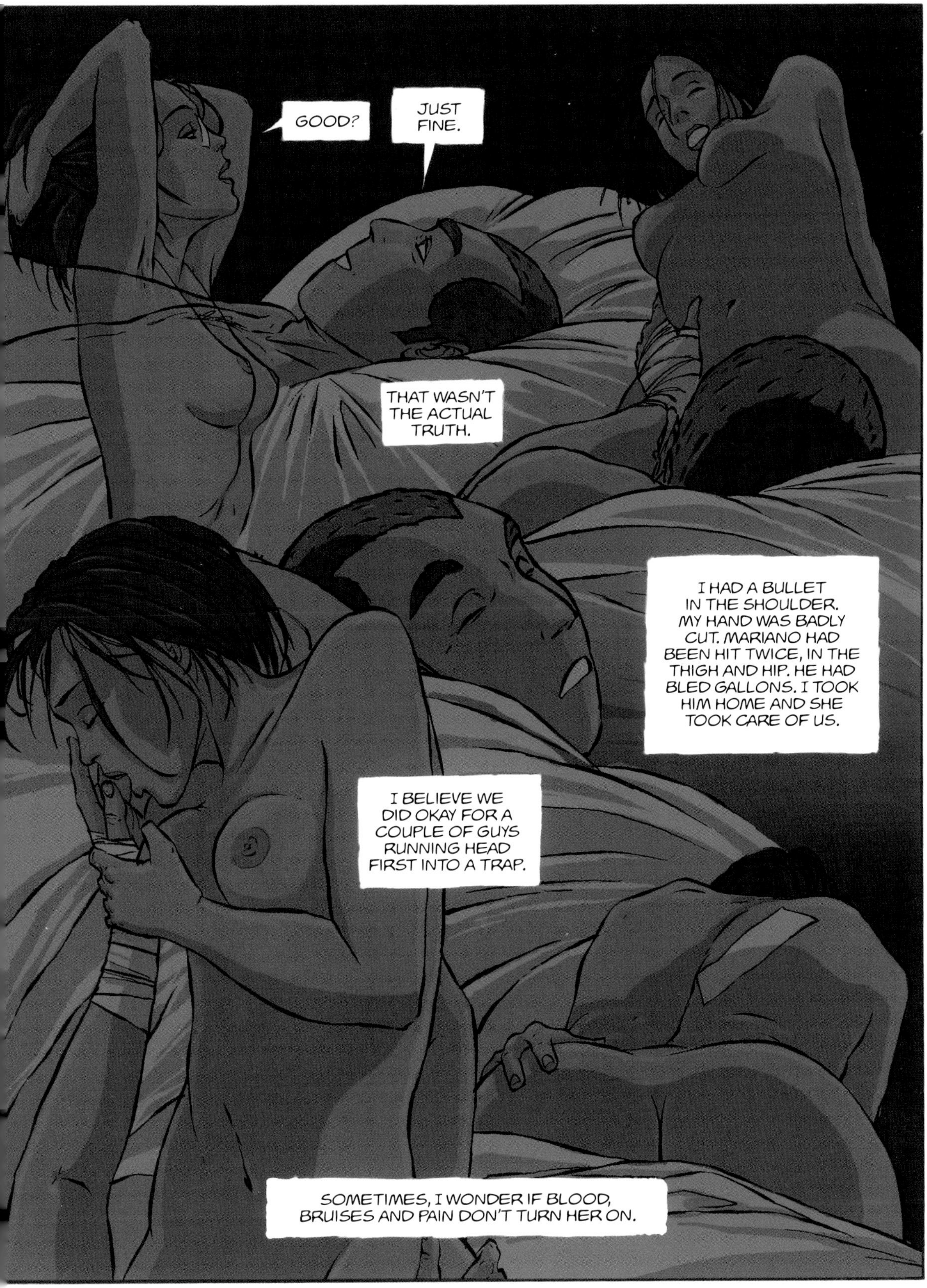
GOOD?
JUST FINE.
THAT WASN'T THE ACTUAL TRUTH.
I HAD A BULLET IN THE SHOULDER. MY HAND WAS BADLY CUT. MARIANO HAD BEEN HIT TWICE, IN THE THIGH AND HIP. HE HAD BLED GALLONS. I TOOK HIM HOME AND SHE TOOK CARE OF US.
I BELIEVE WE DID OKAY FOR A COUPLE OF GUYS RUNNING HEAD FIRST INTO A TRAP.
SOMETIMES, I WONDER IF BLOOD, BRUISES AND PAIN DON'T TURN HER ON.

UNLESS FOR HER, IT'S JUST PART OF A NORMAL LIFE.

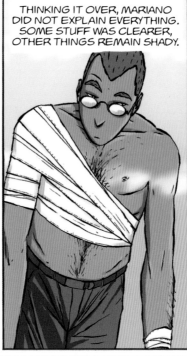

THINKING IT OVER, MARIANO DID NOT EXPLAIN EVERYTHING. SOME STUFF WAS CLEARER, OTHER THINGS REMAIN SHADY.

SOME RICH GUYS WHO DABBLE IN DRUGS WANT TO QUIT WORKING WITH *EL PADRINO*...

... MARTINI, JOUEN AND BISCAY THOUGHT THEY HAD BETTER CARDS TO PLAY.

WHAT CARDS? WHO'D I KILL MARTINI FOR?

EDWARD GAVE ME THAT HIT, AND THEN MOST LIKELY SET ME UP TO SILENCE ME.

EDWARD WON'T BE TALKING ANYMORE. BUT THAT BASTARD HAD TRICKED AND BETRAYED ME FOR MORE THAN JUST *MONEY*.

WHY GIVE ME A JOB AND THEN TAKE ME OUT? WHAT WAS HIS RELATIONSHIP WITH BISCAY?

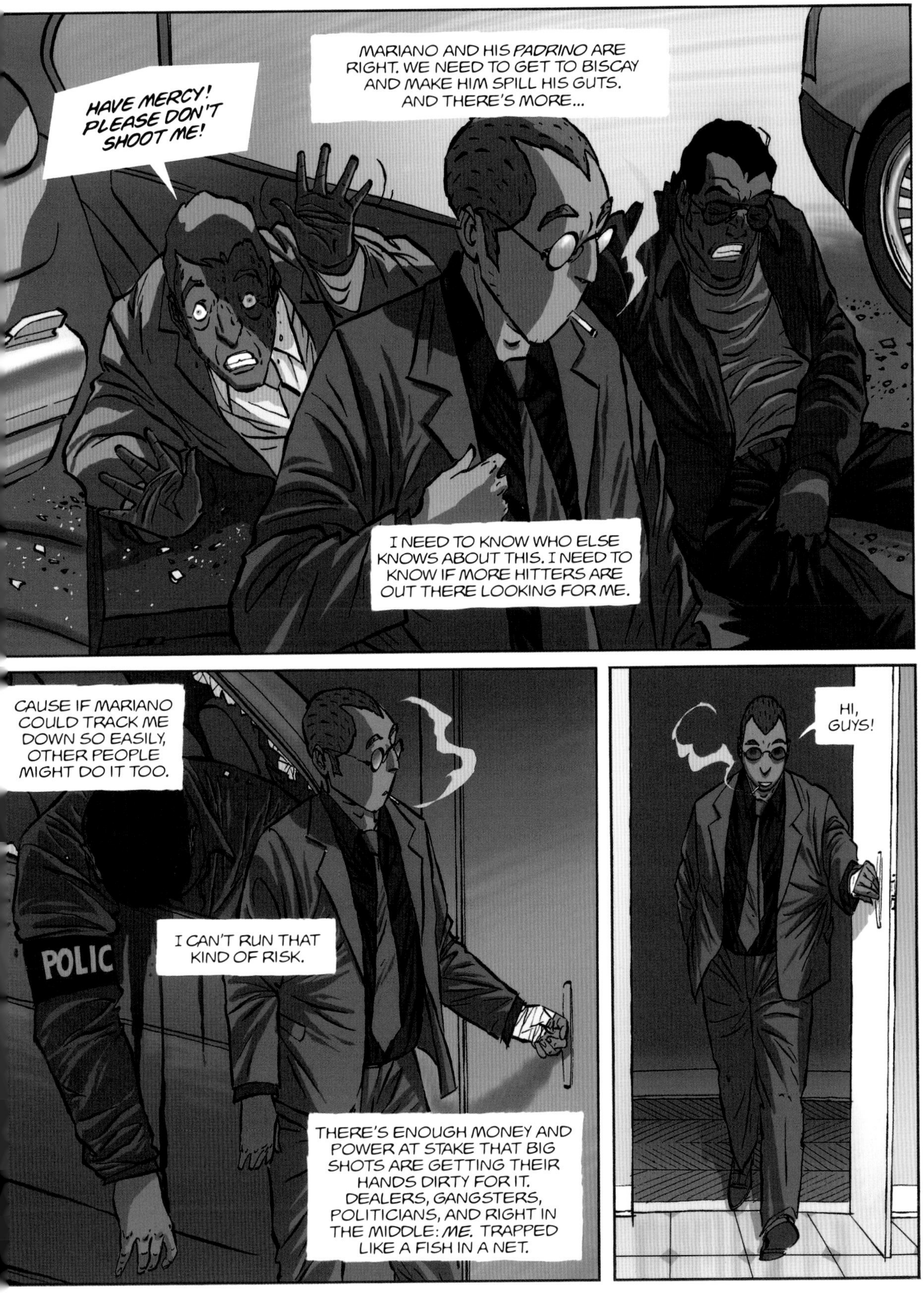
HAVE MERCY! PLEASE DON'T SHOOT ME!
MARIANO AND HIS *PADRINO* ARE RIGHT. WE NEED TO GET TO BISCAY AND MAKE HIM SPILL HIS GUTS. AND THERE'S MORE...
I NEED TO KNOW WHO ELSE KNOWS ABOUT THIS. I NEED TO KNOW IF MORE HITTERS ARE OUT THERE LOOKING FOR ME.
CAUSE IF MARIANO COULD TRACK ME DOWN SO EASILY, OTHER PEOPLE MIGHT DO IT TOO.
POLIC
I CAN'T RUN THAT KIND OF RISK.
THERE'S ENOUGH MONEY AND POWER AT STAKE THAT BIG SHOTS ARE GETTING THEIR HANDS DIRTY FOR IT. DEALERS, GANGSTERS, POLITICIANS, AND RIGHT IN THE MIDDLE: *ME.* TRAPPED LIKE A FISH IN A NET.
HI, GUYS!

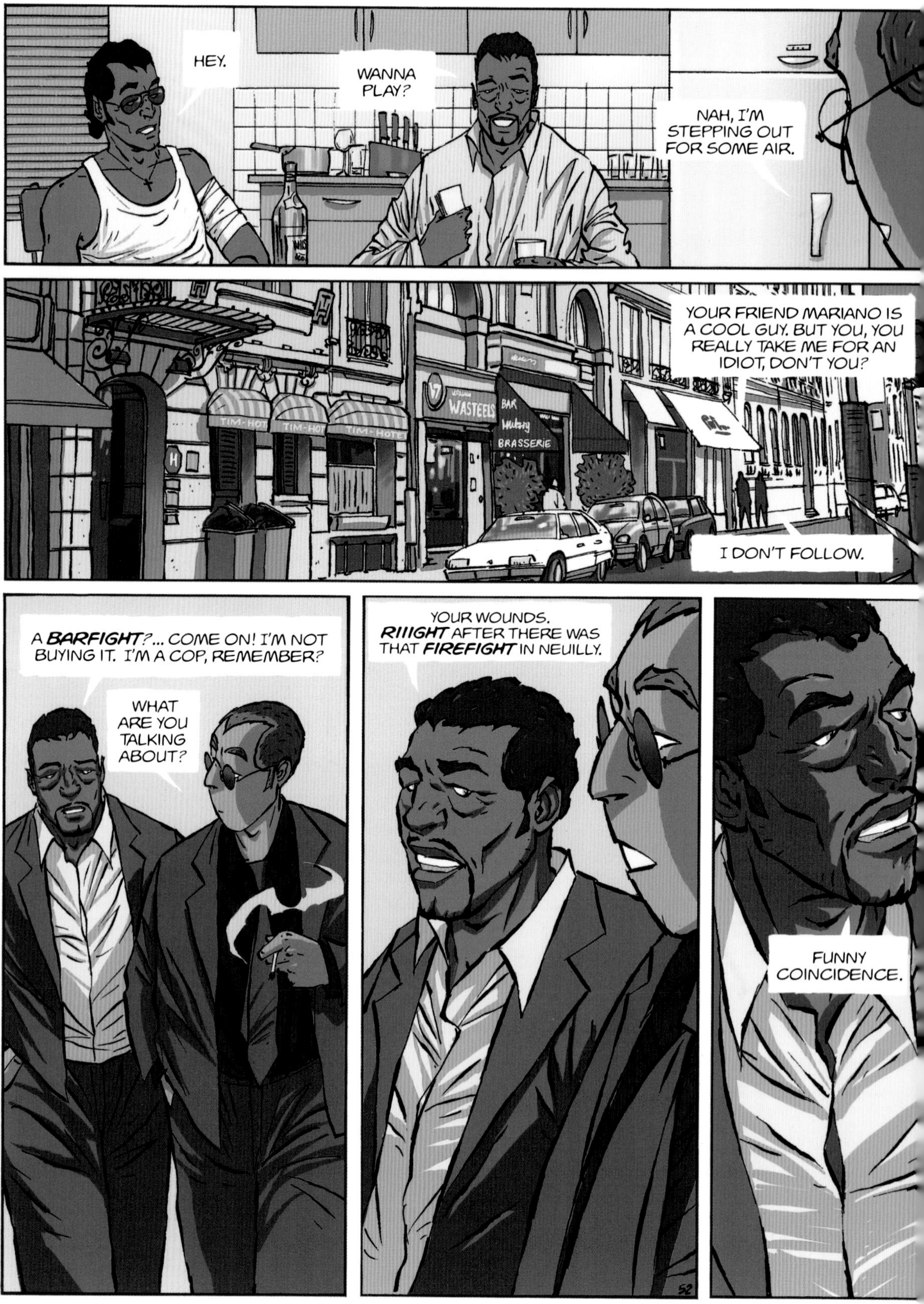
HEY.
WANNA PLAY?
NAH, I'M STEPPING OUT FOR SOME AIR.
YOUR FRIEND MARIANO IS A COOL GUY. BUT YOU, YOU REALLY TAKE ME FOR AN IDIOT, DON'T YOU?
I DON'T FOLLOW.
A BARFIGHT?... COME ON! I'M NOT BUYING IT. I'M A COP, REMEMBER?
WHAT ARE YOU TALKING ABOUT?
YOUR WOUNDS. RIIIGHT AFTER THERE WAS THAT FIREFIGHT IN NEUILLY.
FUNNY COINCIDENCE.

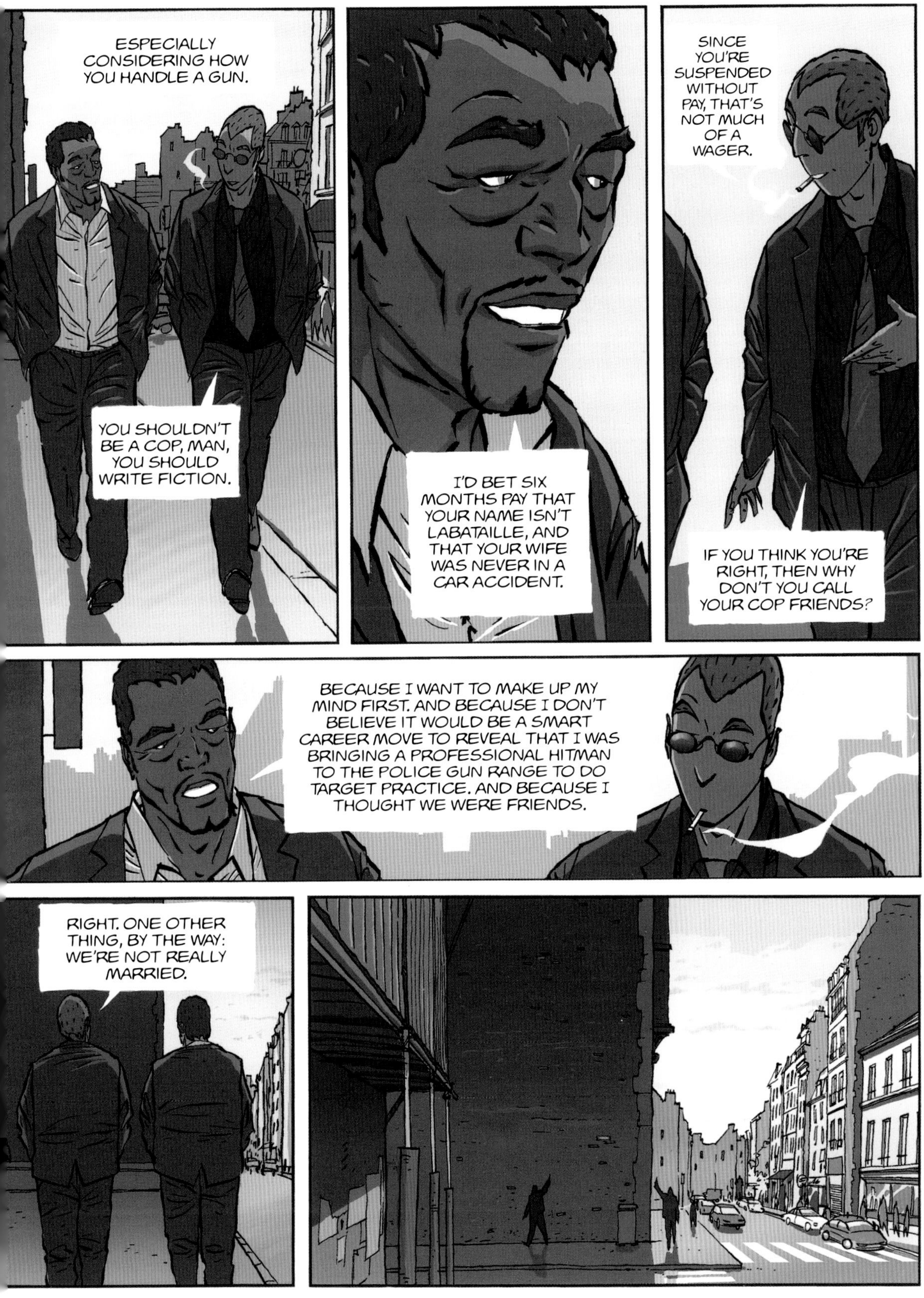
ESPECIALLY CONSIDERING HOW YOU HANDLE A GUN.
YOU SHOULDN'T BE A COP, MAN, YOU SHOULD WRITE FICTION.
I'D BET SIX MONTHS PAY THAT YOUR NAME ISN'T LABATAILLE, AND THAT YOUR WIFE WAS NEVER IN A CAR ACCIDENT.
SINCE YOU'RE SUSPENDED WITHOUT PAY, THAT'S NOT MUCH OF A WAGER.
IF YOU THINK YOU'RE RIGHT, THEN WHY DON'T YOU CALL YOUR COP FRIENDS?
BECAUSE I WANT TO MAKE UP MY MIND FIRST. AND BECAUSE I DON'T BELIEVE IT WOULD BE A SMART CAREER MOVE TO REVEAL THAT I WAS BRINGING A PROFESSIONAL HITMAN TO THE POLICE GUN RANGE TO DO TARGET PRACTICE. AND BECAUSE I THOUGHT WE WERE FRIENDS.
RIGHT. ONE OTHER THING, BY THE WAY: WE'RE NOT REALLY MARRIED.

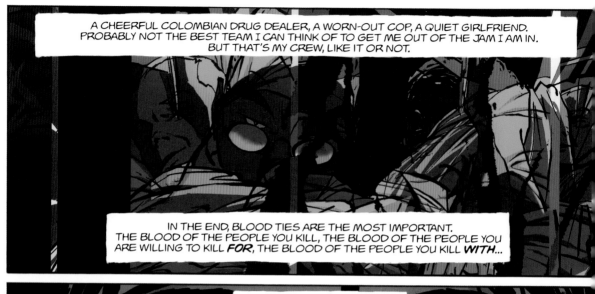

A CHEERFUL COLOMBIAN DRUG DEALER, A WORN-OUT COP, A QUIET GIRLFRIEND. PROBABLY NOT THE BEST TEAM I CAN THINK OF TO GET ME OUT OF THE JAM I AM IN. BUT THAT'S MY CREW, LIKE IT OR NOT.
IN THE END, BLOOD TIES ARE THE MOST IMPORTANT. THE BLOOD OF THE PEOPLE YOU KILL, THE BLOOD OF THE PEOPLE YOU ARE WILLING TO KILL ***FOR***, THE BLOOD OF THE PEOPLE YOU KILL ***WITH***...
...THE BLOOD OF THE PEOPLE YOU ARE READY TO ***DIE*** FOR. OR YOUR OWN BLOOD, BECAUSE NOBODY'S INVULNERABLE...
...AND BECAUSE WE HAVE TO SURVIVE. THAT'S THE ONLY RULE.
BASTILLE
STALINGRAD
NATION
PERE LACHAISE
BOLERO

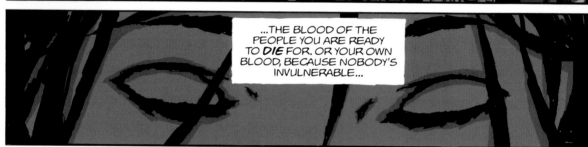

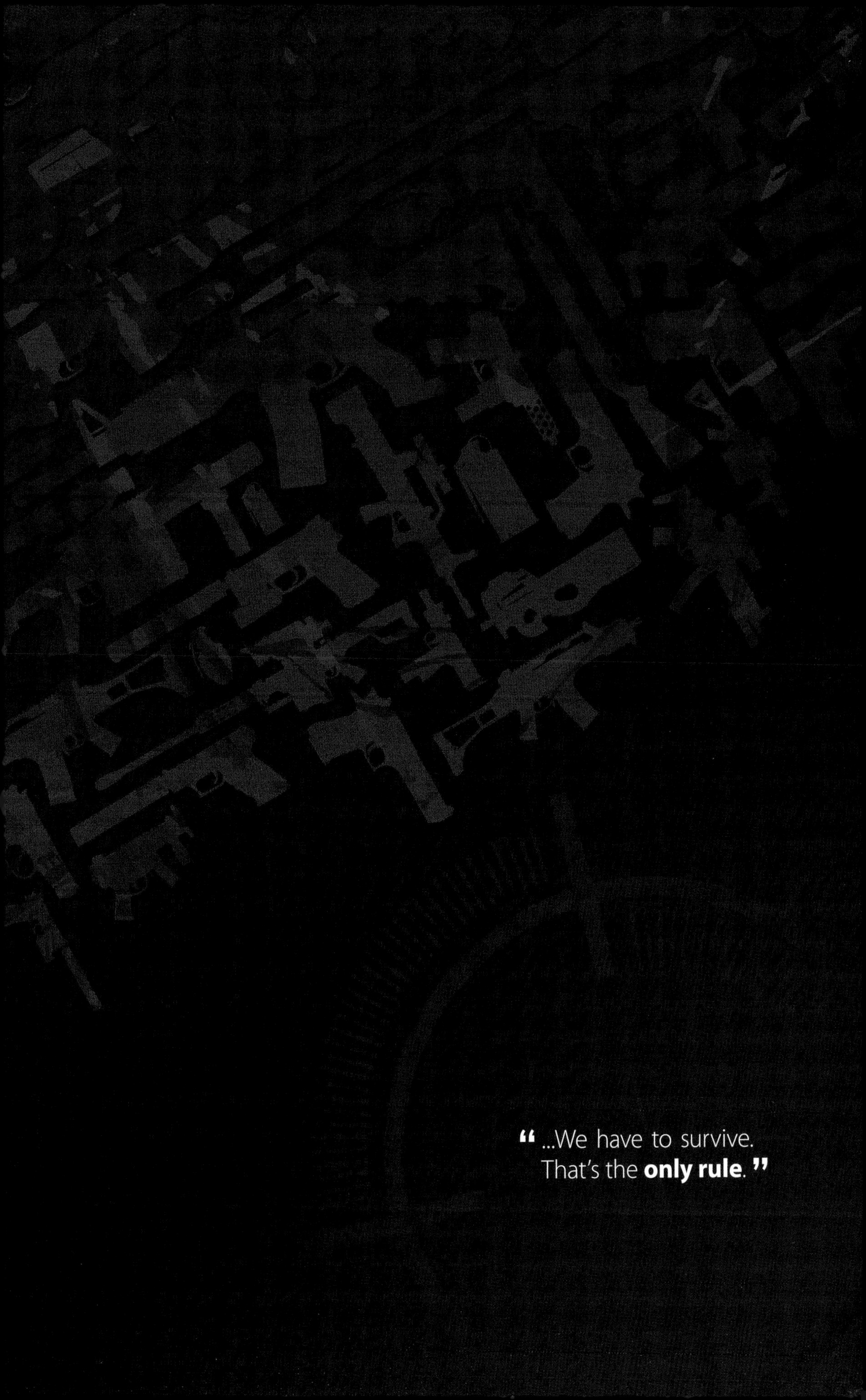
"...We have to survive.
That's the **only rule**."

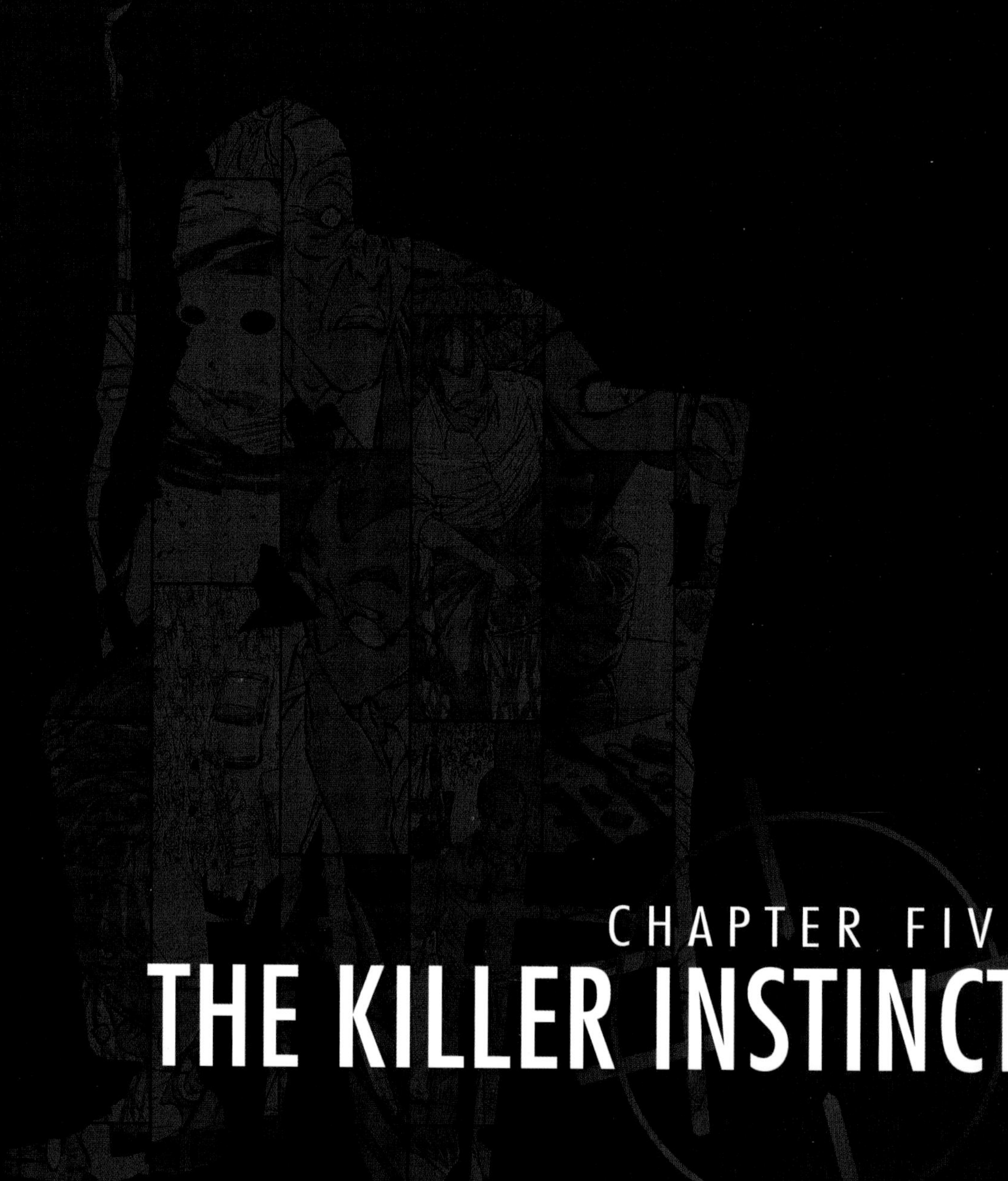

CHAPTER FIVE

THE KILLER INSTINCT

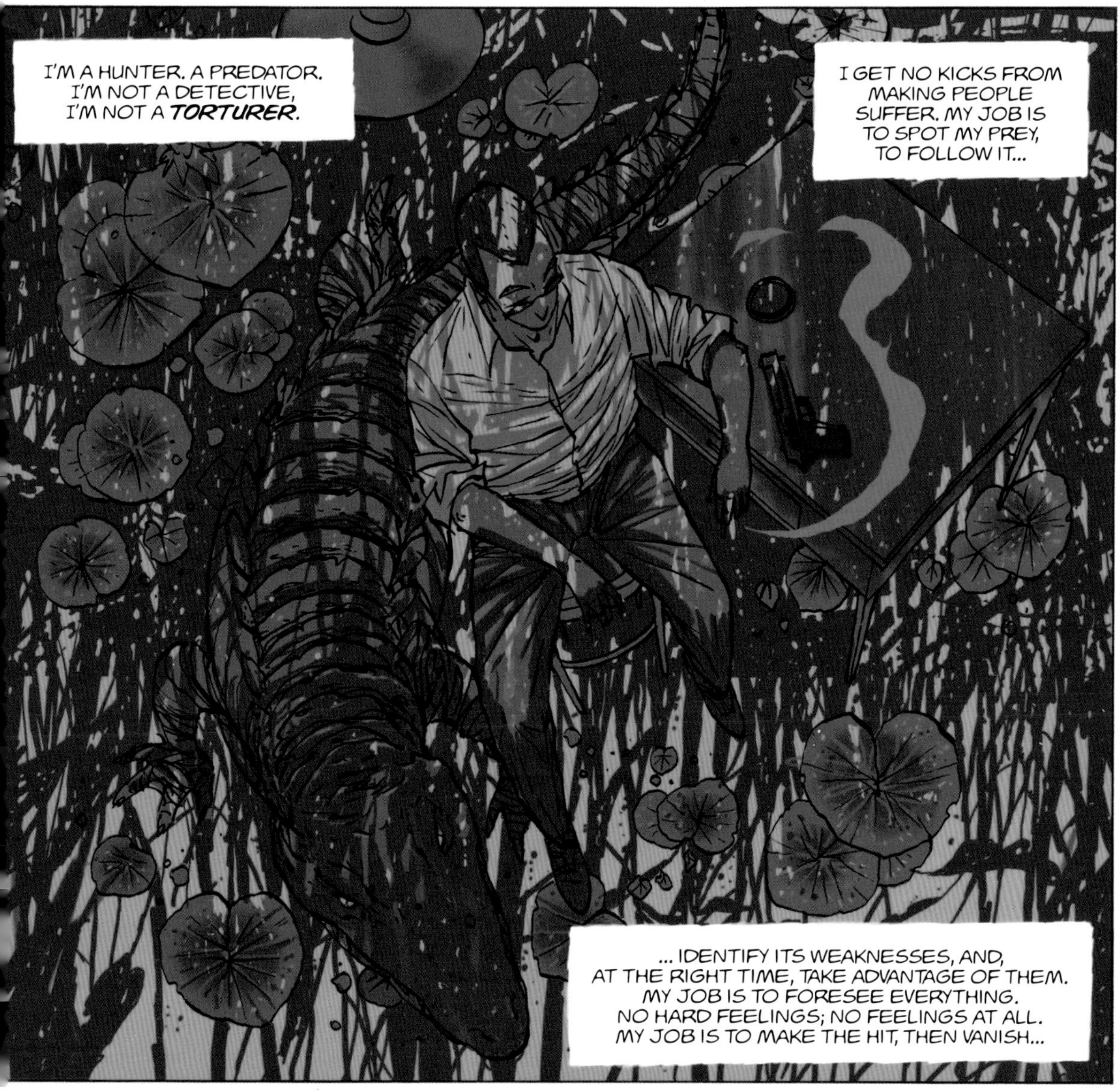
I'M A HUNTER. A PREDATOR. I'M NOT A DETECTIVE, I'M NOT A **TORTURER**.
I GET NO KICKS FROM MAKING PEOPLE SUFFER. MY JOB IS TO SPOT MY PREY, TO FOLLOW IT...
... IDENTIFY ITS WEAKNESSES, AND, AT THE RIGHT TIME, TAKE ADVANTAGE OF THEM. MY JOB IS TO FORESEE EVERYTHING. NO HARD FEELINGS; NO FEELINGS AT ALL. MY JOB IS TO MAKE THE HIT, THEN VANISH...

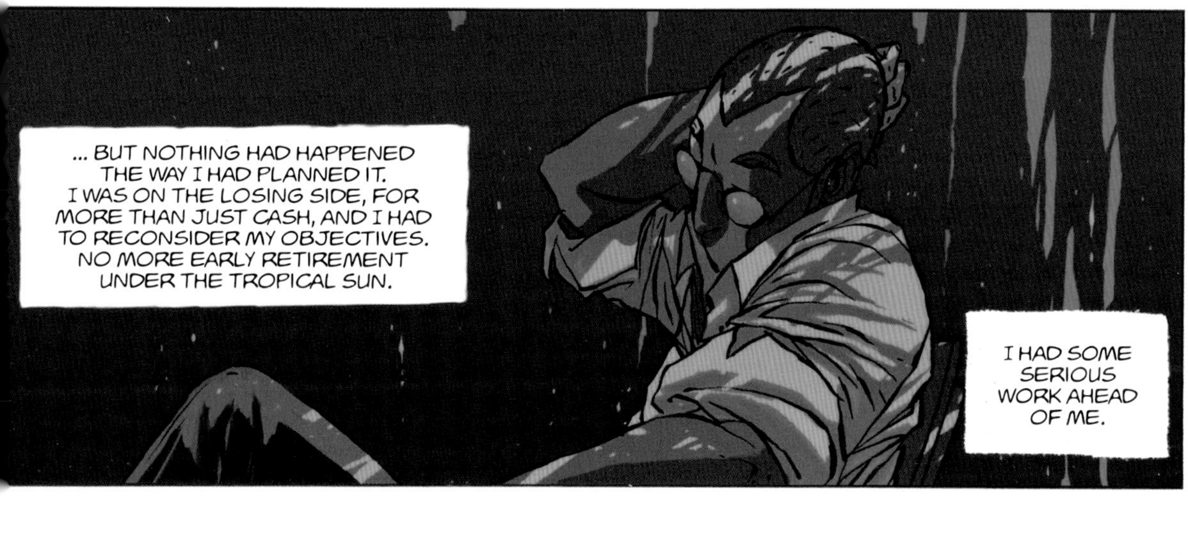
... BUT NOTHING HAD HAPPENED THE WAY I HAD PLANNED IT. I WAS ON THE LOSING SIDE, FOR MORE THAN JUST CASH, AND I HAD TO RECONSIDER MY OBJECTIVES. NO MORE EARLY RETIREMENT UNDER THE TROPICAL SUN.
I HAD SOME SERIOUS WORK AHEAD OF ME.

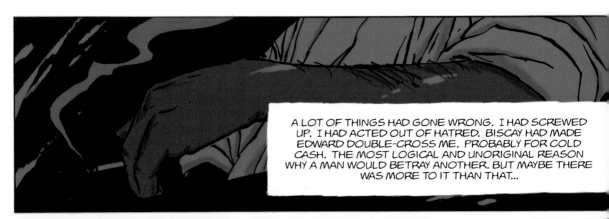

A LOT OF THINGS HAD GONE WRONG. I HAD SCREWED UP. I HAD ACTED OUT OF HATRED. BISCAY HAD MADE EDWARD DOUBLE-CROSS ME. PROBABLY FOR COLD CASH. THE MOST LOGICAL AND UNORIGINAL REASON WHY A MAN WOULD BETRAY ANOTHER. BUT MAYBE THERE WAS MORE TO IT THAN THAT...

... A PIECE OF SOME PIE I WAS APPARENTLY NOT INVITED TO SHARE. NOW, I REALLY WANTED TO KNOW WHAT THAT WAS.

WHAT ARE YOU DOING IN THE DARK, MAN?

JUST THINKING THINGS OVER, MARIANO. THAT'S ALL I SEEM TO DO THESE DAYS.

DON'T SWEAT IT. HE'LL TALK.

I'M NOT WORRIED ABOUT THAT.

MORE WHAT HE'S GOING TO SAY.

WHAT DO YOU MEAN?

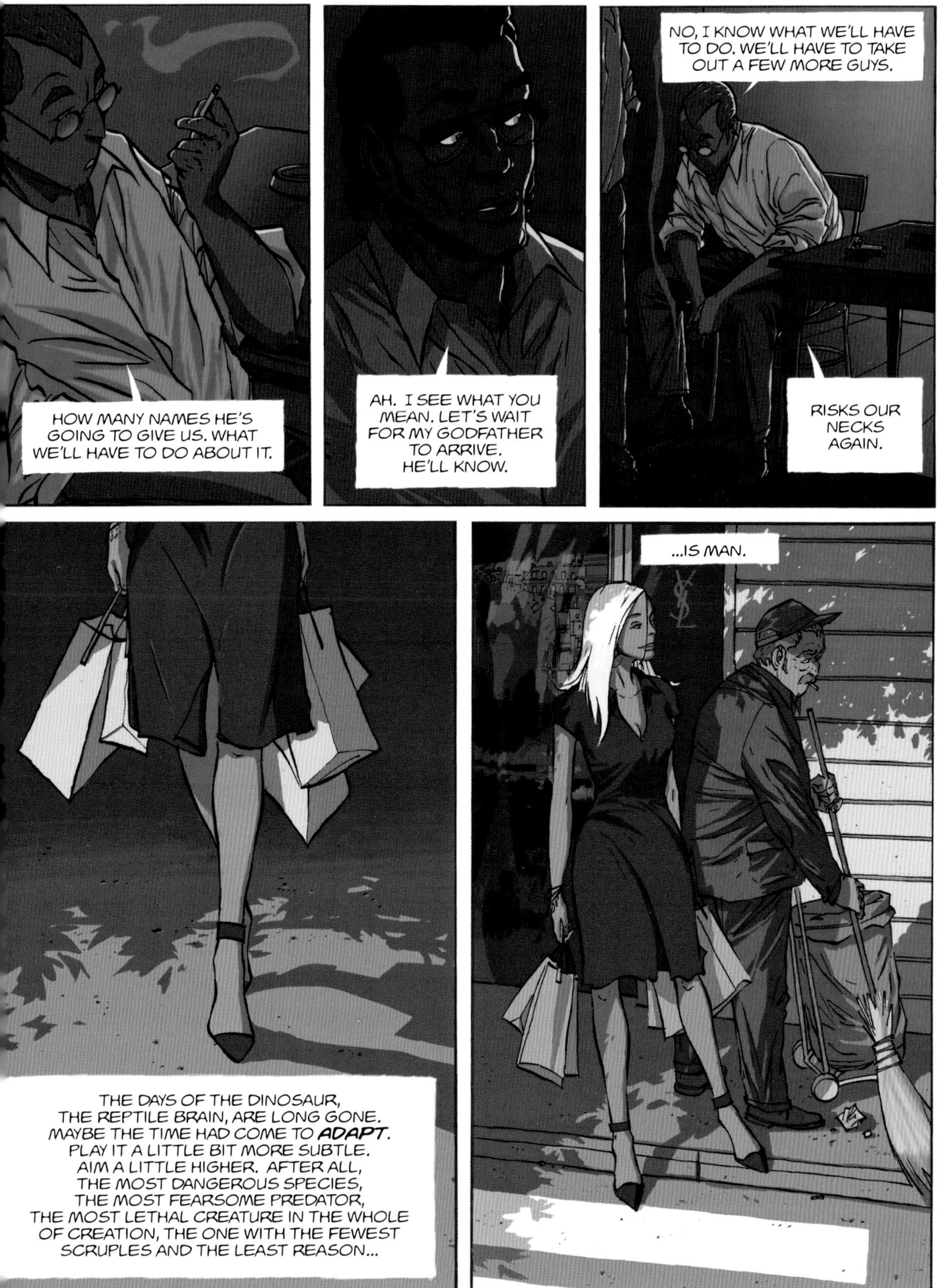
HOW MANY NAMES HE'S GOING TO GIVE US. WHAT WE'LL HAVE TO DO ABOUT IT.
AH. I SEE WHAT YOU MEAN. LET'S WAIT FOR MY GODFATHER TO ARRIVE. HE'LL KNOW.
NO, I KNOW WHAT WE'LL HAVE TO DO. WE'LL HAVE TO TAKE OUT A FEW MORE GUYS.
RISKS OUR NECKS AGAIN.
THE DAYS OF THE DINOSAUR, THE REPTILE BRAIN, ARE LONG GONE. MAYBE THE TIME HAD COME TO ***ADAPT***. PLAY IT A LITTLE BIT MORE SUBTLE. AIM A LITTLE HIGHER. AFTER ALL, THE MOST DANGEROUS SPECIES, THE MOST FEARSOME PREDATOR, THE MOST LETHAL CREATURE IN THE WHOLE OF CREATION, THE ONE WITH THE FEWEST SCRUPLES AND THE LEAST REASON...
...IS MAN.

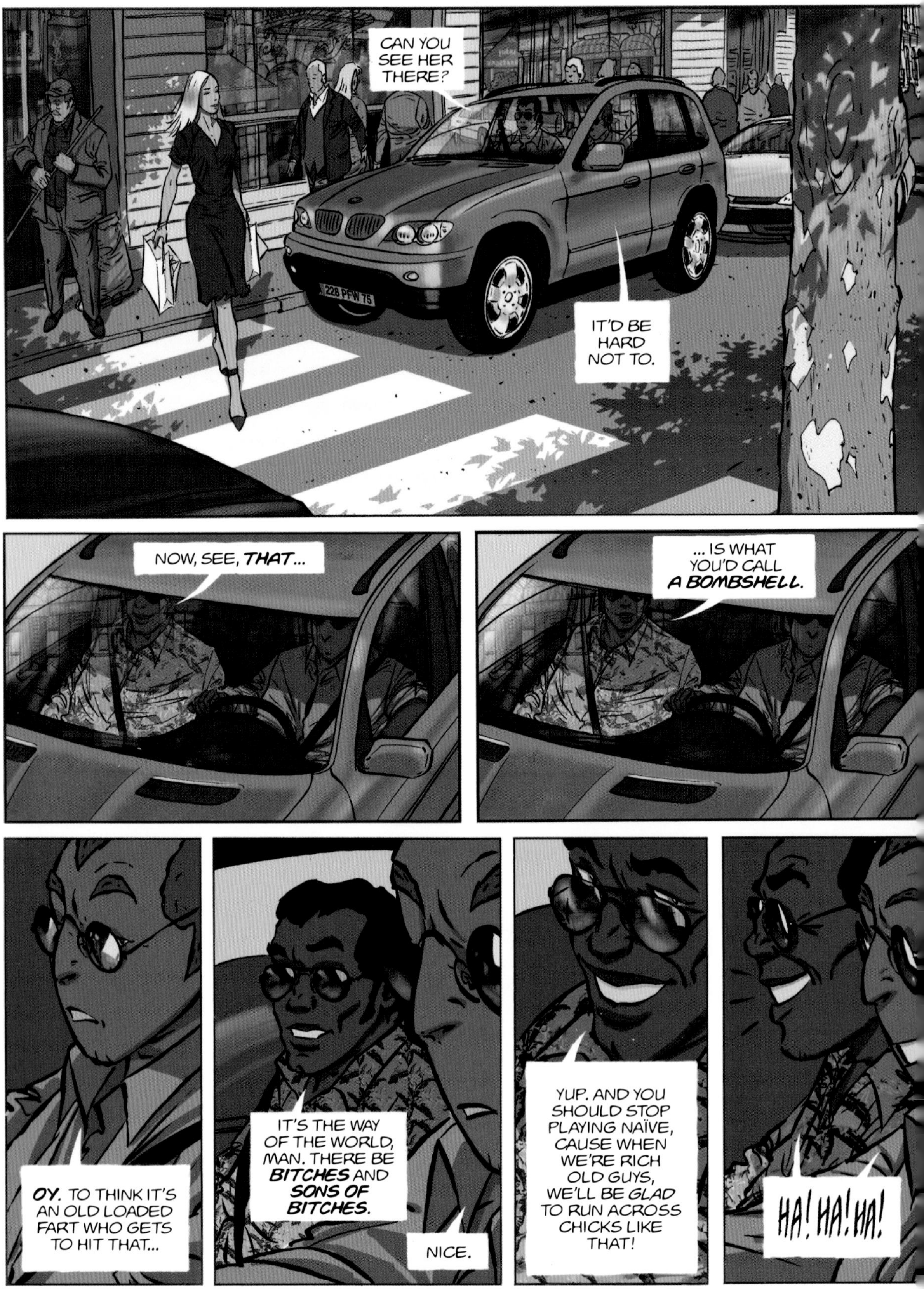
CAN YOU SEE HER THERE?
228 PFW 75
IT'D BE HARD NOT TO.
NOW, SEE, THAT...
... IS WHAT YOU'D CALL A BOMBSHELL.
OY. TO THINK IT'S AN OLD LOADED FART WHO GETS TO HIT THAT...
IT'S THE WAY OF THE WORLD, MAN. THERE BE BITCHES AND SONS OF BITCHES.
NICE.
YUP. AND YOU SHOULD STOP PLAYING NAÏVE, CAUSE WHEN WE'RE RICH OLD GUYS, WE'LL BE GLAD TO RUN ACROSS CHICKS LIKE THAT!
HA! HA! HA!

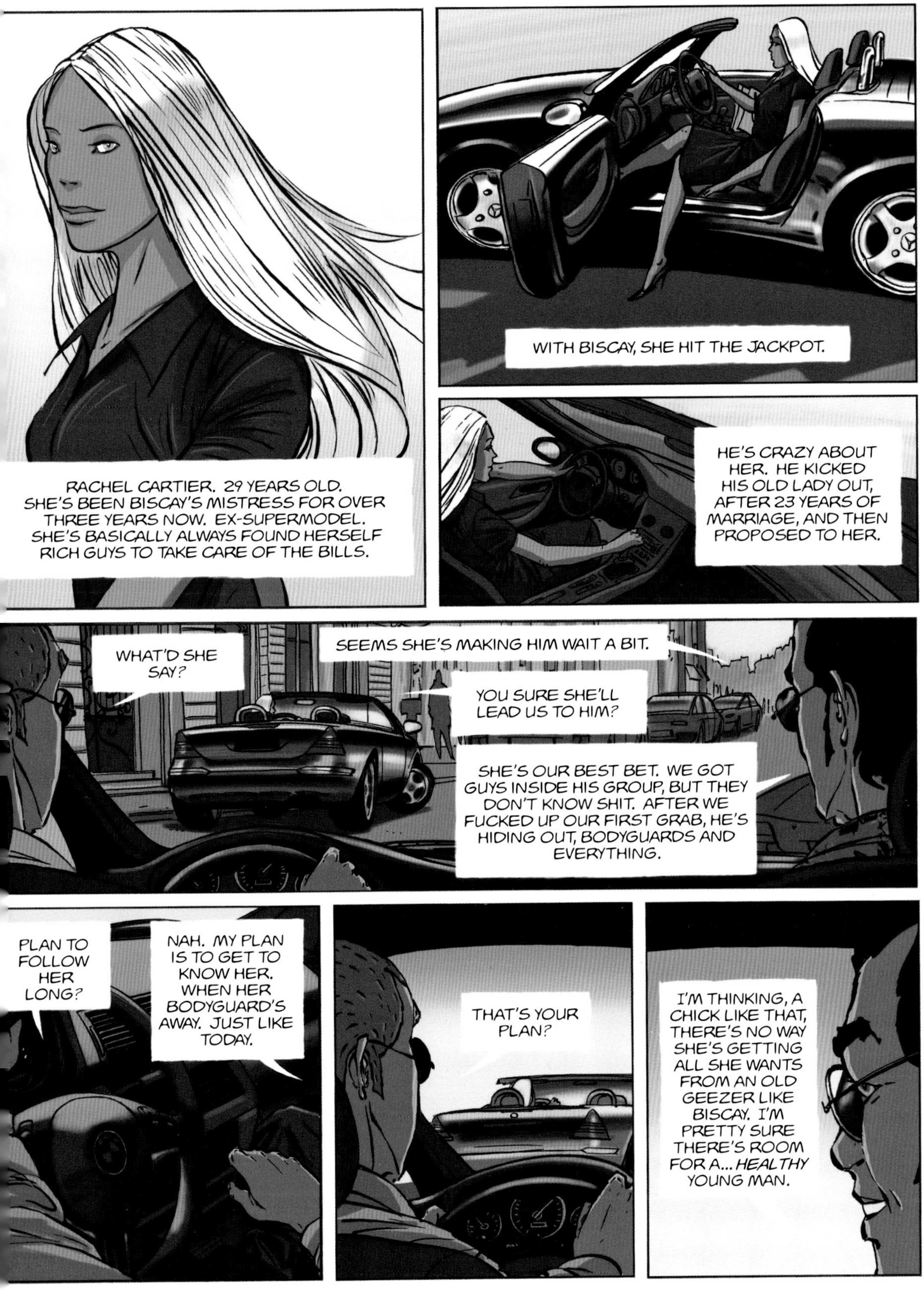
RACHEL CARTIER. 29 YEARS OLD. SHE'S BEEN BISCAY'S MISTRESS FOR OVER THREE YEARS NOW. EX-SUPERMODEL. SHE'S BASICALLY ALWAYS FOUND HERSELF RICH GUYS TO TAKE CARE OF THE BILLS.
WITH BISCAY, SHE HIT THE JACKPOT.
HE'S CRAZY ABOUT HER. HE KICKED HIS OLD LADY OUT, AFTER 23 YEARS OF MARRIAGE, AND THEN PROPOSED TO HER.
WHAT'D SHE SAY?
SEEMS SHE'S MAKING HIM WAIT A BIT.
YOU SURE SHE'LL LEAD US TO HIM?
SHE'S OUR BEST BET. WE GOT GUYS INSIDE HIS GROUP, BUT THEY DON'T KNOW SHIT. AFTER WE FUCKED UP OUR FIRST GRAB, HE'S HIDING OUT, BODYGUARDS AND EVERYTHING.
PLAN TO FOLLOW HER LONG?
NAH. MY PLAN IS TO GET TO KNOW HER. WHEN HER BODYGUARD'S AWAY. JUST LIKE TODAY.
THAT'S YOUR PLAN?
I'M THINKING, A CHICK LIKE THAT, THERE'S NO WAY SHE'S GETTING ALL SHE WANTS FROM AN OLD GEEZER LIKE BISCAY. I'M PRETTY SURE THERE'S ROOM FOR A... *HEALTHY* YOUNG MAN.

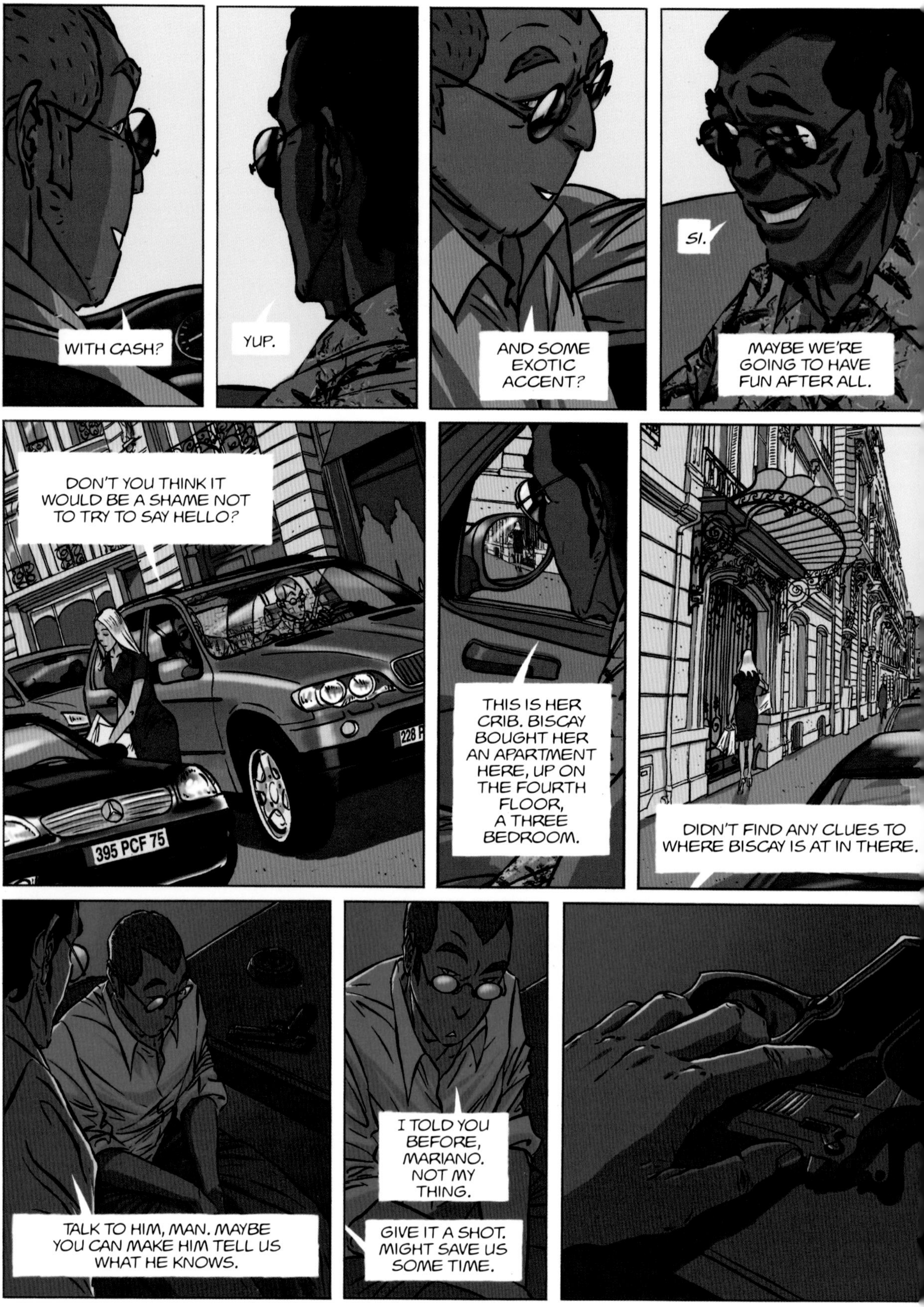
WITH CASH?
YUP.
AND SOME EXOTIC ACCENT?
SI.
MAYBE WE'RE GOING TO HAVE FUN AFTER ALL.
DON'T YOU THINK IT WOULD BE A SHAME NOT TO TRY TO SAY HELLO?
395 PCF 75
THIS IS HER CRIB. BISCAY BOUGHT HER AN APARTMENT HERE, UP ON THE FOURTH FLOOR, A THREE BEDROOM.
DIDN'T FIND ANY CLUES TO WHERE BISCAY IS AT IN THERE.
TALK TO HIM, MAN. MAYBE YOU CAN MAKE HIM TELL US WHAT HE KNOWS.
I TOLD YOU BEFORE, MARIANO. NOT MY THING.
GIVE IT A SHOT. MIGHT SAVE US SOME TIME.

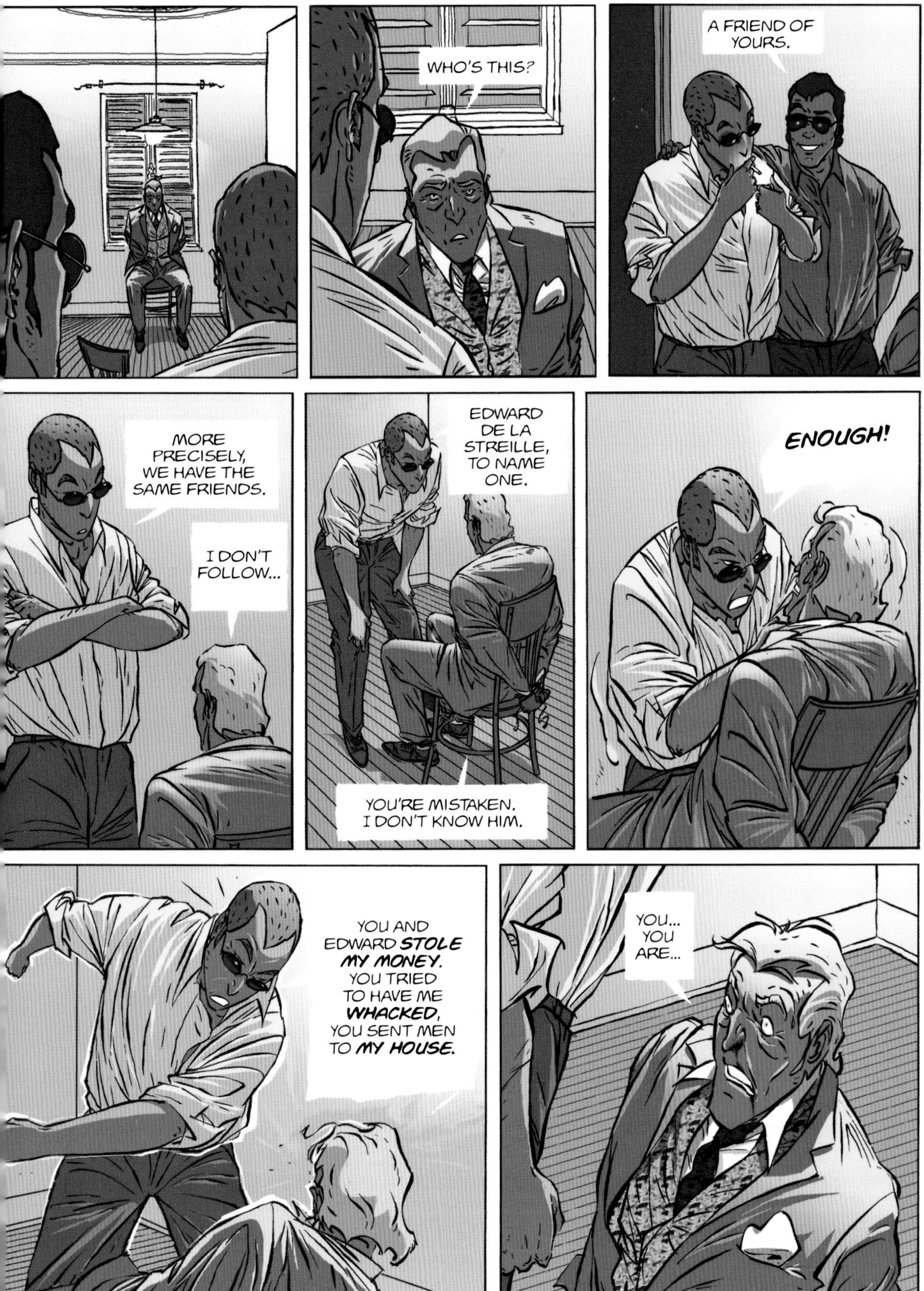
WHO'S THIS?
A FRIEND OF YOURS.
MORE PRECISELY, WE HAVE THE SAME FRIENDS.
I DON'T FOLLOW...
EDWARD DE LA STREILLE, TO NAME ONE.
YOU'RE MISTAKEN. I DON'T KNOW HIM.
ENOUGH!
YOU AND EDWARD STOLE MY MONEY. YOU TRIED TO HAVE ME WHACKED, YOU SENT MEN TO MY HOUSE.
YOU... YOU ARE...

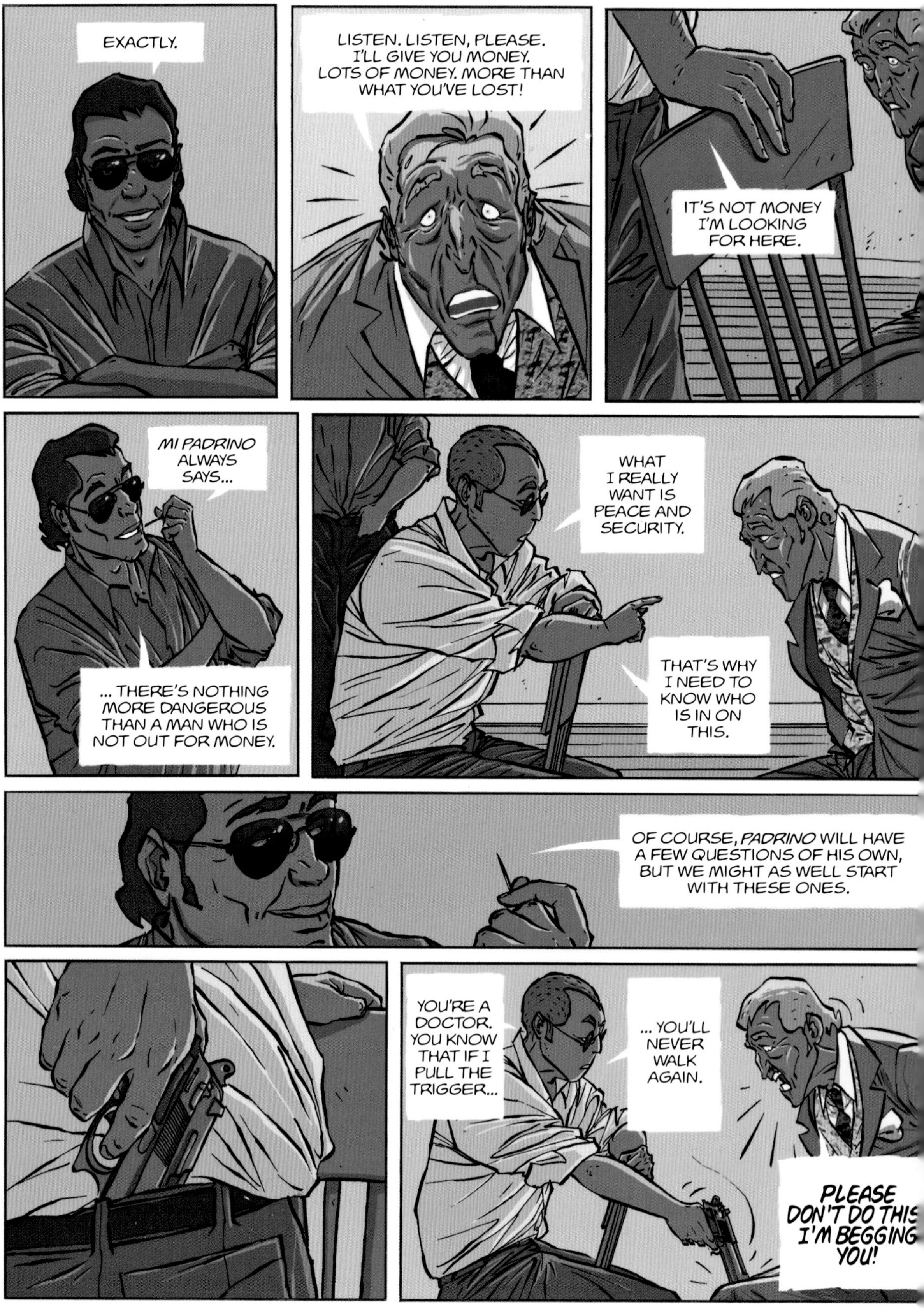
EXACTLY.
LISTEN. LISTEN, PLEASE. I'LL GIVE YOU MONEY. LOTS OF MONEY. MORE THAN WHAT YOU'VE LOST!
IT'S NOT MONEY I'M LOOKING FOR HERE.
MI PADRINO ALWAYS SAYS...
... THERE'S NOTHING MORE DANGEROUS THAN A MAN WHO IS NOT OUT FOR MONEY.
WHAT I REALLY WANT IS PEACE AND SECURITY.
THAT'S WHY I NEED TO KNOW WHO IS IN ON THIS.
OF COURSE, *PADRINO* WILL HAVE A FEW QUESTIONS OF HIS OWN, BUT WE MIGHT AS WELL START WITH THESE ONES.
YOU'RE A DOCTOR. YOU KNOW THAT IF I PULL THE TRIGGER...
... YOU'LL NEVER WALK AGAIN.
PLEASE DON'T DO THIS I'M BEGGING YOU!

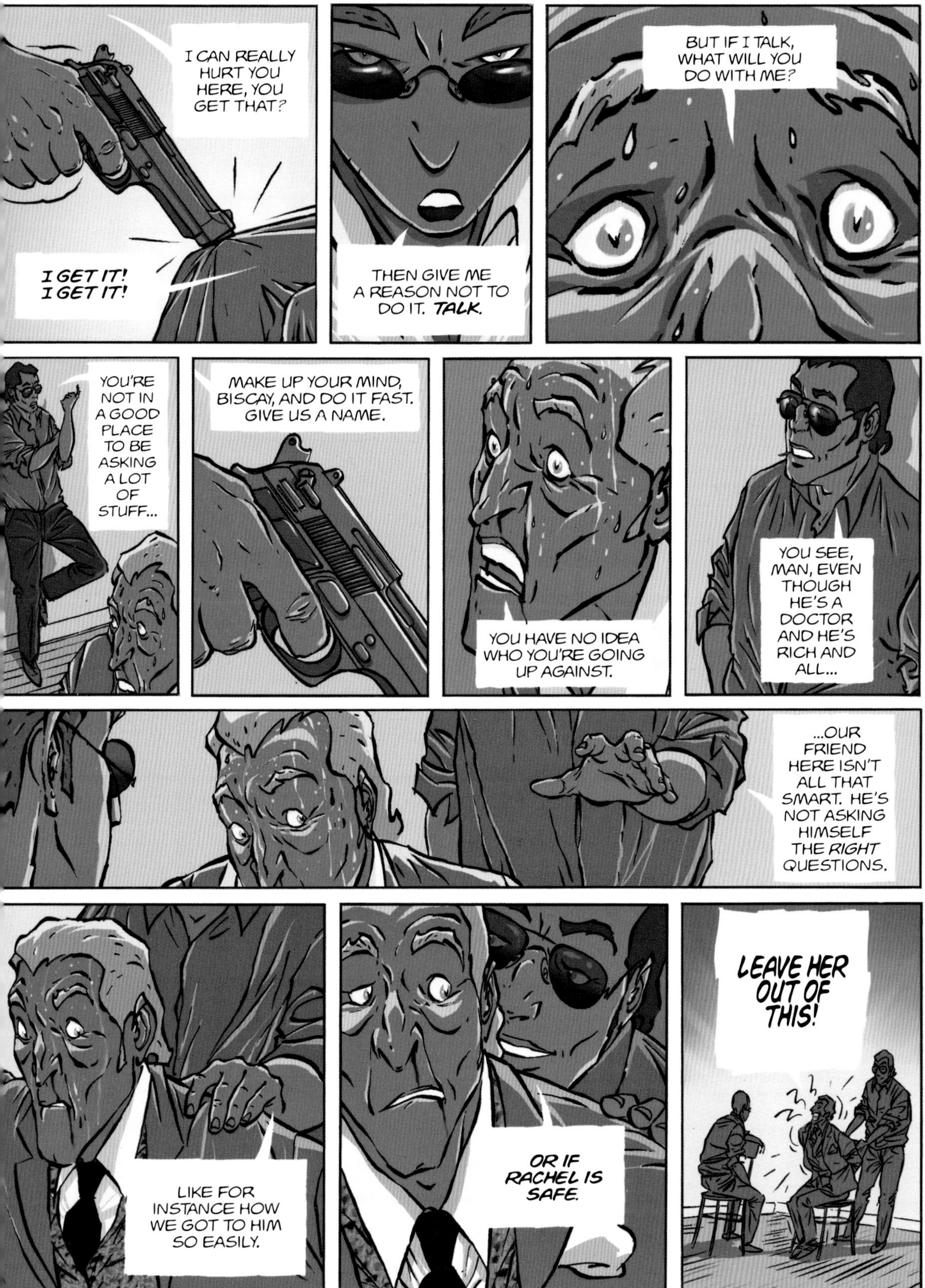
I CAN REALLY HURT YOU HERE, YOU GET THAT?
I GET IT! I GET IT!
THEN GIVE ME A REASON NOT TO DO IT. TALK.
BUT IF I TALK, WHAT WILL YOU DO WITH ME?
YOU'RE NOT IN A GOOD PLACE TO BE ASKING A LOT OF STUFF...
MAKE UP YOUR MIND, BISCAY, AND DO IT FAST. GIVE US A NAME.
YOU HAVE NO IDEA WHO YOU'RE GOING UP AGAINST.
YOU SEE, MAN, EVEN THOUGH HE'S A DOCTOR AND HE'S RICH AND ALL...
...OUR FRIEND HERE ISN'T ALL THAT SMART. HE'S NOT ASKING HIMSELF THE RIGHT QUESTIONS.
LIKE FOR INSTANCE HOW WE GOT TO HIM SO EASILY.
OR IF RACHEL IS SAFE.
LEAVE HER OUT OF THIS!

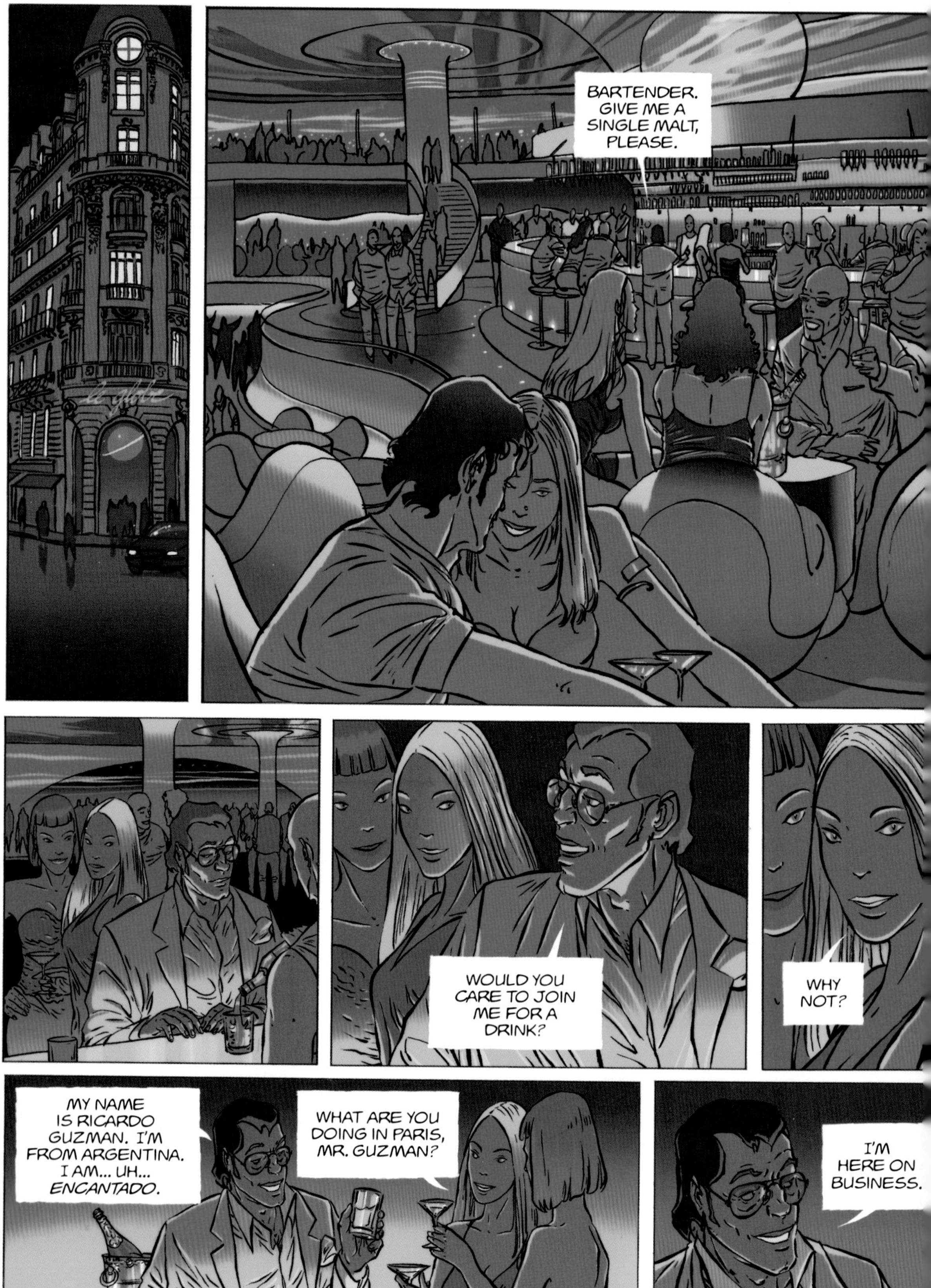
BARTENDER. GIVE ME A SINGLE MALT, PLEASE.
WOULD YOU CARE TO JOIN ME FOR A DRINK?
WHY NOT?
MY NAME IS RICARDO GUZMAN. I'M FROM ARGENTINA. I AM... UH... *ENCANTADO*.
WHAT ARE YOU DOING IN PARIS, MR. GUZMAN?
I'M HERE ON BUSINESS.

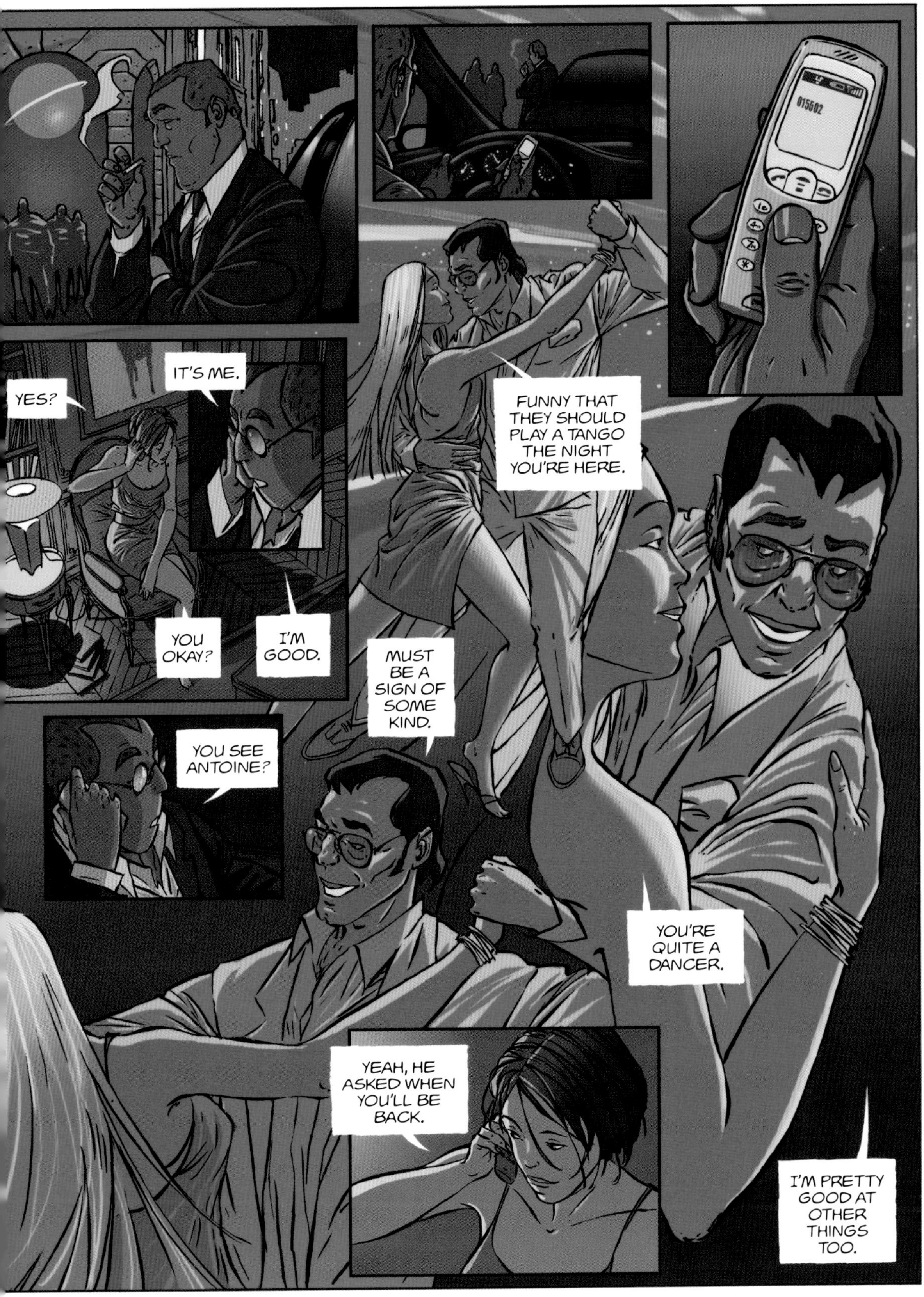
015502
YES?
IT'S ME.
YOU OKAY?
I'M GOOD.
FUNNY THAT THEY SHOULD PLAY A TANGO THE NIGHT YOU'RE HERE.
MUST BE A SIGN OF SOME KIND.
YOU SEE ANTOINE?
YOU'RE QUITE A DANCER.
YEAH, HE ASKED WHEN YOU'LL BE BACK.
I'M PRETTY GOOD AT OTHER THINGS TOO.

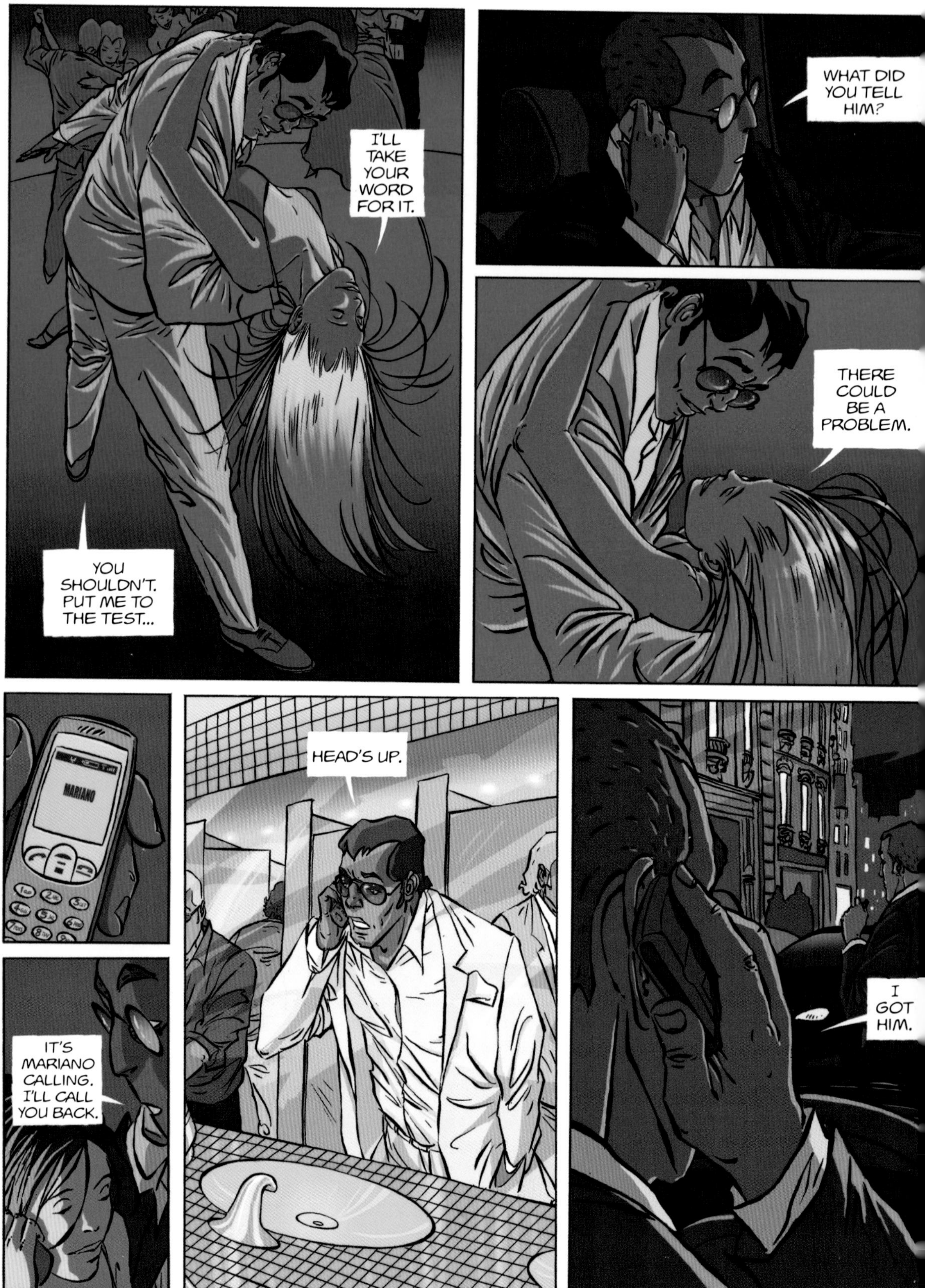
I'LL TAKE YOUR WORD FOR IT.
YOU SHOULDN'T. PUT ME TO THE TEST...
WHAT DID YOU TELL HIM?
THERE COULD BE A PROBLEM.
MARIANO
IT'S MARIANO CALLING. I'LL CALL YOU BACK.
HEAD'S UP.
I GOT HIM.

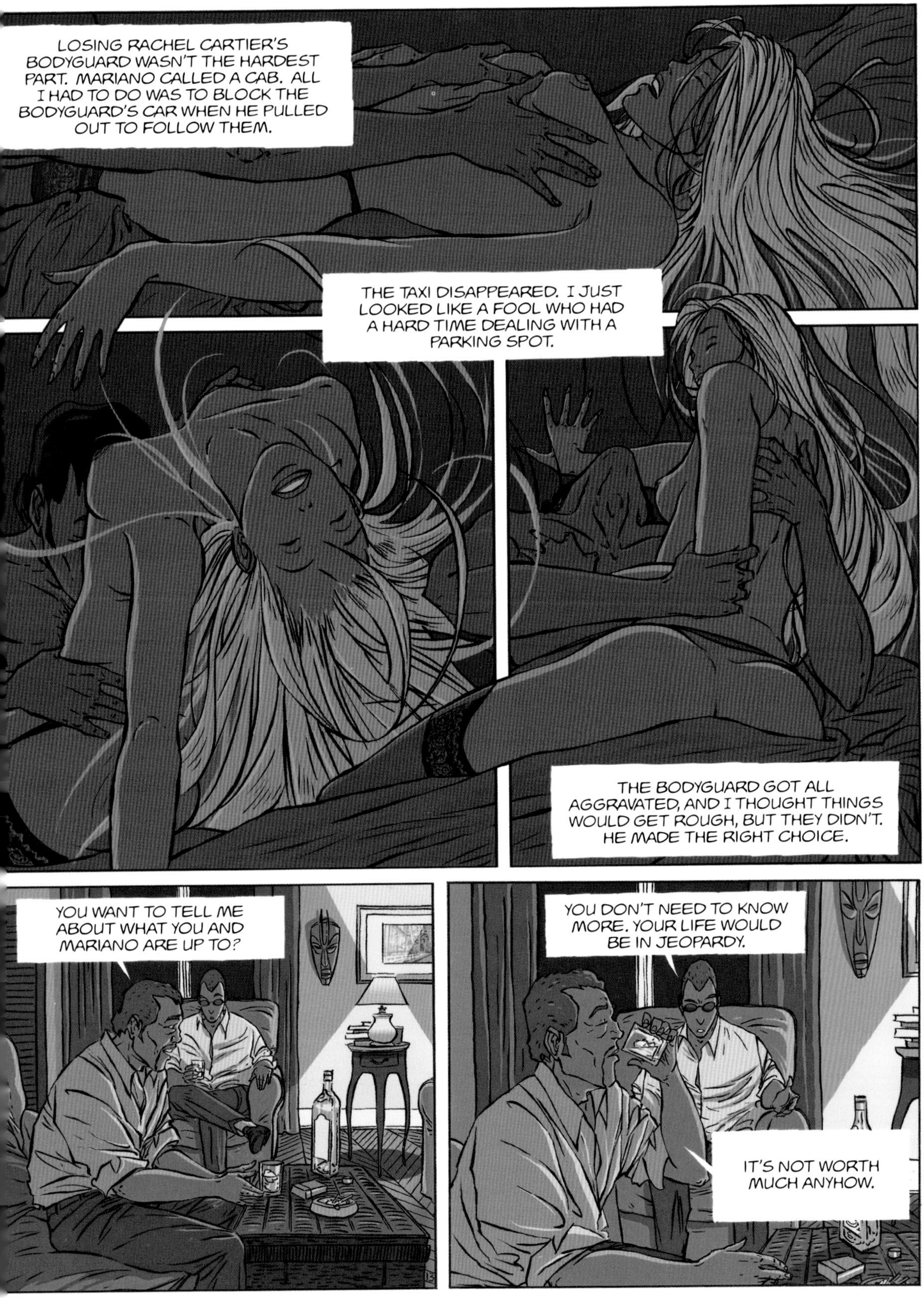
LOSING RACHEL CARTIER'S BODYGUARD WASN'T THE HARDEST PART. MARIANO CALLED A CAB. ALL I HAD TO DO WAS TO BLOCK THE BODYGUARD'S CAR WHEN HE PULLED OUT TO FOLLOW THEM.
THE TAXI DISAPPEARED. I JUST LOOKED LIKE A FOOL WHO HAD A HARD TIME DEALING WITH A PARKING SPOT.
THE BODYGUARD GOT ALL AGGRAVATED, AND I THOUGHT THINGS WOULD GET ROUGH, BUT THEY DIDN'T. HE MADE THE RIGHT CHOICE.
YOU WANT TO TELL ME ABOUT WHAT YOU AND MARIANO ARE UP TO?
YOU DON'T NEED TO KNOW MORE. YOUR LIFE WOULD BE IN JEOPARDY.
IT'S NOT WORTH MUCH ANYHOW.

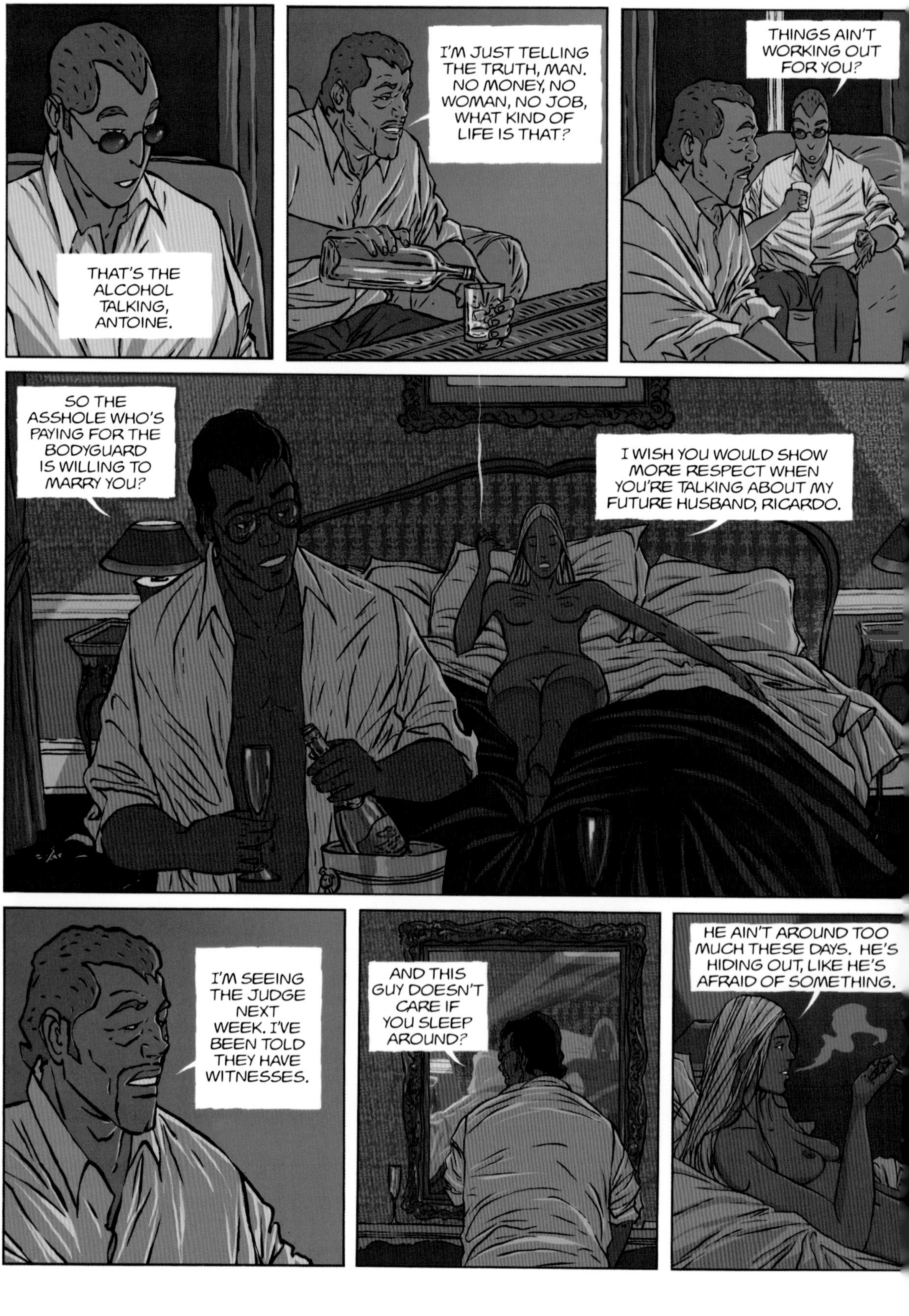
THAT'S THE ALCOHOL TALKING, ANTOINE.
I'M JUST TELLING THE TRUTH, MAN. NO MONEY, NO WOMAN, NO JOB, WHAT KIND OF LIFE IS THAT?
THINGS AIN'T WORKING OUT FOR YOU?
SO THE ASSHOLE WHO'S PAYING FOR THE BODYGUARD IS WILLING TO MARRY YOU?
I WISH YOU WOULD SHOW MORE RESPECT WHEN YOU'RE TALKING ABOUT MY FUTURE HUSBAND, RICARDO.
I'M SEEING THE JUDGE NEXT WEEK. I'VE BEEN TOLD THEY HAVE WITNESSES.
AND THIS GUY DOESN'T CARE IF YOU SLEEP AROUND?
HE AIN'T AROUND TOO MUCH THESE DAYS. HE'S HIDING OUT, LIKE HE'S AFRAID OF SOMETHING.

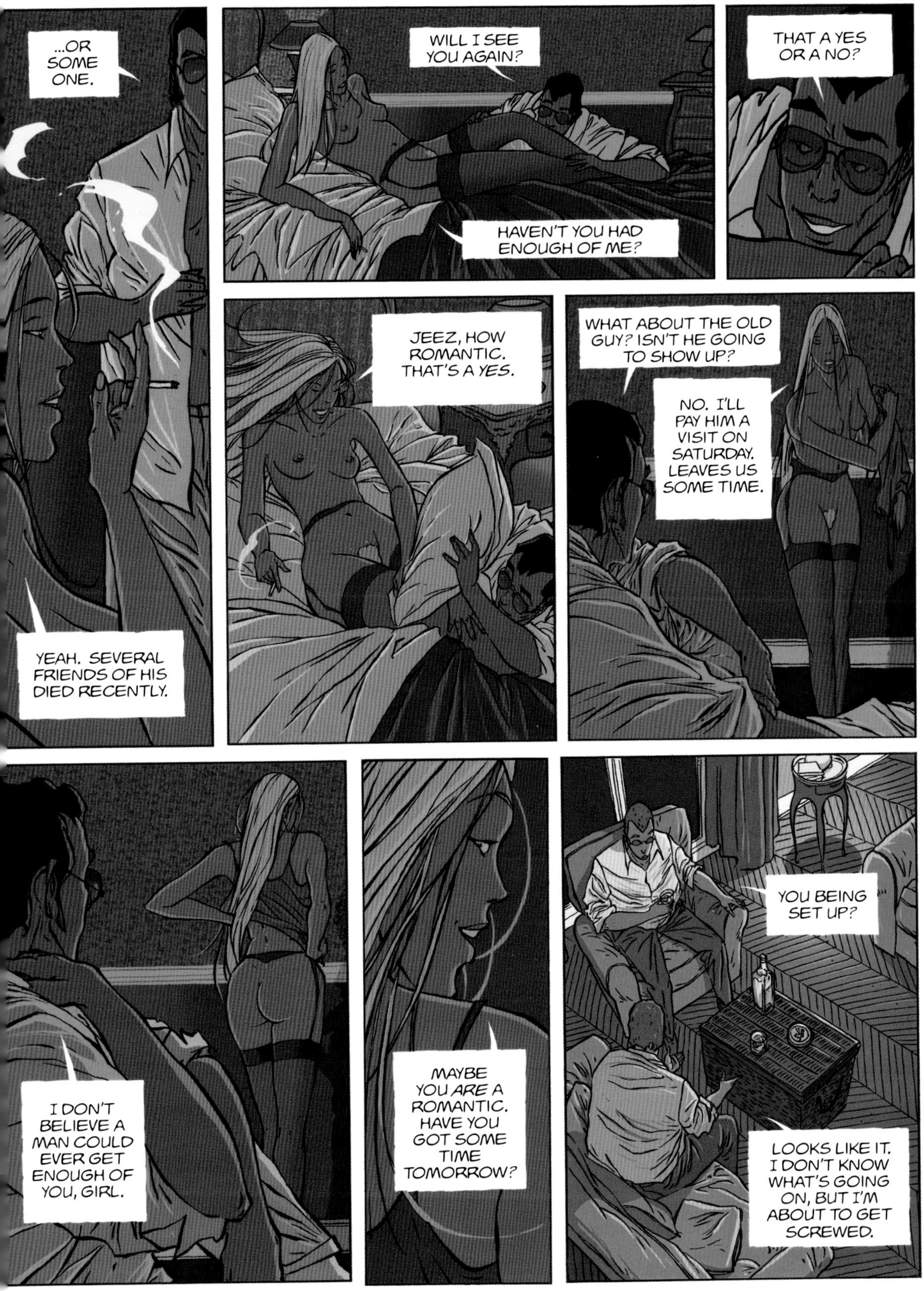
...OR SOME ONE.
YEAH. SEVERAL FRIENDS OF HIS DIED RECENTLY.
WILL I SEE YOU AGAIN?
HAVEN'T YOU HAD ENOUGH OF ME?
THAT A YES OR A NO?
JEEZ, HOW ROMANTIC. THAT'S A *YES.*
WHAT ABOUT THE OLD GUY? ISN'T HE GOING TO SHOW UP?
NO. I'LL PAY HIM A VISIT ON SATURDAY. LEAVES US SOME TIME.
I DON'T BELIEVE A MAN COULD EVER GET ENOUGH OF YOU, GIRL.
MAYBE YOU *ARE* A ROMANTIC. HAVE YOU GOT SOME TIME TOMORROW?
YOU BEING SET UP?
LOOKS LIKE IT. I DON'T KNOW WHAT'S GOING ON, BUT I'M ABOUT TO GET SCREWED.

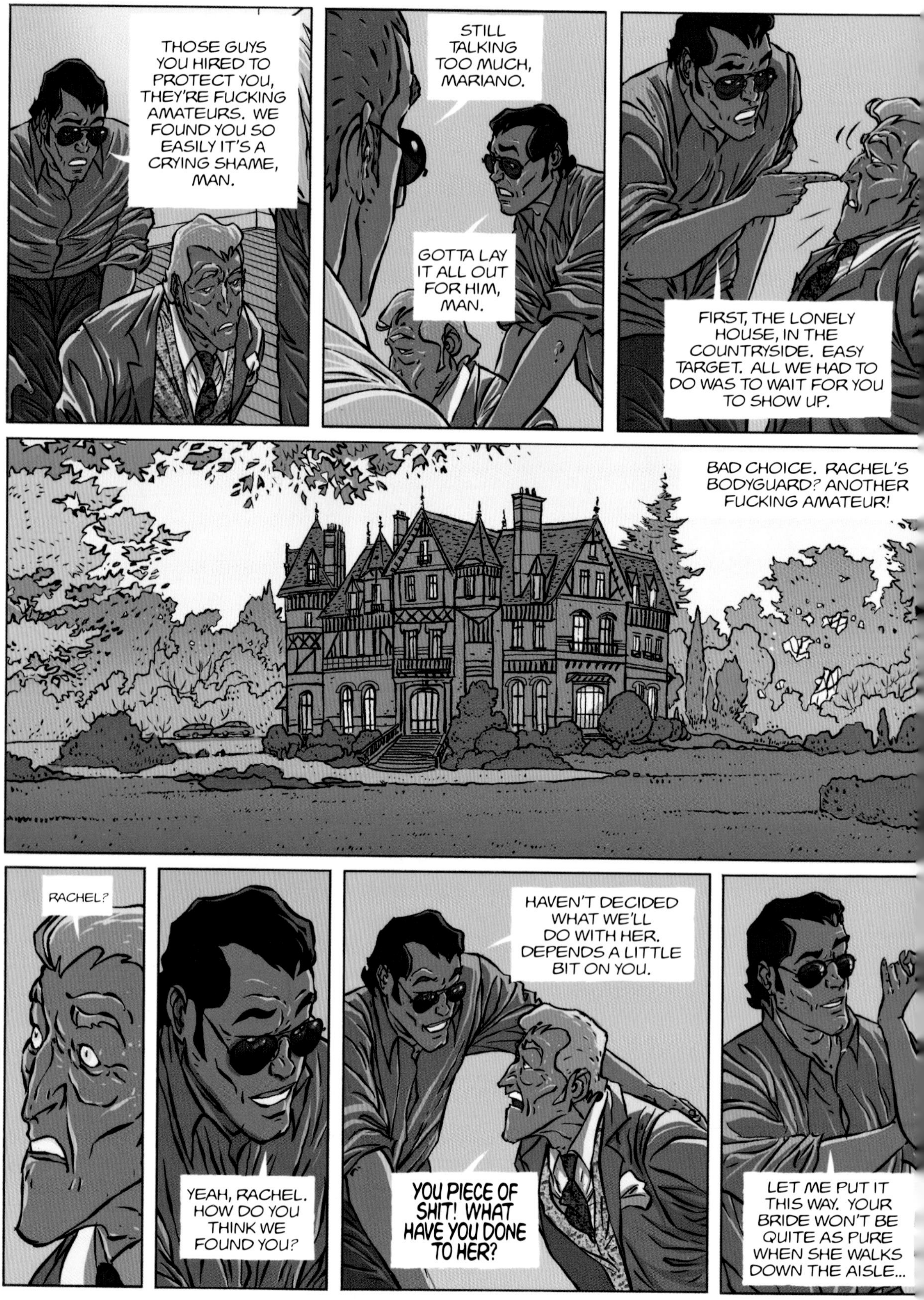
THOSE GUYS YOU HIRED TO PROTECT YOU, THEY'RE FUCKING AMATEURS. WE FOUND YOU SO EASILY IT'S A CRYING SHAME, MAN.
STILL TALKING TOO MUCH, MARIANO.
GOTTA LAY IT ALL OUT FOR HIM, MAN.
FIRST, THE LONELY HOUSE, IN THE COUNTRYSIDE. EASY TARGET. ALL WE HAD TO DO WAS TO WAIT FOR YOU TO SHOW UP.
BAD CHOICE. RACHEL'S BODYGUARD? ANOTHER FUCKING AMATEUR!
RACHEL?
YEAH, RACHEL. HOW DO YOU THINK WE FOUND YOU?
HAVEN'T DECIDED WHAT WE'LL DO WITH HER. DEPENDS A LITTLE BIT ON YOU.
YOU PIECE OF SHIT! WHAT HAVE YOU DONE TO HER?
LET ME PUT IT THIS WAY. YOUR BRIDE WON'T BE QUITE AS PURE WHEN SHE WALKS DOWN THE AISLE...

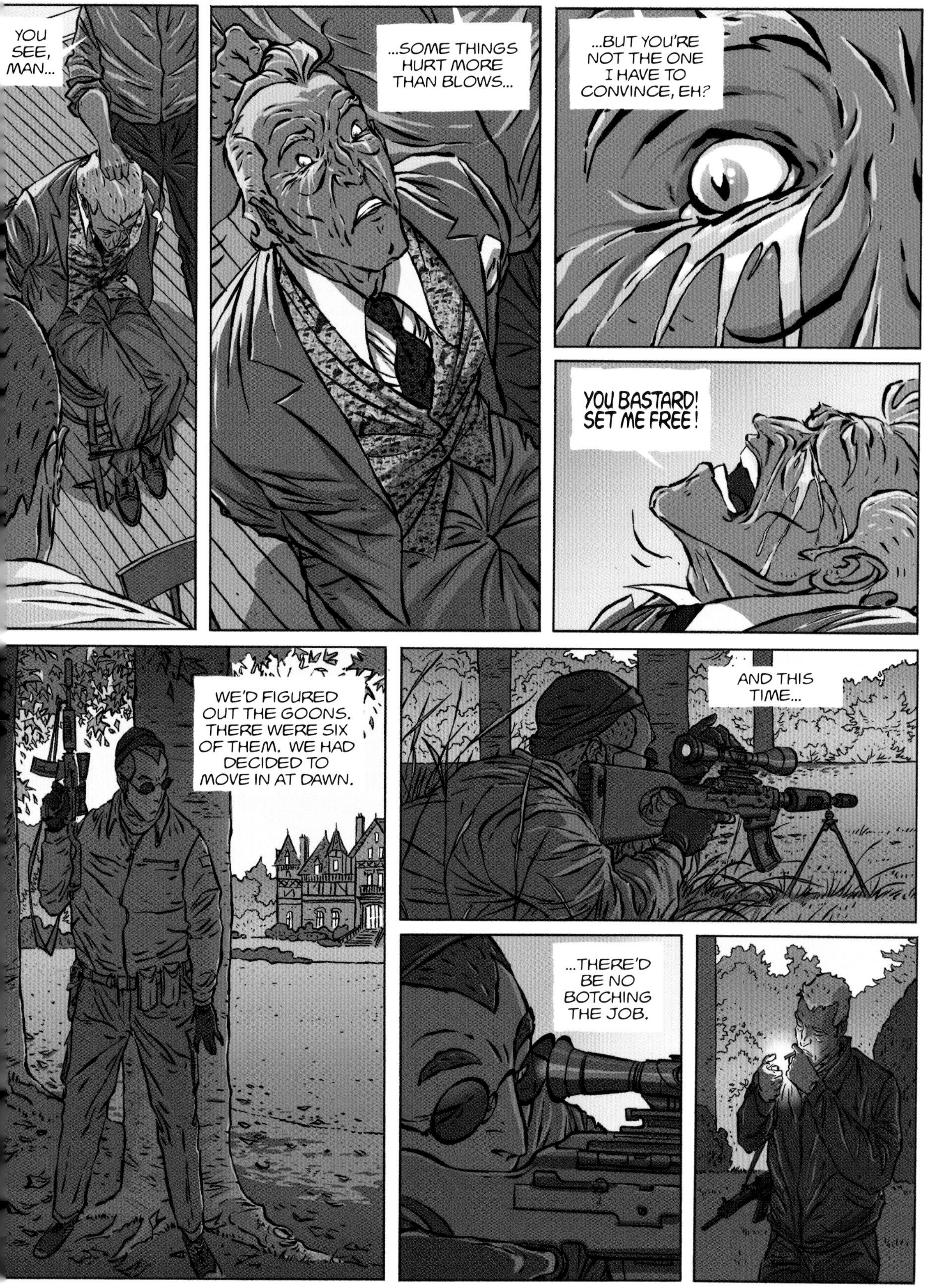
YOU SEE, MAN...
...SOME THINGS HURT MORE THAN BLOWS...
...BUT YOU'RE NOT THE ONE I HAVE TO CONVINCE, EH?
YOU BASTARD! SET ME FREE!
WE'D FIGURED OUT THE GOONS. THERE WERE SIX OF THEM. WE HAD DECIDED TO MOVE IN AT DAWN.
AND THIS TIME...
...THERE'D BE NO BOTCHING THE JOB.

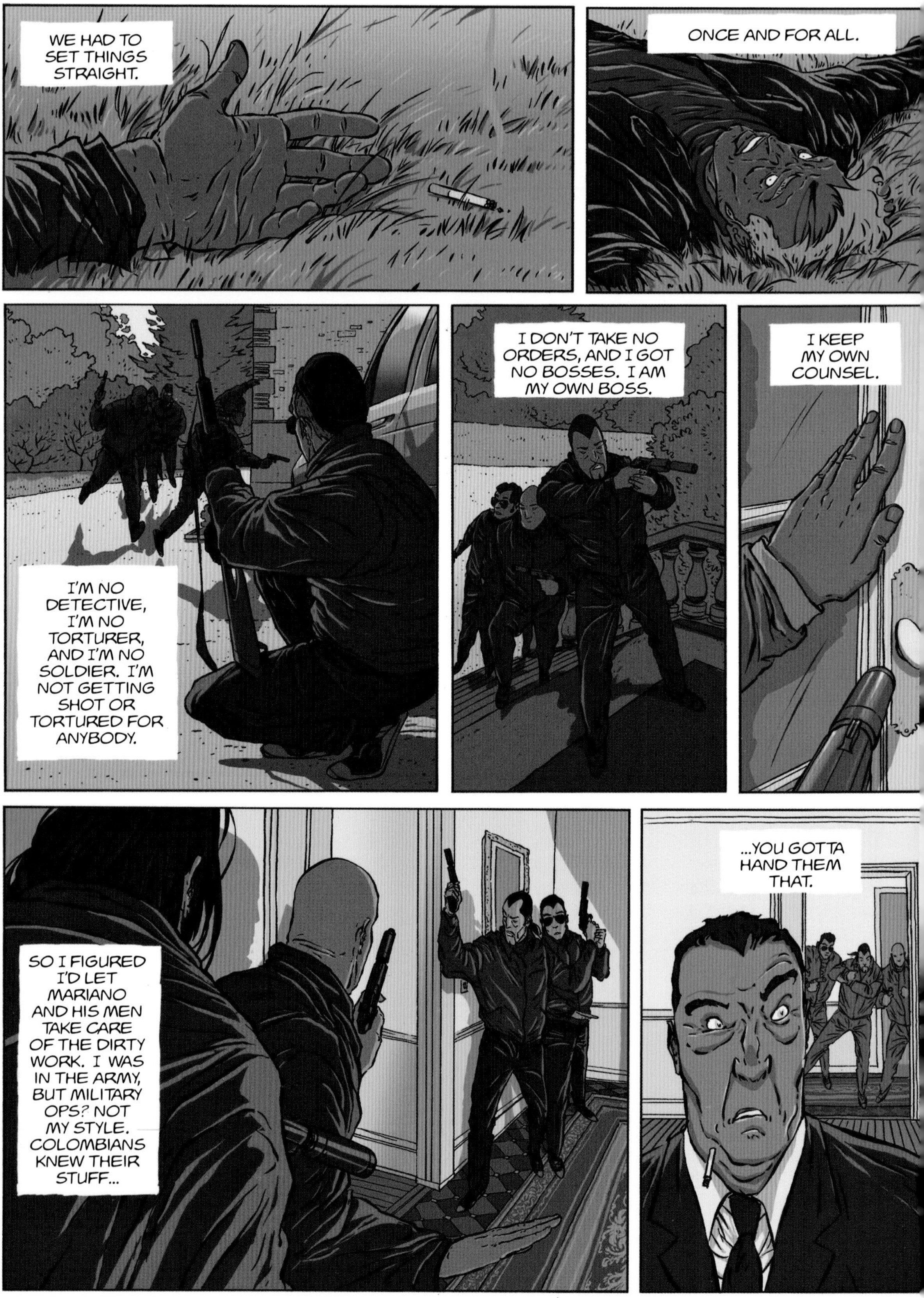
WE HAD TO SET THINGS STRAIGHT.
ONCE AND FOR ALL.
I'M NO DETECTIVE, I'M NO TORTURER, AND I'M NO SOLDIER. I'M NOT GETTING SHOT OR TORTURED FOR ANYBODY.
I DON'T TAKE NO ORDERS, AND I GOT NO BOSSES. I AM MY OWN BOSS.
I KEEP MY OWN COUNSEL.
SO I FIGURED I'D LET MARIANO AND HIS MEN TAKE CARE OF THE DIRTY WORK. I WAS IN THE ARMY, BUT MILITARY OPS? NOT MY STYLE. COLOMBIANS KNEW THEIR STUFF...
...YOU GOTTA HAND THEM THAT.

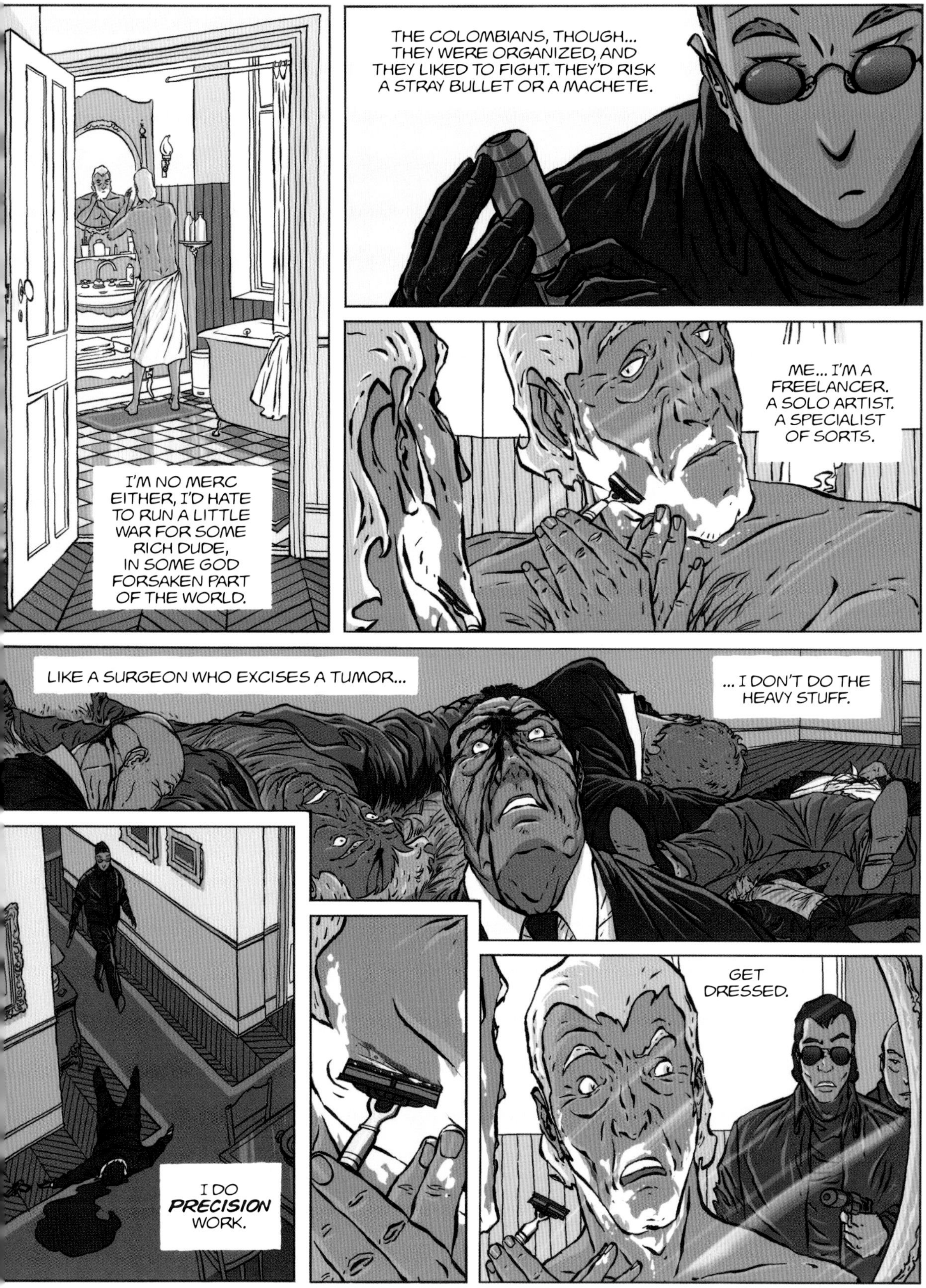
THE COLOMBIANS, THOUGH... THEY WERE ORGANIZED, AND THEY LIKED TO FIGHT. THEY'D RISK A STRAY BULLET OR A MACHETE.
I'M NO MERC EITHER, I'D HATE TO RUN A LITTLE WAR FOR SOME RICH DUDE, IN SOME GOD FORSAKEN PART OF THE WORLD.
ME... I'M A FREELANCER. A SOLO ARTIST. A SPECIALIST OF SORTS.
LIKE A SURGEON WHO EXCISES A TUMOR...
... I DON'T DO THE HEAVY STUFF.
I DO **PRECISION** WORK.
GET DRESSED.

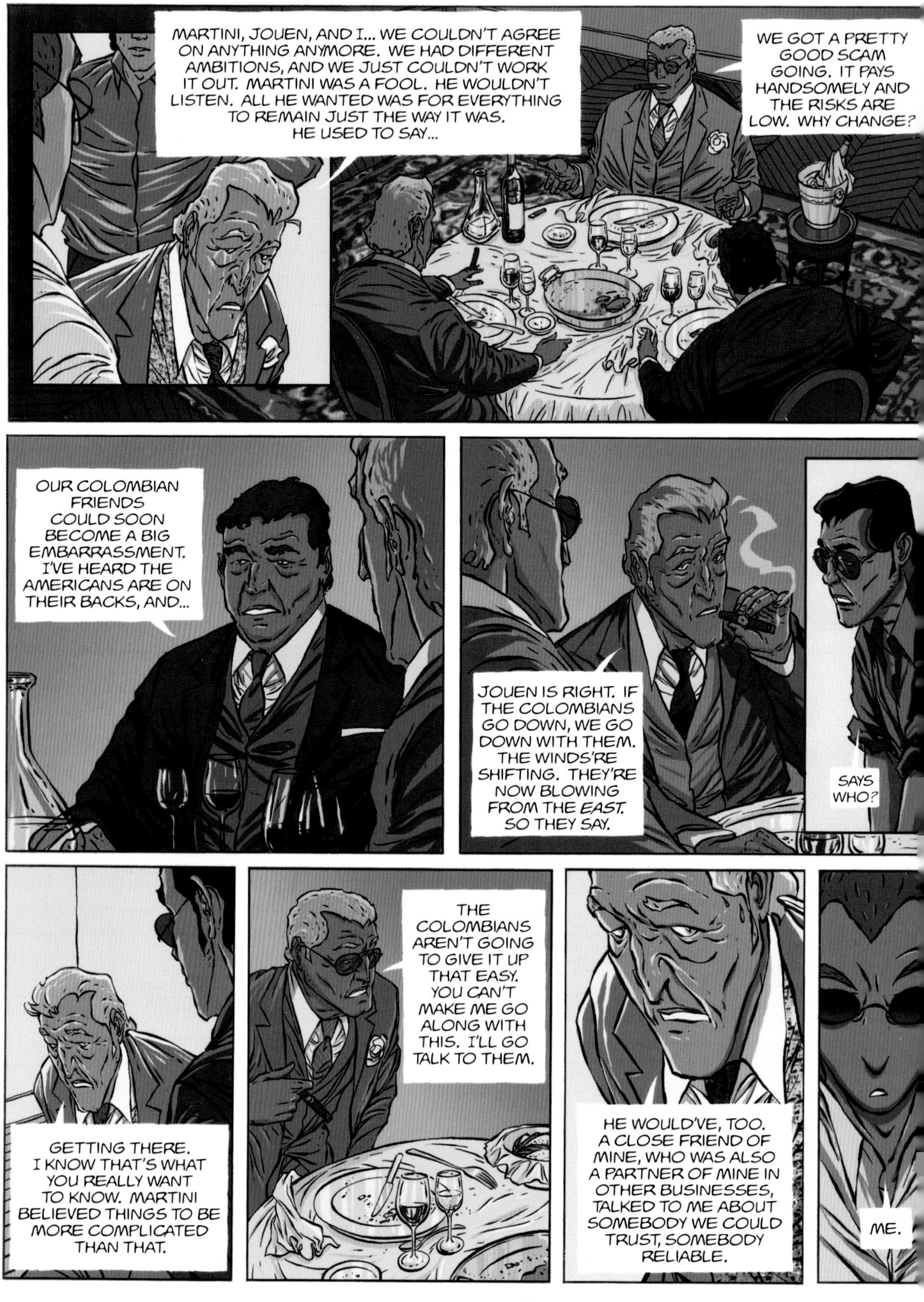
MARTINI, JOUEN, AND I... WE COULDN'T AGREE ON ANYTHING ANYMORE. WE HAD DIFFERENT AMBITIONS, AND WE JUST COULDN'T WORK IT OUT. MARTINI WAS A FOOL. HE WOULDN'T LISTEN. ALL HE WANTED WAS FOR EVERYTHING TO REMAIN JUST THE WAY IT WAS. HE USED TO SAY...
WE GOT A PRETTY GOOD SCAM GOING. IT PAYS HANDSOMELY AND THE RISKS ARE LOW. WHY CHANGE?
OUR COLOMBIAN FRIENDS COULD SOON BECOME A BIG EMBARRASSMENT. I'VE HEARD THE AMERICANS ARE ON THEIR BACKS, AND...
JOUEN IS RIGHT. IF THE COLOMBIANS GO DOWN, WE GO DOWN WITH THEM. THE WINDS'RE SHIFTING. THEY'RE NOW BLOWING FROM THE *EAST.* SO THEY SAY.
SAYS WHO?
GETTING THERE. I KNOW THAT'S WHAT YOU REALLY WANT TO KNOW. MARTINI BELIEVED THINGS TO BE MORE COMPLICATED THAN THAT.
THE COLOMBIANS AREN'T GOING TO GIVE IT UP THAT EASY. YOU CAN'T MAKE ME GO ALONG WITH THIS. I'LL GO TALK TO THEM.
HE WOULD'VE, TOO. A CLOSE FRIEND OF MINE, WHO WAS ALSO A PARTNER OF MINE IN OTHER BUSINESSES, TALKED TO ME ABOUT SOMEBODY WE COULD TRUST, SOMEBODY RELIABLE.
ME.

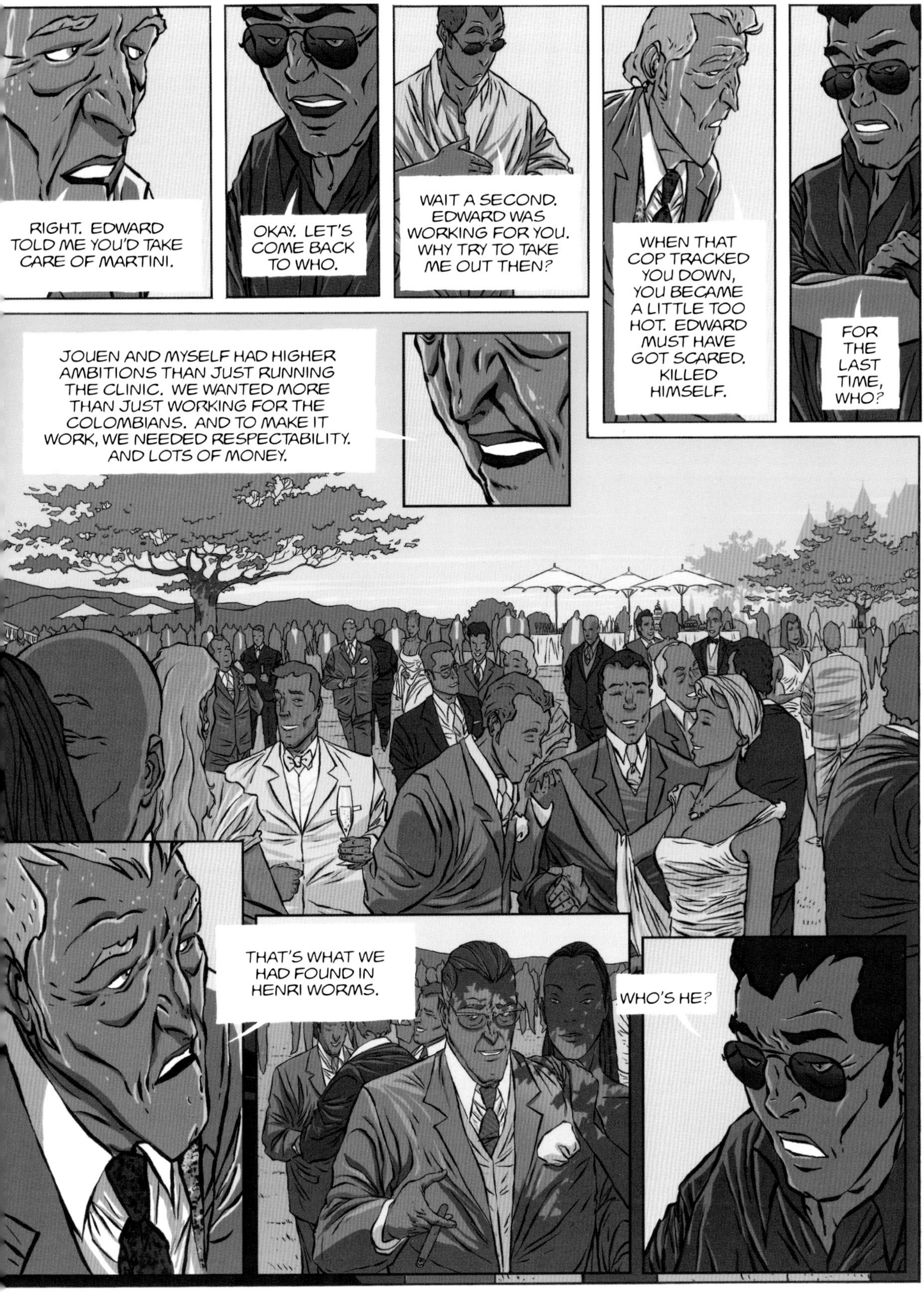
RIGHT. EDWARD TOLD ME YOU'D TAKE CARE OF MARTINI.
OKAY. LET'S COME BACK TO WHO.
WAIT A SECOND. EDWARD WAS WORKING FOR YOU. WHY TRY TO TAKE ME OUT THEN?
WHEN THAT COP TRACKED YOU DOWN, YOU BECAME A LITTLE TOO HOT. EDWARD MUST HAVE GOT SCARED. KILLED HIMSELF.
FOR THE LAST TIME, WHO?
JOUEN AND MYSELF HAD HIGHER AMBITIONS THAN JUST RUNNING THE CLINIC. WE WANTED MORE THAN JUST WORKING FOR THE COLOMBIANS. AND TO MAKE IT WORK, WE NEEDED RESPECTABILITY. AND LOTS OF MONEY.
THAT'S WHAT WE HAD FOUND IN HENRI WORMS.
WHO'S HE?

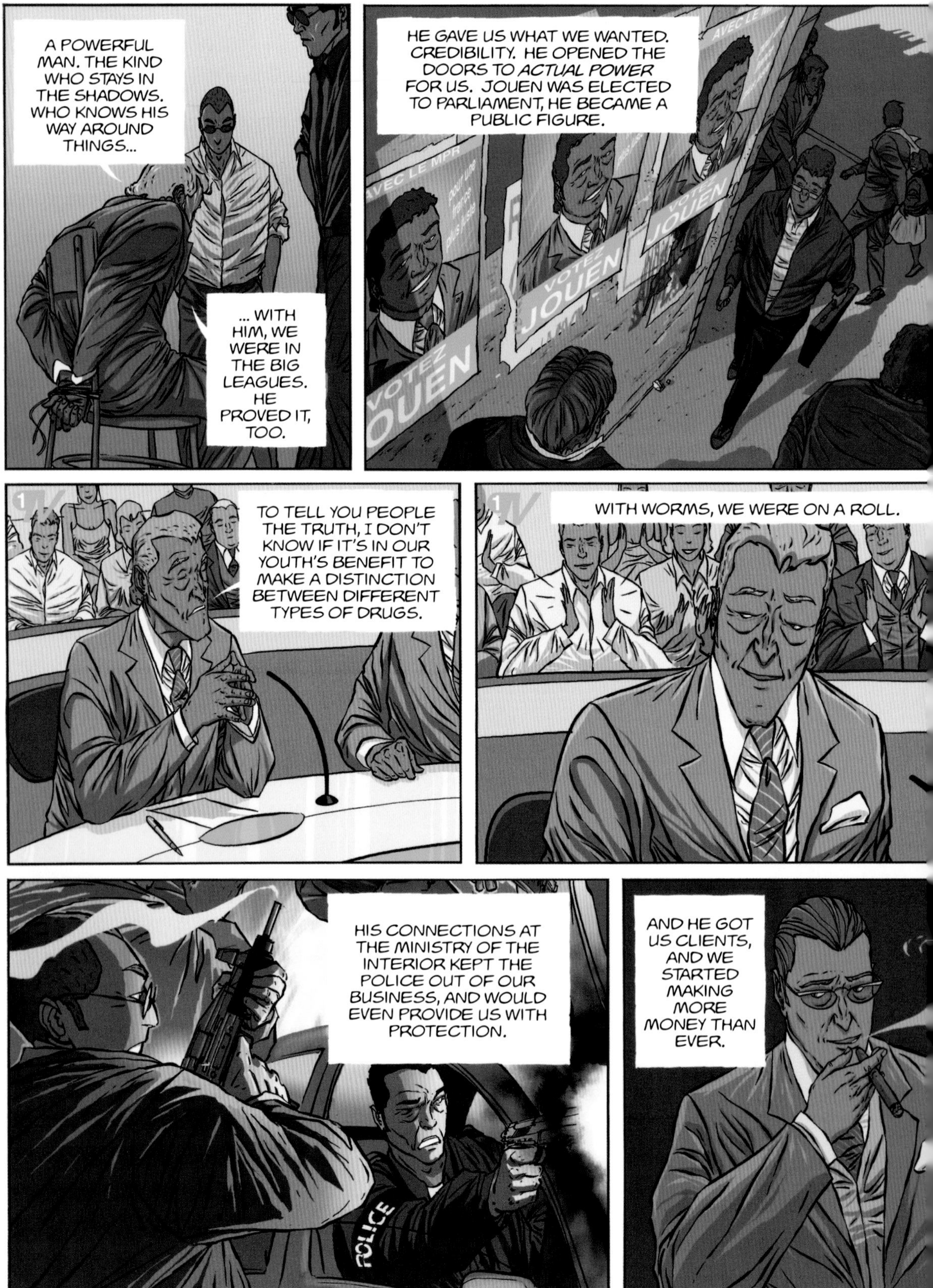
A POWERFUL MAN. THE KIND WHO STAYS IN THE SHADOWS. WHO KNOWS HIS WAY AROUND THINGS...
... WITH HIM, WE WERE IN THE BIG LEAGUES. HE PROVED IT, TOO.
HE GAVE US WHAT WE WANTED. CREDIBILITY. HE OPENED THE DOORS TO *ACTUAL POWER* FOR US. JOUEN WAS ELECTED TO PARLIAMENT, HE BECAME A PUBLIC FIGURE.
AVEC LE MPR
pour une france plus lisse
VOTEZ JOUEN
VOTEZ JOUEN
JOUEN
VOTEZ JOUEN
TO TELL YOU PEOPLE THE TRUTH, I DON'T KNOW IF IT'S IN OUR YOUTH'S BENEFIT TO MAKE A DISTINCTION BETWEEN DIFFERENT TYPES OF DRUGS.
WITH WORMS, WE WERE ON A ROLL.
HIS CONNECTIONS AT THE MINISTRY OF THE INTERIOR KEPT THE POLICE OUT OF OUR BUSINESS, AND WOULD EVEN PROVIDE US WITH PROTECTION.
POLICE
AND HE GOT US CLIENTS, AND WE STARTED MAKING MORE MONEY THAN EVER.

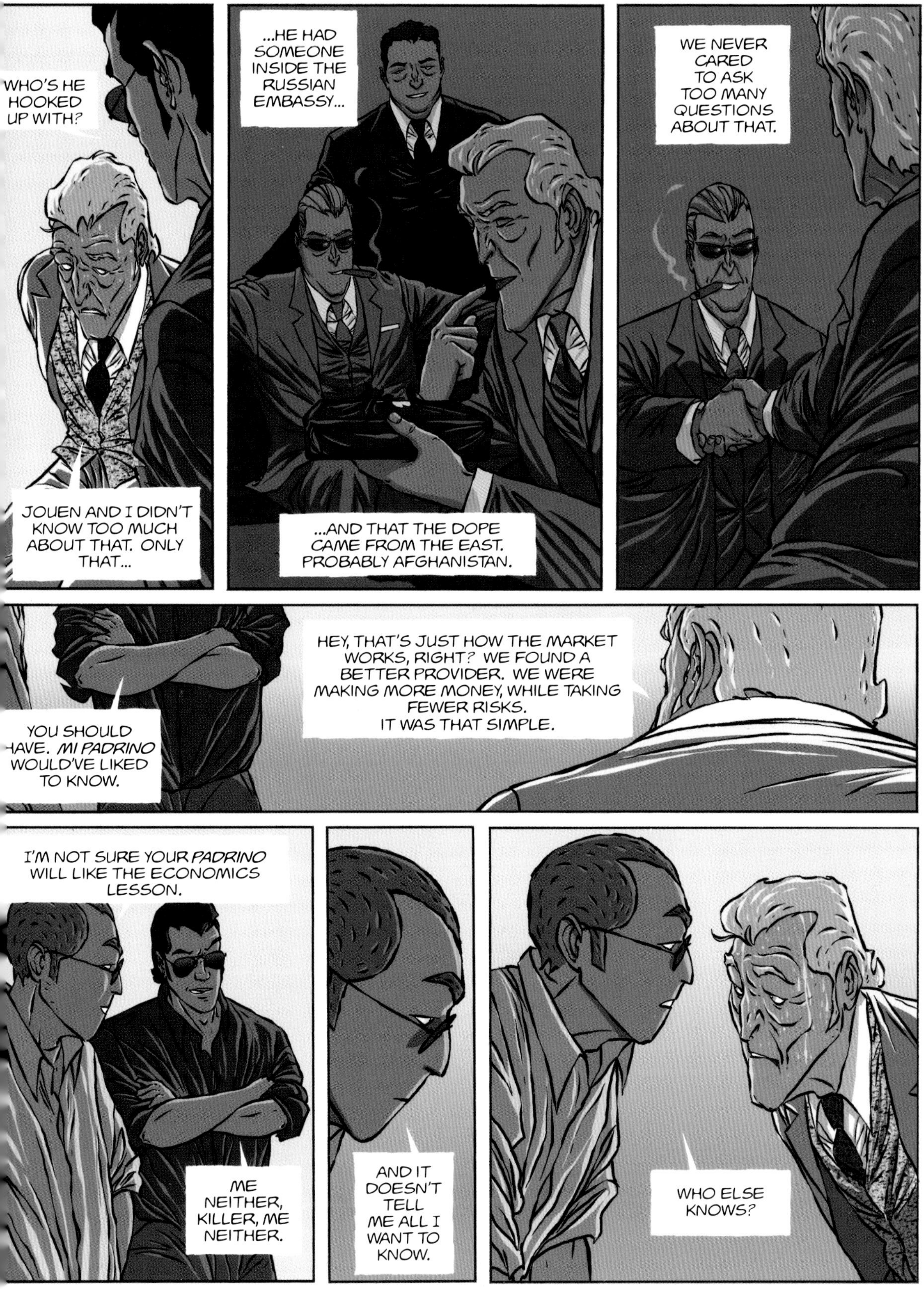
WHO'S HE HOOKED UP WITH?
JOUEN AND I DIDN'T KNOW TOO MUCH ABOUT THAT. ONLY THAT...
...HE HAD SOMEONE INSIDE THE RUSSIAN EMBASSY...
...AND THAT THE DOPE CAME FROM THE EAST. PROBABLY AFGHANISTAN.
WE NEVER CARED TO ASK TOO MANY QUESTIONS ABOUT THAT.
HEY, THAT'S JUST HOW THE MARKET WORKS, RIGHT? WE FOUND A BETTER PROVIDER. WE WERE MAKING MORE MONEY, WHILE TAKING FEWER RISKS. IT WAS THAT SIMPLE.
YOU SHOULD HAVE. *MI PADRINO* WOULD'VE LIKED TO KNOW.
I'M NOT SURE YOUR *PADRINO* WILL LIKE THE ECONOMICS LESSON.
ME NEITHER, KILLER, ME NEITHER.
AND IT DOESN'T TELL ME ALL I WANT TO KNOW.
WHO ELSE KNOWS?

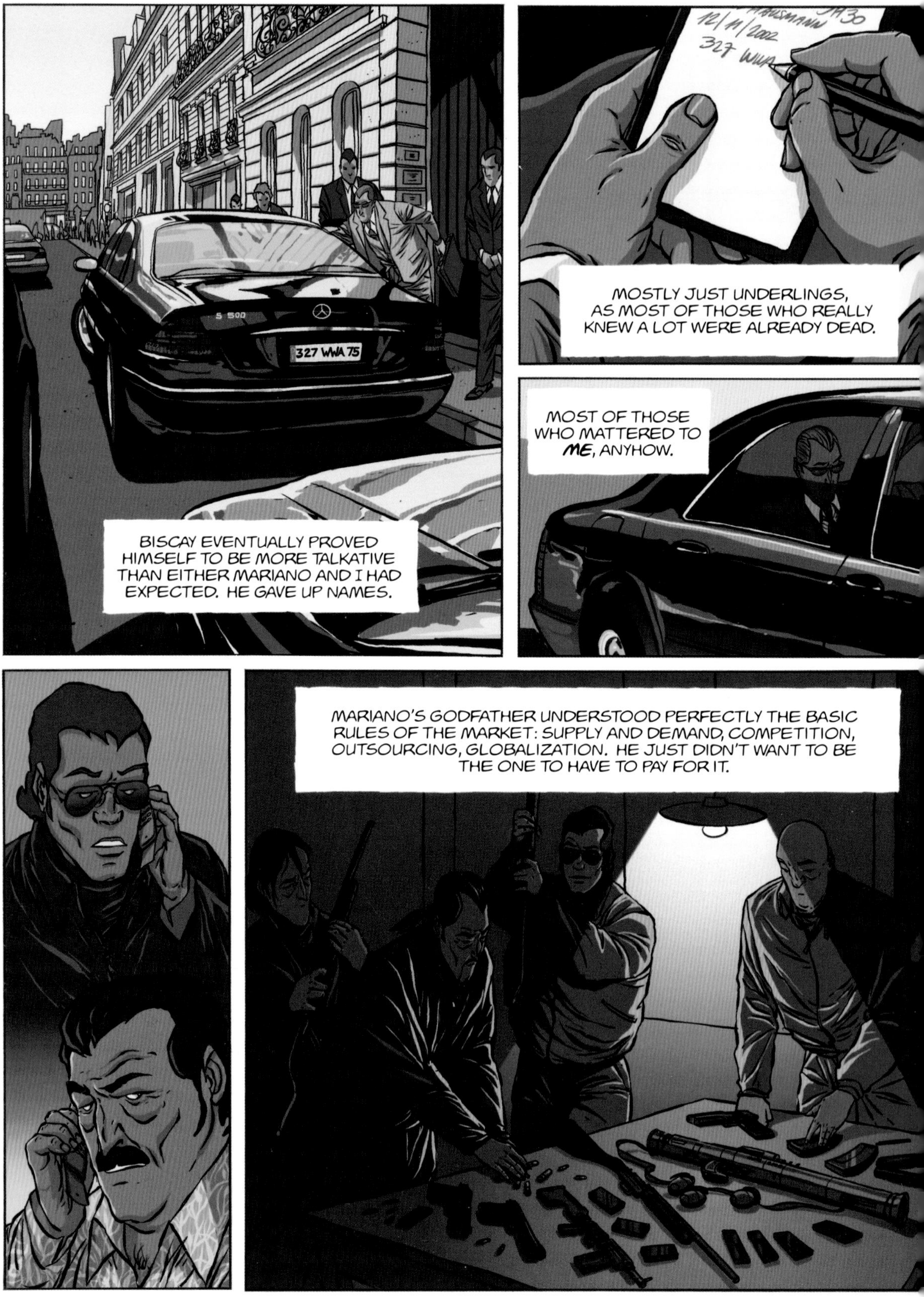
BISCAY EVENTUALLY PROVED HIMSELF TO BE MORE TALKATIVE THAN EITHER MARIANO AND I HAD EXPECTED. HE GAVE UP NAMES.
MOSTLY JUST UNDERLINGS, AS MOST OF THOSE WHO REALLY KNEW A LOT WERE ALREADY DEAD.
MOST OF THOSE WHO MATTERED TO *ME*, ANYHOW.
MARIANO'S GODFATHER UNDERSTOOD PERFECTLY THE BASIC RULES OF THE MARKET: SUPPLY AND DEMAND, COMPETITION, OUTSOURCING, GLOBALIZATION. HE JUST DIDN'T WANT TO BE THE ONE TO HAVE TO PAY FOR IT.

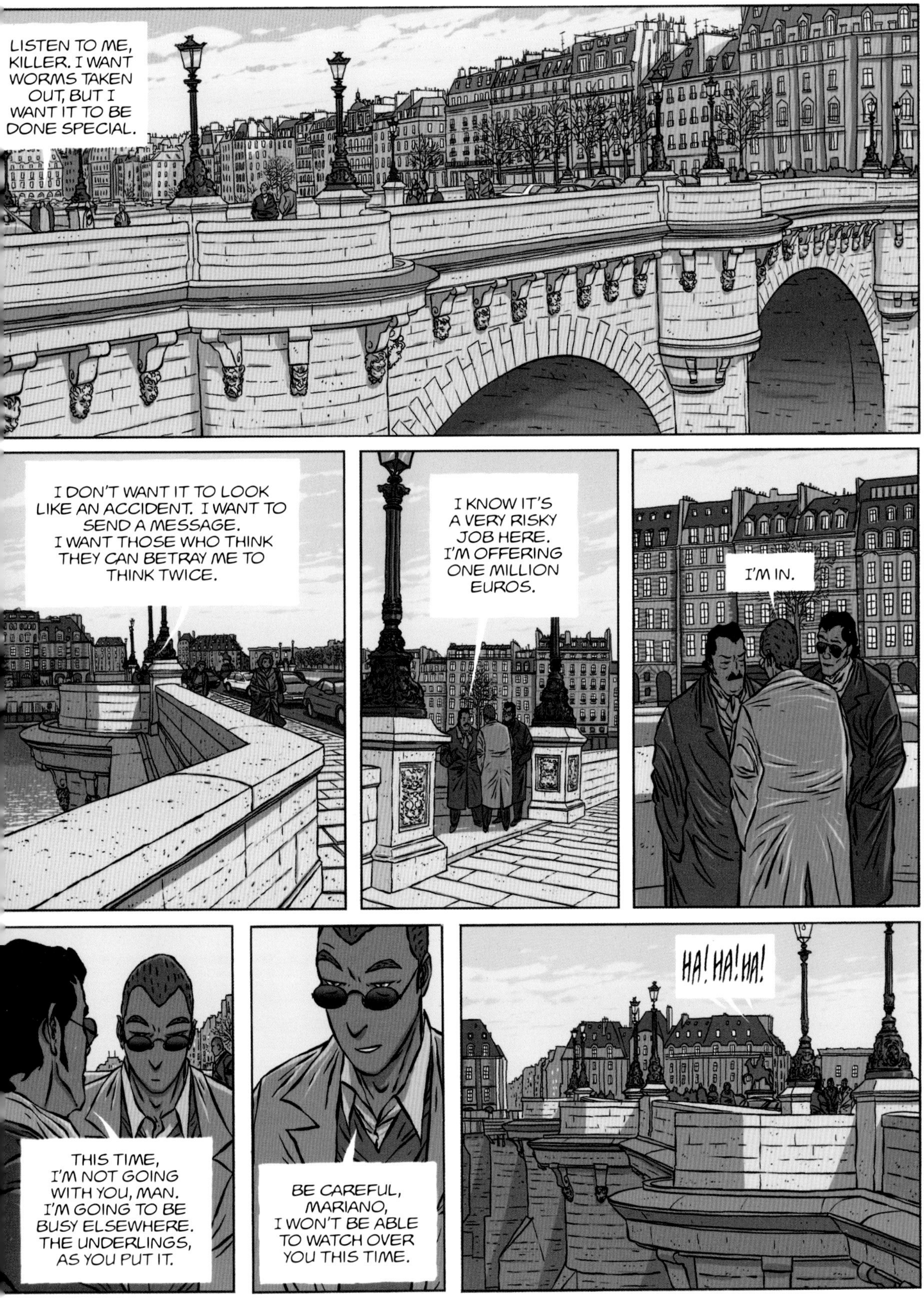
LISTEN TO ME, KILLER. I WANT WORMS TAKEN OUT, BUT I WANT IT TO BE DONE SPECIAL.
I DON'T WANT IT TO LOOK LIKE AN ACCIDENT. I WANT TO SEND A MESSAGE. I WANT THOSE WHO THINK THEY CAN BETRAY ME TO THINK TWICE.
I KNOW IT'S A VERY RISKY JOB HERE. I'M OFFERING ONE MILLION EUROS.
I'M IN.
THIS TIME, I'M NOT GOING WITH YOU, MAN. I'M GOING TO BE BUSY ELSEWHERE. THE UNDERLINGS, AS YOU PUT IT.
BE CAREFUL, MARIANO, I WON'T BE ABLE TO WATCH OVER YOU THIS TIME.
HA! HA! HA!

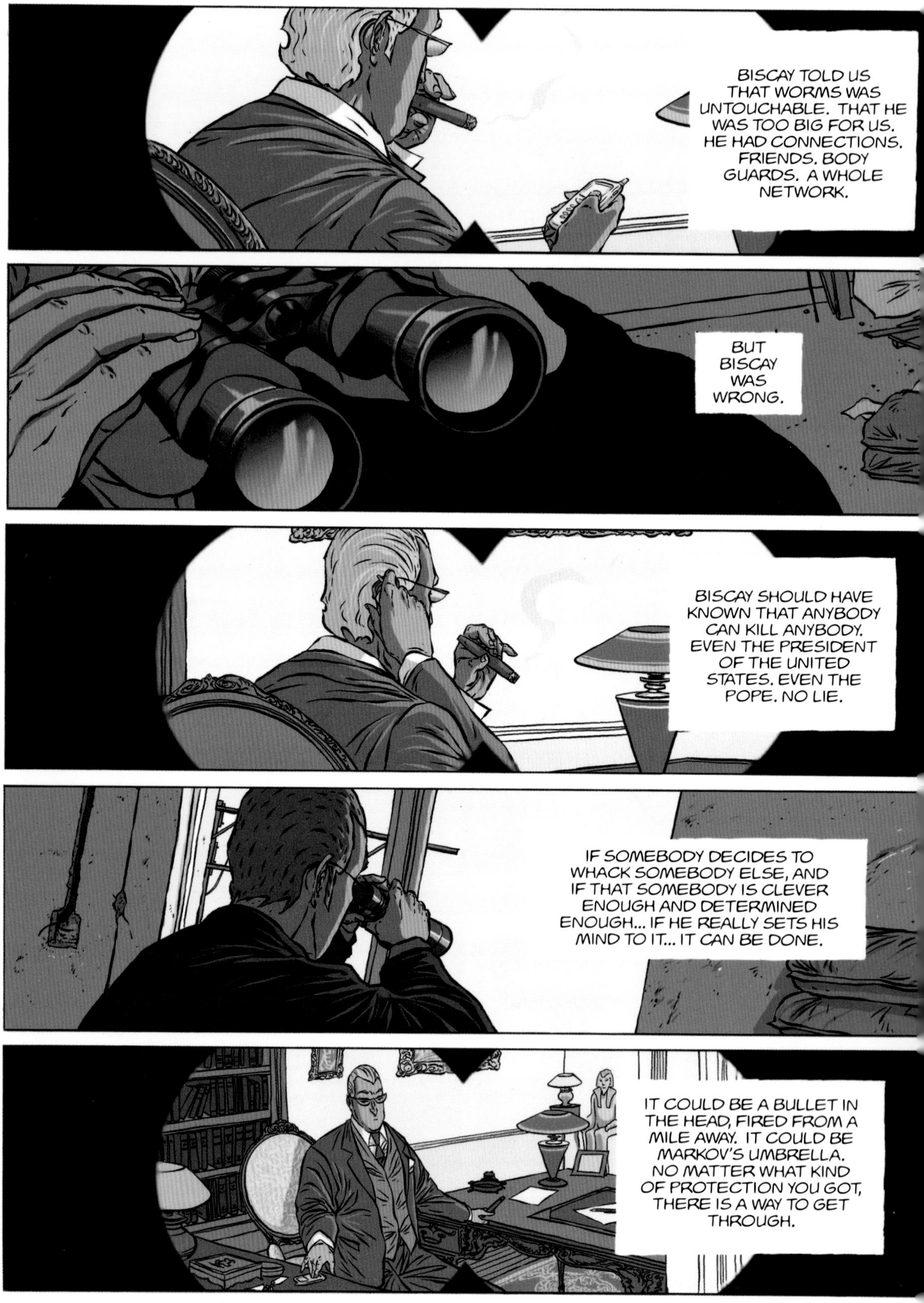
BISCAY TOLD US THAT WORMS WAS UNTOUCHABLE. THAT HE WAS TOO BIG FOR US. HE HAD CONNECTIONS. FRIENDS. BODY GUARDS. A WHOLE NETWORK.
BUT BISCAY WAS WRONG.
BISCAY SHOULD HAVE KNOWN THAT ANYBODY CAN KILL ANYBODY. EVEN THE PRESIDENT OF THE UNITED STATES. EVEN THE POPE. NO LIE.
IF SOMEBODY DECIDES TO WHACK SOMEBODY ELSE, AND IF THAT SOMEBODY IS CLEVER ENOUGH AND DETERMINED ENOUGH... IF HE REALLY SETS HIS MIND TO IT... IT CAN BE DONE.
IT COULD BE A BULLET IN THE HEAD, FIRED FROM A MILE AWAY. IT COULD BE MARKOV'S UMBRELLA. NO MATTER WHAT KIND OF PROTECTION YOU GOT, THERE IS A WAY TO GET THROUGH.

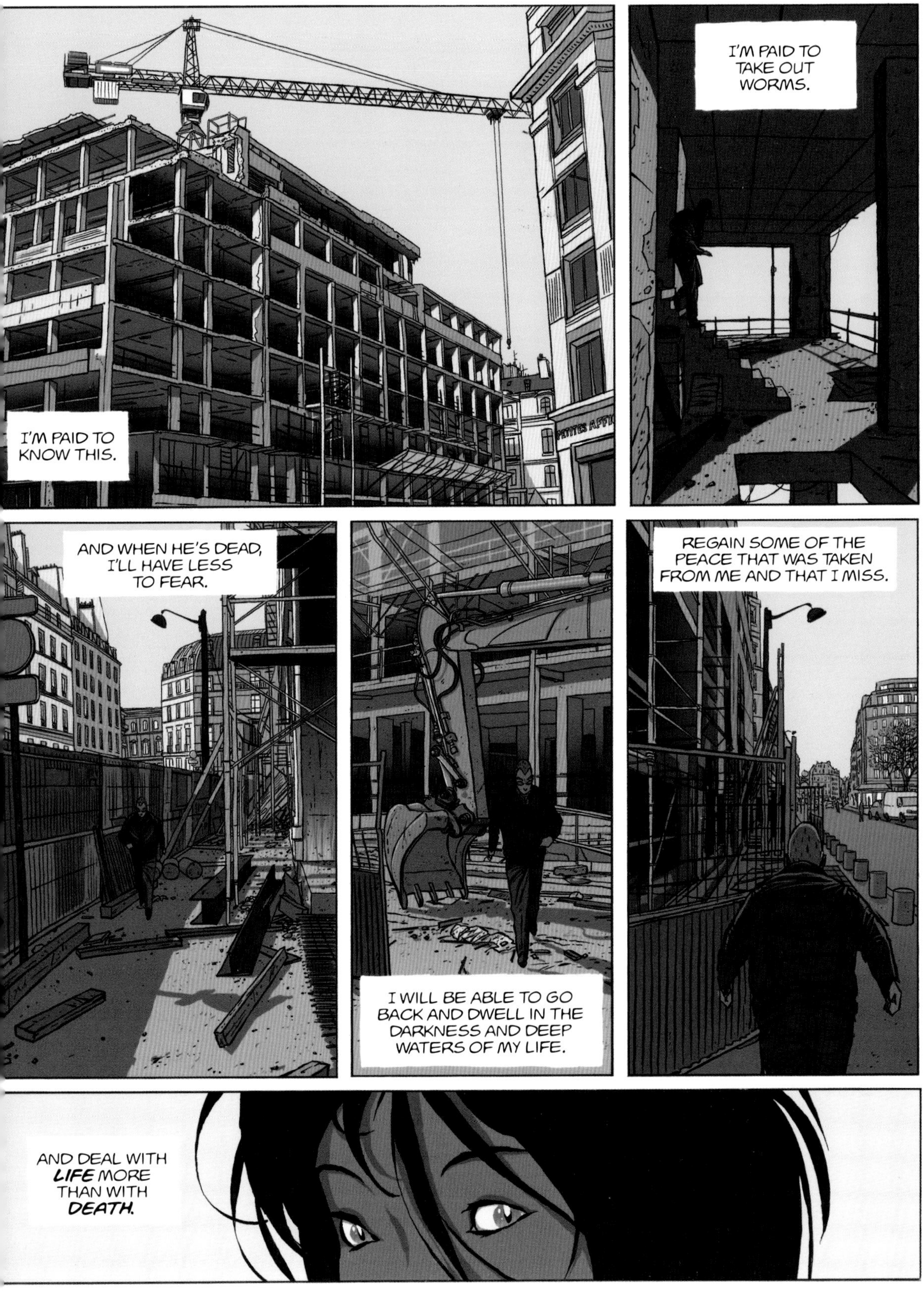
I'M PAID TO KNOW THIS.
I'M PAID TO TAKE OUT WORMS.
PETITES AFFI
AND WHEN HE'S DEAD, I'LL HAVE LESS TO FEAR.
I WILL BE ABLE TO GO BACK AND DWELL IN THE DARKNESS AND DEEP WATERS OF MY LIFE.
REGAIN SOME OF THE PEACE THAT WAS TAKEN FROM ME AND THAT I MISS.
AND DEAL WITH ***LIFE*** MORE THAN WITH ***DEATH***.

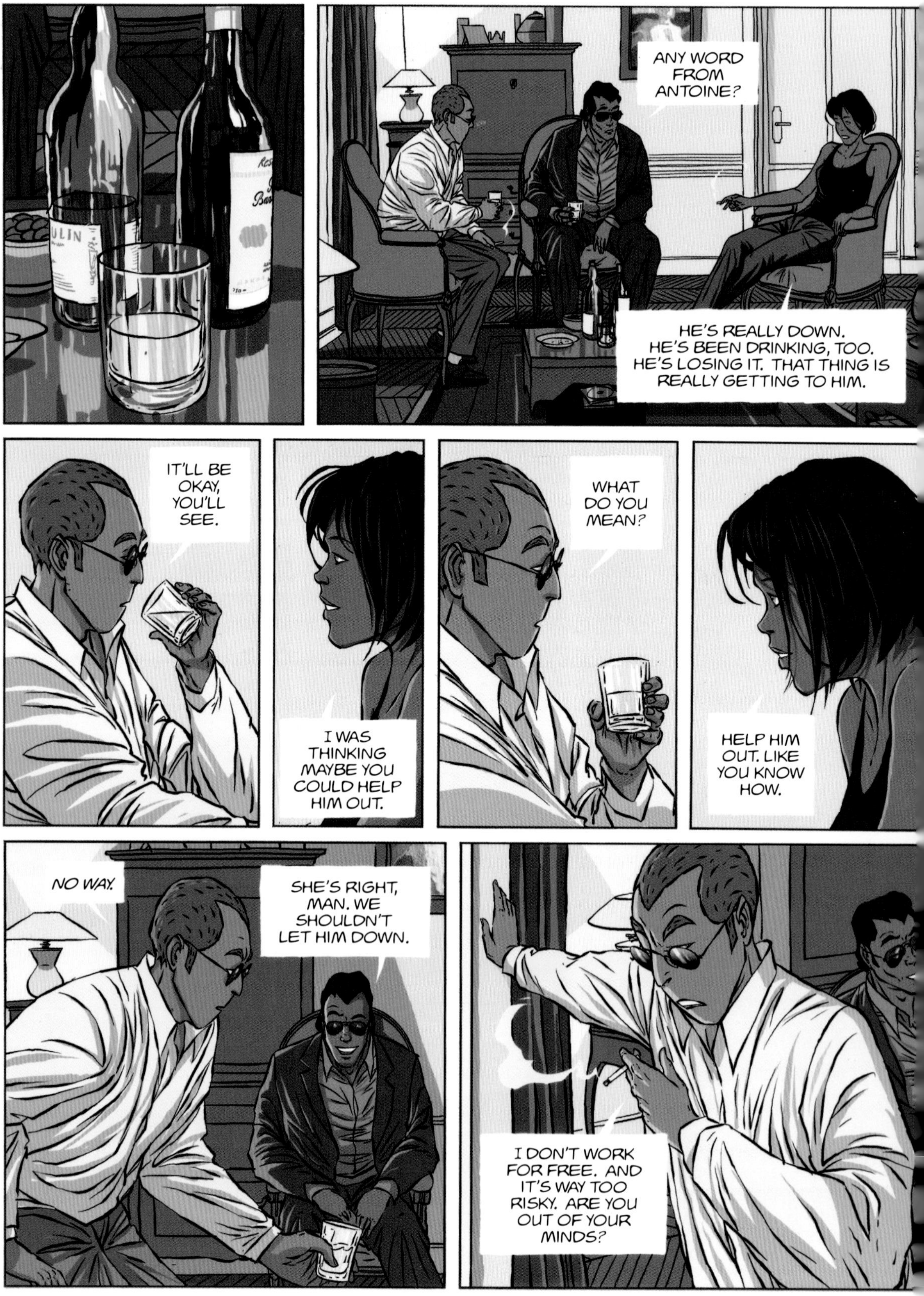
ANY WORD FROM ANTOINE?
HE'S REALLY DOWN. HE'S BEEN DRINKING, TOO. HE'S LOSING IT. THAT THING IS REALLY GETTING TO HIM.
IT'LL BE OKAY, YOU'LL SEE.
I WAS THINKING MAYBE YOU COULD HELP HIM OUT.
WHAT DO YOU MEAN?
HELP HIM OUT. LIKE YOU KNOW HOW.
NO WAY.
SHE'S RIGHT, MAN. WE SHOULDN'T LET HIM DOWN.
I DON'T WORK FOR FREE. AND IT'S WAY TOO RISKY. ARE YOU OUT OF YOUR MINDS?

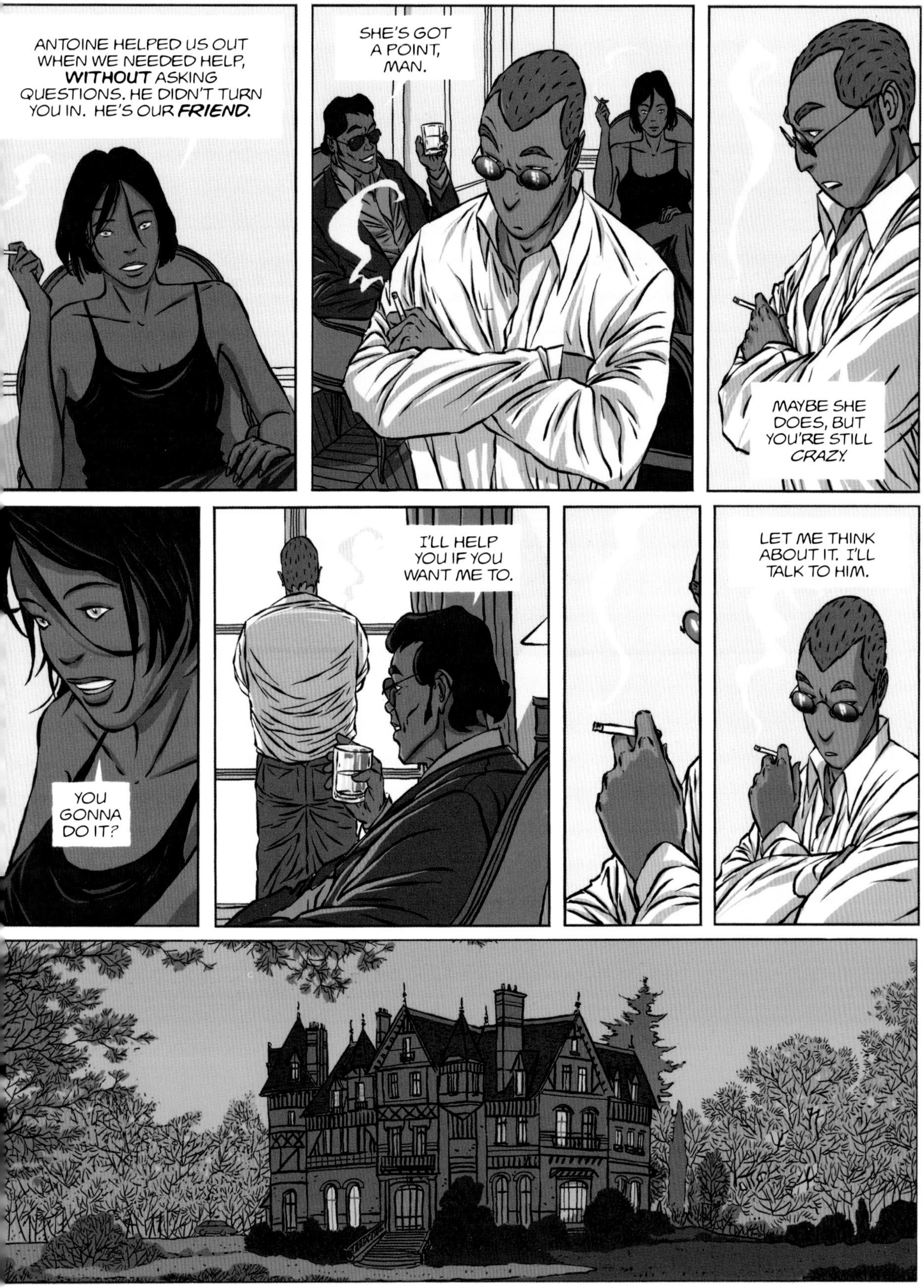
ANTOINE HELPED US OUT WHEN WE NEEDED HELP, **WITHOUT** ASKING QUESTIONS. HE DIDN'T TURN YOU IN. HE'S OUR ***FRIEND.***
SHE'S GOT A POINT, MAN.
MAYBE SHE DOES, BUT YOU'RE STILL *CRAZY.*
YOU GONNA DO IT?
I'LL HELP YOU IF YOU WANT ME TO.
LET ME THINK ABOUT IT. I'LL TALK TO HIM.

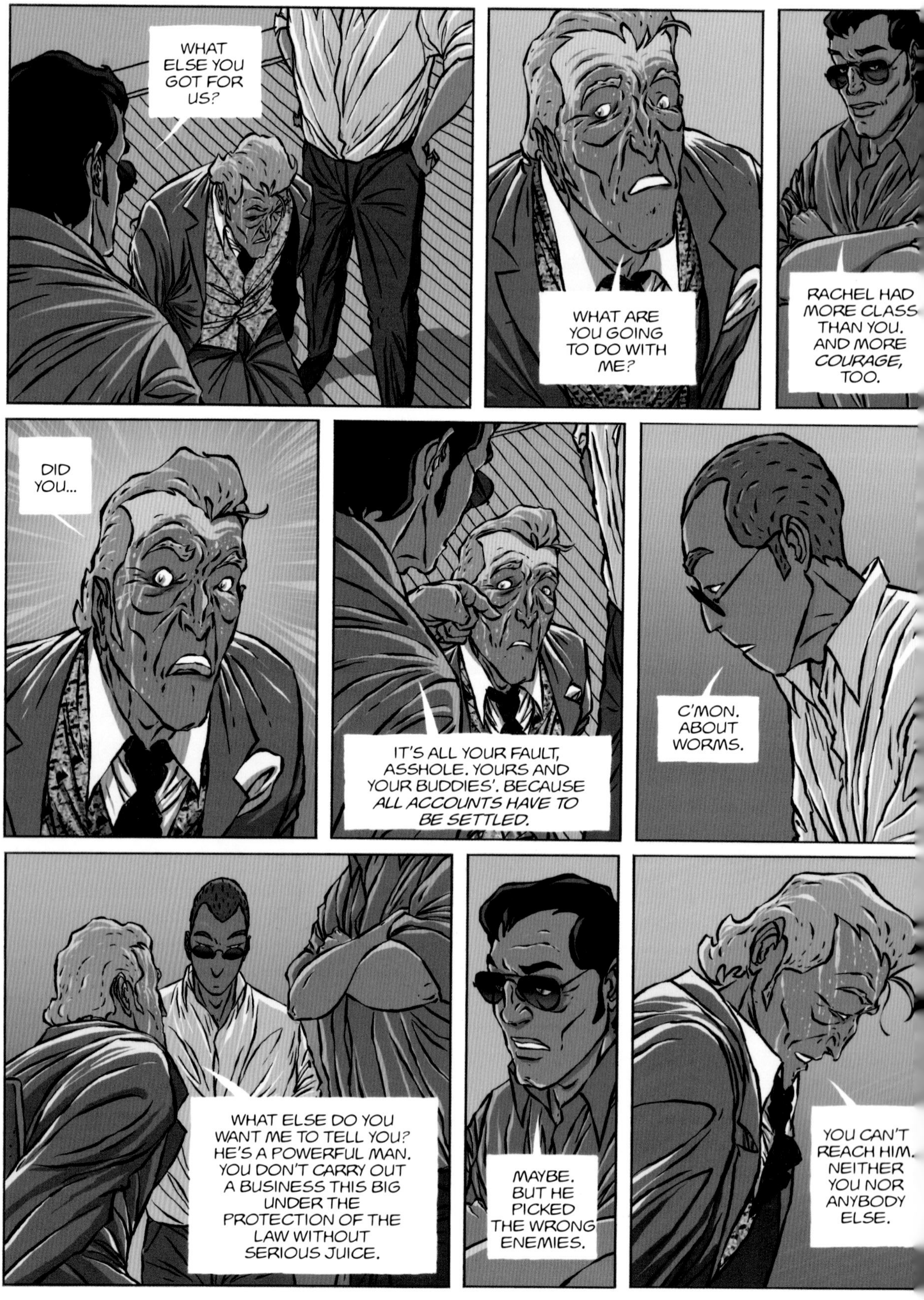
WHAT ELSE YOU GOT FOR US?
WHAT ARE YOU GOING TO DO WITH ME?
RACHEL HAD MORE CLASS THAN YOU. AND MORE *COURAGE*, TOO.
DID YOU...
IT'S ALL YOUR FAULT, ASSHOLE. YOURS AND YOUR BUDDIES'. BECAUSE *ALL ACCOUNTS HAVE TO BE SETTLED.*
C'MON. ABOUT WORMS.
WHAT ELSE DO YOU WANT ME TO TELL YOU? HE'S A POWERFUL MAN. YOU DON'T CARRY OUT A BUSINESS THIS BIG UNDER THE PROTECTION OF THE LAW WITHOUT SERIOUS JUICE.
MAYBE. BUT HE PICKED THE WRONG ENEMIES.
YOU CAN'T REACH HIM. NEITHER YOU NOR ANYBODY ELSE.

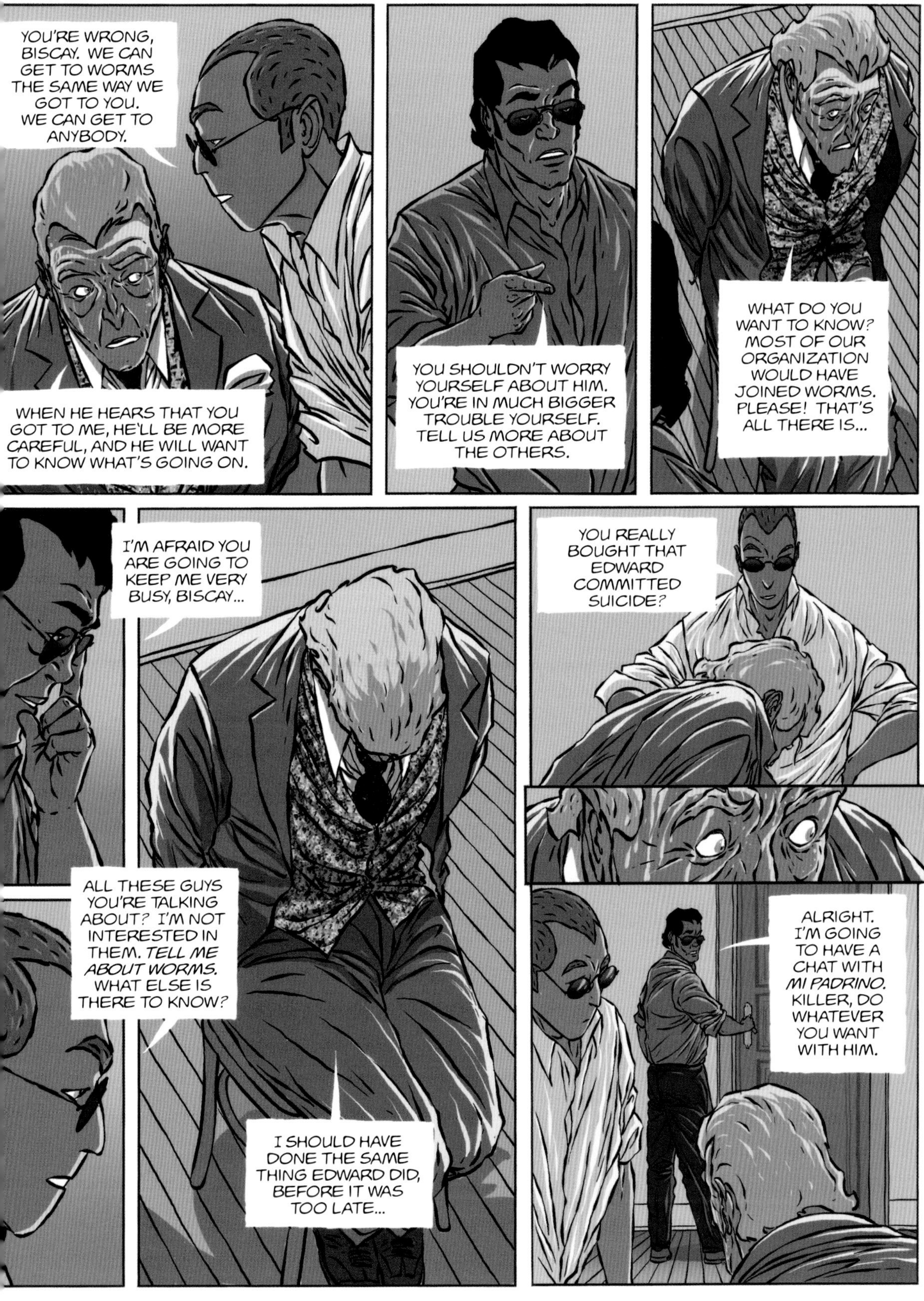
YOU'RE WRONG, BISCAY. WE CAN GET TO WORMS THE SAME WAY WE GOT TO YOU. WE CAN GET TO ANYBODY.
WHEN HE HEARS THAT YOU GOT TO ME, HE'LL BE MORE CAREFUL, AND HE WILL WANT TO KNOW WHAT'S GOING ON.
YOU SHOULDN'T WORRY YOURSELF ABOUT HIM. YOU'RE IN MUCH BIGGER TROUBLE YOURSELF. TELL US MORE ABOUT THE OTHERS.
WHAT DO YOU WANT TO KNOW? MOST OF OUR ORGANIZATION WOULD HAVE JOINED WORMS. PLEASE! THAT'S ALL THERE IS...
I'M AFRAID YOU ARE GOING TO KEEP ME VERY BUSY, BISCAY...
ALL THESE GUYS YOU'RE TALKING ABOUT? I'M NOT INTERESTED IN THEM. *TELL ME ABOUT WORMS.* WHAT ELSE IS THERE TO KNOW?
I SHOULD HAVE DONE THE SAME THING EDWARD DID, BEFORE IT WAS TOO LATE...
YOU REALLY BOUGHT THAT EDWARD COMMITTED SUICIDE?
ALRIGHT. I'M GOING TO HAVE A CHAT WITH *MI PADRINO.* KILLER, DO WHATEVER YOU WANT WITH HIM.

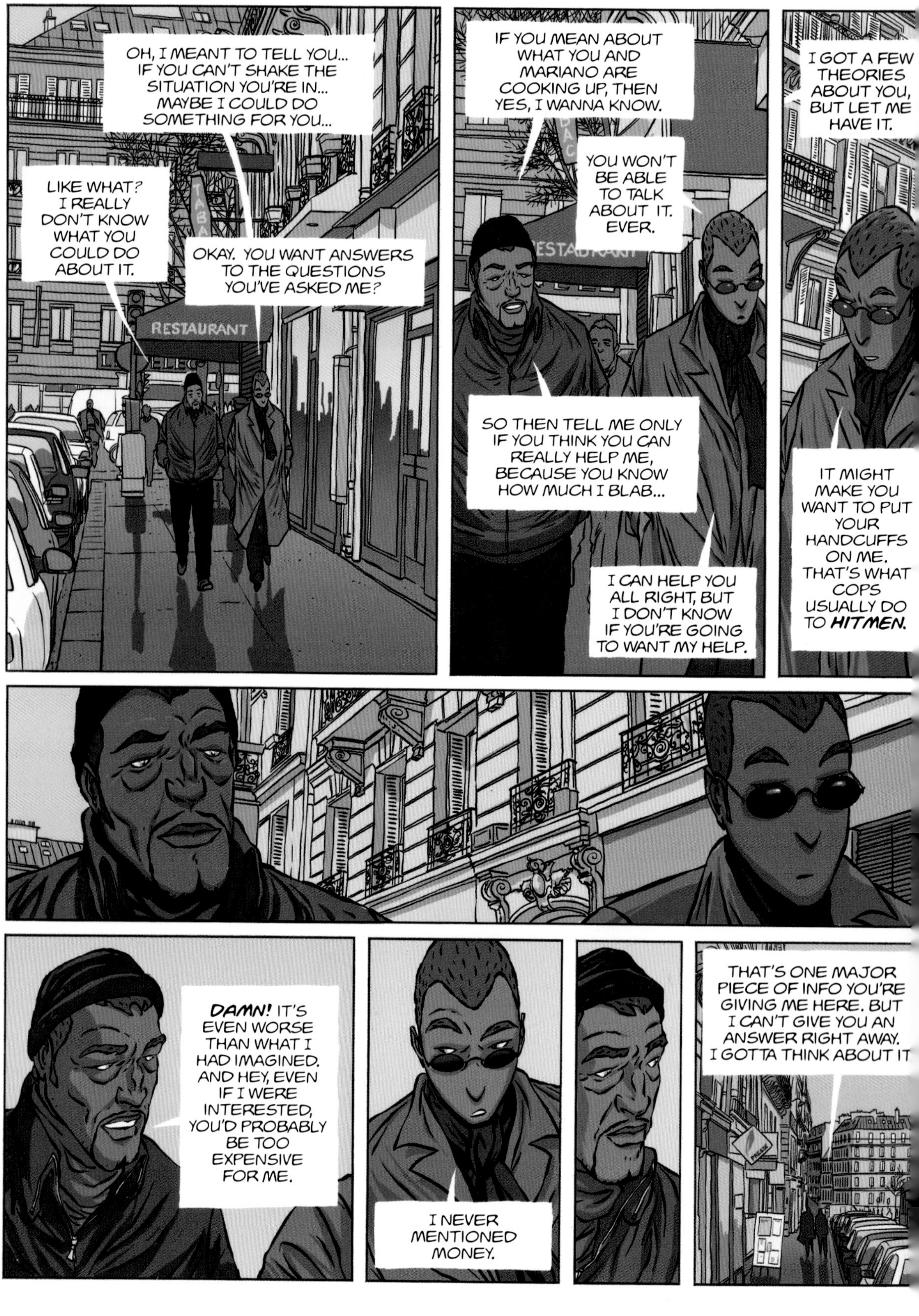
OH, I MEANT TO TELL YOU... IF YOU CAN'T SHAKE THE SITUATION YOU'RE IN... MAYBE I COULD DO SOMETHING FOR YOU...
LIKE WHAT? I REALLY DON'T KNOW WHAT YOU COULD DO ABOUT IT.
OKAY. YOU WANT ANSWERS TO THE QUESTIONS YOU'VE ASKED ME?
RESTAURANT
IF YOU MEAN ABOUT WHAT YOU AND MARIANO ARE COOKING UP, THEN YES, I WANNA KNOW.
YOU WON'T BE ABLE TO TALK ABOUT IT. EVER.
SO THEN TELL ME ONLY IF YOU THINK YOU CAN REALLY HELP ME, BECAUSE YOU KNOW HOW MUCH I BLAB...
I CAN HELP YOU ALL RIGHT, BUT I DON'T KNOW IF YOU'RE GOING TO WANT MY HELP.
I GOT A FEW THEORIES ABOUT YOU, BUT LET ME HAVE IT.
IT MIGHT MAKE YOU WANT TO PUT YOUR HANDCUFFS ON ME. THAT'S WHAT COPS USUALLY DO TO ***HITMEN***.
DAMN! IT'S EVEN WORSE THAN WHAT I HAD IMAGINED. AND HEY, EVEN IF I WERE INTERESTED, YOU'D PROBABLY BE TOO EXPENSIVE FOR ME.
I NEVER MENTIONED MONEY.
THAT'S ONE MAJOR PIECE OF INFO YOU'RE GIVING ME HERE. BUT I CAN'T GIVE YOU AN ANSWER RIGHT AWAY. I GOTTA THINK ABOUT IT

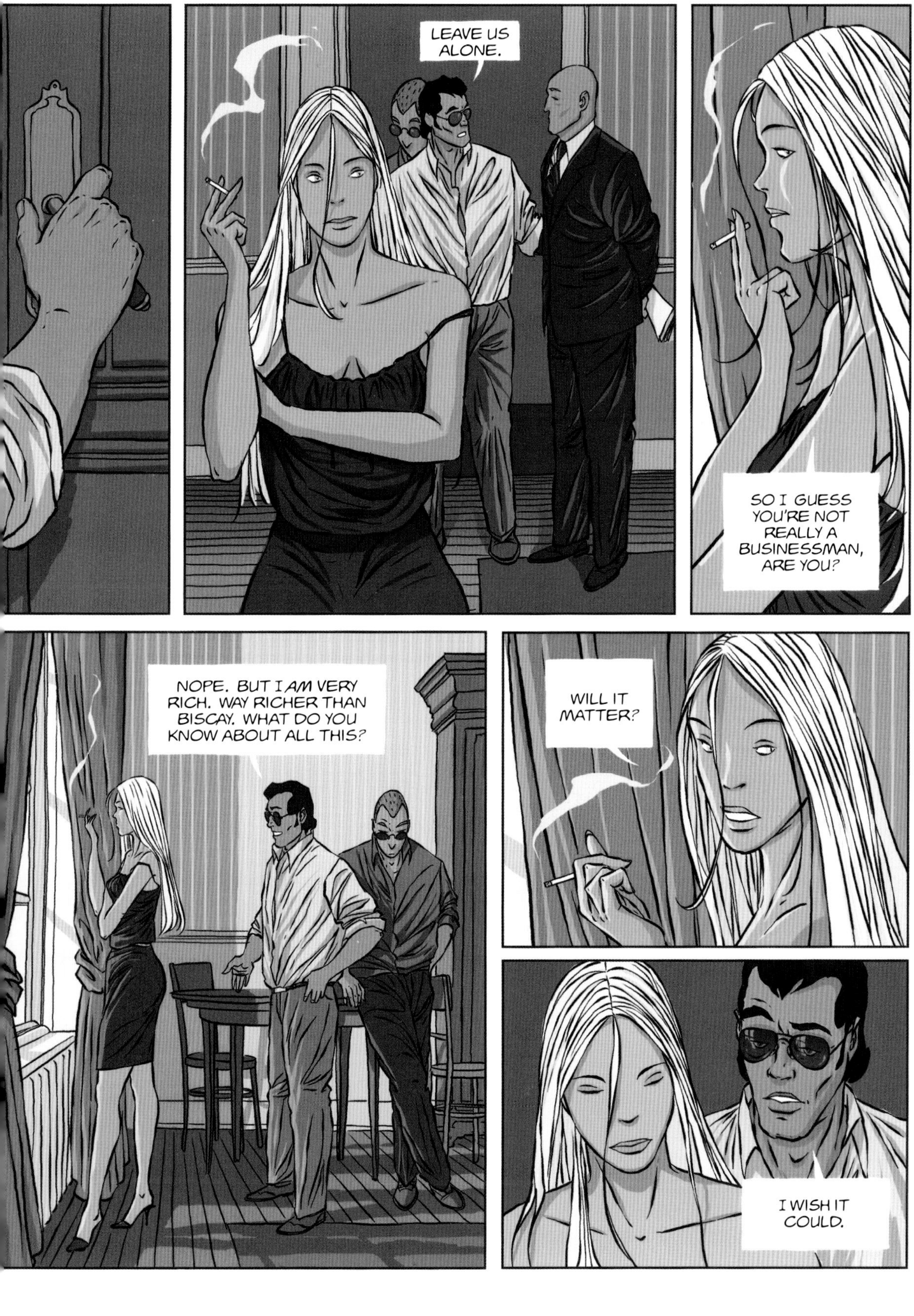
LEAVE US ALONE.
SO I GUESS YOU'RE NOT REALLY A BUSINESSMAN, ARE YOU?
NOPE. BUT I AM VERY RICH. WAY RICHER THAN BISCAY. WHAT DO YOU KNOW ABOUT ALL THIS?
WILL IT MATTER?
I WISH IT COULD.

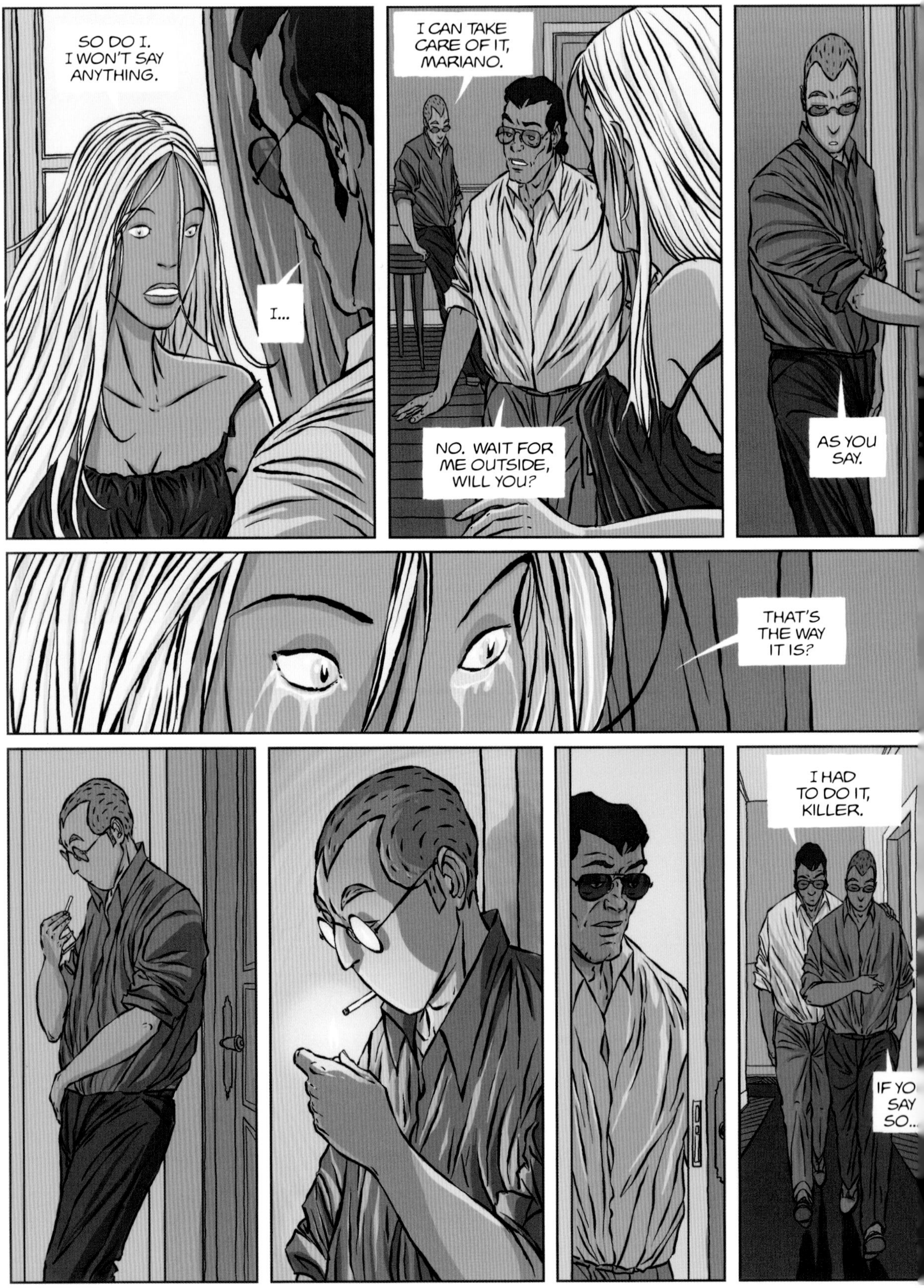
SO DO I. I WON'T SAY ANYTHING.
I...
I CAN TAKE CARE OF IT, MARIANO.
NO. WAIT FOR ME OUTSIDE, WILL YOU?
AS YOU SAY.
THAT'S THE WAY IT IS?
I HAD TO DO IT, KILLER.
IF YO SAY SO...

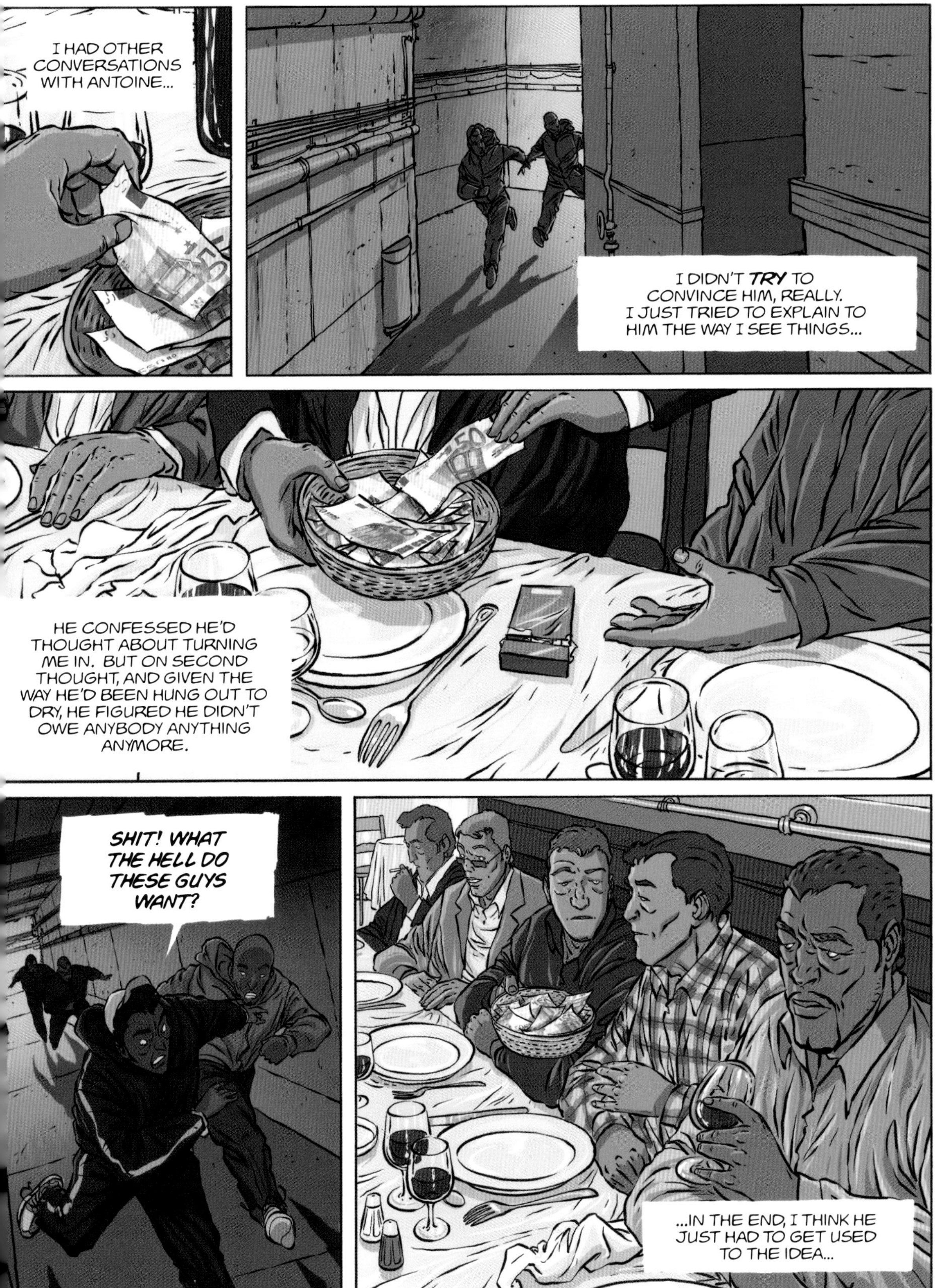
I HAD OTHER CONVERSATIONS WITH ANTOINE...
I DIDN'T **TRY** TO CONVINCE HIM, REALLY. I JUST TRIED TO EXPLAIN TO HIM THE WAY I SEE THINGS...
HE CONFESSED HE'D THOUGHT ABOUT TURNING ME IN. BUT ON SECOND THOUGHT, AND GIVEN THE WAY HE'D BEEN HUNG OUT TO DRY, HE FIGURED HE DIDN'T OWE ANYBODY ANYTHING ANYMORE.
SHIT! WHAT THE HELL DO THESE GUYS WANT?
...IN THE END, I THINK HE JUST HAD TO GET USED TO THE IDEA...

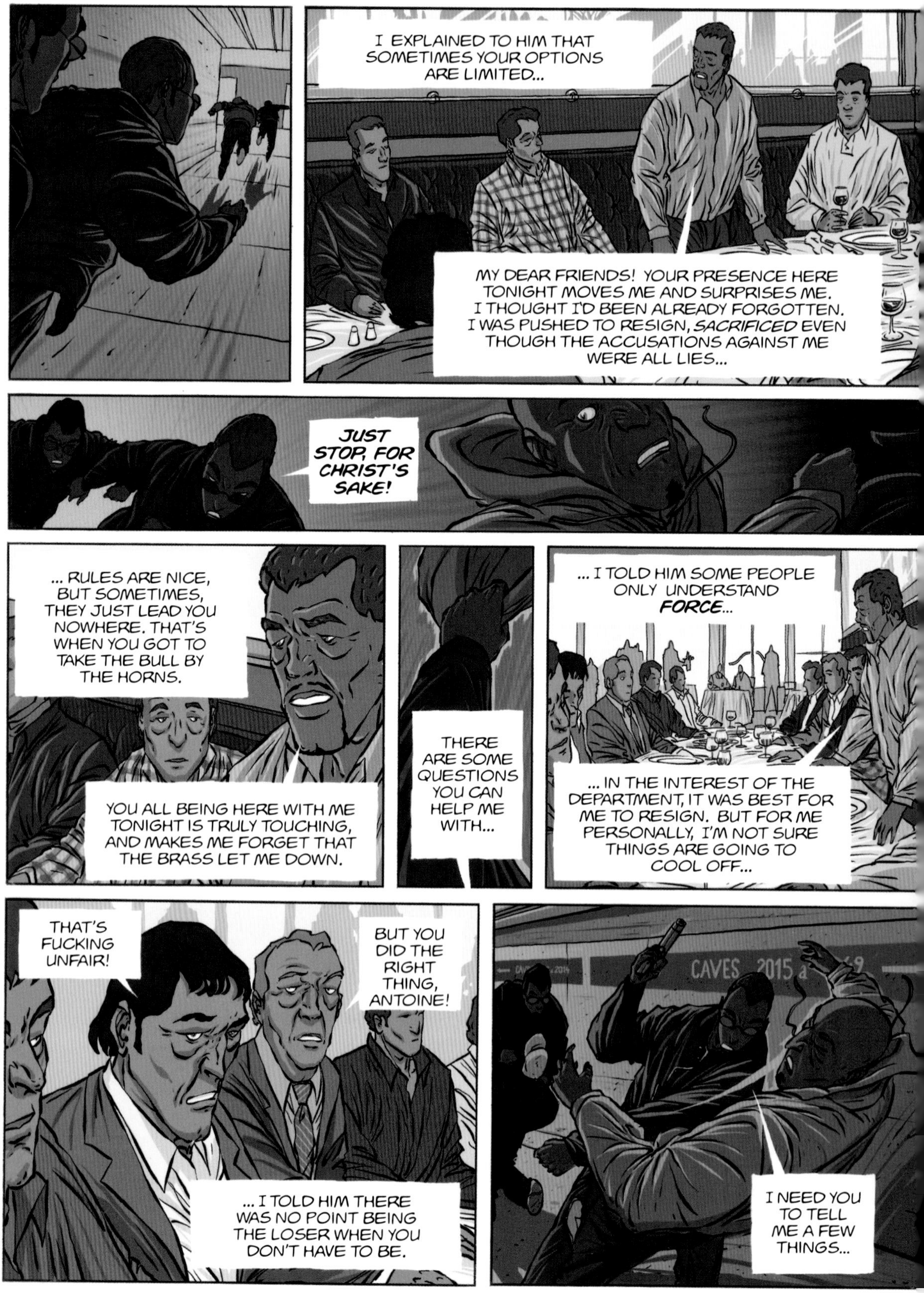
I EXPLAINED TO HIM THAT SOMETIMES YOUR OPTIONS ARE LIMITED...
MY DEAR FRIENDS! YOUR PRESENCE HERE TONIGHT MOVES ME AND SURPRISES ME. I THOUGHT I'D BEEN ALREADY FORGOTTEN. I WAS PUSHED TO RESIGN, *SACRIFICED* EVEN THOUGH THE ACCUSATIONS AGAINST ME WERE ALL LIES...
JUST STOP, FOR CHRIST'S SAKE!
... RULES ARE NICE, BUT SOMETIMES, THEY JUST LEAD YOU NOWHERE. THAT'S WHEN YOU GOT TO TAKE THE BULL BY THE HORNS.
YOU ALL BEING HERE WITH ME TONIGHT IS TRULY TOUCHING, AND MAKES ME FORGET THAT THE BRASS LET ME DOWN.
THERE ARE SOME QUESTIONS YOU CAN HELP ME WITH...
... I TOLD HIM SOME PEOPLE ONLY UNDERSTAND **FORCE**...
... IN THE INTEREST OF THE DEPARTMENT, IT WAS BEST FOR ME TO RESIGN. BUT FOR ME PERSONALLY, I'M NOT SURE THINGS ARE GOING TO COOL OFF...
THAT'S FUCKING UNFAIR!
BUT YOU DID THE RIGHT THING, ANTOINE!
... I TOLD HIM THERE WAS NO POINT BEING THE LOSER WHEN YOU DON'T HAVE TO BE.
CAVES 2015
I NEED YOU TO TELL ME A FEW THINGS...

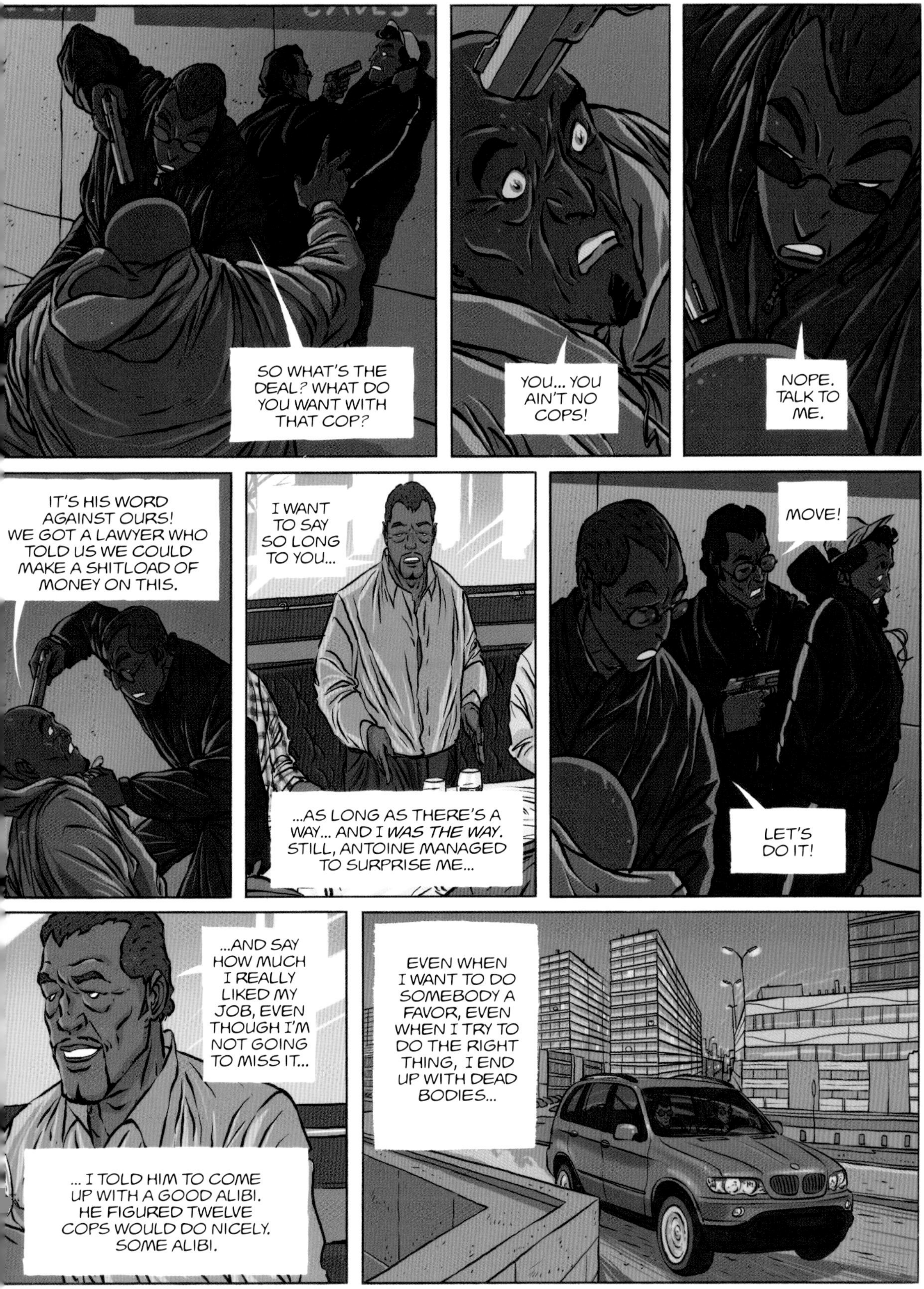
SO WHAT'S THE DEAL? WHAT DO YOU WANT WITH THAT COP?
YOU... YOU AIN'T NO COPS!
NOPE. TALK TO ME.
IT'S HIS WORD AGAINST OURS! WE GOT A LAWYER WHO TOLD US WE COULD MAKE A SHITLOAD OF MONEY ON THIS.
I WANT TO SAY SO LONG TO YOU...
...AS LONG AS THERE'S A WAY... AND I *WAS THE WAY*. STILL, ANTOINE MANAGED TO SURPRISE ME...
MOVE!
LET'S DO IT!
...AND SAY HOW MUCH I REALLY LIKED MY JOB, EVEN THOUGH I'M NOT GOING TO MISS IT...
... I TOLD HIM TO COME UP WITH A GOOD ALIBI. HE FIGURED TWELVE COPS WOULD DO NICELY. SOME ALIBI.
EVEN WHEN I WANT TO DO SOMEBODY A FAVOR, EVEN WHEN I TRY TO DO THE RIGHT THING, I END UP WITH DEAD BODIES...

I FOLLOWED WORMS AROUND. DAY AFTER DAY, NIGHT AFTER NIGHT.

THE EASIEST AND THE SAFEST WOULD HAVE BEEN TO DO IT FROM HERE, WITH A GOOD SNIPER RIFLE. HARD TO MISS, HARD TO GET CAUGHT. BUT I COULDN'T DO THAT...

IT WAS NOT WHAT I WAS ASKED TO DO.

I NEEDED A PUBLIC PLACE. SOMETHING VISIBLE. SOMETHING THAT COULDN'T BE COVERED UP.

IT MEANT MORE RISKS FOR ME.

HE DIDN'T HAVE TOO MANY BODYGUARDS BUT THEY WERE PRETTY GOOD.

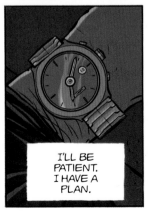

I'LL BE PATIENT. I HAVE A PLAN.

IN THIS LINE OF WORK, YOU HAVE TO STAY IN THE SHADOWS. ALWAYS GO UNNOTICED. IT'S NEVER SPECTACULAR, IT'S NEVER ROMANTIC. THAT IS THE MARK OF A JOB WELL DONE.

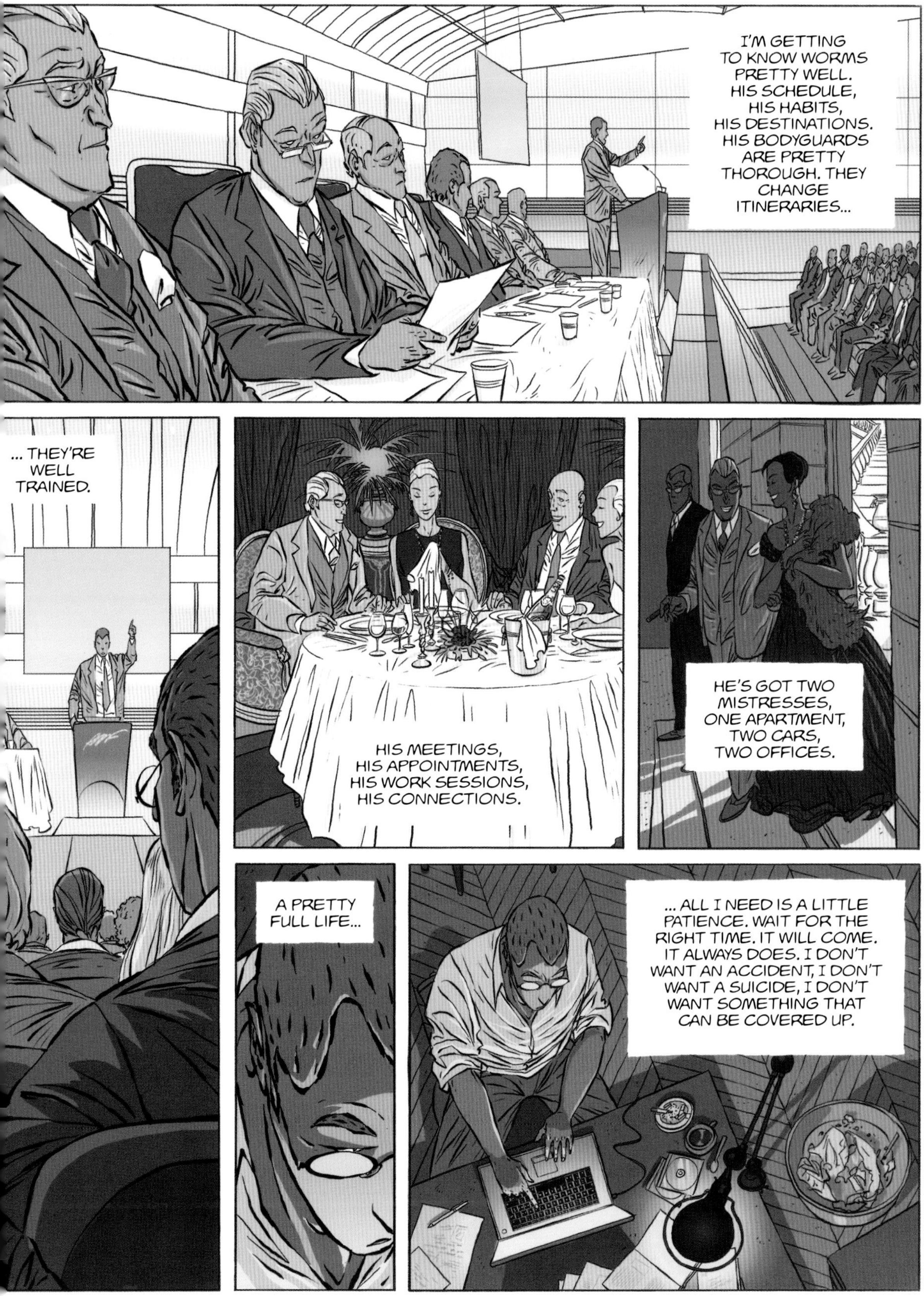
I'M GETTING TO KNOW WORMS PRETTY WELL. HIS SCHEDULE, HIS HABITS, HIS DESTINATIONS. HIS BODYGUARDS ARE PRETTY THOROUGH. THEY CHANGE ITINERARIES...
... THEY'RE WELL TRAINED.
HIS MEETINGS, HIS APPOINTMENTS, HIS WORK SESSIONS, HIS CONNECTIONS.
HE'S GOT TWO MISTRESSES, ONE APARTMENT, TWO CARS, TWO OFFICES.
A PRETTY FULL LIFE...
... ALL I NEED IS A LITTLE PATIENCE. WAIT FOR THE RIGHT TIME. IT WILL COME. IT ALWAYS DOES. I DON'T WANT AN ACCIDENT, I DON'T WANT A SUICIDE, I DON'T WANT SOMETHING THAT CAN BE COVERED UP.

THE UPSIDE OF THIS JOB IS THAT IT MAKES ME LOOK FOR NEW IDEAS AND SOLUTIONS EVERY TIME. I ALWAYS HAVE TO COME UP WITH SOMETHING ORIGINAL.

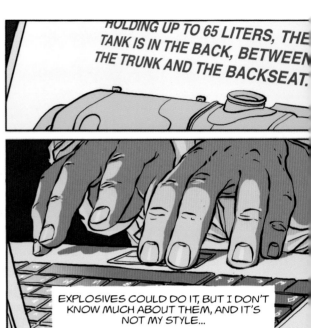

HOLDING UP TO 65 LITERS, THE TANK IS IN THE BACK, BETWEEN THE TRUNK AND THE BACKSEAT.

EXPLOSIVES COULD DO IT, BUT I DON'T KNOW MUCH ABOUT THEM, AND IT'S NOT MY STYLE...

ENTIRELY FABRICATED OF AN ALLOY MADE FROM ALUMINIUM AND STEEL, IT CAN TAKE SHOCKS UP

... COLLATERAL DAMAGE IS TOO HIGH AND USUALLY IMPOSSIBLE TO CONTROL.

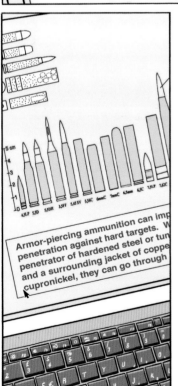

Armor-piercing ammunition can imp
penetration against hard targets. W
penetrator of hardened steel or tun
and a surrounding jacket of coppe
cupronickel, they can go through

BASTARDS WHO KILL PEOPLE RANDOMLY WOULD USE SUCH METHODS...

NITROGLYCERINE

...TERRORISTS' METHODS. BUT THIS IS A *HIT.* AND IT'S NOT THE TIME FOR ME TO CHANGE MY STYLE.

MARIANO

HEY MARIANO, I'M GOING TO NEED SOME LOGISTICS HERE. THINK YOU COULD HELP?

SURE, WHAT DO YOU NEED?

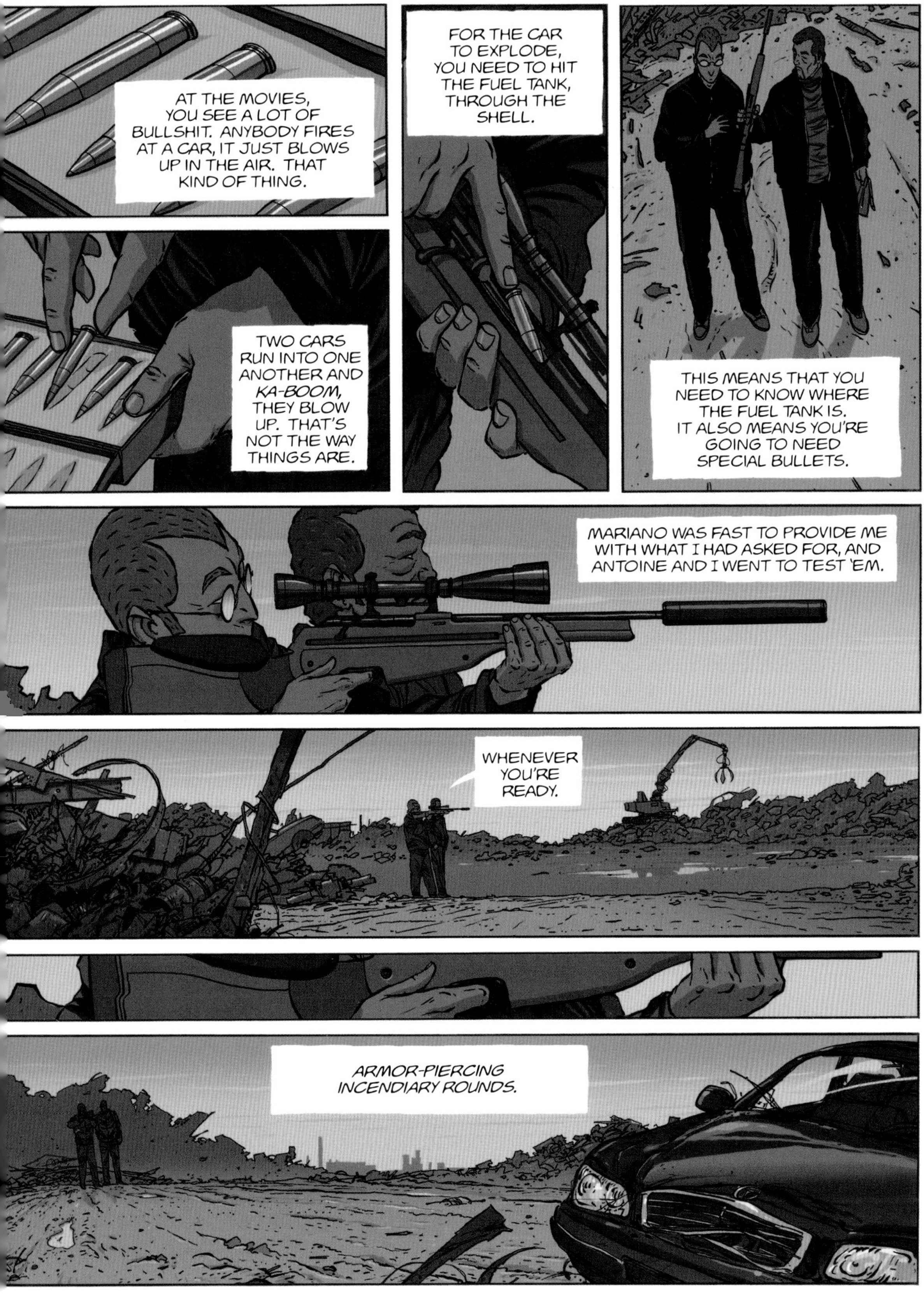
AT THE MOVIES, YOU SEE A LOT OF BULLSHIT. ANYBODY FIRES AT A CAR, IT JUST BLOWS UP IN THE AIR. THAT KIND OF THING.
TWO CARS RUN INTO ONE ANOTHER AND KA-BOOM, THEY BLOW UP. THAT'S NOT THE WAY THINGS ARE.
FOR THE CAR TO EXPLODE, YOU NEED TO HIT THE FUEL TANK, THROUGH THE SHELL.
THIS MEANS THAT YOU NEED TO KNOW WHERE THE FUEL TANK IS. IT ALSO MEANS YOU'RE GOING TO NEED SPECIAL BULLETS.
MARIANO WAS FAST TO PROVIDE ME WITH WHAT I HAD ASKED FOR, AND ANTOINE AND I WENT TO TEST 'EM.
WHENEVER YOU'RE READY.
ARMOR-PIERCING INCENDIARY ROUNDS.

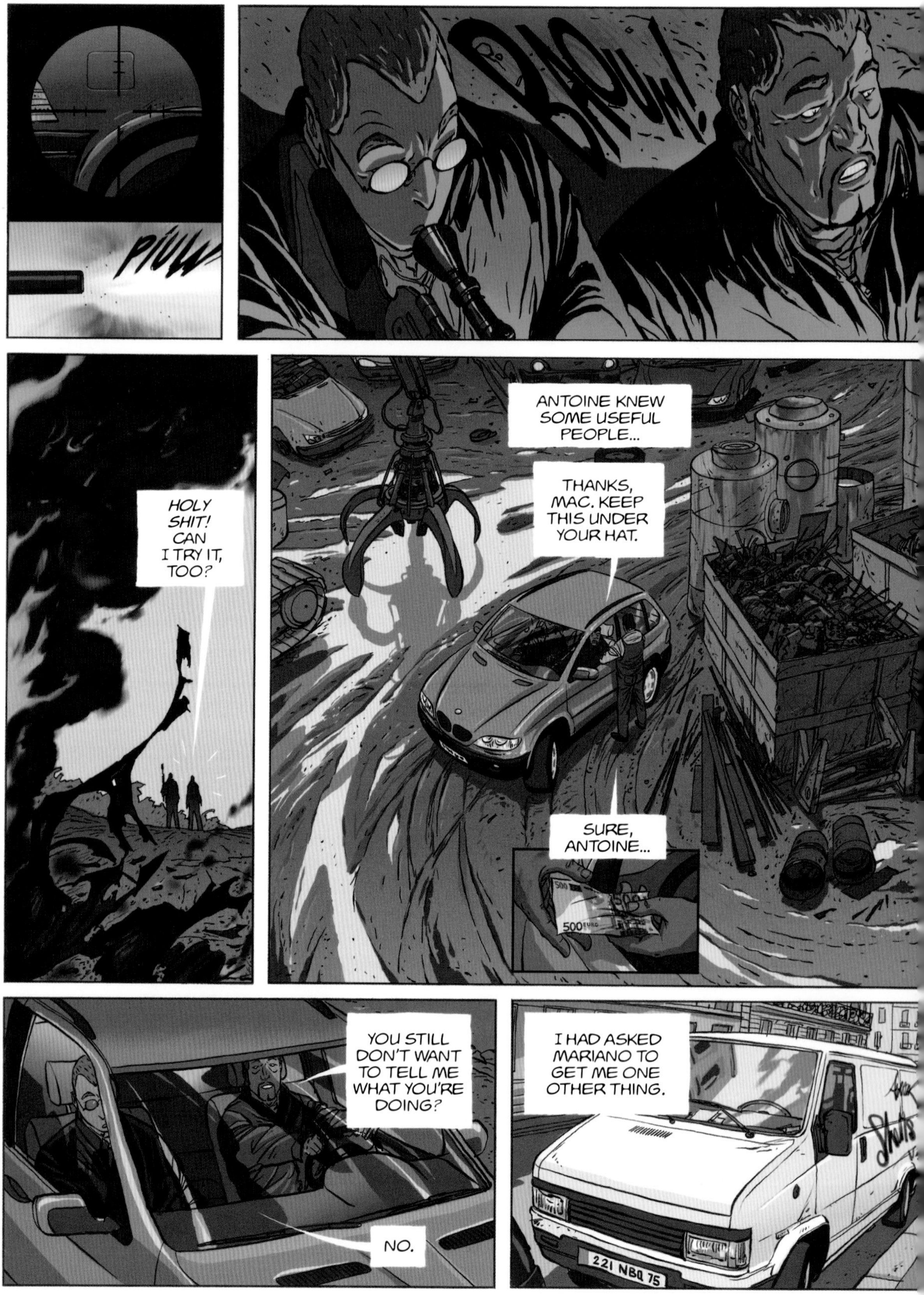
PIUW
BAOUM!
HOLY SHIT! CAN I TRY IT, TOO?
ANTOINE KNEW SOME USEFUL PEOPLE...
THANKS, MAC. KEEP THIS UNDER YOUR HAT.
SURE, ANTOINE...
YOU STILL DON'T WANT TO TELL ME WHAT YOU'RE DOING?
NO.
I HAD ASKED MARIANO TO GET ME ONE OTHER THING.
221 NBQ 75

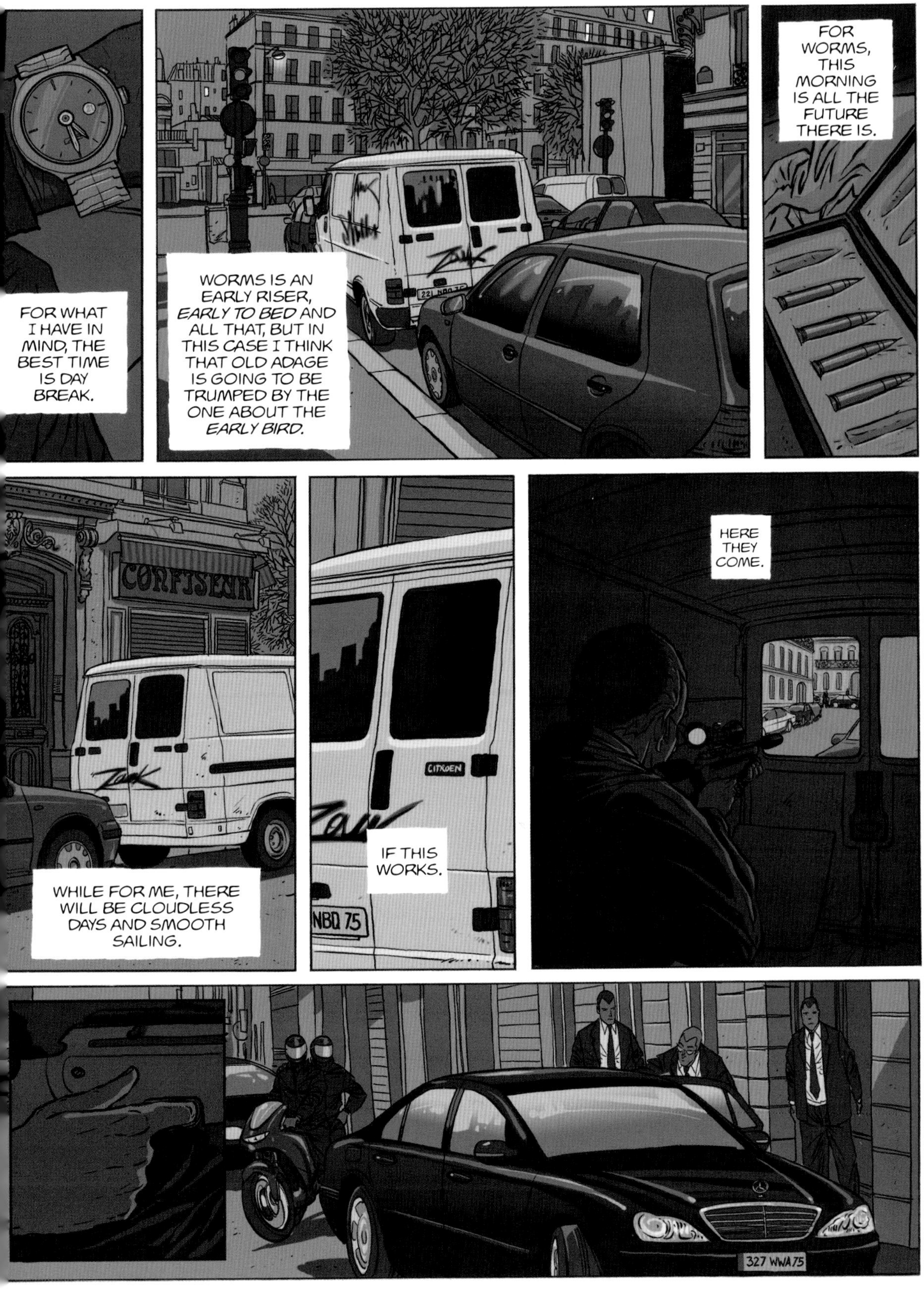
FOR WHAT I HAVE IN MIND, THE BEST TIME IS DAY BREAK.
WORMS IS AN EARLY RISER, *EARLY TO BED* AND ALL THAT, BUT IN THIS CASE I THINK THAT OLD ADAGE IS GOING TO BE TRUMPED BY THE ONE ABOUT THE *EARLY BIRD.*
FOR WORMS, THIS MORNING IS ALL THE FUTURE THERE IS.
CONFISEUR
WHILE FOR ME, THERE WILL BE CLOUDLESS DAYS AND SMOOTH SAILING.
CITROEN
IF THIS WORKS.
NBQ 75
HERE THEY COME.
327 WWA 75

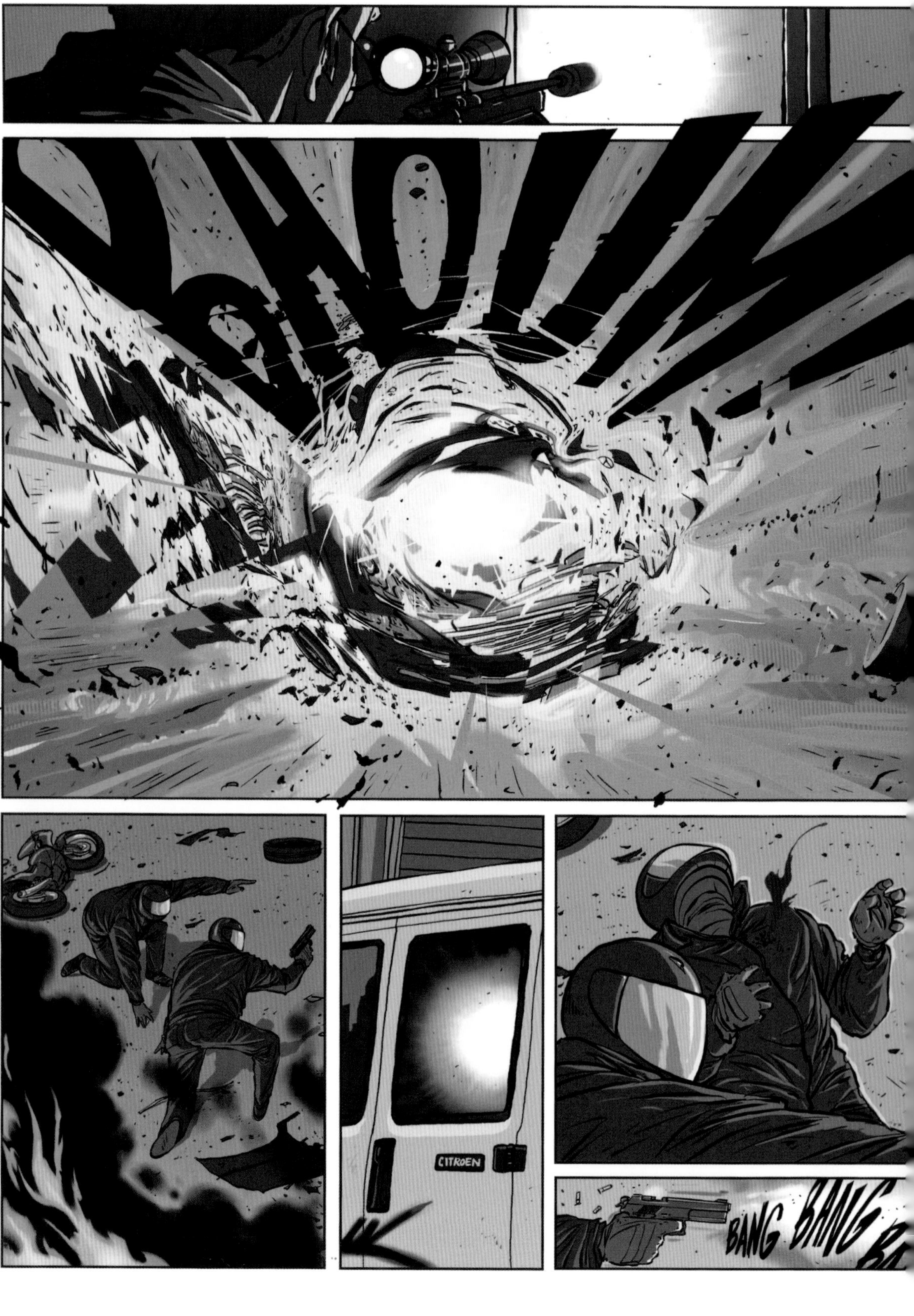
CITROEN
BANG BANG

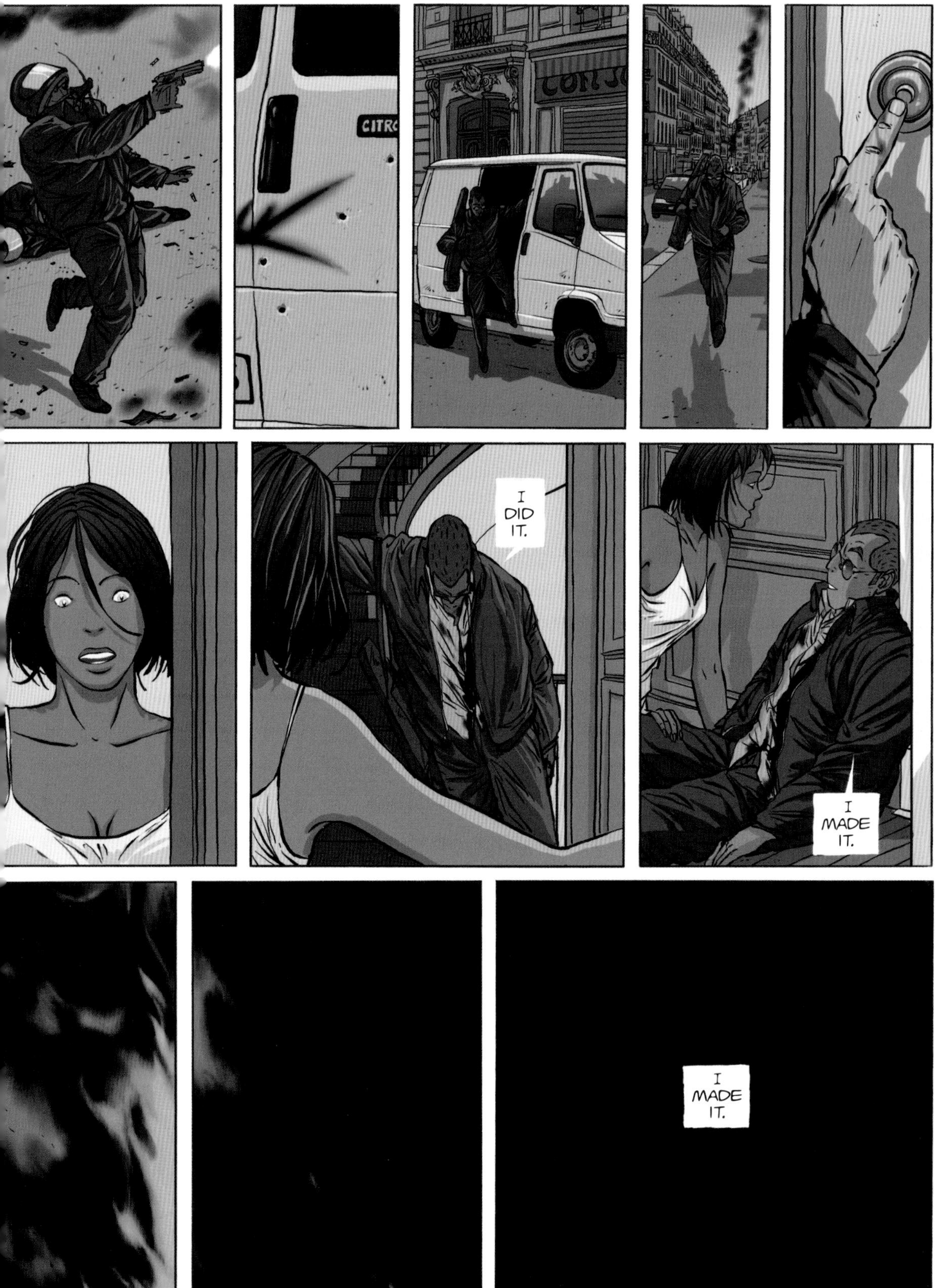
CITRO
I DID IT.
I MADE IT.
I MADE IT.

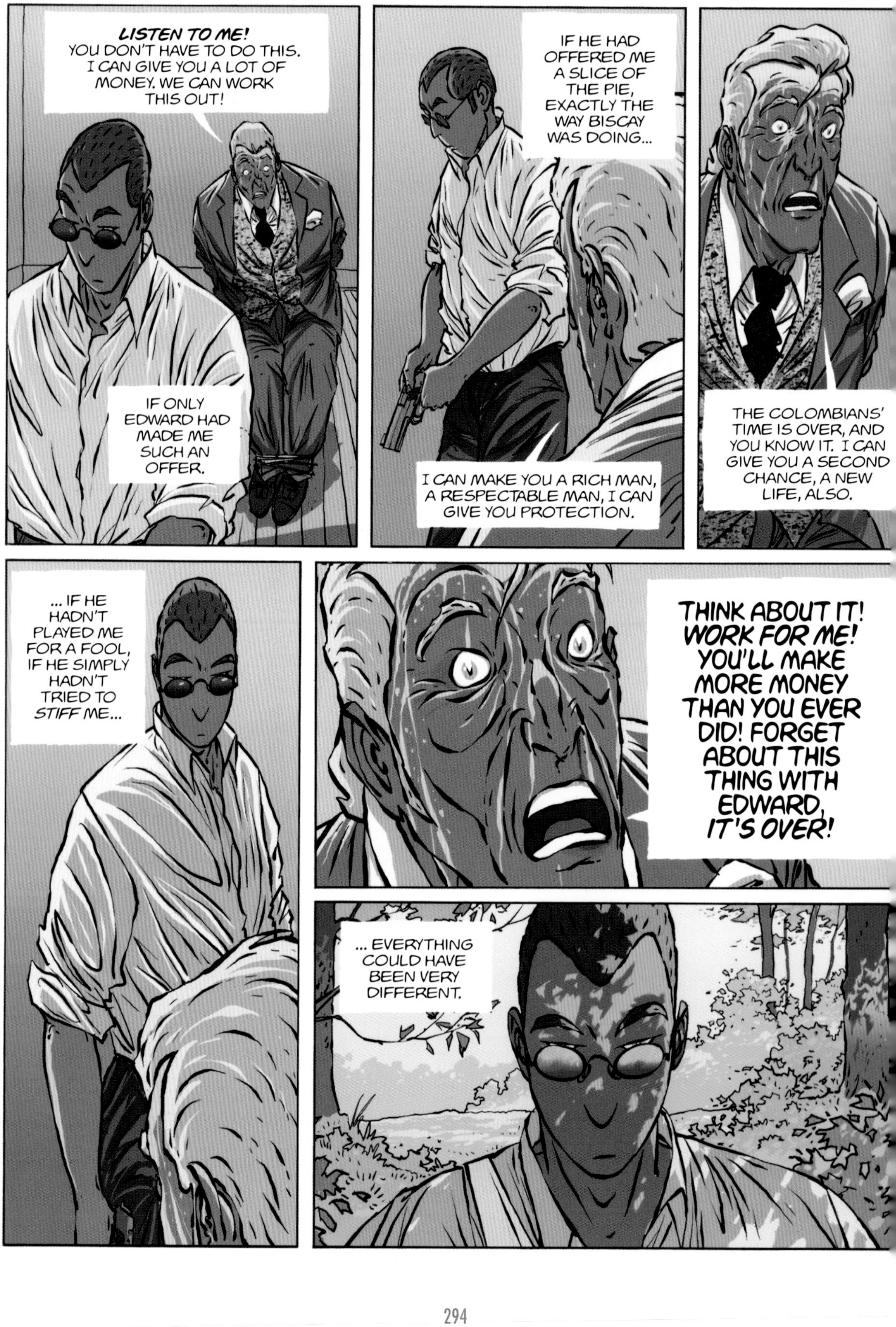
LISTEN TO ME! YOU DON'T HAVE TO DO THIS. I CAN GIVE YOU A LOT OF MONEY. WE CAN WORK THIS OUT!
IF ONLY EDWARD HAD MADE ME SUCH AN OFFER.
IF HE HAD OFFERED ME A SLICE OF THE PIE, EXACTLY THE WAY BISCAY WAS DOING...
I CAN MAKE YOU A RICH MAN, A RESPECTABLE MAN, I CAN GIVE YOU PROTECTION.
THE COLOMBIANS' TIME IS OVER, AND YOU KNOW IT. I CAN GIVE YOU A SECOND CHANCE, A NEW LIFE, ALSO.
... IF HE HADN'T PLAYED ME FOR A FOOL, IF HE SIMPLY HADN'T TRIED TO STIFF ME...
THINK ABOUT IT! WORK FOR ME! YOU'LL MAKE MORE MONEY THAN YOU EVER DID! FORGET ABOUT THIS THING WITH EDWARD, IT'S OVER!
... EVERYTHING COULD HAVE BEEN VERY DIFFERENT.

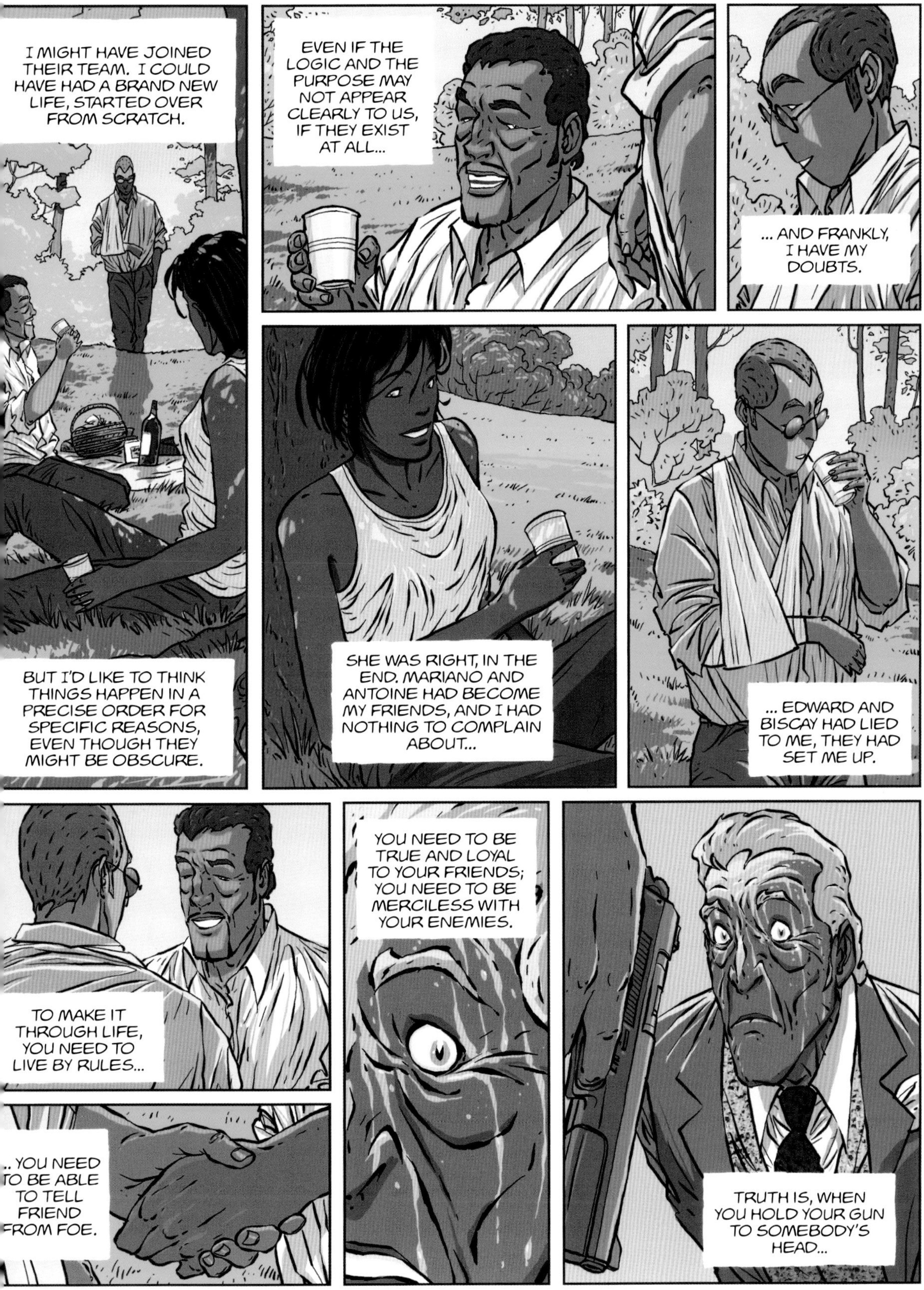
I MIGHT HAVE JOINED THEIR TEAM. I COULD HAVE HAD A BRAND NEW LIFE, STARTED OVER FROM SCRATCH.
BUT I'D LIKE TO THINK THINGS HAPPEN IN A PRECISE ORDER FOR SPECIFIC REASONS, EVEN THOUGH THEY MIGHT BE OBSCURE.
EVEN IF THE LOGIC AND THE PURPOSE MAY NOT APPEAR CLEARLY TO US, IF THEY EXIST AT ALL...
... AND FRANKLY, I HAVE MY DOUBTS.
SHE WAS RIGHT, IN THE END. MARIANO AND ANTOINE HAD BECOME MY FRIENDS, AND I HAD NOTHING TO COMPLAIN ABOUT...
... EDWARD AND BISCAY HAD LIED TO ME, THEY HAD SET ME UP.
TO MAKE IT THROUGH LIFE, YOU NEED TO LIVE BY RULES...
.. YOU NEED TO BE ABLE TO TELL FRIEND FROM FOE.
YOU NEED TO BE TRUE AND LOYAL TO YOUR FRIENDS; YOU NEED TO BE MERCILESS WITH YOUR ENEMIES.
TRUTH IS, WHEN YOU HOLD YOUR GUN TO SOMEBODY'S HEAD...

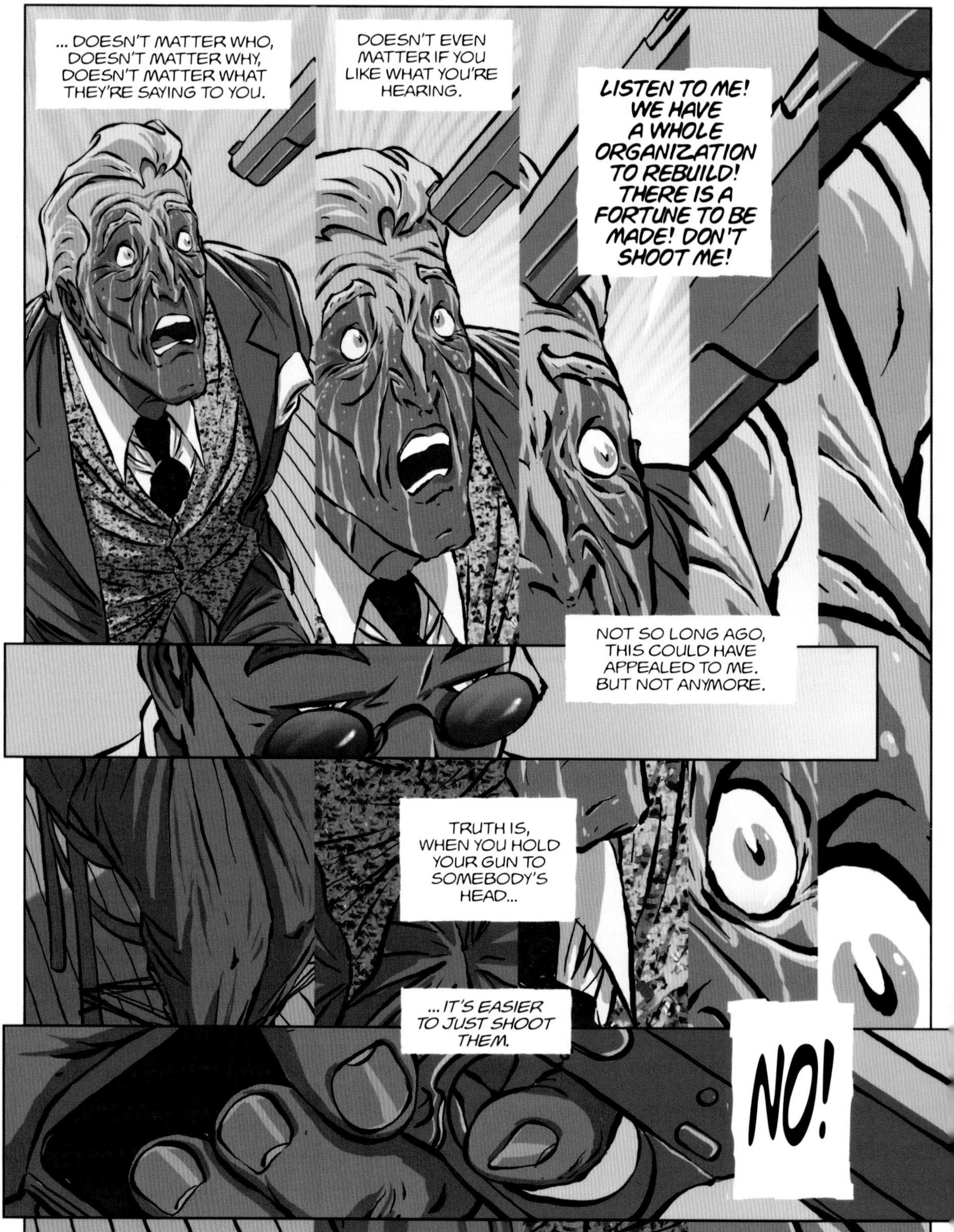
... DOESN'T MATTER WHO, DOESN'T MATTER WHY, DOESN'T MATTER WHAT THEY'RE SAYING TO YOU.
DOESN'T EVEN MATTER IF YOU LIKE WHAT YOU'RE HEARING.
LISTEN TO ME! WE HAVE A WHOLE ORGANIZATION TO REBUILD! THERE IS A FORTUNE TO BE MADE! DON'T SHOOT ME!
NOT SO LONG AGO, THIS COULD HAVE APPEALED TO ME. BUT NOT ANYMORE.
TRUTH IS, WHEN YOU HOLD YOUR GUN TO SOMEBODY'S HEAD...
... IT'S EASIER TO JUST SHOOT THEM.
NO!

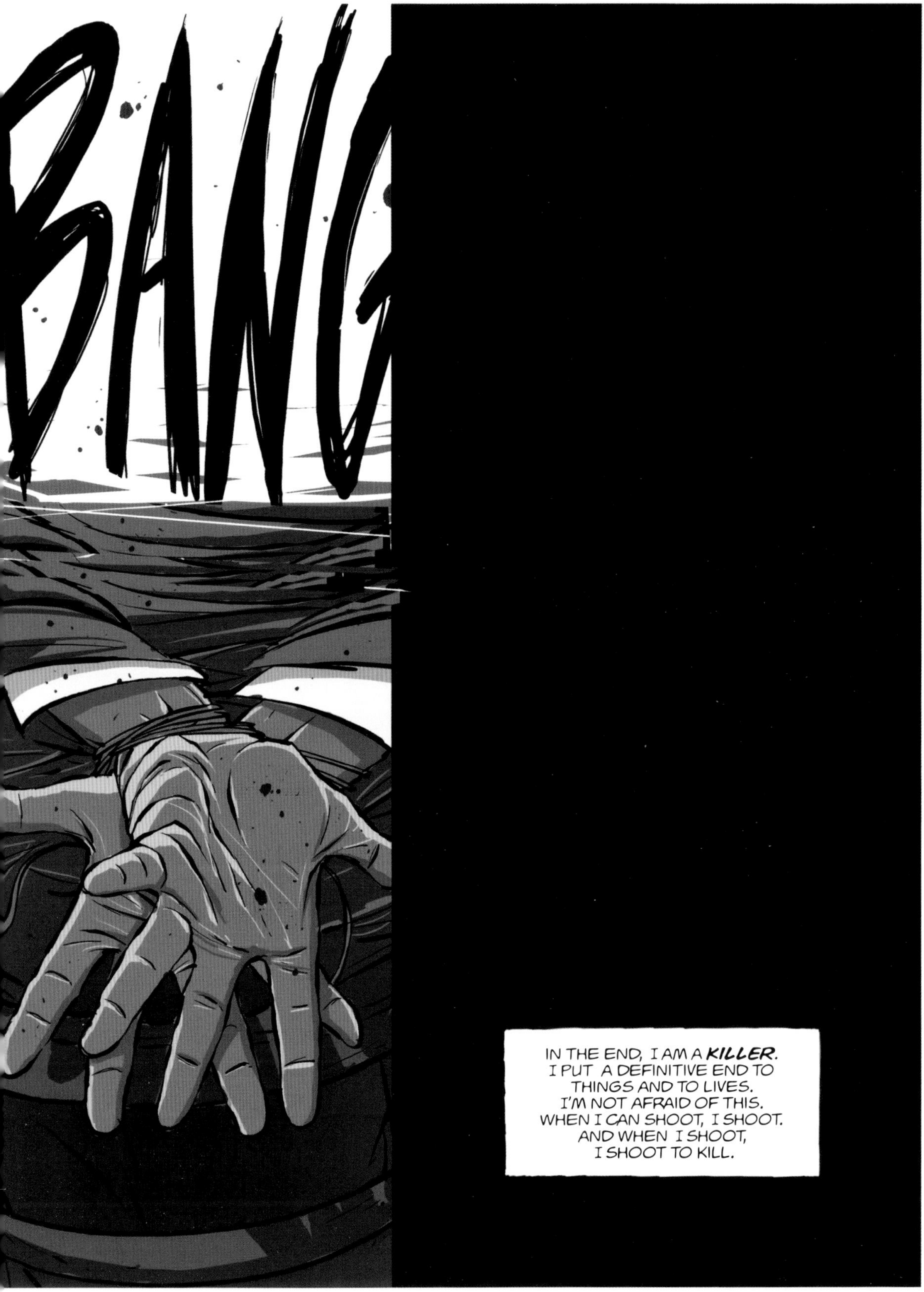
BANG
IN THE END, I AM A **KILLER**. I PUT A DEFINITIVE END TO THINGS AND TO LIVES. I'M NOT AFRAID OF THIS. WHEN I CAN SHOOT, I SHOOT. AND WHEN I SHOOT, I SHOOT TO KILL.

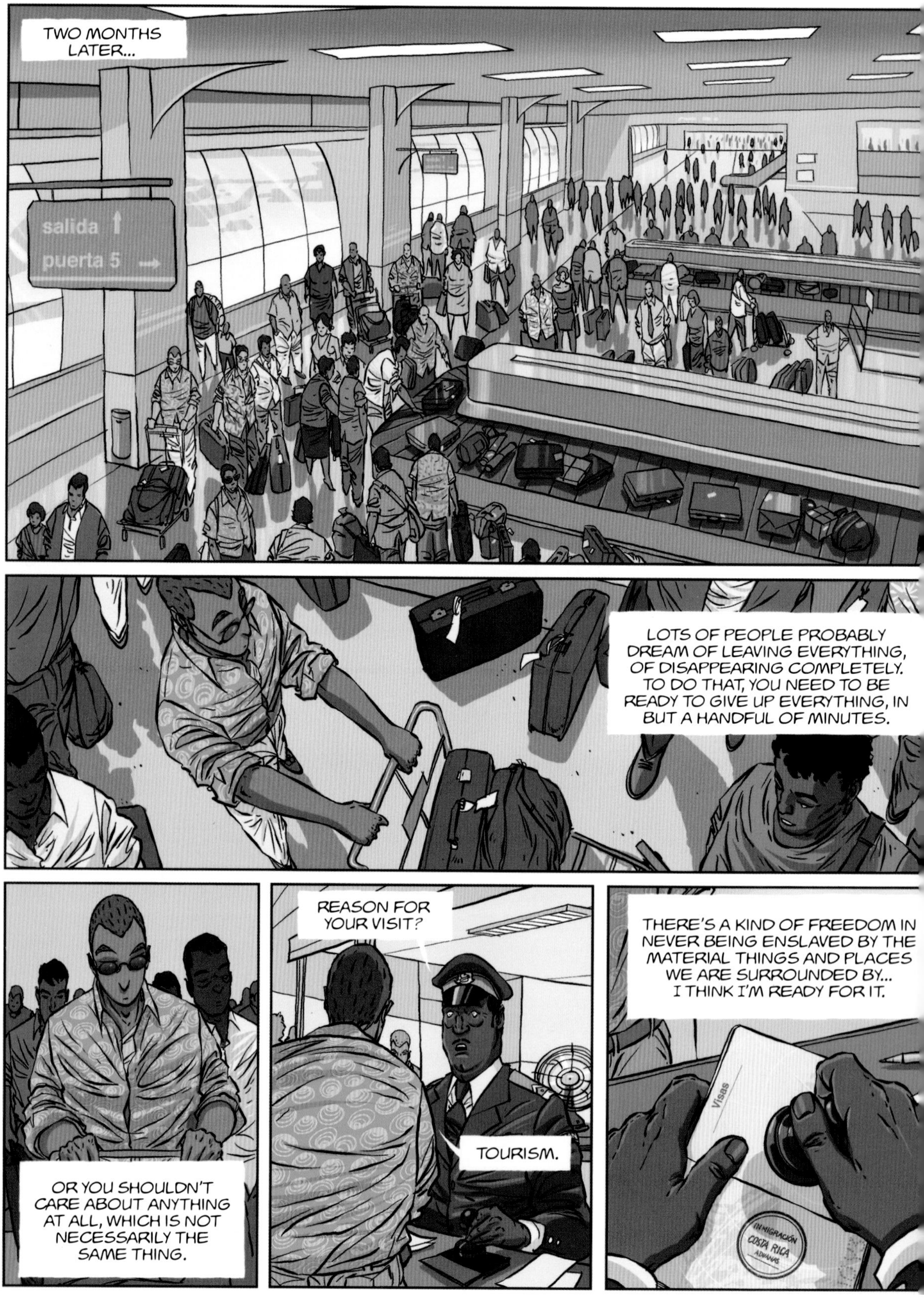
TWO MONTHS LATER...
salida
puerta 5
LOTS OF PEOPLE PROBABLY DREAM OF LEAVING EVERYTHING, OF DISAPPEARING COMPLETELY. TO DO THAT, YOU NEED TO BE READY TO GIVE UP EVERYTHING, IN BUT A HANDFUL OF MINUTES.
OR YOU SHOULDN'T CARE ABOUT ANYTHING AT ALL, WHICH IS NOT NECESSARILY THE SAME THING.
REASON FOR YOUR VISIT?
TOURISM.
THERE'S A KIND OF FREEDOM IN NEVER BEING ENSLAVED BY THE MATERIAL THINGS AND PLACES WE ARE SURROUNDED BY... I THINK I'M READY FOR IT.
Visas
INMIGRACIÓN
COSTA RICA

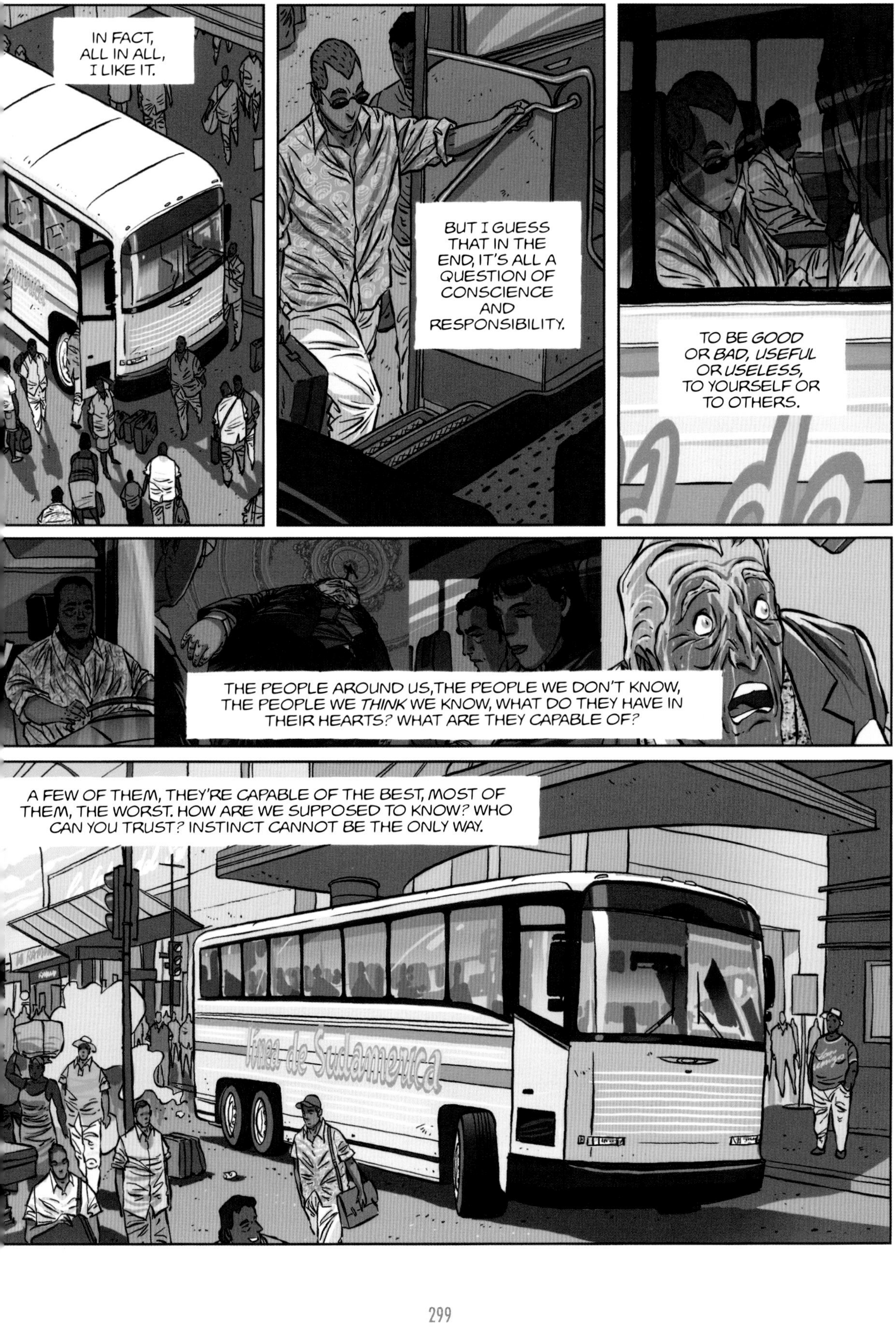
IN FACT, ALL IN ALL, I LIKE IT.
BUT I GUESS THAT IN THE END, IT'S ALL A QUESTION OF CONSCIENCE AND RESPONSIBILITY.
TO BE *GOOD* OR *BAD*, *USEFUL* OR *USELESS*, TO YOURSELF OR TO OTHERS.
THE PEOPLE AROUND US, THE PEOPLE WE DON'T KNOW, THE PEOPLE WE *THINK* WE KNOW, WHAT DO THEY HAVE IN THEIR HEARTS? WHAT ARE THEY CAPABLE OF?
A FEW OF THEM, THEY'RE CAPABLE OF THE BEST, MOST OF THEM, THE WORST. HOW ARE WE SUPPOSED TO KNOW? WHO CAN YOU TRUST? INSTINCT CANNOT BE THE ONLY WAY.

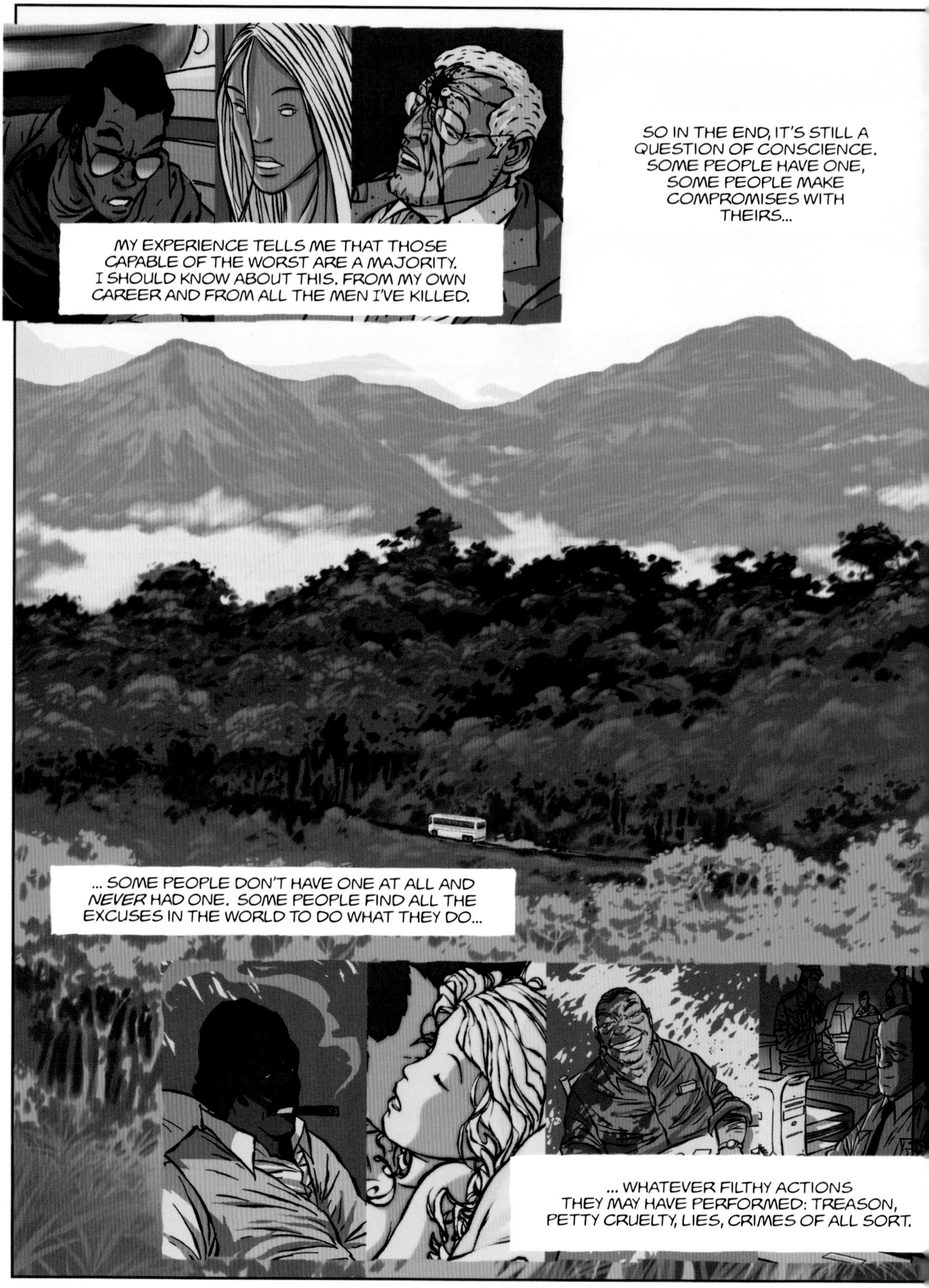
MY EXPERIENCE TELLS ME THAT THOSE CAPABLE OF THE WORST ARE A MAJORITY. I SHOULD KNOW ABOUT THIS. FROM MY OWN CAREER AND FROM ALL THE MEN I'VE KILLED.
SO IN THE END, IT'S STILL A QUESTION OF CONSCIENCE. SOME PEOPLE HAVE ONE, SOME PEOPLE MAKE COMPROMISES WITH THEIRS...
... SOME PEOPLE DON'T HAVE ONE AT ALL AND NEVER HAD ONE. SOME PEOPLE FIND ALL THE EXCUSES IN THE WORLD TO DO WHAT THEY DO...
... WHATEVER FILTHY ACTIONS THEY MAY HAVE PERFORMED: TREASON, PETTY CRUELTY, LIES, CRIMES OF ALL SORT.

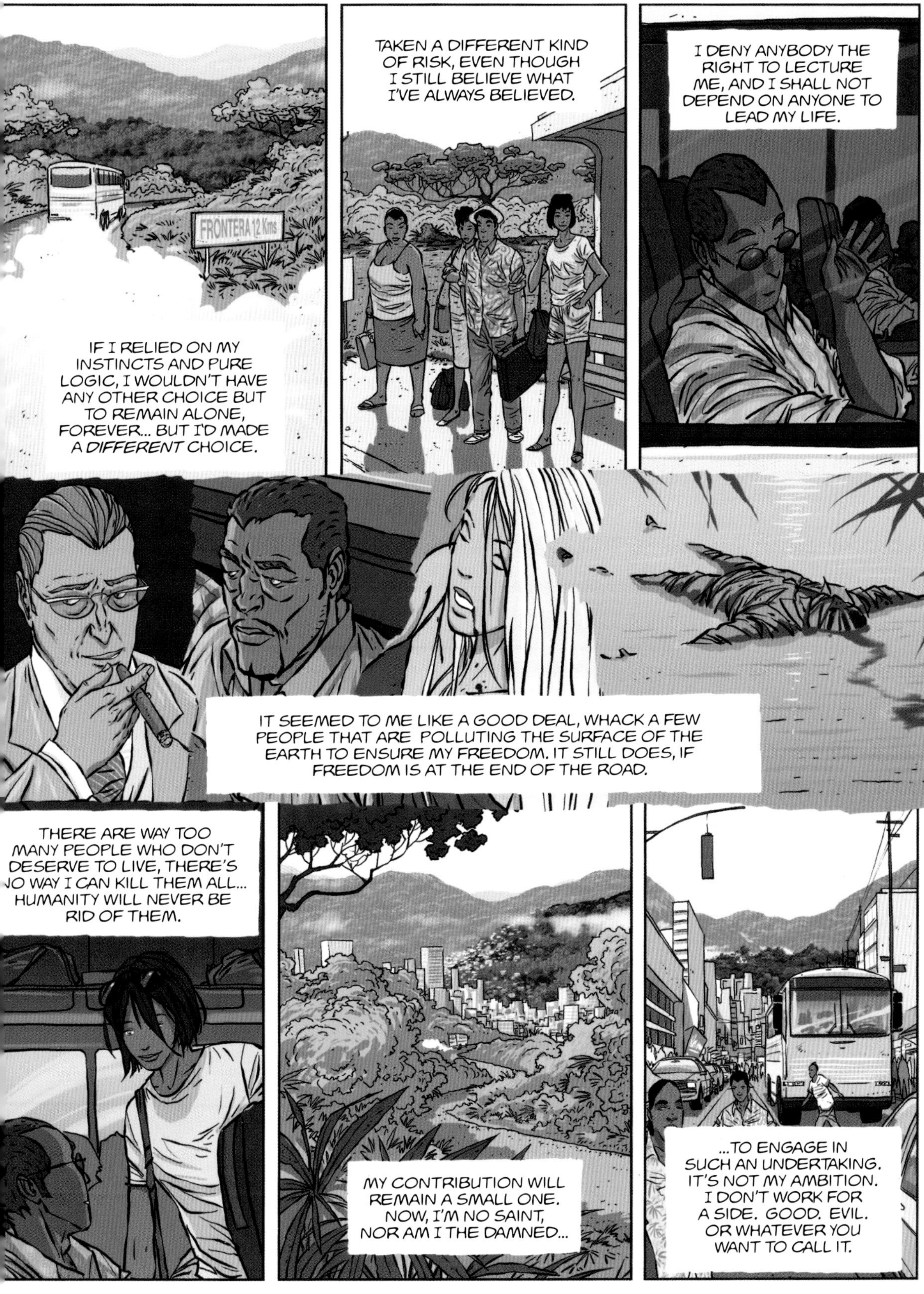
IF I RELIED ON MY INSTINCTS AND PURE LOGIC, I WOULDN'T HAVE ANY OTHER CHOICE BUT TO REMAIN ALONE, FOREVER... BUT I'D MADE A *DIFFERENT* CHOICE.
FRONTERA 12 Kms
TAKEN A DIFFERENT KIND OF RISK, EVEN THOUGH I STILL BELIEVE WHAT I'VE ALWAYS BELIEVED.
I DENY ANYBODY THE RIGHT TO LECTURE ME, AND I SHALL NOT DEPEND ON ANYONE TO LEAD MY LIFE.
IT SEEMED TO ME LIKE A GOOD DEAL, WHACK A FEW PEOPLE THAT ARE POLLUTING THE SURFACE OF THE EARTH TO ENSURE MY FREEDOM. IT STILL DOES, IF FREEDOM IS AT THE END OF THE ROAD.
THERE ARE WAY TOO MANY PEOPLE WHO DON'T DESERVE TO LIVE, THERE'S NO WAY I CAN KILL THEM ALL... HUMANITY WILL NEVER BE RID OF THEM.
MY CONTRIBUTION WILL REMAIN A SMALL ONE. NOW, I'M NO SAINT, NOR AM I THE DAMNED...
...TO ENGAGE IN SUCH AN UNDERTAKING. IT'S NOT MY AMBITION. I DON'T WORK FOR A SIDE. GOOD. EVIL. OR WHATEVER YOU WANT TO CALL IT.

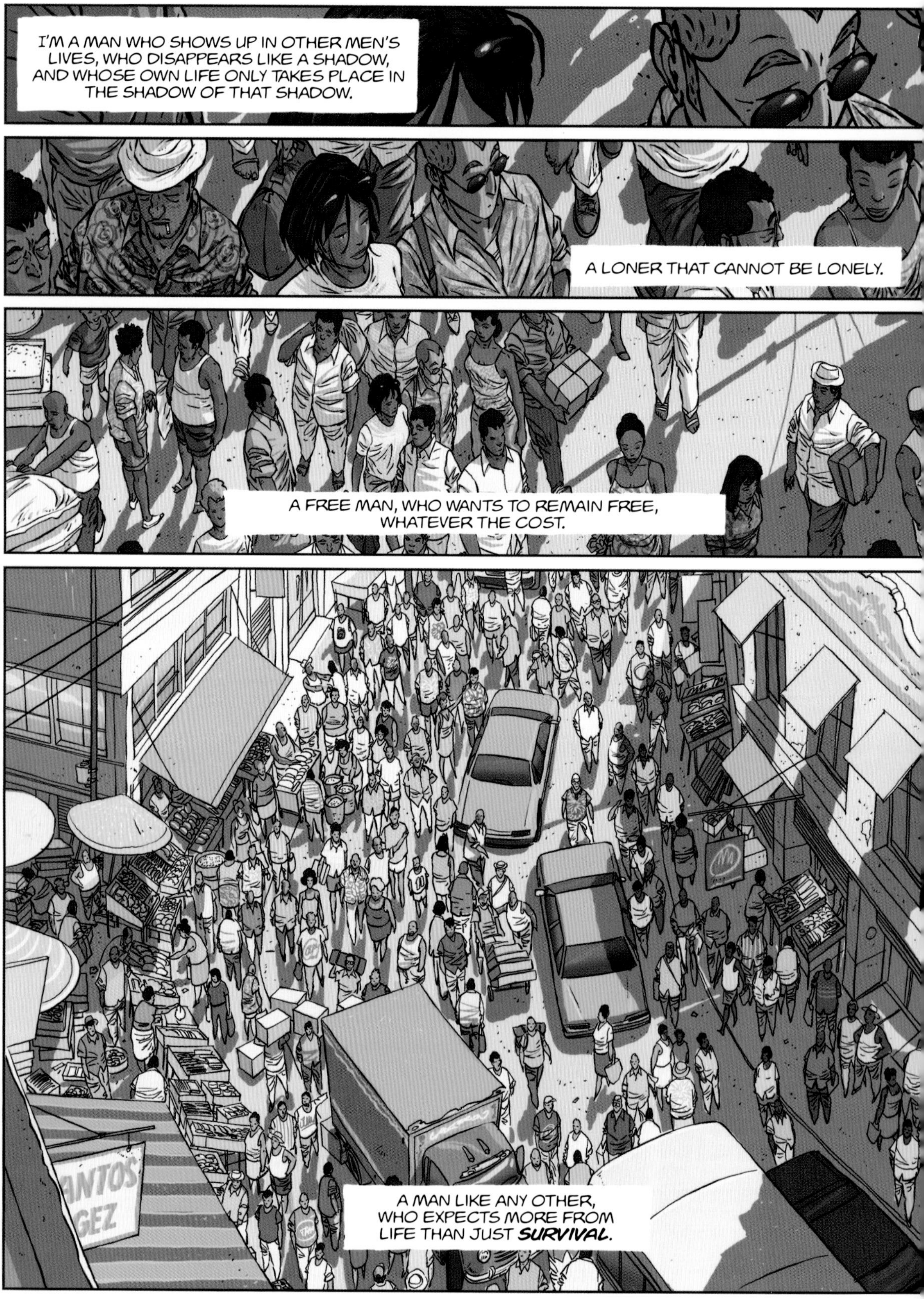
I'M A MAN WHO SHOWS UP IN OTHER MEN'S LIVES, WHO DISAPPEARS LIKE A SHADOW, AND WHOSE OWN LIFE ONLY TAKES PLACE IN THE SHADOW OF THAT SHADOW.
A LONER THAT CANNOT BE LONELY.
A FREE MAN, WHO WANTS TO REMAIN FREE, WHATEVER THE COST.
A MAN LIKE ANY OTHER, WHO EXPECTS MORE FROM LIFE THAN JUST ***SURVIVAL***.

" In the end, I am a **killer**. "

COVER GALLERY

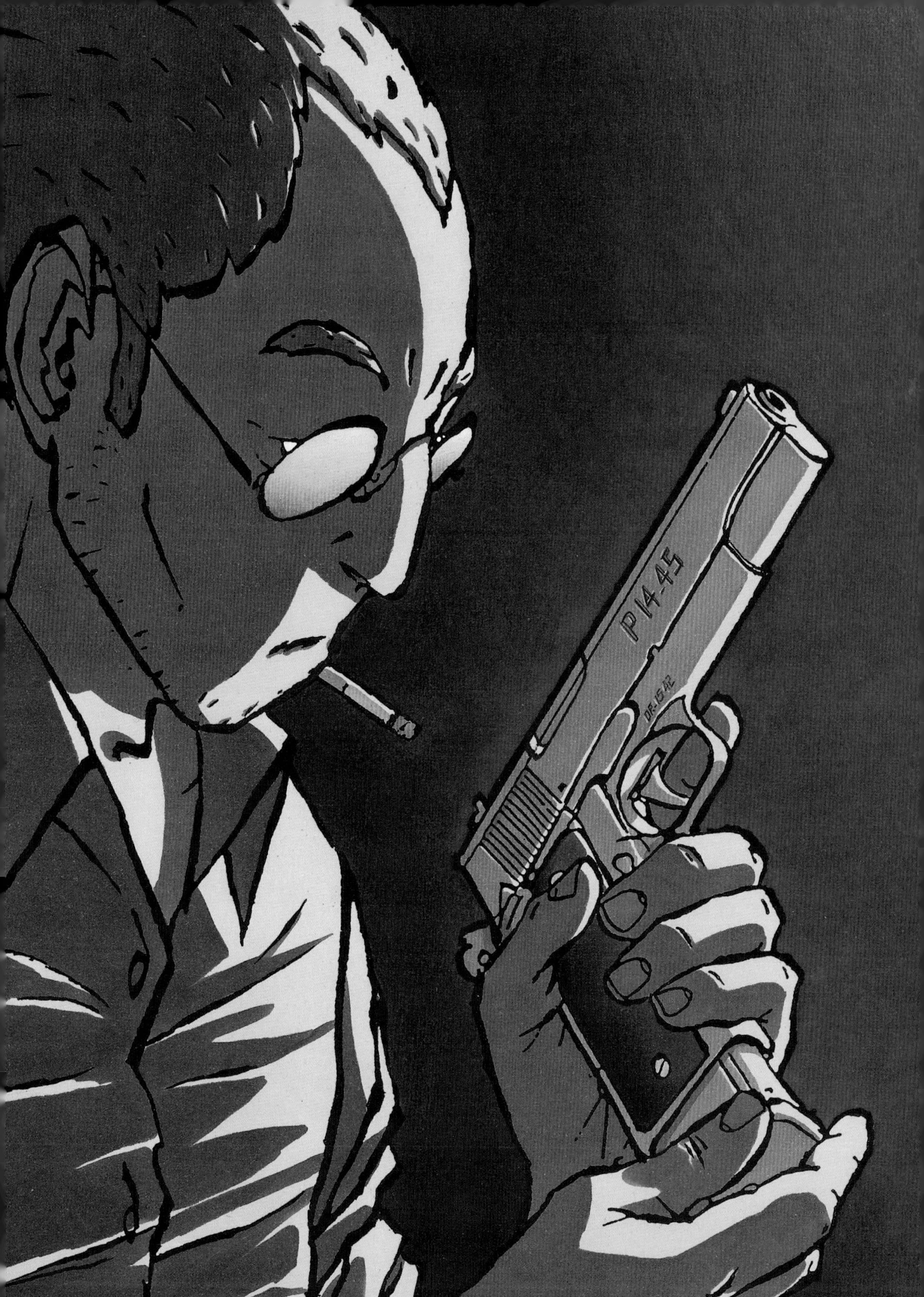
P14.45

CHAPTER ONE **LONG FIRE**

ORIGINAL SERIES COVER

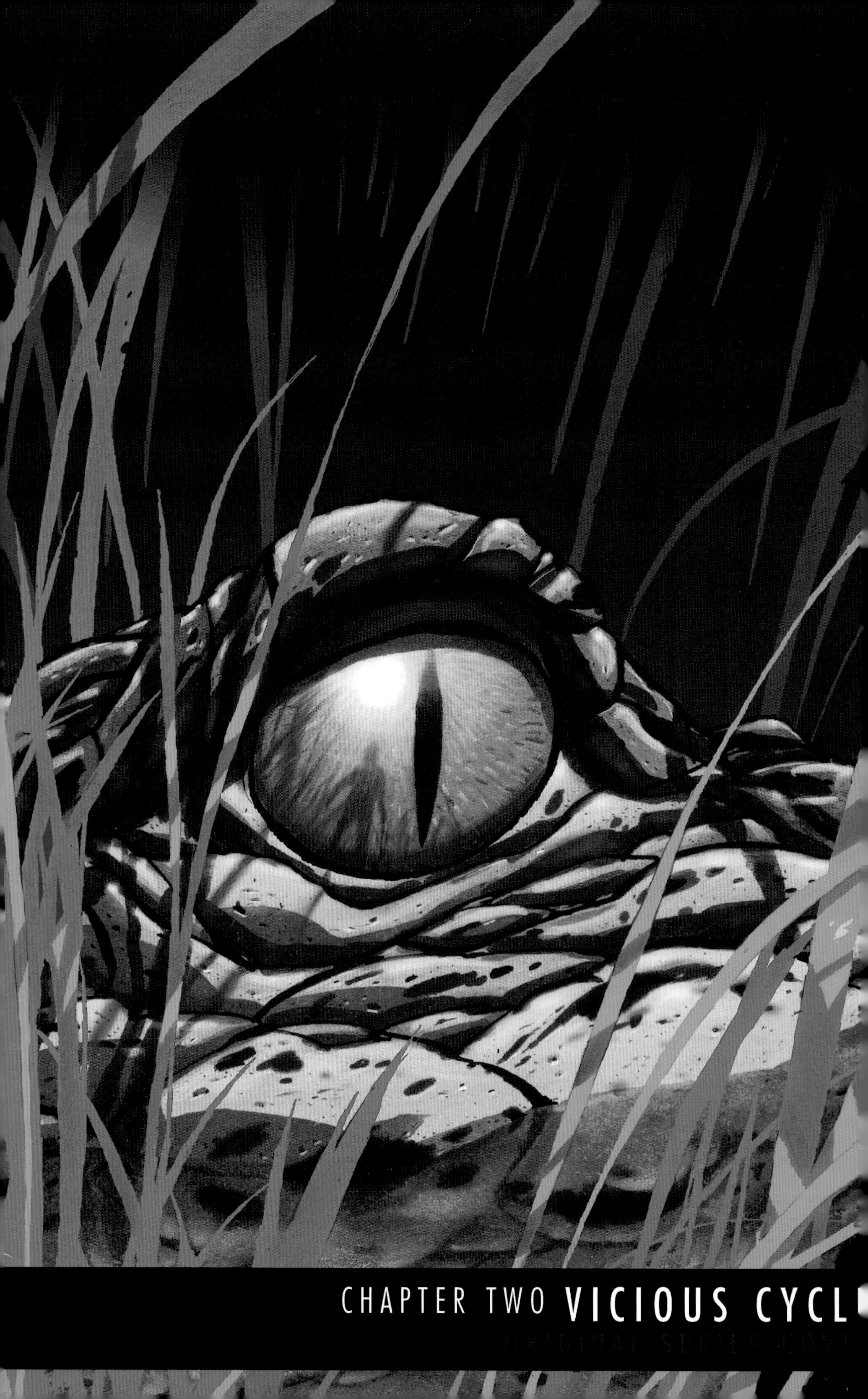

CHAPTER TWO **VICIOUS CYCL**

ORIGINAL SERIES COVE

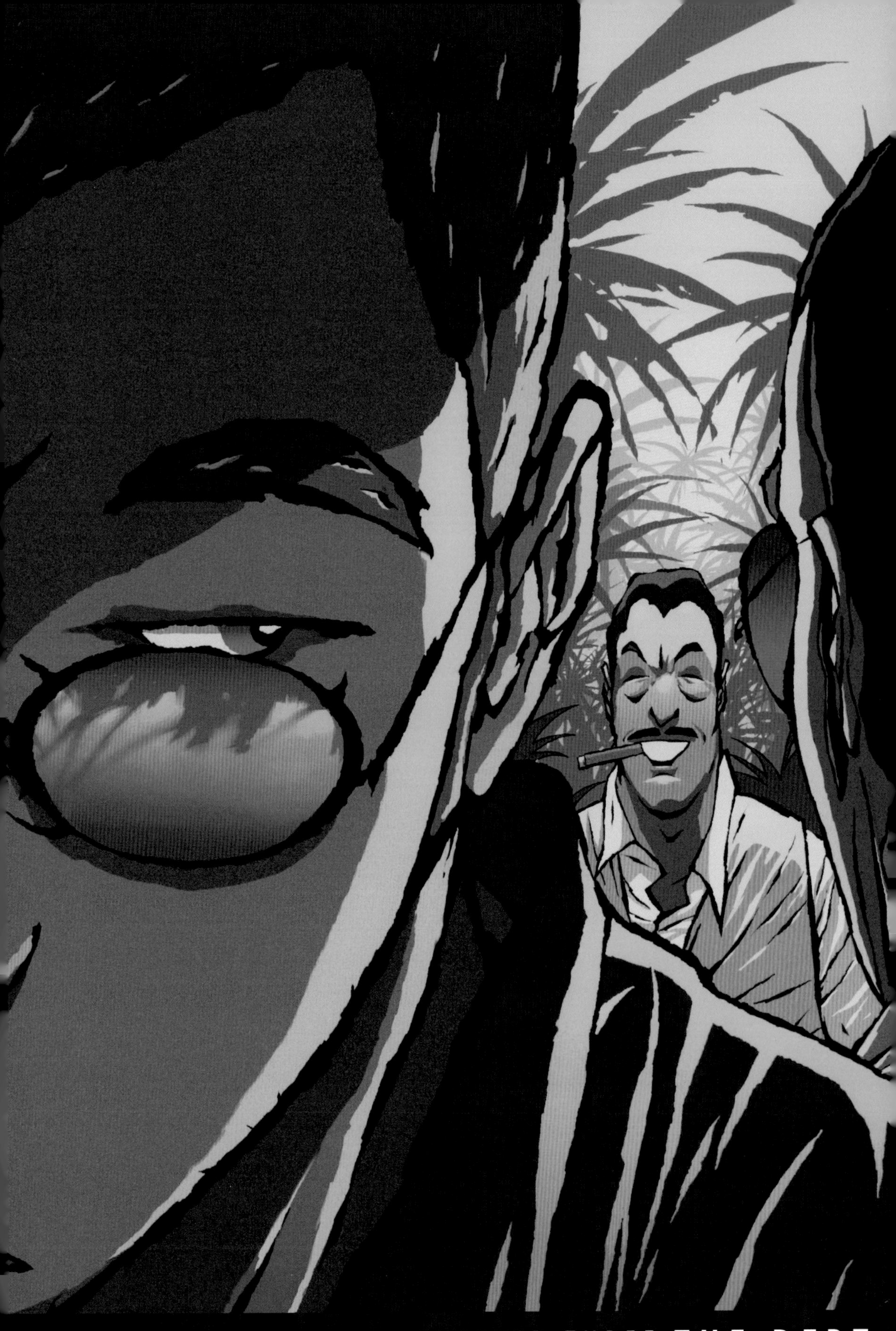

CHAPTER THREE **THE DEBT**

ORIGINAL SERIES COVER

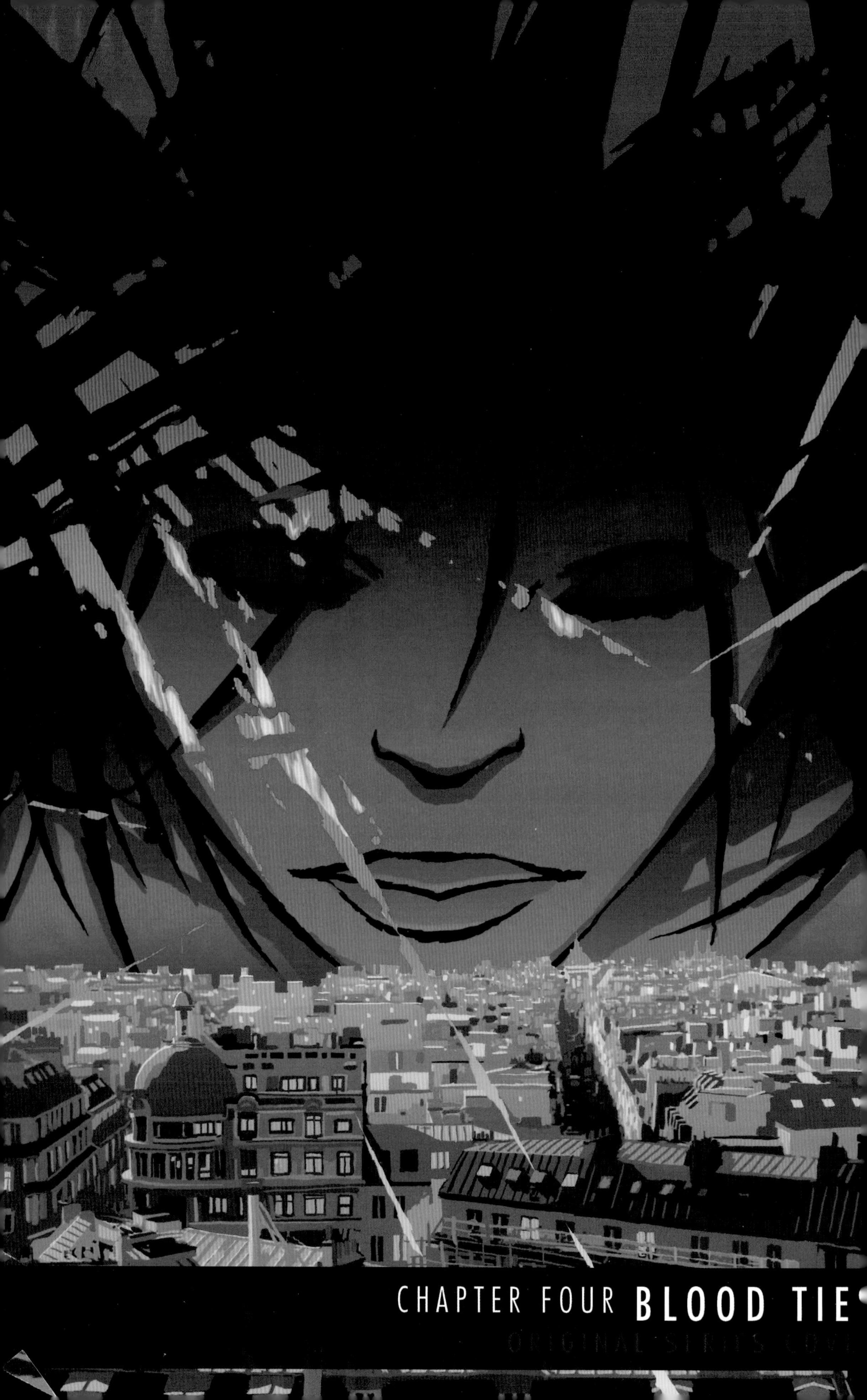

CHAPTER FOUR **BLOOD TIE**

ORIGINAL SERIES COV

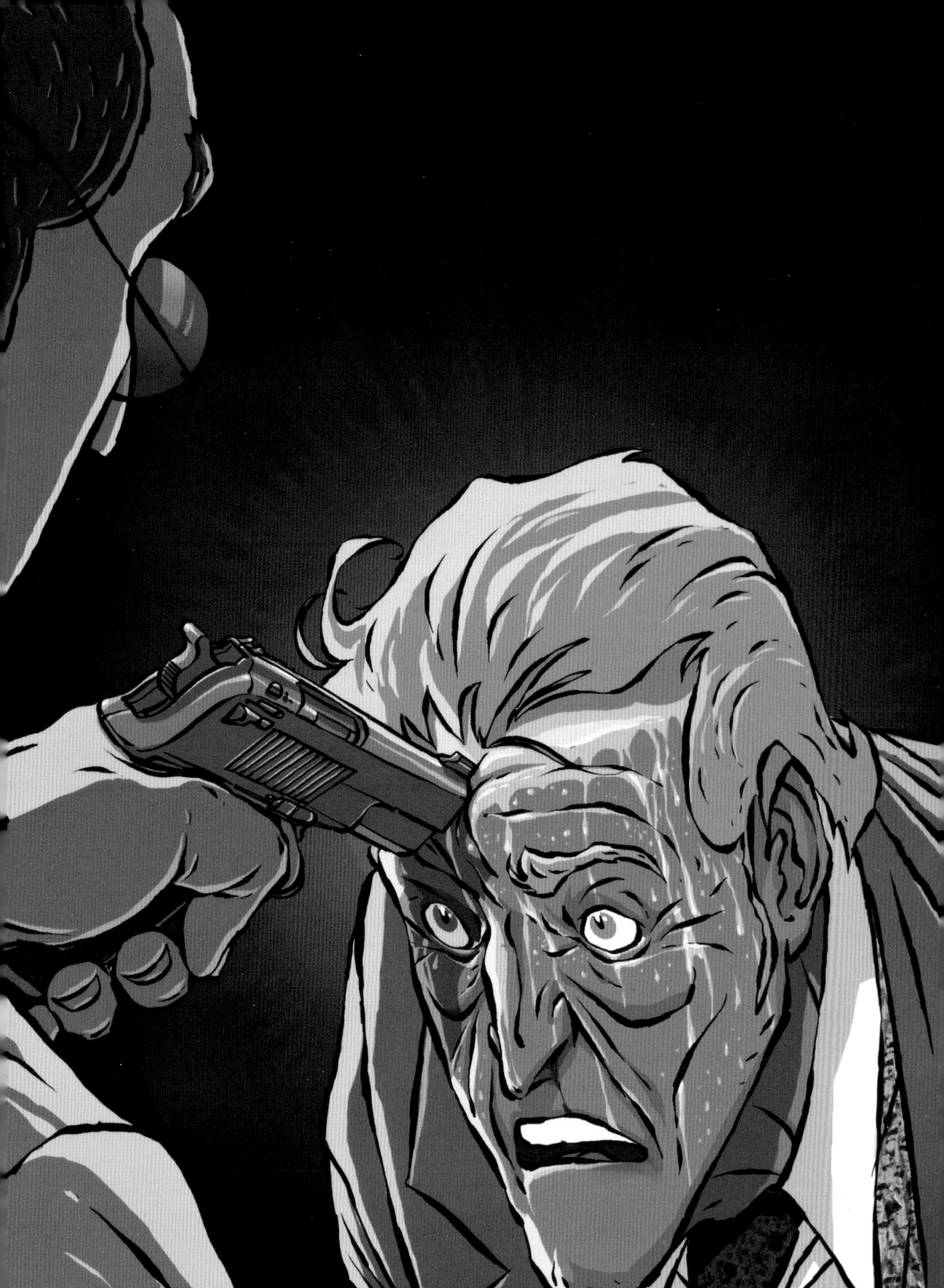

CHAPTER FIVE **THE KILLER INSTINCT**

ORIGINAL SERIES COVER

ABOUT THE AUTHORS

LUC JACAMON honed his drawing skills with an Alfred scholarship in 1986. *LE TUEUR: LONG FEU* was his first published work.

MATZ has published various graphic novels including a near-future sci-fi series called *CYCLOPES* also with artist Luc Jacamon; a thriller, *DU PLOMB DANS LA TÊTE (HEADSHOT)* with renonwned New Zealand artist Colin Wilson; *SHANDY*, with artist Bertail; and *PEINES PERDUES* with artist Chauzy, which was nominated for Best Comic and Audience's Choice at Angoulême in 1993. Matz is also, under his real name, an active writer for videogames, as well as a published novelist.